INTERNATIONAL BUSINESS

Concept, Environment and Strategy

Third Edition

VYUPTAKESH SHARAN

Pearson

Assistant Acquisitions Editor: Nitin Valecha
Associate Production Editor: Ruchi Sachdev
Composition: Sangnee Media Solutions Pvt. Ltd.
Printer:

Published by Dorling Kindersley (India) Pvt. Ltd., licensees of Pearson Education in South Asia.

ISBN: 978-81-317-3251-9

First Impression

Published by Pearson India Education Services Pvt. Ltd, CIN: U72200TN2005PTC057128.

Head Office: 1st Floor, Berger Tower, Plot No. C-001A/2, Sector 16B, Noida - 201 301, Uttar Pradesh, India.
Registered Office: Featherlite, 'The Address' 5th Floor, Survey No 203/10B, 200 Ft MMRD Road, Zamin Pallavaram, Chennai - 600044
Phone: 044-66540100
Website: in.pearson.com, Email: companysecretary.india@pearson.com

Printed in India Saurabh Printers Pvt.Ltd.

To my parents,
Smt Kalyani Devi and Sri Hrishikesh Sharan

Contents

Preface to the Third Edition

The third edition takes into account the changes in the international business environment and strategy taking place during past four or five years. An elaborate discussion of some of the themes makes the text still more meaningful. Some of the important features of this edition are as follows.

- ✓ It incorporates the basic concept and process of globalisation.
- ✓ Strategic alliance has been explained exclusively in a new mould.
- ✓ The theory of trade envelops the theory of intra-industry trade and the theory behind out-sourcing.
- ✓ The inward- and outward-oriented policies of international trade are explained in a wider perspective.
- ✓ The discussion on trade barriers is greatly elaborated.
- ✓ The trade-creating and trade-diverting effects of a regional grouping are more intensively discussed.
- ✓ Some numerical examples of transactions in the foreign exchange market are provided in order to make the concept clearer.
- ✓ The discussion on the taxation issue is more comprehensive.
- ✓ A number of boxes have been inserted in order to show the real-life example.
- ✓ A good number of study topic/case studies have been added to enhance the quality of the text and make it reader friendly.

The valuable opinions from the readers are always welcome.

VYUPTAKESH SHARAN

Preface

The growing acceptance of the policy of economic liberalisation and globalisation has led to fast expansion in international business. International trade and investment as also international transfer of technology have grown at a galloping gait in recent times. All these require trained manpower on a sizeable scale. Perhaps this is the main reason why the subject of international business has gained so much importance among the institutions imparting professional courses all over the world.

I have been writing in this area for over three decades and have been teaching this subject for quite some time. But it is my students who insisted and motivated me to write a textbook on this subject. The credit for this textbook, therefore, should go to them.

At present, there are a number of books on this subject, and I agree that a few of them are really good. But I feel the perspectives of the developing countries have not been stressed upon to the extent it is desired in view of the growing participation of these countries in the international business. I have tried to fill this gap so as to make the book more useful. Again, on an average, the students of business management get less than a month for covering one course. The size of the book has been intentionally kept limited to suit this time framework. Yet again, it is my experience that the students admitted to the professional courses come from various disciplines and they do not have sufficient idea about commerce and economics. Keeping this in mind, all efforts have been made to make the text lucid and intelligible. For readers who would like to go deep into any issue, there is a list of select further readings provided at the end of the respective chapters.

I have greatly benefited from the discussions with my colleagues and professionals working in this field of study. I am thankful to all of them.

I wish to express my sincere thanks to my wife, Roopa Sharan, for the inspiration and encouragement she has provided for preparing this book.

I am sure the readers will find the book useful. Their suggestions, which are most welcome, will surely make the next edition still more useful.

VYUPTAKESH SHARAN

About the Author

Vyuptakesh Sharan, Former Professor and Dean, Faculty of Commerce, Magadh University, is currently a Professor Emeritus at Chandragupt Institute of Management Patna (CIMP) which is an autonomous institution of Government of Bihar. Previously he was Emeritus Fellow at School of International Studies, Jawaharlal Nehru University, New Delhi, UGC Visiting Professor at the MIB Programme, Department of Commerce, Delhi School of Economics, University of Delhi and AICTE Visiting Professor at Global Business Operations Post-Graduate Programme, Sri Ram College of Commerce, University of Delhi.

Professor Sharan teaches international business and international finance. He has delivered special lectures in a number of Indian universities and abroad. He has to his credit six reference books and three text books mostly published by international publishers. He has also contributed a large number of articles to national and international journals, and has chaired more than half a dozen national seminars.

PART

PART 1

Concept of International Business

An exhibition in Pragati Maidan, Delhi, India*

1 Overview of International Business

CHAPTER OBJECTIVES

The chapter acquaints the readers with the nature of international business and how it evolved and developed over time. In particular, it attempts to:

- ✦ Define the meaning and significance of globalisation and international business.
- ✦ Explain how international business is different from domestic business.
- ✦ Delineate the characteristics of an MNC.
- ✦ Discuss the process of evolution of international business and its development.
- ✦ Explain the factors leading to phenomenal growth in international business during the past fifty years.

1.1 THE CONCEPT AND PROCESS OF GLOBALISATION

1.1.1 Meaning

Globalisation is a process through which different economies get inter-woven by way of international trade and investment. They become an integral part of the world economy.

Globalisation is a move towards open economic policies lifting up the restriction imposed on the international economic flows that in turn leads to a sharp increase in the quantum of such flows. The different economies, driven by international trade and investment and aided by information technology, turn this way closely inter-woven and become an indispensable part of the world economy. However, the literature on the subject interprets globalisation in three different ways (Held *et al*, 1999). First of all, the hyper-globalist school feels that globalisation leads to a single global economy transcending and integrating the different economic regions. Supported by technological sophistications and market integration, globalisation leads to denationalisation of strategic economic activities. In the sequel, the flow of global finance exercises a decisive influence on the location and distribution of economic power and wealth. The economy turns borderless. A particular economy has no option rather than to accommodate global market forces.

Secondly, the sceptical view, on the contrary, does not interpret globalisation in terms of emerging and unified international economic activity. It believes in inter-nationalisation where the increasing flow of economic resources takes place among well-defined national economies. In this case, national economic policies remain effective to influence the flow of economic resources.

Thirdly, there are transformationalists who interpret globalisation in terms of a process or a set of processes rather than an end-state. The process embodies a shift in the spatial organisation of social relations from national to transcontinental pattern of human organisation. The economic activities stretch out across frontiers, regions and continents. There is growing interconnectedness among different regions through flow of trade and investment. The flow of trade and investment is so intensive and extensive that the impact of local developments spills over to remotest corners of the globe. In other words, the boundary between the domestic and global affairs turns blurred. The international organisations support and regulate such activities. The transformationalists go on arguing that the very scale of human social organisation extends the reach of power nations across the world's major regions.

Whatever might be the interpretation, the process of globalisation has many dimensions. It has multiple causes and multiple results. There are benefits of globalisation. But it is also true that this process leads sometimes to lack of homogenisation across countries because global economic transactions are influenced by disparity in the economic and political conditions in different countries. However, the divergence is corrected through the process of globalisation depending on the nature of this process.

1.1.2 Evidence

If globalisation fosters close linkages among countries through the flow of goods, labour and capital, it is worth discussing whether it does exist in the real world. In fact, the move towards globalisation was afoot a couple of centuries ago when the European countries, following Industrial Revolution, began exporting their manufactured products and in turn importing necessary raw material. Subsequently, they made foreign investment to ensure continued supply of raw material. As back as in 1870, the merchandise export/GDP ratio in the UK (at 1990 prices) was 12.2 per cent (Maddison, 2000). However, the growing trend towards globalisation was marked only after the Second World War, with the growth in the internationalisation of the US firms. The pace picked up subsequently with the growth of multinational firms in Europe, Japan, the newly industrialising countries and, of late, in the transition economies during 1990s. The foreign direct investment that was barely over $12 billion during 1950s rose to over $200 billion in 1990s and further to around $1.5 trillion during 2007. Similarly, the world trade recorded a jump from $60 billion to over $13.6 trillion during the same period. If one looks at these figures in relation to the gross world product (GWP), the international trade as percentage of GWP rose two-and-half times between 1960 and 2000. Similarly, the foreign direct investment (FDI) rose three-and-half times between 1980 and mid-2000s (Bourdeaux, 2008).

> The evidence of globalisation was found a couple of centuries ago. But it is only since 1950s, and especially in the recent decades that globalisation is distinctly visible.

The process got stimulus from the international institutions. The General Agreement on Tariff and Trade (GATT), established in 1947, created a consensus on axing the tariff and non-tariff barriers over the past five decades which in turn boosted up the world trade. The World Trade Organisation (WTO) substituting GATT implemented the Uruguay Round resolutions and covered many trade-related measures that had remained neglected earlier. Again, the role of the World Bank and the International Monetary Fund was no less significant. During early 1980s, they encouraged different governments to adopt structural adjustment and macro-economic reforms and provided financial assistance for this purpose. Such reforms provided a fillip, among other things, to foreign direct investment. Under the financial sector reforms, the capital market of different countries came to be closely knit, which in turn led to a large-scale flow of financial resources. The foreign portfolio investment, especially in the secondary capital market, which was meagre four or five decades earlier, has turned huge at present. However, the study of Sutcliffe and Glyn (2003) discounts the evidence at least to some extent. In their view, the figures stand exaggerated on account of inappropriate statistical measures and unreliable observations and due to exclusion of counter-globalisation tendencies.

1.1.3 The Impact

The impact of globalisation has been positive as far as rate of economic growth is concerned.

With the process of globalisation picking up the pace and with phenomenal growth in external trade and foreign direct and portfolio investment, there is a marked profound, positive impact on economic growth, labour markets and incomes and the macro and micro-economic policies which the different governments are pursuing. There is a clear indication that this process has weakened the independence of the national economic policies of various governments (Perraton, 2003). Dollar and Kraay (2002) believe that it has reduced poverty. Again, when the markets are highly integrated, the resources are allocated optimally among different markets. The gains accruing in one market are shared by other markets.

Mosley (2000), on the other hand, finds a weak linkage between globalisation and economic growth. Environmental degradation persists. The national governments still holds the key power. The economic chaos and upheavals arising in a country spill easily over to other markets. The US sub-prime crisis is a case in point that engulfed gradually a number of countries. The failure of market forces and inequalities require some kind of governance of the global market so that evils are controlled and the gains from globalisation can be maximised (Stglitz, 2002).

Whatever might be the argument for and against globalisation, some of the figures and analyses suggest the positive impact of globalisation. Gwartney and Lawson (2001) find that in the countries with closed trade policy, the per capita annual income was 13 per cent lower than in the countries opting for an open trade policy. Again, Sachs and Warner (1995) covered in their study 117 countries with both open and closed trade policies and found that in open industrialised countries, the rate of GDP growth was 2.29 per cent compared to 0.74 per cent in closed industrialised world. Similarly, in open developing countries, it was 4.49 per cent compared to 0.69 per cent in closed developing countries. The higher growth rate following globalisation did have a positive impact on other economic and socio-economic variables, such as living standard, life expectancy, low child mortality rate, improved working hours and many other comforts of life (Bourdeaux, 2008).

At the micro level, globalisation has been a boon for the companies. There are thousands of firms that operate, in the first phase, for a small locality or region. They move in due course of time to the national map. If their operations prove successful, they move to one or more countries and finally, they reign over the entire globe. Let us explain here a single example. Proctor and Gamble (P&G) started its operations in 1837 and supplied its products only within a narrow area, known as Cincinnati. By the close of the 19th century, when the rail and road network developed throughout the USA, it produced goods for the entire country. After the Great War of 1914–1918, it consolidated its position through a number of acquisitions and by 1930, it began catering to the overseas demand. After the Second World War and more especially, after 1960, P&G has been operating throughout the world along with its rivals, viz. Colgate-Palmolive, Henkel, Unilever and others. This is not the only case. Such cases are in thousands.

1.2 MEANING AND IMPORTANCE OF INTERNATIONAL BUSINESS

International business means carrying on business activities beyond national boundaries. These activities normally include the transaction of economic resources such as goods, capital, services (comprising technology, skilled labour, and transportation, etc.), and international production. Production may either involve production of physical goods or provision of services like banking, finance, insurance, construction, trading, and so on. Thus, international business includes not only international trade of goods and services but also foreign investment, especially foreign direct investment.

International business means carrying business activities beyond national boundaries. It normally includes the transactions of economic resources such as goods, capital, services (comprising technology, skilled labour, transportation etc.) and international production. Production may either involve production of physical goods or provision of services like banking, finance, insurance, construction, trading and so on.

International business has been playing a crucial role for centuries. In the present-day world, it has become indispensable. Its role has increased significantly, both at the macroeconomic and microeconomic levels. No country—developed, or developing—produces all commodities to meet its requirements. It needs to import items that are not produced domestically. At the same time, it tries to export all items that are produced over and above its domestic requirements, so that its balance of payments may not worsen in the wake of imports. In a developing economy, the range of production is often limited, with the result that import requirements are bigger. On the other hand, such an economy tries to expand its exports in order to earn foreign exchange that could, in turn, meet its import requirements.

Foreign Direct Investment (FDI), which has gained importance in the recent past, is made for a variety of purposes. Acquiring of natural resources, recovery of large expenditure made on research and development, capturing a larger segment of the international market, and earning large profits are some of its important motives. In the case of a developing country with weak balance of payments position, foreign direct investment is very crucial. It helps obtain large foreign exchange resources and latest technology, and also develops managerial capabilities required for economic development programmes. In other words, foreign direct investment is essential as it bridges the resource gap. Thus, whether it is international trade or investment, it is an integral part of a country's economic behaviour.

Corporate wealth is the value of productive assets plus the present value of wealth created by those assets. Alternatively, it is the sum of the value of debt and equity in a firm.

At the microeconomic level, from the viewpoint of maximising corporate wealth, it is in the interest of a firm to export its product to foreign markets and to capture a large share of the markets abroad, especially when the domestic market is saturated. On the other hand, in order to minimise the cost and thereby, maintain a competitive edge, a firm likes to import inputs from least-cost locations. In offshore assembly operations, components involving capital-intensive mode of production are manufactured in a capital abundant economy and exported to a labour abundant economy for their assembly so that the firm can make use of cheap labour. The assembled product is again shipped to the home country and to other markets.

When the demand for a firm's product matures in foreign markets, it is in the interest of the firm to start production in those markets so that the transportation cost and tariffs can be avoided. Manufacturing in a foreign location involves not only investment of capital but also the transfer of technology. The transfer of technology helps improve the firm's competitiveness in markets abroad and at the same time is able to recover the huge cost incurred on research and development. Firms receiving capital and technology are also able to improve their competitiveness.

1.3 DOMESTIC BUSINESS VERSUS INTERNATIONAL BUSINESS

International business differs from domestic business in that the former involves across-the-country transactions or across-the-country production or provision of services, whereas, in the case of domestic business such activities are limited to the length and breadth of the country.

Again, there are many complexities in international business that are not found in case of domestic business. First of all, transactions in international business are mostly intra-firm. Final goods, intermediate goods, and raw material flow between the parent company and the subsidiary, or among different subsidiaries of the same firm. What is unique in such cases is that transactions often involve transfer pricing. This is meant primarily to reduce the overall tax and tariff burden and thereby, maximise the global profit of the firm. But sometimes its purpose is to make necessary adjustments in the cash requirements of different units. This means that the price of the intra-firm export and import is often different from the arm's length prices. The designing of prices is a complex task.

> Transfer pricing is arbitrary pricing of intra-firm transactions at more/less than the arm's-length prices.

International business is different from domestic business. In international business:

- Intra-firm transactions using transfer pricing are common.
- Varying environment—political, legal, economic, socio-cultural and ethical—in host countries, is often not known to the firm.
- Presence of political risk and also of exchange rate risk, sometimes leading to financial risk is marked.
- Varying strategies of business are adopted in different host countries.

Secondly, international business transactions are carried out in unfamiliar conditions prevailing in the host countries. The political and legal environment in the host country may be different, manifesting in different sets of policies, rules, and regulations. The economic environment may be different, manifesting in different levels of income, lifestyle and consumption patterns. For example, a host country having foreign exchange constraints may be adopting exchange control regulations, the financial market in the host country may not be developed, and the social and cultural set-up may be dissimilar, and the social behaviour, language, and the very attitude towards consumption and production may be different in the host countries. Firms involved in international business have to take care of all these factors and chalk out the strategy accordingly. This is not an easy task. It is highly complex when the home country environment differs significantly from the host country environment. The degree of complexity increases if the firm operates simultaneously in many host countries, that is, in multi-environment conditions. Even if the strategy suits the environment of one host country, it may not necessarily suit the other.

If the strategy of the company is not in conformity with the political, social, or economic environment of a particular host country, conflicts arise between the company and the host government. In practice, it is found that the company tries to impose its own business ethics on the host country environment. In some cases it succeeds but in many cases this practice creates problems. For example, firms in USA do not employ child labour. If they operate in India or in some other developing countries, where the social environment is different and where child labour is commonly used, this policy leads to adjustment problems. McDonalds sells beef hamburger in many countries. However, in India beef burgers are not socially acceptable. Again, in many developing countries where tight exchange control measures exist, foreign companies adopt different ways to effect transfer of funds. The host government does not appreciate this and comes into conflict with the company. Thus, there are many occasions on which conflict arises, and conflict management is not an easy task.

Thirdly, international business is prone to various kinds of risks. Political risk is one of them. Nationalisation of foreign firms without providing adequate compensation is common in international business. If the host country government prefers state-run enterprises, the chances for nationalisation are more.

Besides the political risk, international transactions—export and import, borrowing and lending, and other forms of receipts and payments—are subject to exchange rate risk. In a floating rate regime, where market forces determine the exchange rate, changes in the exchange rate are common. Such changes cause losses or gains that in turn lead to fluctuations in profit and give rise to financial risk. Firms involved in international business need to be alert to these risks.

Fourthly, the management function in international business regarding finance and accounting, personnel, marketing, and production differs from that in domestic business. An international firm takes various financial decisions in terms of both domestic currency and host country currency and is more concerned with the hedging of exchange rate risk.

It implements an international accounting system and emphasises on the consolidation of accounts of the various units. The marketing strategy in international firms aims at raising the firm's share in the international market. To this end, the branding strategy, the advertising strategy, the strategy of market segmentation, and so on are quite different. As regards personnel management, it takes into account the utilisation of expatriates. It selects, motivates and rewards the personnel for foreign assignments. Again, as regards product planning, the international firm is more adaptive to differences in technical requirements, consumer preferences, available production skills, sourcing of raw material, and so on. These different decisions make international business really complex.

1.4 MULTINATIONAL CORPORATION

An MNC is an enterprise with a substantial part of its operations in a number of foreign countries.

It is a fact that there are millions of exporting and importing firms that are engaged in international trade. Again, there are numerous firms that make foreign direct investment. But it is the multinational corporations (MNCs) that are responsible for a very large segment of international trade—intra-firm as well as inter-firm—and the largest part of foreign direct investment. Foreign direct investment and MNCs have become synonymous. In view of the significant contribution of the MNCs in international business, it is essential to acquaint the readers with some of their important features.

An MNC is sometimes known as transnational corporation or as supranational corporation. There is no single definition that is widely acceptable. Nevertheless, an MNC is an enterprise that owns or controls production or service facilities outside the country in which it is based (United Nations, 1973). Since there are several small firms that possess these features, it is often said that for qualifying as an MNC, the number of countries where the firm operates must be at least six (Vernon, 1971; United Nations, 1978). At the same time, the firm must generate a sizeable proportion of its revenue from the foreign operation, although no exact percentage is agreed upon. All this means that the firm should be big enough to have its stronghold in many countries through branches and subsidiaries. Looking at the 100 largest multinationals of the world, it is evident that 57.5 per cent of total sales, 48.1 per cent of total assets, and 49.1 per cent of total employment of these companies during 2002 was foreign (United Nations, 2004).

- Deutsche Post AG of Germany is operating in as many as 111 countries.
- The total assets of General Electric of the United States in 2006 amounted to US $697 billion that was greater than the gross domestic product of as many as 164 countries in the world.

Source: Based on: 1. UNCTAD, *World Investment Report*: 2008
2. World Bank, *World Development Indicators*: 2008.

According to Vernon and Wells Jr. (1986), MNCs represent a cluster of affiliated firms located in different countries that:

1. are linked through common ownership
2. draw upon a common pool of resources
3. respond to a common strategy.

All this shows a high degree of integration among different units of the firm.

Based on the strategic features, MNCs are grouped as ethnocentric, polycentric, and geocentric (Perlmutter, 1969; Perlmutter and Heenan, 1974). Ethnocentric firms are those that adopt home market oriented policy and seldom distinguish between domestic operation and global operation policies. On the other extreme, polycentric firms operate in foreign countries just to cater to the demand in those countries. This means that they follow a host market oriented policy. Between the two extremes, geocentric firms maintain a balance between the home market and host market oriented policies. They are in fact closer to real situations. It is this behavioural distinction that influences Punnett and Ricks (1997) to differentiate between a multi-domestic company and a global company. The former is concerned more with the market of the host country where it operates. The latter is concerned with the global market. It finds the world as a single market and plans to cater it through integrated operations.

Again, basing on the behavioural features of MNCs, Bartlett and Ghoshal (1989) differentiate between a multinational company and a transnational company. In the former, decision making is normally decentralised and the activities of the firm in foreign countries are not tightly co-ordinated. In the latter, on the contrary, global business activities of the firm are perfectly configured, coordinated and controlled to achieve global competitiveness. However, in the present text, these different terms are used interchangeably.

Ethnocentric firms are those that adopt home market oriented policy and seldom distinguish between domestic operation and global operation policies. Polycentric firms follow a host market oriented policy. Between the two extremes, geocentric firms maintain a balance between the home market and host market oriented policies.

A **multi-domestic** company is more concerned with the market of the host country where it operates. While a **global company** is concerned with the global market. It considers the world as a single market.

In a **multinational** company, decision making is normally decentralised. While business activities of a **transnational** firm are perfectly configured, coordinated and controlled.

1.5 EVOLUTION AND DEVELOPMENT OF INTERNATIONAL BUSINESS

1.5.1 Process of Evolution

MNCs do not emerge overnight. Domestic firms, after expanding their operation and going through various stages of the evolution process, qualify for being called an MNC. The process of evolution takes place in three successive stages. They are:

1. Trade
2. Assembly or production
3. Integration

Some firms are able to innovate products for which demand gradually develops in foreign markets, leading to export orders. Here begins the first stage of evolution. Initially, the exporting firm takes the help of

The process of evolution of a domestic firm into an MNC involves three successive stages:

1. Trade
2. Assembly or production
3. Integration

some middlemen. But after export becomes a regular phenomenon, an export department is created to substitute middlemen. With growing trade, the firm sets up a branch in importing countries, which gradually evolves into a subsidiary. The subsidiary operates as a marketing aide that helps penetrate the foreign market and collect information regarding the changing tastes of consumers. The two-way traffic gradually becomes easier.

The firm is not satisfied with export alone. It intends to reach the consumers at the lowest possible cost, probably to compete with other suppliers. It may be noted here that the technology involved in the product does not remain the monopoly of the firm in due course of time. Reaching consumers at the least cost is marred by the imposition of tariff and transportation cost. So, the firm decides to assemble the final product in the importing country itself so as to avoid tariff and the transportation cost. In some cases, the firm starts manufacturing of the product in the importing country if necessary facilities are available there. The second phase of the evolutionary process starts here.

Lastly, the firm tries to integrate the activities of its different units. Intra-firm transfer of funds or material takes place in order to maintain an optimal trade-off between liquidity and profitability in the various units located in different countries. It is also undertaken for maximising the global profit. Sometimes, depending upon the cost and the facilities available, various stages of production and assembly of the same product are carried out in different countries. Integration is required in this case too for strengthening and optimising the vertical linkages. The implementation of financial, marketing, production, and personnel strategies too requires foolproof integration among different units. In this way, the third stage of the evolution process is completed and a perfect MNC appears to exist, although internationalisation of business sets in with the beginning of export business.

1.5.2 Early Developments

International trade is many centuries old. In the 16th and the 17th centuries, international trade was carried out by individuals seeking fortunes for themselves. The reward was often great, but the risk of the voyage was also very high. Exotic goods that were traded normally were those that were sold at home at soaring prices. It was the fabulous profits that motivated some firms to operate abroad. The East India Company was among the foreign trading companies that moved to India in the early decades of the 17th century.

> In the wake of Industrial Revolution in Europe, the character of international business changed. International enterprises came to be engaged in extracting, processing, and transporting raw material for industrial plants located in the home country and also in exporting their manufactured goods back to the raw material producing countries.

However, in the wake of Industrial Revolution in Europe, the character of international business changed. International enterprises came to be engaged in extracting, processing, and transporting raw materials for industrial plants located in the home country and also in exporting their manufactured goods back to the raw material producing countries.

In short, their activities were guided by the requirements of the home country industries. During the last quarter of the 19th century through the outbreak of the First World War, the British and other European and American companies operating abroad reached the peak of their trading activities.

After the Great War of 1914–18, the functions of international companies widened. They also came to be engaged in various services that the government of host countries was not able to render efficiently. This was the reason why host governments provided western companies many concessions.

1.5.3 Post-War Developments

By the mid-1940s, the economy of the US turned out to be the strongest. American industries were well developed and needed to acquire new sources of raw material. Moreover, they wanted to capture the largest share of the world market. All this led to rapid internationalisation of US firms since 1950s. During the two decades beginning from 1950, US foreign direct investment grew from $12 billion to $80 billion (Wilkins, 1970).

Since 1960s, many European firms too turned into multinationals, and since 1970s, there was substantial growth in Japanese MNCs. In 1970 only one Japanese MNC was listed among the world's largest 50 companies. By the end of the decade, the number rose to six. By 1980s, the Japanese became the largest producers of automobiles—a position that was enjoyed by the USA until then.

Since 1970s, the firms of developing countries too began operating internationally. There were two sets of developing countries. One was represented by oil exporting countries that had acquired huge foreign exchange reserves in the wake of the oil crisis of the 1970s. The other group was represented by newly industrialising countries that had imported technology from the developed countries and built up their own industrial base. Firms from both types of the developing countries established their affiliates abroad in a big way.

> The US multinationals made a head-way in 1950s, the European ones in 1960s and the Japanese ones in 1970s. The MNCs of developing world appeared in 1970s and those from transition economies made a start in 1990s.

And, of late, multinational firms have come to emerge also among the East European Countries. Although their size is not big, they are expected to grow fast in view of their resource base and also in view of growing opportunities in the 25-member European Union.

If one is to name some of the most prominent MNCs of the Eastern Europe, they are as follows.

1. Primorsk Shipping Corporation of Russian Federation engaged in transportation
2. Zalakeramia Rt. of Hungary engaged in manufacturing of clay product
3. Pliva d.d. of Croatia engaged in pharmaceuticals
4. Novoship Co. of Russian Federation engaged in transportation
5. Policolor S.A. of Romania producing chemicals

On probing the growth of international business during the past five decades or so, its evident that prior to the 1960s, the dominant organisational pattern of international companies was distinctive in the sense that the affiliates were self-contained as far as possible and they were barely small clones of the mother company scattered around the world. It is only since the 1960s that the organisational structure came to be more centralised in the hands of the parent company and this ushered a fast growth in the activities of international companies. But the growing control of the parent company was not relished by the host country governments as it often clashed with their interests. Host country governments began playing a decisive role in the decision making of international firms. They framed various rules and regulations for the conduct of international companies. With the lapse of time, the interest of the various groups became more complex and international business came to be fraught with growing complexities (Robinson, 1981).

1.5.4 Recent Trends

The past couple of decades have witnessed significant growth in international business. It is a fact that international business was greatly constrained by the oil shock and the restrictive policies pursued by many developing countries during the 1970s, but it was resumed by the mid-1980s and it grew in the subsequent period. Statistics show that between 1983 and 1990, FDI outflow grew at an average annual rate of 27 per cent, which was almost four-fold greater than the growth of world output and around three-fold greater than the growth of world exports. During 1990, the amount of FDI outflow stood at US $245 billion, over two-thirds of which were accounted for by only five countries, namely, the United States of America, the United Kingdom, Japan, Germany, and France. There were 170,000 foreign affiliates of over 37,000 parent companies. The worldwide sales of these affiliates were approximately US $5.5 trillion, which was greater than the world export of goods and non-factor services (United Nations, 1993). The fast growth in FDI outflows during the 1980s could be attributed to a host of factors. (1) The growing internationalisation of the Japanese economy resulted in the large explosion of FDI from this country; (2) The phenomenal growth in the demand for services in the wake of growth in per capita real income. Since many services were not tradable, FDI was the only way to participate in foreign markets. (3) This period witnessed more effective moves towards regional integration, as a result of which both intra-bloc and inter-bloc FDI increased.

Table 1.1 shows more recent trends. FDI outflow grew from US $245 billion in 1990 to US $1,150 billion in 2000. However, during 2000, there were ups and downs in the size of the flow. In 2005, it was US $779 billion which increased to US $1,858 billion during 2008. The annual growth rate ascended from 15.7% during 1991–1995 to 35.7% during 1996–2000 but was negative by 5.1% during 2001–2005. In 2006–2007, the outflow increased by around 50% but again in 2008, due to

Table 1.1 Growth in FDI: 1990–2008

	Value at Current Prices (US $ billion)						*Annual Growth Rate (%)*					
Item	*1990*	*2000*	*2005*	*2006*	*2007*	*2008*	*1991–1695*	*1996–2000*	*2001–2005*	*2006*	*2007*	*2008*
FDI inflows	209	1271	916	1411	1833	1697	20.0	40.2	−4.0	47.2	29.9	−14.2
FDI outflows	245	1150	779	1323	1997	1858	15.7			50.2	50.9	−13.5
FDI outward stock	1716	5976	10672	12756	15602	16206	10.7	16.8	10.1	20.4	22.3	−0.1
Cross-border M&As	151	1144	716	1118	1637	673	23.3	51.5	2.2	20.3	46.4	−34.7
Sale of foreign affiliates	5503	15680	22171	25844	31197	30311	10.4	10.9	13.6	22.2	20.7	−4.6
Assets of foreign affiliates	5706	21102	45564	55818	68716	69771	13.7	19.2	15.8	18.6	23.1	−5.0
Employment in foreign affiliates (million)	23.6	45.6	62.0	70	82	77	5.0	14.2	6.5	21.6	16.6	−3.7

Source: Compiled on the basis of figures available from various issues of *World Investment Report.*

international financial crisis, the growth rate in FDI outflow was negative by 13.5%. The FDI outward stock rose from US $1,716 billion in 1990 to US $5,976 billion at the end of 2000 and to US $10,672 billion by 2005 and US $16,206 billion by 2008. The amount of world FDI inflows grew from US $209 billion in 1990 to US $1,271 billion in 2000. During 2000s, the size moved up and down. In 2005, it was US $916 billion which increased to US $1,697 billion during 2008. The total assets of foreign affiliates rose from US $5,706 billion in 1990 to US $21,202 billion by 2000 and to US $45,680 billion by 2005 finally settling to US $69,771 billion at the end of 2008. The sales surged up from US $5,503 billion to US $15,680 billion increasing to US $22,171 billion and US $30,311 billion during the same period. The employment in foreign affiliates increased from 23.6 million to 45.6 million and to US $62 million and US $77 million respectively during this period.

Merger and Acquisition is the combination of two running firms.

What is remarkable is that the mergers and acquisitions (M&As) formed a large part of the FDI outflow. In 1990s, the FDI through cross-border M&As had amounted to US $151 billion which rose to US $1,144 billion.in 2000 but fell to US $716 billion in 2005. During 2008, it was of the order of US $1,205 billion. If one looks at the annual growth rate, it rose from 23.3 per cent in 1991–1995 to 51.5 per cent in 1996–2000 but fell to 2.2 per cent during 2001–2005. In 2006 and 2007, the cross border M&As grew by 20 per cent and 46 per cent, respectively, but in 2008, it was negative at 35 per cent. A deeper probe reveals that the acquisitions were more common.

The other remarkable feature is that owing to the growth of FDI flow in general and the emergence of MNCs in developing as well as in transition countries in a big way, the share of these countries in FDI flow has increased. The figures in Table 1.2/Figure 1.1 show that the share of the developing countries in global FDI inflow moved up and down but remained lower than those for developed countries. The transition economies however, increased their share in global FDI inflow from around 2 per cent in 2000 to around 6 per cent in 2008.

Along with rapid internationalisation of firms, world trade, both intra-firm and inter-firm, grew manifold. The reduction of tariff and non-tariff barriers under the aegis of GATT and now under the WTO umbrella too gave a fillip to international trade. During two and a half decades

Table 1.2 FDI Inflows in Different Groups of Countries US $ Bill.

	1980	*1985*	*1990*	*1995*	*2000*	*2005*	*2006*	*2007*	*2008*
Developed Countries	58	57	162	208	1228	611	973	1359	962
Developing Countries		19	40	106	238	317	434	529	621
Transition Countries				14	26	31	55	91	114

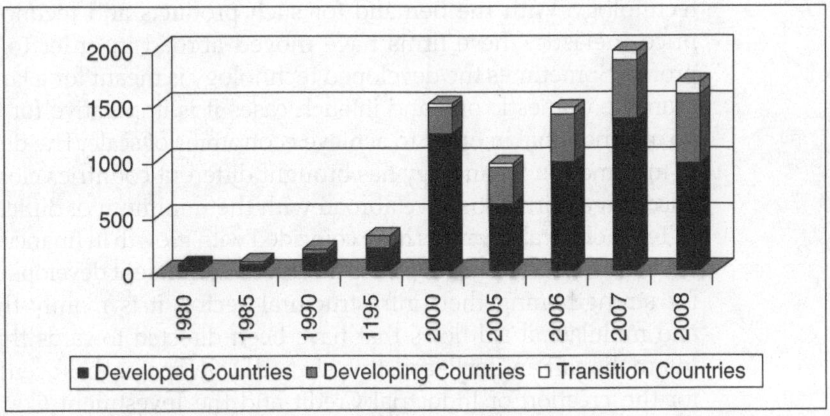

Source: Based on the figures obtained from UNCTAD Database

FIGURE 1.1 FDI Inflows in Different Groups of Countries (US $ Bill.)

beginning from 1980, the value of world trade increased almost five-fold—from US $2,031 billion in 1980 to US $3,486 billion in 1990, to US $6,327 billion in 2000 and to US $10.2 trillion in 2005. The world trade in 2008 was as high as $15.8 trillion. MNCs have a big role in the increasing volume of trade (WTO, 2009). However, in recent decades, the small and medium-sized multinatinals or the so-called mini-multinationals that have come to possess globalising efficiency almost at par with the big organisation, do account for sizeable world trade (UNCTAD, 1993). Again, there has not been any noticeable change in the share of the developed market economies in the world trade. Their share continued to remain at 64 per cent (UNCTAD, 2005). Thus, international business has witnessed a phenomenal growth in the recent past.

Mini-MNCs have large-scale overseas linkages despite their smaller size.

1.6 FACTORS LEADING TO GROWTH IN INTERNATIONAL BUSINESS IN RECENT DECADES

It is a fact that the desire to expand sales and revenue, to acquire inputs at the least cost, and to minimise business and financial risk through geographic diversification has led to the growth of MNCs; yet there are some other factors too that provided them a congenial atmosphere to expand their activities at a very fast rate. These factors are:

1. Rapid technological advancement
2. Emergence of supportive institutions
3. Openness of economic policies among large number of countries
4. Break-up of the former USSR
5. Increase in competition

The past few decades have witnessed rapid advancement in product and process technology and in information technology. Many firms have emerged up with innovated products or with improved process technology. With the demand for such products and technology being price-inelastic, these firms have moved abroad in order to reap large profits. Sometimes the developed technology is meant for a larger market than the domestic one and in such cases it is imperative for the firm to go international in order to achieve economies of scale. The development of information technology has brought different countries closer and has encouraged firms to move abroad with the minimum of difficulties.

Technological advances have coincided with growth in financial and other infra-structural facilities. Besides the efforts of different developing countries for strengthening their infrastructural sector, it is mainly the bilateral and multilateral aid flows that have been directed towards this end. The International Bank for Reconstruction and Development has been responsible for the creation of Industrial Credit and the Investment Corporation of India and similar financial institutions in many other developing countries. Similarly, one of the primary objectives of the American aid programme has been to build up necessary infrastructure in developing countries so that American business could flourish in these countries. Whatever might be the reasons, developing countries have witnessed fast growth in their infrastructure, which has paved the way for international business.

Structural adjustment refers to macroeconomic policy reforms with an emphasis on liberalisation and globalisation.

The other factor responsible for the growth of international business, especially since 1980s, has been the structural adjustment and macroeconomic reforms in many developing countries. Many countries were facing huge trade deficit and severe external debt problems. In such cases, they have gone for economic adjustments or reforms, in turn improving their export sector and substituting external loans with foreign investment. The natural consequence is the growing volume of international business.

After the break-up of the former Soviet Union, there emerged a number of independent economies. They pursued a market-oriented economic policy substituting their closed economic and centrally planned economic policy. It was an outward-looking trade and investment policy. As a result, they added to the growing volume of international business.

Last but not least, it is the growing competition that has led to the growth of international business in the past few decades. With increasing competition, firms have preferred not only to source raw material and intermediate goods from the least-cost country but also to set up their units in different countries, which minimises the cost of operation and reduces financial risk. The growing concept of cost minimisation and risk reduction, with a view to surviving in a competitive environment, has thus led to rapid growth of the internationalisation process.

1.7 STRUCTURE OF BOOK

In view of the growing size and complexity of international business, the subject has now become an independent branch of study. This book deals with the various aspects of the subject and analyses the complex issues related to this branch of study.

The discussion is divided into three parts. The first part deals with the basic conceptual framework that forms a background for the discussions in the remaining two parts. To be precise, it delineates the process of globalisation and in this context the broad features of international business and its development, especially over past few decades; discusses different modes of international business and their comparative merits and demerits; presents the theoretical framework of international trade and foreign direct investment; and analyses the different aspects of balance of payments, which serves as a mirror showing the ultimate impact of international business on the economy as a whole.

> The discussion is divided into three parts. The first part deals with the basic conceptual framework that forms a background for the discussions in the remaining two parts.

It has already been mentioned that international business is different from domestic business insofar as it is normally carried on in an unfamiliar environment. It is thus rather imperative to acquaint the readers with the various types of environment in which international business is carried on. They are the regulatory environment dealing with the trade and FDI regulations at the national level as well as at the international level and the economic integration schemes in different parts of the globe. There are also the political, legal, economic, socio-cultural and ethical environment that differ from one country to the other, in turn, influencing the international business. Besides, the international financial environment is also important, as trade and investment involve different currencies and also funds that are borrowed and lent in different currencies and in different segments of the international financial market. Thus, the second part of the book deals essentially with the various types of environment influencing international business.

> The second part of the book deals essentially with the various types of environment influencing International Business

A study of international business is not limited to the study of the heterogeneous environment influencing it. Framing and implementing of strategies in order to fulfil the basic objective of maximising corporate wealth is also very significant. Although this aspect is significant for both domestic and international firms, it is more crucial for international business, in view of the far greater complexity in the case of the latter. The third part of the book, therefore, embraces the various strategies that an international firm adopts or should adopt. The discussion of strategies begins with the very distinctive organisational structure, planning, and control, and moves ahead covering the vital issues of technology and production, marketing, and human resource management. The financial strategy is no less important in this area of business. So the discussion regarding strategy also embraces financial strategy. In the end, the discussion is devoted to doing business in different sets of countries as the politico-economic and other conditions differ among them. The situations are different between an industrialised country and a less developed country. They are different in the European Union from those in industrialised countries in general. Again, the situations are different in transition economies. International business strategy needs at least some modifications for these different sets of the host countries. The study will be concluded with a discussion of international business strategy for heterogeneous groups of countries.

> The third part of the book embraces the various strategies that an international firm adopts or should adopt.

SUMMARY

- Globalisation is a process through which different economies comes closer to one another by way of trade and investment. There is clear-cut evidence of globalisation in so far as there is a phenomenal growth in international trade and investment in recent decades. This process has led ultimately to a higher economic growth rate.
- International business includes international transaction of economic resources, international production of goods, and provision of services. The broad forms of internationalisation of business are, therefore, trade, technical collaboration, and investment.
- International business is different from domestic business. Domestic business is limited to national frontiers, while international business spreads beyond them. International business involves many complexities that are related to intra-firm transactions and to unfamiliar host-country environment—regulatory, economic, and financial, political and legal, socio-cultural, ethical, and many others. Moreover, the very management function in international business differs from those in domestic business. These differences are visible mainly in the area of accounting and finance, personnel, marketing, and production.
- The most significant participant in international business is the MNC. It operates simultaneously in many countries. Its different units are linked through common ownership and they respond to a common strategy, although the degree of integration varies from case to case.
- International business did not emerge overnight, and has in fact, developed over several centuries. The earliest phase was manifested in trade. Then followed international production. The element of integration is the latest addition. Centuries ago, international business manifested itself in the trade of exotic goods. In the wake of the Industrial Revolution in England and other European countries, international production made a beginning but it was limited mainly to exploration of minerals and production of primary commodities. The purpose was to provide the Empire with necessary inputs and to find market abroad for the goods produced at home. However, it is only during the past three to four decades that MNCs have registered phenomenal growth. International trade too has expanded fast. The reasons for this are mainly rapid growth in technology, supportive institutions, openness of the different economies, and increased competition.

REVIEW QUESTIONS

1. What do you mean by international business? Is it true that international business has to face greater complexities than domestic business?
2. Discuss the process of evolution of international business.
3. Distinguish between ethnocentric, polycentric, and geocentric multinational firms.
4. Elaborate on the factors contributing to rapid growth in international business during the past four decades.
5. What do you mean by globalisation? Is this process working now?

OBJECTIVE TYPE QUESTIONS

1. Mark True or False:
   (a) International business includes international production.
   (b) Foreign direct investment is one of the forms of international business.
   (c) Most transactions in international business are intra-firm.
   (d) Transfer pricing is the same as the arm's length pricing.
   (e) International business carries no exchange rate risk.
   (f) Multinational corporations are the most important vehicle for international business.
   (g) A multinational company and a transnational company are both of the same nature.
   (h) A multi-domestic company and a global company are both different in nature.
   (i) Japanese MNCs began flourishing in the 1950s.
   (j) Some MNCs are headquartered in developing countries.

2. Choose the most suitable answer:
   (a) The successive stages in the process of evolution of international business are:
      (i) Integration, assembly, and trade
      (ii) Trade, assembly, and integration
      (iii) Assembly, integration, and trade
      (iv) None of these
   (b) International business is fraught with:
      (i) Only exchange rate risk and no other risk
      (ii) Both political and exchange rate risk
      (iii) Neither political risk nor exchange rate risk
      (iv) None of these
   (c) Ethnocentric firms are those that are:
      (i) Compatible with host country market oriented policy
      (ii) Compatible with home country market oriented policy
      (iii) Compatible with no specific orientation, either towards home country or towards host country market
      (iv) None of these
   (d) Polycentric firms are:
      (i) Compatible with host country market oriented policy
      (ii) Compatible with home country market oriented policy
      (iii) Compatible with no specific orientation, either towards home country or towards host country market
      (iv) None of these
   (e) Geocentric firms are:
      (i) Compatible with host country market oriented policy
      (ii) Compatible with home country market oriented policy
      (iii) Compatible with no specific orientation, either towards home country or towards host country market
      (iv) None of these
   (f) FDI outflow in 2003 amounted to:
      (i) US $1150 billion

(ii) US $500 billion
(iii) US $612 billion
(iv) None of these

(g) Mergers and acquisitions in total FDI outflow in 2003 accounted for:
(i) 20%
(ii) 48.5%
(iii) 10.5%
(iv) None of these

(h) Fast growth in international business in recent decades is attributed to:
(i) Technological advancement
(ii) Inward looking policy of host governments
(iii) Greater political risk in host countries
(iv) None of these

CASE STUDY

India's Overseas Investment

India's overseas investment dates back to 1970s. But since the policy was contained within the ambit of the then existing FERA, it was not very liberal and failed to give a big push to overseas investment. In fact, the objective was limited only to help raise exports through the Indian ventures overseas and to play a role in the South-South co-operation. At the end of 1991, there were only 245 ventures, of which 161 were in operation and 84 were under different stages of implementation. Total investment in the equity of foreign concerns stood at Rs. 1.209 billion or $49.4 million at the then existing exchange rate.

But then the policy turned liberal. In October 1992, procedural formalities were simplified. The ceiling for investment in form of cash was raised. Automatic approval system, of course with specific conditions, was introduced. Again, in 1995, the ceiling for investment in cash was raised further. A "fast-track" system for approval was introduced besides the "normal-track" system. The policy turned more liberal in the following years. All this yielded positive results.

At the end of September 1999, there were 831 active wholly-owned subsidiaries (WOSs) involving $1368 million of investment. It is revealed that 64 per cent of the ventures had moved only to four countries viz. USA, UK, Singapore and Mauritius. Again, around 90 per cent of the ventures were found in non-financial services alone. As regards the contribution of the WOS to the balance of payments, one finds that the cumulative amount of foreign exchange earnings on account of dividend, fees, and export stood at Rs. 14.907 billion.

Similarly, there were 912 active non-WOS ventures abroad involving an investment of $1150 million at the end of September 1999. The geographic/sectoral concentration was not high in this case. Top four countries, viz. USA, UK, UAE and Sri Lanka hosted only one-third of the Indian ventures. They were primarily in non-financial service sector. The cumulative flow of foreign exchange earnings in this case amounted to Rs. 17.351 billion up to September 1999.

During 2000s, fresh incentives were provided by the Government to encourage the overseas operation of the Indian firms. The Indian firms could use ADR/GDR proceeds or the external commercial borrowings to fund their overseas operations. The ceiling for investment during a particular financial year was raised from $50 million to $100 million. In case of Nepal and Bhutan and other South Asian countries, the limits were raised further. A special economic zone unit could open foreign branches and also a foreign currency account with a foreign bank. The RBI's approval could not remain mandatory for investment overseas by way of a share swap or for providing short-term credit to the subsidiaries abroad. The Government eased the investment in foreign financial sector through lifting up the provision of a Rs. 150 million net worth required earlier for the investor in such cases.

These policy incentives did work and the overseas investment stock rose to $16.395 billion by February 2006. It is true that this amount did not compare favourably with the overseas investment of a number of countries, such as Hong Kong, Taiwan, Singapore, China mainland, Brazil, Malaysia, Mexico and Korea. But there was definitely a fast growth in such investments.

As the figures reveal, 32 per cent of India's investment at the end of February 2006 was directed to the developed countries, mainly the European Union and the North America. The other 51 per cent was directed to the developing countries and the rest 17 per cent to the transition economies of the South East Europe and CIS. In fact, the modified technology and products by the Indian firms were more attractive among the developing world. Again, the investment was more pronounced in the manufacturing sector and the non-financial services sector. The former accounted for 58 per cent of the investment and the latter absorbed 36 per cent. The Indian firms relished greater participation in the overseas equity. In 70 per cent of the cases, the equity participation was 75 per cent and above.

The liberal policy of the Indian Government was definitely congenial for the country's investment abroad. The RBI doubled the remittances limit to US$2 million and permitted the Indian Companies to invest up to 400% of net worth in overseas joint-ventures. By the end of FY 2007–08, the amount of the overseas investment stock touched $17.4 billion and further to $23.07 billion by July 2008. At the end of FY 2007–08, the structure of overseas investment was equity-dominated as over 61 per cent of the investment was in equity form, 11 per cent in loan form and the rest 28 per cent in the form of guarantee. The automatic route was the commonest form of investment as it accounted for 99.6 per cent of the proposals and 96.4 per cent of the investment during FY 2007–08. The receipt of foreign exchange on account of dividend, royalty, etc. was as large as $916 million during this financial year. It is evient from the figures that India's investment stood highly concentrated among a few countries. At the end of FY 2007–08, Singapore accounted for 35 per cent, the Netherlands shared 23 per cent and British Virgin Islands received 7 per cent of the investment. This means around two-thirds of the investment were destined to only three countries. Besides, the sectoral concentration too was there. The manufacturing sector shared 43 per cent. In this sector, electronic equipment, fertilisers, agricultural and allied products, gems and jewellery were significant. The non-financial services sector, which was the next important sector, included mainly telecommunication and medical services, software development services and trading. To probe deeper, the Indian ventures moved in the area where highly sophisticated technology was not required. Again, in services, for example, computer software, India possesses competitive advantage and so there were large number of joint ventures and wholly-owned subsidiaries of Indian firms in this area. The international financial crisis did affect India's investment abroad. During the first nine months of FY 2008-2009. India's investment abroad dipped by 11.0 per cent over the corresponding period of FY 2007-2008.

Source: Based on: 1. *RBI Bulletin*, April 2009 and *RBI Bulletin*, July 2009

2. V. Sharan and I. N. Mukherji (2001), *India's External Sector Reforms*, New Delhi; Oxford University Press.

QUESTIONS

1. What has prompted Indian firms to operate abroad?
2. What are the broad areas showing liberalisation in policy towards overseas investment?
3. How have Indian firms helped improve the country's balance of payments?

REFERENCES

Books

Bartlett, C. A. and S. Ghoshal (1989), *Managing Across Borders: The Transnational Solution* (Boston: Harvard Business School Press).

Boudreaux, D. J. (2008), *Globalisation*, Westport (Greenwood Press).

Caselli, F. and J. Feyrer (2008), "The Marginal Product of Capital", *Quarterly Journal of Economics*, 122 (May), 535–68.

Dollar, D. and A. Kraay (2002), "Spreading the Wealth", *Foreign Affairs*, 81 (1), 120–33.

Gwartney, J. and R. Lawson (2001), *Economic Freedom of the World Annual Report 2001* (Vancouver: Fraser Institute).

Held, D.A. et al (1999), *Global Transformations: Politics, Economics and Culture* (Cambridge: Polity Press).

Maddison, A. (2000), *The World Economy: A Millennial Perspective* (Paris: OECD).

Mosley, P. (2000), "Globalisation, Economic Policy and Convergence", *World Economy*, 23, 613–34.

Perraton, J. (2003), "The Scope and Implications of Globalisation" in J. Michie (ed.), *The Handbook of Globalisation* (Northampton: Edward Elgar).

Punnett, B. J. and D. A. Ricks (1997), *International Business* (Oxford: Blackwell Business), Chap.1.

Sachs, J. and A. Warner (1995), "Economic Reform and the Process of Global Integration, *Brookings Papers on Economic Activity*, Vol. 1.

Stiglitz, J. (2002), *Globalisation and Its Discontents* (London: Penguin Press).

Sutcliffe, B. and A. Glyn (2003), "Measures of Globalisation and Their Misinterpretation" in J. Michie (ed.), *The Handbook of Globalisation* (Northampton: Edward Elgar).

UNCTAD (1993), *Small and Medium-sized Transnational Corporation: Executive Summary and Report of the Osaka Conference*, Geneva.

Vernon, R. (1971), *Sovereignty at Bay: The Multinational Spread of United States Enterprises* (New York: Basic Books).

_______ and L. T. Wells Jr, (1986), *Manager in the International Economy* (Englewood Cliffs: Prentice-Hall).

Wilkins, M. (1970), *The Emergence of Multinational Enterprise: American Business Abroad from the Colonial Era to 1914* (Cambridge Mass.: Harvard University Press).

Journals and Reports

Perlmutter, H. V. (1969), "The Tortuous Evolution of the Multinational Corporation", *Columbia Journal of World Business*, IV (Jan.–Feb.), 9–18.

_______ and D. A. Heenan (1974), "How Multinational Should Your Top Manager Be", *Harvard Business Review*, LII (Nov.–Dec.), 121–32.

Robinson, R. D. (1981), "Background Concepts and Philosophy of International Business from World War II to the Present", *Journal of International Business Studies*, XII (Spring-Summer), 13–21.

United Nations (1973), *Multinational Corporation in World Development*, New York, p. 23.

_______ (1978), *Transnational Corporations in World Development: A Re-examination*, New York, pp. 154–63.

UNCTAD (2001), *Handbook of Statistics*: 2001, New York and Geneva.

_______ (1998), *World Economic and Social Survey*, New York.

_______ (1999), *World Investment Report: Foreign Direct Investment and the Challenges of Development*, New York.

_______ (2001), *World Investment Report: Promoting Linkages*, New York.

_______ (2004), *World Investment Report*, New York.

_______ (2006), *Trade and Development Report: 2006*, New York.

WTO (2009), *Annual Report: 2008*, Geneva.

SELECT FURTHER READINGS

Ball, D. A. and W. H. McCulloch, Jr. (1982), *International Business* (Plano, Tex.: Business Publications).

McCarthy, D. M. P. (1994), *International Business History* (Westport, Conn.: Praeger).

---

* India Trade Promotion Organisation (ITPO), located at Pragati Maidan, is the nodal agency of the Government of India for promoting the country's external trade. ITPO, during its existence of nearly three decades, in the form of Trade Fair Authority of India and Trade Development Authority, has played a proactive role in catalysing trade, investment and technology transfer processes. Its promotional tools include organising of fairs and exhibitions in India (depicted in the picture is one such exhibition) and abroad, Buyer-Seller Meets, Contact Promotion Programmes, Product Promotion Programmes, Promotion through Overseas Department Stores and Market Surveys and Information Dissemination.
Photo by Ivan Lam

New York Stock Exchange, New York, USA*

2 Modes of International Business

CHAPTER OBJECTIVES

The present chapter discusses the various modes through which international business is operated. In particular, the chapter attempts to:

- ✦ Explain the factors influencing the choice of a particular mode of international business.
- ✦ Describe the features, merits, and demerits of direct and indirect trade as well as counter-trade.
- ✦ Evaluate various forms of contractual entry mode.
- ✦ Distinguish between foreign direct investment and foreign portfolio investment.
- ✦ Explain the nature and forms of mergers and acquisitions and the motivations behind such moves.
- ✦ Present a comparative picture of trade vis-à-vis FDI.
- ✦ Compare between FDI and contractual entry mode.
- ✦ Present a comparative analysis of green-field investment, and mergers and acquisitions.

The preceding chapter has already explained the nature of international business. Yet it could be better explained if one discusses, at some length, the different modes through which international business is carried on. Moreover, since huge amount of funds are involved in international business, the choice of a particular mode or modes is very significant for carrying on business across national borders. The present chapter acquaints the readers with these modes, such as international trade, contractual entry mode, and investment mode, and also with their relative suitability.

The choice of entry mode is also significant in view of the fact that different firms prefer different levels of involvement in international business. If a firm is in favour of least involvement, only trade may suffice the purpose. On the contrary, if a firm is in favour of maximum involvement in international business, the investment mode will be most suitable. But the question is whether the firm is capable of making investment. Even if it is capable of making investment, the host country environment may not be congenial for making investment. So a firm may go for different entry modes in different countries. The choice of entry mode takes a number of factors into account. Some of the more important factors need some explanation before beginning any discussion of the different modes.

2.1 DETERMINANTS OF ENTRY MODE

A firm adopts various modes for its entry into business transaction across borders. Which particular mode a firm should adopt depends, at least, upon four factors. They are:

1. Subservience of the corporate objective
2. Corporate capability
3. Host country environment
4. Perceived risk

> A firm adopts various modes for its entry into business transaction across borders. Which particular mode a firm should adopt depends, at least, upon four factors. They are:
> 1. Subservience of the corporate objective
> 2. Corporate capability
> 3. Host country environment
> 4. Perceived risk

When the objective of a firm spreading internationally is simply to earn profits and not necessarily to maintain control over the entire operation, only trading activities will serve its purpose. But if control is the primary objective, the investment mode, and especially investment in a wholly owned foreign subsidiary, will be the best course of action. Thus, a particular mode is selected in tune with the very objective of the firm behind international business.

> In a **wholly owned subsidiary** the entire equity capital is owned by the parent company.

The corporate objective shaping the entry mode must be supported by the company's capability to select the particular entry mode. For example, if the company' financial position is not strong enough to make large investment abroad, it will be difficult for the company to make such investment even if it is desirable on the grounds of fulfilling corporate objectives. Thus, the choice of the entry mode depends, to a considerable extent, on the capability of the company going international.

The host country environment too influences the entry mode. It includes many aspects, such as the regulatory environment; cultural environment; political and legal environment; economic environment, especially the size of the market and the production; the shipping cost, and so on (Root, 1987). When the managers of a firm are not well acquainted with the values, beliefs, customs, language, religion, and other aspects of the target market, the firm does not prefer to invest there. Rather, it limits its business only to trading activities in such cases. The company starts operation in the host country only when the managers are acquainted with the cultural environment in the host countries. Again, if the political conditions are not congenial in the target market or if the legal formalities are lengthy, large investment is often avoided. Sometimes, when the host government bans certain types of investment, foreign investors cannot make such investments even if they wish to make them. In India, in 1973, the government had fixed a ceiling on foreign equity participation. Foreign companies that did not favour the ceiling dismantled their operations in India (Sharan, 1992). Yet again, it is the size of the market in the host country that influences the entry mode of foreign firms. When the market is large and ever expanding, foreign firms prefer to enlarge their involvement through investment. But if the size of the market remains small, trade is the only suitable option. Last but not least, if the cost of production in the host economy is lower than in the home country, the host country attracts foreign investment. In fact, this is one of the important reasons that companies from the developed world have moved to developing countries. If the shipping cost is also low, it is possible that the firm may shift the entire production process to the low cost host country and may ship the output back to the home country for meeting the domestic demand. If, on the other hand, the host country does not represent cost effectiveness, trading remains the only way out.

Besides these factors, it is risk involved in the different modes of entry that influences the decision of a firm in this respect. Different modes involve varying degrees of risk. The lesser the amount of control in a particular mode, the lower the risk. If trading activities are ranked on the lowest rung of the ladder from the viewpoint of control, it carries the least risk. On the contrary, if investment in a wholly owned subsidiary possesses the largest element of control, it is supposed to be highly risky. Thus, the choice of the entry mode depends, among other things, upon the control-risk consideration of the firm.

In **direct export**, a company takes full responsibility for making its goods available in the target market by selling directly to the end-users.

Indirect export takes place when the exporting company sells its products to intermediaries, who in turn sell the same products to the end users in the target market.

2.2 TRADE MODE

2.2.1 Direct and Indirect Export

The trade mode presents the first step in international business. It includes export and import. Export may be either direct or indirect. In case of direct export, a company takes full responsibility for making its goods available in the target market by selling directly to the end users, normally through its own agents. Direct export is feasible when the exporter desires to involve itself greatly in international business; and at the same time possesses the capacity to do so. There are also some commodities where direct export is more convenient. They are, for example, air crafts and similar industrial products.

When an EMC functions as a distributor, it takes title to goods, sells them on its own account, and assumes the trading risk. Alternatively, when it acts as an agent, it charges a commission. Trading companies provide services to exporters, in addition to exporting activities.

When the exporting company does not possess the necessary infrastructure to involve itself in direct exporting, indirect export takes place. It takes place when the exporting company sells its products to intermediaries, who in turn sell the same products to the end-users in the target market.

It is a fact that the nature of intermediary differs in direct export or import from that in an indirect export and import. However, when one talks about intermediaries, export management companies (EMCs) and trading companies cannot be ignored. When an EMC functions as a distributor, it takes title to goods, sells them on its own account, and assumes the trading risk. Alternatively, when it acts as an agent, it charges a commission. Sometimes it acts as an agent for one client and as a distributor for the other. Trading companies, on the other hand, provide services to exporters, in addition to exporting activities, such as storage facilities, financing services, and so on. These companies originated in Europe but are now common in Japan and South Korea.

Apart from the intermediaries, there are trade facilitators. They are independent entities supplying information and knowledge to the exporter but definitely not participating in the transactions. They exist both in the public and private sectors. Various commodity boards and export promotion councils can be grouped as trade facilitators. There are also government organisations working under the Ministry of Commerce, such as trade development authority, that act as trade facilitator.

2.2.2 Counter-trade

Counter-trade is a sort of bilateral trade where one set of goods is exchanged for another set of goods.

Counter-trade is a sort of bilateral trade where one set of goods is exchanged for another set of goods. In this type of external trade, a seller provides a buyer with deliveries and contractually agrees to purchase goods from the buyer equal to the agreed percentage of the original sale contract value (US Department of Commerce, 1978). Counter-trade is classified broadly as:

1. Commercial counter-trade such as classical barter, counter-purchase and pre-compensation.
2. Industrial counter-trade such as buy-back agreements, develop for import arrangements, and framework agreements.

Commercial Counter-trade: Classical barter is one of the oldest modes of commercial counter-trade. It involves a once-only exchange of goods on the terms agreed upon between the buyer and the seller. The quantum, quality, and value of goods to be exchanged are well defined. Naturally, the trade flows in one direction are fully compensated by those in the reverse direction. There is no need for bridging finance. Negotiating parties are often governments. The exchange of Iranian oil for New Zealand's lamb or the exchange of Argentine wheat for Peruvian iron pillets are examples of classical barter (Banks, 1983).

In case of counter-purchase, which is also known as parallel barter, the contracts are often separate for import and export. The type and price of goods traded are generally not specified at the time of signing of the contract. The exporter of goods agrees to accept, in return, a wide range of goods from the importer. Balancing of the value of export and import is done every three to five years. If the two sides are not equal, the balance is paid in cash.

In case of pre-compensation, the value of exports is entered into an evidence account and imports are made on that basis. This means that payments for imports are not made immediately.

Industrial Counter-trade: Being a form of industrial counter-trade, buy-back agreements normally involve a larger amount corresponding to the sale of industrial equipment or turnkey plants in exchange for the products manufactured by these industrial plants. Naturally, the contract period is longer, varying from 10 to 20 years. The United Nations Economic Commission for Europe (1979) mentions the case of Austria selling pipeline equipment and related material to the then Soviet Union so that the latter could develop certain gas fields and could pipe a part of the output back to Austria. In case of developing countries, such agreements are common as they suffer from the technology gap on a large scale.

Develop-for-import arrangements are also a variant of the buy-back agreement where the exporter of the plant and machinery participates in the capital of the importing firm and, thereby, takes a share in the profits thereof. This means the involvement of the exporting firm is deeper than in a general buy-back arrangement. Japanese investment in an Australian firm developing gunpowder copper mine is an apposite example (Nameth, 1984).

Framework agreements are the long term protocol or bilateral clearing agreement normally concluded between governments. Trade is balanced after a long period as mentioned in the agreement. If the trade is not equal in value, the debtor sells the agreed upon commodity in the international market and the creditor is paid off. For example, Mexico sold cocoa to the United States of America to pay for its excess import from Malaysia (Far Eastern Economic Review, 1983).

Growth of Counter-trade: Barter trade was the mode of international trade in the eighteenth century when there was no sufficient monetisation. During the twentieth century, especially during the inter-War years, the West german government had resorted to bartering for strategic raw material (Banks, 1983). In the post-War period, counter-trade was initiated on a large scale by East European countries while trading with western countries and developing countries because they did not relish multilateral trade. In the wake of the oil crisis of 1970s, oil was exchanged for Soviet arms. The share of counter-trade in the world trade rose from around two per cent in 1964 to 20–30 per cent by the late 1980s (Debroy, 1987), although accurate estimates cannot be made on account of unavailability of figures. There is also region-wise difference as far as the volume of counter-trade is concerned.

Merits of Counter-trade: It is true that the multilateral trading system is beneficial, but the gains from it are limited in view of imposition of trade barriers. In such cases bilateral trade plays a vital role. First of all, it is a good option for meeting import requirements, especially in case of developing countries whose export faces high barriers.

Secondly, counter-trade helps stabilise export earnings because it predetermines the size of export and import. It also helps stabilise the terms of trade as the ratio between export and import prices is predetermined. Through stabilising export earnings and terms of trade, it transfuses stability in the development process.

Thirdly, it helps in trade diversification and, thereby, reduces the risk of geo-political chaos. Diversification of exports allows greater outlets for exportable goods, which in turn creates a more competitive market, increases export earnings, and reduces import costs.

Fourthly, counter-trade augments the flow of technology to developing countries, especially when they suffer from a serious technology gap. Buy-back agreements are particularly helpful in such cases.

Fifthly, when the counter-trade agreement is long term, the importing country gets the same advantage as it gets from loans. This means that counter-trade serves the purpose of loans and at the same time does not impose the burden of interest payment.

Sixthly, despite the fact that balancing of trade sometimes poses a problem, it reduces the net currency outflow and, thus, helps avoid foreign exchange problems.

Seventhly, developing countries often face distortions caused by unsuitable exchange rate policies. For example, overvaluation of currency tends to make export uncompetitive despite its impact in form of reduced import cost. Counter-trade helps correct such distortions. Goods can be exported at less than the quoted price and this can act as an export subsidy.

All this shows that counter-trade helps avert the problem of foreign exchange, which is endemic to developing countries. In fact, this has been a major factor for resorting to counter-trade. To quote a few examples, Brazil and Mexico opted for counter-trade in 1979 when their external balance was disturbed. So was the case with Indonesia in 1981. India was ready to exchange various raw materials for wheat and other agricultural commodities from the USA only after its foreign exchange crisis in the late 1950s.

Counter-trade

Merits
- Absence of tariff barriers
- Stabilisation of export earnings
- Scope for benefits from trade diversification
- Possibility for flow of technology, especially in buy-back agreements
- Some advantages similar to those of loans
- No need for foreign exchange for making imports
- Avoiding distortions caused by unsuitable exchange rate policy

Demerits
- Non-conforming with the norms of the multilateral trading system
- Absence of multilateral surveillance leading to distortions in markets and price
- Lack of encouragement for quality improvement
- Lack of double coincidence of goods to be traded
- Balancing of trade sometimes turns difficult

Demerits of Counter-trade: It is maintained that counter-trade goes against the norms of multilateral trade and so countries opting for it, abstain from reaping gains, from the multilateral trading system. There is always the possibility of market distortions because of the lack of multilateral surveillance. Distortions can take place in many ways. The price of the import may be very low and hence may harm domestic industries. If it is abnormally high, terms of trade will deteriorate. Once caught in counter-trade, the weak trading partner is coerced by the strong counterpart.

Again, difficult to sell products are sometimes traded. This means the country exporting such goods never tries to improve its efficiency. This negatively influences the export performance in the long run.

Yet again, there is always a difficulty of double coincidence of traded goods with the result that the trade earnings become unstable.

Last but not least, the balancing of trade poses a serious problem both at the micro level and at the macro level. Experience shows that micro level balancing is often more cumbersome. The problem also occurs at the macro level when exports face supply constraints. This happened in Indonesia during 1982 and 1983, when the country faced serious problems in balancing trade (Miramon, 1985).

2.3 CONTRACTUAL ENTRY MODES

Contractual entry modes are found in case of intangible products such as technology, patents, and so on. When a company develops a particular technology through its own research and development programme, it likes to recover the cost of research and development. To this end, it sells the technology either to a domestic firm or to a foreign firm. But in this

Contractual entry modes are found in case of intangible products such as technology, patents, and so on. When a company develops a particular technology through its own research and development programme, it likes to recover the cost of research and development. To this end, it sells the technology either to a domestic firm or to a foreign firm.

case, the secrecy of technology is not maintained and the firm's ownership advantage is always at stake. Thus, in order to maintain the ownership advantage, a firm passes on the technology only to its own subsidiary located abroad. But if the host government does not permit any foreign investment, the subsidiary of the firm in that host country cannot exist. Transfer of technology through contractual deals is the only way out. The contractual entry mode, often known as technical collaboration or technical joint-venture, is very common. It is preferred in many cases where:

1. The licensor does not possess enough capital for investment, nor does it possess the requisite knowledge of the foreign market for the purpose of export.
2. The licensor wishes to exploit its technology in the foreign market.
3. The licensor finds the host country market too small to make any investment for reaping economies of scale.
4. Nationalisation is feared in the host country.
5. Foreign investment in the host country is restricted.

Technical collaboration normally takes four forms. They are:

1. Licensing
2. Franchising
3. Management Contracts
4. Turnkey Projects

These different forms of the contractual mode are explained here (Figure 2.1).

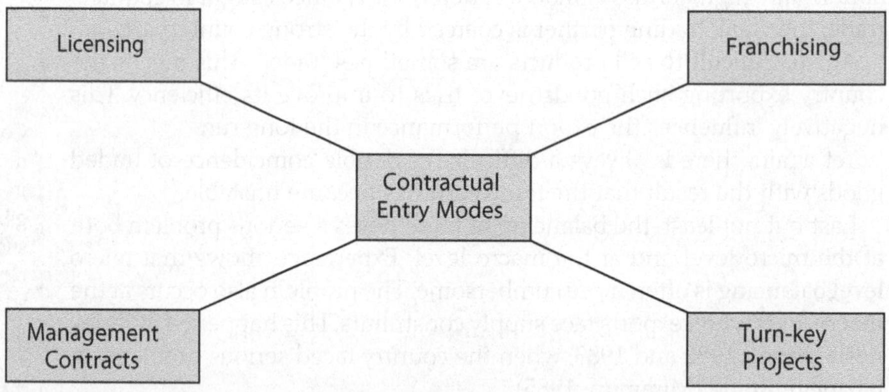

FIGURE 2.1 Different Forms of Contractual Entry Mode

2.3.1 Licensing

Nature and Forms: Licensing is an arrangement by which a firm transfers its intangible property such as expertise, know-how, blueprints, technology, and manufacturing design to its own unit, or to a firm, located abroad. It is also known as technical collaboration. The firm transferring technology, and so on is known as the licensor. The firm receiving technology, at the other end, and so on is known as the licensee. The arrangement is meant for a specific period. The licensor gets technical service fee from the licensee. The licensee, on the other end, does not have to make a huge investment on research and development. Thus both the parties reap the benefits of licensing.

A licence can be exclusive, non-exclusive, or cross. In an exclusive licence, the arrangement provides exclusive rights to produce and market an intangible property in a specific geographic region. On the contrary, a non-exclusive licence does not grant a firm sole access to the market. The licensor can grant even more companies the right to use the property in the same region. Cross licensing is reciprocal where intangible property is transferred between two firms, both of them being the licensor and the licensee at the same time. In the early 1990s there was cross licensing between Fujitsu of Japan and Texas Instruments of the USA. Both the companies used each other's technology for a given period.

Licensing is an arrangement by which a firm transfers its intangible property such as expertise, know-how, blueprints, technology, and manufacturing design to its own unit, or to a firm, located abroad. It is also known as technical collaboration.

A licence can be exclusive, non-exclusive, or cross.

Delhi-based Precision Pipes and Profiles, having already three tie-ups—a technical collaboration with Tokai Kogyo of Japan, a manufacturing and marketing agreement with Power Data Corporation of Australia and a licensing agreement with Nissen Chemitec of Japan, supplies automobile sealing system and auto-exterior products to Maruti Suzuki, General Motors (India), Toyota Kirloskar Motors and Honda SIEL and many others. It has already five manufacturing centres with a combined capacity of five million tonnes. However, in order to bring down the cost and to absorb minor cost fluctuations, it is setting up green-field unit at NOIDA to manufacture auto parts, major part of which will be exported to Australia and Japan under a buy-back plan.
Source: Based on the news published in *Business Standard*, 17.12.2007.

Advantages and Disadvantages: There are many advantages in a licensing arrangement. A licensor can expand its operation in different countries by exploiting its innovative technology, without making any investment. In other words, it can reap benefits from its technology without making any investment abroad. Secondly, it is less risky than the investment mode because it does not commit any investment. Even if there is an unfavourable political climate in the host country, the licensor is not going to lose anything except for some amount of technical fees. But in case of investment, the loss may be huge. Thirdly, licensing can be advantageous to the licensee too as it is able to upgrade its production technology and can develop its competitiveness in the international market.

However, there is the fear that licensing can reduce the global consistency of the quality and marketing of a licensor's product in different national markets, especially if different licensees operate in their own way. Again, the secrecy of technology is known to the licensee the moment the licensing agreement is made. In this way, a licensing arrangement hampers the very competitive advantage possessed by the licensor. During 1960s, RCA transferred technical know-how for the production of colour televisions to Sony and Matsushita for a handsome price. The licensees assimilated the technology and left RCA far behind in the competition in the world market.

2.3.2 Franchising

Franchising is a form of technical collaboration in which the franchisee makes use of intellectual property rights, like trademarks, copyrights, business know-how, managerial assistance, geographic exclusivity, or of a specific set of procedures of the franchiser for creating the product in question.

Meaning and Forms: In this form of technical collaboration, the franchiser is the entrant and the franchisee is the host country entity. The franchisee makes use of intellectual property rights, like trademarks, copyrights, business know-how, managerial assistance, geographic exclusivity, or of specific set of procedures of the franchiser for creating the product in question. In the literature available on this subject, a few experts have established similarities between licensing and franchising. Oman (1984) suggests that "franchising may be regarded as a particular type of licensing". Root (1987) too feels that franchising is a form of licensing in which the franchiser licenses a business system and other property rights to a franchisee. On the contrary, there are views to suggest that these two are different. Perkins (1987) is of the view that while franchising encompasses transfer of the total business function, licensing concerns just one part of business, including transfer of right to manufacture or distribute a single product or process. Again, franchising differs from licensing in that the former gives a company greater control over the sale of the product in the target market. When the franchisee fails to abide by the set of procedures, the franchiser takes back the franchise. Yet again, licensing is common in manufacturing industries, whereas franchising is more common in service industries where the brand name is more important.

Franchising may take different forms. In direct franchising, the franchiser frames policy and monitors and directs the activities in each host country from its home-country base. But in case of indirect franchising, there are sub-franchisers between the original franchiser and the host country units. The sub-franchiser possesses the exclusive right to exploit the original franchiser's business package within a defined geographic area.

Advantages and Disadvantages: The merit of franchising is that it allows the franchiser to maintain consistency of its standard products in different target markets. Moreover, it is a very low-risk mode of entry in different markets. However, there is often the problem of controlling a large number of franchisees in different markets. To avoid this problem, a master franchisee is established in a particular market to monitor the operation of individual franchisees in that market.

On the other hand, franchising is not cost-free. There are different types of costs involved in it. The costs are search costs, servicing costs, property right protection costs, and monitoring costs. The search cost is involved in evaluating, selecting and contacting a foreign party. The servicing cost includes the cost of codifying the franchise format appropriately, the cost of providing managerial and technical assistance, support, and ongoing training. The property right protection cost occurs in the process when the franchiser takes steps to safeguard its ownership advantage embodied in the franchise format. Last but not least, the franchiser needs to police and supervise the activities of the franchisee in order to maintain its brand image. The cost of policing and supervision is known as monitoring cost.

2.3.3 Management Contracts

Nature of Management Contracts: In a management contract, one company supplies the other with managerial expertise. Such agreements are normally signed in case of turnkey projects where the host country firm is not able to manage day to day affairs of the project, or in other cases where the desired managerial capabilities are not available in the host country. The transfer includes both technical expertise and managerial expertise.

In a **management contract**, one company supplies the other with managerial expertise. Such agreements are normally signed in case of turnkey projects where the host country firm is not able to manage day-to-day affairs of the project, or in other cases where the desired managerial capabilities are not available in the host country. The transfer includes both technical expertise and managerial expertise.

Merits and Demerits: It is through management contracts that many developing countries are able to utilise specialised expertise in different areas of their economy. But the moment local talent is developed, management contracts lose their significance.

Management contracts often supplement the licensing agreement insofar as they help the firm reap the advantages of licensing. Suppose a firm gets improved technology but lacks managerial inputs for better marketing, its products will remain unsold and the ultimate impact of the licensing agreement will be zero.

The transfer of managerial know-how is very easy as the licensor has to simply overstretch its management resources and make them available to the licensee. But the problem is that there is often misunderstanding between the foreign managers and the local managers, ultimately effecting productivity. Again, if foreign managers work only for a short period and do not train the local personnel, managerial efficiency will not be up to the mark. This will lead to problems when they go back to their home country.

2.3.4 Turnkey Projects

Meaning: In a turnkey project agreement, a firm agrees to construct an entire plant in a foreign country and make it fully operational. It is known as turnkey because the licensor starts the operation and hands over the key of the operating plant to the licensee. Agreements for turnkey projects normally take place where the initial construction part of the plant is more complex than the operational part. Such projects are either self-engineered or made to specifications. In case of the former, it is the licensor who decides the design of the project. In the latter, it is the licensee who takes such decision. In both cases, the contract involves either a fixed price or a cost-plus price. In a fixed-price contract, the risk of cost overruns lies with the licensor.

In a **turnkey project** agreement, a firm agrees to construct an entire plant in a foreign country and make it fully operational. It is known as turnkey because the licensor starts the operation and hands over the key of the operating plant to the licensee.

Advantages and Disadvantages: Turnkey projects allow firms to specialise in their core competencies, which they could not have done in the absence of such contracts. Moreover, such contracts allow the host government to obtain world class designs for its infrastructure projects.

Turnkey projects are also advantageous in cases where the host government restrict the inflow of capital. For example, many oil exporting countries did not permit foreign direct investment in the oil sector. Foreign firms entered these markets through turnkey projects. But the suppliers of turnkey projects often fall back on their own monopoly position in the international market.

2.4 FOREIGN INVESTMENT

2.4.1 Foreign Portfolio Investment and Foreign Direct Investment

Foreign portfolio investment is an investment in the shares and debt securities of companies abroad in the secondary market merely for sake of returns and not in the interests of the management of the company.

Foreign direct investment in form of green-field investment is an investment in the equity capital of a company abroad for the sake of the management of the company or investment abroad through opening of the branches.

M&As are either outright purchase of a running company abroad or an amalgamation with a running foreign company.

Foreign investment takes two forms. One is foreign portfolio investment, which does not involve the production and distribution of goods and services. It is not concerned with the control of the host country enterprise. It simply gives the investor, a non-controlling interest in the company. Investment in securities on the stock exchanges of a foreign country or under the global depository receipt mechanism is an example of foreign portfolio investment. On the other hand, foreign direct investment (FDI) is very much concerned with the operation and ownership of the host country firm. It is often said that even in case of FDI, if a company acquires around 10 per cent of the equity in a foreign firm, it should be treated as foreign portfolio investment as the investing or the acquiring firm does not have a say in the affairs of the target company (United Nations, 2000).

FDI is found in form of either green-field investment (GI) or mergers and acquisitions (M&As) or brown-field investment. Green-field investment takes place either through opening of branches in a foreign country or through foreign financial collaborations—meaning investment in the equity capital of a foreign company, in the majority of cases a newly established one. If the firm buys the entire equity shares in a foreign company, the latter is known as the wholly-owned subsidiary of the buying firm. In case of purchase of more than 50 per cent shares, the latter is known as a subsidiary of the buying firm. In case of less than 50 per cent purchase, it is known simply as an equity alliance. Sometimes an equity alliance is reciprocal, meaning that both companies invest in the equity capital of each other.

M&As are either outright purchase of a running company abroad or an amalgamation with a running foreign company. The term "brown-field" investment is used to denote a combination of green-field investment and M&As. It is found in cases when a firm acquires another firm; and after the acquisition, it completely replaces the plant and equipment, labour, and product line (Meyer and Estrin, 1998).

Again, FDI is either horizontal or vertical. Horizontal FDI is said to exist when a firm invests abroad in the same operation/industry. Suzuki's investment in India to manufacture cars is an example of horizontal FDI. On the contrary, vertical FDI is found when a firm invests abroad in other operations either with a view to have control over the supply of inputs or to have control over marketing of its product. British Petroleum and Royal Dutch Shell have invested abroad in the production of oil. Volkswagen has acquired a number of US dealers in order to sell its cars to consumers in the USA. These two are examples of vertical FDI. However, the first example is an example of a backward vertical FDI, where FDI assures the supply of inputs for its production at home. The second one is an example of forward vertical FDI in which it helps the sale of domestically produced goods in the host country. It may be noted that the forward vertical FDI is not as common as the backward vertical FDI.

Brown-field investment refers to mergers and acquisition followed by fresh doses of green-field investment. FDI is either horizontal or vertical. Horizontal FDI is said to exist when a firm invests abroad in the same operation/industry.

On the contrary, vertical FDI exists when a firm invests abroad in other operations either with a view to have control over the supply of inputs or to have control over marketing of its product.

Last but not least, based on the motives of the MNCs, FDI may be classified as: (1) market-seeking FDI, (2) resource-seeking FDI, (3) efficiency-seeking FDI and (4) strategic-asset-seeking FDI. Market-seeking FDI moves to a country where per capita income and the size of the market are large.

Suzuki Motor of Japan and many others like Hyundai Motor of the Republic of Korea, Toyota Motor and Honda Motor of Japan and General Motors and Ford Motor of the USA—all have invested and are going to expand their operations in India in view of large market. These investments can be categorised as market-seeking FDI.

The resource-seeking FDI flows to the host country where raw material and manpower are in abundance. The raw material may be related either to agriculture, forestry and fisheries or to non-renewable resources, such as energy minerals and metallic and non-metallic minerals. The share of extractive industries in global inward FDI stock was around 9.0 per cent at the end of 2005. In absolute terms, FDI in primary goods sector increased five times in 1970s, three-and-half times during 1980s and four times in 1990s.

Again the efficiency-seeking FDI moves to a country where the abundance of resources and presence of large market helps MNCs to improve their efficiency.

Last but not least, strategic-asset-seeking or created-asset-seeking FDI is meant to acquire next technologies in order to improve productivity.

2.4.2 Mergers and Acquisitions (M&As)

Forms of M&As: As mentioned above, FDI takes place also through mergers and acquisitions (M&As) that are not a start-from-scratch mode or a greenfield investment. Broadly speaking, M&As take two forms. One is the acquisition where one firm acquires or purchases another firm. The former is known as acquiring company and the latter is known as target company. No new firm comes into existence after the merger. The other form manifests in consolidation or amalgamation where two merging firms lose their identity into a new firm that comes to exist representing the interest of the two.

The M&As are either horizontal, or vertical, or conglomerate. Horizontal M&As are found where two or more firms engaged in similar lines of activities join hands. For example, if two firms manufacturing automobiles merge, it will be called a horizontal merger. Horizontal M&As help create economies of scale because the size of the firm becomes larger to reap such gains. On the other hand, vertical M&As occur among firms

Forms of M&As

- **Based on corporate structure:**
  1. Acquisition
  2. Amalgamation/consolidation
- **Based on financial relationship:**
  1. Horizontal
  2. Vertical
  3. Conglomerate
- **Based on technique:**
  1. Hostile
  2. Friendly

involved in different stages of the production of a single final product. If an oil exploration firm and a refinery unit merge, it will be called a vertical integration. It reduces cost of transportation, and of communicating and coordinating of production. Uncertainty over input supply is overcome as also the marketing of goods of a particular unit is assured through backward and forward linkages. Again, a conglomerate merger or consolidation involves two or more firms in unrelated activities. Three types of conglomerate M&As are often found. Product-extension combination broadens the product lines of the firm. Similarly, a geographic market extension merger involves two firms operating in different and non-overlapping geographic areas. The size of the market expands after the merger. Lastly, conglomerates representing neither of the two are known as pure conglomerate mergers. There are financial conglomerates where a financial company manages the financial functions of other companies in the group. Similarly, there are managerial conglomerates combining the management of several companies under one roof.

M&As are either hostile or friendly.

Again, from the viewpoint of technique, M&As are either hostile or friendly. In the hostile takeovers, the time devoted to negotiations is minimised as much as possible because it is just the discreet purchase of the shares of the target company. There are two ways to acquire shares. One is known as dawn raid, where the acquiring company makes a sudden purchase of shares of the target company. The other is by securing an irrevocable call option over someone else's shares. After the initial stake is finalised, the acquiring company makes a bid. In order to grab the shares it quotes a much higher price, which deters other parties from making bid. Such a bid is called as pre-emptive strike. On the other hand, if the company does not see a formidable competitor, it quotes a very low bid, often lower than the worth. This is done in order to gain more and this is called low-ball offer.

As far as friendly takeovers are concerned, there are a lot of negotiations. The take-over deal is not disclosed until it is finalised. To this end, the acquiring company signs confidentiality letter whereby it promises not to disclose the fact to any third party. When the negotiation is on and all the

Sun Pharmaceuticals bid for the assets of an Israeli company, Taro Pharmaceuticals was considered as the first ever hostile takeover by an Indian company for the control of a global company. Alkaloida, a subsidiary of Sun Pharma started a tender offer for all outstanding ordinary shares of Taro for $7.75 per share in cash on the June 30, 2008. This bid would bypass Taro's management and minority shareholders including Brandes Investment Partners and Franklin Templeton Asset Management.
Source: Based on the news published in *Hindustan Times Business*, 1.7.2008

relevant issues are sorted out, a letter of intent is signed. Finally, after the formal announcement is made to the press, a contract is signed.

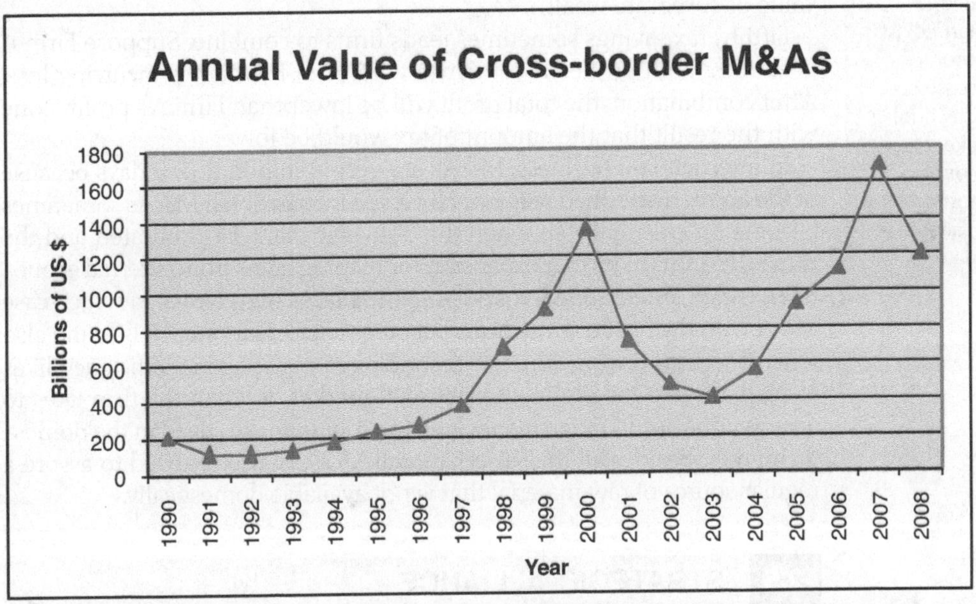

Source: Based on the figures obtained from UNCTAD Database

Motivations behind M&A: M&A is preferable to other modes of investment or the start-from-scratch mode of investment. Firstly, the M&A provides a synergistic advantage. This means that the firms operating individually do not reap the benefits that they are able to reap when they are combined. This occurs because the combination allows firms to derive the economies of scale on different counts, especially on the count of production, technological research, management, finance, and marketing. For example, when the fixed cost in Firm A does not cross the relevant range even after it acquires Firm B, the combination will lead to saving of the fixed cost that Firm B was previously incurring. This would result in lower cost of production. Similar savings would occur in other relevant areas. These economies are most likely to occur in case of horizontal combinations where opportunities exist for avoiding duplicate facilities.

Secondly, M&A enables overnight growth of the firm. At the same time, the very risk of competition reduces after merger. However, emergence of monopolistic character has some amount of disadvantage for consumers when the price is unwarrantedly raised.

Thirdly, M&A reduces financial risk through greater amount of diversification. More particularly in case of conglomerates, assets of completely different risk classes are acquired and consequently there is the possibility of negative correlation between the rates of return from these different classes of assets. If so, the return from total portfolio of assets would be comparatively stable.

International M&A is preferred additionally where: 1. domestic market is saturated, 2. high tariff exists in host country, 3. firm possesses superior technology to take a lead in host country, and 4. host country is a regular source of raw material.

Fourthly, M&A leads to diversification, which raises the debt capacity of the firm. Because of greater stability in the rates of return or in the cash flow after merger, the firm goes ahead to employ leverage in the capital structure. This helps the cost of capital move downward and raises the value of corporate wealth.

Fifthly, tax savings sometimes leads firms to combine. Suppose Firm A is earning high profits. It combines with Firm B which is incurring loss. After combination, the total profit will be lower than Firm A's profit alone with the result that the amount of tax would be lower.

In international business, M&As are very common now a days because of the above mentioned reasons. However, international M&As sometimes become an essential step when the domestic market is saturated and the firm is desirous of further expansion for reaping gains from external economies. Again, international marketing often faces high tariffs, in which case M&A with the host country firms becomes a necessary step. It is found also when the firm having superior technology or managerial efficiency likes to reap advantages in the international market or when the firm likes to acquire improved foreign technology in order to make a lead in the domestic market. Besides all this, international M&A is also resorted to assure a regular source of raw material that is not available domestically.

2.5 STRATEGIC ALLIANCE

Strategic alliance is technical/financial collaboration with very specific objectives.

It has already been discussed that investment in the equity capital of a company registered abroad is known as equity alliance or foreign financial collaboration or financial joint venture. It is different from technical collaborations/joint ventures where only technology is transferred and not the capital. Strategic alliances too represent joint ventures. They take the form of either licensing, franchising, management contracts or equity alliance involving the flow of capital. But they are different from the general kind of financial and technical collaborations in so far as the purpose or the goal for which strategic alliances are made is very specific.

More commonly, the goal or purpose for which strategic alliances are made is as follows:

1. **Development of technology:** Apple Computers and IBM formed an alliance for the development of hardware and software technology for desktop computers.

2. **Increase in the size of market:** Ranbaxy formed a strategic alliance with a Japanese firm to grab the Japanese market for its generic drugs. Tata Tea's alliance with Tetley helped the former in the marketing of tea abroad.
3. Achieving economies of scale in production.
4. Reducing risk and promoting stability.
5. Multiple goal incorporating the above goals simultaneously.

Besides, involving a specific purpose, strategic alliance allows the partner firms to remain independent. But in such cases, there is uncertainty as to what one party is counting on the other party to do. Sometimes M&As are treated as a form of strategic alliance. But it is inconsistent with the very concept of alliance in so far as the acquired or merged firm does not depend on two or more existing organisations for its survival as does an alliance.

Inkpen (2001) mentions different types of strategic alliance. They are: (1) industry consortium, (2) technical training, (3) supply/buyback arrangement, (4) production/assembly arrangement, (5) patents licensing, (6) franchising, (7) know-how licensing, (8) management/marketing service agreement, (9) non-equity co-operative agreements and (10) equity joint-ventures.

Strategic alliances are assumed better than other modes in so far as they involve lower transaction costs. They are more economically feasible and involve a less irreversible commitment than an acquisition. Since there is no transfer of ownership rights, the partners may terminate alliance with a relatively low cost.

2.6 FDI COMPARED WITH TRADE

> FDI is better than trade because:
> 1. Different markets can better be served with differentiated products
> 2. FDI overcomes tariff and transport cost involved in trade
> 3. It is a better means to acquire resources from the host county
> 4. It reduces financial risk through greater diversification
> 5. It creates harmonious political relations.

In the very beginning of the discussion on FDI, it is worth examining whether it is better than trade especially when the fulfilment of major international business objectives is concerned. Let us assume the objectives to be:

1. Expansion in sales and, thereby, in revenue
2. Acquisition of resources
3. Minimisation of risk through diversification
4. Political motive

Sales can be expanded also through greater magnitude of exports. But there are cases when export has only a limited scope. In such cases, FDI is made to generate sales. FDI overcomes the transportation cost involved in export. It is true that if the same product is exported to different markets, the firm produces more, exports more, and achieves economies of scale that largely compensates the transport cost. But when the product is differentiated, depending upon varying consumption pattern in different markets, economies of scale cannot be achieved. FDI is a better alternative in the sense that products with dissimilar features are produced in different countries in order to meet the specific demands of consumers there. It is the only way to generate sales.

Again, it is not only transport cost but also tariff and non-tariff barriers that are overcome by FDI. The generation of export is often handicapped by high tariff or non-tariff barriers imposed by importing countries. But if the exporting firm begins production in the importing country, trade barriers do not come in the way. The product becomes cheaper in the hands of the host country consumers. The firm finds itself in a competitive position and is able to raise its sales.

Apart from the generation of sales and revenue, the issue of the acquisition of resources is also important. Resources can be imported, but the import is possible only when the exporter agrees to export. On the other hand, FDI is a more reliable means to acquire resources. In the last quarter of the 19th century and the early decades of the 20th century, a good number of the British firms were engaged in mining activities. Even today, we find that Digital Equipment has made investments in India in order to access Indian software talent. Again, a large number of firms from industrialised countries have moved to developing countries to reap the benefit of cheap labour in the host countries. Suzuki produces cars with cheap Indian labour and exports them to the international market at competitive rates. Sometimes it is the cheap raw material that attracts FDI. Indian firms have moved to Sri Lanka for the manufacture of rubber products and to Nepal for the manufacture of herbal products. Thus FDI is more effective than other modes for the purpose of acquisition of resources. The resource acquisition process becomes easier, especially in a cross-border vertical set-up where the firm of an industrialised country uses cheap labour of a labour abundant economy through an off shore assembly operation.

Maximisation of return cannot be thought of in isolation of risk. With a given level of return, the risk has to be minimised. It can no doubt be minimised through the diversification of trade among larger number of countries. But the diversification process is easier in case of FDI. A firm can make investment in different countries; can source inputs from different countries, and can market its products in different countries. It is possible that the currency of a country from where the inputs are imported appreciates or it may be that the political relations with that country deteriorates. In such cases, risk can be reduced through diversifying the sources of inputs. Again, it is possible that the sales performance in a particular market is not good in a particular year; it may be diversified. Similarly, if returns from different ventures are negatively correlated, there will be stability in earnings and financial risk would be low. But all this is possible through diversification of the firm's operation.

FDI is a better instrument to develop harmonious political relationship with other countries. It is a fact that political motive is not the primary motive behind FDI, but it is definitely complementary to more important economic motives. The USA has made huge investments in some of Caribbean countries. One of the reasons is that these countries were opposed to the Cuban communist regime.

2.7 FDI COMPARED WITH CONTRACTUAL ENTRY MODE

It is true that, in almost all the cases, FDI also involves the transfer of technology with the result that the contractual entry mode can go side by side with FDI. But the two are different in nature. While FDI involves flow of funds or investment in the equity capital of a foreign company, contractual entry mode does not involve such investment. As a result, the contractual mode does not confer controlling power to the management of the company to which licenses/management know-how/trade mark, and so on are provided. Thus, from the viewpoint of control, FDI is superior to contractual entry mode.

Again, FDI is a broader form of joint venture compared to the contractual entry mode. It is because it involves capital investment and also, when required, the transfer of technical and managerial know-how. The investor can earn dividend and also charge royalty and technical service fees. Dividend is not payable to a licensor or a franchiser. This is why investors prefer FDI to the contractual entry mode.

It is true that FDI has an edge over the contractual entry mode, but even then there are cases when the contractual entry mode is preferred. It is preferred when the host government imposes restrictions on the inflow of FDI. Contractual mode is the only way out, apart from trade, to enter a foreign market. Again, it carries lesser risk of operating in a foreign land compared to FDI, especially when the investor is unaware of the political, legal, economic and socio-cultural environment prevailing in the host country. In such cases, firms enter a foreign market only gradually—first through trade, then through the contractual entry mode, and finally through making investment in the equity. In short, the two modes are to a large extent complementary rather than being competitive.

> **FDI** is a broader form of joint venture compared to the contractual entry mode. But contractual entry mode is preferred when the host government imposes restrictions on the inflow of FDI. It carries lesser risk of operating in a foreign land compared to FDI, especially when the investor is unaware of the political, legal, economic and socio-cultural environment prevailing in the host country.

2.8 GREENFIELD INVESTMENT (GI) VERSUS M&As

2.8.1 Substitutability between GI and M&As

The trends of international investment show that the share of M&As in total FDI outflow registered an increase from 60 per cent to 95 per cent and more during 1990–2000 (United Nations, 2001). This raises a very pertinent question whether M&As are an alternative to the greenfield investment (GI). It is often said that GI and M&As are the substitutes of each other. It may be correct if the level of economic development, institutional framework, and the FDI policy in the two countries—home country and the host country—are similar. Moreover, in the developed world, where financial markets are quite developed, M&As may serve as an alternative to GI. Again, as far as the impact of these two modes on the development in the host country is concerned, they are more or less the same and so they may be treated as an alternative to each

> Greenfield investment and M&As are not the substitutes of each other if the host country is a developing one. The two are found different from each other. On account of: 1. availability of financial resources, 2. technology considerations, 3. employment considerations, 4. building of export competitiveness, and 5. their impact on market , structure and competitiveness.

other. But in a developing country, M&As should not be treated so. The reason is that:

1. The level of technology and management expertise is different from that in a developed country.
2. There are still governmental restrictions on the M&As, despite the liberalisation of economic policies.
3. Asset market is underdeveloped and accounting standard is poor, with the result that the assets of target companies are often undervalued, causing them to incur loss.

In short, the GI and the M&As are not the alternatives in the true sense of the term. Moreover, there are reasons to believe that the two differ in details. The difference is manifest in many ways.

2.8.2 Differing Impact of GI and M&As

The preceding section makes it clear that greenfield investment and M&As are not the substitutes of each other if the host country is a developing one. There are many viewpoints from which the two are found different from each other. Some of the more important viewpoints are discussed here.

Availability of Financial Resources: First of all, from the viewpoint of the inflow of the financial resources into the host economy it can be said that the financial resources provided under M&As do not necessarily add to the capital stock required for production. It is because they involve transfer of the ownership of the local assets to foreign hands normally in return for some amount of disposable shares. However, in case of distress sale when the target company is on the verge of bankruptcy and is not able to get financial resources from any of the sources, M&A adds to the foreign exchange resources of the host country. There are cases to show that during the Asian crisis, many firms could be saved in crisis-hit countries through cross-border M&As. Moreover, M&As often lead to currency appreciation of the host country insofar as the investment inflow is often lumpsum and immediate. GI does not lead to such effects because the investment inflow spreads over time and in most cases it is in kind. Similarly, outflow of resources in the form of dividend repatriation in case of M&As is sooner than in case of GI. Again, the GI essentially represents an investment in the plant; on the contrary, the M&As consideration value is fungible and can be used also for non-productive purposes.

The Technology Considerations: From the viewpoint of the transfer, upgrading, and diffusion and generation of technology, the two modes differ to some extent. Since M&As involve working with an existing facility and the GI is concerned with setting up a new one, the latter is more likely to involve newer equipment from the very beginning. However, this is not always the case. Caves (1998) finds that since the technology gap between a developed and a developing country is large, M&As too are found injecting new technology in the target firm and additionally, they help preserve the technology developed by the acquired firm.

As far as technological upgrading is concerned, it depends more upon the market orientation of the investment, local skills and capabilities in the host country, and the corporate strategy, and not much on the entry mode. However, empirical studies have shown that FDI through M&As has led to considerable technological upgrading (United Nations, 2000).

Apart from transfer and upgrading of technology, diffusion of technology is greater in case of M&As insofar as the acquired firms enjoy greater linkages with the local economy, whereas it takes time to develop such linkages in the case of GI. However, in the context of innovation or generation of technology, the views are different. It is true that if the R&D in the acquired firm is uneconomic, the acquiring firm's sword falls on it. But there is nothing wrong if uneconomic R&D is substituted by an economic one. If the existing R&D in the acquired firm is economic, there is no reason for its substitution. Rather, in case of efficiency seeking or created asset seeking foreign direct investment, the acquired company avails of the R&D capabilities within no time. In case of GI, it takes a long time to develop R&D activities.

Employment Considerations: From the viewpoint of quantity and quality of employment, the two modes—M&As and GI—differ substantially. GI generates new employment, while M&As transfers responsibility for existing employees who may be laid off by the new owner on the grounds of efficiency or over-staffing. In fact, the impact of M&A on employment generation depends on the motivation behind it as also on the characteristics of the acquired firm. First, if the M&A is a market seeking move, the impact on the employment generation is expected to be neutral or, to some extent, positive in the short run and medium term, as the existing employees are retained to work for the new market. Second, if the M&A is strategic asset seeking, employment in the acquired firm is expected to expand as the employees possess valuable skills and capabilities. Third, if the M&A is efficiency seeking, employment in the acquired firm may decrease if it has substantial excess capacity or has a duplication of functions. Cross-border M&As in automotive, financial, and service industries during the 1980s and 1990s led to cut in employment despite increase in output (United Nations, 2000). Fourth, if the motive is financial, employment may decrease owing to restructuring or asset-stripping. Fifth, if the motive is to privatise a public-sector unit, employment may decrease as a result of restructuring. Evidences from cross-border M&As in seven countries of Central and Eastern Europe support this phenomenon (United Nations, 1999). But if the acquired firm had been liquidated in the absence of an M&A, the M&A would have been employment conserving, even if there was a partial lay-off to some extent.

This is all about the impact of M&As on direct employment generation. There may be positive impact on indirect employment generation following forward and backward linkages of the acquired firm with other enterprises in the economy.

Turning to the qualitative aspects of employment, it is often found that both greenfield investment and M&As provide better-quality employment. But in specific circumstances, wages may be lowered and facilities may be cut on the grounds of cost reduction.

Building of Export Competitiveness: Greenfield investment is more useful for building export competitiveness when the host country firm does not possess large export potential. However, the experience varies from case to case. In Hungary, M&As were less export oriented than greenfield investment. In the Czech Republic, the export potential of M&As was the same as that of greenfield investment (United Nations, 2000). Again, when greenfield projects have weak linkages with local firms and depend more on imported inputs, imports tend to rise.

Impact on Market Structure and Competition: It is normally believed that greenfield Investment adds to the number of enterprises and reduces market concentration. But this is not always true. If the investing firms were present earlier in the market through other modes, new firms will not be created. Again, if the new foreign affiliate offsets the dominant market positions of incumbent firms or takes a dominant market position itself, the market will be more concentrated.

On the contrary, cross-border M&As may have a positive impact on the market structure if an ailing firm is acquired, which would have otherwise been forced out of the market. But if it is a monopolising or quasi-monopolising M&A, the market structure will turn more concentrated. In India, when Hindustan Lever Limited, the Indian subsidiary of Unilever, acquired its main rival, Tata Oil Mills Company, the market for toilet soaps and detergents became concentrated (Mehta, 1999). However, when market is open to imports and to foreign investment, the domestic concentration level may not necessarily make a difference to effective competition.

SUMMARY

- The choice of entry mode depends on the objective, extent, and capability of a firm's involvement in international business on the one hand, and the host country environment and the magnitude of risk involved on the other.
- The broad modes of international business are:

  1. Trade, including direct and indirect trade, and counter-trade;
  2. Contractual mode, including licensing, franchising, management contracts, and turnkey jobs; and

3. Foreign direct investment, including greenfield investment and mergers and acquisitions.

- Direct trade means direct involvement of the firm in trade, while indirect trade is conducted through any other agency. In countertrade, one set of goods is exchanged for the other set of goods.
- Contractual modes are found in case of intangible products such as technology, patents, and so on.
- Foreign direct investment possesses essentially the element of control and this way it is different from foreign portfolio investment. Foreign direct investment that serves some of the international business objectives in a better way may be greenfield investment through foreign branches and subsidiaries. Alternatively, it can take the form of M&As.
- M&As may be horizontal, vertical, or conglomerate. They may be either hostile or friendly. There are a number of motives behind M&As, such as reaping of synergistic advantage, overnight growth of the firm, risk minimisation, tax savings, and so on. In cross-border M&As, exchange rate changes, tax rate differentials, financial leverage norms, and so forth too come in the picture.
- Strategic alliance is financial technical collaboration with specific objective.
- A comparative analysis of greenfield investment and M&As shows that in developed countries where the asset market is developed, they may substitute each other. But in the case of developing countries, substitution is not feasible. Moreover, the two methods are different in their impact with respect to the availability of financial resources, transfer, upgradation, diffusion and generation of technology, employment generation, building of export potential, and market structure and competition.

REVIEW QUESTIONS

1. "Choice of entry mode is crucial for international business". Discuss. Explain the determinants of entry mode.
2. What are the different forms of countertrade? Is it preferable to multilateral trade?
3. Present a comparative picture of the different forms of contractual entry mode of international business.
4. Explain different forms of M&As. In what ways are they different from green-field investment?
5. Write a note on strategic alliance.

OBJECTIVE TYPE QUESTIONS

1. Mark True or False:
   (a) A particular mode of international business depends on the extent of involvement of the firm.

(b) Host country environment does not at all influence the mode of international business.
(c) Both direct and indirect trade involve intermediaries.
(d) Counter-trade and bilateral trade are synonyms.
(e) Contractual entry mode is found normally in the case of intangible products, such as technology.
(f) While franchising involves transfer of total business function, licensing is concerned with a single product or process.
(g) Sub-franchisers exist in case of direct franchising.
(h) In a turnkey job, the host-country constructs the entire plant.
(i) Foreign portfolio investment is concerned with the operation and ownership of the host country firm.
(j) Vertical M&As occur among firms involved in different stages of the production of a single product.

2. Choose the most suitable answer:

(a) Financial conglomerates are those where:
  (i) A financial company manages the financial functions of all the companies in the group.
  (ii) The different companies of the group are financially independent.
  (iii) The different companies of the group have their own geographic area.
  (iv) None of these.

(b) Amalgamation is a form of M&As where:
  (i) The acquiring and the acquired firms cease to exist and a new firm comes up in their place.
  (ii) The acquiring firm ceases to exist, but the acquired firm continues to operate.
  (iii) The acquired firm loses its existence and the acquiring firm continues to operate.
  (iv) None of these.

(c) The impact of greenfield investment and M&As differs in case of a developing country insofar as:
  (i) Asset market is well developed.
  (ii) The level of technology is not so well developed.
  (iii) The government adopts liberal economic policies.
  (iv) None of these.

(d) In strategic asset seeking M&As, employment in an acquired firm is expected to increase because:
  (i) Employees possess valuable skills and capabilities.
  (ii) Excess capacity exists.
  (iii) Restructuring and asset-stripping tend to occur.
  (iv) None of these.

(e) Turnkey projects are found in cases where:
  (i) The initial construction of the plant is complex and its operation is simple.
  (ii) The initial construction of the plant is simpler than its operation.
  (iii) The initial construction and the operation are both simple.
  (iv) None of these.

(f) Buy-back agreements are a form of:
  (i) Commercial counter-trade.
  (ii) Industrial counter-trade.

(iii) Both industrial and commercial counter-trade.
(iv) None of these.

CASE STUDY

Alok Mukherji was serving as an accountant in a private sector bank at Kolkata. Since the environment in which he was working was not congenial to him, he preferred to go for voluntary retirement. He had a good amount of money that he planned to invest in a restaurant business. A real estate dealer helped him in getting a piece of land. Its location was attractive in as much as it was barely 15 kilometres east of Kolkata, on the corner of two roads—one of them was under construction.

Mr. Mukherji built up a small restaurant in 1998 and began serving traditional home-cooked food apart from beverages. There were plenty of customers as the construction was going on and they liked the food also. Within a couple of years, he earned a large amount of money. The brand name was established by then. So he set up two more restaurants within a radius of 20 kilometres under the same brand name. The two new restaurants too did a good business. But by 2002, the construction work was over, as a result of which there was a sudden drop in the number of customers. The business did not remain economical and he had to close down the restaurant business there.

In 2003, he came across a new opportunity. The Government of Bangladesh had already liberalised its foreign investment policy. He was advised by his friends to grab this opportunity and to set up a restaurant just on the other side of the border in Bangladesh. The new area was connected through the newly built road.

Mr. Mukherji had four alternatives. The first was to set up a new restaurant at this new location. The second was to purchase an existing restaurant already functioning in that area. The third was to go for a joint venture with the local partner in Bangladesh who had an idea of the food habits of the persons living there and could be able to use the brand name of Tasty Food. The fourth option was the combination of all these three.

Let us sketch in brief the cost and benefit of all these options. A green-field investment would require site selection, finances and legal assistance to cope with the local laws and the employment of a completely new manpower. Mr. Mukherji had an idea of starting new restaurant that would cost approximately Rs. 15 million. The labour cost might be lower in that country but taking into account the cost of environment there, this option did not look feasible. The tax rates were not a problem in so far as the rates of taxes were not very different in the two countries.

As far as the acquisition is concerned, the cost was expected to be still lower than the green-field investment. The potential availability of the existing staff was very much attractive. But the quality of staff—both the new and the existing ones—was never guaranteed. It was difficult to manage the brand image in such cases.

Again, in a joint venture, the cost would have been still lower. But the risk was large as the partner might not be reliable. In such cases, the management of the joint venture would have been a troubling affair.

Yet again, the franchising would have been the least costly. But it was uncertain whether the franchisee would be able to maintain the quality of Tasty Food. Again, there would have been a combination but it was not certain as to how far the legal provisions in Bangladesh would be favourable. It was necessary for Mr. Mukherji to study the plus and minus points of all these possibilities and to choose a particular mode.

QUESTIONS

1. Was it beneficial for Tasty Food to move to Bangladesh?
2. Compare between acquisition and green-field investment in this case.
3. Do you think that franchising agreement would have been the best solution?
4. Which of the modes will confer on Mr. Mukherji the largest benefit in monetary terms?

REFERENCES

Books

Inkpen, A. C. (2001), "Strategic Alliance" in A. M. Rugman and T. L. Brewen, *The Oxford Handbook of International Business* (Oxford: Oxford University Press).

Root, F. R. (1987), *Entry Strategies for International Markets* (Lexington, M. A.: Lexington Books).

Journals and Reports

Banks, G. (1983), "The Economics and Politics of Countertrade", *The World Economy,* VI (2), 159–82.

Caves, R. E. (1998), "Industrial Organisation and New Findings on the Turnover and Mobility of Firms", *Journal of Economic Literature,* XXXVI (4), 1947–82.

Debroy, B. (1987), "Counter-trade", *The Economic Times,* 12th May and 13th May.

Far Eastern Economic Review (1983), 27th August.

Jacques de Miramon (1985), "Countertrade: An Illusory Solution", *The OECD Observer,* Paris, May, 24–25.

Mehta, P. S. (1999), "Foreign Direct Investment, Mega-mergers and Strategic Alliances: Is Global Competition Accelerating Development or Heading towards World Monopolies ?", *The Role of Competition Policy for Development in Globalising World Markets,* UNCTAD Series on Issues in Competition Law and Policy (Geneva: United Nations).

Meyer, K. and S. Estrin (1998), "Entry Mode Choice in Emerging Markets: Greenfield, Acquisition and Brownfield", *Centre for East European Studies,* Copenhagen Business School, Working Paper no. 18.

Nameth, L. (1984), "Offsets under Fire Down Under", *Multinational Monitor,* V (1), 3.

Oman, C. (1984), *New Forms of International Investment* (Paris: OECD).

Perkins, J. S. (1987), "How Licensing, Franchising Differ", *Les Nouvelles,* XXII (4), 15.

Sharan, V. (1992), "Foreign Investments in India: Trends, Problems and Prospect", *Foreign Trade Review,* XXVII (1), 74–84.

_______ United Nations (1999), *World Investment Report*, 1999, (New York and Geneva: UNCTAD).
_______ (2000), *World Investment Report*, (New York and Geneva: UNCTAD).
_______ (2001), *World Investment Report*, (New York and Geneva: UNCTAD).
United Nations Economic Commission for Europe (1979), *Countertrade Practices in the ECE Region*, Geneva, Trade R. 385, p. 22.
United States Department of Commerce (1978), *East-West Countertrade Practices*, Washington, D.C.

SELECT FURTHER READINGS

Beamish, P. W. (1985), "The Characteristics of Joint Ventures in Developed and Developing Countries", *Columbia Journal of World Business*, XX (Fall), 13–19.
Contractor, F. J. (1990), "Contractual and Co-operative Forms of International Business: Towards a United Theory of Modal Choice", *Management International Review*, XXX (1), 31–54.
Hill, C. W. L. *et al* (1990), "An Eclectic Theory of the Choice of International Entry Mode", *Strategic Management Journal*, XI (2), 117–28.
Lecraw, D. J. (1989), "'The Management of Counter-trade: Factors Influencing Success", *Journal of International Business Studies*, XX (1), 41–59.
Oman, C. (1984), *New Forms of International Investment in Developing Countries* (Paris: OECD).
United Nations (2000), *World Investment Report: 2000* (New York and Geneva: UNCTAD).
Welch, L. S. and A. Pacifico (1990), "Management Contracts: A Role in Internationalisation", *International Marketing Review*, VII (Summer), 64–74.

* The **New York Stock Exchange (NYSE)** is located at 11 Wall Street in lower Manhattan, New York City, USA. It is the world's largest stock exchange by market capitalisation of its listed companies at US$28.5 trillion as of May 2008. Average daily trading value was approximately US$153 billion in 2008.

The NYSE is operated by NYSE Euronext, which was formed by the NYSE's 2007 merger with the fully electronic stock exchange Euronext. With more than 8,000 listed issues, NYSE Euronext is home to the world's leading companies providing access to the global liquidity they need to collaborate, compete and grow.

France*

3 Theories of International Trade

CHAPTER OBJECTIVES

The present chapter explains the theoretical basis of international trade. The focus, in particular, is to:

- ✦ Explain the various theories of international trade, ranging from the mercantilist version to classical theories of absolute and comparative cost advantage, the factor endowment theory, neo-factor proportions theory, country similarity theory, intra-industry trade, trade in intermediate products and services, and finally, Porter's theory of national competitive advantage.
- ✦ Discuss the static and dynamic gains from trade.
- ✦ Explain terms of trade and their various forms.

The preceding chapter makes it evident that trade is an important mode of international business. And so a very pertinent question arises in the very beginning as to what, how much and with whom a country should trade. The answer to the question lies in the explanation given by different economists during different periods. The explanation has taken the form of theories of international trade. The present chapter thus deals with the various trade theories. In the beginning, the conventional theories are discussed and then the post-Heckscher-Ohlin developments forming a part of modern theories will be analysed.

3.1 MERCANTILISTS' VERSION

> Mercantilism was a school of economic thought prevalent in 17th and early 18th centuries that advocated for trade surplus.

Mercantilism stretched over about three centuries ending in the last quarter of the eighteenth century. It was the period when the nation-states were consolidating in Europe. For the purpose of consolidation, they required gold that could best be accumulated through trade surplus. In order to achieve trade surplus, the governments monopolised the trade activities, provided subsidies and other incentives for export. On the other hand, it restricted imports. Since the European governments were mainly the empire, they imported low-cost raw material from the colonies and exported high-cost manufactures to the colonies. They also prevented colonies from producing manufactures. All this was done in order to generate export surplus. Thus, in short, increasing gold holding through export augmentation and import restriction lay at the root of the Mercantilist theory of international trade.

> Trade surplus can be defined as excess of export over import.

However, the later versions of the Mercantilist doctrine explained that trade surplus was not an everlasting phenomenon. A positive trade balance led to an increase in the commodity prices relative to other countries. The increase in commodity prices caused a drop in export and thereby an erosion in trade surplus.

Again, the Mercantilists had a static view of the world economy. They did not realise that the gains from trade of a particular country were possible only at the expense of the other country. In fact, trade should promote the welfare of the world economy and not simply of a particular nation.

Moreover, the exponents of this theory ignored the concept of production efficiency through specialisation. In fact, it is the production efficiency that brings in gains from trade (Heckscher, 1935).

3.2 ABSOLUTE AND COMPARATIVE ADVANTAGE

The classical economists refuted the Mercantilist notion of precious metals and specie being the source of wealth. They thought domestic production was the prime source of wealth. And so they took into account the productive efficiency as the motivating factor behind trade. Two such theories need to be mentioned here—one propounded by Adam Smith and the other propounded by Ricardo.

3.2.1 Theory of Absolute Advantage

Adam Smith was one of the forerunners of the classical school of thought. He propounded a theory of international trade in 1776 that is known as the theory of absolute cost advantage. He is of the opinion that the productive efficiency among different countries differs because of diversity in the natural and acquired resources possessed by them. The difference in natural advantage manifests in varying climate, quality of land, availability of minerals, of water and other natural resources; while the difference in acquired resources manifests in different levels of technology and skills available. A particular country should specialise in producing only those goods that it is able to produce with greater efficiency, that is at lower cost; and exchange those goods with other goods of their requirements from a country that produces those other goods with greater efficiency or at lower cost. This will lead to optimal utilisation of resources in both the countries. Both the countries will gain from trade in so far as both of them will get the two sets of goods at the least cost.

Absolute cost advantage theory explains that a country having absolute cost advantage in the production of a product on account of greater efficiency should specialise in its production and export.

Adam Smith explains the concept of absolute advantage in a two-commodity, two-country framework. Suppose Bangladesh produces 1 kg of rice with 10 units of labour or it produces 1 kg of wheat with 20 units of labour. On the other hand, Pakistan produces the same amount of rice with 20 units of labour and produces the same amount of wheat with 10 units of labour. Each of the countries has 100 units of labour. Equal amount of labour is used for the production of two goods in absence of trade in the two countries.

In absence of trade, Bangladesh will be able to produce 5 kg of rice and 2.5 kg of wheat. At the same time, Pakistan will produce 5 kg of wheat and 2.5 kg of rice. But when trade is possible between the two countries, Bangladesh will produce only rice and exchange a part of the rice output with wheat from Pakistan. Pakistan will produce only wheat and exchange a part of the wheat output with rice from Bangladesh. The total output in both the countries will rise because of trade. Bangladesh, which was producing 7.5 kg of food-grains in absence of trade, will now produce 10 kg of

Table 3.1 Theory of Absolute Cost Advantage

Amount of Production in Absence of Trade			*Amount of Production after Trade*		
	Rice	*Wheat*		*Rice*	*Wheat*
Bangladesh	5 kg	2.5 kg	Bangladesh	10 kg	Nil
Pakistan	2.5 kg	5 kg	Pakistan	Nil	10 kg
Total output in two countries: 15 kg			Total output in two countries: 20 kg		

food-grains. Similar will be the case with Pakistan where 10 kg of food-grains will be produced instead of 7.5 kg (Table 3.1).

The theory of absolute cost advantage explains how trade helps increase the total output in the two countries. But it fails to explain whether trade will exist if any of the two countries produces both the goods at lower cost. In fact, this was the deficiency of this theory that led David Ricardo to formulate the theory of comparative cost advantage (Haberler, 1950).

3.2.2 Ricardian View of Comparative Advantage

Comparative cost advantage theory explains that a country should specialise in the production and export of a commodity in which it possesses greatest relative advantage.

Ricardo focuses not on absolute efficiency but on the relative efficiency of the countries for producing goods. This is why his theory is known as the theory of comparative cost advantage. In a two-country, two-commodity model, he explains that a country will produce only that product which it is able to produce more efficiently. Suppose Bangladesh and India, each of the two has 100 units of labour. One half of the labour force is used for the production of rice and the other half is used for the production of wheat in absence of trade. In Bangladesh, 10 units of labour are required to produce either 1 kg of rice or 1 kg of wheat. On the contrary, in India, 5 units of labour are required to produce 1 kg of wheat and 8 units of labour are required for producing 1 kg of rice. If one looks at this situation from the viewpoint of absolute cost advantage, there will be no trade as India possesses absolute advantage in the production of both the commodities. But Ricardo is of the view that from the viewpoint of comparative advantage, there will be trade because India possesses comparative advantage in the production of wheat. This is because the ratio of cost between Bangladesh and India is 2:1 in case of wheat, while it is 1.25:1 in case of rice. Because of this comparative cost advantage, India will produce only 20 kg of wheat with 100 units of labour and export a part of wheat to Bangladesh. On the other hand, Bangladesh will produce only 10 kg of rice with 100 units of labour and export a part of rice to India. The total output of foodgrains in the two countries, which was equal to 26.25 kg prior to trade, rises to 30 kg after trade. Thus it is the comparative cost advantage that leads to trade and specialise in production and thereby to increase in the total output in the two countries (Table 3.2).

Table 3.2 Theory of Comparative Cost Advantage

Amount of Output in Absence of Trade			*Amount of Output after Trade*		
	Rice	*Wheat*		*Rice*	*Wheat*
Bangladesh	5 kg	5 kg	Bangladesh	10 kg	Nil
India	6.25 kg	10 kg	India	Nil	20 kg
Total output in two countries: 26.25 kg			Total output in two countries: 30 kg		

Despite being simple, the classical theory of international trade suffers from a few limitations. Firstly, it takes into consideration only one factor of production, that is labour. But in the real world, there are other factors of production too that play a decisive role in production. Similarly, the theory does not take into account the transportation cost involved in trade.

Secondly, the theory assumes the existence of full employment, but in practice, full employment is a utopian. Normally, the entire resources in a country are not fully employed. In such cases, the country puts restrictions on the import in order to employ its idle resources, even if these resources are not to be employed efficiently.

Thirdly, the theory stresses too much on specialisation that is expected to improve efficiency. But it is not always the case in real life. The countries may pursue some other objectives too that may not be necessarily the productive efficiency. It is because when the country specialises in the production of a particular good, changes in the technology make the economy highly vulnerable.

Fourthly, the classical economists feel that the resources are mobile domestically and immobile internationally. But neither of the two assumptions is correct. Within the country, it is difficult for the labour to move from one occupation to another, especially when the job is highly technical. On the contrary, labour and capital move easily across nations.

Nevertheless, the empirical tests carried on by MacDougall (1951), Stern (1962) and Balassa (1963) supported the Ricardian hypothesis. It would not be wrong to say that the classical theory holds good even today insofar as it suggests how a nation could achieve the consumption level beyond what it could do in absence of trade. This is in fact the reason why the countries stress upon expansion in the world trade (Haberler, 1950).

3.2.3 Comparative Advantage based on Opportunity Cost

Later writings did not remain confined to a single factor of production, labour. They explained comparative advantage based on opportunity cost. Opportunity cost is the amount of a commodity foregone to get the other commodity. Recalling the earlier example, if 6.25 kg of rice are foregone to get 10 kg of wheat in India, the marginal rate of transformation (MRT) in India will be −0.625 kg of rice for 1 kg of wheat. Similarly, in Bangladesh, 5 kg of rice are foregone to get 5 kg of wheat, the MRT in Bangladesh will be −1 kg of rice for 1 kg of wheat. In terms of equation,

> MRT is the amount of one product that a country must forego to produce each additional unit of the other product.

$$\text{MRT} = \Delta\ \text{Product A}/\Delta\ \text{Product B} \qquad \text{....(3.1)}$$

Comparing the MRT in both the countries, it is found that India has lower opportunity cost of wheat for rice and so India has comparative advantage in the production of wheat.

Now trade is possible only when demand exists in each country for the commodity produced in other country. If demand is intense, the country may pay a higher price for imports. Suppose that there is demand for wheat in Bangladesh as a result of which it likes to import wheat from India. But now the question is at what price India will be ready to export wheat. If MRT in India is −0.625 kg rice/1 kg wheat, it will not accept less than 0.625 kg of rice for 1 kg of wheat. Rather it will like to get a better price. On the other hand, Bangladesh will not be ready to forego more than 1 kg of rice for 1 kg of wheat. Rather it will prefer to forego less rice for 1 kg of wheat. Thus the price will lie between the MRT existing in the two countries. If Bangladesh is ready to forego more rice than MRT in India, the terms of trade will move in favour of India because the same amount of export will fetch more imports for India. Suppose, Bangladesh is ready to forego 0.80 kg of rice for 1 kg of wheat in view of strong demand for it. In that case, India will get 0.80 kg − 0.625 kg or 0.175 kg more rice that what it could get in case of no trade. Bangladesh has still to forego less rice for wheat that it could have foregone in absence of trade.

3.2.4 Production Possibilities Schedule

The gains from trade can be explained through production possibilities frontier (PPF). PPF represents various combinations of two goods produced in a country with fully employed factors of production. We assume for the moment constant opportunity cost with the result that PPF is a straight line. The PPF existing in the two countries is given here in Figure 3.1(a) and Figure 3.1(b).

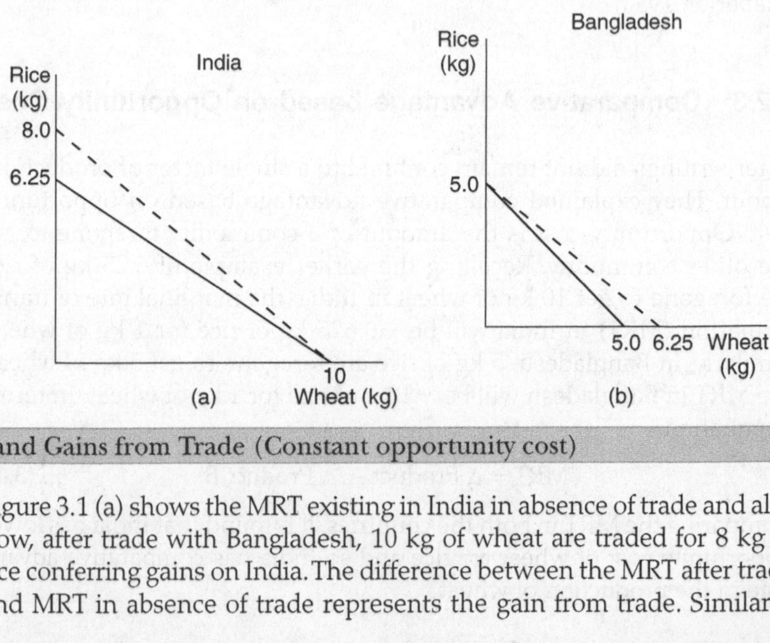

FIGURE 3.1 PPF and Gains from Trade (Constant opportunity cost)

Figure 3.1 (a) shows the MRT existing in India in absence of trade and also how, after trade with Bangladesh, 10 kg of wheat are traded for 8 kg of rice conferring gains on India. The difference between the MRT after trade and MRT in absence of trade represents the gain from trade. Similarly,

Figure 3.1 (b) shows the MRT existing before trade and after trade in Bangladesh and also how this country gains through trade.

3.2.5 Static and Dynamic Gains from Trade Re-examined

The above analysis has shown gains from trade. They are in fact production gains and consumption gains both of static nature. Trade leads to specialisation and thereby growth in output in both the countries. Similarly, with larger production and trade, there will be ample opportunity for increased consumption. How much one of the two countries will share the gains depends on the terms of trade which was not explained systematically by Ricardo. Ricardo set a limit within which the terms of trade lay. He did not explain the role of demand that influences the terms of trade. The larger the demand, the greater the price a country will be willing to pay. And this will influence the terms of trade. The country is able to share more gains in whose favour the terms of trade will move.

Static gains manifest in larger production and consumption. The share of the trading country in total gains depends on the terms of trade.

Dynamic gains manifest in contribution of trade to economic growth.

However, there are dynamic gains too in form of contribution of trade to economic growth. The productivity theory of international trade explained by Hla Myint (1958, 1977) relates economic growth to the country's foreign trade. It is because trade encourages innovations, overcomes technical indivisibilities and raises labour productivity. These are nothing but dynamic gains. Leibenstein (1966) is of the view that free trade may lead to promote X-efficiency which means better use of inputs so as to reduce the real costs per unit of output. The cost reduction is definitely the dynamic gains from trade.

First of all, when resources are employed more efficiently based on comparative advantage, GDP is bound to rise. Income grows; saving grows and then investment grows.

Secondly, increasing production of specific commodities helps the producers to achieve economies of scale and thereby to reduce the cost per unit. The process makes the producers more competitive in the international market. Greater competition enhances efficiency.

Thirdly, import of lower cost goods compels the domestic producers to improve efficiency. All round efficiency will certainly be beneficial for the process of economic growth.

3.3 FACTOR PROPORTIONS THEORY

Almost after a century and a quarter of the classical version of the theory of international trade, the two Swedish economists, Eli Heckscher and Bertil Ohlin, propounded a theory that is known as the factor endowment theory or the factor proportions theory. In fact, it was Eli Heckscher (1919) who mooted the notion of a country's comparative advantage (disadvantage) based on relative abundance (scarcity) of factors of production.

Later on, his student, Bertil Ohlin (1933) developed this notion of relative factor abundance into a theory of the pattern of international trade.

3.3.1 Heckscher-Ohlin Theorem

Factor endowment theory explains that a country should produce and export a commodity that primarily involves a factor of production abundantly available within the country.

The theory explains in a two-country, two-factor and two-commodity framework: (1) What determines the comparative advantage? (2) How trade influence the income of the factors of production?

The theory believes that different countries are endowed with varying proportions of different factors of production. Some countries have large population and large labour resource. The others have abundance of capital but short of labour resource. Capital-abundant country presents a higher capital/labour ratio than what a labour-abundant country presents. Thus a country with large labour force will be able to produce those goods at lower cost that involve labour-intensive mode of production. Similarly, the countries with large supply of capital will specialise in those goods that involve capital-intensive mode of production. The former will export its labour-intensive goods to the latter and import capital-intensive goods therefrom. After the trade, both the countries will have both types of goods at the least cost (Ohlin, 1933).

All this means that the theory holds good if the capital-abundant country has a distinct preference for the labour-intensive goods and the labour-abundant country has a distinct preference for capital-intensive goods. If it is not, the theory may not hold good. Again, the theory does not hold good if the labour-abundant economy is technologically advanced in capital-intensive goods or if the capital-abundant economy is technologically advanced in the production of labour-intensive goods.

3.3.2 Factor Price Equalisation

The effect of free trade among nations would be to increase the overall welfare by equating not only the prices of goods exchanged but also the prices of factors of production involved in the production of those goods in different countries. For example, in absence of trade, the price of capital in a capital-abundant economy of the USA will be much lower than that in case of a labour-surplus economy of India. But after trade is established between the two countries, more capital-intensive commodities will be produced in the USA. As a result, the price of capital will increase in the USA and the existing differential in this respect between the two countries will be lower. Similarly, more labour-intensive commodities will be produced in India. Wage level will increase in India with the result that the wage differential between the two countries will be narrower (Samuelson, 1948, 1949).

Now the question is whether the factor prices will be the same in two countries. Heckscher-Ohlin theory is affirmative. But in the real world, the answer is in negative in view of imperfections in the factor market.

3.3.3 Leontief Paradox

Leontief (1954) put this theory to empirical testing and found in case of the US trade during 1947 that this country was exporting less capital-intensive goods even when it had abundance of capital compared to labour. Had the factor proportions theory been true, the USA would have exported more of capital-intensive goods. This is really a paradox and so it is known as *Leontief Paradox*. However, Leontief himself re-examined this issue and found that the paradox disappeared if the natural resource industries were excluded. Moreover, he found that the USA exported more of labour-intensive goods because the productivity of labour in this country was higher than in many labour-abundant countries. Even in case of labour-abundant economies, he viewed, different countries differ in the sense that some countries possess skilled labour pool, whereas in other countries, the labour resource may be unskilled. The country with skilled labour force will be able to manufacture the same labour-intensive product in a more capital-intensive fashion and will be able to export that product to those labour-abundant countries where improved skill is not employed in the manufacture of the same product. Thus it is not only that the factor endowments are not homogeneous, but also they differ along parameters other than the relative abundance. Leontiefs later views find support from a couple of studies. The studies of Hufbauer (1966) and of Gruber, Mehta and Vernon (1967) reveal that improved technology was involved in the US export of labour-intensive goods that characterised US exports as technology-intensive rather than labour-intensive.

Leontief paradox refers to the empirical evidence based on US export of labour intensive goods challenging the factor endowment theory.

Soon after Leontiefs study, Tatemoto and Ichimura (1959) found that in case of US-Japan trade, Japan exported labour-intensive goods to the USA and imported capital-intensive goods therefrom. Similarly, Bharadwaj (1962) found in case of Indo-US trade that India imported mainly capital-intensive goods from the USA and exported labour-intensive goods to this country in 1951. These two empirical tests support the Heckscher-Ohlin theory of international trade.

3.3.4 Distribution of Income

Since labour and capital are fully employed before and after the trade, it is natural for the real income of both the factors to move up along with the rise in their prices. It means that the share of capital in national income will tend to rise in a capital-abundant economy compared to the share of labour in national income. In a labour-surplus economy, the share of labour in the national income will rise compared to that of capital. In all, this means that trade will lead to inequality of income within a country. This view is confirmed by Stopler-Samuelson theorem which states that trade does not necessarily leads to equal distribution of income in the country.

3.4 NEO-FACTOR PROPORTIONS THEORIES

Neo-factor proportion theories also consider the third factor, such as human skill, skill intensity, economies of scale and R&D.

Extending Leontief's view, some of the economists emphasise on the point that it is not only the abundance (scarcity) of a particular factor but also the quality of that factor of production that influences the pattern of international trade. The quality is so important in their view that they analyse the trade theory in a three-factor framework instead of two-factor framework taken into account by Heckscher and Ohlin. The third factor manifests in the form of:

1. Human capital
2. Skill-intensity
3. Economies of scale
4. Research and development (R&D) including technological innovation

As Kravis (1956) suggests, human capital which is the result of better education and training, should be treated as factor input like physical labour and capital. A country with improved human capital maintains an edge over other countries in regard to the export of commodities produced with the help of improved human capital.

The skill-intensity hypothesis is similar as the human capital hypothesis as both of them explain the capital embodied in human beings. It is only the empirical specifications of these two hypotheses that differ. Keesing (1965, 1971) computed the direct skill requirements for production of 1957 manufactured exports and imports for nine countries and 15 manufacturing sectors. The study revealed that labour is a non-homogeneous factor and it is the differing quality of labour in terms of skills that determines the pattern of international trade.

The scale-economies hypothesis explains that with rising output, unit cost decreases. The producer achieves internal economies of scale. A country with large production possesses an edge over other countries as regards to export. However, even a small country can reap such advantages if it produces exportables in large quantity.

Last but not least, R&D activity is positively associated with the competitive ability of the manufacturing industries. It is a proxy for trade advantage meaning that a country with large expenditure on R&D possesses a comparative trade advantage. Krugman and Obstfeld (1994) deal with both the process innovation and the product innovation. The process innovation hypothesis examines how different countries are ranked on the basis of technological level and how goods are ranked by technological intensity. The higher-ranked countries do always maintain an absolute advantage over the low-ranked countries. Again, their model with product innovation demonstrates that the process of innovation goes on continuously. A technologically advanced country exports newly innovated goods where its innovation continues to remain as its monopoly. It imports "old" goods where the technology has already been imitated by the producers in other countries.

3.5 COUNTRY SIMILARITY THEORY

Different from the classical argument or the factor proportions theory, Linder (1961) did not emphasise on the supply side or the cost of production. He rather stressed on the demand side meaning that trade is dependent upon the preference of the consumers. The pattern of consumption depends upon the level of income. And so, the consumers in the developed countries demand for sophisticated goods in contrast with the consumers in the less developed countries that demand for less sophisticated goods. Whenever an entrepreneur manufactures a particular commodity, it designs the product keeping in view the taste of the domestic consumers. It is because that the meeting of demand of the domestic consumers is the primary concern. The manufacturer expands the production in order to achieve the economies of scale and then only it is able to export the product. The export is made to similar countries or the countries with the same level of income because it will not be accepted in the countries with different levels of income. In other words, international trade in manufactured goods is influenced by the similarity of demand. For example, if the level of income between the US and the UK is similar, the US-manufactured goods will be exported to the UK or the latter's goods will be exported to the US. The goods of the US may not be in demand in Bangladesh because the living standard and the consumption pattern there is quite different from that in the US. In the words of Linder, "the more similar the demand structures of two countries, more intensive, potentially is the trade between these two countries" (p. 98). If the two countries have the same pattern of demand, their items of export and import will be the same, although they will vary on the basis of product-differentiation that in turn depends upon the degree of specialisation.

Linder has tested his theory empirically through the use of a matrix of trade intensities for a sample of 32 countries. He finds that most of high trade intensities lie closer to the diagonal meaning that the countries with similar per capita income record most of the greater trade intensities. Using Linder's data, Sailors et al (1973) have tested the theory with the help of rank correlation between absolute differences in per capita income and trade intensities for 31 countries. Their findings are generally in support of Linder's hypothesis.

3.6 INTRA-INDUSTRY TRADE

3.6.1 Nature of Intra-industry Trade

Ricardo's comparative advantage theory and Heckscher-Ohlin theorem both had conceived of inter-industry trade. But during the past few decades, intra-industry trade has attained huge proportions. Let us first explain intra-industry trade. The goods produced in the same industry, irrespective of the fact whether they are identical from every angle or differentiated on account of brand, etc. come under the purview of intra-industry trade. Now the question is how one defines a particular industry. Pen, pencil and sharpener may constitute a single industry under the banner of "stationery". Alternatively, they may be looked at as three different industries. In case of the latter, the size of intra-industry trade will be the minimal.

Grubel and Llyod (1975) classify the goods based on similarity of input and substitutability in use. The first group includes those goods with similar input requirements but low substitutability in use. The second one includes goods with low similarity in input requirements but high substitutability in use. The third group contains goods with similarity in input requirements and high substitutability in use. The trade in commodities of the first two groups can be explained to some extent by the conventional theories. But the third one needs a new theory dealing with intra-industry trade.

Intra-industry trade is found both in homogeneous products and the differentiated products.

The commodities belonging to the third group can further be compartmentalised as homogeneous products and differentiated products. A country may export and import homogeneous products. Suppose a company supplies its products to different countries in a region. The demand is such that it involves frequent orders. In such cases, the company sets up its warehouse in one of the countries of that region, from where the products are shipped to different countries on demand. Thus, the country, where warehouse is located, imports and exports the same commodity. This type of trade is known as entrepot trade. The entrepot trade is shown in Figure 3.2.

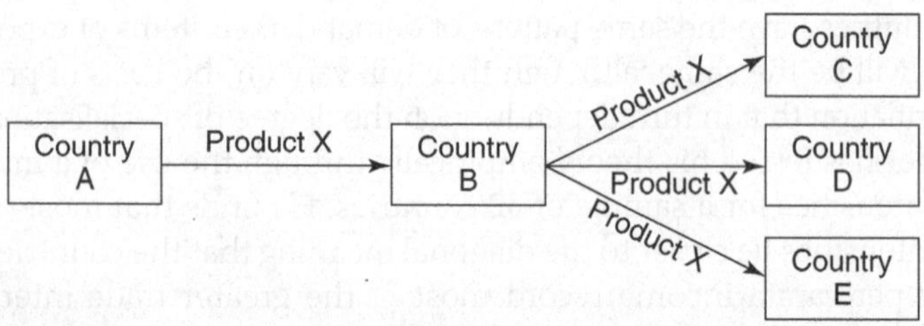

FIGURE 3.2 Entrepot Trade (Homogeneous Product)

Sometimes, trade in homogeneous products takes place because of heavy weight of that product. Suppose cement factories are located in northern part of India. They cater to the domestic as well as international market. But if a factory located in the extreme southern part of the country needs cement, it is easier and economical to import cement from Sri Lanka. In such cases, India will be exporting and importing the same product. Such cases are, however, not usual.

Intra-industry trade occurs mostly in differentiated products. The products are either vertically differentiated or horizontally differentiated. Vertically differentiated goods have different physical features and different prices. On the contrary, horizontally differentiated goods have similar prices. In fact, the trade of such goods takes place under imperfect market conditions. The market conditions may take varying form, such as monopoly, duopoly, oligopoly, monopolistic competition, etc. The prices tend to vary in different forms of markets. A country can export and import the same product with varying brands depending on the varying preferences of the consumers for different brands of the same product. The US is a manufacturer and exporter of automobiles but at the same time it imports car from Japan. It is because a good number of the American consumers have preference for Japanese make. Intra-industry trade in differentiated products is shown in Figure 3.3.

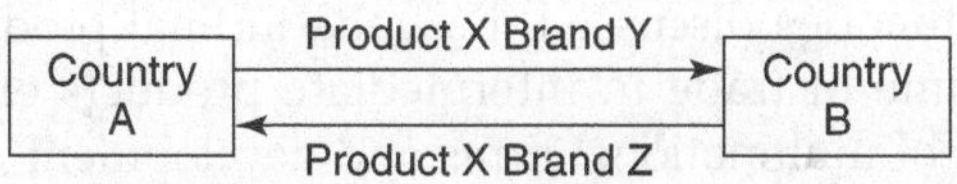

FIGURE 3.3 Intra-industry Trade in Differentiated Products

3.6.2 Measures of Intra-industry Trade

The size of intra-industry trade can be measured based on Grubel-Lloyd index. Grubel-Lloyd Index,

$$GLI = 1 - \{(Xi - Mi)/Xi + Mi\} \quad ....(3.2)$$

The index for any industry is calculated by taking the absolute value of trade balance and dividing it by the sum of export and import of the same industry and then subtracting the ratio from 1. If the export and import of an industry are equal to each other, the index will be one which means that the entire trade of the industry is intra-industry. On the other extreme, if index is zero, the industry does not have intra-industry trade. The evidences suggest that the index is normally high in (1) high-technology industries where frequent creation of new products leads to product differentiation; (2) industries with few trade barriers and (3) high-income countries.

3.6.3 Gains from Intra-industry Trade

When the manufacturers of the same product compete among themselves, they try to cut the cost through different means. The benefit of the cost reduction reaches the consumers in form of lower price. In case of inter-industry trade, it is not guaranteed that if the import price falls, export price too will fall. But if it is intra-industry trade, the export and the import prices fall simultaneously normally in the sequel of internal economies benefiting in turn the consumers in both the countries.

> The gains from intra-industry trade may appear in form of variety of a single product available to consumers at lower price. The gains may lead to employment and income generation.

The consumers get an added advantage. It is that their choice is not limited to a specific variety of a product. They use many varieties/brands of a single product. It is because the different brands have some unique product features.

Any fall in export and import prices leads to emergence of new firms in that particular industry. The income and employment get a boost up. Trade in the two countries moves upward in the sequel of less restrictive measures. The reason is that intra-industry trade occurs normally among the countries of similar income level and of similar factor endowment.

3.7 TRADE IN INTERMEDIATE PRODUCTS AND SERVICES: OUTSOURCING

The conventional theories discussed the trade in final products. But in view of large volume of trade in intermediate products emerging on account of growth of multinational firms and development of transport and communication in recent decades, the very concept behind such trade needs to be discussed. Today, with a view to acquire larger share in the domestic as well as international market, firms are trying to slice their value chain and to get the different parts of their production process performed in different countries so that the cost of production be the minimum. For example, if labour is cheap in labour-surplus developing country, the firms of the industrialised countries locate their assembly units in these countries. In other words, the firms are "outsourcing" their assembly operation to a developing country. Here it may be mentioned that it is not only manufacturing activities where outsourcing is found. It is now common in services too. Thus the concept of outsourcing and its potential gains need to be discussed.

3.7.1 Outsourcing and Off-shoring

> Outsourcing occurs when a firm locates a part of production process in some other countries Intra-firm outsourcing is off-shoring.

Outsourcing may be a domestic one. Domestic outsourcing occurs when a firm uses in its manufactured product some components manufactured by some other domestic firms. But here we are concerned with international outsourcing. In this case, a firm locates its specific parts of production process in some other countries depending on the availability of labour force and on the cost-cutting possibilities.

In this context, two terms are used—one is outsourcing and the other is off-shoring. When a firm outsources some of the functions to its own affiliates in some other countries, it is off-shoring. In other words, intra-firm outsourcing is known as off-shoring. Inter-firm outsourcing is known simply as outsourcing. For example, many automobile firms import components from India. Maruti Udyog buys components from local producers. In the initial years, Maruti-Suzuki was importing automobile engines from its parent company in Japan. These three examples are respectively of international outsourcing, domestic outsourcing and off-shoring.

3.7.2 Bases of Outsourcing

In order to have a full view of outsourcing, we may divide the manufacturing of a product into different phases. The consecutive phases are as follows:

1. Research and development
2. Production of components
3. Assembly
4. Marketing and sales

Now the question is which of these four functions will be performed in the domestic unit and which of them shall be outsourced to a foreign location. In fact, this decision depends upon the availability of the skilled labour force and the level of wages. Since the skilled worker asks for higher wage than unskilled or semi-skilled labour, only those functions need to be assigned to the skilled labour force that cannot be performed by the unskilled or semi-skilled labour force. The other functions should naturally be assigned to the semi-skilled or unskilled labour force. This way, the cost of production can be minimised.

Again, it is found that the developing world has a large reservoir of unskilled and semi-skilled labour force who is satisfied with lower wages. On the other hand, developed countries possess large number of skilled labourers. Thus it is natural for the firms located in the industrialised world to outsource those functions to the developing world that can be performed by the semi-skilled and unskilled workers at low cost. In the four functions mentioned above, production of components and their assembly should be outsourced, and the R&D and marketing and sales should be performed at the domestic unit located in the industrialised world. Similarly, the firms headquartered in the developing countries import R&D from the developed world. The newly industrialising countries of the developing world have a long history of technology import. They import technology and subsequently modify it in order to make it suitable for their own economy. In some cases, they export the modified technology to the developed world. Nevertheless, as far as the latest and sophisticated technology is concerned the firms of the developing world outsource R&D to the developed world. They also outsource the sophisticated components when they lack skilled workers to produce them. The computer industry in India is found outsourcing many such components.

3.7.3 Gains from Outsourcing

The gains from outsourcing can better be explained through PPF. We base our analysis on two factors—R&D involving skilled workers and component production involving unskilled and semi-skilled workers. Suppose a firm located in an industrialised country produces a final product without outsourcing, the quantity of final product, F_1 will be produced with components, Q_C and R&D, Q_R, as shown in Figure 3.4, at Point *A*. This is the point where the relative price line, *P* or Q_C/Q_R meets the PPF and Isoquant F_1 is tangent to PPF. Point *A* indicates the maximum output using a combination Q_C and Q_R.

But if the company outsources components to a labour-surplus developing country, the relative price line, P_1 meets the PPF at Point *B* on account of cheaper component. At Point *C*, a new isoquant, F_2 is tangent to PPF which shows the final product with outsourcing. The difference between F_2 and F_1 shows the additional output or the gain from outsourcing.

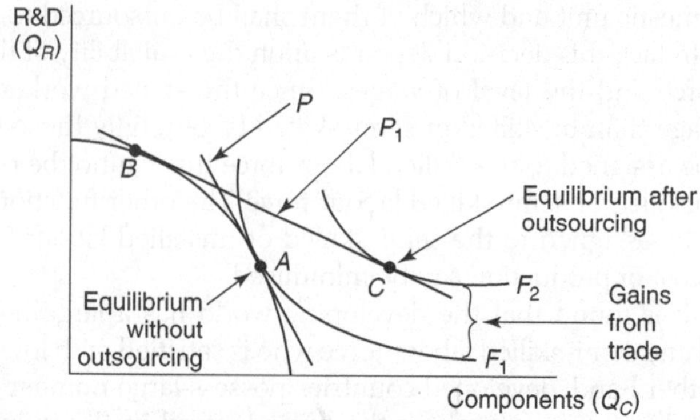

FIGURE 3.4 Outsourcing and Gains from Trade

Diamond of national advantage refers to the factors responsible for maintaining a nation' s competitive advantage, as explained by Porter. The factors are:

1. Factor conditions
2. Demand conditions
3. Related and supporting industries
4. Firm strategy, structure, and rivalry

However, there are two additional factors, such as governmental policy and chance of events that do influence the "Diamond".

3.7.4 Outsourcing of Services

The outsourcing of services is comparatively a new phenomenon but the size of services outsourced is huge and variety of outsourced services is wide (WIR, 2004). Although the same objective of cost reduction works behind it, yet it is not simply the availability of skilled manpower that is important but also it is the strong communication infrastructure which has been an important factor. Why is India a good host for outsourcing? It is because the communication system here is highly developed; Indians have English-speaking skill; and above all, software industry is highly developed.

3.8 THE NATIONAL COMPETITIVE ADVANTAGE

It is a fact that Porter (1990) never focussed primarily on the factors determining the pattern of trade, yet his theory of national competitive advantage does explain why a particular country is more competitive in a particular industry. If, for example, Italy maintains competitive advantage in the production of ceramic tiles and Switzerland possesses the competitive advantage in watches, it can be interpreted that the former will export ceramic tiles and the latter will export watches and both of them will import those goods in which their own industry is not competitive.

Why is this difference? Porter explains that there are four factors responsible for such diversity. He calls those factors as the"diamond of national advantage". The diamond includes the following (Figure 3.5):

1. Factor conditions
2. Demand conditions
3. Related and supporting industries
4. Firm strategy, structure and rivalry

These factors have been more or less taken into account by the earlier economists. What is crucial in Porter's thesis is that it is the interaction among these factors that shapes the competitive advantage.

Factor conditions show how far the factors of production in a country can be utilised successfully in a particular industry. This concept goes beyond the factor proportions theory and explains that availability of the factors of production per se is not important, rather their contribution to the creation and upgradation of product is crucial for the competitive advantage. This is possible if labour force is well-skilled and better-trained. Skill and training in Porter's view is an advanced factor which is essential for maintaining competitive advantage. If one says that Japan possesses competitive advantage in the production of automobiles, it is not simply because Japan has easy access to iron ore but this country has skilled labour force for making this industry competitive.

Secondly, the demand for the product must be present in the domestic market from the very beginning of production. Porter is of the view that it is not merely the size of the market that is important, but it is the intensity and sophistication of the demand that is significant for the competitive advantage. If consumers are sophisticated, they will make demand for sophisticated products and that in turn will help the production of sophisticated products. Gradually, the country will achieve competitive advantage in such production.

Thirdly, the firm operating along with its competitors as well as its complementary firms gathers benefit through close working relationship in form of competition or backward and forward linkages. If competition is acute, every firm will like to produce better-quality goods at lower cost in order to survive in the market. Again, if there is agglomeration of complementary units in a particular region, there may be strong backward and forward linkages. All this will help attain national competitive advantage.

Fourthly, the firm's own strategy helps in augmenting export. There is no fixed rule regarding the adoption of a particular form of strategy. It depends upon a number of factors present in the home country or the importing country and it differs from one point of time to the other. Nevertheless, the strategic decisions of the firm have lasting effects on their future competitiveness. Again, equally important is the industry structure and rivalry among the different companies. The greater the rivalry, the greater will be the competitive strength of the industry.

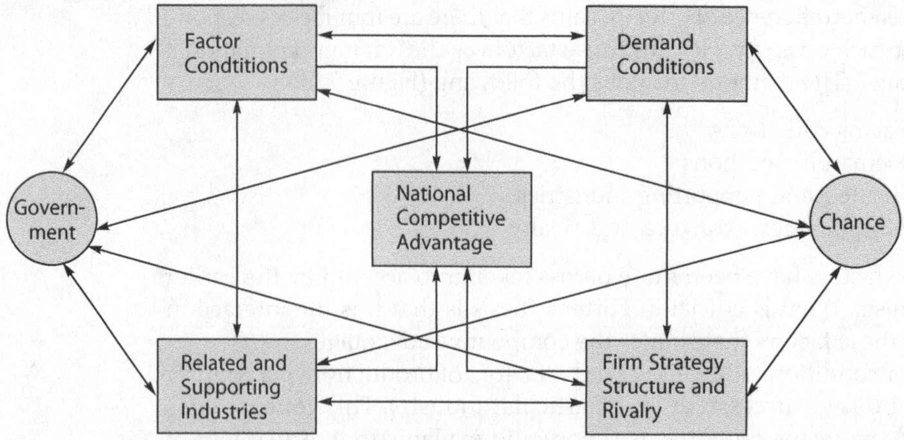

FIGURE 3.5 Porter's Diamond of National Advantage

Besides the four factors, Porter gives weightage to a couple of factors such as, governmental policy and the role of chance of events. The governmental policy influences all the four factors through various regulatory/deregulatory measures. It can control the availability of various resources or change the pattern of demand through taxes, etc. It can encourage/discourage the supportive industries through various incentives/disincentives. Similarly, chance of events such as, war or some unforeseen events like inventions/innovations, discontinuities in the supply of inputs, etc. can eliminate the advantages possessed by the competitors.

However, there are various criticisms put forth against Porter's theory. First, there are cases when the absence of any of the factors does not influence much the competitive advantage. For example, when a firm is exporting its entire output, the intensity of demand does not matter. Secondly, if the domestic suppliers of inputs are not available, the backward linkage will be meaningless. Thirdly, Porter's theory is based on empirical findings covering 10 countries and four industries. Majority of the countries in the world have different economic background and do not necessarily support the finding. Fourthly, availability of natural resources, according to Porter, is not the only condition for attaining competitive advantage and there must be other factors too for it. But the study of Rugman and McIlveen (1985) shows that some of the Canadian industries emerged on the global map only on the basis of natural resource availability. Fifthly, Porter feels that sizeable domestic demand must be present for attaining competitive advantage. But there are industries that have flourished because of demand from foreign consumers. For example, a lion's share of Nestle's earnings comes from foreign sales. Nevertheless, these limitations do not undermine the significance of Porter's theory.

3.9 TERMS OF TRADE

The concept of terms of trade is important in view of ascertaining the gains from trade. It is based on"what you get for what you give". If you get more than what you give, the terms of trade move in your favour and the trade brings in gain to you. For example, the raising of oil prices in 1973 by the OPEC nations improved their terms of trade and worsened the terms of trade of the oil-importing countries. In order to explain this phenomenon, if the import price rises relatively to the export prices, it means that one physical unit of the export will buy fewer physical units of import than before. It will be nothing but deterioration in the terms of trade. For a comparative analysis of the trend in the export and the import prices, one constructs the price index for exports and imports in the same fashion that the consumer price index is constructed.

Net barter terms of trade index is defined as Export price index divided by import price index.

Gross barter terms of trade index refers to export quantity index divided by import quantity index.

Income terms of trade index is defined as net barter terms of trade index multiplied by the index of the size of export.

There are different measures of terms of trade, such as net barter terms of trade, gross barter terms of trade, income terms of trade, factoral terms of trade, utility terms of trade and the real cost terms of trade (Meier, 1965). However, the first three measures are more commonly used for empirical analysis. Net barter terms of trade represent the ratio between the export price index and the import price index. In form of an equation,

$$\text{Net barter terms of trade} = P_x/P_m \qquad \text{.... (3.3)}$$

Where P_x is the export price index, and
P_m is the import price index.

For example, if in India in 2001, the export price index is 183 and the import price index is 224 (1980 = 100), the net barter terms of trade in 2001 will be unfavourable at 0.817 showing a decline by 18 per cent over the base year.

In case of gross barter terms of trade, the index of import quantity and the index of export quantity are computed and then the ratio between the two is found out. Since the quantity of different commodities cannot be easily added up, it is the value of export and import that is taken into account for this purpose. Gross barter terms of trade are favourable if a given quantity (value) of export is able to import a larger quantity (value) of import. In other words, gross barter terms of trade are reciprocal of the net barter terms of trade. In form of an equation,

$$\text{Gross barter terms of trade} = Q_x/Q_m \qquad \text{.... (3.4)}$$

Where Q_x is export quantity index, and
Q_m is the import quantity index.

If in India in 2001, the quantity of export index and quantity of import index are respectively 110 and 105 with base year as 1980, the gross barter terms of trade in 2001 will be unfavourable at 1.048 showing a decline of 4.8 per cent over the base year.

The computation of the income terms of trade is also important. With a fall in the export prices over a period, the net barter terms of trade will tend to deteriorate, but if the demand is highly price-elastic, the export earnings will rise at a greater rate that is beneficial from the viewpoint of country's foreign exchange earnings. If this is the situation, the income terms of trade will tend to improve despite deterioration in the net barter terms of trade. The computation of income terms of trade is very simple. The net barter terms of trade index is multiplied by the index of the size of export.

$$\text{Income terms of trade} = (P_x/P_m) \times V_x \quad ....(3.5)$$

Here V_x *is the index of the value of total export.*

Example

A country exports three items and imports three items, the volume and value during the base year (2000–2001) and the current year (2006–2007) being indicated below. The weight of a particular commodity in a particular year depends on the value of export/import. Find out the net barter, gross barter and income terms of trade.

Export					*Import*				
Item	*2000–2001*		*2006–2007*		*Item*	*2000–2001*		*2006–2007*	
	Volume (tonnes)	*Value $*	*Volume (tonnes)*	*Value $*		*Volume (tonnes)*	*Value $*	*Volume (tonnes)*	*Value $*
A	600	30000	800	36000	D	400	8000	400	12800
B	800	24000	500	20000	E	400	16000	400	18000
C	100	6000	200	16000	F	800	16000	1000	15000

1. **Net barter terms of trade in 2006–2007 (Base Year = 100):**
   Weighted average unit price of export:
   2000–2001:
   $50 \times 0.5 + 30 \times 0.4 + 60 \times 0.10 = \$43$
   2006–2007:
   $45 \times 0.5 + 40 \times 0.28 + 80 \times 0.22 = \$51.30$
   Price index for export in 2006–2007
   $51.30/43.00 \times 100 = 119.30$
   Weighted average price for import:
   2000–2001:
   $20 \times 0.2 + 40 \times 0.4 + 20 \times 0.4 = \$28$
   2006–2007:
   $32 \times 0.28 + 45 \times 0.39 + 15 \times 0.33 = \$31.46$
   Price index for import in 2006–2007:
   $31.46/28 \times 100 = 112.36$
   Export price index/import price index = 119.30/112.36 = 106.18
   Net barter terms of trade have improved by 6.18%.
2. **Gross barter terms of trade in 2006–2007 (Base Year = 100):**
   Export value index in 2006–2007:
   $\$(36000 + 20000 + 16000)/(30000 + 24000 + 6000) \times 100 = 120$

Import value index in 2006–2007:
$ (12800 + 18000 + 15000)/(8000 + 16000 + 16000) × 100 = 114.50
Export value index/import value index = 120/114.50 = ***104.80***
Gross barter terms of trade have turned unfavourable by 4.80%.

3. **Income terms of trade in 2006–2007 (Base Year = 100):**
Net barter terms of trade index × Export value index = 106.18 × 120/100 = 127.42
Income terms of trade have improved by 27.42%.

SUMMARY

- The theories of trade explain that goods produced competitively and more efficiently in a given country are exported. As a corollary, it means that those products that cannot be produced efficiently at home should be imported. The advocates of mercantilism argued for trade surplus that would in turn add to the country's stock of gold and the country's wealth, while the classical economists based their theories on the principle of cost advantage. Adam Smith talked about absolute advantage in a two-commodity, two-country framework. But his theory failed to explain the possibilities for trade when a single country possessed absolute advantage in both the commodities. Ricardo explained that trade could occur even in such cases if one country possessed comparative advantage in one of the two products. The classical theory was simple, but suffered from many limitations. So the comparative advantage explained through the opportunity cost is free from those limitations.
- After about a century and a quarter of the classical approach, Heckscher and Ohlin propounded the factor proportions theory of international trade. It is the factor endowment in a particular country that confers on it the competitive advantage. A labour-surplus country will produce and export labour-intensive goods, while a capital-abundant economy should produce and export capital-intensive products. This way the prices of factors of production tend to equalise among the trading countries. Leontief found in his empirical study that the USA being a capital-abundant economy exported labour-intensive goods. But he was of the view that such possibilities could not be ruled out because the US was able to produce labour-intensive goods in a bit capital-intensive fashion. The proponents of neo-factor proportions theories extend Leontief's idea and are of the view that it is not simply the abundance of labour or capital in a country that helps determine the pattern of trade, but importantly, it is the quality of the factors of production. The quality of factors of production manifests in human capital, skill intensity, economies of scale and R&D including product and process innovation.
- Linder's view is, however, different. He opines that large amount of trade today takes place among the industrialised countries because they share similar market segments. His theory also explains intra-industry trade that did not find a place in the conventional analysis. Besides, it is the outsourcing of intermediate products that brings in gains from trade.
- Last but not least, Porter's theory of national competitive advantage believes that countries seek to improve their national competitiveness through developing successful industries.

The success of targeted industries depends upon a host of factors that is termed as diamond of national advantage.
- Again, favourable terms of trade lead to gains from trade. There are different forms of terms of trade, yet more commonly used forms are net barter terms of trade, gross barter terms of trade and the income terms of trade.

REVIEW QUESTIONS

1. Explain the comparative cost advantage theory of international trade. Is it an improvementover the theory of absolute cost advantage?
2. Examine the factor proportions theory of international trade.
3. What do you mean by national competitive advantage as explained by Porter?
4. Distinguish between static and dynamic gains from trade.
5. Explain:
   (i) net barter terms of trade
   (ii) gross barter terms of trade
   (iii) income terms of trade
   (iv) outsourcing and off-shoring
6. Explain the comparative advantage theory based on opportunity cost.
7. What do you mean by intra-industry trade? Describe the possible gains from such trade.

OBJECTIVE TYPE QUESTIONS

1. Mark True or False:
   (a) Mercantilism had coincided with then consolidation of the nation-states in Europe.
   (b) Absolute cost advantage theory is based on the concept of productive efficiency.
   (c) The concept of productive efficiency does not form the basis of comparative cost advantagetheory.
   (d) Leontief paradox explains the validity of factor endowment theory of trade.
   (e) Free trade leads to equalisation of factor prices among the trading countries.
   (f) Neo-factor proportions theory discusses trade in a three-factor framework.
   (g) Trade between two countries, according to Linder, is influenced by similarity of demand.
   (h) "Diamond of national advantage" includes factor conditions as well as demandconditions.
   (i) Gains from trade can be interpreted only in static, and not in dynamic, framework.
   (j) Gross barter terms of trade depend on export/import price index.
2. Choose the most suitable answer:
   (a) Net barter terms of trade show:
      (i) The ratio between export price index and import price index

(ii) The ratio between export quantity index and import quantity index
(iii) Both of the above

(b) Income terms of trade mean:
(i) Net barter terms of trade multiplied by the index of export size
(ii) Gross barter terms of trade multiplied by the index of export size
(iii) None of the two

(c) Free trade:
(i) Leads to promote X-efficiency
(ii) Retards X-efficiency
(iii) has nothing to do with X-efficiency

(d) In Porter's view, trade depends on:
(i) Availability of factors of production alone
(ii) Contribution of the factors of production to create and upgrade output
(iii) Both of the above

(e) In Porter's view, backward and forward linkages are promoted through:
(i) Agglomeration of complementary units
(ii) Deglomeration of complementary units
(iii) None of the two

(f) According to the factor proportions theory, capital intensive goods are exported by:
(i) Capital abundant countries
(ii) Labour abundant countries
(iii) Both of the above

CASE STUDY

Lower Cost of Labour behind India's Jewellery Export

In the jewellery industry, the labour cost in the western industrialised countries is $21 per hour compared to around $120 per month in India. Such a big difference is nothing new between a capital-abundant economy and a labour-abundant economy. This is the reason that Indian firms producing labour-intensive goods, such as jewellery, enjoy an advantage over the firms in the USA and Europe.

Normak Fashions Pvt. Ltd., a manufacturers and exporters of Estelle brand jewellery, is one of such Indian firms. It enjoys 10 per cent share in the Indian organised fashion jewellery market estimated at Rs. 6,000 million. The firm possesses the unique distinction of being a preferred supplier for leading fashion brands in the West including Disney, Givenchy, Tommy Hilfiger, Jones New York and Napier.

Normak Fashions has a factory in Hyderabad which is a 100 per cent export-oriented unit and the capacity of which is 3.6 million units per year. It markets its products to the USA, the UK, Canada, Australia and Hong Kong.

(Continued)

The firm has set up recently another factory with a capacity of 2.4 million units that caters to the need of the domestic consumers. In the near future, the capacity is being expanded by 100 per cent to meet the growing demand abroad and to increase its share in the Indian fashion jewellery market which is expected to expand from the present level of Rs. 6.0 billion to Rs. 15.0 billion by 2010. The expansion will be made not at the cost of quality. The firm meets strict quality specifications. For example, in kids' jewellery, the lead content should not exceed 0.02 per cent. It follows this norm and so it is better known as the supplier of kids' jewellery. Moreover, in order to maintain the quality standard, it uses imported inputs and imported machinery. Its technicians visit the factories of some international brands, especially with which it has developed linkages.

Source: Based on the reports published in *Financial Express*, 24.7.2008

QUESTIONS

1. Is Normak's export of fashions jewellery commensurate with the factor endowment theory of international trade?
2. What are the reasons for its good export performance?
3. Why do the globally known brands prefer supply of fashion jewellery from Normak?

STUDY TOPIC

Recent Trends in India's Terms of Trade

The following table shows variation in the unit value of India's exports and imports that has influenced in turn the net barter terms of trade. The net barter terms of trade figure has moved up and down depending upon the changes in the ratio of import and export unit prices. The gross barter terms

(1978–79 = 100)

FY	Unit Value Index		Volume Index		Terms of Trade Index		
	Exports	*Imports*	*Exports*	*Imports*	*Gross*	*Net*	*Income*
1991–92	369.5	309.1	208.6	228.0	109.3	119.5	249.3
1992–93	421.5	331.0	222.9	282.0	126.5	127.3	283.8
1993–94	474.1	327.2	257.5	329.1	127.8	144.9	373.1
1994–95	494.6	324.6	292.7	408.3	139.5	152.4	446.0
1995–96	484.2	351.0	384.3	514.8	134.0	137.9	530.0
1996–97	504.7	399.8	411.8	511.8	124.3	126.2	519.7
1997–98	589.4	404.2	386.0	562.1	145.8	145.8	562.8

FY	Unit Value Index		Volume Index		Terms of Trade Index		
	Exports	Imports	Exports	Imports	Gross	Net	Income
1998–99	611.7	407.8	399.2	644.2	161.4	150.0	598.8
1999–00	604.5	450.5	461.0	704.8	152.9	134.2	618.7
2000–01	624.3	487.5	571.4	697.7	122.1	128.1	732.0
2001–02	618.0	492.9	592.7	732.8	123.6	125.4	743.2
2002–03	619.6	545.6	721.6	802.4	111.2	113.6	819.7
2003–04	672.4	545.1	764.8	970.4	126.9	123.4	943.5
2004–05	732.0	663.0	899.0	1113.0	110.0	124.0	991.0
2005–06	881.0	988.0	1307.0	1095.0	67.0	90.0	662.0
2006–07	863.0	608.0	1,164.0	2,047.0	176.0	142.0	1,653.0
2007–08	939.0	575.0	1,227.0	2,603.0	212.0	163.0	2,000.0

Source: Government of India, *Economic Survey: 2006–2007*, (New Delhi: Ministry of Finance).

of trade have also shown variations among different years. The reason is that the size of trade has moved up and down depending upon the varying requirements for imports and also the demand and supply constants influencing the size of exports. However the income terms of trade have normally increased over the years at a greater rate which shows that the decline in export prices has led to an increase in demand for India's export.

REFERENCES

Books

Bharadwaj, R. (1962), *Structural Basis of India's Foreign Trade*, Bombay: Bombay University Press.

Grubel, H. G and P. J. Lloyd (1975), *Intra-industry Trade: The Theory and Measurement of International Trade in Differentiated Products*, London: Macmillan.

Haberler, G. (1950), *The Theory of International Trade*, London: William Hodge.

Heckscher, E. (1919), "Foreign Trade and Income Distribution, *Economisk Tidskrift*, translated in Ellis, H. S. and L. A. Metzler, *eds*. (1950), *Readings in the Theory of International Trade*, London: Allen & Unwin.

——— (1935), *Mercantilism*, London: George Allen & Unwin.

Hufbauer, G. (1966), *Synthetic Materials and the Theory of International Trade*, Cambridge MA: Harvard University Press.

Krugman, P. and Maurice Obstfeld (1994), *International Economics: Theory and Policy*, New York: Harper Collins.

Linder, S. B. (1961), *An Essay on Trade Transformation*, New York: Wiley.

Meier, G. M. (1965), *International Trade and Development*, New York: Harper & Row.

Ohlin, B. (1933), *Interregional and International Trade*, Cambridge Mass.: Harvard.

Porter, M. E. (1990), *The Competitive Advantage of Nations* (New York: Free Press).

Rugman, A. M. and J. McIlveen (1985), *Megafirms: Strategies for Canada's Multinationals* (Toronto: Methuen/Nelson).

Journals

Balassa, B. (1963),"An Empirical Demonstration of Classical Comparative Cost Theory", *Review of Economics and Statistics*, XLV (3), 231–38.

Gruber, W. H., D. Mehta and R. Vernon (1967),"The R&D Factor in International Trade and International Investment of the United States Industries", *Journal of Political Economy*, LXXV (1), 20–37.

——— (1971),"Different Countries' Labour Skill Coefficients and the Skill Intensity of International Trade Flows", *Journal of International Economics*, I (4), 443–52.

Keesing, D. B. (1965),"Labour Skills and International Trade: Evaluating Many Trade Flows with a Single Measuring Device", *Review of Economics and Statistics*, XLVII (3), 287–94.

Kravis, I (1956), "Availability and Other Influences on Commodity Compositions of Trade", *Journal of Political Economy*, LXIV (2), 143–55.

Leibenstein, H. (1966), "Allocative Efficiency versus X-Efficiency", *American Economic Review*, LVI (3), 392–415.

Leontief, W. W. (1954)," Domestic Production and Foreign Trade: The American Capital Position Re-examined", *Economia Internazionale*, VII (1), 9–45.

MacDougall, G. D. A. (1951),"British and American Export: A Study Suggested by the Theory of Comparative Costs", *Economic Journal*, LXI (244), 697–724.

Myint, H. (1958), "The Classical Theory of International Trade and the Underdeveloped Countries", *Economic Journal*, LXVIII (270), 317–37.

Meier (1977),"Adam Smith's Theory of International Trade in the Perspective of Economic Development", *Economica*, VIL (175), 231–48.

Sailors, J. W. et al (1973),"Empirical Verification of Linder's Trade Thesis", Southern Economic Journal, XL (2), 262–68.

Samuelson, R. A. (1948), "International Trade and the Equalisation of Factor Prices", *Economic Journal*, LVIII (230), 163–84.

——— (1949), "International Factor Price Equalisation: Once Again", *Economic Journal*, LIX (233), 181–97.

Stern, R. M. (1962),"British and American Productivity and Comparative Costs in International Trade", *Oxford Economic Papers*, XIV (3), 275–96.

Tatemoto, M. and S. Ichimura (1959),"Factor Proportions and Foreign Trade: The Case of Japan", *Review of Economics and Statistics*, XLI (4), 442–46.

* **France** is the world's sixth-largest agricultural producer and the second-largest agricultural exporter, after the United States. However, the destination of 70% of its exports is other EU member states. Wheat, beef, pork, poultry and dairy products are the principal exports. A member of the G8 group, its economy is the fifth largest in the world in nominal terms, behind the United States, Japan, China and Germany and the eighth largest by purchasing power parity.

Stroget, Copenhagen, Denmark*

4

Theoretical Framework of Foreign Direct Investment

CHAPTER OBJECTIVES

This chapter discusses the motivation for FDI in what forms it occurs, and what impact it leaves on the home and host countries both at the economy's level and at the firm's level. The chapter discusses also how the MNCs' operations should be controlled so as to minimise the cost of FDI. In particular, the objectives are to:

- ✦ Discuss various theories of FDI.
- ✦ Show how different theories of FDI are applicable in case of FDI from developing countries.
- ✦ Analyse the benefits and costs of FDI from the viewpoint of both the home country and the host country.
- ✦ Evaluate the impact of M&As on the value of the firm.
- ✦ Discuss the measures of control of MNCs' operations.

The preceding chapter deals with the theories of international trade. Therefore, it is befitting to discuss the theoretical aspects of FDI in the present chapter especially, the basic theories in this respect and the impact of FDI, both in macroeconomic and microeconomic perspectives. It also discusses how the cost FDI can be minimised through control of MNCs.

4.1 THEORIES OF FDI

There are a number of theories explaining FDI. Except for the MacDougall-Kemp hypothesis, FDI theories are primarily based on imperfect market conditions. A few among them are based on imperfect capital market. The others take non-economic factors into account. Still others explain the emergence of MNCs exclusively among developing countries.

4.1.1 MacDougall-Kemp Hypothesis

Investment flows from a capital-abundant economy to a capital-scarce economy until the marginal productivity of capital in both of them is equal or till the returns from investment is greater than the loss of output in the home country.

One of the earliest theories was developed by G.D.A. MacDougall (1958) and subsequently elaborated by M.C. Kemp (1964). Assuming a two-country model—one being the investing country and the other being the host country—and the price of capital being equal to its marginal productivity, they explain that capital moves freely from a capital abundant country to a capital scarce country and in this way the marginal productivity of capital tends to equalise between the two countries. This leads to improvement in efficiency in the use of resources that leads ultimately to an increase in welfare. Despite the fact that the output in the investing country decreases in the wake of foreign investment outflow, national income does not fall insofar as the country receives returns on capital invested abroad, which is equivalent to marginal productivity of capital times the amount of foreign investment. So long as the income from foreign investment is greater than the loss of output, the investing country continues to invest abroad because it enjoys greater national income than prior to foreign investment. The host country too witnesses increase in national income as a sequel to greater magnitude of investment, which would not have been possible in the absence of foreign investment inflow.

4.1.2 Industrial Organisation Theory

The industrial organisation theory is based on oligopolistic or imperfect market conditions in which the investing firm operates. Market imperfections arise in many cases, such as product differentiation, marketing skills, proprietary technology, managerial skills, better access to capital, economies of scale, government-imposed market distortions, and so on. Such advantages confer on MNCs an edge over their competitors in foreign locations and, thus, help compensate the additional cost of operating in an unfamiliar environment.

One of the earliest theories based on the assumptions of an imperfect market was propounded by Stephen Hymer (1976). To Hymer, a multinational firm is a typical oligopolistic firm that possesses some sort of superiority and that looks for control in an imperfect market with a view to maximising profits. Despite the fact that the international firm is posted disadvantageously in a foreign host country where it has no intimate knowledge of language, culture, legal system, and consumers' preference, it possesses certain specific advantages that outweigh the disadvantages. The firm-specific advantages in Hymer's view are mainly the technological advantages that help the firm to produce a new product different from the existing one. It is in fact related to the possession of knowledge, which helps in developing special marketing skills, superior organisational and management set-up, and improved processing. What is significant in this theory is that these advantages are transmitted more effectively from one unit to the other irrespective of their geographical distance. Since the market is imperfect, rival firms do not avail of the technological advantage. International firm harvests huge profits. Graham and Krugman (1989) found empirically that it was the technological advantage possessed by European firms that had led them to invest in the USA. Caves (1971) feels that firm-specific advantages are transmitted more effectively if the firm participates effectively in the production in the host country than through other ways such as export or licensing agreements.

Firm-specific advantage refers to technological and similar other advantages possessed by a firm that enable it to produce new, differentiated products.

4.1.3 Location-specific Theory

Hood and Young (1979) stress upon the location-specific advantages. They argue that since real wage cost varies among countries, firms with low cost technology move to low wage countries. Again, in some countries, trade barriers are created to restrict import. MNCs invest in such countries in order to start manufacturing there and evade trade barriers. Sometimes it is the availability of cheap and abundant raw material that encourages the MNCs to invest in the country with abundant raw material. Dabur has moved to Nepal in as much as varieties of herbs to be used in medicine are available in plenty in that country.

Location-specific advantage refers to advantages like cheap labour, abundantly available raw material, and so on for the production of a commodity to be established in a particular location or country.

4.1.4 Product Cycle Theory

Hymer explained "why" foreign investment takes place. Hood and Young explained "where" foreign investment takes place. It was Raymond Vernon (1966) who added "when" to "why" and "where", based on data obtained from US corporate activities. Raymond Vernon's theory is known as the product cycle theory.

Vernon feels that most products follow a life cycle that is divided into three stages. The first is known as the "innovation" stage. In order to compete with other firms and to have a lead in the market, the firm innovates a product with the help of research and development. The product is manufactured in the home country primarily to meet the domestic demand, but a portion of the output is also exported to other developed

Innovation stage is a stage in the product cycle when the product is in demand because of its new and improved quality, irrespective of its price.

countries. The quality of the product, and not the price, forms the basis of demand because the demand is price-inelastic at this stage.

Maturing product stage is a stage in the product cycle when the demand for the innovator's product is price-elastic in view of availability of similar products in the market.

The second stage is known as "maturing product" stage. At this stage, the demand for the new product in other developed countries grows substantially and it turns price-elastic. Rival firms in the host country itself begin to appear at this stage to supply similar products at a lower price owing to lower distribution cost, whereas the product of the innovator is often costlier as it involves the transportation cost and tariff that is imposed by the importing government. Thus in order to compete with rival firms, the innovator decides to set up a production unit in the host country itself, which would eliminate transportation cost and tariff. This leads to internationalisation of production. The imposition of tariff in the host country encouraging foreign direct investment is confirmed by Uzawa and Hamada, but they feel that entry of foreign capital in protected industry reduces welfare in the host country (Kojima, 1978).

Standardised product stage is a stage in the product cycle when technology does not remain the exclusive possession of the innovator. Competition turns stiffer.

In the final or "standardised product" stage, a standardised product and its production techniques are no longer the exclusive possession of the innovating firm, rival firms from the home country itself, or from some other developed countries, put stiff competition. This is not unusual because the follow-the-leader theory developed by Knickerbocker (1973) suggests that there is a tendency among followers to snatch the benefits of international production from the innovator. At this stage, price competitiveness becomes even more important; and in view of this fact, the innovator shifts the production to a low cost location, preferably a developing country where labour is cheap. The product manufactured in a low cost location is exported back to home country or to other developed countries.

Dematuring stage is a a stage when technological development breaks down product standardisation.

Literature on the subject identifies one more stage in the product's life cycle. It is known as "dematuring" stage, when development in technology or in the consumers' preference breaks down product standardisation. Sophisticated models of the product are manufactured again in technology advanced, high income countries so that the firm can have a close linkage with consumers' tastes and with the basic infrastructure required for production. Cheap labour does not matter much at this stage as sophisticated models involve a capital intensive mode of production. Globerman (1986) has explained the four stages with a simple example of television set that was first produced in the United States of America and then in other advanced countries. Technology became standardised. Production became concentrated in Japan owing to the cheap labour cost. Lastly, the dematuring stage appeared when sophisticated models were developed and produced in the USA itself.

The product cycle theory clearly explains the early post-Second World War expansion of US firms in other countries. But with changes in the international environment, different stages of the product life cycle did not necessarily follow in the same way. Vernon (1979) himself has pointed out this limitation in his later writing, showing how in the second stage itself firms were found moving to the developing world to reap the advantages of cheap labour. This was possible with the narrowing of the information gap.

Again, the assumptions of the theory that the "export threat" causes a firm to set up a subsidiary in that country are not always true. If this is true, all US firms should have set up subsidiaries abroad in countries to which they had been exporting (Bhagwati, 1972). Yet again, development in the second stage and in the third stage is contradictory in the sense that the former is anti trade oriented vis-à-vis the latter, which is trade-oriented. In fact, it is this difference that characterises US firms and differentiates them from the Japanese ones (Kojima, 1985).

4.1.5 Internalisation Approach

Buckley and Casson (1976) too assume market imperfection, but imperfection, in their view, is related to the transaction cost that is involved in the intra-firm transfer of intermediate products such as knowledge or expertise. In an international firm, technology developed at one unit is normally passed on to other units free of charge. This means that the transaction cost in respect of intra-firm transfer of technology is almost zero, whereas such costs in respect of technology transfer to other firms are usually exorbitantly high putting those firms at a disadvantage. Coase (1937) too believes that MNCs bypass the regular market and use internal prices to overcome the excessive transaction cost of an outside market. Thus, it is the internalisation benefit manifesting in the cost-free intra-firm flow of technology or any other knowledge that motivates a firm to go international. It can be said that the views of Buckley and Casson are more or less in common with the contents of the appropriability approach of Magee (1979) that emphasises on potential returns from technology creation as a prime mover behind internationalisation of firms.

Internalisation benefit is cost free intra-firm flow of technology developed by the parent unit.

There are, of course, critics who argue that intra-firm transaction cost may not necessarily be low. If subsidiaries are located in an unfamiliar or uncongenial environment, the transaction cost is generally high. Kogut and Parkinson (1993) are of the view that if the transfer of intermediate goods involves substantial modification of well established practice, transaction cost is very large. Franke, Hofstede, and Bond (1991) opine that if the cultural differences between the home country and the host country are wide, the internalisation process will be a costly affair.

Again, the internalisation theory, says Rugman (1986), is a general theory explaining FDI and so it lacks empirical content. However, in a subsequent study, he feels that with a precise specification of some additional conditions successful testing is possible. Buckley (1988) himself is suspicious of the very limitation, but is hopeful of getting satisfactory results from a rigorous and precise test.

4.1.6 Eclectic Paradigm

Dunning's eclectic paradigm is a combination of the major imperfect market-based theories of FDI, that is, industrial organisation theory, internalisation theory and location theory. It postulates that, at any given time, the stock of foreign assets owned by a multinational firm is determined by a combination of firm specific or ownership advantage (O), the extent of location bound endowments (L), and the extent to which these advantages are marketed within the various units of the firm (I). Dunning is conscious that configuration of the O-L-I advantages varies from one country to the other and from one activity to the other. Foreign investment will be greater where the configuration is more pronounced.

Again, he introduces a "dynamised add-on" variable to his theory. This is nothing but a variable of strategic change, which may be either autonomous or a strategy-induced change. International production during a particular period would be the sum of the strategic responses of the firm to the past configuration of O-L-I and to changes in such configuration as a sequel to exogenous and endogenous changes in environment. The example of autonomous change in strategy may be that a firm makes foreign investment more in innovatory activities because of greater O-advantage, or it invests more in a particular country because of L-advantage or it adopts a different marketing strategy depending upon the greater amount of I-advantage. Similarly, the strategy induced change may be evident from the fact that a market seeking investment has a different O-L-I configuration from that of a resource based investment. And ultimately, it is the varying configuration that shapes the direction and the pattern of FDI (Dunning, 1980, 1993).

The eclectic approach thus, has wider coverage. It has also been empirically tested by Dunning himself with satisfactory results.

4.1.7 Currency based Approaches

> Firms from a strong-currency country move out to a weak-currency country.

The currency based theories are normally based on imperfect foreign exchange and capital market. One such theory has been developed by Aliber (1971). He postulates that internationalisation of firms can best be explained in terms of the relative strength of different currencies. Firms from a strong-currency country move out to a weak-currency country. In a weak-currency country, the income stream is fraught with greater exchange risk. As a result, the income of a strong-currency country firm is capitalised at a higher rate. In other words, such a firm is able to acquire a large segment of income generation in the weak-currency country corporate sector.

The merits of Aliber's hypothesis lie in the fact that it has stood up to empirical testing. FDI in the United States of America, Canada, and the United Kingdom has been found to be consistent with the hypothesis. However, the theory fails to explain why there is FDI in the same currency area.

Another theory based on the strength of currency has been developed by Kenneth Froot and Jeremy Stein (1989). The view is that depreciation in the real value of currency of a country lowers the wealth of domestic residents vis-à-vis the wealth of foreign residents. As a result, it is cheaper for foreign firms to acquire assets of domestic firms. The authors have found that this factor has been one of the determinants of foreign investment in the United States of America.

Yet another theory in this context has been propounded by Richard Caves (1988) in one of his later writings. Caves mentions a couple of channels through which exchange rate influences FDI. First, changes in exchange rate influence the cost and revenue stream of a firm. If the domestic currency depreciates, the import bill will inflate, diminishing in turn the net income. But, if export expands in the wake of currency depreciation, income will rise. Secondly, exchange rate changes influence FDI by giving rise to capital gains. Depreciation in the value of currency, which is expected to be reversed in the near future, will lead to capital gains following appreciation. In lure of capital gains, foreign capital will flow in. This theory has been tested empirically by Caves himself, who finds a negative correlation between the level of exchange rate and the level of FDI in the USA.

4.1.8 Politico-economic Theories

The politico-economic theories concentrate on political risk. Political stability in the host countries leads to foreign investment therein (Fatehi-Sedah and Safizedah, 1989). Similarly, political instability in the home country encourages investment in foreign countries (Tallman, 1988). However, Schneider and Frey (1985) believe that the theory underlying the political determinants of FDI is less well developed than those involving economic determinants. The political factors are only additive ones influencing foreign investment.

> Political stability in the host countries leads to foreign investment therein. Similarly, political instability in the home country encourages investment in foreign countries.

4.1.9 Modified Theories for Third World Firms

The theories discussed above also apply to international firms headquartered in developing countries, but they need some modifications. These firms have long been importing technology from industrialised countries. But since imported technology is mainly designed to cope with a large market, firms export a part of their output after meeting the domestic demand. The products become gradually mature and then the firms set up units in the product importing countries. But it is different from the product cycle theory insofar as the firms do not necessarily innovate the product; rather they modify the product to suit the consumers' needs in different countries. The modification is of scaling-up kind when it concerns the consumers in the developed countries. For the low income consumers, it is a scaling-down modification. However, it cannot be denied that modification of these types confers upon the firms a sort of firm-specific advantage (Sharan, 1985). Winlee Ting (1982) cites an example of a Taiwanese firm manufacturing pressure cookers and table fans. The firm modified the imported technology and set up units not only in the developing countries but also in the country from where it had originally imported the technology.

> Developing country MNCs possess firm-specific advantage in form of modified technology. They move abroad also to reap advantages of cheap labour and abundance of natural resources.

Some Recent Acquisitions by MNCs of Developing and Transition Economies

- China's National Petroleum Corporation acquired PetroKazakhstan in 2005 for $4.1 billion.
- China's Sinopec bought the Russian-United Kingdom joint venture Udmurtneft in 2006 for $3.5 billion.
- Mittal Steel Group, a company of Indian origin headquartered in the Netherlands acquired a European steel company, Arcelor in 2006 for $32.0 billion.
- The Indian Tata Group acquired the British/Dutch Corus Group in 2006 for $9.0 billion.
- Russian Aluminium acquired a part of Swiss Glencore International in 2006 for $2.5 billion.
- Sterlite Industries (India) Ltd., a subsidiary of UK-based Vedanta Resources Plc. acquired a US-based Asarco LLC in 2008 for $2.6 billion.

Source: Based on the reports published in *World Investment Report, 2007* and *Financial Express*, June 1, 2008

Again, the firms in developing countries possess a pool of cheap labour that accompanies the investment. On the other hand, the developing host country possesses, in some cases, abundance of natural resources, which attracts investment from other developing countries. This is very much in common with the location-specific theory of FDI discussed above. Thus, the theories discussed so far applies also to MNCs of the developing world.

Joint Venture

India's leading tractor maker Mahindra & Mahindra's American arm, Mahindra's USA Inc, decided to set up an assembly unit in Canada to locally produce and market a range of low-horsepower cab tractors with features like AC, heater, personal stereo and even a sun-roof.

The firm was also to source cab tractors from Japan's Mitsubishi and Tong Yang of South Korea, and market them in Canada under the Mahindra badge.

Again, in response to rising US demand, Mahindra USA opened a second assembly plant and distribution centre in Georgia.

Source: Adapted from TOI report.

4.2 BENEFITS AND COSTS OF FDI

When direct investment flows from one country to another, it creates benefits both for the home country and the host country. At the same time, it involves some costs too. Thus, when a firm decides to make FDI, it takes into consideration the benefits and costs to be accrued, not only to its home country but also to the host country. The host country perspective is no less significant, because cooperation from the host government depends upon the benefits derived by the host country.

In the present section, the benefits and costs of FDI are mentioned from the point of view of the home country as well as the host country. Since the host country perspective is more sensitive, it will be discussed first.

4.2.1 Benefits to the Host Country

Availability of Scarce Factors of Production: FDI helps attain a proper balance between different factors of production through the supply of scarce factors and fosters the pace of economic development. FDI brings in capital and supplements the domestic capital. This is a significant contribution where the domestic savings rate is too low to match the warranted rate of investment. FDI brings in scarce foreign exchange, which activates the domestic savings that would not have been put into investment in the absence of foreign exchange availability. It happens when the investment outlay possesses a foreign exchange component and in absence of foreign exchange, domestic savings remain idle. It also happens when local investors are afraid of the large risk involved in the investment project. In case of FDI, foreign investors share the risk and the investment project is implemented.

FDI brings in capital (scarce foreign exchange), skilled personnel, strategic raw material and improved technology.

One can say that a country can get scarce foreign exchange also through foreign borrowing and other forms of investment. But FDI is superior to all of them. It is because FDI, which takes a longer-term view of the market, is more stable than non-FDI flows. Statistics reveal that the coefficient of variation of real FDI was on an average 0.94 and 0.63, respectively, during 1980–1989 and 1990–1997, compared to 1.96 and 1.76 for non-FDI flows during the corresponding period (United Nations, 1999). Moreover, it does not create debt. Profit is repatriated only when it actually exists.

Sometimes FDI is accompanied by labour force that performs jobs that the local labour force is either not willing to do or is incapable of doing on account of lack of desired skill. Besides, the foreign labour force infuses non-traditional mental attitudes among the local labour force.

Besides, foreign investors make available raw material and improved technology. Raw material is normally not a very important consideration for the host country, but this factor becomes significant when the question of some vital raw material is concerned. At the same time, host countries often encourage FDI inflow because they procure improved technology; and more importantly, an ongoing access to continued research and development programmes of the investing country. Statistics reveal that over 90 per cent of the R&D activities giving rise to the creation of new product and process technology are concentrated in seven industrialised countries. Other countries reap the benefit from these innovative activities when they are transferred to them in the form of FDI through MNCs. The transfer takes two forms—one is internalised to the affiliates under the same ownership and control and the other is externalised to other firms in form of franchises, licenses, sub-contracting, and so on. Externalised transfer is found in cases where technology is simple and secrecy considerations are not very important, but it is often costly. Internalised transfer is often cheaper and can be made at different levels of operation. Whatever may be the mode of transfer, it benefits the recipient. In the short term, the benefit manifests in the form of increased productivity, new products, and lower costs. In the long term, it depends on how much the recipient learns from the technology and is able to deepen and develop its own capabilities. For the economy as a whole, the benefits also include the diffusion of technology and its spillovers to other firms.

As regards diffusion, it depends on how intense the linkages are in the host country. Since MNCs prefer to establish linkages with foreign firms, local linkages are often poor. However, such trends are gradually changing. Mani (1999) points out that Japanese MNCs have been transplanting their traditional *keiretsu* links from their home country to host countries. Again, Kumar (1998) found in the case of US and Japanese MNCs operating in a sample of 74 host countries that the affiliate R & D intensity was positively and significantly related to the scale of R & D activity and the availability of scientists and engineers in the host country.

FDI improves balance of payments through its contribution both to current account and capital account.

Improvement in the Balance of Payments: FDI helps improve the balance of payments of the host country. The inflow of investment is credited to the capital account. At the same time, the current account improves because FDI helps either import substitution or export promotion. The host country is able to produce items that were being imported earlier. FDI is able to augment export because foreign investors bring in the knowledge of exporting mechanics and of foreign markets. They bring in improved technology to produce goods of international standards and at a lower cost. They possess a world-reputed brand name, which is helpful in promoting export. They are also more capable of availing export credits from the cheapest source in the international financial market. In the United States of America, for example, MNCs—both local and foreign combined—accounted for three-fourths of the total export in 1996. They have done well in the export of natural resources, processed agricultural products, and of services, but they have done far better in the export of manufactured goods. In fact, they pursue the export activities not only in the existing pattern of comparative advantage, but more importantly they exploit this advantage (Helleiner, 1973). These MNCs operate in low technology activities and derive competitive strength in export on the basis of cheap labour or cheap raw material. In cases of medium and high technology activities, they are able to export well on the basis of their vertical set-up or because of their involvement in large scale processing of natural resources. They bring in dynamism in the sense that they move on to the next level of technological complexity. In a primary goods exporting country, dynamism means launching of simple manufactured products. In case of countries with simple manufactured exports, they move to higher value added products. An UNCTAD study shows a positive correlation between FDI and export dynamism in the developing world (United Nations, 1999).

Building of Economic and Social Infrastructure: When foreign investors invest in sectors such as basic economic infrastructure, social infrastructure, financial markets, and marketing system, the host country is able to develop a support system that is required for rapid industrialisation. Even if there is no investment in these sectors, the very presence of foreign investors in the host country creates a multiplier effect. A support system develops automatically.

Fostering of Economic Linkages: Foreign firms have forward and backward linkages. They make demand for various inputs, which in turn helps develop input supplying industries. They employ labour force, which helps raise the income of employed people, which in turn raises the demand and industrial production in the country. In all, the total investment in the host country increases by more than the amount of FDI. This is nothing but the "crowding-in effect" of FDI. An empirical study of Borensztein et al (1995) shows that the crowding-in effect of FDI is very common.

Crowding-in effect is the increase in total amount of investment in the host country by more than the amount of FDI on account of backward and forward linkages.

Table 4.1

Foreign Affiliate-Local Firm Relationship

Backward linkages	**Forward linkages**
Short-term	Short-term
–Normal Purchase	–Normal sales
–Short-term purchase contract	–Short-term sales contract
Long-term	Long-term
–Long-term contract	–Long-term sales contract
–Sub-contracting	–Outsourcing
–Joint-venture	–Joint-venture arrangement
–arrangement	–Setting up of distributional affiliate

As shown in Table 4.1, the backward and forward linkages may be a short-term phenomenon. They may also represent a long-term relationship between the foreign company and the local company. The short-term relationship is manifested in pure market purchase or sale transactions. Sometimes, there is a short-term or medium term contract for purchase and sale between the two parties. On the contrary, in case of long-term linkages, there may be long-term contract for purchase and sale. Alternatively, for the backward linkages, there may be sub-contracting of the production of final or intermediate product. In case of forward linkages, there may be outsourcing from domestic firms to foreign affiliates. In some cases, there is joint-venture arrangement between the foreign affiliate and the domestic firm.

Sona Koyo supplies power steering system to Maruti and also to Mahindra & Mahindra passenger car segment. It is because of the huge supply of power steering system that the operating profit of Sona Koyo grew 33.1 per cent to Rs 17.7 crore in the second quarter of 2007–08. Its net sales too grew 18.8 per cent to Rs 164.6 crore during this period.
Source: Based on the reports published in *Business Standard*, 25.11.2007

Strengthening of Government Budget: Foreign firms are a source of tax income for the government. They pay not only income tax but also the tariff on their import. At the same time they help reduce governmental expenditure requirements through supplementing the government's investment activities. All this eases the burden on the budget.

4.2.2 Benefits for Home Country

FDI benefits the home country too. The country gets the supply of necessary raw material if the investor makes investments in the exploration of a particular raw material. The balance of payments improves insofar as the parent company gets dividend, royalty, technical service fees, and other payments. It is also because of the rising export of the parent company to the subsidiary. If FDI takes place in order to develop a vertical set-up abroad, the export is quite significant. When persons accompany the investment, it results in greater employment of the nationals. The parent company gains access to new financial markets through investment abroad.

Moreover, the government of the home country generates revenue by taxing the dividend and other earnings of the parent company. There is also revenue from tariff on imports of the parent company from its subsidiary abroad. Again, since FDI is a complement to foreign aid, it helps develop a closer political tie between the home country and the host country, which is beneficial for both countries.

4.2.3 Cost to the Host Country

It is a fact that the inflow of foreign investment helps improve the balance of payments, but the outflow on account of imports and the payments of dividend, technical service fees, royalty, and so on deteriorates the balance of payments. There is evidence to prove that such outflows have exceeded the investment inflows in some of the years in India (Sharan, 1978). Based on the latest figures supplied by RBI, it is evident that the export of the foreign direct investment companies in India continued to remain largely at 11.1–16.4 per cent of their total sales during FYs 2001–08. The import-export ratio of these firms moved between 123.2 per cent and 158.5 per cent during FYs 2004–08. Added to it was the payment on account of royalty, technical fees and dividend that resulted in negative foreign exchange earnings. The three-year average of net foreign exchange earnings moved from Rs. (–) 34.26 billion in FY 2003–04 to as large as Rs. (–) 272.32 billion in FY 2006–07.

This is not only the case of balance of payments. Raw materials are exploited keeping in view the interest of the home country, which sometimes mars the interest of the host country. Again, the parent company supplies the technology to the subsidiary, but normally does not disseminate it to the host market. The result is that the host country remains dependent on the home country for the technology, which is often received at an exorbitant price. Sometimes the technology is inappropriate for the local environment and in that case, the loss to the host country is large.

As far as employment of the locals is concerned, MNCs normally show reluctance to train local people. Technology is normally capital intensive, which does not assure larger employment.

Sometimes, manufacturing by the foreign investors does not abide by the pollution norms, the norms regarding optimal use of natural resources, or the norms regarding location of industries. All this goes against the interest of the host country.

Foreign investors are generally more powerful. Domestic industrialists do not compete with them, with the result that the domestic industry fails to grow. This is nothing but the "crowding-out" effect of FDI. The study of Kumar and Pradhan (2002) finds that in 29 out of 83 cases, there was a clear-cut crowding-out effect. Foreign companies in such cases, charge higher prices for the product in view of their oligopolistic position in the market. Higher prices hamper the interest of the consumers as well as lead to inflationary pressure. Foreign companies infuse foreign culture into the industrial set-up and also in the society. Sometimes, they are so powerful that they are able to subvert the government.

4.2.4 Cost to Home Country

The cost accruing to the home country is only little. However, it cannot be denied that investments abroad takes away capital, skilled manpower, and managerial professionals from the country. Sometimes the outflow of these factors of production is so large that it hampers the home country's interest.

The MNCs operate in different countries in order to maximise their overall profit. To this end, they adopt various techniques that may not be in the interest of the host country. This leads to a tussle between the host government and the home government, leading to deterioration bilateral relations.

Thus, FDI is not an unmixed blessing. It does possess bright features, but at the same time, it has dark spots too. Thus, global benefit can be achieved only if it is carefully handled.

4.3 M&As AND THE VALUE OF THE FIRM

M&A is a gainful strategy only when the value of the combined firm is greater than the sum of the value of the two firms computed individually in absence of a merger. In form of an equation,

$$\text{Gain} = V_{AB} - (V_A + V_B) \quad \text{...(4.1)}$$

However, the gain so derived has to be compared with the cost of M&A, which is arrived at after deducting the value of the target firm from the price that the acquiring firm pays to the target company. This means that the net gain from M&A accruing to the acquiring firm exists only when:

$$[V_{AB} - (V_A + V_B)] > (\text{Price} - V_B) \quad \text{...(4.2)}$$

Thus, in this context, it is significant to know what price the acquiring firm should pay to the target firm for acquisition and what would be the impact of the changes in price on the post-merger value of the firm. The price is known as the consideration value fixed within the two extremes. One is the floor price for the package, any price below which is not acceptable by the

Consideration value refers to the price that the acquiring firm pays to the target firm.

target company. It is basically the market value of the shares of the target company. For example, if Firm *A* acquires Firm *B* and if the market value of Firm *B's* share is \$15, the consideration value must at least be \$15. In practice, it is more than \$15, as the premium will attract Firm *B* for acquisition.

P/E Ratio is the ratio between market price of a share and the earning per share.

However, it does not mean that the amount of premium will swell infinitely. If it moves up beyond a certain limit, the value of the acquiring firm will reduce and the very objective of the acquiring firm behind the merger will be marred. This limit is known as the ceiling price, where the EPS of the acquiring firm in the post-merger period is equal to that in the pre-merger period. In other words, the ceiling price would be equal to the product of the EPS of the target firm and the *P/E* ratio of the acquiring firm.

Suppose the financial data of the two firms is as follows:

	Firm *A*	Firm *B*
Present earnings (\$)	20,000.00	8,000.00
Shares (no.)	5,000.00	3,000.00
EPS (\$)	4.00	2.67
Market value of shares (\$)	32.00	16.00
Price-earning ratio	8.00	6.00

At the floor price, the value of Firm *B* in the post-merger period will be the same as during the pre-merger period. The owners of Firm *B* will get 16/32 × 3,000 or 0.5 share in Firm *A* for one share in Firm *B*. Thus, the wealth of Firm *B* in the post-merger period will be \$32 × 1500 shares or \$48,000, which is equal to \$16 × 3,000 shares during the pre-merger period.

At this floor price paid, the EPS of Firm *A* after the merger will increase to \$(20,000 + 8,000)/(5,000 + 1,500 shares) or to \$4.31. Assuming a price-earning ratio of 8.0, the value of one share of Firm *A* after the merger will be \$4.31 × 8.0 or \$34.48 and the value of the merged firm will be \$34.48 × 6,500 shares = \$224,120, which is higher than the sum of the value of the two firms in the pre-merger period. Using equation 4.1, the net gain from merger will be:

$$\$\{224,120 - (160,000 + 48,000)\} - (48,000 - 48,000) = \$16,120.$$

The greater the price than the floor price, the lower the gain to the acquiring firm as well as the higher the gain to the target company. However, Firm *A* may pay a large premium to Firm *B* in order to allure the latter for acquisition. The ceiling will reach where the price will be equal to the product of the EPS of the target company and the price-earning ratio of the acquiring firm. In the above example, it is \$2.67 × 8 = \$21.36. At this price, Firm *B* will receive 0.6675 share in Firm *A* in lieu of one share or in all 2,003 shares in Firm *A*, meaning that there will be in all 7,003 shares in the merged firm. The EPS will be \$28,000/7,003 shares = \$4.0, which is equal to the pre-merger EPS in Firm *A*. Assuming the price-earning ratio of 8, the value of the merged firm will be \$32 × 7,003 shares or \$224,096. Thus, at both the ceiling price and the floor price, the value of the merged firm is almost the same. But at the ceiling price, the net gain to the acquiring firm would just be zero because the gain from the merger will be reaped entirely by the target company.

Consideration Value

- Floor price = Market price of the share of the target firm
- Ceiling price = EPS of the target firm × Price-earning ratio of the acquiring firm
- Actual consideration value existing between floor and ceiling price is influenced by bargain between the acquiring firm and the target firm

In practice, the actual price is determined between these two limits, depending upon the bargaining power of the acquiring firm and the target firm; and accordingly, the net gain is shared partially by the acquiring firm and partially by the target firm. Suppose, the consideration value is $20 per share of Firm *B*. In this case, Firm *A* will issue 0.625 share for each share in Firm *B*, which will be in all 1,875 shares. The value of owners' wealth in Firm *B* would now be $32 × 1,875 shares or $60,000, as compared to $48,000 in the pre-merger period. The EPS of the merged firm would be $28,000/6,875 shares or $4.07. Assuming a price-earning ratio of 8, the value of the merged firm will be $32.56 × 6875 shares or $223,850, which is higher than the sum of the value of the two firms in the pre-merger period. The net gain to the acquiring firm as per equation 4.1 will be:

$ {223,850 – (160,000 + 48,000)} – (60,000 – 48,000) = $3,850

Thus, at a price agreed upon between the floor and the ceiling, both the acquiring firm and the target firm will reap the benefits; and as a result, both will agree to the merger. However, there are cases when the acquiring firm goes for acquisition even when its net gain is zero. But this is done if some other significant benefits are going to accrue to the acquiring firm.

The consideration value has so far been discussed in the absence of any changes in the international environment. But in international M&A, such changes cannot be overlooked. One of such changes is change in the exchange rate. The lower the existing spot rate of the currency of the country to which target company belongs the lower the price to be paid by the acquiring firm. If it is higher, the salvage value will be higher from the viewpoint of the acquiring firm. If the future spot rate is expected to be higher, the acquiring firm will receive a larger cash flow.

In international M&As, consideration value is influenced also by: 1. changes in exchange rate, 2. cost of capital being different in different countries, 3. debt-equity norm in different countries, and 4. legal and regulatory formalities in the target company country.

Secondly, it is the required rate of return that influences the value of the acquisition. It is because the cost of capital varies from one country to another. This is why the acquisition of a particular country's firm may be more beneficial than that in another country.

Thirdly, the value of acquisition differs in case of different countries because the ability to use financial leverage varies among countries. Since acquisition is financed mostly through borrowings, acquisition of firms in a country where flexibility to borrow is large is more common. For example, in the United States, a high debt ratio is not preferred, and the acquiring firm does not get much incentives on this count.

Last but not least, there are legal formalities regarding tax and accounting. If they are favourable, they create competitive advantages for acquiring firms. This means that when these rules are more favourable and liberal, the acquiring firm may bid a higher price for acquisition.

4.4 CONTROL OF MNCs

Since a lion's share of FDI is accounted for by MNCs, their positive contribution to the economy of the home country/host country is represented by the benefits derived by them from the FDI. The benefits have already been discussed in the present chapter, which means that the operation of MNCs is conducive for economic development, not only in the home country/host country but in the global economy as well. However, the problem is that MNCs are more interested in their own good, and frame and implement strategies accordingly, with the result that their strategy comes into conflict with the interest of the home country/host country. This is why it is often argued that the activities of MNCs need to be controlled so that the interest of the home country/host country is better served.

4.4.1 Conflicts with Home Country and Measures of Control

It is found that a large number of multinational corporations shift their profits to a tax haven and from there make further investment in different host countries. Again, they hide their actual profit through the transfer pricing technique in order to evade taxes. It is true that they do it in order to minimise their tax burden, but it is a loss of foreign exchange and income to the state exchequer.

Sometimes R&D activities are spread over a number of subsidiaries. It is true that the requirements of the host countries are taken into consideration but the home country remains deprived of such facilities. This creates a negative impact on the employment of scientific and technical personnel.

Again, MNCs enjoy economies of scale on account of their large production, with the result that they charge low prices for products that are priced high in the domestic market. Consequently, domestic manufacturers are thrown out of the market in their home country.

More often, under competitive pressures, MNCs locate a part of their operation in resource rich/labour cheap countries under a vertical set-up. This helps cut costs and enables the company to enjoy competitive advantage but causes loss of employment generation and full use of the locally available resources in the home country.

> The home government can: 1. prohibit any investment in a particular host country, 2. design fiscal and monetary disincentives, 3. tighten approval rules and 4. introduce extra-territoriality provisions to interfere with foreign subsidiaries.

These are the major reasons for conflict of interest between the home country government and MNCs. In the sequel, the home country takes up a number of measures. It is easier for the domestic government to take up restrictive measures insofar as the home country executives as well as the home country shareholders may support the government's move.

First of all, the home government can prohibit any investment in, or any technical collaboration with, a particular host country. For example, the US Government had not allowed the transfer of the latest computer technology to East European countries during 1980s. Secondly, it can design fiscal and monetary disincentives to deter any outflow of investment. Discriminatory tax can be levied. Exchange control mechanism can be implemented. When the US balance of payments was sailing through rough weather during late 1950s and early sixties, the Government had restricted the outflow of its currency for overseas investment. Thirdly, the home government can tighten the approval rules and regulations ultimately restricting FDI outflow. In India, during 1970s and 1980s, the Government had permitted foreign joint venture and also capital investment, but the policy was restrictive. Fourthly, the government can introduce extra-territoriality provisions and can interfere with the activities of its MNC's foreign subsidiary, although this option is rarely exercised. Last but not least, the home government can design an anti-trust law that can trim its MNCs wings and restrict its operations in foreign markets.

4.4.2 Conflict with the Host Government and the Measures of Control

The conflict between MNCs and the home government is not as severe as it is with the host government. There is often a feeling in the host country that the MNCs are taking advantage of cheap resources available there and share the largest share of the resultant profits. As a result, is that the government imposes high tax on the profits of the MNCs. MNCs do not like this because they feel that they are utilising unused resources, catering to the demand of the local population, and giving employment to the local population.

Trade unions oppose multinationals because they do not find themselves in a bargaining position, in view of manoeuvrability power of the firm during strikes. Again, when senior positions are filled up by expatriates, it causes loss of employment which is detrimental to the host country interests.

Local firms competing with MNCs also do not favour them. The cost structure in local industries is often high, in view of poor technology and lower size of production. Local firms cannot market goods at a low price as the MNCs are able to. The result is that they are easily driven out of the market.

Sometimes consumers resent the existence of the MNCs. It is often found that after MNCs are able to drive out local manufacturers from the market on account of cheaper and more cost-effective products, they enjoy a monopolistic position. They raise the price abnormally and exploit consumers.

MNCs charge an abnormally large price for the transfer of technology. They bring their own inputs imported from the home country or a sister unit in some other country at a high price. They use transfer pricing on a large scale. All this adds to the balance of payments of the host country. In India, for example, it was found that the balance of payments was severely affected by the operation of the MNCs during 1970s (Sharan, 1978).

Last but not least, MNCs adopt unethical practices, such as manufacturing health-hazard products, bribing the officials, encouraging cross-border transfer of funds circumventing the exchange control regulations in the host country, and so on, in many cases. In a few cases, by bribing

The government in the host country insists normally on:
1. appointing government representatives on the management board and on manning the senior positions with local personnel
2. domestic participation in the equity share capital
3. purchase of inputs from local sources
4. checking unwarranted activities.

the politicians, they cause threat to the very political set-up in the host country (Boatright, 1993).

Thus, with a view to limit the malpractices of MNCs, the host government tries to implement some measures. First, the government insists on appointing government representatives on the management board and on manning the senior positions with local personnel who are expected to work in the interest of the host country. Recruitment for low grade job with locals may lead to employment generation.

Secondly, the government insists on domestic participation in the equity share capital. The profits are distributed among the local shareholders, minimising the outflow of scarce foreign exchange. Moreover, in such cases, there is every possibility of policy design, keeping intact the interest of the host country.

Thirdly, the government insists on the purchase of inputs from local sources. The practice provides stimulus to local industries supplying input, helps conserve scarce foreign exchange, and also curbs the possibility of transfer pricing.

Fourthly, the host government puts in restrictive clauses in the import rules and encourages strict surveillance in order to check unwarranted activities.

Last but not least, the host government expropriates the assets of MNCs lying in its own country. Sometimes it pays the compensation, but at other times it does not. Even if compensation is paid, the amount is normally inadequate, and it usually takes a long time to be realised. However, it is the last resort, especially when MNCs do not at all abide by the host country rules and regulations.

4.4.3 Code for Control at the International Level

For the first time in 1971, the Group of 77 resolved to have surveillance on the activities of MNCs so that the balance of payments of the low income countries is not strained on account of greater outflow. Again, it was reiterated at the Non-aligned Conference of 1972 that foreign investment should be in conformity with the national development objectives in the host country. During 1970s, the UN Commission on Transnational Corporations prepared a code of conduct for MNCs. The code requires an MNC to abide by the rules and regulations of the host country, adhere to its economic policy and socio-cultural objectives, share information with the host government and not to engage in unethical activities.

The codes drafted at the international level are only suggestive and not binding on MNCs, with the result that they are not very effective.

Again, in 1977, the International Labour Organisation adopted a code that was concerned with employment, training, working conditions and industrial relations. The code stressed the need for consultation between the MNCs' management and the employees for a meaningful negotiation on a particular issue of discord.

The UNCTAD too issued two codes with respect to the operation of MNCs. The first code issued in 1980 was concerned with the prevention of restrictive business practices. The second code issued in 1983 related to the transfer of technology. Emphasis was given on a reasonable payment for the technology received, especially by developing countries and on the building up of technological capabilities in the technology receiving developing countries.

There are thus a number of mechanisms for controlling MNCs' operation both at the national and the international levels. The mechanisms at the national level are better implemented. But those at the international level are only suggestive and not binding on MNCs, with the result that they are not very effective. The need of the day is to make the international codes legally binding.

SUMMARY

- FDI involves movement of factors of production into operating facilities abroad. It may be either in the form of investment in foreign branches or in subsidiaries, or in the form of a merger with, and acquisition of, a foreign firm.
- There are a number of views explaining why a firm moves abroad. First, capital moves from a capital abundant economy to capital scarce economy and it continues moving until the marginal productivity of capital in the two countries becomes equal. Both the countries gain from this movement. Second, firms having some sort of ownership advantage find themselves in an oligopolistic position and move abroad in order to reap advantages from their oligopolistic position. Third, it is believed that firms move to a foreign country to take the advantage of cheap raw material or cheap labour there so as to minimise the cost of production. Fourth, there are different stages of manufacturing operations that differently influence the movement of a firm abroad. Fifth, it is the arbitrary pricing of intra-firm transfer of intermediate products that encourages a firm to move to a foreign market. Sixth, there are some approaches based on the strength of the home country currency vis-à-vis the host country currency that explain the movement of firms across borders. Seventh, there are a few politico-economic theories that suggest that economic and political stability is an important factor influencing the movement of capital from one country to the other.
- The above theories have been developed normally in the context of MNCs headquartered in developed countries. However, they are also applicable to MNCs headquartered in the developing world, of course, with minor modifications.
- FDI is beneficial to both the host country and the home country. The host country gets scarce factors of production. FDI helps improve the balance of payments, creates econ omic and social infrastructure, fosters economic linkages, and improves the gover nment budget. The home country gets returns on the capital employed, gets a market for its products, and is able to employ its surplus manpower in foreign operations.
- However, there are costs too. When the outflow of different payments is large, it entails upon the external balance of the host country. The technology imported is often inappropriate. There is no dissemination of technology with the result that the host country remains dependent on the foreign technology. Sometimes foreign firms create undue competition that is often not congenial for the domestic producers. In the home

country too, problems arise if an unduly large volume of capital flows out and if the investing firms take actions that are not in the interest of the home country.

- The impact of FDI, and especially the M&As, can be assessed in terms of maximisation of corporate wealth. Corporate wealth depends upon the consideration value that the acquiring firm gives to the target firm. In case of cross border M&As, there are a host of factors that influence the consideration value.
- If the operations of an MNC are not in the interest of the home/host countries, they can be controlled through different measures so as to minimise the cost of FDI.

REVIEW QUESTIONS

1. Comment on some major theories of FDI. Are they applicable to the MNCs headquartered in developing countries?
2. "FDI is an unmixed blessing". Discuss this statement from the viewpoint of both the home country and the host country.
3. "The consideration value given by the acquiring firm to the target firm determines the value of the combined firm". Discuss and show how the consideration value is computed.
4. Is it true to say that the MNCs do not always operate in the interest of the home/host country? Explain and suggest measures for controlling their operation.

OBJECTIVE TYPE QUESTIONS

1. Mark True or False:
   (a) Firm-specific advantages, in Hymer's view, are generally technological advantages.
   (b) MacDougall and Kemp were of the view that capital flows from a capital abundant economy to a capital deficit country till the marginal productivity of capital is higher in the latter.
   (c) A country with cheap raw material and cheap labour attracts FDI.
   (d) At the "innovation stage", demand for the product is inelastic.
   (e) At the "standardised product stage", demand for product is inelastic.
   (f) The income of a strong-currency country firm is capitalised at a high rate.
   (g) There is often a positive correlation between FDI and export dynamism in the developing world.
   (h) M&A is advocated where the value of the combined firm is greater than the value of the two firms computed individually.
   (i) The floor price the acquiring firm gives to the target firm is equal to the market value of the latters shares.
   (j) The greater is the gain to the acquiring firm if it pays higher than the floor price to the target firm.
   (k) The mechanisms to control MNCs' operation framed at the international level have been found better implemented than those framed at the national level.

2. Choose the Most Suitable Answer:
   (a) Crowding-in effect of FDI means:
      (i) Permeation of FDI in different sectors of the economy
      (ii) Greater production in foreign controlled companies
      (iii) Stronger backward and forward linkages in the host country
   (b) The price given by the acquiring firm to the target firm is normally:
      (i) Lower than the market value of the shares of the target firm
      (ii) Higher than the market value of shares of the target firm
      (iii) Higher than the product of EPS of the target firm and the price-earning ratio of the acquiring firm.
   (c) FDI involves the transfer of:
      (i) Capital only
      (ii) Technology only
      (iii) Both capital and technology
   (d) The payment for the use of the trademark is in the form of:
      (i) Royalty
      (ii) Technical service fees
      (iii) Dividend
   (e) Internalisation benefits manifest in form of:
      (i) Cost-free intra-firm flow of technology
      (ii) Intra-firm flow of funds
      (iii) Both of the above
   (f) Firms from developed countries move out to developing countries in order to:
      (i) Take advantage of cheap labour
      (ii) Take advantage of cheap raw material
      (iii) Both of the above
   (g) At the"maturing-product" stage, the demand for the product is:
      (i) Price-inelastic
      (ii) Price-elastic
      (iii) Only with limited price elasticity

CASE STUDY 1

Gujarat Ambuja Teams up with Holcim to Bid for ACC

It's an investment banker's dream come true—a complex, multilayered deal which culminates with a big buy-out. Swiss giant Holcim, the world's second-largest cement maker, is teaming up with Gujarat Ambuja Cements Ltd. (GACL) to bid for India's second-largest cement maker, ACC. At an open offer price of Rs 370 per share, the deal is estimated to be worth Rs 2,400 crore.

In a four-stage deal, Holcim will first acquire 40% ownership from the private equity investors in ACIL—AIG and GIC, the private equity arm of the Government of Singapore—for

$200 million. In the second stage, the Zurich-based cement maker will invest $600 million in ACIL and hike its ownership to 67%. The remaining stake will be held by GACL with a put option to sell it to Holcim after sometime. The acquirer will also subscribe to preference shares worth Rs 810 crore which can be redeemed after two years.

In the third stage, ACIL will make an open offer for 36.21% (6.92 crore shares) of ACC to hike its shareholding to 50.1%. In the fourth stage, it will invest the remaining Rs 79 crore to buy the minority shareholders out of ACEL at Rs 70 per share.

In all, Holcim will bring in FDI of $800 million in India, the biggest investment by a foreign cement major in the coutnry. Once the transaction is completed, Gujarat Ambuja will double its indirect ownership to 16.5% in ACC from the current 8.5% and Holcim will gain majority control with 33.5%.

As per the deal, Holcim will control ACC's 18.2 million cement capacity and GACL will manage the 2 million tonne capacity of ACEL.

After the deal, 70% of the Indian cement market will be under the control of five companies and multinationals will control close to 20% of the market.

Post-transaction, both Holcim and GACL will compete in the country's western and the northern markets. ACC, with a market share of 14%, is the second largest domestic cement producer with a capacity of 18.2 million tonnes spread across 15 plants, next to Grasim-Ultra Tech combine at 30 million tonnes and commanding a share of 26%. With a capacity of 3.5 million tonnes and market share of 12%, Ambuja is the third largest cement producer in India. India has a total production capacity of 140 million tonnes.

Meanwhile the Reserve Bank of India notified that no further purchase of equity shares of Gujarat Ambuja Cement Ltd (GACL) should be made on behalf of foreign institutional investors without its prior permission.

No purchases should be made through primary or secondary market as Gujarat Ambuja had reached the trigger limit of 28% of its paid up capital as the contribution from FII, the reserve Bank of India said in a press release.

Source: Based on report published in TOI.

QUESTIONS

1. How did market react to Holcim GACL deal with ACC?
2. Explain the process of the acquisition deal.
3. What was the impact of acquisition on the market share of Holcim and GACL?
4. Why did RBI prohibit purchase of equity shares of GACL by FIIs?

Case Study 2

Backward Linkages of Japanese Firms in Select Host Countries

In almost all host countries, local-content requirements have compelled the MNCs operating there to go for backward linkages with the local suppliers. If the components are more technology-intensive, the linkage helps in upgrading the technological skill of the local employees. In either case, the local employment is generated; there are frequent information flows that lead to quality improvement; and over and above, the local cluster of suppliers enjoys the competitive advantage.

The backward vertical linkage can be measured by the local content of manufacturing operations. It is expressed in terms of local content ratio which is equal to the local procurement divided by the sales. Normally, it is stated that the Japanese firms abroad do not relish backward linkages with the host-country suppliers. But the case study of 272 Japanese electronics manufacturing affiliates operating in as many as 24 countries suggests that those affiliates did have some kind or the other backward linkages with the local suppliers. The extent of the linkages, of course, differed from one case to the other and from one host country to the other. Table 1 shows the top ten largest local content ratios in the host countries.

Table 1: Number of Japanese Affiliates and Average Local Content Ratio by Country

Host country	*No. of affiliates*	*Local content ratio*
Mexico	2	0.95
Israel	1	0.88
India	4	0.87
Brazil	10	0.86
USA	44	0.81
Belgium	2	0.80
Taiwan	34	0.74
Spain	4	0.73
Indonesia	5	0.72
Canada	5	0.71

It is evident from the empirical findings that the affiliates of technology-intensive parent firms located in the developing countries had lower local content ratio. But the same firms operating in the developed countries did have larger local content ratio. The apparent reason is that the local suppliers in many developing countries were not capable of producing inputs of the desired quality.

Secondly, the local content ratio depended also on the entry mode. It was found that in case of acquisitions, the local content ratio was 47 per cent higher than in case of wholly-owned subsidiaries. The joint ventures had 0.07 per cent higher local content ratio than the greenfield affiliates. The reason is obvious. In a wholly-owned subsidiary, the managerial decisions are influenced more by the parent unit objectives.

Thirdly, the extent of vertical linkages depended on the extent of trade barriers. Among the affiliates established to circumvent the trade barriers or, in other words, in case of the tariff-jumping FDI, the local content ratio was lower by 0.14 points. The reason is that the very objective of the firms behind operating abroad was not to use the locally produced cheap inputs.

Fourthly, the local content ratio depended on the availability of improved infrastructure in the host country. The host countries with poor infrastructure were associated with low local content ratio. The reason is that the absence of desired infrastructure failed to encourage the development of input-supplying clusters.

Fifthly, the strictness of local content regulations did influence the backward linkages. It is because the strictness of the government on the use of local inputs limited the freedom of the foreign companies. The study finds that the maximum effect of local content regulations was around 0.13 points.

Sixthly, the local content ratio depended on the very motivations behind operating overseas. If the host country allows MNCs for meeting the domestic market requirements, the local content ratio would certainly be higher. But if, on the other hand, the motivation is to encourage export, the local content ratio may not be higher. The study found higher ratio in the first group of affiliates.

Source: Based on: Belderbos, *et al* (2001), "Backward Vertical Linkages of Foreign Manufacturing Affiliates: Evidence from Japanese Multinationals", *World Development*, 29 (1), 189–208.

QUESTIONS

1. What are the factors responsible for varying local content ratio among different host countries?
2. Is it true that the technology-intensive MNCs have a low local content ratio in a developing host country?
3. Do you agree that the joint ventures and acquisitions mode involve a higher local content ratio than in case of wholly-owned subsidiaries?
4. Do you feel that improved infra-structure is a pre-requisite for a successful backward linkage of an MNC with the local suppliers?

REFERENCES

Books

Aliber, R.Z. (1971), "The Multinational Enterprise in a Multiple Currency World" in J.H. Dunning (*ed.*), *The Multinational Enterprise* (London: George Allen & Unwin), pp. 49–56.

______ (1993), *The Globalisation of Business* (London: Routledge).

Boatright, J. R. (1993), *Ethics in the Conduct of Business* (Englewood Cliffs: Prentice-Hall).

Buckley and Mark Casson (1976), *The Future of the Multinational Enterprise*, New York: Holmes and Meier.

Globerman, S. (1986), *Fundamentals of International Business Management* (Singapore: Prentice-Hall).

Graham, E.M. and P. R. Krugman (1989), *Foreign Direct Investment in the United States* (Washington D.C.: Institute of International Economics).

Hood, N. and S. Young (1979), *The Economics of Multinational Enterprise* (London: Longman).

Hymer, S.H. (1976), *The International Operations of National Firms: A Study of Direct Investment* (Cambridge Mass.: MIT Press).

Julius, D. (1990), *Global Companies and Public Policy: The Growing Challenge of Foreign Direct Investment* (London: Pinter).

Kemp, M.C. (1964), *The Theory of International Trade* (Ithaca: Prentice-Hall).

Knickerbocker, T. (1973), *Oligopolistic Reaction and the Multinational Enterprise* (Boston: Harvard Graduate School of Business Administration).

Kogut, B. and D. Parkinson (1993), "The Diffusion of American Organising Principles to Europe" in B. Kogut (ed.), *Country Competitiveness and the Organisation of Work* (London: Oxford University Press), pp. 17–28.

Kojima, K. (1978), *Direct Foreign Investment; A Japanese Model of Multinational Business Operations*, London: Croom Helm, pp. 73–76.

Kumar, N. (1999), *Globalisation and Quality of Foreign Direct Investment: A Quantitative Analysis of the Role of Multinationals in Industrialisation*, Export–*Expansion and Innovation in Host Countries* (London and New York: Routledge).

Kumar, N. and I. P. Pradhan (2002), *Foreign Direct Investment, Externalities and Economic Growth: Some Empirical Explorations and Implications for WTO Negotiations on Investment*, New Delhi: RISNODC.

Magee, S.P. (1979), "Information and the Multinational Corporation; An Appropriability Theory of Direct Foreign Investment" in D.R. Lessard (ed.), *International Financial Management* (Boston: Warren Gorham & Lamont), p. 57.

Mani, S. (1999), *Public Innovation Policies and Developing Countries in a Phase of Economic Liberalisation*, (Maastricht: United Nations University, Mimeo).

Safarian, A.E. (1993), *Multinational Enterprise and Public Policy; A Study of the Industrial Countries*, Aldershot: Edward Elgar, pp. 467–70.

Shapiro, A. C. (1995), *Multinational Financial Management* (New Delhi: Prentice-Hall of India).

Journals and Reports

Bhagwati, J. (1972), "Book Review: Raymond Vernon, Sovereignty at Bay: The Multinational Spread of US Enterprises, 1971", *Journal of International Economics*, XIV (4), 455–59.

Borensztein, E. et al (1995), *How Does Foreign Direct Investment affect Economic Growth* (Cambridge M.A.: NBER), Working Paper no. 5057.

Buckley, P.J. (1988), "The Limits of Explanation: Testing of Internalisation Theory of the Multinational Enterprise", *Journal of International Business Studies*, XIX (2), 181–93.

Caves, R.E. (1971), "International Corporations: The Industrial Economics of Foreign Investment", *Economica*, XXXVIII (1), 5–6.

_______ (1988), *Exchange Rate Movements and Foreign Direct Investment in the United States*, Harvard Institute of Economic Research, Discussion Paper No. 1383.

Coase, R.H. (1937), "The Nature of the Firm", *Economica*, IV (4), 386–405.

Dunning, J.F. (1980), "Towards an Eclectic Theory of International Production", *Journal of International Business Studies*, XI (1), 9–31.

Fatehi-Sedah, K. and M.H. Safizedah (1989)), "Association between Political Instability and the Flow of Foreign Direct Investment", *Management International Review*, XXIX (1), 23–36.

Franke, R.H. et al (1991), "Cultural Roots of Economic Performance: A Research Note", *Strategic Management Journal*, XII (2), 165–73.

Froot, K.A. and J.C. Stein (1989), *Exchange Rates and Foreign Direct Investment: An Imperfect Capital Market Approach* (Cambridge Mass: NBER), Working Paper No. 2914.

Helleiner, G.K. (1973),"Manufactured Exports from Less Developed Countries and Multinational Firms", *Economic Journal*, LXXXIII (1), 21–47.

______ (1985),"Japanese and American Direct Investment in Asia: A Comparative Analysis", *Hitotsubhashi Journal of Economics*, XXVI (1), 1–36.

MacDougall, G.D.A. (1958),"The Benefits and Costs of Private Foreign Investment Abroad: A Theoretical Approach", *Economic Record*, XXXVI (1). 13–35.

Rugman, A.M. (1986),"New Theories of Multinational Enterprise: An Assessment of Internalisation Theory", *Bulletin of Economic Research*, XXXVIII (1), 101–118.

Schneider, F. and B.S. Frey (1985),"Economic and Political Determinants of Foreign Direct Investments", *World Development*, XIII (2), 161–75.

Sharan, V. (1978),"Multinational Corporations and Balance of Payments Problems in a Developing Host Country: An Indian Experience", *Indian Economic Journal*, XXVI (Dec.), 199–215.

______ (1985),"Internationalisation of Third World Firms: An Indian Case Study", *International Marketing Review*, II (Summer), 63–71.

Tallman, S.B. (1988),"Home Country Political Risk and Foreign Direct Investment in the United States", *Journal of International Business Studies*, XIX (2), 219–34.

Ting, W. (1982), "The Product Development Process in NIC Multinationals", *Columbia Journal of World Business*, XVII (1), 76–81.

United Nations (1993), *World Investment Directory 1992* (New York: Department of Economic and Social Development).

______ (1999), *World Investment Report 1999*, New York and Geneva, UNCTAD.

______ (2000), *World Investment Report 2000*, New York and Geneva: UNCTAD.

Vernon, R. (1966), "International Investment and International Trade in the Product Cycle", *Quarterly Journal of Economics*, LXXX (May), 190–207.

Vernon, R. (1979),"The Product Cycle Hypothesis in a New International Environment", *Oxford Bulletin of Economics and Statistics*, LXI (2), 255–67.

SELECT FURTHER READINGS

Earl, P. and Fisher, F.G. (1986), *International Mergers and Acquisitions* (London: Euromoney Publications).

Reuber, G. L. (1973), *Private Foreign Investment in Development* (Oxford: Clarendon Press).

Sharan, V. (1995),"Theories of International Business: A Review of Literature", *Foreign Trade Review*, XXX (3), 315–331.

United Nations (1999), *World Investment Report 1999* (New York and Geneva: UNCTAD).

United Nations (2000), *World Investment Report 2000* (New York and Geneva: UNCTAD).

* **Strøget** is a carfree zone in Copenhagen, Denmark. This popular tourist attraction in the centre of town is the longest pedestrian shopping area in Europe. Created in 1960's, about 2,50,000 people use Strøget every day at the height of tourist season in summer, and about 1,20,000 do on a winter day. Many of the city's most famous and expensive stores, such as Illums Bolighus, Magasin du Nord, the Royal Copenhagen Porcelain Manufactory, and chain stores, are located along the strip. There are also a multitude of souvenir shops and fast food outlets.

Gold Souk in Diera, Dubai, UAE*

5

Balance of Payments

CHAPTER OBJECTIVES

The chapter acquaints the readers with the structure of the balance of payments, balance of payments disequilibrium and with how disequilibrium is adjusted. In particular, it attempts to:

- Discuss the structure of balance of payment (BOP) focussing on the current and capital account transactions.
- Show how official reserves account is related to BOP disequilibrium.
- Explain BOP equilibrium and disequilibrium.
- Discuss various approaches to BOP adjustment – beginning from the classical approach to the elasticity approach, Keynesian approach and monetary approach.

Whatever the mode of international business, it involves cross-border movement of funds. The movement of funds is reflected in a country's balance of payments. In other words, balance of payments shows the financial impact of international business. It is from this point of view that it is essential to acquaint the readers with the basic concept of balance of payments.

5.1 STRUCTURE OF BALANCE OF PAYMENTS

Balance of payments is a macrolevel statement showing inflow and outflow of foreign exchange.

Balance of payments is a statement listing receipts and payments in the international transactions of a country. In other words, it records the inflow and the outflow of foreign exchange. The system of recording is based on the concept of double entry book keeping, where the credit side shows the receipts of foreign exchange from abroad and the debit side shows payments in foreign exchange to foreign residents. Disequilibrium does occur, but not from accounting point of view because debit and credit balances equal each other if the various entries are properly made. The concept of accounting equilibrium is discussed later in this chapter.

Again, receipts and payments are compartmentalised into two heads: one being the current account and the other being the capital account. The basic distinction between the two is that the former represents transfer of real income, while the latter accounts only for transfer of funds, without effecting a shift in real income.

5.1.1 Current Account Transactions

Current account is part of BOP statement showing flow of real income or foreign exchange transactions on account of trade of goods and invisibles.

The current account records the receipts and payments of foreign exchange in the following ways. They are:

Current account receipts:

1. Export of goods
2. Invisibles:
   (a) Services
   (b) Unilateral transfers
   (c) Investment income
3. Non-monetary movement of gold

Current account payments:

1. Import of goods
2. Invisibles:
   (a) Services
   (b) Unilateral transfers
   (c) Investment income
3. Non-monetary movement of gold

Export of goods effects the inflow of foreign exchange into the country, while import of goods causes outflow of foreign exchange from the country.

The difference between the two is known as the balance of trade. If export exceeds import, balance of trade is in surplus. Excess of import over export means deficit balance of trade. Table 5.1 shows the balance of payments figures released by the Reserve Bank of India. During 2007–08, the statement shows a deficit balance of trade for US $119.403 billion.

There is another item in the current account, known as non-monetary movement of gold. It may be noted that there are two types of sale and purchase of gold. One is termed as monetary sale and purchase that influences the international monetary reserves. The other is non-monetary sale and purchase of gold. This is for industrial purposes, and is shown in the current account, either separately from, or along with, the trade in merchandise. In some of the years, the balance of payments statement prepared by the Reserve Bank of India has shown the non-monetary movement of gold, separately from the trade in the merchandise account. But now this item stands included in the trade in merchandise.

Besides, trade in services embraces receipts and payments on account of travel and tourism, financial charges concerning banking, insurance, transportation, and so on. Investment income includes interest, dividend and other such receipts and payments.

Similarly, unilateral transfers include pension, remittances, gifts, and other transfers for which no specific services are rendered. They are called unilateral transfers because they represent the flow of funds in only one direction. They are unlike export or import, where goods flow in one direction and the payment flows in the other.

Trade in services, investment income and the unilateral transfers form the "invisibles", which is a significant item in the current account, shown separately from the trade in the merchandise account. There may be an inflow or outflow of foreign exchange on account of invisibles, and accordingly credit and debit entries are made.

Invisibles refer to trade in services, investment income, and unilateral transfers.

The debit and the credit sides of two accounts—trade in merchandise and the invisibles—are balanced. If the credit side is greater than the debit side, the difference shows the current account surplus. On the contrary, the excess of debit side over the credit side indicates current account deficit. Table 5.1 shows current account surplus for US $29.817 billion during 2007–08.

5.1.2 Capital Account Transactions

Similarly, capital account transactions take place in the following ways:

Capital account is a part of BOP statement showing flow of foreign loans/investment and banking funds.

Capital account receipts:

1. Long term inflow of funds
2. Short term inflow of funds

Capital account payments:

1. Long term outflow of funds
2. Short term outflow of funds

The flow on capital account is long-term as well as short-term. The difference between the two is that the former involves maturity over one year, while the short-term flows are effected for one year or less. The credit side records the official and private borrowing from abroad net of repayments, direct and portfolio investment and short-term investments into the country. It records also the bank balances of the non-residents held in the country. The debit side includes disinvestment of capital, country's investment abroad, loans given to foreign government or a foreign party and the bank balances held abroad. When credit side of the current account along with the credit side of the long-term capital account transactions is compared with the transactions on the debit side of the current account and the long-term capital account, the difference is known as the *basic balance* which may be negative or positive. As per the practice adopted by Reserve Bank of India, basic balance is not shown in the balance of payments statement.

Balance of Payments

- Balance of trade = Export of goods – Import of goods
- Balance of current account = Balance of trade + Net earnings on invisibles
- Balance of capital account = Foreign exchange inflow – Foreign exchange outflow, on account of foreign investment, foreign loans, banking transactions, and other capital flows
- Overall balance of payments = Balance of current account + Balance of capital account + Statistical discrepancy

The capital account balancing is not complete with the basic balance. The debit and the credit sides of the short-term capital account transactions are added to their respective sides. Then the two sides are compared. The difference is known as the capital account balance. Table 5.1 shows a surplus balance in the capital account for US $9.146 billion.

Statistical discrepancy refers to estimate of foreign exchange flow on account of either variations in the collection of related figures or unrecorded illegal transaction of foreign exchange.

Errors and omissions, which is also termed as "statistical discrepancy", is an important item on the balance of payments statement, and is taken into account for arriving at the overall balance. As per Table 5.1, it stands at US $591 million during 2007–08. It may be noted that the statistical discrepancy arises on different accounts. Firstly, it arises because of difficulties involved in collecting balance of payments data. There are different sources of data, which sometimes differ in their approach. In India, trade figures compiled by the Reserve Bank of India and those compiled by the Director-General of Commercial Intelligence and Statistics differ. Secondly, the movement of funds may lead or lag the transactions that they (funds) are supposed to finance. For example, goods are shipped in March, but the payments are received in April. In this case, figure compiled on 31st March, the financial year end, will record the shipment that has been sent, but its payment would be recorded in the following year. Such differences lead to the emergence of statistical discrepancy. Thirdly, certain figures are derived on the basis of estimates. For example, figures for earning on travel and tourism account are estimated on the basis of sample cases. If the sample is defective, there is every possibility of error and omission. Fourthly, errors and omissions are explained by unrecorded illegal transactions that may be either on the debit side, or on the credit side, or on both the sides. Only the net amount is written on the balance of payments. When the country is politically or economically stable, credit balance is normally found because unrecorded inflows of funds occur. But in the reverse case, there is capital flight and the amount is normally negative. The experiences reveal that when Iraq invaded Kuwait, the US balance of payments witnessed such flows, in large measure, on the credit side. This was so because there was substantial capital flight from the Middle East to the USA.

After the statistical discrepancy is located, the overall balance is arrived at. The overall balance represents the balancing between the credit items and the debit items appearing on the current account, capital account, and the statistical discrepancy. Table 5.1 shows an overall balance that is surplus by US $20.080 billion during 2007–08.

If the overall balance of payments is in surplus, the surplus amount is used for repaying the borrowings from the IMF and then the rest is transferred to the official reserves account. On the contrary, when the overall balance is found in deficit, the monetary authorities arrange for capital flows to cover up the deficit. Such inflows may take the form of drawing down of foreign exchange reserves or official borrowings or purchases (drawings) from the IMF. From this point of view, capital inflows are bifurcated into autonomous and accommodating ones. If the inflow of funds on the capital account is for meeting the overall balance of payments deficit, it is termed as accommodating or compensatory capital flow. In other words, accommodating capital inflows aim at putting the balance of payments in equilibrium. On the other hand, autonomous capital flows take place regardless of such considerations. A foreigner paying back the loan or the inflow of foreign direct investment is an apposite example of autonomous capital inflow. This is why autonomous capital inflow goes "above-the-line", while accommodating capital inflow goes "below-the-line".

Accommodating capital flow is the inflow of foreign exchange to meet the balance of payments deficit, normally from the IMF.

Autonomous capital flow refers to flow of loans/investment in normal course of a business.

5.1.3 Official Reserves Account

Official reserves are held by the monetary authorities of a country. They comprise of monetary gold, SDR allocations by the IMF, and foreign currency assets. Foreign currency assets are normally held in form of balances with foreign central banks and investment in foreign government securities. If the overall balance of payments is in surplus, the surplus amount, as it is mentioned above, adds to the official reserves account. But if the overall balance of payments is in deficit, and if accommodating

SDRs allocation is the creation of international reserve assets by the IMF, and their allocation among member countries in order to improve international liquidity.

Table 5.1 India's Overall Balance of Payments

Item	*US $ million*
	2008–09
A. Current Account	
1. Exports, f.o.b.	1,75,184
2. Imports, c.i.f.	2,94,587
3. Trade Balance	–1,19,403
4. Invisibles, Net	89,586
(a) 'Non-factor' services *of which*:	49,818
software services Exports	47,000
(b) Income	–4,511
(c) Private Transfers	44,047
(d) Official Transfers	232
5. Current account balance	–29,817
B. Capital Account	
1. Foreign Investment, Net (a + b)	3,462
(a) Direct investment *of which*:	17,496
i. In India	34,982
Equity	27,809
Re-invested earnings	6,426
Other capital	747
ii. Abroad	–17,486
Equity	–13,558
Re-invested earnings	–1,084
Other capital	–2,844
(b) Portfolio investment	–14,034
In India	–13,855
Abroad	–179
2. External Assistance, Net	2,638
Disbursements	5,042
Amortisation	–2,404
3. Commercial Borrowings	8,158
Disbursements	15,382
Amortisation	–7,224
4. Short term credit, net	–5,795
5. Banking capital *of which*:	–3,397
NRI deposits, Net	*4,290*
6. Rupee Debt Service	–101
7. Other Capital, Net	4,181
8. Total Capital Account	9,146
C. Errors & omissions	**591**
D. Overall balance [A(5) + B(8) + D]	**–20,080**
E. Monetary movements (F + G)	**20,080**
F. IMF, Net	**0**
G. Reserves and monetary gold	**20,080**
[Increase (–), Decrease (+)]	

Source: *RBI Annual Report: 2008–09*

capital is not available, the official reserves account is debited by the amount of deficit.

Table 5.1 shows that US $20.080 billion was drawn from the official reserves account.

5.2 EQUILIBRIUM, DISEQUILIBRIUM AND ADJUSTMENT

5.2.1 Accounting Equilibrium

Since the balance of payments is constructed on the basis of double entry book keeping, credit is always equal to debit. If debit on the current account is greater than the credit side, funds flow into the country, which are recorded on the credit side of the capital account. The excess of debit is wiped out. Thus, the concept of balance of payments is based on the concept of accounting equilibrium, that is,

$$\text{Current account} + \text{Capital account} = 0 \qquad (5.1)$$

The accounting balance is an *ex post* concept. It describes what has actually happened over a specific past period. There may be accounting disequilibrium when the two sides of the autonomous flows differ in size. But in such cases, accommodating flows bring the balance of payments back to equilibrium.

5.2.2 Disequilibrium and the Focus of Adjustment

In economic terms, balance of payments equilibrium occurs when surplus or deficit is eliminated from the balance of payments. However, normally, in real life, such equilibrium is not found. Rather it is the disequilibrium in the balance of payments that is a normal phenomenon.

There are external economic variables influencing the balance of payments and giving rise to disequilibrium. But domestic economic variables are more important for causing disequilibrium. Some important variables are:

1. National output and national spending
2. Money supply
3. Exchange rate
4. Interest rate

If national income exceeds national spending, the excess amount (saving) will be invested abroad, resulting in capital account deficit. Conversely, excess of national spending over national income causes borrowings from abroad, pushing the capital account into a surplus zone.

Disparity in national income and national spending influences the capital account via the current account as well. If national output exceeds national spending, the difference manifests in export, causing current account surplus. The surplus is invested abroad, which means capital account deficit. The excess of national spending over national output leads to import. Deficit appears on the current account. The country borrows to meet the current account deficit. The borrowing results in capital account surplus.

Similarly, increase in money supply raises the price level and exports turn uncompetitive. Fall in export earnings leads to deficit in the current account. The higher prices of domestic goods make the price of imported commodities competitive and imports rise, leading to enlargement of deficit in the current account.

If the currency of a country depreciates, exports become competitive. Export earning improves. On the other hand, imports become costlier. If, as a result, imports are restricted, the trade account balance will improve. But if imports are not restrained, deficit will appear in the trade account. Infact, the net effect depends upon how far the demand for export and import is price-elastic.

Last but not least, the increase in domestic interest rate causes capital inflow in lure of higher returns. Capital account runs surplus. The reverse is the case when the interest rate falls.

However, diseqilibrium becomes a cause for concern when it is associated with the current account. This is because current account represents a shift in real income; and at the same time, any adjustment in this account is not very easy. Even in the current account, it is the balance of trade account that is largely responsible for disequilibrium. If the balance of trade is in surplus, its correction is not difficult. The surplus amount is used either for meeting the deficit on invisible trade account, or it may be invested abroad. But if the balance of trade is in deficit zone and if the deficit is large, so as not to be covered by invisible trade surplus, current account deficit will occur. Correcting it is not easy, insofar as the autonomous and accommodating capital flows are not so smooth. Again, if the deficit on the current account continues to persist, official reserves will be eroded. If a country borrows large amounts to meet the deficit, it may fall into a vicious debt trap. This is why adjustment measures are primarily aimed at correcting disequilibrium in the trade account.

5.3 DIFFERENT APPROACHES TO ADJUSTMENT

5.3.1 The Classical View

Price-specie-flow mechanism deals with relationship between flow of specie, money supply, prices, and foreign trade.

The issue of linkage between domestic economic variables and the balance of payments responsible for disequilibrium in the latter, as well as its adjustment, has been investigated by a number of experts. Classical economists were aware of the balance of payments disequilibrium, but they were of the view that it was self adjusting. Their view, which was based on the price-specie-flow mechanism—stated that an increase in money supply raises domestic prices, where by exports become uncompetitive and export earnings drop. Foreign goods become cheaper, and imports rise, causing the current account balance to go into deficit in the sequel. Precious metal leaves the country in order to finance imports. As a result, the quantity of money lessens, that lowers the price level. Lower prices in the economy lead to greater export and trade balance reaches equilibrium once again. In this manner, the classical version of the balance of payments adjustment was a refutation of the mercantilist belief that a country could achieve a persistent balance of trade surplus through trade protection and export promotion.

5.3.2 Elasticity Approach

After the collapse of the gold standard, the classical view could not remain tenable. The adjustment in the balance of payments disequilibrium was thought of in terms of changes in the fixed exchange rate, that is through devaluation or upward revaluation. But its success was dependent upon the elasticity of demand for export and import. Marshall and Lerner explained this phenomenon through the "elasticity" approach (Marshall, 1924; Lerner, 1944).

The elasticity approach is based on partial equilibrium analysis where everything is held constant, except for the effects of exchange rate changes on export or import. It is also assumed that elasticity of supply of output is infinite so that the price of export in home currency does not rise as demand increases, nor does the price of import fall with a squeeze in demand for imports. Again, the approach ignores the monetary effects of variation in exchange rates. Based on these assumptions, devaluation helps improve the current account balance only if:

$$E_m + E_x > 1 \tag{5.2}$$

Where E_m is the price elasticity of demand for import and

E_x is the price elasticity of demand for export.

If the elasticity of demand is greater than unity, the import bill will contract and export earnings will increase as a sequel to devaluation. Trade deficit will be removed. However, the problem is that the trade partner may also devalue its own currency as a retaliatory measure. Moreover, there may be a long lapse of time before the quantities adjust sufficiently to changes in price. Till then, trade balance will be even worse than that before devaluation. This is nothing but the J-curve effect of devaluation. In Figure 5.1, trade balance moves deeper into the deficit zone immediately after devaluation. But then it gradually improves and crosses into surplus zone. The curve resembles the alphabet, J and so, it is known as the J-curve Effect.

> When the devaluation of currency leads to a fall in export earnings in the initial stage and then a rise in export earnings, making the earning curve look like the alphabet, J it is called J-curve effect

The weakness of the elasticity approach is that it is a partial equilibrium analysis and does not consider the supply and cost changes as a result of devaluation as well as the income and the expenditure effects of exchange rate changes. In this context, it may be mentioned that it was Stern (1973) who incorporated the concept of supply elasticity in the elasticity approach. According to him, devaluation could improve balance of payments only when:

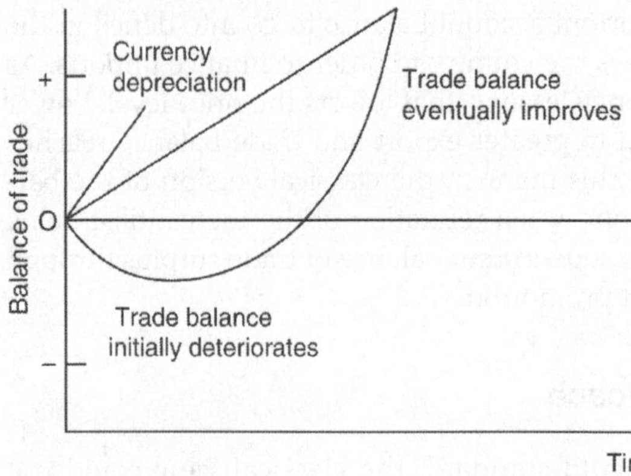

FIGURE 5.1 J-curve Effect

$$X\left[\frac{(ED_X-1)}{\left(1+\frac{ED_X}{ES_X}\right)}\right]+M\left\{\frac{\left[ED_m\times\left(1+\frac{1}{ES_m}\right)\right]}{\left(\frac{ED_m}{ES_m}+1\right)}\right\}>0 \qquad (5.3)$$

Where X and M are exports and imports,
ED_x is elasticity of demand for exports,
ES_x is elasticity of supply for exports,
ED_m is elasticity of demand for imports, and
ES_m is elasticity of supply for imports.

It is not only elasticity of demand but also the elasticity of supply for export and import that influences balance of trade.

Based on the figures of British exports and imports, Stern came to the conclusion that the balance of trade would improve if:

1. the elasticity of demand for exports and imports is high and is equal to one coupled with elasticity of supply both for imports and exports, which could be either high or low.
2. the elasticity of demand for imports and exports is low but the elasticity of supply for imports and exports is lower.

On the contrary, if low elasticity of demand is matched with high elasticity of supply, the balance of trade should worsen.

Absorption approach deals with how changes in total income and absorption, meaning consumption, investment and governmental spending influence the trade balance.

5.3.3 Keynesian Approach

The Keynesian view takes into consideration primarily the income effect that was ignored under the elasticity approach. Here the readers are being acquainted with three different views that are based on the Keynesian approach.

Absorption Approach: The absorption approach explains the relationship between domestic output and trade balance and conceives of adjustment in a different way. Sidney A. Alexander (1959) treats balance of trade as a residual given by the difference between what the economy produces and what it takes for domestic use or what it absorbs. He begins with the contention that the total output, Y is equal to the sum of consumption, C, investment, I, government spending, G, and net export, $(X - M)$. In form of an equation,

$$Y = C + I + G + (X - M)$$

Substituting $C + I + G$ by absorption, A, it can be rewritten as:

$$Y = A + X - M$$

or
$$Y - A = X - M \tag{5.4}$$

This means that the amount by which total output exceeds total spending or absorption is represented by export over import or the net export, which means a surplus balance of trade. This also means that if $A > Y$, deficit balance of trade will occur. This is because excess absorption in the absence of desired output will cause imports. Thus, in order to bring equilibrium to the balance of trade, the government has to increase output or income. Increase in income without corresponding and equal increase in absorption will lead to improvement in balance of trade. This is called the expenditure switching policy.

In case of full employment, where resources are fully employed, output cannot be expanded. Balance of trade deficit can be remedied through decreasing absorption without equal fall in output. This is known as the expenditure-reducing policy. On the contrary, where full employment is yet to be achieved, output can be increased or/and absorption can be reduced in order to bring about equilibrium in the trade balance. It may be noted that the validity of the absorption approach depends upon the operation of the multiplier effect, which is essential for accelerating output generation. It also depends on the marginal propensity to absorb, which determines the rate of absorption.

J. Black ignores governmental expenditure, G, and equates $X - M$ with $S - I$.

J. Black (1959) explains absorption in a slightly different manner. He ignores governmental expenditure, G, and equates $X - M$ with $S - I$ (where S is saving and I is investment). He is of the opinion that when balance of trade is negative, the country has to increase savings on the one hand and to reduce investment on the other. In case of full employment, he suggests redistribution of national income in favour of profit earners who possess greater propensity to save.

Let us now look at the effects of devaluation/depreciation in the framework of absorption approach. The effects fall upon both the income and absorption. There are three types of effect on income—idle resource effect, terms of trade effect, and resource allocation effect. As a sequel to devaluation, imports turn costlier and demand for home produced goods increases, which helps use of idle resources and, thereby, in output expansion. This is idle-resource effect. Terms-of-trade effect is subject to the elasticity of supply for export and import. If terms of trade improve, income improves and then so does the balance of payments. Again, if productivity is lower in the non-traded goods sector and if devaluation takes place, resources will shift from the lower to higher productivity sector. Income will naturally improve. This is the resource allocation effect.

The effect of devaluation on absorption manifests in rising import cost and the consequent upsurge in the cost and price of home produced goods. High price goods lower consumption.

Mundell-Fleming Approach: Mundell-Fleming (1962) approach, developed in the Keynesian framework, focuses through IS–LM curve on how the internal and external balance is influenced by fiscal and monetary policies. The IS curve for an open economy shows various combinations of output and interest rate. It shows that:

$$S + M = I + G + X \tag{5.5}$$

The left side of the equation is known as the leakages and the right side is known as the injections. Savings include autonomous savings plus savings on account of risen income based on marginal propensity to save. Imports include autonomous imports plus imports on account of risen income based on marginal propensity to import. Investment is assumed to be an inverse function of rate of interest. Exports and governmental expenditure are autonomous with respect to interest rate and the level of national income. The relationship between leakages and income can be shown with an upward sloping line, whereas the injection schedule is downward sloping—from left to right.

The L–M schedule shows various combinations of level of income and rate of interest under the assumption that the supply of money is equal to demand for money meaning that the money market is in equilibrium. Money is demanded either for transaction purposes or for speculative purposes. The larger is the income, the bigger is the money held for transaction purposes meaning that transaction demand for money is a positive function of income. The demand for money for speculative purposes has an inverse relationship with the rate of interest. Taking together these two forms of demand, L–M schedule is upward sloping from left to right because the income levels require comparatively bigger transaction balances than the speculative balances.

The balance of payments (BP) schedule shows various combinations of rate of interest and income accruing in the balance of payments. As far as current account is concerned, export is assumed to be independent of the level of national income and then rate of interest. But import is assumed to be positively related to income which means higher income, higher the imports and deficit is the current account. Current account deficit, if any, is offset by surplus in the capital account. Net capital account flow is positively related to the rate of interest, which means higher interest rate in the country attracts inflow of capital. Thus, the current account and capital account schedules slope downward from left to right.

The balance of payments is in equilibrium because IS and LM schedules intersect at a point on the BP schedule corresponding to a given interest rate and the level of income, as shown in Figure 5.2 a.

If the income and imports increase and interest rates decrease following an expansionary monetary policy, the balance of payments

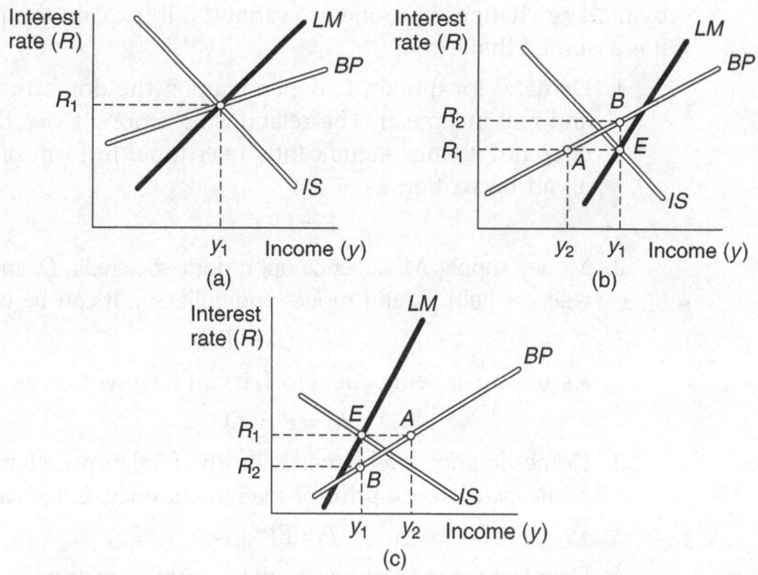

FIGURE 5.2

will turn deficit and BP schedule will shift leftward (Figure 5.2 b). On the contrary, during contractionary monetary policy regime, the balance of payments will turn surplus and the BP schedule will shift rightward (Figure 5.2 c).

New Cambridge School Approach: This is a special case of absorption approach. It takes into account savings (*S*), investment (*I*), taxes (*T*), and government spending (*G*), and their impact on the trade account. In form of an equation, it can be written as:

$$S + T + M = G + X + I$$

Or $\quad (S - I) + (T - G) + (M - X) = 0$

Or $\quad (X - M) = (S - I) + (T - G) \quad (5.6)$

The theory assumes that $(S - I)$ and $(T - G)$ are determined independently of each other and of the trade gap. $(S - I)$ is normally fixed as the private sector has a fixed net level of saving. And so the balance of payments deficit or surplus is dependent upon $(T - G)$ and the constant $(S - I)$. In other words, with constant $(S - I)$, it is only the manipulation of $(T - G)$ that is necessary and a sufficient tool for balance of payments adjustment.

5.3.4 Monetary Approach

Monetarists believe that the balance of payments disequilibrium is a monetary and not a structural phenomenon (Connolly, 1978). The adjustment is automatic unless the government is intentionally following an inflationary policy for quite a long period. Adjustment is brought about by making changes in monetary variables. To explain the phenomenon, it is assumed that:

1. Demand for money, L, depends upon the domestic price level, P, and real income, Y. The relationship among these three variables does not change significantly over time. In form of an equation, it can be written as

$$L = kPY \tag{5.7}$$

2. Money supply, M, depends upon domestic credit, D, and international reserves held, R, and money multiplier, m. It can be written as

$$M = (R + D)m$$

Assuming m being equal to 1, it can be rewritten as

$$M = R + D \tag{5.8}$$

3. Domestic price level depends on the foreign price level, P^*, and the domestic currency price of foreign currency, E, we can write it as

$$P = EP^* \tag{5.9}$$

4. Demand for money equals the supply of money because there is held an equilibrium in the money market, which is

$$L = M \tag{5.10}$$

In **fixed exchange rate regime**, monetary authorities set the external value of the currency vis-a-vis another currency/SDRs/a basket of currencies.

The process of adjustment varies among the types of exchange rate regime the country has opted for. In a fixed exchange rate regime or in gold standard, if the demand for money, that is the amount of money people wish to hold, is greater than the supply of money, the excess demand would be met through the inflow of money from abroad. On the contrary, with the supply of money being in excess of the demand for it, the excess supply is eliminated through the outflow of money to other countries. The inflow and the outflow influence the balance of payments. To explain it further, with constant prices and income and, thus, constant demand for money, any increase in domestic credit will lead to outflow of foreign exchange as the people will import more to lower excessive cash balances. Consequently, the balance of payments will turn deficit. Conversely, a decrease in domestic credit would lead to an excess demand for money. International reserves will flow in to meet the excess demand and balance of payments will improve.

Floating rate regime refers to the exchange rate which is not fixed but varies, depending upon the forces of demand and supply.

However, in a floating rate regime, the demand for money is adjusted to the supply of money via changes in the exchange rate. Especially in a situation when the central bank makes no market intervention, the international reserves component of the monetary base remains unchanged. The balance of payments remains in equilibrium with neither surplus nor deficit. The spot exchange rate is determined by the quantity of money supplied and the quantity of money demanded.

When the central bank increases domestic credit through open market operations, the supply of money is greater than the demand for it. Households increase their imports and with increased demand for imports, the domestic currency will depreciate and it will continue depreciating until the supply of money equals the demand for money. Conversely, with decrease in domestic credit, the households reduce their import.

Domestic currency will appreciate and it will continue appreciating until supply of money equals demand for money.

In case of managed floating, the central bank often intervenes to peg the rates at a desired level. Therefore, this case is a mix of fixed and floating rate regimes. It means that changes in the monetary supply and demand not only influence the exchange rate, but also the quantum of international reserves.

Different Approaches to BOP Adjustment

- Classical view: Self-adjusting process. Trade deficit → outflow of gold → decreased money supply → lower prices → higher exports → elimination of trade deficit.
- Elasticity Approach (Marshall/Lerner's view): Trade deficit → devaluation → (demand for export and import being price-elastic) exports cheaper abroad and higher export earnings + costlier imports and squeezed import bill → elimination of trade deficit. Stern added the concept of supply elasticity, meaning that supply elasticity for import and export must be favourable.
- Absorption Approach (Alexander's view): Trade deficit → decrease in absorption (consumption + investment + government expenditure) so that total output > absorption → elimination of trade deficit. Black suggests increasing saving and reducing investment in order to eliminate trade deficit.
- Mundell-Flemming view through adjustment in interest rate and income: Rise in interest rate → lower income → lower import → elimination of trade deficit. Again, rise in interest rate → inflow of foreign investment → improvement in capital account to absorb trade deficit.
- New Cambridge School Approach: Greater taxes + lower governmental expenditure → lower income → lower import → elimination of trade deficit.
- Monetary Approach:
  - Fixed exchange rate: Reduction in credit creation → decreased supply of money → lower import → falling trade deficit.
  - Floating exchange rate: Size of credit → size of money supply → exchange rate → balance of trade.

SUMMARY

- The balance of payments is a statement showing a country's commercial transaction with the rest of the world. It shows inflow and outflow of foreign exchange. It is divided into current and capital accounts. The former records the transaction in goods and services. The latter incorporates the flow of financial assets.
- The major economic variables influencing the balance of current and capital accounts are national output, national spending, money supply, exchange rate, and interest rate. The concept of disequilibrium is normally associated with the current account, and that too with the trade account.

- There are various approaches to adjustments in the balance of payments disequilibria. Classical economists believed in automatic adjustment through the flow of precious metals. Neo-classical economists emphasised on devaluation for improvement in the balance of trade. The focal point of the Keynesian approach is the income effect. Different views have been expressed in the Keynesian framework. One view, known as the absorption approach, suggests a proper alignment between output and absorption. Mundell-Fleming approach incorporates interest rate also and analyses the impact of interest rate changes, both on the current account and the capital account. The views of the New Cambridge school highlight taxes minus government spending as a tool for balance of payments adjustment. The monetarists, on the other hand, argue for changes in the monetary variables for adjustment in the balance of payments.

REVIEW QUESTIONS

1. What are the items listed in the current and the capital accounts?
2. Distinguish between:
   (a) monetary movement of gold and non-monetary movement of gold
   (b) autonomous capital flow and accommodating capital flow
   (c) capital account and current account
3. Explain statistical discrepancy.
4. Mention the macroeconomic variables that influence balance of payments.
5. "The adjustment in the balance of payments is automatic". Discuss this statement from the viewpoint of classical economists.
6. Explain elasticity approach to the adjustment in balance of payments.
7. Explain the Keynesian approach to the balance of payments adjustment.
8. Explain the monetary approach to balance of payments adjustment.

OBJECTIVE TYPE QUESTIONS

1. Mark True or false:
   (a) Unilateral transfers are entered in the capital account.
   (b) Any increase in revenue from tourism helps improve the balance of trade.
   (c) Direct and portfolio investments are entered in the capital account.
   (d) Interest on loans is a part of the capital account.
   (e) Overall BOP deficit adds to the official reserves account.
   (f) Spontaneous flow of capital goes below the line.
   (g) The J-curve effect is in no way related to the elasticity of demand for export.
   (h) Balance of payments adjustment can be brought about through changes in monetary variables.
2. Choose the most suitable answer:
   (a) According to the Elasticity Approach, trade balance should improve if:
      (i) Demand for export and import is price-elastic

(ii) Demand for export and import is price-inelastic
(iii) None of these

(b) According to the Absorption Approach, BOP adjustment in a situation of full employment can be brought about through:
(i) Increase in output
(ii) Decrease in absorption
(iii) None of these

(c) Classical economists believed that BOP adjustment:
(i) Was automatic
(ii) Was possible through devaluation
(iii) None of these

(d) Accommodating capital flow goes:
(i) Above the line
(ii) Below the line
(iii) None of these

(e) Invisibles influence:
(i) Trade balance
(ii) Balance of current account
(iii) None of these

3. Find the balance of trade, balance of current account, and the overall balance of payments with the help of the following figures:

Item	*Debit ($ mill.)*	*Credit ($ mill.)*
Trade in goods	55383	38285
Services, such as travel, transport & others	11865	15721
Statistical discrepancy	-	323
Unilateral transfer	34	12672
Foreign investment	7123	12240
External assistance	2183	3074
External commercial borrowings	2874	3207
Investment income	5490	1931
Banking capital	8532	11259
Rupee debt service	711	-
Other capital transactions	2510	4018

STUDY TOPIC

Recent Trends in India's Balance of Payments

Any discussion of recent trends in India's balance of payments essentially involves the impact of structural adjustment and macroeconomic reforms that were adopted in the country in mid-1991. The reforms in trade—in the form of import liberalisation, export promotion, exchange rate rationalisation, and steps to improve invisible earnings—did have an impact on the current account. At the same time, the liberal foreign investment policy and declining emphasis on foreign loans led to improvement in the capital account.

Current Account

During 1991–94 or the initial years of reform, the trade deficit shrank to US $2.8–5.4 billion annually from a figure of US $9.4 billion during 1990–91. The net invisible earnings too improved. The deficit on the current account was slightly over one billion US dollars in 1991–92 and 1993–94, although it was around US $3.5 billion in 1992–93. However, since 1994–95, with the slow pace of export, trade deficit began to grow and touched US $14.3 billion during 1996–97 and US $16.3 billion during 1997–98. The fast rising earnings on the invisible account, mainly due to a spurt in remittances saved the position from going worse and the deficit on current account moved in the range of US $3.4 to 6.5 billion annually. On the whole, the impact of reform can be said positive in the sense that the current account deficit as percentage of GDP dipped from 3.2 in 1990–91 to a bracket of 0.4 to 1.7 annually during 1991–98.

India's Balance of Payments (Current Account)

Millions of US $

Year	Import	Export	Trade Balance	Invisibles (net) Total	Invisibles (net) Investment Income	Invisibles (net) Remittances	Balance of Current Account
1991–92	21,064	18,266	–9,049	1,620	–3,830	3,798	–1,178
1992–93	24,316	18,869	–5,447	1,921	–3,423	3,865	–3,526
1993–94	26,739	22,683	–4,056	2,898	–3,270	5,287	–1,158
1994–95	35,904	26,855	–2,798	5,680	–3,431	8,112	–3,369
1995–96	43,670	32,311	–11,359	5,460	–3,205	8,539	–5,899
1996–97	48,063	33,764	–14,294	10,638	–3,250	11,139	–3,631
1997–98	51,126	34,849	–16,277	9,804	–3,457	11,830	–6,473
1998–99	47,544	34,298	–13,246	9,208	–3,544	10,587	–4,038
1999–2000	55,383	38,285	–17,098	12,935	–3,559	12,638	–4,163
2000–01	59,264	44,894	–14,370	12,106	–3,918	12,798	–2,264
2001–02	57,618	44,915	–12,703	14,054	–2,654	12,125	1,351
2002–03	65,474	53,000	–12,474	16,182	–4,882	14,448	3,708
2003–04	79,658	62,952	–16,706	25,425	–4,703	19,444	8,719
2004–05	118,779	82,150	–36,629	31,229	–3,814	20,253	–5,400
2005–06	156,334	104,780	–51,554	40,942	–5,599	24,095	–10,612
2006–07	191,995	127,090	–64,905	55,296	–4,282	27,415	–9,609
2007–08	2,48,521	1,58,461	–90,060	72,657	–5,239	40,778	–17,409
2008–09	2,94,587	1,75,184	–1,19,403	89,586	–4,511	44,047	–29,817

Sources:

1. Government of India (1998), *Economic Survey 1997–98* (New Delhi: Ministry of Finance).
2. Reserve Bank of India (1999), *Reserve Bank of India Bulletin*, May 1999.
3. www.rbi.org.in

During 1998–99, the imports fell, as a sequel to which the trade deficit reduced even further to US $13.246 billion; and taking into account the invisibles, the deficit on current account was also lower, at US $4.038 billion. But in the following year, the trade deficit increased to US $17.098 billion due to greater increase in the import bill by US $7.839 billion vis-à-vis an increase in the export earnings only by US $3.987 billion. Fortunately, the invisibles earnings were greater and so the current account deficit rose barely to US $4.163 billion. During 2000–01, the trade deficit amounted to US $14.370 billion, which was lower than during the preceding financial year; and the invisibles earnings (net) during this period being almost constant, compared to the preceding fiscal years, the current account deficit shrank to US $2.264 billion. During the following six-year period, the trade deficit moved up consistently to $ 64.9 billion in 2006–07, but since the invisibles showed large earnings, the current account turned either surplus or deficit within a limited range.

During 2007–08 and 2008–09, the trade deficit increased fast but at the same time, the total invisible earnings also rose. However, the increase in invisible earnings could not reduce the trade deficit much and as a result, the current account deficit widened to US $29,817 million during 2008–09.

Capital Account

The picture of capital account transactions was satisfactory to a great extent. The net inflow of foreign investment was sizeable—rising from US $133 million in 1991–92 to over US $5.8 billion in 1996–97. The amount dropped to US $5.0 billion in 1997–98 and to US $2.312 billion in 1998–99, but again crossed the US $5 billion mark in 1999–2000. During 2000–01, the net foreign investment inflow was lower and stood at US $2.911 billion. But then it grew large. In 2005–06, it was as large as $18.2 billion although it shrank to $15.5 billion during 2006–07. The following fiscal year foreign investment inflow was as large as US $44.8 billion although during FY 2008–09, on account of international financial crisis, it shrank to barely US $3.5 billion.

Net external assistance on the whole showed a declining trend, except for some marginal rise in a few years. Almost similar was the case with commercial borrowings, which remained confined within a low range, except for 1997–99, 2000–01, 2006–07 when they were large. Owing to a strong capital account position, IMF funds that had been borrowed in the initial phases of economic reform were repaid in instalments. Moreover, the deficit on current account was met by capital account transactions. The rest of the flow added to the official reserves. The size of the foreign currency assets, which was just over one billion US dollars during May–June 1991, inflated to US $42.281 billion at the end of March 2001. In the following five years, the net inflow on capital account was larger, with the result that foreign exchange reserves shot up fast and reached the $199 billion by March 2007 and US $299.23 billion by March 2008, although on account of international financial crisis they plummeted to US $241.426 billion by March 2009.

Capital Account Transactions during the Period of Reform (Millions of US$)

	External Assistance (Net)	*Commercial Borrowings (Net)*	*IMF Funds (Net)*	*Foreign Investment (Net)*	*Total Capital Account (Net)*	*Foreign Currency Assets at the Year End*
1991–92	3,031	948	786	133	3,777	5,631
1992–93	1,856	–1,445	1,288	567	2,936	6,434
1993–94	1,896	–84	187	4,235	9,695	15,068
1994–95	1,518	1,517	–1,143	4,807	9,156	20,809
1995–96	867	1,334	–1,715	4,604	4,678	17,044
1996–97	1,101	1,855	– 975	5,834	10,454	22,367
1997–98	877	4,010	– 618	4,993	11,924	25,975
1998–99	799	4,367	393	2,312	8,565	29,522
1999–2000	891	333	–260	5,117	10,242	35,058

(Continued)

	External Assistance (Net)	Commercial Borrowings (Net)	IMF Funds (Net)	Foreign Investment (Net)	Total Capital Account (Net)	Foreign Currency Assets at the Year End
2000–01	410	4,016	–26	2,911	7,487	42,281
2001–02	1,204	–1,147	–	5,925	9,545	51,049
2002–03	–2,460	–1,698	–	4,555	12,638	71,890
2003–04	–2,661	–1,853	–	14,492	22,122	112,959
2004–05	1,923	5,040	–	12,147	31,027	141,514
2005–06	1,438	1,591	–	18,222	24,693	151,622
2006–07	1,770	16,084	–	15,499	44,944	199,122
2007–08	2,114	22,165	–	44,806	1,08,031	2,99,230
2008–09	2,638	8,158	–	3,462	9,146	2,41,426

Sources:

1. Government of India (1998), *Economic Survey 1997–98* (New Delhi: Ministry of Finance).
2. Reserve Bank of India (1999), *Reserve Bank of India Bulletin*, May 1999.
3. www.rbi.org.in

QUESTIONS

1. Can you say why India's trade deficit took a downtrend during 1999–2003?
2. "Investment income has shown a negative balance". What reasons do you attribute to it?
3. Explain why India experienced a surplus balance of current account despite deficit trade balance during 2001–04.
4. Why have foreign currency assets risen fast during 2000–2007?

REFERENCES

Books

Connolly, M. (1978), "The Monetary Approach to an Open Economy: The Fundamental Theory" in Putnam, R. *et al.* (eds.), *The Monetary Approach to International Adjustment* (New York: Praeger), pp. 46–59.

Lerner, A. P. (1944), *The Economics of Control* (New York: Macmillan), Chaps. 28–29.

Marshall, A. (1924), *Money, Credit and Commerce* (London: Macmillan), Book, III.

Mundell, R. A. (1968), *International Economics* (New York: Macmillan).

Stern, R. M. (1973), *The Balance of Payments* (London: Macmillan).

Journals

Alexander, Sidney A. (1959), "Effects of a Devaluation: A Simplified Synthesis of Elasticity and Absorption Approaches", *American Economic Review*, I L (1), 22–42.

Black, J. (1959), "Saving and Investment Approach to Devaluation", *Economic Journal*, LXIX (273), 267–74.

SELECT FURTHER READINGS

Daniels, J. and D. Vanhoose (1999), *International Monetary and Financial Economics* (New York: International Thomson Publishing Company).

Melvin, M. (1985), *International Money and Finance* (New York: Harper Row), Chap.6.

* **Dubai Gold Souk** is a traditional market located in the heart of eastern Dubai's commercial business district in Deira. By some estimates, approximately 10 tons of gold is present at any given time in the souk. In 2003, the value of trade in gold in Dubai was approximately Dh. 21 billion (US$ 5.8 billion), while trade in diamonds was approximately Dh. 25 billion (US$ 7 billion) in 2005. India is Dubai's largest buyer of gold, accounting for approximately 23% (2005) of the emirate's total gold trade in 2005.

PART

PART 2

International Business Environment

Freight Station, Hamburg, Germany*

6

National Regulation of International Business

CHAPTER OBJECTIVES

International business is normally subject to various kinds of regulatory environment. The present chapter discusses the regulation of international business at the national level. In particular, the objective is to:

- Examine the merits of free trade versus trade protection.
- Explain the forms of trade regulation—trade restrictions and trade liberalisation.
- Examine the rationale behind regulation of FDI from the viewpoints of both the home country and the host country.
- Discuss the modalities of FDI regulation in both, the home country and the host country.

It has already been mentioned that international business is carried on in a multiplicity of environments insofar as the environment differs from one country to the other. This part of the book, therefore, acquaints the readers with the various kinds of environments. A beginning is made with the regulatory environment at the national level.

Regulation does not simply mean restrictions on foreign trade and investment, but also encouragement to them. The two divergent processes—restrictions vis-a-vis encouragement, determine essentially the quantum and pattern of international trade and investment in two different directions. The present chapter presents the relative merits of these two divergent processes and then discusses the different forms of regulation.

6.1 FREE TRADE VERSUS PROTECTION

6.1.1 Case for Free Trade

Free trade refers to absence of restrictions on export and import.

Protection is restricting import in order to protect domestic industries.

If regulation aims at *liberalisation of trade*, it is definitely a move towards *free trade*. If, on the contrary, it is meant for restriction of trade, it is nothing but protection. It is better to mention the arguments sometimes given in favour of free trade before any discussion of regulation of trade.

First of all, the argument for free trade rests primarily on the belief that it leads to specialisation, which helps increase output and the gains from the increased output is shared by the trading partners. It may be noted that output can also be increased through acquiring greater resources or through improving the quality of the factors of production. But, international trade is the least painful of the three measures for increasing output. Moreover, trade facilitates the other two types of the measures.

Secondly, free trade generates competition, which in turn promotes efficiency in production. Increased productive efficiency leads to improvement in quality and in lowering of prices. All this benefits both the producers and the consumers.

Thirdly, free trade leads to the generation of economies of scale. There are some industries that can achieve minimum average cost only through a bigger amount of sale, which is possible only when goods are exported to a global market. For example, the aeroplane-manufacturing industry cannot achieve economies of scale when its has only domestic customers.

Fourthly, free trade helps check inflation through the application of the one-price principle. It maximises the welfare of trading countries, and consequently, global welfare.

6.1.2 Arguments for Protection

It is a fact that free trade has a sound theoretical base, but it has only limited empirical support. Moreover, in real life, free trade is a utopian ideal. There are economic as well as non-economic arguments for regulating

Table 6.1 Arguments for Trade Protection

Economic Factors	*Non-economic Factors*
1. Protection of infant industry	1. Maintenance of essential industries
2. Promotion of industrialisation	2. Relations with unfriendly countries
3. Retaliatory action	3. Preservation of culture and national identity
4. Balance of payments adjustment	4. Preservation of community health
5. Price control and terms of trade	5. Preservation of national security
6. Employment generation	

trade (Table 6.1). The economic arguments are normally concerned with strengthening industrialisation in the country or with protecting balance of payments from any deterioration. The non-economic arguments are mainly political in nature. Whenever any government regulates foreign trade, there is normally a combination of factors behind it. Here it is relevant to discuss some of the major arguments behind protection of international trade.

Economic Factors:

1. The **infant industry** argument presents the most important justification behind the regulation of international trade. Newly born firms are generally not strong enough to compete with well established firms. Global firms enjoy economies of scale and are able to sell goods at a lower price. On the other hand, newly born domestic firms have high costs and cannot sell their products at low prices, at least in the short run. If the import of such products is not restricted, consumers will demand the imported product and not the domestically produced high cost goods. The result will be that in absence of demand, domestic firms producing such goods will have to close down their operations. Thus, if such firms have to be developed at home, import restriction becomes a necessity.

   This concept is not new. As far back as in 1930s, several industries in India were given protection against imports from the UK and other countries. It is often said that the sugar industry in India is a child of protection. However, there are a few problems that arise in such cases. First, it is very difficult to decide which industry has to be protected. Second, protection, once given, cannot easily be lifted because the producers, workers, and consumers tend to oppose it. Third, there is every possibility that the infant industry becomes dependent on the protection. If this is the case, it can never stand on its own feet and become competitive. Fourth, protection often causes greater economic harm than good insofar as the consumers have to pay higher prices for the product. Thus, whenever imports are restricted to help develop the infant industry, it should be a short-run phenomenon.

2. The **industrialisation promotion** argument is also important. In many countries, import substituting industries are developed to achieve self-reliance and to give a boost to other industries. This means that import restrictions lie at the very root of industrialisation. Sometimes, it is also said that when the government restricts imports, foreign investors boost up their investment in that country. This is because they get a sheltered market where they can make huge profits. Daniels and Radebaugh (2000) cite an example where Japanese automobile manufacturers began investing in the United States of America following restrictions on automobile import by the US Government. If this is the case, it means that import restrictions lead to foreign investment inflow and, thereby, strengthens the process of industrialisation.

   Again, sometimes the government restricts imports in order to help revive an already existing industry that is not in its infancy but is quite old. This is because such industries get a breathing space for revival in the absence of competition from imported products. This argument holds good in Canada where footwear imports are restricted because this is a traditional industry in Canada.

3. Sometimes, **retaliatory actions** need import restrictions. Such measures are taken when exporters adopt unfair trade practices. In order to capture the market, exporters sell goods in foreign countries, even at a lower price than their cost structure justifies. Such practices disrupt the very industrial structure in the importing countries. In order to counteract this move of exporters, the government in the importing country imposes restrictions on imports. However, it is very difficult to prove unfair trade practices in some cases. Moreover, retaliatory measures often turn to be unending and they prove harmful for trading countries.

4. **Balance of payments adjustment** is another justification, either for imposing restrictions on import or for export encouragement or both. In developing countries, axing the trade deficit lies at the root of import restrictions. In India, when the balance of trade was in a very bad shape during the early 1990s, import restriction measures were adopted quite intensively. Again, the import restriction measures are often accompanied by export encouragement measures. But sometimes it is found that import restrictions considerably hamper the export potential since the exporting industries do not get the desired amount of raw material or they get it only at a higher cost. So, import restrictions are only a short-term measure. They cannot be long-term, especially when they affect the exporting industries.

5. **Price control** is another objective behind the regulation of international trade. It is often found in cases where the exporting country is in a monopolistic or oligopolistic position with respect to a particular commodity. The exporting government shapes the price of the export in such a way that it provides for maximum profit. When the demand for the product is price inelastic, the exporting government raises the price of the product far beyond the cost of production. But if, on the contrary, the demand for export is price-elastic and the importing government imposes duty on the import, the price of the product will be unusually high in the hands of the consumers. As a result, the supplier will be forced to cut the price in order to maintain demand for the product. With a cut in the price, the ratio between the import price and the export price will be lower for the importing countries, improving in turn the terms of trade. An improvement in the terms of trade means accruing of gains from trade.
6. Protection of trade helps **generate employment** in the importing country. In macroeconomic terms, protection helps generate balance of payments surplus, which in turn increases income and employment. But if the additional income is used for imports, surplus in the balance of payments is eroded. On the contrary, the microeconomic employment case for protection starts with the fact that imposition of tariff may raise the demand for labour in a particular industry where import substituting goods are produced. But if labour is not mobile among industries, this effect may not be felt.

Non-economic Factors:

1. Among the non-economic factors, **maintenance of essential industries** is a guiding factor behind the regulation of trade. Each and every country tries to develop some essential industries so that in case of an extra-ordinary situation, the supply of essential products is not completely hampered. In order to protect these industries, the government regulates the export and import of these products. Again, in some other cases where the producers need the assurance of an uninterrupted supply of raw material, the government regulates the export and import of raw material. For example, the US Government subsidises the domestic production of silicon, which is made easily available to the computer industry.
2. **Trade with unfriendly countries** needs to be regulated. If the political relations are not friendly between two governments, trade is not encouraged between them. In cases where minimum trade is conducted, there is often the possibility of non-payment. So in such cases, trade is highly regulated in terms of commodities and price.

3. **Preservation of national culture and identity** is one of the factors behind regulating trade. For example, France imposes partial curb on the import of foreign films. This is out of fear that those films may affect badly the French culture and identity. In Canada too, there are restrictions on the import of entertainment products from the United States.
4. **Preservation of community health** is of utmost importance. The essence of health and sanitary regulations is to import only those products that do not adversely affect consumers' health. This is why food products are checked by health authorities the moment they enter ports
5. Trade regulation is necessary in order to preserve **national security.** Industries considered important for national security are often subjected to export or import regulations. The export and import of defence related products are cases in point.

6.1.3 Move from Inward-looking to Outward-looking Trade Policy Regimes

Neither of the two extremes–completely free trade on the one hand and complete trade restriction on the other–is found in the real life. The real scenario over past couple of decades shows that majority of the developing countries have moved from an inward-looking trade policy regime to an outward-looking one. Here the readers should be acquainted with the nature of these two policy regimes.

> ILP regime discriminates against imported products through imposing trade barriers
>
> OLP regime liberalises imports and provides incentives for encouraging exports

Inward-looking Policy: The inward-looking policy (ILP) regime represents a situation when a country tries to establish its domestic market for its own products through discriminating against the imported products by way of imposing trade barriers. Normally, this policy is known as import-substitution policy (ISP).

ISP was widely in use after the Second World War untill 1980s. The argument behind the use of this policy during the initial years was that the industrialisation in the developing world could not be financed through the export of primary commodities because the prices of these commodities tended to languish over the period that led to shrinkage in foreign exchange earnings (United Nations, 1949; Prebisch, 1950). Moreover, this policy helped the infant industries to grow (Hirschman, 1968). A number of tools were employed to serve the policy objective, such as tariff and quantitative restrictions, multiple exchange rates and different kinds of subsidies. However, it was never an easy sail. High tariff on intermediate goods harmed the final goods producers using those inputs. Balassa (1980) has cited some cases of Argentina and Hungary where the export industries using imported inputs had suffered a lot and the effective rate of protection is quite higher than the nominal rate of protection if the domestic value addition is not sizeable. The empirical study of Little et al (1970) shows that the effective rate of protection in India and

Pakistan was 200 per cent higher than the nominal rate of protection and it was 100 per cent higher in Argentina and Brazil. Moreover, the protected industries gain at the cost of unprotected ones. It leads to malallocation of resources and also to price distortions over time. Taylor (1998) finds quite substantial price distortions in terms of black market premium on foreign exchange among the inward-looking countries during 1950–1980. Again, the growth rate in the ISP countries lagged behind the growth rate in non-ISP countries. Maddison (1995) finds that in India, an ISP country, the growth rate in per capita GDP was lower than in six non-ISP countries of Latin America during the same period. The ISP scenario was thus subject to multiple maladies which led the different governments to make a good-bye to this policy by 1980s.

Outward-looking Policy: The outward-looking policy (OLP) regime is based on the export-oriented strategy where imports are liberalised and other incentives are provided to boost up exports. This strategy came into light when some East Asian countries shifted from ISP to outward-looking policy encouraging manufactured exports and recorded faster growth since 1960s. The policy requires a supportive macroeconomic environment and suitable macroeconomic incentives. The incentive may take the form of investment incentives, softer form of export credit, fiscal incentives for research and development and setting up of export-processing zones.

The outward-looking policy is found successful in so far as foreign demand is often larger in size and especially more stable than the domestic demand. The exports tend to reduce in many cases the foreign exchange constraints on growth (Krueger, 1990); and also, they encourage larger size of production and thereby the economies of scale. The economies of scale influence productivity in a positive way (Girma et al, 2004).

It is the success of the outward-looking policy in many parts of the world that has made this policy an integral component of the development policy throughout the world.

The Global Enabling Trade Report 2008 evaluates the trade policy of 118 countries and presents a cross-country analysis of measures stimulating trade. The higher the score is, the greater is the outward-orientation or the liberalisation in the trade policy. Hong Kong and Singapore have the highest score of, respectively, 6.04 and 5.71 because they have the most hassle-free customs procedures alongwith an equally open business environment. Among the other eight top-scorer countries are Sweden, Norway, Canada, Denmark, Finland, Germany, Switzerland and New Zealand. China is positioned on the 48th rank as this country has a near-closed import market characterised by tariff and non-tariff barriers. India ranks 52nd in the sample in view of cumbrous customs procedures and corrupt border administration resulting in hampered market access.
Source: Based on reports published in *Outlook Business*, 29/6–12/7, 2008.

Soren Kjeldsen-Kragh (2001) distinguishes between inward-looking policy and the outward-looking policy on the basis of effective exchange rate (EER) for the export and the import sectors. The EER for the export sector,

$$EER_X = ER(1 - t_x + s_x)$$

where t_x is export tariff that needs to be deducted from the world market price before the export proceeds are received by the producers; and s_x is the subsidy that the export sector gets.

Similarly, ERR for import sector,

$$EER_M = ER\ (1 + t_m)$$

where t_m is the trade barriers supporting domestic producers to compete with imports.

Now outward-looking policy is found where $EER_X = EER_M$ because there is no discrimination either against the importer or against the exporter. But if $EER_M > EER_X$, it is an indicator of the inward-looking policy because the government discriminates to the advantage of the import-competing industries.

6.2 FORMS OF TRADE REGULATION AT THE NATIONAL LEVEL

It may be emphasised at the very beginning that regulation of trade at the national level is not simply confined to the restriction of trade—export and import. It also includes different measures that act as stimuli to trade—import liberalisation and export encouragement. In all, trade regulation embraces:

1. Restriction of imports
   (a) Imposition of tariff and non-tariff barriers
   (b) Currency controls, such as restrictions on the convertibility of the currency into convertible currencies
   (c) Administrative delays in respect of licences and customs valuation
2. Restriction of exports
   (a) Putting export product on negative/restricted list
   (b) Imposing tariff on export
   (c) Imposing quota on export
3. Import liberalisation
   (a) Tariff cut
   (b) Reduction/abolition of quota and other non-tariff barriers
   (c) Shifting of import items from prohibited/restricted list to open list
4. Export augmentation
   (a) Passing on information or advising the exporters
   (b) Financial support, such as production subsidy and guarantees
   (c) Marketing support, especially provision of export subsidy

(d) Establishment of export-processing zones/special economic zones Since the EPZ units import inputs duty-free, they are able to sell the products in international market at competing prices.

6.3 INSTRUMENTS OF TRADE REGULATION

There are a number of tools that are applied by a government for regulating trade. More importantly, they are tariff. They are non-tariff barriers, such as quota, customs valuation, embargo and the technical barriers, such as classification, labelling requirements, testing standards, voluntary export restraints and buy-local legislation. Subsidy is another tool to augment export. In this section, they need discussion at some length.

6.3.1 Tariff

Tariff means duty levied by the government on imports. When assessed on a per unit basis, tariff is known as specific duty. But when assessed as a percentage of the value of the imported commodity, tariff is called *ad valorem* duty. When both types of tariff are charged on the same product, it is known as compound duty. Sometimes tariff is imposed to counter unfair trade practices, such as subsidy of the trading partner. In such cases, tariff is known as countervailing duty. Whatever may be the form of tariff, it reduces the quantum of import as the imported product turns costlier after the imposition of tariff. How much deeper the effect of tariff will be on the import restriction depends not only on the nominal rate of tariff but, more importantly, on the effective rate of protection.

> Specific duty refers to duty based on units of goods.
>
> **Ad valorem** duty is duty based on the value of goods.
>
> Compound duty is duty based on both the unit and the value.
>
> Countervailing duty refers to duty to negate the impact of unfair business practices, such as subsidy.

Effective rate of protection may be much lower/much higher than the nominal rate of tariff. This is because many goods are produced with imported raw material or intermediate products. Suppose a ball-point pen produced in India costs Rs. 25, of which Rs. 10 represents imported ink and the rest, Rs. 15, represents the value addition in the country. If tariff on an imported ball-point pen is 30 per cent and the tariff on the import of ink is 5 per cent, the effective rate of protection comes to 46.6 per cent compared to a nominal tariff rate of 30 − 5 or 25 per cent. This difference is because the entire production process is not protected, but only the value addition is protected. So, the effective rate of protection can be unusually high if any, or all, of the following conditions prevails.

The conditions are:

1. tariff on imported input is very low or zero
2. tariff on the final product to be imported is very high
3. value addition to the imported input is only insignificant

The effective rate of protection is

$$erp = \frac{(T - a_m T_m)}{(1 - a_m)} \qquad ...(6.1)$$

Where T is the nominal tariff rate,
a_m is the percentage of the final product that is imported,
$1 - a_m$ is percentage value added in the country, and
T_m is tariff on the imported component of production.

Based on the above example, the effective rate of protection will be:

$$\frac{0.3 - 0.05 \times 0.4}{0.6} = 0.466 \text{ or } 46.6\%$$

Impact of Tariff Under Partial Equilibrium Analysis: The effect of tariff, especially in a country that is not in a position to dictate the terms at which it trades, is presented in Figure 6.1. Assume in the beginning that there is no trade. The country produces 50 motorcycles and sells them at Rs. 28,500 each. Later on, it opens its domestic market to foreign suppliers. Motorcycles are available at an international price equivalent to Rs. 24,000 each. Lower price raises the demand for 80 motorcycles out of which 20 are domestically supplied and 60 are imported. Openness of the market raises the gains accruing to the consumers. But when the government imposes a tariff of Rs. 3,000 per motorcycle, price of motorcycle is higher at the consumers' end leading to a cut in demand to 60 out of which 40 are supplied by the domestic producers and 20 are imported. A part of the gains enjoyed by the consumers in absence of tariff shifts away from them after the imposition of tariff.

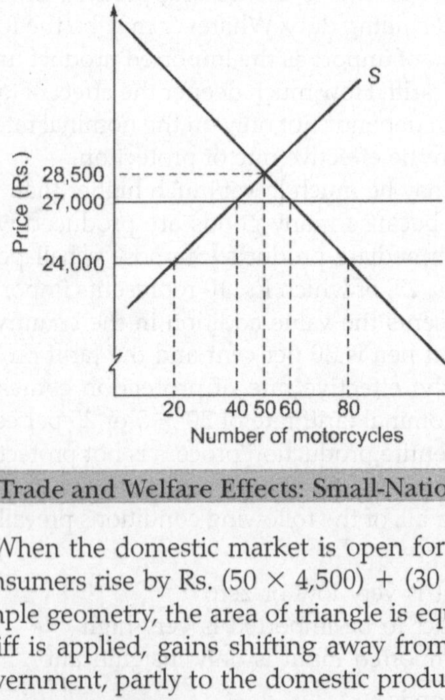

FIGURE 6.1 Tariff Trade and Welfare Effects: Small-Nation Model

When the domestic market is open for the foreign supplier, gains to consumers rise by Rs. (50 × 4,500) + (30 × 4,500/2) = 2,92,500 (as per simple geometry, the area of triangle is equal to height × base/2). When tariff is applied, gains shifting away from the consumers partly to the government, partly to the domestic producers and partly as deadweight loss are as follows:

1. Government's income effect = Rs. 3,000 × (60 – 40) = 60,000.
2. Consumption effect as deadweight loss = Rs. 3000 × [(80 – 60)/2] = 30,000.

3. Protective effect encouraging inefficient producers as deadweight loss = Rs. 3,000 × {(40 – 20)/2} = 30,000
4. Redistributive effect shifting net gains to producers = Rs. (3,000 × 40) – 30,000 as protective effect = 90,000.

A large country is different from a small country in so far as the former is in a position to change the world price of the commodity. Through the imposition of tariff, it influences the foreign suppliers to cut prices. The reduced price of import turns the terms of trade in favour of the importing country. The favourable terms of trade confers gain on the importing country, as a result of which the welfare increases. Here, it may be noted that a small importing country is not in a position to influence the world price and so it does not reap terms of trade gains through tariff imposition.

The impact of tariff on a large importing country can be explained through Figure 6.2. In case of autarky, 50 thousand motorcycles are supplied and demanded in the country at the rate of Rs. 28,500 each. But when the country begins to trade with no restrictions, the supply schedule changes to S_{D+F}. The schedule is upward-sloping in view of the fact that the price of imports can be changed. The price of the imported motorcycles is Rs. 24,000 each. As a result of the lower price of import, the demand moves up to 75 thousand motorcycles. The domestic producers supply 15 thousand of them and rest 60 thousand of them are imported.

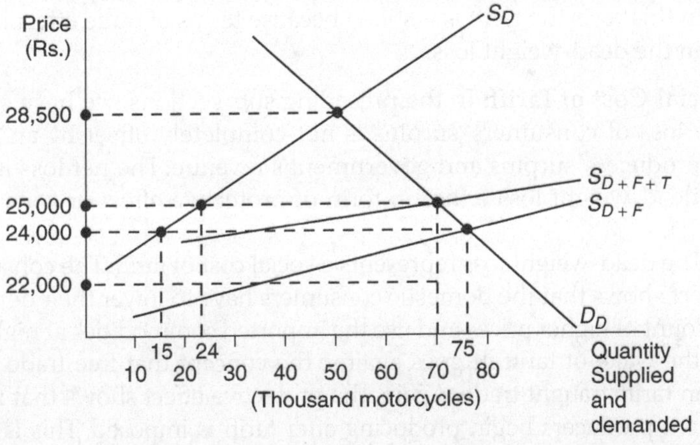

FIGURE 6.2 Welfare Impact of Tariff: The Case of a Large Nation

At a later stage, the country imposes tariff at a rate of Rs. 3,000 per motorcycle. Since the importing country is a very large buyer and it can influence the world price, the price of the imports in the hand of the domestic consumers rises not by the amount of tariff but only by Rs. 1,000. The rest Rs. 2,000 are shared by the foreign supplier which is manifested in the reduced price of import. To be specific, the imported price per motorcycle is Rs. 22,000 and the domestic consumers get the import for Rs. 25,000 each. Again, in the sequel of rising price in the hands of consumers, the supply schedule changes as S_{D+W+T} and the demand slips to 70 thousand motorcycles, out of which 24 thousand are supplied by domestic producers and the rest 46 thousand of them are imported.

On the basis of the above facts, the various effects of tariff will be as follows:

1. Redistributive effect shifting from consumers to domestic producers = Rs. (1,000 × 15) + Rs. 1,000 × {(24 – 15)/2} = Rs. 19,500
2. Dead-weight loss
   (a) Consumption effect = Rs. 1,000 × {(75 – 70)/2} = Rs. 2,500
   (b) Protective effect = Rs. 1,000 × {(24 – 15)/2} = Rs. 4,500
3. Income effect reaped by government = Rs. 3,000 × (70 – 24) = Rs.1,38,000

The income effect in case of a large importer is divided into domestic revenue effect and terms of trade effect

The income effect can be grouped into two compartments. One is the domestic revenue effect which is equal to Rs. 1,000 × 46 = Rs. 46,000. The other is the terms of trade effect which is equal to Rs. 2,000 × 46 = Rs. 92,000.

1. The nation's welfare increases if terms of trade gains > dead-weight loss
2. The nation's welfare decreases when terms of trade gains < dead-weight loss
3. The nation's welfare remains constant if terms of trade gains = dead-weight loss

In this case, the tariff is justified because terms of trade effect is greater than the dead-weight loss.

Social Cost of Tariff: In the preceding sub-sections, we have seen that the loss of consumers' surplus is not completely offset by an increase in producers' surplus and government's revenue. The net loss is known as dead-weight loss either in form of protective effect or consumption effect.

The dead-weight loss represents a social cost of tariff. The consumption effect shows that the domestic consumers have to lower their demand on account of higher prices and use the imported commodities at higher price in the wake of tariff. It goes against the concept that free trade is better than tariff-fraught trade. Again, the protective effect shows that the inefficient producers begin producing after tariff is imposed. This is nothing but the misallocation of resources because, in absence of tariff, these resources would have been used for exportable goods in which the country possessed comparative advantage. However, if there is less than full employment, the imposition of tariff may help create employment when the inefficient producers begin production. If this is true, the protective effect will be lower. Nevertheless, if exporters of the commodity take retaliatory measures, it would be difficult to measure the employment-generating effect and the imposition of tariff involves administrative cost that must be deducted from the government revenue from tariff.

Concept of Optimal Import Tariff: The imposition of tariff by a large country has two effects. The first one is a dead-weight loss manifesting in the decline in the volume of trade which reduces in turn the nation's welfare. The second one is apparent in improving terms of trade that in turn improves the nation's welfare. If the country imposes small tariff, it helps to increase nation's welfare because the terms of trade gain exceed the dead-weight loss. With the raising of tariff, the excess of terms of trade gains over the dead-weight loss goes on increasing, enhancing the nation's welfare. But this upward move is only to a certain point. Beyond this, if the tariff is raised, the excess of terms of trade gain goes on shrinking and a time will come when the net gain will come down to a no-trade position or a position where no import is made on account of very high tariff. Thus, a large country should impose tariff only to that extent where the excess of terms of trade gains over the dead-weight loss is the highest or, in other words, the net increase in welfare is the maximum. In fact, this rate of tariff is the optimal tariff rate (de Graff, 1949).

However, the imposition of optimal tariff may not be suggested. It is because the other trading partner will face a twin problem of loss of the volume of trade and at the same time a deteriorating terms of trade. In the sequel, it may retaliate and the gains from trade reaped may be lower.

Now, the question is whether an optimal tariff exists in a small country. A small country does not reap the terms of trade gain. Any tariff leads to a dead-weight loss with the result that optimal tariff rate does not exist.

Impact of Tariff under General Equilibrium Analysis: Since the effect of tariff spills over to other sectors of the economy, a general equilibrium analysis is required to assess the impact of tariff. The impact falls in a variety of ways. They are as follows:

First, tariff causes an increase in domestic production. Even those domestic producers start meeting the domestic demand that were not capable of producing goods at the international price of the product. It is because tariff makes the domestic market a sheltered market for the producers. It is not only an increase in production but also a shift in the production structure in the economy that is marked in the sequel of tariff imposition. The resources shift from other industries to the industry where tariff is imposed to reap the advantage of a sheltered market.

Secondly, with the rising production, the income of the factors of production rises, especially of those factors that are used intensively in the production of the product. A rise in income generates demand and thereby output and employment in the country.

Thirdly, tariff helps to reduce consumption because the imported goods turn costlier. Lower income or lower consumption means lower welfare. However, if the government uses the tariff income for providing various services to the community, the loss of consumption would be offset partly or wholly. Again, as the Metzler's paradox explains, since the marginal propensity to import in the tariff-imposing country is often very low, the price of the imported commodity may drop in the world market more than the amount of tariff. This means that the imported commodity in the tariff-imposing country may be cheaper. Cheaper imports may not have an adverse impact on consumption.

Fourthly, tariff helps to lower the volume of trade. The reason is that tariff leads to a rise in the domestic production of that commodity. The imports turn costlier on account of tariff. The domestic availability of gods at a lower price helps to cut the volume of imports. If the tariff is very high, it is possible that the import of the commodity in question comes down to a zero level. Such tariff is known as a prohibitive tariff.

Fifthly, when the tariff imposing country is large enough to influence the world demand and prices, the imposition of tariff compels the foreign suppliers to reduce the price of the product. The lower price of the import helps to improve the terms of trade. The terms of trade gains leads to a further boost for the economy.

6.3.2 Quota

> Quota is a quantitative restriction on import. It may be global or country-specific. Additionally, it may be tariff-rate quota.

Quota is an instrument to put quantitative restrictions on import. It may take different forms. One is the outright limitation on the quantity of import. Limitation may be either a global one or specific to a country. For example, if the government permits the import of only 2,000 bicycles without mentioning a particular country, it will be global quota. But if the government limits the import of 500 bicycles from the USA, it will be country-specific quota or selective quota. Since the global quota is based on first-come-first-served, the importing country has to accept those supplies that are made earlier irrespective of their quality and source.

Sometimes, the government fixes quota for the import and at the same time imposes tariff. Up to the quota limit, the rate of tariff is lower, but if the imports are made beyond the quota, a higher rate of tariff is applicable for the additional import. The tariff-rate quota is a subtler form of quota that permits the import beyond the quota limit, although at a higher rate of tariff.

> Import licensing requirement and voluntary export restraints may be treated as quota.

The other form of quota is import licensing requirement. If obtaining licence from the government to import a particular commodity is mandatory, the commodity can be imported only to the extent it is specified in the licence. The government issues licence for import based on the required size of import. It is true that the import licensing requirement is a less transparent form of quota than the outright limitation on the size of import, but it is a common instrument. By 1980s, it was used as a major tool for protecting industries in Mexico. In India too, it was used more frequently till 1980s.

Still the other form of quota is known as voluntary export restraint (VER). In this case, the exporting country is asked by the importing country to limit the supply of a particular commodity. The restriction is imposed by the exporting country and not by the importing country. There are many examples of VER negotiated by the USA to restrict the

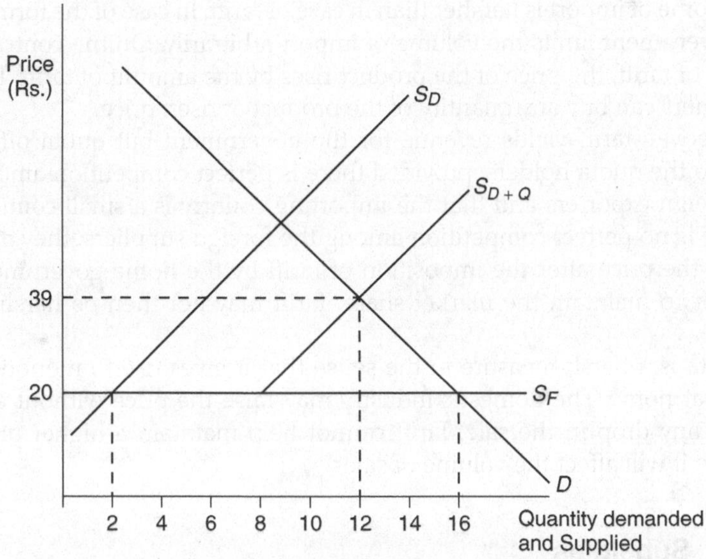

FIGURE 6.3 Welfare Impact of Import Quota

import of textiles, automobiles and other products from Japan, Korea and other countries.

Welfare Impact: Import quota leaves a definite impact on the welfare of the country. The impact is explained in Figure 6.3. Suppose, India's total demand for edible oil is 16 million tonnes, out of which it produces only 2 million tonnes. The rest is imported from Italy under a free trade scenario. There are two supply schedules—one for home, S_D showing availability of 2 million tonnes of the commodity and the other for Italy, S_F where the supply is perfectly elastic. The price of the commodity is equal in both the countries, which is equivalent to Rs. 20 per tonne of oil.

Now, the Indian Government restricts import up to 6 million tonnes under the provisions of quota. The supply schedule will now change showing limited availability of this product. The new supply line, S_{D+Q} intersects the demand line at a higher point meaning that the price of edible oil gets higher at Rs. 39 on account of the imposition of quota. The consumers' surplus and thereby the nation's welfare decreases. The decrease is equal to:

1. Redistributive effect = {(Rs. 39 – Rs. 20) × 2 mn tonnes} + {(Rs. 39 – Rs. 20) × 4 mn tonnes)/2 = Rs. 76 mn
2. Protective effect = {(Rs. 39 – Rs. 20) × 4 mn tonnes}/2 = Rs. 38 mn
3. Consumption effect = {(Rs. 39 – Rs. 20) × 4 mn tonnes}/2 = Rs. 38 mn
4. Revenue effect = {(Rs. 39 – Rs. 20) × 6 mn tonnes} = Rs. 114 mn

Difference between Quota and Tariff: Quota and tariff both restrict imports. But the impact of the two is different. In short, the axe of quota on the volume of import is harsher than in case of tariff. In case of the former, the government limits the volume of import arbitrarily. On the contrary, in case of tariff, the price of the product rises by the amount of tariff. The consumers can buy any quantity of the product at risen price.

Moreover, tariff yields revenue for the government but quota offers gains to the quota holders, provided there is perfect competition among the foreign exporters and that the importing country is a small country. If there is no perfect competition among the foreign suppliers, they may reduce the price after the imposition of tariff by the home government in order to maintain the market share. Tariff may not then be harsh in effect.

Quota is a harsh measure in the sense that it gives rise to monopoly power at home. The domestic industry may raise the price without any fear of any drop in the sale. Tariff cannot help maintain a higher price because it will affect the volume of sales.

6.3.3 Subsidies

Subsidies are other form of non-tariff barriers. Subsidies take many forms, such as cash assistance given by the government, tax concessions, loans at lower than market rate of interest arranged by the government and such others. In this way, they allow the domestic producers to produce at prices lower than warranted by the actual cost or profit considerations.

> Subsidies may be either domestic subsidy given normally to producers of import-competing goods or they may be export subsidy given to exporters to make them internationally competitive.

Domestic Subsidy: With domestic subsidy, inefficient producers begin production at a price compatible with the international price. As a result, domestic production rises and import falls with a given demand for the product. As per Figure 6.4, in absence of trade, the domestic production and domestic demand, Q_1 meets each other at price, P_1. When the country opts for trade, the commodity is available at lower price, P_3. At the lower price, the demand rises to B, out of which OQ_2 is supplied domestically and Q_2Q_3 is imported. But when subsidy is given to domestic producers,

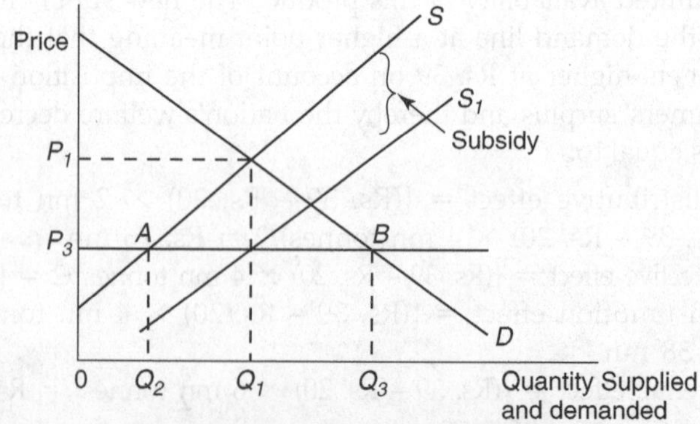

FIGURE 6.4 Welfare Impact of Domestic Subsidy

the supply schedule changes from S to S_1 and domestic output increases from Q_2 to Q_1 negating any import to that extent. The net price to the producers of the commodity equals the sum of international price and the amount of subsidy. The financial burden on government is equal to the amount of subsidy multiplied by OQ_1. This additional domestic production in the sequel of subsidies may be termed as protective effect of subsidies.

Domestic subsidies are better than tariff and quota. It is because the subsidies do not force consumers to lessen their demand and there is no dead-weight loss in the form of consumption effect. But, at the same time, subsidies fall on the state exchequer and enlarge the fiscal deficit.

Export Subsidy: Export subsidy is confined to those producers that produce for export. In this case, the domestic price of the commodity is higher than the foreign price. It is true that the volume of export rises thereby increasing the total export earnings, but the net barter terms of trade worsens as a result of the fall in price. Figure 6.5 shows that in free trade, Q_1 commodity is supplied at price, P_2. When subsidy is given to exporters, supply schedule tends to change from S to S_1 that leads in turn to greater volume of export at Q_2. But, at the same time, the price of the export falls to P_1 worsening in turn the terms of trade. How far a fall in price will augment export depends on the price elasticity of demand. But it is true that the domestic consumers have to pay a higher price at P_3, which is equal to the sum of foreign price and the amount of subsidy.

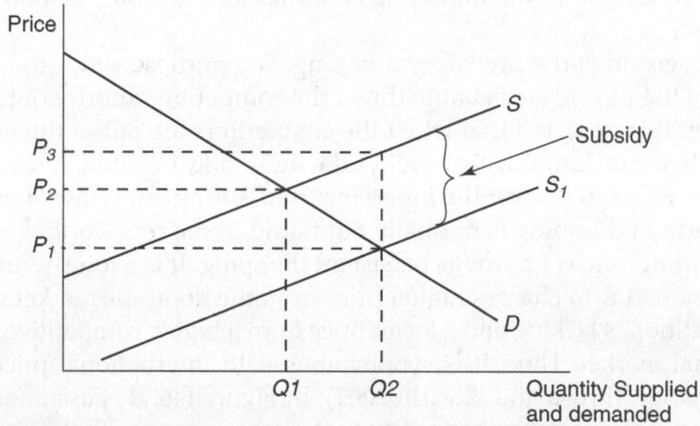

FIGURE 6.5 Welfare Impact of Export Subsidy

Huge Subsidisation of Chinese Exports

The share of Chinese exports in the world trade moved up from 4.7 per cent to 10.8 per cent between 2000 and 2006. The most important reason is that the Chinese goods are highly price-competitive in the international market on account of ample subsidies provided to producers and exporters in variety of ways. The subsidies are diversely spread and the government uses fancy names for the subsidies, such as market exploration fund, export

credit insurance, offshore processing trade project, etc. with the result that it is very difficult to quantify them. However, there are some more important forms of subsidies. First of all, cash grant is given to the manufacturers in the form of technology and research promotion. Secondly, there are equity infusions by the government. Thirdly, preferential loans are given. Fourthly, it is the tax exemptions. Fifthly, it is the supply of power at a subsidised rate. Last but not least, the government has put the value of Renminbi well below its market-determined value. According to some estimates, Renminbi is undervalued by 35–55 per cent.
Source: Based on the reports of *Outlook Business*, 18–31 May, 2008

6.3.4 Dumping

Dumping is a form of price discrimination in favour of foreign consumers. The same product is sold to foreign buyers at a lower price than what the domestic buyers have to pay. Dumping also occurs when goods are sold in the overseas market at a price below the average cost of production.

Dumping may take different forms depending upon the purpose for which it is done. The first is distress dumping or the sporadic dumping. In this case, a firm clears its unsold stock at a lower price in overseas market. It is true that it hurts the competing exporters in other countries or the producers in the importing countries, but it is only a short-term problem.

The second is the predatory dumping. The purpose is not the clearance of the unsold stock but to throw the competing exporter out of the market. It is expected that when the competitors are out of the market and when the dumping firm enjoys the monopoly position, it raises the price in order to recover the losses incurred during dumping. However, this form of dumping is normally not found in the real world.

The third one is known as persistent dumping. It is a long-term phenomenon. A firm charges higher price from the domestic market where competition is lacking and a lower price from a highly competitive international market. Thus, it is synonymous with international price discrimination (Prusa and Skeath, 2001). In Figure 6.6, it is assumed that the firm enjoys monopoly position at home meaning that any additional sale of the product is possible only at a reduced price. The result is that the marginal revenue curve will slope downwards. On the other hand, there are many suppliers in the foreign market with the result that the firm has to charge the prevailing market price for the product, irrespective of the amount of sale. In the sequel, the marginal revenue curve is a horizontal straight line. The slope of the average and marginal cost is based on the increasing return initially and then diminishing return to scale. The equilibrium is achieved where marginal revenue in the domestic market, marginal revenue in the foreign market and marginal cost are equal or,

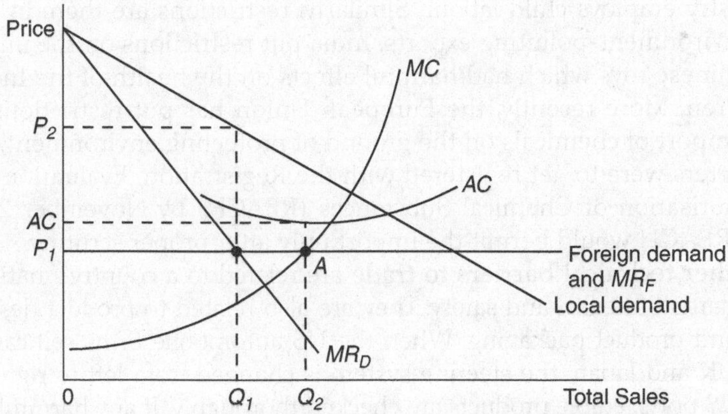

FIGURE 6.6 Persistent Dumping and International Price Discrimination

$$MR_D = MR_F = MC \qquad \ldots\ldots(6.1)$$

In Figure 6.6, MR_F and MC are equal at Point A which represents the total sale, Q_2 at a price P_1. But the entire sale is not directed to the foreign market. A part of it, Q_1 is sold in the domestic market at a higher price, P_2. Q_1 lies at Point B where MR_D is equal to MR_F. We find that even if the price in foreign market is lower than the average cost, the higher price at home not only compensates the loss in the foreign market but also, over and above, yields profit.

6.3.5 Some Other Forms of Non-tariff Barriers

Among other non-tariff barriers, we here discuss some of their important forms, such as buy-local legislation, social regulations, health and sanitary regulations, etc.

Buy-local legislation is enacted to force the domestic producers to buy the inputs first in the domestic market. It also forces the consumers to buy locally-made goods. Such legislation is treated as a trade barrier because it discriminates against low-cost foreign suppliers in favour of domestic suppliers. Costly inputs raises the cost of production and thereby the price of the product and lowers the consumers' surplus. It causes dead-weight welfare losses in the form of consumption effect and protective effect.

During the international financial crisis of 2008 and 2009, the US Government emphasised on the local purchase of iron and steel for the infrastructural projects. It entailed upon the export performance of the Indian economy during FY 2009–2010.

Social regulations apply to specific social problems, environmental issues and other related issues. The US Government has put restrictions on the import of carpet from India because the Indian carpet industry employs child labour. Similarly, restrictions are there in case of environment-polluting exports. India put restrictions on the import of Chinese toys which had harmful effects on the health of the Indian children. More recently, the European Union has put restrictions on the import of chemicals on the ground of protecting environment. The exporters were to get registered with the Registration, Evaluation and Authorisation of Chemical Substances (REACH) by November 2008. The REACH would permit the import only after proper scrutiny.

Other technical barriers to trade are related to a country's national standards of health and safety. They are also related to product designing and product packaging. When the US automobile firms sell cars in the UK and Japan, the steering system is changed from left to right. At the US ports, edible products are checked thoroughly. If any harmful live bacterium is found in any packet of the product, the ship is returned on the ground of preserving health in the country. Similarly, packaging is very important to protect the product from getting rancid. So goods with improper packaging are not accepted at the port of many countries.

The details of some of the major NTMs that are maintained against Indian exports are as under:

Country	*Item*	*Details of NTM*
United States	Marine products	Increased inspections under the Bio-Terrorism Act, Customs Bond requirement, Mandatory labeling discriminating "farm raised" and "wild" with punitive fines and non-recognition of EIC certification
United States	Paper products	Non scientific quarantine restrictions, customs surcharges, eco labeling stipulations and food safety/health standards exist on paper products exports
United States	Tobacco	A TRQ regime restricts imports
United States	Food products	Detailed labeling requirements are stipulated with extensive product and content description
Argentina	Processed Marine Products, Matches, Insecticides, Fungicides, Plastics, Rubber, Leather, Wood and Paper Products, Textiles and Clothing, Headgear, Footwear, Articles of Iron and Steel, Mechanical and Electrical Machinery, two wheelers, optical instruments, furniture, toys, miscellaneous manufactured articles	A new regulation (57 and 58/2007 dated 24.08.2007) wherein minimum import price has been established for specified product imports from India and some other countries. Under this the Argentine Customs authorities can ask for validation of Indian customs invoice with a full set of original documents if they suspect that the invoiced value is less than the minimum import price established
Argentina	Pharmaceuticals	There is delay in registration leading to non-viability of exports

Australia	Mangoes	Australia maintains ban on the pretext of the presence of fruit flies and stone weevils
Armenia	Agro chemicals and pharmaceuticals	Armenia stipulates registration requirements and mandates permission for imports and exports.
Bangladesh	Poultry products	Bangladesh continues to ban imports despite India gaining the avian influenza free status
Brazil	Pharmaceuticals	Procedural delays occur in the clearances, inspections and registration by the Brazilian Health Surveillance Agency (ANVISA)
Canada	Paper products	Non scientific quarantine restrictions, customs surcharges, eco labeling stipulations and food safety/health standards exist on paper product exports
Chile	Wheat, wheat flour and sugar	A complex price band system wherein a minimum import price (well above the international price and domestic prices) is stipulated. On account of a WTO dispute decision, this band would be lowered by 2% every year from 2008 to 2014 after which a Presidential review would be undertaken
China	Agricultural products	Opacity of sanitary and phytosanitary (SPS) measures and delays in giving clearances
Colombia	Pharmaceuticals	The registration by Colombian Drugs Control and Certification takes 11 to 12 months, inspections are undertaken for environmental compliance and a 10% price preference is granted for French pharmaceutical companies under a bilateral agreement
European Communities	Bovine meat	Standards are more stringent than OIE (World Organization for Animal Health) Terrestrial Animal Health Code, a ban is maintained on account of Foot and Mouth Disease (FMD) and prolonged delay in upgradation of India's status to GBR1 (No risk of BSE)
European Communities	Marine products	Rejection and subsequent destruction of consignments with chloramphenicol/nitrofuran residues, rejections in Italy and France due to the presence of vibrio parahaemolyticus without judging the virulence factors, rejection due to alleged presence of bacterial inhibitors/antibiotic residues without any confirmatory tests
European Communities	Chemicals	The Registration, Evaluation and Authorisation of Chemicals (REACH) legislation increases cost of compliance by € 85,000 to € 325,000 per chemical product

(*Continued*)

Country	*Item*	*Details of NTM*
European Communities	Engineering and Electronics	The stipulation of CE (originally known by the French term Conformité Européenne) marking to indicate conformity with the essential health and safety requirements increases cost for small and medium enterprises
Japan	Footwear	The tariff rate quota (TRQ) restricts imports to the quantum of the quota
Korea	Chemicals, pharmaceuticals, computer and medical equipment	Certification requirements (including prior approval) add on to the cost of exports
New Zealand	Paper products	Non scientific quarantine restrictions, customs surcharges, eco labeling stipulations and food safety/health standards exist on paper products exports
Norway	Marine products	The pathogen analysis is carried out by the NMKL method which is not accepted internationally
Russia	Meat products	Standards for bovine meat are more stringent than the OIE Terrestrial Animal Health Code, EIC Conformity certificates are not recognised and certification with respect to swine fever and FMD are insisted upon for poultry exports which are not relevant
Ukraine	Bovine meat, coffee, tea, spices, pharmaceuticals, cosmetics, plastics, leather products, textiles and clothing	A compulsory certification with the option of either (a) certificate of acceptance of foreign certification by Derzh Standard or (b) Conformance certificate by the Ukrainian agency. Though ISO 9000 standards are adopted by Derzh Standard, foreign certification recognition exists only to the extent of international treaty obligations of Ukraine
Uzbekistan	All products	Registration and certification, a custom processing fee @ 0.7% of value and lengthy procedure for conversion of hard currency as well as profit repatriation

Source: *GOI website vb*

6.4 REGULATION OF FDI

FDI is regulated both at the national and international levels. At the national level, the home country government as well as the host country government provides various kinds of incentives in order to encourage FDI flow. But it does not mean that governments let loose their rein of control. Various checks are maintained so as to reap maximum advantage from the FDI flow. Similarly, at the international level, it is the WTO that regulates FDI under the aegis of TRIMS.

6.4.1 Rationale behind Regulation

Host-country Perspective: It is clear from the earlier section of this chapter that there are certain benefits to be reaped by the host country from FDI inflow. They are, for example, availability of scarce foreign exchange, improvement in the balance of payments, accelerated rate of economic development through warranted rate of investment and through the creation of economic linkages, and so forth. In fact, these are the factors responsible for the adoption of a favourable FDI inflow policy by the host country government. But at the same time, FDI inflow is subject to checks because it often produces negative impact on the host economy, such as deterioration in its balance of payments on account of larger imports, payment of dividend and other fees, and continued dependence on the imported technology. These issues have already been discussed and so do not need repetition. Nevertheless, it may be mentioned that since the subsidiary sources its inputs either from the parent unit or from a third country unit of the firm, FDI inflow fails to help build what Porter calls a "cluster". In such cases, the developmental impact of FDI is very little. Moreover, in such cases of sourcing, transfer pricing is very common. This means over-invoicing of imports of the subsidiary, which in turn channels out scarce foreign exchange from the country and entails upon the balance of payments. The host government encourages local sourcing. If foreign sourcing is indispensable, the government scrutinises the invoicing procedure.

Again, it is true that a high tariff wall motivates tariff-jumping FDI. But in such cases, the foreign firms are able to raise the price of the product to the extent of tariff imposed on the import of similar products. It happens in cases where demand for the product is price-inelastic and local substitutes are not available. Consumers are then forced to bear the price rise. In order to avoid such a situation host country governments often encourage FDI inflow through lowering of tariff.

Tariff-jumping FDI is an FDI made in a country just to evade its high tariffs.

It is not only the consumers in the host country that are affected through tariff-jumping FDI, domestic producers face tough competition from foreign manufacturers. They ask the government to put some sort of restriction on foreign investors so that the domestic market can be sheltered. It is perhaps from this viewpoint that the European Union limits the market share for Japanese car manufacturers (Safarian, 1993).

The host country government controls the operation of foreign investors not only on economic grounds, but it is also on the grounds of defence and national security. The US government justifies prohibition or restrictions on foreign investment in air transport, coastal shipping, commercial fisheries, communications, and energy resources. This is simply on the grounds of national security.

Extra territoriality issue refers to the issue concerning a company implementing its home country rules and regulations for its foreign subsidiaries.

Apart from reasons of national security there is the issue of extraterritoriality. When foreign ownership results in extraterritorial application of laws and the regulatory mechanism of the firm's home country to its activities in the host country, the host country government does not relish it and imposes certain restrictions. The US anti-trust law is applicable not only to the US owned firms but also to foreign-country firms. Developing countries do not like the use of inappropriate technology or technologies that do not help develop local skills by foreign firms. If it is so, they impose various types of restrictions.

Home country Perspective: It is also the home country government that regulates FDI on, both, economic and political grounds. It encourages investment abroad when such investment is beneficial to the home country. But when foreign investment outflow is not conducive to the economy, the home country government imposes restrictions on it. Similarly, FDI is encouraged/restricted depending upon the political relationship with the host country. Readers are suggested to go through the positive and negative impact of FDI on the home country discussed earlier. Infact, these are also the reasons behind either encouraging or discouraging FDI outflow.

6.4.2 Modalities of Regulation in Host Country

There are different tools for regulating FDI. The first is concerning ownership. In India, when the government proposed to restrict FDI in 1973, the Foreign Exchange Regulation Act was amended to limit the equity owned by foreign investors to 40 per cent. But when it tried to encourage FDI in 1991, this ceiling was abolished. Now foreign investors can have 100 per cent equity in an Indian enterprise in special cases.

Secondly, the government opens different sectors of the domestic economy for FDI. This happened in India in 1991. But when the purpose is to restrict FDI, it is not allowed in many sectors of the domestic economy. In 1968 and again in 1973, the Indian government limited the scope for FDI inflow.

Thirdly, the government restricts the repatriation of dividend, royalty, and other fees to the home country. Alternatively, it introduces the balancing requirements where the foreign enterprise has to export a certain amount of its product, which could balance its payments for imports or other payments.

Fourthly, the host government provides financial incentives and infrastruc-tural facilities to foreign investors in order to attract such investment. The financial incentives normally include tax or tariff incentives. The infrastructural incentives include free or subsidised provision of land, electricity, transport, and so on. In India, foreign investors get such facilities if they operate in an export processing zone/special economic zone.

6.4.3 Modalities of Regulation in Home Country

When the home country government intends to encourage FDI outflow, it provides insurance cover to the investors against political risk in the host country. Sometimes it grants loans to the investors for investment abroad or guarantees loans provided by financial institutions. Again, it provides tax rebates on the inflow of dividend and other fees. Last but not least, it puts pressure on the host country government to relax restrictions, if any.

When the home country government intends to restrict FDI outflow, it withdraws the facilities given to the investors and increases the tax rates on profits earned. In extreme cases, it imposes outright sanctions that prohibit making any foreign investment.

SUMMARY

- Free trade, no doubt, has merits. But in real life, international trade is regulated. It is regulated at the national level as well as by international authorities. A number of arguments—economic as well non-economic—are given for regulation at the national level. The economic factors are mainly the protection of infant industries, promotion of industrialisation, retaliation, balance of payments adjustment, price control, and generation of employment. Among the non-economic factors are mainly the maintenance of essential industries, relations with the unfriendly countries, preservation of culture and national identity, community health, and national security.
- Over past few decades, countries have moved away from inward-looking policy regime to outward-looking policy regime.
- Regulation at the national level is found in the form of import restriction, import liberalisation, export restriction, and export liberalisation. Tariff and non-tariff measures have an important role to play in this process, although some other measures are also applied for this purpose.
- In view of the benefits and costs of FDI, it is regulated both by the home country and the host country governments. In order to encourage it, various incentives are provided by the government. But if the objective is to restrict FDI, incentives are withdrawn and restrictions are imposed. The home country government may impose sanctions. The host country government may put restrictions on the ownership pattern as well as it may limit the area of operation open to foreign investors.

REVIEW QUESTIONS

1. What is the rationale behind trade protection? What are the ways of restricting export and import?
2. Distinguish between inward-looking and outward-looking policy regimes.
3. Do you agree with the statement that import liberalisation is a prerequisite for export promotion? What are the ways of augmenting export?
4. Explain effective rate of protection. What are the factors responsible for the difference between the nominal rate of tariff and the effective rate of tariff?
5. Discuss the impact of tariff.
6. What do you mean by quota? Describe its impact.
7. What do you mean by subsidy? Discuss its impact.
8. Write a note on dumping.
9. Is regulation of the MNCs essential? What are the modalities to regulate them?

Objective Type Questions

1. Mark True or False:
   (a) Free trade leads to specialisation and thereby to increase in output.
   (b) Free trade creates hurdles in achieving economies of scale.
   (c) Import restriction helps new industries.
   (d) Import restrictions are both long term and short term measures of balance of payments adjustment.
   (e) Trade protection helps generate employment in importing countries.
   (f) Specific duties mean tariff imposed on the basis of value of goods.
   (g) The purpose of countervailing duty is to counter unfair trade practices.
   (h) Effective rate of protection depends inter alia on the tariff levied on the import of the final product.
   (i) Subsidies are a form of tariff levied on the import of agricultural products.
   (j) Extraterritoriality in the context of FDI means the application of the home country rules and regulations for the activities of foreign subsidiaries.

2. Choose the Most Suitable Answer:
   (a) Free trade means:
      (i) Greater competition that, in turn, improves efficiency
      (ii) Development of newly born industries
      (iii) Incentives for imports and exports
   (b) Trade protection aims at:
      (i) Preservation of cultural and national identity
      (ii) Specialisation in production
      (iii) None of the above
   (c) Imports can be restricted through:
      (i) Currency control
      (ii) Establishment of EPZs
      (iii) Tariff cut
   (d) Exports are augmented through:
      (i) Raising tariff rate
      (ii) Providing subsidies
      (iii) Both of the above
   (e) FDI inflow can be augmented by:
      (i) Opening different sectors for FDI inflow
      (ii) Providing foreign investors a greater stake in the equity
      (iii) Both of the above
   (f) Effective rate of protection depends upon:
      (i) Tariff on the imported input
      (ii) Tariff on the final product
      (iii) Both of the above

CASE STUDY

Regulation of Foreign Trade in India

India's foreign trade has been under constant regulation. Beginning from the early 1960s, several export promotion schemes were announced and implemented, but till mid-1980s, the trade policy remained primarily inward oriented. During 1980s, a few measures were taken to liberalise imports. But since mid-1991, when structural adjustment and macroeconomic reforms were initiated in the country, the trade policy structure became clearly outward oriented.

Redesigning of the foreign trade policy covers quite a broad area and a variety of measures. During the period of reform, some new measures have been added to, and a few of them have been withdrawn from, the policy package from time to time depending upon the changing performance and position of this sector. The measures that have been taken in this regard can broadly be grouped under four heads. They are:

1. rationalisation of exchange rate policy;
2. import liberalisation;
3. export incentives and
4. simplification of procedural formalities and fostering of transparency.

Rationalisation of Exchange Rate Policy: In the first week of July 1991, the rupee was depreciated by around 20 per cent vis-à-vis a basket of five currencies, that is, the US dollar, Deutsch mark, British pound, French franc, and Japanese yen. The purpose was to bridge the gap between the real and the nominal exchange rates that had emerged on account of rising inflation and, thereby, make exports competitive. In March 1992, the Liberalised Exchange Rate Management System (LERMS) was introduced. It provided for a dual exchange rate system under which 40 per cent of the export proceeds were to be surrendered at the official exchange rate and the remaining 60 per cent were to be converted at market determined rates. The units in the export-processing zones (EPZs), 100 per cent export oriented units (EOUs) and the units in the electronics technology park were allowed to convert their entire foreign exchange earnings at the market rate. The system was further liberalised in March 1993 when full convertibility was introduced, meaning that the entire export proceeds were convertible at market determined exchange rates. By August 1994, the entire current account earnings came to be convertible at market rates.

The unification of exchange rate beginning from March 1993 is an added step. The rupee is on a managed float, meaning that its value is determined by the forces of supply and demand, although the Reserve Bank possesses the right to intervene in the market for the purpose of stabilising the exchange rate. The monetary policy, announced from time to time, takes care of stabilising the value of the rupee. The RBI has often opted for intervention selling and purchasing of US dollars so that the value of rupee could be stablised.

Liberalisation of Imports: The reform measures seek to arrest trade deficit, not through massive import restrictions but through export expansion for which import liberalisation is a prerequisite. Initially, automaticity was injected into the process of import by introducing a freely tradable instrument, known as Eximscrip, which provided import entitlement up to a certain percentage of export value. But with the introduction of LERMS, the provision of exim-scrip was withdrawn. Under LERMS, capital goods and intermediates came to be imported freely, subject to normal tariff and availability of foreign exchange from the free market.

Beginning from 1992–93, tariff rates were gradually axed with the result that peak tariff rates dipped from a level of over 300 per cent during the pre-reform period to 40 per cent within a few years of reform. For a couple of years, this percentage was subject to a surcharge of 5.0 per cent, which in effect raised the peak tariff rates to 45 per cent. But the budget proposals for 1999–2000 discontinued the surcharge with the result that it came to be 40 per cent once again. The import of capital goods witnessed a preferential rate. In this case, the import weighted custom duty rates came down from 97.0 per cent in 1990–91 to 30.0 per cent in 1998–99. There is also a provision known as Export Promotion Capital Goods scheme. This scheme provides for duty free imports of capital goods. A number of sectors such as agriculture and allied sectors, industries manufacturing electronic items, gems and jewellery, sports and leather goods, the toys, food-processing industry, specific bio-technology industries, small scale engineering industries, and so forth have been enjoying this scheme. There was a threshold limit for this privilege but it was completely removed under the Exim policy for 2000–01. Again, as a member of the World Trade Organisation, the Indian government bound about two-thirds of its tariff lines and made a phased reduction in these bound levels, which will be complete by the year 2005. The budget proposals for 1999–2000 took back some commodities from the zero-duty scheme, but taking into account the non-applicability of special additional duty in these cases, the tariff continues to remain only nominal. Thus, the overall picture shows lower tariff, which means lower cost of production and enhanced export competitiveness.

Apart from tariff cuts, quantitative restrictions were removed from the import of many items, especially capital goods and intermediates. The Indian government submitted a detailed proposal to the World Trade Organisation for curbing quantitative restrictions. It unilaterally removed quantitative restrictions on imports of around 2,300 items from SAARC countries. Moreover, there is delicensing of a large number of imports. The negative list of imports has sizeably been pruned. On the other hand, the open general licence (OGL) list has been broadened. The April 1998 Exim Policy alone delicensed 340 items of import by moving them out from the restricted list to the OGL list. The Exim policy for 2000–01 took out as many as 714 of 1,429 products to the OGL list. Many imports previously made through specified public sector agencies stand decanalised.

The system of advance licence further liberalised imports. The Exim Policy of 1997–2002 abolished value-based advance licence scheme, but the quantity based advance licence scheme was to continue. The Exim Policy of April 1998 further simplified the provisions of advance licences.

The special import licence is another chain in this series. Only certain categories of exporters are given this licence, many items have been added to this list. For the electronic sector, the entitlement has been raised under this scheme. However, the Exim policy for 2000–01 abolished the special import licence scheme.

Encouragement to Exporters: Reform measures strengthen the channels of export. In this context, EPZs, EOUs, export houses, trading houses, star trading houses, and so on have got a number of incentives. They get a special import licence and tax holiday for a ten-year period. They can also get 100 per cent foreign equity participation. The EOU scheme is extended to agriculture and allied activities and trading. The Exim Policy of 1997–2002 allowed EOU/EPZ units in agriculture and allied sectors to sell one half of their production in the domestic tariff area. The government has now permitted setting up of private software technology parks.

The policy has sizeably pruned the negative list of exports. Infact, it is based on strategic considerations, environmental and ecological grounds, and on the grounds of essential domestic requirements and the socio-cultural heritage.

The reform measures ensure easy availability of export credits, both, in domestic and foreign currencies. Interest rates on such credits have been reduced. The budget proposals for 1999–2000 provided credits to exporters at internationally competitive rates in order to enable them to compete in the international market. Export under all export promotion schemes is exempted from the applicability of 4.0 per cent special additional duty (SAD). SAD is taken into account for establishing duty drawback rates. Exporters are given the facility of forfeiting. With the strengthening of foreign exchange reserves, exporters are now permitted to retain up to 50 per cent of their foreign exchange receipts in an account designated as an Exchange Earners' Foreign Currency account. This percentage is as high as 100 in case of EPZ units and EOUs. This facility protects exporters from inconveniences related to conversion cost while making payments for imports. The Exim policy for 2000–01 proposed the establishment of special economic zones that could help augment export and provided for adherence to the norms of multilateral trade negotiations.

Simplification of Procedural Formalities and Fostering of Transparency: The reform measures have ensured transparency and simplified procedures from the very beginning. The trade and customs classification stands greatly harmonised. The number of duty rates has been gradually reduced to only five. The processes are computerised so as to ensure speedy disposal of applications. Legal requirements have been eased. Now manufacturer-exporters with a good record are permitted to furnish a legal undertaking instead of bank guarantees against import of duty free raw material. The Exim Policy of 1997–2002 represents not only a micro-management approach for specific commodities but also a macro-management approach making the entire scenario quite liberal. The Exim Policy announced in April 1998 provided for the automatic issue of advance licences on the basis of information furnished by importers. Moreover, the licensing functions are being decentralised so as to make them more smooth. Presently, the Ministry of Commerce is thinking of integrating all export promotional schemes into one so as to ensure greater transparency. It is also to bring about reduction in transaction costs related to foreign trade licensing, tax procedures, and the banking system. The Exim Policy for 2000–01 aimed at decentralisation and simplification of the procedures such as rationalisation of duty drawback scheme and simplification of second-hand capital goods imports.

Foreign Trade Policy of FYs 2002–07: Maintaining the broad contours of the liberal trade policy, the Government announced in March 2002 a medium-term policy for 2002–07. Among other things, the policy first sought to strengthen special economic zones (SEZs) through setting up of off-shore banking units, hedging of commodity price rise and through simplification of sub-contracting procedures. Second, it sought to raise agricultural exports through setting up of agri-EPZs and through providing them non-actionable subsidies. Third, value-added garment export was to be augmented in view of lifting of quota from 2005. Fourth, the policy abolished licensing related to rough diamond import in order to boost up gems and jewellery export. Fifth, status holders were provided strategic packages. And sixth, trade procedures were simplified through restructuring of commodity classification.

In January 2004, additional measures were introduced reducing the peak tariff rate to 20 per cent. Special additional duty was abolished. Customs duty on project imports was reduced to 10 per cent. Price Stabilisation Fund was created to benefit the export of tea, coffee and marine products. The interest-free period for warehouse goods was increased. Round-the-clock filing of customs document was introduced. The service sector exports were encouraged through the introduction of duty-free import facilities in specific cases. EPCG scheme was made more flexible. Duty-free replenishment certificate scheme was extended to deemed exports. Labour and insurance laws related to SEZs were relaxed.

Last but not least, the foreign trade policy announced in April 2005 emphasised on almost doubling India's share in world trade by 2009. To this end, the policy suggested further simplification of procedural formalities. Greater initiative is to be taken for the development of highly labour-intensive products that would help generate export, and at the same time, create employment in the country. The export obligation under the Export Promotion Capital Goods scheme stands waived off subject to specific conditions. Again, the policy suggested for the establishment of Service Export Promotion Council in view of growing trade in services.

Trade Policy Measures in FY 2008–2009: Interest subvention of 2.0 per cent to labour-intensive exports, full refund of claims of CST, excise duty, etc. on deemed exports, back-up guarantee made available to ECGC to a fixed extent, support to textiles sector for technological upgradation, elimination of export duty on iron ore, elimination of import duty on specific products, such as naptha, zirconia, etc. were some of the evidences of liberalised policy. The RBI too took measures to improve liquidity (including foreign exchange liquidity) so as to ease credits to traders. The term for export credits was also enhanced.

Source: *Government of India, Economic Survey, Various Issues.*

QUESTIONS

1. How did the Government rationalise the exchange rate policy?
2. What was the basic purpose of import liberalisation? What steps were taken in this respect?
3. In what ways did the export policy turn liberal?
4. Explain the broad features of the Exim policy 2002–07.
5. What are the priority areas for development suggested by the foreign trade policy of April 2005?

STUDY TOPIC

Indian Special Economic Zones

In April 2000, the Indian Government announced the Special Economic Zones (SEZs) policy to make then existing export processing zones (EPZs) even more effective and to set up new SEZs in the context of the country's export promotion programme. The policy emphasised on the quality infrastructure alongwith an attractive fiscal package, both at the centre and the state level, and on the minimum possible regulations.

Special Economic Zones Act, 2005

In order to make the SEZs a reality, the government enacted Special Economic Zones Act, 2005 in June 2005, which came into effect on February 10, 2006, providing for drastic simplification of procedures and for single window clearance on matters relating to central as well as state governments. The main objectives of the SEZ Act are as follows:

1. Generation of additional economic activity
2. Promotion of exports of goods and services
3. Promotion of investment from domestic and foreign sources
4. Creation of employment opportunities
5. Development of infrastructure facilities

The Act envisages key role for the state governments in export promotion and the creation of related infrastructure. A Single Window SEZ approval mechanism has been provided through a 19-member inter-ministerial SEZ Board of Approval (BoA). The applications duly recommended by the respective state governments/UT administration are considered by this BoA periodically. All decisions of the BoA are with consensus.

The SEZ Rules, 2006

The SEZ rules created subsequently provide for minimum land requirement for different classes of SEZs. Every SEZ is divided into a processing area wherealone the SEZ units would come up and the non-processing area where the supporting infrastructure is to be created. To be precise, the SEZ rules provide for:

1. simplified procedures for development, operation and maintenance of the special economic zones and for setting up units and conducting business in SEZs,
2. single window clearance for setting up of a SEZ,
3. single window clearance for setting up a unit in a SEZ,
4. single window clearance on matters relating to central as well as state governments and
5. simplified compliance procedures and documentation with an emphasis on self certification.

The developer submits the proposal for establishment of SEZ to the concerned state government. The state government has to forward the proposal with its recommendation within 45 days from the date of receipt of such proposal to the Board of Approval constituted by the central government. The applicant has the option to submit the proposal directly to the Board of Approval.

The functioning of the SEZs is governed by a three-tier administrative set up. The Board of Approval is the apex body and is headed by the secretary, Department of Commerce. The Approval Committee at the zone level deals with approval of units in the SEZs and other related issues. Each zone is headed by a development commissioner, who is the ex-officio chairperson of the Approval Committee.

Once a SEZ has been approved by the Board of Approval and the central government has notified the area of the SEZ, units are allowed to be set up in the SEZ. All the proposals for setting up of units in the SEZ are approved at the zone level by the Approval Committee consisting of development commissioner, customs authorities and representatives of the state government. All post-approval clearances including grant of importer-exporter code number, change in the name of the company or implementing agency, broadbanding diversification, etc. are given at the zone level by the development commissioner. The performance of the SEZ units are periodically monitored by the Approval Committee and the units are liable for penal action under the provision of Foreign Trade (Development and Regulation) Act, in case of violation of the conditions of the approval.

Incentives Offered to SEZs Units

The units in the SEZs get:

1. duty free import/domestic procurement of goods for development, operation and maintenance purposes,
2. 100% income tax exemption on export income for first 5 years, 50% for next 5 years thereafter and 50% of the ploughed back export profit for the next 5 years,
3. exemption from minimum alternate tax,
4. external commercial borrowing up to US $500 million in a year without any maturity restriction through recogniged banking channels.
5. exemption from central sales tax,
6. exemption from service tax,
7. single window clearance for central and state level approvals and
8. exemption from state sales tax and other levies as extended by the respective state governments.

Number of SEZs

There were 15 EPZs operating before the enactment of the SEZs Act. All of them were converted into SEZs. Moreover, 260 new were added to the list till September 2008. Of the new 260 units, 56 were set up in Andhra Pradesh, 42 in Tamil Nadu, 38 in Maharashtra, 24 each in Karnataka and Haryana, 23 in Gujrat and the rest were set up in other states and union territories.

SEZs and the growth of labour intensive manufacturing industry

Out of the 531 formal approvals given till September 2008, 174 approvals were for sector specific and multi product SEZs for manufacture of textiles and apparels, leather footwear, automobile components, engineering, etc. which would involve labour-intensive manufacturing. SEZs are going to lead to the creation of employment for large number of unemployed rural youth. Nokia and Flextronics electronics hardware SEZs in Sriperumbudur are already providing employment to 14,577 and 1,058 persons, respectively. Hyderabad Gems SEZ for jewellery manufacturing in Hyderabad has already employed 2,145 persons, majority of whom are from landless families, after providing training to them. They have a projected direct employment for about 2,267 persons. Apache SEZ being set up in Andhra Pradesh will employ 20,000 persons to manufacture 10,00,000 pairs of shoes every month. Current employment in Apache SEZ is 5,536 persons. Brandix Apparels, a Sri Lankan FDI project would provide employment to 60,000 workers over a period of 3 years. Even in the service sector, 12.5 million sq meters space is expected in the IT/ITES SEZs, which as per the NASSCOM standards translates into 12.5 lakh jobs. By the end of June 2008, SEZs helped create 3.49 lakh jobs, out of which 2.14 lakh jobs were created after February 2006. It is, therefore, expected that establishment of SEZs would lead to faster growth of labour intensive manufacturing and services in the country.

SEZs and Exports

Benefit derived from SEZs is evident also from the exports generated. During the past five financial years, the exports rose almost five-fold—from Rs. 139 billion in FY 2003–2004 to Rs. 666 billion in FY 2007–2008. The performance of the SEZs on this count was sizeable during FY 2007–2008 as there was 92 per cent increase in the quantum of the export earnings.

Financial Year	*Value (Rs. in billion)*	*Growth Rate (over previous year)*
2003–2004	138.54	39%
2004–2005	183.14	32%
2005–2006	228.40	25%
2006–2007	346.15	52%
2007–2008	666.38	92%

Source: Government of India, *Ministry of Commerce and Industry Annual Report*, various issues.

QUESTIONS

1. How are the SEZs different from EPZs?
2. What are the broad provisions of the SEZ rules?
3. Do you feel that the SEZs have led to the growth of employment?
4. Comment on the issue that SEZs are export promoters.

REFERENCES

Books

Balassa, B. (1980), "The Process of Industrial Development and Alternative Development Strategies", *Essays in International Finance*, 141 (Princeton: Princeton University Press).

Daniels, J. D. and L. H. Radebaugh (2000), *International Business: Environments and Operations* (New Delhi: Addison Wesley Longman (Singapore) Private Limited).

Girma, S., D. Greenaway and and R. Kneller (2004), "Does Exporting Increase Productivity? A Micro-econometric Analysis of Matched Firms", *Review of International Economics*, 12(5), 855–66.

Hirschman, A.O. (1968), "The Political Economy of Import Substitution", *Quarterly Journal of Economics*, 82 (1), 1–32.

Kjeldsen-Kragh, S. (2001), *International Trade Policy* (Copenhagen: Copenhagen) (Business School Press).

Krueger, A. O. (1990), "Trends in Trade Policies of Developing Countries" in C. S. Pearson and James Riedel (*eds.*), *The Direction of Trade Policy* (Cambridge, MA.: Basil Blackwell).

Little, I. T. Scitovsky and M. Scott (1970), *Trade and Industry in Some Developing Countries* (Oxford: Oxford University Press).

Maddisson, A. (1995), *Monitoring the World Economy: 1870–1992* (Paris: OECD Development Centre).

Prebisch, R. (1950), *Economic Development of Latin America and Its Principal Problems*, UN Doc. E/CN 12/89.

Safarian, A.E. (1993), *Multinational Enterprise and Public Policy; A Study of the Industrial Countries* (Aldershot: Edward Elgar), pp. 467–70.

Taylor, A.M. (1995), "On the Costs of Inward-looking Development: Price Distortions, Growth and Divergence in Latin America", *The Journal of Economic History*, 58(1), 1–28.

The World Bank (1998), *India 1998: Macroeconomic Update*, Washington D. C.

United Nations (1949), *Post-War Price Relations in Trade between Under-developed and Industrialised Countries*, Doc. E/CN. 1/Sub 3/W. 5.

Journals

Sharan, V. (1981), "Non-tariff Barriers in International Trade and India's Exports", *Journal of Social and Economic Studies*, IX (2), 295–304.

SELECT FURTHER READINGS

Kotabe, M. and M. R. Czinkota (1992), "State Government Promotion of Manufacturing Exports: A Gap Analysis", *Journal of International Business Studies*, XXIII (Winter), 637–58.

Milner, H. V. (1989), "An Alternative to Free Trade or Protectionism: Why Corporations Seek Strategic Trade Policy", *California Management Review*, XXXI (4), 111–31.

* Located in the North of Germany at Elbe River, Hamburg is the trade and transport hub of Northern Europe. It offers an outstanding transport infrastructure and most advanced logistical support for passenger and freight transport. Everyday 170–180 goods trains ply the rails between the Port of Hamburg and inland areas. They convey 4,000 goods wagons which are delivered and collected daily from around 1,000 sidings and loading points around the port. In the domestic battle between carriers for long-distance traffic to and from Hamburg, the rail has a market share of over 70%.

City of London, UK*

7 Multilateral Regulation of Trade and Investment

CHAPTER OBJECTIVES

The purpose of the chapter is to discuss the regulation of trade and investment at the international level. The focus of discussion lies on GATT/WTO and UNCTAD. In particular, the objective is to:

- Discuss the basic principles of multilateral trade negotiations.
- Acquaint the readers with the GATT and its various rounds prior to the Uruguay Round.
- Delineate the broad features of, and major agreements concluded at, the Uruguay Round.
- Present the main features of the WTO, in comparison to GATT, and the organisational structure and the functions of the WTO.
- Show how the dispute settlement mechanism works at the WTO.
- Mention the major challenges before the WTO.
- Explain India's relationship with the WTO.
- Introduce the readers to UNCTAD, especially about its origin, its status compared to GATT/WTO, and the major areas of negotiations at UNCTAD.
- Evaluate some of the more recent trends in UNCTAD's role in the area of international trade and development.

Trade regulation at the national level was found as far back as during mercantilism. But the regulation of trade at the international level is of recent origin. The creation of the General Agreement on Tariffs and Trade (GATT) in 1947 was the beginning of multilateral regulation in international trade. The creation of GATT was an interim arrangement and so with the evolution of consensus at the international level, the World Trade Organisation (WTO) came into being in 1995. The WTO substituted GATT for providing more effective stimuli to the multilateral trading system. It also regulates foreign direct investment through TRIMS. The present chapter discusses the basic principles of multilateral trade negotiations under the GATT/WTO umbrella, the long journey from the creation of GATT to the creation of WTO and the present challenges that this new organisation is facing. It also includes a brief discussion of the functioning of the United Nations Conference on Trade and Development (UNCTAD), which looks after the interests of developing countries in particular.

7.1 BASIC PRINCIPLES OF MULTILATERAL TRADE NEGOTIATIONS

GATT was an international institution set up in 1947 to encourage multilateral trade.

The GATT will always be remembered for conferring upon the world trading system a multilateral character as also for making world trade more restriction-free. The WTO has stepped into the same shoes with more vibrant measures. It would thus be worthwhile to explain what actually formed the basis for multilateral trade negotiations during the past five decades. Hockman and Kostecki (1995) refer to four such principles (Figure 7.1). They are:

1. Non-discrimination
2. Reciprocity
3. Market Access
4. Fair Competition.

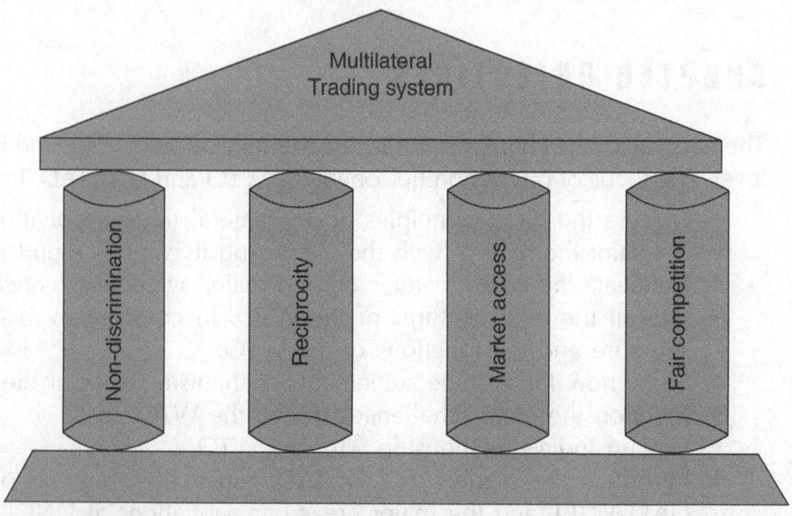

FIGURE 7.1 Principles of Multilateral Trading System

In the **most-favoured nation's treatment** any tariff reduction will be applicable equally to all member countries irrespective of economic status of the member country.

First of all, the principle of non-discrimination which is referred to in the very preamble of the GATT, is amplified in two key provisions, they are, Article I, adopting the principle of "Most-favoured Nation's Treatment (MFNT)" and Article III, adopting the principle of national treatment. MFNT requires that any tariff reduction negotiated between two member countries will be extended immediately and unconditionally to all member countries. This means that MFNT provides for equal, and not any special treatment irrespective of the economic status of a member country. However, there are a few bilateral features that have continued to exist. For example, trade concessions negotiated between the United States of America and Canada remained bilateral. A few safeguard clauses also continued to remain bilateral. For example, any country facing a balance of payments problem could impose restrictions on import from a specific country. Similarly, manufactured products of the less developed world continued to enjoy preferential status in the developed world under the Generalised Scheme of Preferences (GSP) initiated during the 1970s. Again, the trade concessions applicable to the members of a regional trade bloc are also examples of exceptions.

At the national level too, the government has to give equal treatment to a foreign product and an identical domestic product as far as taxes and regulations are concerned. Once foreign products are subjected to import duty, no additional burden can be imposed through internal taxes or internal regulations where domestic producers of the same product do not bear the same burden. In this way the principle of non-discrimination makes it very difficult for a member country to prevent foreign products from entering its domestic market. Both foreign suppliers and domestic buyers are assured of a transparent regulatory environment in which they operate.

Principle of reciprocity is based on *quid pro quo*, that is, any concession given by one country has to be matched by the other.

Secondly, the principle of reciprocity implies *quid pro quo*. Any reduction in the level of protection of one member country has to be matched by an equivalent reduction in the level of protection given to the other country. The reciprocity criteria may be interpreted in two ways. One involves the exchange of similar concession, that is tariff concession against tariff concession. The other provides for the exchange of dissimilar concessions such as tariff concession as against removal of quota. Again, reciprocity criteria may be product specific or it may be an across-the-board trade barrier reduction, usually meaning reduction in average tariff rate. Here it may be mentioned that the initial GATT round discussions were confined to bilateral concessions, but since the Kennedy Round, the concessions became mainly multilateral in character.

Thirdly, the concept of market access is based on an open trading system where competition prevails among suppliers located in different countries. A country cannot raise tariff beyond the bound level for limiting access to its market. If it does, it will have to compensate the affected parties.

Dumping refers to selling goods abroad at a price lower than the domestic price.

Fourthly, competition should be fair and it should not harm the trading partner. The WTO maintains transparency in its own dealings and likes its members to maintain transparency in their trade policies and procedure. This is why the GATT rules have provided for imposing anti-dumping duty in order to counter any move for unwarranted dumping. The importing governments may intervene if the imports are injurious to domestic industries or to the balance of payments of the country.

7.2 GATT AND ITS EARLY ROUNDS

The process of the evolution of GATT was not very smooth. In fact, the pursuance of beggar-thy-neighbour policy, including competitive devaluation, tariff imposition, and discriminatory trade barriers resulting in shrinkage in world trade during 1930s and early 1940s led resolutions during the Bretton Woods Conference in 1944 to create the International Trade Organisation (ITO). The first discussion on then proposed ITO was held at the 1946 United Nations Conference on Trade and Employment. A preparatory committee was formed, which had various meetings and the final charter was agreed upon at Havana. But in the wake of the refusal of the United States Congress to ratify the Charter, the GATT, designed as a multilateral treaty to regulate the world trade, came into being as an interim arrangement (Table 7.1).

Table 7.1 GATT Rounds

Round	*Year*
• Geneva Round	1947
• Annecy Round	1949
• Torquay Round	1951
• Geneva Round	1951–56
• Dillon Round	1960–61
• Kennedy Round	1962–67
• Tokyo Round	1973–79
• Uruguay Round	1986–94

Beginning from 1947, GATT endeavoured its best to promote multilateral trading system for almost five decades. The number of member countries, which was 23 in 1947, rose to 124 by the 1990s and to 149 by 2005. It covered eight rounds of meeting of its members during which it negotiated primarily for the axing of trade barriers. The first round, at Geneva in 1947, led to the creation of the General Agreement and to some 45,000 tariff concessions covering around one half of world trade. The following two rounds—one at Annecy in France in 1949 and the other at Torquay in the UK in 1951—were largely concerned with accession negotiations and tariff reduction was only modest. By the Geneva Round of 1951–56, the number of members had reached 33. During this round too, the negotiations for tariff reductions were modest compared to those in the first round. The average cut in tariff for the United States of America, which was 21.1 per cent in 1947, ranged between 1.9 per cent and 3.5 per cent (Baldwin, 1986). During the Dillon Round of 1960–61, tariff adjustments were made following the creation of the European Common Market and some tariff reduction negotiations were held.

However, the tariff cut negotiated at the Kennedy Round (1962–67) was sizeable. An across-the-board formula was adopted for tariff reduction on industrial products, resulting in a tariff cut of 35 per cent on such products. Even some of the non-tariff barriers were negotiated for the first time. It witnessed the conclusion of an anti-dumping code and an agreement on the US customs valuation procedures for specific products.

In the Tokyo Round (1973–79), 99 countries participated, representing around 90 per cent of the world trade. The negotiations spared 33,000 tariff lines with the result that the average import weighted tariff on manufactured goods dropped to around 6 per cent. There were also a few specific agreements such as preferential treatment for exports of developing countries into the developed market, specific non-tariff measures, like subsidies and countervailing measures, customs valuation, product standards, import licensing procedures, and a revision of the Kennedy Round anti-dumping code.

7.3 URUGUAY ROUND

7.3.1 Main Features

The Uruguay Round (1986–94), or the eighth round, was of great significance, especially in view of its broad coverage.

1. The unfinished agenda of the Tokyo Round had to be completed. They were primarily: (a) **reforms** in the **safeguard measures** that were adopted by some of the member countries to restrict import on the pretext of protecting balance of payments or domestic industries and (b) **reforms in agriculture** that had remained outside the mainstream of the GATT rules.
2. Besides including the traditional tariff axing measures that brought down the average level of tariff to 3.9 per cent by the mid-1990s, compared to about 40 per cent during late 1940s (Jackson, 1989; Wall Street Journal, 1993), the Uruguay Round discussions aimed at doing away with, or smoothening of, some of the important **non-tariff barriers.**
3. The constitution of a **trade policy review mechanism (TPRM)** for examining the trade policy of member countries was stressed on so that reforms could be brought about in the trade policy and procedures of the individual member countries.
4. Some **new aspects related to international trade,** such as trade-related investment measures (TRIMS), trade-related intellectual property rights (TRIPS), and general agreement on trade in services (GATS) were also covered.

5. **Refurbishment of the dispute settlement system** so as to make it more effective and to provide relief to the affected member countries within a prescribed time framework was dealt with.
6. GATT was conferred with a legal status through the **creation of** WTO.

7.3.2 Agreements at the Uruguay Round

Plurilateral agreements are agreements binding only on signatories as opposed to multilateral agreements that are binding on all members.

The contracting parties at the Uruguay Round concluded 18 separate agreements: 14 were multilateral in character and the remaining four were plurilateral in character. It may be noted that multilateral agreements are binding on all members, while plurilateral agreements are binding only on their signatories.

Agriculture: The agreement on agriculture included three aspects: market access, domestic support, and export subsidies. The market access provision included imposing tariff for non-tariff barriers and gradual reduction of such tariffs by 36 per cent in case of developed countries over a period of six years and by 24 per cent in case of developing countries over a ten-year period. Domestic support to farmers was to be cut by 20 per cent by developed countries over a six year period and by developing countries over a 10 year period. Similarly, export subsidies were to be cut by 36 per cent by developed and developing countries, respectively, over six years and ten years. No such measures were proposed in case of the least developed countries. Finally, the agreement sought to set up a committee on agriculture.

Uruguay Round Agreements

Multilateral: agriculture, sanitary and phytosanitary measures, textiles and clothing, technical barriers to trade, TRIMS, anti-dumping practices, customs valuation, pre-shipment inspections, rules of origin, import licensing procedures, subsidies and countervailing measures, safeguards, GATS, TRIPS, dispute settlement, and trade policy review mechanism (TPRM).

Plurilateral: public procurement, trade in civil aircraft, international dairy products, and international bovine meat.

Sanitary and Phytosanitary Measures: Although sanitary and phytosanitary measures were covered under GATT, the Uruguay Round set out detailed guidelines in the sense that such measures should not be arbitrary and discriminating, but they should be more transparent and justified on scientific grounds. A committee in this area has been set up to monitor the agreement.

Textiles and Clothing: Textile and clothing, trade had been taken away from the GATT purview by the 1974 Multi-fibre Arrangement. The Uruguay Round brought it back to the GATT fold. The restrictions under this arrangement were to be reduced in four phases. The first phase started in January 1995 and required member states to integrate into GATT 16 per cent of the total volume of such imports effected in 1990. The second phase began in January 1998 and covered a further 17 per cent of such imports. The third phase started from January 2002, covering an additional 18 per cent of such imports and the remaining share of imports are to be phased out by January 1, 2005. Safeguard measures can be adopted by importers, but only in exceptional cases of injury to domestic industries and only for a maximum of three years. These measures are subject to monitoring by the Textiles Monitoring Body.

Technical Barriers to Trade: The agreement on technical barriers to trade was meant for the protection of the environment. It says that member countries have the right to introduce regulations and standards that ensure health and protect the environment. The agreement sought to establish a committee on technical barriers to trade.

TRIMS: Regarding TRIMS, it was stated that no member country should attach conditions to foreign direct investment, which could in turn restrict or distort the trade. The conditions were related to purchases from the domestic country, a specific import-export ratio in the enterprise, and restrictions on export. The developed countries, developing countries, and the least developed countries were to adhere to these norms within two years, five years, and seven years, respectively. The agreement sought to set up a committee for monitoring TRIMS.

Anti-dumping Practices: The GATT had permitted imposing of anti-dumping duties. The agreement at the Uruguay Round provided greater clarity to this issue. A "sunset" clause was introduced for the review of anti-dumping actions every five years. Moreover, it sought to establish a committee on anti-dumping practices.

Customs Valuation: Fraudulent practices normally involved in customs valuation were taken care of during the Tokyo Round. The agreement in the Uruguay Round re-emphasised that the basis for the valuation of goods for customs purposes should be at the maximum of the transaction value of the goods. It provided the customs authorities some additional power to obtain further information from the importer and to establish the customs value through recourse to alternative methods. It sought to establish a committee in this respect.

Pre-shipment Inspection: It involves the use of specialised private companies to check shipment details, such as the price, quality, and quantity of goods. The agreement sought to introduce greater transparency and so it was in favour of an independent review procedure that could resolve any dispute between the inspecting agencies and the exporter.

Rules of Origin: Origin means "nationality" of a product. It is important, particularly in case a product is manufactured in more than one country. This is because the origin of a product determines the amount of tariff to be imposed in the importing country. The agreement at the Uruguay Round sought to ensure transparency in this respect. It provided that the Committee on Rules of Origin, along with a technical committee, would supervise the harmonisation of different countries' procedures in this context.

Import Licensing Procedures: The agreement tried to bring in transparency to the import licensing procedure. It emphasised on the publication of the licensing rules in the importing countries and on avoidance of unnecessary delays in granting licence.

Subsidies and Countervailing Measures: The agreement went a few steps further than what was agreed upon at the Tokyo Round and it governed "specific subsidy" that was available to an enterprise or an industry. It prohibited subsidies that were related to export performance but the least developed countries and developing countries below $1000 per capita income continued to remain outside the scope of this provision. The ad valorem subsidisation of a product exceeding 5 per cent or a subsidy given in order to prop up a loss-making industry was subject to be taken to the dispute settlement body. But the subsidy assisting industrial research was not questionable. The agreement introduced new rules for the computation of the value of subsidies.

Safeguards: In case of safeguards involving protective measures to save the domestic industry from injury, the agreement limited the scope and duration of the safeguard measures. All the grey area measures, such as voluntary export restraint agreements and orderly market arrangements were to be phased out by the end of 1999. If at all safeguard measures were adopted, their life was set at four years with the possibility of one four year extension.

GATS: The agreement involved reduction and elimination of barriers in international trade in services and the establishment of the MFNT principle in this area. This means that WTO members are now obliged to offer MFN status and provide market access, ensuring transparency to all service providers from countries bound by the GATT in the form of transparent rules and regulations and administrative actions. The GATS framework is made up of 29 articles. A Council for Trade in Services was established to protect trade in services.

TRIPS: The Uruguay Round agreement covered TRIPS in view of the fact that practices like counterfeiting, copying, and piracy on a large scale had come in the way of fair trade. It was estimated that the loss incurred by EU on account of copyright piracy was around 10 per cent of the value of its export. The agreement aimed at regulating and standardising international intellectual property rights in order to prevent these abuses.

It provided greater protection to trademarks and industrial designs and introduced patent protection for pharmaceutical and chemical products. It also set up a Council for TRIPS to oversee the smooth running of the agreement.

Dispute Settlement: A dispute settlement procedure existed in the pre-Uruguay Round GATT but it was handicapped by the refusal of countries—mainly developed countries—to respect its final rulings. But the Uruguay Round agreement made the ruling binding on the parties to the dispute and made the procedure more effective.

TPRM: The purpose of TPRM is to monitor trade policies and practices of member countries and to achieve a greater degree of transparency in their trading policies. The Uruguay Round agreement authorised the WTO to make such reviews.

Plurilateral Trade Agreements: Besides the multilateral agreements that the member countries have to abide by, there were four plurilateral agreements concluded at the Uruguay Round. They are the agreements whose acceptance is not a prerequisite to WTO membership. The first is the agreement concerning public procurement. This means that the foreign suppliers must be given equal treatment in government procurement just as the domestic suppliers. A Committee on Government Procurement has been established under the supervision of the WTO General Council. The second agreement concerns trade in civil aircrafts, which aims at the elimination of import duties on all aircrafts. The third concerns international dairy products. This agreement tries to introduce greater stability in the market by seeking to limit surpluses, shortages, and fluctuations in price. The International Dairy Council has been established under the supervision of the WTO General Council. The fourth agreement concerns international bovine and meat products. Its purpose is to regulate such trade.

7.4 WORLD TRADE ORGANISATION

The WTO was officially launched on January 1, 1995 replacing the GATT, which take care of the agreements contained in the final act of the Uruguay Round.

The greatest success of the Uruguay Round discussions was evident in the creation of the World Trade Organisation (WTO). The WTO, which was officially launched on January 1, 1995, replaced the GATT. Naturally, the GATT members became the members of WTO. It administers the agreements contained in the Final Act of the Uruguay Round.

7.4.1 Basic Difference between GATT and WTO

Although the WTO replaced the GATT, there are a few similarity and disimilarity in agreements between the two.

It is a fact that the WTO replaced the GATT and so the purpose of these two institutions is the same. Nevertheless, there is some dissimilarity between the two. First of all, GATT allowed the continuance of some side agreements concluded between specific members during different GATT rounds. But WTO administers a unified package of agreements to which all members are committed.

Secondly, the coverage of the WTO is bigger as it includes TRIPS, GATS, etc. under its purview. Moreover, the environment has come up as a major issue on the agenda for the first time.

Thirdly, WTO contains an improved version of the original GATT rules in relation to the trade in goods. And so it is more effective than the GATT.

Fourthly, the grey area measures such as textiles and clothing and agriculture remained to exist outside the GATT purview. But they are now under WTO.

Fifthly, the membership of the GATT was not as large as that of WTO. WTO members had 153 members during July 2008 and so its jurisdiction is far wider.

Finally, the settlement of the disputes between the member countries was not easy during the GATT regime as the members used to block decisions arrived at under the dispute settlement mechanism. But it is not possible under WTO. Moreover, there is a fixed time framework during which the dispute has to be settled.

7.4.2 Organisational Structure

The Ministerial Conference is the apex body in the WTO's organisational structure meeting every two years. It is composed of the representatives of the member governments—one representative from each member. It is the chief policy-making body. Any major policy change requires its approval.

Below the Ministerial Conference lies the General Council. Its composition is similar to that of the Ministerial Conference. Its principal functions are: to act as a dispute settlement body; to administer the TPRM; and to supervise the functioning of trade in goods, GATS, TRIPS, as well as all the trade committees. There is no fixed timing for its meeting, but normally it meets every two months. For day-to-day functioning, it delegates its responsibility to three subordinate councils meant for trade in goods, trade in services, and intellectual property rights. The General Council can appoint a working group to deal with specific issues. The report of the working group is placed before the Heads of Delegation meeting. The findings and the suggestions are approved by the General Council.

The three councils just below the General Council have to look after the functioning of different committees constituted for specific areas. For example, the Council for Trade in Goods looks after the functioning of committees on market access, agriculture, specific non-tariff barriers, TRIMS, and the Textile Monitoring Body. The Council for Trade in Services looks after the committees established in the area of services. The Council for TRIPS manages the operation of the TRIPS agreement.

The Trade Committees looking after specific areas of the multilateral trade agreements are the lowest wing in the WTO structure. The committees are established in two ways. Those established under the terms of the

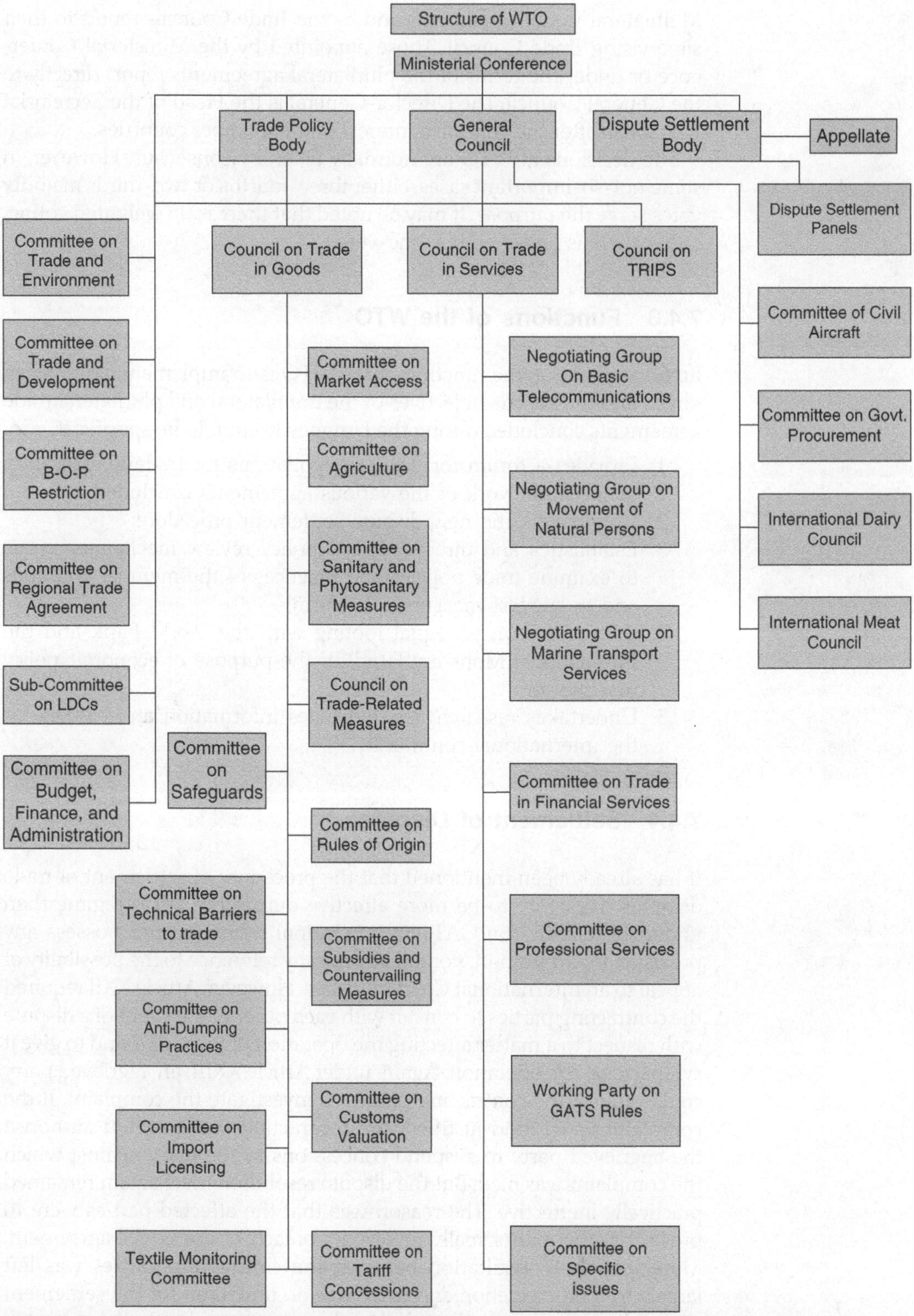

FIGURE 7.2 Structure of the World Trade Organisation

Multilateral Trade Agreements and by the Trade Councils report to their supervising Trade Council. Those appointed by the Ministerial Conference or under the terms of the plurilateral agreements report directly to the General Council. The Director-General is the Head of the Secretariat who looks after the collective interest of the member countries.

The decisions at WTO are normally taken by consensus. However, in some not-so-important cases, either three-fourths or two-thirds majority votes serve the purpose. It may be noted that there is no weighted voting, rather there is one-member, one-vote.

7.4.3 Functions of the WTO

Broadly speaking, the function of the WTO is to implement, administer, direct, and further the objectives of the multilateral and plurilateral trade agreements concluded during the Uruguay Round. To be specific, it:

1. Provides a forum for further negotiations for trade liberalisation in the framework of the various agreements concluded;
2. Administers the new dispute settlement procedure;
3. Establishes and directs a trade policy review mechanism so as to examine trade policies and practices of the member countries and to suggest measures of reform;
4. Cooperates on an equal footing with the World Bank and the International Monetary Fund for the purpose of economic policy making; and
5. Undertakes research and publishes information and studies for the international community.

7.4.4 Settlement of Disputes

It has already been mentioned that the procedure of settlement of trade disputes has come to be more effective during the WTO regime than under the GATT. The GATT in its original terms did not possess any provision for arbitration, nor did it make any reference to the possibility of appeal to an International Court of Justice. However, Article XXII required the contracting parties to consult with each other in the event of a dispute with respect to a matter affecting the operation of the GATT and to give it sympathetic consideration. Again, under Article XXIII, an aggrieved party could request the contracting parties to investigate the complaint. If the complaint was found justified, the contracting parties could authorise the aggrieved party to suspend concessions to the party against which the complaint was filed. But the dispute resolution mechanism remained practically ineffective. The reason was that the affected parties were to prove that the matter really involved a breach of the GATT agreement. Moreover, the consultation between the contracting parties was left largely to their discretion and there was no time limit for the settlement of the dispute. In case the aggrieved party was a developing country, it did not have the resources and expertise to negotiate effectively during consultations. On the contrary, the other party could block the negotiation indefinitely, with ultimately no settlement of the dispute. Even if disputes were settled, the decision was not binding on the parties.

DSB Cuts US Anti-dumping Duty and Cash Guarantee on Indian Shrimps

It was in August 2004 when the US authorities imposed 10.54 per cent anti-dumping duty on the import of Indian shrimps on the ground that the price was lower than that from any other country. The additional problem for the Indian exporters was that they had to deposit cash guarantee to cover any increase in anti-dumping duty usually at the same rate. The bonds got to be renewed every year for three years.

The entire matter was referred to the Disputes Settlement Body (DSB) which examined the entire issue. In January 2006, after the first review, the duty was cut to 7.22 per cent. Again, the second review was made in January 2007 and the duty was further cut to 1.69 per cent. The third review was made in March 2008 and the duty was expected to be slashed to 1.06 per cent.

The slash helped Devi Seafoods Ltd. to save the cash guarantee it had to pay. It is the largest Indian shrimp exporter accounting for over 15.0 per cent of the shrimp exports from the country. In its case, the burden of duty has fallen to 0.35 per cent. Since the exporter has not to deposit cash guarantee if duty is below 0.5 per cent, it is able to save that amount.

As many as 68 shrimp exporters, who had moved to the DSB for doing away with the cash guarantee scheme, welcomed DSB's decision in India's favour. Now, they will reap the benefit from the DSB judgement. But over 200 Indian shrimp exporters will not gain as they were not the party to the representation made to the DSB. They have still to pay 10.54 per cent duty along with the cash guarantee.

Source: Based on the reports published in *Mint*, 12.7.2008

But the settlement of disputes under WTO is effective and is possible within a prescribed time framework. This is the reason that during the first two years of the new dispute settlement regime, 74 dispute cases were reported compared to only 300 cases during the entire 48 year history of GATT (Anderson, 2000). In the WTO framework, there is Dispute Settlement Body (DSB) that has the authority to establish panels, adopt panel reports, scrutinise the implementation of recommendations, and to authorise retaliatory measures, if necessary. The coverage of the dispute settlement mechanism is broader, and includes not only the trade in goods, but also trade in services and intellectual property.

The dispute settlement mechanism is time-bound and phase-wise. In the first phase, stress is given on consultation and mediation. If the parties do not arrive at any conclusion within 60 days, the matter is referred to a panel to be established by the DSB. The panel members are normally the retired international civil servants well acquainted with the trade matters. The panel hears the arguments, prepares a report along with recommendations and submits it with the DSB. The panel report is adopted by the DSB within 60 days. If a party does not agree with the panel report, it may appeal to the Appellate Body. The appeal proceedings have to be complete within 60 days.

The parties have to abide by the decision of the Appellate Body within a reasonable period of time. They go for a negotiation to compensate the aggrieved party. If it is not done, DSB may ask for retaliatory action.

7.4.5 Challenges before WTO

It has already been discussed that after the inclusion of the Uruguay Round agreements, the WTO came to be the strongest authority regulating global trade. According to an estimate, the WTO discipline covers around 40–50 per cent of the world GDP compared to only 25–30 per cent under the GATT discipline in 1993 (Messerlin, 2000). But, at the same time, it is also true that there is still a long way for the WTO to go in view of the conflicting interest of the developed and the developing countries.

First of all, let us talk about the trade barriers. The tariff is not a problem as its level is quite low. As per a United Nations study, the effectively applied tariffs have come down by 33.7–50.6 per cent among the developing countries and by 51.5–53.2 per cent among the developed countries during 1994–2005 (United Nations, 2006). Moreover, some of the NTBs have been brought under control. If the trade barriers are fully brought

Simulating the Environmental Impact of Trade Liberalization

Mexico: Beghin, Roland-Holst, and van der Mensbrugghe calibrated the OECD GREEN model for Mexico and used it to model the environmental impact of three policy scenarios: trade liberalization, implementation of piecemeal environmental policies (i.e. abatement taxes to reduce emissions), and trade liberalization *cum* emission reduction. When trade liberalization is accompanied by pollution abatement measures, GDP growth is accompanied by a decline in pollution emissions.

Indonesia: Lee and Roland-Holst analyse the environmental impact of trade liberalization in Indonesia. Trade liberalization results in an expansion in Indonesia's trade of about 6 per cent and a corresponding increase in GDP of about 0.9 per cent. But liberalization also leads to pollution rising at a rate greater than the increase in output. This is because liberalization leads to Indonesia specializing more towards environmentally 'dirty' industries. The paper then simulates both trade liberalization and implementation of a uniform emission tax to reduce pollution. The simulation shows that Indonesia is able to achieve both an increase in output (0.3 per cent) and a reduction in emissions.

United Kingdom: The paper by Espinosa and Smith is notable for incorporating the negative externalities associated with air pollution into a CGE model. Reducing trade barriers in durable manufacturing in the UK still results in an overall increase in welfare despite the rise in morbidity and mortality from more emissions. The increase in morbidity and mortality rates from increased air pollution reduces welfare by only 0.09 per cent of GDP.

Source: World Trade Report 2004.

under control and the merchandise trade is fully liberalised, the welfare gains on this account may touch $ 280 billion a year by 2015, out of which $ 86 billion will accrue to the developing countries (Hertel and Winters, 2006). But the trade barriers are still quite high. The overall trade restrictiveness index (OTRI) in 2005 was 11 per cent in high-income countries, down from 12 per cent in 2002. It was higher at 20 per cent among the low-income and least developed countries (The World Bank, 2006). The important reasons are that the use of NTBs in form of technical barriers almost doubled from 31.9 per cent to 58.5 per cent during 1994–2004 and the anti-dumping measures were more frequently used by developing and developed countries (United Nations, 2006).

To be specific for agricultural products where NTBs have been substituted by a transparent tariff system in many cases, the level of tariff is very high. As per an estimate, the level of protection in case of these commodities is more than ten times the average on other merchandise (Anderson, 2000). The primary reason is that there is disagreement on domestic support regarding which the WTO draft recommends a modification of Blue Box subsidies (production limiting) that allows an extension of subsidies. The USA supports this view but the developing countries are arguing for elimination/capping of subsidies. The argument of the developing countries is that the agricultural sector in majority of them accounts for a very large share of GDP and employment. Moreover, subsidies elicit overproduction that causes world price to fall. Again, there is disagreement on the issue of cotton. The WTO considers cotton as a part of the agricultural group of products. But a large number of developing countries argue for treating cotton as a separate group. Moreover, the production and trade of cotton is highly distorted on account of government support programme in developed countries. The US Farm Bill, 2007, does not promise for removal of government support to cotton.

> The protection level in textiles and clothing and agricultural products is more than ten times the average on other merchandise.

Secondly, as far as the issue of the market access of non-agricultural products (NAMA) is concerned, the tariff level is low. But since the developing countries with cheap labour maintain an edge over the developed countries, especially in case of the products involving labour-intensive mode of production, the developed countries have employed different techniques to restrict the import of such goods. They talk about the "social issues" and the "environmental issue" in order to defend themselves. They know that the developing countries use cheap child labour that lowers the cost of production. They also know that the developing countries seldom use environment-protection measures and are thus able to arrest the cost of production. So if the developed countries are rigid on these two issues, they can restrict imports of manufactures and thereby can protect their own industry. It is because of their rigid attitude that the issue has remained unsolved so far.

> "Social issues" and "environmental issues" are yet to be solved.

Thirdly, as far as the Singapore issue is concerned, many governments still lack transparent policies on TRIMS. The private sector policies in many countries are non-competitive. The developing countries know that their domestic industry cannot compete with the large-size foreign enterprises. So they are insisting on dropping this issue from the WTO agenda. But the developed countries are very keen on TRIMS so that their MNCs should get a lasting ground in the developing countries.

The Singapore issues are still to be solved. GATS is not effective. TRIPS goes against free trade.

Fourthly, regarding GATS, the efforts of the WTO are not very pin-pointed, although they cover all modes of services and all forms of barriers (Snape, 1998). Moreover, in the sequel of the revolution in the digital technology, some of the services have become tradable, blurring the national demarcation in many cases. They account for 20–25 per cent of total cross-border trade. According to a study by the Coalition of Services industries in the USA, the liberalisation of services trade under the Doha Development Agenda (DDA) may result in global welfare gains equalling US $ 1.7 trillion. The WTO rules and modalities need to be very effective.

Fifthly, the case of TRIPS is not very different. Bhagwati (2000) feels that the WTO provisions concerning TRIPS are tilted against the interest of the consumers and go against the concept of free trade. There are many small countries where the government is not in a position to tune the intellectual property rights regulations in conformity with those of the WTO. The TRIPS agreement does not embrace the provisions for protecting traditional knowledge, genetic resources and folklore because they fall under the public domain meaning that they are not innovations and so they cannot be patented. It is this reason that has made developing countries to argue for amending the TRIPS provisions.

In India, the situation has improved. The Indian Patent Office granted 15,262 patents during FY 2007–2008 compared to 1911 in FY 2004–2005. India is willing to share with its digital knowledge library on 1,70,000 traditional medicines with the USPTO and its European counterpart on the condition that it should not be put in the public domain. It is to launch a campaign to rope in universities and the scientific community. The government likes more men to have been trained at the World Intellectual Property Organisation.
Source: Based on the news published in *Financial Express*, 22/23.04.2008.

Representation by transition countries and least developed countries is still meagre. The accession procedure at the WTO is very slow.

Sixthly, despite efforts of the WTO to confer the benefits of freer trade among large number of countries, there are a number of countries, especially the low-income and least developed ones that are still not its member. The reason is that the procedure of accession is lengthy. It is a fact that bureaucracy in many countries is not equipped to pursue the accession process. In others, the government does not enjoy political support on the accession issue. But the WTO is definitely held responsible for a slow process. A number of experts feel that the WTO is still a developed countries' club. Accession of large number of developing countries would mean a slap on their proportionate representation. Moreover, the political and economic interest of the developed countries is not served with a rapid accession process. For example, China, after its accession to the WTO, enjoys many privileges. The developed countries do not relish it (Anderson, 1997). However, in recent past, Cambodia, Nepal and Tonga became member to the WTO as a result of which the least developed countries have started representing at this institution. But at the end of 2005, there were as many as 29 such countries knocking at the door of WTO for accession.

It is not only that only a few of the least developed countries (LDCs) are the WTO member, the solution of their problems is not very easy for the WTO. They number around one-fourth of the total number of countries, but they share not even 1 per cent of the global merchandise trade. In view of this asymmetry, DDA pledged to integrate these countries with the multilateral trading system through providing them duty-and-quota-free market access and extending them economic aid to improve trade. The Hong Kong Ministerial declaration reiterated this objective. But, contrary to the assertion, the US move to exclude some of the products from this facility may jeopardise the whole initiative. For example, Bangladesh and Cambodia are doing well in textiles and clothing. But they do not have the desired response from many developed countries. Again, among the developing countries, it is only Brazil that has offered this facility to the LDCs, but in that country itself, there is a powerful lobby against this initiative.

The creation of regional trading blocs is a major challenge before the WTO as such arrangements can result in trade and investment diversion.

Seventhly, the creation of the regional trading blocs and the conclusion of bilateral agreements at a fast growing speed has become a problem for the WTO. In January 2005, there were around 170 notified regional trade agreements, up from 24 in 1990 "that went up to 387 by July 2007". Many more are in the process of notification. As a result, they have come to account for approximately one-third of the world trade. In some cases, for example, on account of the scheme of generalised system of preferences, the exports of the developing countries have increased. In 2005, the European Union liberalised this scheme through covering more products and extending more liberal treatment for vulnerable economies as well as sub-Saharan countries. But these trade agreements being not non-discriminatory, block the way for growing multilateralism of trade. Such trade agreements, it is found, help divert trade rather than creating trade. The gainers are usually the rich countries and not the poor ones. It is true that Article XXIV of WTO permits such arrangements but it does not contain the diversion effects. Moreover, bilateral investment agreements lie outside the scope of this chapter.

Eighthly, it is true that the dispute settlement mechanism has improved under the WTO system. The developing countries can get redressed their grievances. It is this reason that, in 2005, they brought 64 per cent of the complaints to the DSB. But the problem is that the decision of the dispute settlement body is not fully implemented by the developed/economically stronger countries. Nothing substantial can be achieved if the developed countries do not change their attitude.

DSB decision/the Appellate Body report is not fully implemented by the concerned countries.

Now the question is how far the WTO has taken care to meet these challenges. We know that the Ministerial Conference meets at least once during a two-year period. It met at Singapore in 1996, at Geneva in 1998, at Seattle in 1999, at Doha in 2001, at Cancun in 2003 and at Hong Kong in 2005. In the first three Ministerial Conferences, nothing substantial could be achieved insofar as both the developed and the developing countries harped on their own tune. However, at Doha, both groups agreed on a declaration. Important elements at Doha Round included the mandate to sharply reduce trade-distorting agricultural subsidies that had kept many developing countries out of international market, to reduce tariff peaks and tariff escalation particularly on the products of special interest of developing countries, to fine-tune WTO rules in areas like anti-dumping, to deal with services in conformity with Article XIX of GATS, to strengthen the relationship between trade and development and to promote trade facilitation programmes.

The successive meetings focussed on the Doha declarations. But nothing substantial could be achieved. Although at Hong Kong, the members showed their willingness to agree at least on some measures. They were concerning:

- Cutting subsidies on agriculture completely by 2013
- Reaching an agreement on cotton
- Restriction-free market access for the least developed countries
- A beefed-up framework for full modalities in agricultural and non-agricultural products
- A text on services for forward negotiation

The Hong Kong summit also set a foundation for a new "aid-for-trade" package. It was to address the supply constraints, to raise the training level and to improve the infrastructure. The purpose was to integrate the developing countries more fully in the global trading system. As per a World Bank study, the implementation of the Hong Kong measures may lead to a global gain of $ 95–120 billion. The General Council along with different committees is making efforts to transform these decisions into ground reality. The meeting at Davos in 2007 was held to review the progress. But even though, there nothing could be done to free the LDCs' export from quota and tariff and to eliminate subsidies on developed countries' agricultural export by 2013.

7.5 WTO AND INDIA

India was a founder member of the GATT and so is one of the original members of the WTO. The country was an active participant of the Uruguay Round discussions, and is bound to abide by the resolutions taken up there and incorporated in the Final Act. Over the years, India has been tuning its external sector policy in conformity with WTO principles. Some of the specific cases in this respect are listed below.

1. India has bound around two-thirds of its **tariff lines** compared to only 5 to 6 per cent of its tariff lines bound prior to the WTO. The ceiling has come to be 25 per cent for intermediate goods, 40 per cent for manufactured and 100 per cent in the case of agricultural goods. The period under which the tariff has to be phased out is 10 years, beginning March 1995. However, the Indian government has clarified its stand that if the agreements on

textiles and clothing do not materialise during this period, it may revert to pre-Uruguay Round duties. Moreover, it has not made any commitment on the issue of market access and on subsidies.

2. As far as **quantitative restrictions** are concerned, they are still maintained on the grounds of balance of payments inquiry. But, in May 1997 the Indian Government presented a detailed plan for the elimination of these restrictions in a phased manner over a period of 9 years. The length of the period was not acceptable to some of the importing countries. Therefore, it was reduced to six years, to which several countries, except the United States of America, have given their consent.
3. India has agreed to abide by the agreement on the **intellectual property rights**, ensuring non-discrimination and transparency in this regard. In March 2005, the Indian parliament passed the patent bill in order to tune its provisions with those of the WTO.

   However, on the issue of public health, India still maintains that the Doha mandate should not be diluted to restrict the scope of definition of disease to just infection disease, as desired by the United States of America.
4. Under the **trade related investment measures**, India has already notified its stand. It has also assured establishment and administration of national standards and technical regulations in conformity with the MFN principle.

   However, there are many areas of special interest for India where it has tabled its conditional offer for liberal moves on the part of developed countries.
5. India has agreed to offer **entry to foreign service providers** in 33 lines of activities, which is more than the average for individual developing countries.

   In view of this very argument, India has made a couple of submission to the Negotiating Group of Rules: first, there should be special and differential treatment for developing countries during anti-dumping and countervailing duty investigation; second, there should be greater transparency in the rules related to regional trade agreements and fisheries subsidies; third, there should be more discussion on substantive issues under GATT Article XXIV.

   The WTO made a third review of India's trade policy in June 2002. It was satisfied with the trade and FDI liberalisation policy of the country, although it was of the view that the tariff regime was still complex, containing numerous exemptions. It also raised concerns about large subsidies in the agricultural sector and about anti-dumping provisions.
6. The Indian government has amended the **customs valuation rules** to bring them in line with the provisions of WTO.

On the other hand, India expects from the other members of the WTO, especially the developed countries to strengthen the multilateral trading system in true spirit. It is of the view that the provisions of the agreement on textiles and clothing have not been implemented meaningfully as desired market access has not been granted to developing countries. It is also of the view that the safeguard clauses that permit any country to impose NTBs should be interpreted in a different way for developing countries insofar as the balance of payments scenario is quite different in developing countries, as compared to that in developed countries. Again, as regards subsidies, India is of the view that the stage of industrial development in developing countries is quite different. As a result, subsidies form an essential part of maintaining industrial development in these countries.

Taking a bold initiative, India hosted Ministerial Conference in September 2009. In the following Conference, it reiterated its commitment to uphold development dimension, especially the need of the poor. At the successive meetings, India sought to strengthen anti-dumping duties, rules concerning the sunset reviews and mandatory application of lesser duty.

7.6 UNITED NATIONS CONFERENCE ON TRADE AND DEVELOPMENT (UNCTAD)

7.6.1 Origin of UNCTAD

UNCTAD is an international institution set up in 1964 to promote trade and development, especially of developing countries.

The UNCTAD, which came into being in 1964 is a significant international institution shaping international trade and development in the developing world. It was the absence of a desired remedy to the trade problems of the developing world in the hands of the GATT that led to the establishment of the UNCTAD. GATT had no doubt led to multilateral trade negotiations and, thereby, to large growth in international trade, but its principle of non-discrimination and reciprocity did not suit the interest of developing countries. This is because the developed countries and the developing countries stood on different footings. The latter were never in a position to reciprocate with the former. Moreover, the GATT negotiations were heavily tilted towards developed countries, as only products that suited their interest were covered under negotiations and not those that were significant from the viewpoint of developing countries. Again, GATT failed to limit the use of non-tariff barriers imposed by developed countries on their imports from the developing world under the guise of "safeguard" measures. The greatest victims were the manufactured exports of developing countries, which enjoyed comparative cost advantage on account of their labour-intensive mode of production. The aftermath was evident in lop-sided world trade. During 1950s and early 1960s, world trade rose over two-fold, but the export from the developing countries increased only by half, with the result that their share in world trade fell from nearly one-third in 1950 to around one-fifth by the early 1960s. Between 1950 and 1961, the terms of trade of the developing countries deteriorated by around 17 per cent. All this led to growing trade deficit, especially at a time when they needed a large amount of foreign exchange for their economic development programmes (Cutazar, 1985).

The weak bargaining position was highlighted by a number of economists. The Latin American economist, Raul Prebisch, explained the theory of trade and development that had pinpointed the shortcomings of the GATT and this was one of the factors for third world countries to consolidate, especially in the form of the Group of 77. Various meetings were held at regional and the global levels; and finally, the Economic and Social Council and the General Assembly took a decision to convene the first United Nations Conference on Trade and Development in 1964. Subsequently, the UNCTAD was set up as an organ of the General Assembly, for deliberations and negotiations in the field of trade and development. With the setting up of the UNCTAD, developing countries got a platform from where they could build pressure on developed countries for granting them relief in matters of trade and development finance (Table 7.2).

7.6.2 Major Areas of Negotiations

The negotiations and deliberations at different rounds covered a wide area of trade and development, which has been of special interest from the viewpoint of developing countries. These rounds have taken place at regular intervals and at different places.

Table 7.2 UNCTAD Rounds

Round	*Year*	*Place*
UNCTAD I	1964	Geneva, Switzerland
UNCTAD II	1968	New Delhi, India
UNCTAD III	1972	Santiago, Chile
UNCTAD IV	1976	Nairobi, Kenya
UNCTAD V	1979	Manila, Philippines
UNCTAD VI	1983	Belgrade, Yugoslavia
UNCTAD VII	1987	Geneva, Switzerland
UNCTAD VIII	1992	Cartagena, Colombia
UNCTAD IX	1996	Midrand, South Africa
UNCTAD X	2000	Bangkok, Thailand
UNCTAD XI	2004	Sao Paulo, Brazil
UNCTAD XII	2008	Accra, Ghana

Broadly speaking, the negotiations pinpointed at the following issues:

1. Stabilisation in export earnings, especially of the primary goods exporters,
2. Improvement in market access for the goods of developing countries,
3. Increase in development finance and initiation of debt relief measures,
4. Preferential treatment for least developed countries, and
5. Code of Conduct for international shipping.

Commodity Stabilisation Programmes: The commodity stabilisation programme primarily included international commodity agreements on ten core and eight additional commodities of special interest to developing countries. The ten core commodities were sugar, coffee, cocoa, tin, tea, cotton, hard fibres (sisal), jute and jute products, rubber, and copper. The eight additional commodities were bananas, bauxite and alumina, manganese, iron ore, beef, phosphate, tropical timber, and vegetable oils. The purpose of the commodity agreement was to regulate the supply of, and demand for, these commodities and fixing up the floor and ceiling prices so as to bring stability in the export proceeds.

In order to regulate the supply, stress was laid on the creation of an international buffer stock. However, funds are required to finance such stocks, and so, the second aspect of the commodity stabilisation programme was the creation of the Common Fund.

Despite conclusion of the international commodity agreements and the creation of the Common Fund, it was feared that the primary goods exporting countries might face oscillations in their export earnings. In case of a sudden drop in export earnings, there was IMF's Compensatory Financing Facility through which exporting countries could get balance of payments support. Nevertheless, the stress was on making the IMF's facility more meaningful by adding up a complementary financing facility.

This issue was raised at the UNCTAD II and the UNCTAD III but nothing significant could emerge. It was only at the UNCTAD IV that these issues were agreed upon. The developed countries were quite aware of the price rise of food-stuff and raw material, which was evident between mid-1972 and mid-1974, and they were afraid of the collective action of developing countries as in case of oil. The developing countries, on the other hand, had already formulated the Integrated Programme for Commodities (IPC), which had been approved by the Manila Declaration of 1976. However, the move towards integrated commodity agreements was very slow. Agreements were concluded only with respect to cocoa, sugar, natural rubber, jute and jute products, tropical timber, tin, olive oil, and wheat. The Common Fund could not take its originally envisaged shape for want of required financial support, although its establishment provided financial backing for the operation of international stocks and for R&D projects in the field of commodities. The IMF too did not set up any complementary mechanism to the existing compensatory financing facility.

> GSP is the provision to allow duty free import of manufactured goods form developing countries into the market of developed countries.

The Market Access Issue: UNCTAD negotiations emphasised on increasing the market access for products from developing countries, especially those going into developed market economies. To this end, diversification of the export structure in favour of manufactured export was suggested. In order to help develop processing in the developing world, the negotiation favoured the creation of the second window of the Common Fund, which could provide financial assistance for this purpose. Again, to help manufactured exports enter the markets of the developed world, the UNCTAD suggested removal of duty by developed countries on their import of manufactured and semi-manufactured goods from the developing world. The issue was raised at UNCTAD I. But since the United States of America clung to the principle of non-discrimination and reciprocity, no headway could be made in this direction. It was only in April 1967 that the United States of America changed its stand, and then it was easy for UNCTAD II to reach an agreement. This scheme, known as the Generalised System of Preferences (GSP), was first introduced by the European Union in 1971, which was followed by many other countries. As a result, over US $70 billion of export from the developing world, per year, received preferential treatment under this scheme. However, the creation of the second window of the Common Fund for encouraging processing in developing countries could not take concrete shape for want of the required resources.

As far as the expansion of trade among developing countries is concerned, the UNCTAD helped reach an agreement on the Global System of Trade Preferences (GSTP) among developing countries in 1989. Under this agreement, a developing country provides preferences on its imports from another developing country.

GSTP refers to import liberalisation scheme among developing countries.

Development Finance and Debt Relief: The UNCTAD was of the view that reform in the trading system was essential for financing the foreign exchange component of the development outlays in developing countries. But this was not enough. The export earnings were to be supplemented by concessional finance flowing from both bilateral and multilateral sources. The UNCTAD was of the view that 0.7 per cent of the GNP of developed countries should come out in form of concessional assistance, either bilaterally or through multilateral sources, out of which 0.15 per cent should be earmarked exclusively for least developed countries. It is a fact that the ratio of concessional assistance in the total flow of development finance increased, but the 0.7 per cent target was never achieved.

Again, the UNCTAD's move led to the evolution of many debt relief measures such as writing-off of debt, debt refinancing, and rescheduling. It helped in the creation of guidelines for international action in the area of debt rescheduling in 1980. In 1978, the Trade and Development Board resolved to agree to retroactive adjustment of the terms of the ODA debt of low-income developing countries, under which more than 50 such countries benefited from debt relief for debts valued over US $6.5 billion.

Preferential Treatment for Least Developed Countries (LDCs): The UNCTAD has played a significant role in mobilising international support for LDCs. In 1981, the Special New Programme of Action (SNPA) was created to help generate faster growth in these countries. A similar programme was created for their development during the 1990s. In 1995, an agreement was signed for improving the transport system in the land-locked countries. In all, the purpose is to bridge the gap between the LDCs and other developing countries.

Code of Conduct for Liner Conferences: The UNCTAD helped in the adoption of the United Nations Convention on a Code of Conduct for Linear Conferences in 1974, which helped developing countries to get an equitable share in merchant fleets in the ocean carriage of their trade. This convention was followed by many other conventions that related to international multi-modal transportation of goods, conditions for registration of ships, and also to maritime liens and mortgages.

7.6.3 Some Recent Developments

The UNCTAD is making consistent efforts to attain its objectives. Through its Division on Investment, Technology, and Enterprise Development (DITE), it tries to encourage the flow of FDI, including technology, and plays a leading role in the area of enterprise internationalisation. Since UNCTAD X in Bangkok in 2000, DITE has undertaken research and policy analysis in the field of FDI. It is delivering policy advice on institution capacity building. It has organised seminars/symposia and undertaken fact-finding studies. As a result, 160 bilateral investment treaties have been concluded since then (UNCTAD, 2004).

UNCTAD XI at Sao Paulo, Brazil, in June 2004, proposed, among other things, to ensure coherence between the national development strategies and global economic development as a means to foster sustainable trade and development, especially in the developing world. Fortunately, there was a general consensus on this issue between the developed and the developing countries, although there were some contentious issues between them that need to be resolved. The developed countries interpreted good national governance in the framework of economic liberalisation and globalisation, but the developing countries stressed on the cooperation to be shown by the developed world with respect to trade, debt, transfer of technology, and making investments.

Here it may be pointed out that UNCTAD XI focussed on trade and development from a gender-and-women-in-development perspective. It identified 'trade and gender" as a major issue along with the issue of "trade and poverty" and "trade creating industries and development". Several of discussions were held and a consensus evolved on this issue, although it is still entirely not clear what actions will be taken in this respect in the coming years.

Last but not least, UNCTAD XII held at Accra, Ghana addressed the opportunities and challenges of globalisation for development. It called for coherence between economic development and poverty alleviation, enhancing the enabling environment to strengthen productive capacity, trade and investment and for enhancing the role of UNCTAD and its institutional effectiveness. Its role in respect of commodities, including agriculture was also felt especially in the face of the crisis provoked by surging prices for basic food items.

In other words, the Accra Accord highlighted the challenges facing many developing countries as they strive to integrate successfully into the international economic and financial system. It set out detailed agenda for economic and social development spanning over areas ranging from commodities, trade and debt to investment and new technologies. While welcoming the strong economic growth rates that global trade and investment flows have brought in many of the developing countries, UNCTAD XII autioned that these advances have not been shared by all and also have been accompanied by new difficulties, most notably the current crises in food prices and financial markets, as well as growing income inequalities.

SUMMARY

- Multilateral regulation of trade began with the GATT, which came into being in 1947 and was substituted by the WTO in 1995. The GATT/WTO believes in the multilateral trading system, which is based on the principle of non-discrimination, reciprocity, full market access, and fair competition.
- The GATT endeavoured to axe trade barriers, mainly the tariff barriers, during its first seven rounds. Its eighth round, known as the Uruguay Round, was much broader in coverage. Besides resolving to cut tariff and NTBs, it stressed on reforming safeguard measures and trade in agricultural products, constitution of TPRM, inclusion of some new aspects such as TRIMS, TRIPS, GATS, and so on, and on an effective trade dispute settlement system. As many as 18 agreements were concluded, of which 14 were multilateral in character and the other 4 were plurilateral. The WTO administers these agreements and maintains an effective dispute settlement mechanism. Still, there are several challenges before the WTO.
- India has been a member of the GATT/WTO. Its external trade policy is considerably well tuned with those of the WTO. This means it has bound a significant part of its tariff lines and has been phasing out quantitative restrictions. It has agreed also to abide by the provisions of TRIPS, TRIMS, and GATS. However, in case of subsidies, it has its own viewpoint.
- The UNCTAD is yet another international institution that was set up in 1964. It believes that the two unequal trade partners—developed and developing—cannot be treated equally and so developing countries should get preferential treatment. In this way it is different from the WTO, and yet it has been an important recommending body with respect to international trade benefiting the developing world.
- During its twelve rounds so far, the UNCTAD has made vital recommendations. Prominent among them are stabilisation of export earnings, especially of primary goods exporting countries; improvement in the market access for the goods of the developing countries; increase in the flow of development finance, investment and technology preferential treatment for least developed countries; and framing a code of conduct for international shipping.

REVIEW QUESTIONS

1. What are the principles on which the GATT/WTO's multilateral trade negotiations are based? Do the same principles guide the UNCTAD's recommendations?
2. Is the WTO different from the GATT? Explain the organisational structure of the WTO.
3. What are the major agreements concluded at the Uruguay Round, which the WTO now administers? Briefly mention the major challenges that the WTO is currently facing in this regard.
4. Do you agree that the dispute settlement mechanism is more efficient under the WTO than it was under the GATT? How is a dispute settled?
5. Comment on the broad achievements of the UNCTAD.

OBJECTIVE TYPE QUESTIONS

1. Mark True or False:
   (a) Across-the-board trade barrier reduction usually means reduction in average tariff rates.
   (b) It is because of the GATT rounds that the average level of tariff fell from 40 percent in late 1940s to 3.9 per cent by mid-1990s.
   (c) TRIMS and GATS were discussed for the first time in the Tokyo Round.
   (d) GATS, TRIMS, and TRIPS were covered under plurilateral agreements.
   (e) Under the provisions of TRIMS, no country can attach conditions that could distort the flow of FDI.
   (f) Safeguard measures restrict imports in order to save domestic industry from injury.
   (g) The UNCTAD follows the principle of non-discrimination and reciprocity.
   (h) Under the WTO regime, the rulings of the Dispute Settlement Body are binding on the concerned parties.
   (i) The acceptance of the plurilateral agreements is a pre-condition to WTO membership.
   (j) Under the Kennedy-Round negotiations, stress was given on the reduction of non-tariff barriers.

2. Choose the Most Suitable Answer:
   (a) MFNT is based on:
      (i) The principle of non-discrimination
      (ii) More favoured treatment with a particular member
      (iii) None of the above
   (b) The reciprocity criterion of multilateral trade involves the exchange of:
      (i) Tariff concessions for tariff concessions only
      (ii) Tariff concessions for removal of quota only
      (iii) Both of the above
   (c) Under a multilateral trade system, a nation:
      (i) Cannot raise tariff beyond the bound level

(ii) Can raise tariff beyond the bound level
(iii) Can raise tariff beyond the bound level, but in that case it has to compensate the affected party

(d) The Uruguay Round discussed:
(i) Safeguard measures only
(ii) Reforms in trade in agriculture only
(iii) Both of above

(e) Rules of origin means:
(i) The rules and regulations of the exporting countries
(ii) The nationality of product especially when it is manufactured in more than one country
(iii) None of the above

(f) TRIPS cover:
(i) Trade in services
(ii) Counterfeiting, copying and piracy affecting fair trade
(iii) Both of the above

(g) The UNCTAD emphasises more on:
(i) Developed countries
(ii) Developing countries
(iii) Both of the above

CASE STUDY

Resolution of Trade Conflicts under the WTO's Dispute Settlement Understanding

European Communities—Anti-dumping duties on Imports of Cotton-type Bed Linen, [Complaint by India (WT/DS-141)]

The dispute concerns the imposition of anti-dumping duties by European Communities on the imports of cotton-type bed linen from India. India argued that the European Communities acted inconsistently with various obligations under Articles 2, 3, 5, 6, 12, and 15 of the Anti-dumping Agreement.

At its meeting on 27 October 1999, the DSB established a panel. Egypt, Japan, and the United States of America reserved their third party rights. The panel concluded that the European Communities did not act inconsistently with its obligations under Articles 2.2, 2.2.2, 3.1, 3.4, 3.5, 5.3, 5.4, and 12.2.2 of the Anti-dumping Agreement in (a) calculating the amount for profit in constructing the normal value; (b) considering all imports from India (and Egypt and Pakistan) as dumped in the analysis of injury caused by dumped imports; (c) considering information for producers comprising the domestic industry, but not among the sampled producers, in analysing the state of the industry; (d) examining the accuracy and adequacy of the evidence prior to initiation; (e) establishing industry support for application; and (f) providing public notice of its final determination. The panel, however, also concluded that the European Communities acted inconsistently with their obligations under Articles 2.4.2, 3.4, and 15 of the

Anti-dumping Agreement in: (a) determining the existence of margins of dumping on the basis of a methodology incorporating the practice of zeroing; (b) failing to evaluate all relevant factors having a bearing on the state of the domestic industry and specifically all the factors set forth in Article 3.4; (c) considering information for producers not part of the domestic industry, as defined by the investigating authority in analysing the state of the industry; and (d) failing to explore possibilities of constructive remedies before applying anti-dumping duties.

The panel report was circulated to all WTO members on 30 October, 2000. On 1 December, 2000, the European Communities notified the DSB of its intention to appeal certain issues of law covered in the Panel report and legal interpretations developed by the Panel.

On 22 May 2002, the DSB agreed to refer this dispute, if possible, to the original panel pursuant to Article 21.5 of the DSU. On 29 November 2002, the Panel circulated its Report to Members, concluding that the European Communities had implemented the recommendation of the original panel and the Appellate Body, as adopted by the DSB, to bring its measure into conformity with its obligations under the Anti-Dumping Agreement.

On 8 January 2003, India notified the DSB of its decision to appeal the Panel Report of 29 November 2002 and filed a Notice of Appeal with the Appellate Body. On 8 April 2003, the Appellate Body circulated its Report to Members. The Appellate Body upheld the Panel's finding that India's claim under Article 3.5 of the Anti-Dumping Agreement was not properly before the Article 21.5 Panel. The appellate Body reversed the Panel's finding that the European Communities did not act inconsistently with Articles 3.1 and 3.2 of the Anti-Dumping Agreement. The Appellate Body found, instead, that, in respect of import volumes attributable to exports or producers that were *not examined individually* in the investigation, the European Communities had failed to determine the "volume of dumped imports" on the basis of "positive evidence" and an "objective examination", as required by Articles 3.1 and 3.2. The Appellate Body found that the Panel had properly discharged its duties under Article 17.6 of the Anti-Dumping Agreement and Article 11 of the DSU. The Appellate Body recommended that the DSB request the European Communities to bring its measure into conformity with its obligations under the Anti-Dumping Agreement.

On 24 April 2003, the DSB adopted the Report of the Appellate Body and the corresponding Panel Report, as modified by the Appellate Body Report.

Source: *Based on WTO Annual Report 2001.*

QUESTIONS

1. What forms the basis of the dispute?
2. What process was followed at the WTO?
3. What was the finding of the Appellate body?

Study Topic

Anti-dumping Duties and the WTO

Article VI of GATT 1994 authorises WTO members to impose AD duties in addition to other tariffs, if they find that (1) the price of imports of a specific product is less than the normal value and (2) the imports cause injury to a domestic industry. The article lays guidelines for determining if dumping has occurred, for identifying the "normal value" of the targeted product and for assessing the dumping margin. It also provides for conducting injury investigations. The imposition of AD duties must expire after five years of the date of imposition, unless an investigation shows that ending the measure would continue to result in injury.

Since the number of AD initiations has turned large especially since 1995, there is pressure on WTO to find an amicable way to keep these measures well within limits. The issue was significant at Doha Declaration in November 2001 and at the Hong Kong Declaration during December 2005. According to statistics, the total number of AD initiations rose sharply after 1994 and peaked at 366 in 2001. There was marginal decline in the initiation in the following years perhaps because of the on-going DDA negotiations.

To be precise, India initiated 412 AD petitions during January 1995–June 2005, followed by the USA (358), the European Union (318), Australia (174), Canada (133) and New Zealand (46). Other developing countries leading initiators of AD actions included Argentina (193), South Africa (191), Brazil (119), China (110) and Turkey (97). The leading exporter targets of AD initiations during the above period were China (434), the European Union (363), Korea (212) and the USA (158). The most important victims were inputs used in the manufacturing process, including steel and chemical products.

WTO members are obliged to inform the WTO of their anti-dumping legislation. By the end of 2007, the EU members and the other 95 members had submitted notifications regarding anti-dumping legislation and/or regulations. The review of members' notifications of legislation takes place at the regular meetings of the Committee on Anti-Dumping Practices. The Committee has two subsidiary bodies—the Working Group on Implementation and the Informal Group on Anti-Circumvention. These bodies normally meet twice a year in regular session, in conjunction with the regular meetings of the committee. The Working Group on Implementation considers, principally, technical issues concerning the agreement. At its meetings in April and October 2007, the Working Group continued discussions on a series of topics referred to it by the committee based on papers submitted by WTO members, draft recommendations prepared by the WTO secretariat and information submitted by the members concerning their own practices. In the Informal Group on Anti-Circumvention, the members discuss the matters referred to the committee by the ministers in the 1994 Ministerial Decision on Anti-Circumvention. The Informal Group met in April and October 2007, continuing to discuss: "what constitutes circumvention", "what is being done by members confronted with what they consider to be circumvention" and "to what extent can circumvention be dealt with under the relevant WTO rules and what other options may be deemed necessary?"

The data available indicate that 159 new anti-dumping investigations were initiated by WTO members from July 1, 2006 to June 30, 2007. WTO members initiating 10 or more new investigations were India (29), the European Communities (18), Brazil (14) and China (11). The United States initiated nine new investigations and Argentina, Egypt, Korea and Malaysia each initiated eight new investigations. Australia, Canada, Chile, Colombia, Japan, Mexico, New Zealand, Pakistan, Peru, South Africa, Chinese Taipei, Thailand and Turkey each initiated seven or fewer new investigations. As of June 30, 2007, 28 members reported anti-dumping measures (including undertakings with exporters) in force. Of the 1,274 measures reported, 18 per cent were maintained by the United States, 13 per cent by India, 12 per cent by the European Communities, 8 per cent each by China and Turkey, and 5 per cent each by Argentina, Mexico and South Africa. The products exported from China were the subject of the most anti-dumping investigations (53) initiated from July 1, 2006 to June 30, 2007, followed by products exported from Korea (11), Chinese Taipei (10), the European Communities and Indonesia (9 each), Japan (8) and the United States (7). The remaining members exporting products subject to investigation were each subject to fewer than seven new investigations. The following figures show the countrywise details.

Reporting WTO member	*Initiations*	*Provisional measures*	*Definitive Duties*	*Price undertakings with exporters*	*Measures in force on 30 June 30, 2007*
Argentina	8	5	10	0	62
Australia	2	3	3	1	46
Brazil	14	3		0	50
Canada	3	6	3	0	40
Chile	2	1	1	0	1
China	11	10	14	0	103
Colombia	5	9	3	0	6
Costa Rica	0	1	1	0	1
Egypt	8	0	6	0	31
EU	18	11	13	2	149
India	29	20	18	0	162
Indonesia	0	0	1	0	15
Israel	0	0	3	1	6
Jamaica	0	0	0	0	Not Reported
Japan	4	0	0	0	2
Korea	8	3	7	2	29
Malaysia	8	8	0	0	16
Mexico	5	5	0	0	69
New Zealand	6	1	2	0	10
Pakistan	3	4	4	2	17
Paraguay	0	0	0	0	1
Peru	1	1	2	0	33
Philippines	0	0	0	0	1
South Africa	5	1	5	0	61
Taipei	4	1	2	2	7
Thailand	3	1	0	0	24
Trinidad & Tobago	0	0	0	0	4
Turkey	3	0	13	0	99

USA	9	8	6	0	229
Total	159	102	118	10	1274

Source: Based on WTO, Annual Report: 2008

Thus, it is clear that the WTO has taken due consideration of the anti-dumping duties. It is expected, they will be well within limits.

QUESTIONS

1. What do you mean by AD duties? When are they imposed?
2. Why has its management become more significant?
3. Describe the steps taken at the WTO in this respect.

REFERENCES

Books

Anderson, K. (2000),"The Future Agenda of the WTO", in WTO, *From GATT to the WTO: The Multilateral Trading System in the New Millenium* (The Hague: Kluwer Law International,) pp. 7–33.

Bhagwati, J. (2000),"Fifty Years: Looking Back, Looking Forward", in WTO, *op. cit.,* pp. 57–66.

Cutazar, M. Z. ed. (1985), *UNCTAD and the South-North Dialogue: The First Twenty Years* (Oxford: Pergamon Press).

Hertel, T. and L. A. Winters eds. (2006), *Poverty and the WTO: Impacts of the Doha Development Agenda* (Washington D.C.: The World Bank and Palgrave Macmillan).

Hockman, B. M. and M. M. Kostecki (1995), *The Political Economy of the World Trading System* (Oxford: Oxford University Press).

Jackson, J. H. (1989), *The World Trading System* (Cambridge MA: MIT Press).

Messerlin, P. A. (2000),"The WTO's New Horizons", in WTO, *op.cit.,* pp. 83–96.

Puche, J. S. (2000),"Regionalism and the WTO", in WTO, *op. cit.,* pp. 123–35.

Snape, R. H. (1998),"Reading Effective Agreements Covering Services", in A. O. Krueger, ed., *WTO as an International Organisation* (New York: Oxford University Press) pp. 279–96.

The World Bank (2006), *The Global monitoring Report, 2006,* Washington D.C.

United Nations (2006), *Trade and Development Report: 2006,* Geneva: UNCTAD.

Journals

Anderson, K. (1997),"On the Complexities of China's WTO Accession", *World Economy,* XX (5), 749–72.

Baldwin, R. (1986), "Towards More Efficient Procedures for Multilateral Trade Negotiations", *Aussenwirtschaft,* XLI (3), 379–94.

Wall Street Journal (1993), *The Uruguay Round's Key Results,* December 15, p. A6.

SELECT FURTHER READINGS

Bhagwati, J. (1991), *Protectionism* (Cambridge MA: MIT Press).

Cutazar, M. Z. (1985), *UNCTAD and the South-North Dialogue: The First Twenty Years* (Oxford: Pergamon Press).

Krueger, A. O. (1998), *WTO as an International Organisation* (New York: Oxford University Press).

Qureshi, A. H. (1996), *The World Trade Organisation: Implementing International Trade Norms* (Manchester: Manchester University Press).

WTO (2000), *From GATT to the WTO: The Multilateral Trading System in the New Millenium* (The Hague: Kluwer Law International).

* The city of London is recognised as one of the key "world cities". Located in a small area within Greater London, England, it is often referred as the city or Square Mile. Today the city is a major business and financial centre, ranking on a par with New York City as the leading centre of global finance. It accounted for 4% of UK's GDP in 2008.

LNG plant at Bontang, East Kalimantan, Indonesia*

8

Regional Economic Integration

CHAPTER OBJECTIVES

The purpose of this chapter is to acquaint readers with the basics of regional economic integration and how integration influences international business. In particular, the objective is to:

- ✦ Describe the different levels of regional economic integration.
- ✦ Discuss the benefits and costs of regional economic integration from the viewpoint of international trade and FDI.
- ✦ Acquaint the readers with some regional economic integration schemes presently followed in different parts of the globe.

International trade is also regulated at the regional level through the creation of regional integration schemes. Regional economic integration scheme, opines Balassa (1973), is a process as well as a state of affairs. As a process, it means the removal of discrimination between different states. As a state of affairs, it means the absence of different forms of discrimination. While the former is a dynamic concept, the latter is a static concept. While intra-region trade is normally tariff-free, tariff is imposed on imports from outside the region. Again, there is often no restriction on the intra-region movement of capital and labour that also regulates other forms of international business. In view of trade and business regulation of this kind, the present chapter discusses the major specialities of the integrative arrangements that do influence the business decisions of international managers.

8.1 LEVELS OF ECONOMIC INTEGRATION

Economic integration or regional economic grouping represents some kind of preferential economic arrangement among member countries, where they cooperate with one another in many ways and eliminate restrictions on the intra-region flow of goods, services, capital, and labour. The member countries normally belong to a particular geographic region, with the result that they have common history and similar awareness to the regional problem. However, belonging to a specific geographic region is not an essential qualification for regional grouping. Cuba was a member of the Council for the Mutual Economic Assistance (COMECON) before the break-up of the former USSR, despite the fact that it was quite distantly located.

The different forms of regional economic integration schemes differ from each other. One of the reasons is that they represent different levels of economic integration. Based on the varying levels, the integration schemes are known as:

1. Free Trade Area
2. Customs Union
3. Common Market
4. Economic Union
5. Political Union

Free Trade Area refers to a situation where intra-region trade is duty-free but there is variation in tariff structure for import from a third country.

Free Trade Area: In a free trade area, which involves the least integration, member countries abolish tariff and non-tariff barriers on intra-region trade but they are free to impose tariff on their import from a third country at different rates. Thus tariff abolition is a preferential economic arrangement that aims at encouraging intra-region trade. European Free Trade Association (EFTA) and North American Free Trade Agreement (NAFTA) are apposite examples of this type of economic integration.

Customs Union refers to free trade within the union along with a uniform tariff structure for import from a third country.

Customs Union: The second form of economic integration is known as customs union where the member countries abolish tariff and non-tariff barriers on intra-region trade just as in case of a free trade area. But, the member countries maintain a common tariff wall on imports from a third country. Thus, it is different from the free trade area, which does not involve a common external tariff. The European Union in its initial stage was a customs union.

Common Market: The third form is known as common market where the degree of integration is further one step ahead. The common market involves common external tariff that is found in a customs union. Over and above, it also involves free movement of factors of production such as labour, capital, enterprise, and technology among the member states. As a result, there are chances for best allocation of resources in a common market leading to maximisation of benefits from resource utilisation among the member states.

Common Market is a customs union along with free intra-union movement of factors of production.

Economic Union: The fourth form is known as an economic union where all the features of a common market exist. But additionally, the member states try to harmonise monetary, fiscal, and other economic policies. Thus, the content of integration is the maximum in this case. This may mean that the member states surrender, at least to some extent, their national sovereignty for the harmonisation of economic policies. The European Union, after the Maastricht Treaty, has come to be an economic union.

Economic Union is a common market along with a common economic and monetary policy.

Political Union: Political union represents the highest level of integration. Although it is not a pure form of economic integration, it does indicate the logical outcome of increased economic integration among a group of nations. In this case, the member countries lose their national identity and come under a single state. East Germany joined West Germany to form a political union.

Political Union is a single political sovereignty.

These are the five stages through which the process of economic integration moves further. The time span for the movement from one stage to the other may vary widely depending upon the subservience of the economic goal amongthe member states. In Europe, it took around four decades to enter a complete economic union. In South Asia, the first stage is not complete even after oneand a-half decades of the formation of the South Asian Association of Regional Co-operation (SAARC).

Policy Action	*Type*				
	Free Trade Area	*Customs Union*	*Common Market*	*Economic Union*	*Political Union*
1. Removal of tariff and quota	Yes	Yes	Yes	Yes	Yes
2. Common external tariff	No	Yes	Yes	Yes	Yes
3. Factor mobility	No	No	Yes	Yes	Yes
4. Harmonisation of economic policies	No	No	No	Yes	Yes
5. Total economic and political unification	No	No	No	No	Yes

8.2 BENEFITS AND COST OF ECONOMIC INTEGRATION

8.2.1 Trade Creation and Trade Diversion

Locus of production shifting from high cost to low cost centre within the union, leading to productive efficiency is trade creation. Trade diversion is the opposite of trade creation.

It was Jacob Viner (1950) who discussed the benefits and costs of economic integration for the first time, in terms of trade creation and trade diversion. While the trade creation has beneficial welfare implications, trade diversion may be injurious. Explaining the difference between the these two terms, Viner says that when the locus of production shifts from a high cost point to a low cost point, the resources will tend to move from a less efficient use to a more efficient use. This would be a trade creating effect. On the contrary, the movement of production and resources in the opposite directions leads to trade diversion. Suppose the price of a single commodity X in three countries, *A*, *B*, and *C* at existing exchange rates is respectively, \$36, \$25, and \$20. In the absence of any regional integration scheme, Country *A* imposes a tariff of 100 per cent, which is sufficient to protect its own industry. But, if Country *A* forms a customs union with Country *B*, it will prefer to import that commodity from Country *B* instead of using its own product inasmuch as import will be cheaper. This would lead to a movement of resources from Country *A* to Country *B* or from a high cost point to a low cost point, and would be treated as trade creation. Had there been a different rate of tariff, the trade pattern would have been different. For example, if Country *A* imposes 50 per cent tariff on the import of commodity X, this commodity would be imported from Country *C* in absence of any customs union. But when there is a customs union between Country *A* and Country *B*, the commodity will be imported from Country *B* as there is no tariff imposed on intra-region trade. In this case, the source of supply shifts from a low-cost point to a higher-cost point, that is from Country *C* to Country *B*, and this will cause trade diversion. The concept of trade creation and trade diversion can be explained with the help of a diagram. Figure 8.1 shows the trade-creating effect of a customs union. Suppose D_X and S_X are, respectively, the demand and supply of Commodity X in Country *A*. Prior to the formation of a customs union, Country *A* imposes tariff of 100 per cent in order to protect its own industry from the cheaper imports from Country *B*. The tariff-inclusive price is Rs. 4. The total demand for the product in Country *A* following the imposition of tariff is 71, out of which 23 are produced domestically and 48 are imported from Country *B*. Country *A* does not import the product from a third country in as much as the tariff-inclusive price is higher than Rs. 4.

Suppose, further that a customs union is formed between Country *A* and Country *B*. The tariff is now zero on the trade between the two countries. The price of the product in absence of the tariff falls to Rs. 2. In the wake of the falling price, the demand for the product rises to 85, out of which

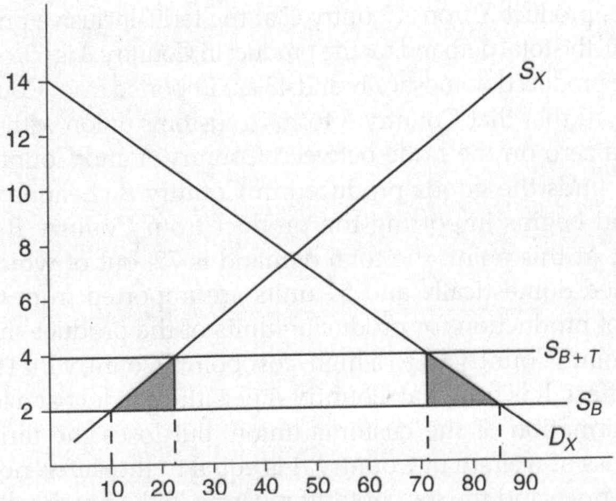

FIGURE 8.1 Trade-creating Effect of Customs Union in Country A

10 are produced domestically and 75 are imported from Country *B*. Here, Country *A* imports 27 more units from Country *B* that substitutes the domestic production in Country *A*. In other words, the locus of production for producing 27 products shifts from a high-cost point in Country *A* to a low-cost point in Country *B*. This is the trade-creating effects of a customs union. The gains accruing to Country *A* are:

$$[\{(23 - 10)/2\} + \{(85 - 71)/2\}] \times (4 - 2) = \text{Rs. } 27$$

As far as trade diversion is concerned, Figure 8.2 shows that D_X and S_X are the demand and supply of product *X* in Country *A*. S_B and S_C are the perfectly elastic supply line, respectively, in Country *B* and Country *C*. In order to protect its own industry, Country *A* imposes tariff of 100 per cent on its import

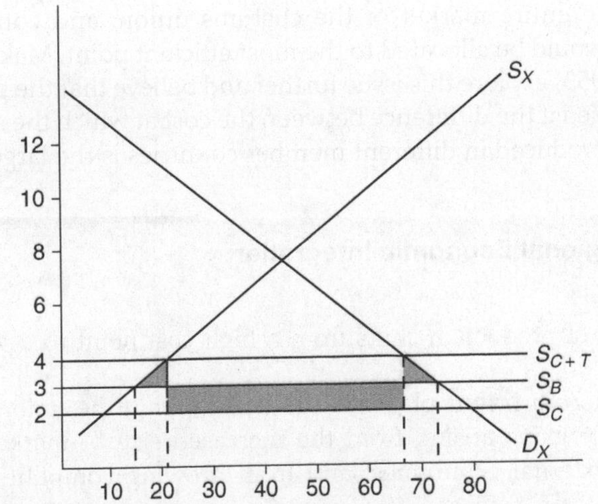

FIGURE 8.2 Trade-diverting Effect of Customs Union in Country A

and imports product *X* from Country *C* at the tariff-inclusive price of Rs. 4. At this point, the total demand for the product in Country *A* is 65, out of which 22 units are produced domestically and 43 are imported from Country *C*.

Suppose, further that Country *A* forms a customs union with Country *B*. The tariff is zero on the trade between Country *A* and Country *B*. Now, Country *A* finds the goods produced in Country *B* cheaper in absence of tariff and begins importing the product from Country *B* instead of Country *C*. At this point, the total demand is 72, out of which 15 units are produced domestically and 57 units are imported from Country *B*. The locus of production for producing units of the product shifts from a low-cost point (Country *C*) to a high-cost point (Country *B*). This is trade diverting effect. It is true that Country *A* gets the product at a lower price after the formation of the customs union, but loses the tariff income. Thus, the loss of welfare in Country *A* is equal to the difference between the gain in price and the loss of tariff revenue. To be precise, it is:

$$\{(65 - 22) \times (3 - 2)\} - [\{(22 - 15)/2\} + \{(72 - 65)/2\}] \times (4 - 3)$$

$$= \text{Rs. } 43 - 7 = 36$$

However, Meade (1956) is not satisfied with Viner's explanation. In his view, it is not the difference of the total volume of trade on which costs have been raised from the total volume of trade on which costs have been lowered that indicates the net gain or loss. Rather, it is the extent to which the costs have been lowered on each unit of the newly created trade that indicates the trade creating effect. This effect should, of course, take into account the loss of revenue to the State Exchequer on account of abolition of tariff on intra-region trade, unless other taxes are raised to compensate such losses.

Viner is very particular regarding the choosing of a union member so that the gains could be maximised. He prefers partners that are competitive, and not complementary, in the range of commodities protected by tariff. This is because in this case, the most efficient partner would capture the entire market of the customs union; and consequently, resources would be allocated to the most efficient point. Makeower and Morton (1953) explore this issue further and believe that the gains could be maximised if the difference between the cost at which the same commodity is produced in different member countries is the largest.

Regional Economic Integration

Benefits:

- Trade creation when locus of production shifts from a high cost point to a low cost point.
- Inter-commodity substitution in favour of goods produced within the union.
- Dynamic effects in form of gains arising from the increased size of market, from economies of scale and external economies, and from growing competition and technological change

- Development of collective self-reliance among member countries, especially through harmonisation of economic policies.
- Increased foreign direct investment within the union and from outside the union, especially in view of the larger market.

Costs:

- Trade diversion when locus of production moves from a low-cost point to a high cost point.
- Trade deflection when outside goods enter a free trade area through a member country having lowest tariff.
- Polarisation of benefits from integration moving away from the weaker partner in favour of the economically stronger partner, leading to intra-region inequality

8.2.2 Inter-commodity Substitution and Consumption Gains

Viner's analysis is limited to the inter-country substitution of goods. But, as Meade (1956), Gehrels (1956), and Lipsey (1960) believe, there exists also the scope for inter-commodity substitution. The induced changes in the relative prices, as a result of customs union, may have an influence on the consumption pattern. It is expected that the union members will increase their consumption of commodities imported from the member countries, which will supplement their reduced consumption of goods imported from a third country. This sort of intra-union trade will raise the welfare gains and partly offset any loss from trade diversion. Gehrels and Lipsey observed that even if the country does not shift its import from a third country, the higher price of the commodity in question will force consumers to shift their demand in favour of a cheaper substitute produced domestically or imported from a member country. This effect may outweigh the unfavourable effects of trade diversion and cause a net rise in welfare. The basic premise of their argument is that the relative price between the imports from the member country and domestic goods are made conform with the real rates of transformation, which tends to raise welfare. But, if the relative price between the imports from within the region and the imports from a third country tends to move away from being equal to the real rates of transformation, welfare would decrease.

The induced changes in the relative prices, as a result of customs union, may have an influence on the consumption pattern.

8.2.3 Trade Deflection in a Free Trade Area

The theory of customs union may not be completely applicable to a free trade area as the latter does not have a common external tariff. Trade

Trade deflection refers to goods produced in a third country entering a free trade area through a member country having lowest tariff.

deflection, which is not a problem in a customs union, may emerge in a free trade area. Since the member countries in a free trade area have their own external tariff wall, the goods produced in a third country find their way into the free trade area via the member country that has the lowest tariff. This kind of trade deflection negates the protective efforts of a market integration scheme. This is why some of the free trade areas have a provision known as the rules of origin, which necessitates that a certain minimum percentage of the price of the goods should be represented by the cost of the material produced in the region. This provision performs the function of a common external tariff to a certain extent and minimises the effects of trade deflection. Nevertheless, as Shibata (1967) feels, a few differences do exist between a customs union and a free trade area. For instance, consumers of a product in a country with the lowest tariff are not worse off with the formation of a free trade area; but in a customs union, they have to face a higher common union price till the common external tariff is brought down to the lowest previous duty. Again, with increasing cost of area-origin inputs, free trade area manufacturers with no access to non-region-origin inputs are at disadvantage. On the contrary, in a customs union, the common external tariff makes all manufacturers competitive, provided the assumption of perfect mobility of factors of production holds good. Yet again, highly specialised member countries prefer a free trade area as they do not require protection through common external tariff. Last but not least, countries that complement each other prefer to have a free trade area, while those that are competitive prefer to form a customs union.

Countries that complement each other prefer to have a free trade area, while those that are competitive prefer to form a customs union.

8.2.4 Dynamic Effects

The dynamic benefits include the gains arising from the widening of the size of the market, economies of scale and external economies, growing competition, and technological change lead to economic growth.

Besides the issue of trade creation, trade diversion, and trade deflection, which are all more or less of static nature, there are some dynamic benefits from regional grouping. The dynamic benefits include the gains arising from the widening of the size of the market, economies of scale and external economies, growing competition, and technological change. The regional groupings reap gains that induce production and lead to economic growth (Balassa, 1962; Scitovsky, 1958). However, as Thorbecke (1963) feels, the dynamic effects may sometimes outweigh the static effects and help move the terms of trade against the union. The argument is that the economic growth, as a sequel to the dynamic effects, may raise the demand for imports via real income effect as also the productive efficiency may reduce the cost of production that, as a combined effect, may influence the terms of trade in an unfavourable direction.

The dynamic effects of a regional integration scheme are more significant in the case of a developing country. This is one of the reasons that the dynamic effects have been exclusively discussed in the context of developing countries (Dell, 1963; Bhambri, 1962; Mikesell, 1963; Balassa and Stoutjesdijk, 1975; Dosser, 1972). It is generally believed that the national market in developing countries is often too small to allow manufacturers to achieve economies of scale and fully utilise their capacities. Regional cooperation schemes help widen the market, facilitate larger production, and permit large size plants with greater specialisation. This is why the cost of protection is often lower in a regional grouping than in an individual country. Mikesell feels that the widening of market creates new opportunities for innovation and brings about changes in the investment pattern, which constitutes the dynamic elements of growth. He attaches importance to the issue of economies of scale in view of the fact that the investment as well as intermediate goods cannot be economically produced if the market is small. Balassa and Stoutjesdijk have statistically shown that no national market of any developing country is sufficiently large for this purpose. Economic integration is naturally a viable alternative in this context. Firms reaping the benefits of scale are able to supply goods at a lower cost within the region as well as outside. The export base of the region as a whole widens.

Again, the competition generated by the formation of economic integration scheme often leads to a healthy competitive environment. Mikesell is of the opinion that it is primarily the emergence of impersonal competitive forces. Firms that previously had an oligopolistic or monopolistic position in an individual country will now have to face competition from other firms in the region. Consequently, they employ cost reducing methods. The improvement in the competitive position of firms leads to an increase in their export outside the region. Larger export leads to larger production and investment, and greater specialisation at home. This may push the relative prices and consumption pattern towards optimum conditions.

8.2.5 Collective Self-reliance

Member countries of a regional grouping are able to develop collective self-reliance through intra-region trade, movement of factors of production, harmonisation of economic policies, and they need not depend on the wishes of other countries. This is very important in the case of developing countries that have to depend on developed countries for their economic needs. Economic integration provides them with greater strength while bargaining collectively with others.

8.2.6 Increased Foreign Direct Investment

Economic integration leads to larger market and thereby to greater demand and increased intra-bloc and inter-bloc FDI.

The trade liberalisation aspects of regional economic integration have a positive influence on foreign direct investment (FDI) especially on the flow of intra-bloc FDI. Economic integration leads to a larger market and, in turn, to greater demand. Consequently, inter-bloc as well as intra-bloc FDI flows to respond to the increased demand. Regional firms move abroad (within the bloc) to operate at the least-cost location. When integration results in the convergence of regulatory regimes of member countries or when pressure is built on non-member countries to converge their policies in tune with the member countries, FDI will definitely be promoted.

In fact, it was experienced in case of Bulgaria and Romania that during the process of convergence preceding their accession to the European Union on January 1, 2007, the magnitude of FDI inflow into these two countries increased considerably. Bulgaria's rank in the UNCTAD FDI performance index moved up to 7th during 2004–2006 from 92nd in 1990–1992. Romania's ranking improved from 101st to 21st during the same period (Based on WIR, 2007).

Strange (1997) explains six different motivations behind FDI that are stimulating in the wake of regional economic integration. (i) when firm-specific factors such as technology are available in the host country, which is not transferable to the home country, FDI flows to the host country. (ii) when the host-country government provides various incentives to foreign investors, the inflow of FDI begins to rise. (iii) when the motive is to gain access to one another's product ranges, there is often mutual investment in different member countries of the regional grouping. (iv) when firms intend to secure access to customers in the host country, they make investment in those countries. (v) the high tariff wall of a regional integration scheme often discourages imports from a third country. In such cases, companies of the third country begin to operate in the regional bloc in order to avoid the tariff barrier. Such FDI is often known as tariff-jumping FDI. (vi) when there is international competition among similar products, technical change often shifts comparative advantage in favour of foreign firms. The host country makes greater imports. In such cases, foreign firms collaborate with the host country firms in order to meet the greater demand for the product.

8.2.7 Polarisation of Benefits

> In the ANDEAN Pact, the distribution of national income during 1960s and early 1970s was obviously unequal.

There is one school of thought that believes in the reduction of inequality in income and wealth through economic integration. It is perhaps because increased trade should reduce disparity between factor prices (Edel, 1969; Samuelson, 1949). But this argument is refuted on the grounds that the introduction of monopoly elements and trade through unequal exchanges lead to intra-region inequality. Vaitsos (1978) has presented some empirical findings to show that despite special consideration to distributional aspects in the ANDEAN Pact, the distribution of national income during 1960s and early 1970s was obviously unequal. Around 40 per cent of the population within this region received 9 to 13 per cent of the national income, whereas the top 5 per cent of the population had 40 per cent of overall earnings.

Bird (1965) too feels that the polarisation forces, that is growth in one part of the region attracts further growth in that part, are often more prominent than the spread of growth in other parts. In the developed world, where even the least advanced country possesses the minimum industrial impulses, polarisation forces are not very apparent. But in the developing world, where such impulses are lacking, the formation of a regional integration scheme is fraught with such problems. Bird maintains that the emergence of economies of scale and the operation of external economies push down the cost. Trade creating forces tend to appear shifting the productive resources and factors of production away from high cost centres. Industrial agglomeration gets an impetus, which further gives rise to external economies, encouraging, in turn, further industrial agglomeration in specific parts of the region. There are of course social costs associated with this trend, but private entrepreneurs hardly care for them.

Polarisation forces become active when a particular member country does not augment export but simply shifts its imports from a low cost source to a high cost source. This leads to deterioration in terms of trade. Besides, large imbalances appear on the payments count due to large intra-region trade imbalances. However, Balassa and Stoutjesdijk feel that such imbalances may be offset by changes in extra-region trade.

Polarisation forces become active when a particular member country does not augment export but simply shifts its imports from a low cost source to a high cost source. This leads to deterioration in terms of trade. Besides, large imbalances appear on the payments count due to large intra-region trade imbalances.

Whatever may be causes for polarisation, its continuance leads to heterogeneity among member economies with respect to the level of income and industrial development. Weaker countries feel dissatisfied with such developments that affect cordial relations within the region. The members oppose harmonisation of economic policies, which negates the very objective of economic integration. Germanico Salgado Penaherrera (1980–81) gives an account of such a situation in a few regional groupings and of equalisation mechanisms that have followed to correct the imbalances and differences. He finds that such mechanisms have a very low success rate.

8.3 SOME ECONOMIC INTEGRATION SCHEMES

8.3.1 The European Case

Early Attempts: The first exercise towards economic integration was made in 1948 when the Organisation for European Economic Cooperation (OEEC) was established for the purpose of administering the Marshall Plan aid meant for the reconstruction of the war devastated economies. In 1952, six European countries, that is, West Germany, France, Italy, Belgium, the Netherlands, and Luxembourg formed the European Coal and Steel Community (ECSC). The purpose was to establish a common market for coal and steel among the member countries.

European Union: A major step towards regional grouping was manifest in the creation of the European Economic Community (EEC) among the ECSC countries in 1957 under the Treaty of Rome. It was basically a common market that had a customs union along with a provision for free internal movement of goods, services, labour, and capital. The process of abolition of internal tariff began in 1959 and was completed by 1968.

The Common Agricultural Policy (CAP) established in 1962 incorporated various measures of tariff and price support and helped restrict the import of agricultural products in the interest of domestic agriculture and the farmers engaged in it. In 1967, the ECSC, EEC, and the European Atomic Energy Community (EAEC) were merged under a new banner of the European Community (EC). Denmark, Ireland, and the United Kingdom joined the EC in 1973. Greece joined it in 1981; Portugal and Spain in 1986; and Austria, Finland, and Sweden in 1995. The size of the European Union increased in 2004 when ten new countries joined it. The new members were: Cyprus, the Czech Republic, Estonia, Hungary, Lativa, Lithuania, Malta, Poland, Slovakia, and Slovenia. Two more countries, viz. Bulgaria and Romania joined the EU subsequently. The number of member countries rose to 27.

In 1987, the Single European Act was implemented in order to add more vigour to the EC as it provided for harmonising product standards throughout the region and removing barriers to internal trade and the flow of financial services.

The members of the EC met in 1991 at Maastricht, the Netherlands, to plan for more advanced stages of economic integration. The Maastricht Treaty, which was signed in February 1992 and came into force from November 1993, renaming the EC as the European Union (EU), called for a close link between the European economic union and the European monetary union. It set up monetary and fiscal targets for the countries participating in the monetary union. Of the then 15 EU members, there were only 11 members of the EMU as Greece and Sweden were not able to meet the convergence criteria and Denmark and the United Kingdom are still opposed to the single currency, Euro replacing their currency by 2002. However, Greece joined the Euro club in January 2001, raising the number of Euro club members to 12. Again, it called for political union among the members, that is, to include a common defence and foreign policy and a common citizenship.

The organisational structure of the EU primarily embraces five institutions. The European Commission initiates proposals for legislation and executes the policies. The European Parliament has legislative powers and it supervises the executive decisions. It is rather a consultative body that debates and amends legislation proposed by the European Commission. The Council of Ministers composed of the ministers from the member countries votes on the passage of the law. The Court of Justice, composed of one justice from each member country, hears the case when a country does not abide by the rules framed by the Union or when the Commission or the Council does not perform its duties well. The Court of Auditors looks after the management of the EU budget.

These five institutions are flanked by five other important bodies. They are: (1) the European Economic and Social Committee looking after economic and social issues; (2) the Committee of the Regions, expressing the views of the regional authorities; (3) the European Central Bank, responsible for the management of monetary issues; (4) the European

Ombudsman, dealing with citizens' complaints; and (5) European Investment Bank, responsible for financing investment projects.

European Economic and Monetary Union: The European Economic and Monetary Union was born in the mid-1970s with the creation of the "snake in the tunnel", which took a more concrete shape in the form of the European Monetary System (EMS) in 1979. The European Currency Unit (ECU) was then the monetary unit of the EMS. ECUs were created and allocated among the EMS member countries. It was a composite monetary unit made up of a basket of a specified amount of the currencies of the 12 EU member countries. The specified amount was determined on the basis of the country's GDP and foreign trade. One unit of the ECU was equal to the sum of the fixed amount of such currencies.

"Snake in the tunnel" refers to an attempt towards monetary integration among six West European nations in 1972, the purpose of which was to narrow the fluctuation in those currencies.

ECUs were created by revolving three-month swaps of gold and US dollars between the members' central banks and the European Monetary Co-operation Fund (EMCF). The EMCF was renamed as the European Monetary Institute (EMI) in 1994 and again, with greater functions and powers, as the European Central Bank, in 1998. The central bank of a member country, if it had held ECUs more than the allocated amount, got interest on the additional amount. If its holdings of ECUs were lower than the allocated amount, it had to pay interest.

ECU helped determine the parity grid or the grid of bilateral rates of exchange. This meant that the exchange rate between the two currencies was fixed through their share in the ECU valuation. Any fluctuation in the bilateral parity grid was not unexpected in view of the widely differing macroeconomic variables in the different member countries. So, a fluctuation band was prescribed that was initially +/– 2.25 per cent, except for the Italian lira, where it was 6.00 per cent. Any fluctuation beyond the prescribed limit was restricted through intervention by the central banks. In practice, intervention was made much before the prescribed limit had reached. This type of optional intervention prevented any compulsory intervention that had to be made when the prescribed limit had been reached.

Again, there was a provision for monetary support. It originated from the EMCF or the EMI, now the European Central Bank, and had varying maturity limit. The very short term credit was to assist central banks in intervention. Short term credit met the balance of payments deficit. The medium term credit was meant for a medium term balance of payments support. Besides all these, there was also a provision for medium term financial support for fostering convergence between economically weak and the economically strong member countries. Such credits flowed from the European Investment Bank.

Exchange rate stability, which could not be achieved completely over the years, was to be achieved by reducing disparity in the macroeconomic performance of the member countries. This was possible through the convergence of economic policies among the members. In order to bring about a greater degree of convergence, the Committee for the Study of Economic and Monetary Union, 1989, put forth a three-stage plan. This was commonly known as the Delors Plan approved at Maastricht in February 1992.

The first stage, which was formally to begin from July 1990, emphasised on currency convertibility through removal of exchange control and through encouraging free capital movement. The second stage, beginning from January 1994, focused on institutional development. The European System of Central Banks (ESCB) was to be set up for the purpose of envisaging a common monetary policy. Exchange Rate Mechanism (ERM) was to be hardened through narrowing the exchange rate fluctuation band. The time-table for the third stage was to begin from January 1999. In the first year, budgetary coordination was to be brought about. The EMI, now the European Central Bank (ECB), was responsible for fostering monetary coordination in the then proposed framework of the new European currency, the euro, that was created in January 1999. In the following three years, the exchange rate of member currencies was to be irrevocably pegged to one another. From 2002, the national currencies of the member countries were to retire in favour of the euro.

The Delors Plan suggested a full convergence of economic and monetary policies, focussing specifically on the size of inflation, interest rates, fiscal deficit, and government debt. However, it is difficult to say how far the convergence criteria will be met.

In January 1999, the Euro was created as the currency of the EMU. It replaced the ECU on a one-for-one basis, with the result that the ECU ceased to exist. One unit of euro comprised of 100 euro cents. The exchange rate between euro and the members' currency came to be fixed. This was done with a view to avoid fluctuation in the bilateral parity grid. Table 8.1 shows the Euro-member currency rates.

Table 8.1 Intra-EMU Exchange Rate

As on 1 January, 1999

Member's Currency	*Value per unit of Euro*
DM	1.95583
French franc	6.55957
Italian lira	1936.27
Spanish peseta	166.386
Dutch guilder	2.20371
Belgian franc	40.3399
Austrian shilling	13.7603
Portuguese escudo	200.482
Finnish markka	5.94573
Irish pound	0.787564
Luxembourg franc	40.3399

Note: Cyprus and Malta joined on 1 January, 2008 and on 1 January, 2009, Slovakia joined the EMU

On this count, the post-euro regime is different from the pre-euro regime. The bilateral parity grid is not expected to be constrained because the European System of Central Banks (ESCB), composed of the central banks of the participating countries, and the ECB will frame and implement a common monetary policy in all the member countries. However, the exchange rate between the euro and the non-member currency is subject to market forces. When the euro came into being, its value in relation to the US dollar was US $1.1665/euro.

On January 1, 2002, Euro notes and coins were introduced in the 12 member countries. By the end of February 2002, the euro completely replaced members' currencies. Euro bank notes are issued by both the European Central Bank and the national central banks with full understanding between them. Out of the total size of the issue, 8 per cent are allocated to the ECB. The coins are minted by the national authorities.

Euro has some benefits: 1. No transaction cost involved in exchange of currencies, 2. Price transparency, 3. No exchange rate exposure in intra-EU trade, 4. Market imperfections being minimum, 5. No problem in consolidation of accounts by MNCs.

The euro has some benefits, but at the same time, there may be costs too. First of all, the benefits manifest in eliminating transaction costs that occur on account of exchanging one member currency for another. Secondly, goods produced in different member countries are priced in a single currency, which leads to price transparency and encourages market integration. Thirdly, there is no exchange rate changes and, thereby, no foreign exchange exposure in intra-union trade. With no exchange rate exposure, intra-union trade will expand, leading to increase in capital productivity and national income. Fourthly, the existence of a single currency is expected to minimise market imperfections that will be apparent more in financial services. In a nearly perfect financial market, the number of participants will increase. All this will help develop the financial market within the Union. Fifthly, there will be no problem in the consolidation of accounts by multinational corporations operating within the Union as translation of currency will not be required. But, on the other hand, in the absence of a multiple currency system, the number of transactions exchanging one currency for another will significantly reduce bankers' income.

Again, as far as the use of the euro for invoicing of trade with a third country is concerned, its success depends upon the stability of its value in the foreign exchange market and on the demand for it in international transactions. In fact, this is the reason that the US dollar is invariably the currency of invoice even where the United States of America is not involved in the trade. If one looks at the figures, it is found that 37 per cent of world trade is invoiced in the EU member countries' currency as against 48 per cent of the world trade invoiced in the US dollar. On this basis, one can be confident about the successful use of the euro in international transactions. Moreover, there is an indication that the Bank of Japan is holding euros in its reserves. If it is followed by the central bank of other countries, euro has a good prospect. Presently, the bonds denominated in EMU member currencies account for around one-half of dollar-denominated bonds. If these currencies retire in favour of the euro, euro-denominated bonds will be commonly used.

However, the experience in the two years after the euro came into being was not very impressive. It depreciated against the US dollar during this period. The reasons were perhaps the larger current account deficit in the EMU than in the United States of America and the falling rate of industrial production in the EMU compared to that in the United States of America. Nevertheless, these trends were not permanent. In recent past, euro has appreciated against the US dollar. If the macroeconomic variables of EMU improve, the euro definitely has good prospects.

European Free Trade Association (EFTA): There were some countries in Europe during late 1950s that did not relish the idea of relinquishing national sovereignty despite favouring free intra-group trade. They did not join the EEC at the time, rather they formed the EFTA under the Stockholm Convention of May 1960 where they adopted free trade within the group but maintained their own tariff while trading with third countries. Originally, there were seven member countries in the EFTA, namely, Austria, Denmark, Norway, Portugal, Sweden, Switzerland, and the United Kingdom. However, in due course of time some of them left and joined the EU, while a few countries joined EFTA. Presently, there are only four members, namely Iceland, Liechtenstein, Norway, and Switzerland.

8.3.2 The American and Caribbean Schemes

The American continent has also witnessed economic integration schemes. They are either between two developed countries, between two or more developing countries, or between developed and developing countries. Some of them have not been successful, while others are doing well.

US-Canada Free Trade Agreement: In January 1989, a free trade agreement was signed between Canada and the United States of America with a view to eliminate tariff from bilateral trade in three stages during one decade. A tribunal was established to settle disputes in this respect. It was expected that in the wake of tariff reduction or elimination, trade would rise; and it did rise by over 60 per cent during the first decade. In 2000s, Canada's trade with the USA was as large as around 50 per cent of the former's GDP.

North American Free Trade Agreement (NAFTA): The NAFTA, embracing three member countries, namely, the United States of America, Canada, and Mexico, came into force from January 1994. In the wake of peso devaluation during 1995, there were some problems, but since 1996 it has regained strength. The grouping aims at dismantling trade barriers and liberalisation of government procurement rules and the rules concerning trade in services, intellectual property rights, and environment. The US and Canadian firms have reaped advantage from the cheap surplus labour of Mexico. This is one of the reasons that there has been large flow of investment from the US and Canada to Mexico. Moreover, intra-union trade has multiplied. Mexico became the largest user of US goods, only next to Canada. Mexican export to these countries rose primarily on account of intra-firm trade. However, there were strict local content requirements in case of trade availing of duty free provisions.

Andean Community: The Andean Community, initially known as the Andean Pact, was created in 1969 only after the Latin American Free Trade Association (LAFTA) failed to meet its desired objective. Initially, five countries, namely, Bolivia, Chile, Colombia, Ecuador and Peru were its members. Venezuela joined the community in 1973 but subsequently, Chile left the community. During the first two decades, the grouping did not fare well on account of political differences among the member countries. But in 1990, there was a revival as the members planned to create a free trade area by 1992, a customs union by 1994, and a common market by 1995. It is a fact that the implementation of these decisions is only partial, covering only a limited number of members and products, yet there has been expansion in trade with the revival of the integration scheme.

Southern Common Market (MERCOSUR): Initially, in 1991, the two members, namely, Argentina and Brazil, formed MERCOSUR, which expanded subsequently to cover Paraguay, Uruguay, Bolivia, and Chile; the last two being only associate members. It covers a large area and over one-half of the total economic output of Latin America. The group implemented common external tariff in 1995 and abolished tariff on intra-group trade in 1996. It is doing well as intra-group trade and investment has increased manifold.

Central American Common Market (CACM): The CACM was created in 1960 by the Treaty of Managua, with Costa Rica, El Salvador, Guatemala, Honduras, Nicaragua, and Panama as its members. The member countries had contemplated establishing a common market, but it could not be done due to civil war and bloody conflict between the Honduras and El Salvador. However, since 1991, the member countries have started stressing more on industrial deregulation, harmonisation of economic policies, and so on.

Free Trade Areas of Americas (FTAA): The scheme is still in the making, but when complete, it will cover the entire American continent, from extreme north to the extreme south, except Cuba. It will be the biggest regional grouping in the world covering different sets of economies. Around 30 countries have shown interest but the chances for comprehensive trade agreement are very little.

Caribbean Community and Common Market (CARICOM): Created in 1973, CARICOM gives special emphasis on the free movement of factors of production and free movement of tourists within the region that covers Antigua and Barbuda, Bahamas, Barbados, Belize, Dominica, Grenada, Guyana, Haiti, Jamaica, Montserrat, St Kitts-Nevis, St Lucia, St Vincent, Suriname, and Trinidad and Tobago. Some of the member countries have eliminated tariff and established a common external tariff. But the process is yet to be completed.

8.3.3 Integration Schemes in Africa and the Middle-East

Economic Community of West African States (ECOWAS): The ECOWAS was formed in 1975, but remained quite inactive for the first one and a-half decades. It was only in 1992 that fresh initiatives were taken to establish a customs union and then a common market. It includes Benin, Burkina Faso, Cape Verde, Cote d'Ivoire Gambia, Ghana, Guinea, Guinea-Bissau, Liberia, Mali, Nigeria, Senegal, Sierra Leone, and Togo. Guinea and Niger were suspended, respectively, in 2008 and 2009. The group is striving to give a final shape to its integration scheme, but the low rate of economic development and other economic problems in these countries are hindering the process.

Besides ECOWAS, there are some other regional grouping schemes in Africa. They are the Afro-Malagasy Economic Union, the East Africa Customs Union, the West African Economic Community, the Maghreb Economic Community, the Organisation of African Unity, the Southern African Development Community, and so on. All of them face the same fate, with poor economic infrastructure and low rate of economic development marring their progress.

Gulf Cooperation Council (GCC): The GCC was formed in 1980 by Bahrain, Kuwait, Oman, Qatar, Saudi Arabia, and the United Arab Emirates as a defensive measure to counteract the expected threat from Iraq-Iran War. Its purpose was to deal with the regional groups of Europe such as EU and EFTA. It permits the citizens to move freely and own property freely within the region. It is more a political union than an economic union.

8.3.4 Economic Co-operation Schemes in Asia and Pacific

Association of South East Asian Nations (ASEAN): The ASEAN was formed in 1967 by Indonesia, Malaysia, the Philippines, Singapore, and Thailand. Brunei joined in 1984, Vietnam in 1995, Laos and Myanmar in 1997, and Cambodia in 1999. The group officially formed the ASEAN Free Trade Area in 1993. It was decided that the tariff on intra-region trade was to be cut to 5 per cent by 2007, although the poorer countries could take even more time. The main objective of this grouping is to promote economic, social, and cultural development and safeguard political and economic stability in the region. The financial crisis during late 1990s had dampened the spirit of the member countries towards cooperation, but the recovery has definitely helped this grouping to perform well and achieve its objectives.

Asia-Pacific Economic Co-operation (APEC): Formed in 1989, it now covers 21 countries of Asia and the Pacific region, namely, Australia, Brunei, Canada, Chile, China, Hong Kong, Indonesia, Japan, Malaysia, Mexico, New Zealand, Papua New Guinea, Philippines, Singapore, South Korea, Taiwan, Thailand and the United States of America. It expects to have free trade and investment by 2010, although the poorer countries may abide this norm by 2020. It has softened the restrictions on the movement of professionals in the region and has started simplifying custom procedures.

Association for South Asian Regional Co-operation (SAARC): The SAARC is a regional grouping scheme among seven South Asian countries, namely, Bangladesh, Bhutan, India, Maldives, Nepal, Pakistan, and Sri Lanka. The need for a economic cooperation scheme for this region had long been felt. As far back as in September 1978, the MargaInstitute of Colombo initiated discussions on the prospect of economic cooperation in this region. In 1980, the then President of Bangladesh, Zia-ur-Rahman proposed to hold a regional summit and circulated a paper to other member governments on the modalities for creating an institutional mechanism aiming at a common regional approach to international developmental issues and at removing regional disparities. The foreign secretaries of the seven countries met in Colombo in April 1981 and agreed on some basic principles of regional cooperation. They agreed to focus on matters of common interest, excluding from its ambit bilateral and contentious issues. A Study Group was set up for identifying the areas for possible cooperation. A long term programme of action was chalked out to assess the needs and resources, to prepare specific projects of regional nature, and to finalise the financing modalities.

The Heads of the seven States adopted the SAARC charter in Dhaka in December 1985, and the SAARC came into being with a secretariat at Kathmandu.

The second meeting of the Secretaries was held in Islamabad during August 1982. It endorsed the recommendations of the Study Group and resolved to ensure their speedy implementation. At the following three meetings in Dhaka and New Delhi, some preparatory steps were taken, leading to the meeting of the Foreign Ministers. The Foreign Ministers signed the Declaration on South Asian Regional Cooperation comprising the basic objectives and provisions for institutional and financial arrangements. On their recommendations, the Heads of the seven States adopted the SAARC charter in Dhaka in December 1985, and the SAARC came into being with a secretariat at Kathmandu.

At different annual summits, different issues related to economic development in the region were taken up and the necessary follow up actions were taken. In December 1995, the SAARC Preferential Trading Arrangement (SAPTA) became operational. During the first round of the SAPTA, the seven governments offered a consolidated schedule of 226 items for tariff concession. The depth of tariff cut ranged between 10 per cent and 100 per cent. At SAPTA II, which became effective from June 1997, the number of products involving tariff concession increased to 2013. At SAPTA III, which became operational from June 1999, concessions were multi-lateralised in all cases except those availed by the least developed countries of this region (Bangladesh, Bhutan, Maldives, and Nepal).

In January 2004, it was agreed that the South Asian Free Trade Area would function from 2006. A charter on social issues was signed and investment cooperation agreement was also signed.

The Ninth SAARC Summit held in Male during 1997 constituted the Group of Eminent Persons (GEP) for the purpose of a comprehensive appraisal of SAARC and to suggest measures to redress its functioning.

The GEP recommended, among other things, the creation of a South Asian Free Trade Area by 2008, a South Asian Customs Union by 2015, and a South Asian Economic Union by 2020. It also recommended, for the development of a common investment area, known as SAARC Investment Area, the establishment of the South Asian Development Bank; augmentation of the size of the South Asian Development Fund; coordination of the macroeconomic policies of the member governments, and many other plans for the socio-economic development of the region. However, the required political will is lacking owing to strained bilateral relations between some of the members. The 12th Summit of the SAARC, which was scheduled to be held in November 1999, was postponed sine die. Nevertheless, in January 2004, the SAARC Summit could be held in Islamabad, where some important decisions could be taken. The agreement on the South Asian Free Trade Area was concluded and it was agreed to implement it from 2006. A charter on social issues was also signed, which attempts inter alia to eradicate poverty from this region. Again, an investment cooperation agreement was signed, which should encourage intra-region investment in the near future.

The 13th Summit was held at Dhaka in November 2005 where poverty alleviation was stressed upon and the implementation of the SAFTA was ensured. The South Asian Free Trade Area (SAFTA) came into operation on the first day of 2006. The member countries have begun tariff reduction, which is expected to be complete within a decade. But it will not do much unless and until other problems relating to transportation, customs and infra-structure, etc. are sorted out. It is marked that over one thousand trucks are lined up at the Indo-Bangladesh border for four to five days simply for paper work. Indian goods take a sea-route to enter Pakistan. All this adds to the transportation cost. According to an UNCTAD estimate, the transaction cost in intra-SAARC trade is the highest in the world. It is around 15 per cent compared to only 3 per cent in ASEAN and EU. In fact, these are the reasons that the intra-region trade in South Asia is only 6 per cent of the total trade of the region compared to 70 per cent in Western Europe, 53 per cent in East Asia and Pacific, 40 per cent in North America, 18 per cent in Sub-Saharan Africa and 16 per cent in Latin America and Caribbean (Hindustan Times, 9.4.2007).

More recently, at the 14th SAARC Summit in New Delhi, the member countries agreed on a 25-point charter. The more important among them are establishment of a South Asian University, incorporation of trade in services into SAFTA, operation of a $ 300-million SAARC Development Fund, establishment of a telemedicine network, rationalisation of telecom tariff, taking up of basic issues, such as energy, food, environment, etc. Moreover, because Afghanistan is the eighth member of this regional grouping.

The 15th Summit held at Colombo in August 2008 resolved for initiating people-centric projects and for reviewing the SAARC Development

Goals by 2009. It also resolved for looking into the non-tariff barriers and para-tariff barriers so as to foster the objectives of the SAFTA.

SAARC: A Calendar of Events

1981 – Colombo	First formal meeting of the foreign secretaries of the region for venturing into institutionalised regional cooperation was held.
1983 – New Delhi	The second stage towards regional cooperation was marked with the convening of the meeting of the foreign secretaries. The Integrated Programme of Action (IPA) was launched here through the declaration of the South Asian Regional Cooperation (SARC).
1985 – Dhaka	The first SARC Summit was held and the heads of state or government decided to establish South Asian Association for Regional Cooperation (SAARC). For the first eight years of its existence, hardcore economic issues, such as trade, industry, money and finance were to be kept outside the scope of cooperation under SAARC.
1991 – Colombo	An Inter-Governmental Group (IGG) was set up to formulate an agreement to establish a SAARC Preferential Trading Agreement (SAPTA) by 1997.
1993 – Dhaka	The framework agreement on SAPTA was finalised. SAARC and UNCTAD signed a Memorandum of Understanding too.
1995 – New Delhi	SAPTA formally came into existence, well in advance of the date stipulated by the Colombo Summit. The SAPTA provided for a transition to a South Asian Free Trade Area (SAFTA). Earlier it was envisaged that SAFTA would be achieved by the year 2005. Three rounds of negotiations have taken place under SAPTA. In the last round of negotiations, a total of 3456 commodities were offered for tariff concessions.
1997 – Male	At the Summit, the heads of state or government decided to bring forward the date of achieving SAFTA to 2001.
1998 – Colombo	The tenth Summit decided that deeper tariff concessions should be extended to products which are being actively traded or are likely to be traded among members, in order to accelerate the progress in the next round of SAPTA negotiations.
2004 – Islamabad	Agreement on SAFTA, a charter on social issues and an investment co-operation agreement were signed.
2005 – Dhaka	Stress on Poverty alleviation and on the implementation of SAFTA.
2007 – New Delhi	Agreement on a 25-point programme.
2008 – Colombo	Taking up of people-centric projects and review of SAARC Development Goals by 2009. Resolution of NTBs and PTBs in order to make SAFTA more effective.

SUMMARY

- Trade and investment is also regulated at the regional level through the creation of regional economic cooperation/integration schemes. The economic integration may be of varying intensity/levels such as free trade area, customs union, common market, economic union, and political union.
- Regional integrative schemes make a definite impact on the intra-region trade and investment, although the impact varies slightly depending upon the nature and intensity of integration. Trade is created and diverted through inter-country and inter-commodity substitution. There are also dynamic benefits from regional integrative schemes such as widening of the size of the market, reaping of the economies of scale, etc. Building up of self-reliance among the member countries and increased foreign direct investment are the other benefits. However, if the different member countries are of varying economic strata, benefits may be polarised in favour of the well-off member countries leadings to intra-region inequality.
- Regional cooperation schemes are found almost in all parts of the globe. It was started in Europe during the 1950s. The European Union, including the European Monetary Union, is the biggest and the most important regional integrative scheme. These schemes have also been created in America, Africa and the Asia.

REVIEW QUESTIONS

1. Explain the different levels of regional economic integration.
2. Discuss some more important benefits and costs of regional economic grouping.
3. Comment on the recent developments in the European economic and monetary integration scheme.
4. Distinguish between trade creation and trade diversion as explained by Jacob Viner.

OBJECTIVE TYPE QUESTIONS

1. Mark True or False:
   (a) Trade creation and trade diversion, both, have beneficial welfare implications.
   (b) Regional partners should be competitive, and not complementary, for the purpose of most efficient use of economic resources within a customs union.
   (c) Gains from regional groupings can be maximised if the cost of producing a particular commodity is the same among different member countries.
   (d) In a customs union, imports are substituted by the goods produced within the union.

(e) Polarisation of benefits from regional grouping favours economically weak members.
(f) The European community came to be known as European Union after the Maastricht Treaty.
(g) EFTA was formed under the Stockholm Convention of May 1960.

2. Choose the Most Suitable Answer:
(a) The problem of trade deflection arises in:
 (i) Customs union alone
 (ii) Free trade area alone
 (iii) Both of the above
(b) The net benefit from trade creation and trade diversion, according to Meade, depends on:
 (i) Total volume of trade created or diverted
 (ii) The extent to which cost on each unit of newly created trade falls
 (iii) Both of the above
(c) Regional grouping encourages:
 (i) Inter-country substitution of goods
 (ii) Inter-commodity substitution of goods
 (iii) Both of the above
(d) Member countries that complement one another prefer to have:
 (i) Free trade area
 (ii) Customs union
 (iii) None of the above
(e) Tariff-jumping FDI in a regional grouping takes place when:
 (i) Foreign investors take advantage of high tariff wall on imports from a third country
 (ii) Foreign investors do not have pay tariff on the imports from the home country
 (iii) None of the above
(f) ASEAN was formed as a free trade area in:
 (i) 1967
 (ii) 1993
 (iii) 2003

CASE STUDY

SAPTA: Its Impact on Indo-Bangladesh Trade

SAPTA Concessions

It is true that Indo-Bangladesh trade agreement was signed as back as in March 1972 and a few subsequent agreements were signed between the two countries to boost up the trade, but it was the South Asian Preferential Trading Arrangement (SAPTA), signed under the aegis of SAARC in 1993 and implemented at the end of 1995 that provided a big fillip to the bilateral trade. Under the four rounds of negotiations held under SAPTA, India offered concessions on 2927 six-digit HSC products of which 2450 products were offered exclusively to Bangladesh and the other least developed countries (LDCs) of the region. To be precise, there were 62, 514 and 1,874 products in the first, second and the third rounds, respectively. On the other hand, Bangladesh offered concessions on 564 products to non-LDCs of this region that included India. Again, after continued request by Bangladesh, India offered it 100 per cent tariff concessions on 16 product groups consisting of 40 tariff lines during the trade review talks in April 2002. Duty-free access was announced also for items of other 39 tariff lines during March 2003. Now, the question is whether these tariff concessions have really helped augment Indo-Bangladesh trade.

Increase in the Size of Indo-Bangladesh Trade

Let us first have the annual figures of trade. As per the direction of trade statistics of the International Monetary Fund, the annual average of India's export to, and import from, Bangladesh stood respectively at $333.5 million and $20.5 million during the first ten years of the SAARC regime. On the contrary, during the ten-year period of SAPTA, beginning from 1996 to the end of 2005, the respective figures were as large as $1,138.4 million and $63.8 million. It simply means that during the SAPTA regime, India's export to Bangladesh increased by 241.4 per cent and its import from Bangladesh moved up by 211.2 per cent. The combined figure taking export and import both increased by 239.6 per cent.

The Commodity-wise Impact

The impact of SAPTA on the Indo-Bangladesh trade will be more revealing if one analyses the commodity-wise details. Let us first analyse the growth in India's overall import under different commodity categories between FY 1997–1998 and FY 2005–2006. The figures in Table 1 reveal that despite overall growth of 198 per cent, there were three commodity groups that showed negative growth in the range of 9.57 per cent and 90.58 per cent. These commodity groups represented wood pulp and paper, transport equipment and works of art and antiques. On the contrary, foodstuffs and beverages, vegetable products, mineral products, footwear and mechanical appliances presented phenomenal growth between 16,491 per cent and 4,240 per cent. In other cases, the increase was recorded between 19 per cent and 577 per cent.

Table 1: Commodity-wise Distribution of India's Imports from Bangladesh

Rs. million

Sec.	*Commodity Group*	*Chapters*	*Total Imports*		
			1997–98	2005–06	*% change*
1	2	3	4	5	6
I	Live Animals and Animal Products	01–05	391.85	467.29	19.25
II	Vegetable Products	06–14	1.53	129.78	8,382.35
III	Fats and Oils	15	-	107.88	
IV	Foodstuffs and Beverages	16–24	0.77	127.75	16,490.91
V	Mineral Products	25–27	1.14	70.31	6,067.54

VI	Chemicals and Allied Products	28–38	580.13	1,802.83	210.76
VII	Plastics and Rubber and their Products	39–40	12.46	84.32	576.72
VIII	Raw Hides and Skin and their Products	41–43	47.39	107.02	125.83
IX	Wood Articles	44–47	-	0.14	-
X	Wood Pulp and Paper	47–49	5.85	5.29	−9.57
XI	Textiles and Textile Products	50–63	797.87	2,289.01	186.89
XII	Footwear, Feathers and Artificial Flowers	64–67	0.20	8.68	4240
XIII	Articles of Stones, Glass Products	68–70	1.00	2.82	182
XIV	Pearls and Precious Stones	71	-	-	-
XV	Base Metals and Articles thereof	72–83	-	223.04	-
XVI	Machinery and Mechanical Appliances	84–85	3.21	172.85	5,284.73
XVII	Vehicles and Transport Equipment	86–89	3.01	0.95	−68.44
XVIII	Optical and Photographic Articles	90–92	-	0.22	-
XIX	Arms and Ammunitions	93	-	-	-
XX	Miscellaneous Manufactures	94–96	0.20	21.63	10715
XXI	Works of Art and Antiques	97–99	25.68	2.42	−90.58
	Total		1,888.45	5,624.01	197.81

Note: Difference of total is due to rounding off.
Source: Govt. of India, *Monthly Statistics of Foreign Trade of India*, Calcutta: DGCIS, March 1998 and March 2005.

On the side of India's export to Bangladesh, the commodity-wise picture is presented in Table 2. It is found that in three commodity groups comprising of chemicals and allied products, stone and glass products and pearls and precious stones, there was shrinkage in the trade value ranging between 41 per cent and 98 per cent. In other cases, the trade expanded on account of SAPTA measures. The increase was as meagre as 47 per cent in case of textiles and textile products but as large as 335 per cent in case of vegetable products.

Table 2: Section-wise Distribution of India's Exports to Bangladesh

Rs. in million

Section	Commodity Group	Chapters	Total exports		
			1997–98	2005–06	% Change
1	2	3	4	5	
I	Live Animals and Animal Products	01–05	-	761.85	-
II	Vegetable Products	06–14	4,553.83	19,822.90	335.30
III	Fats and Oils	15	26.31	110.84	321.28
IV	Foodstuffs Beverages	16–24	894.40	2,462.95	175.37
V	Mineral Products	25–27	2,472.75	8,145.59	229.41
VI	Chemicals and Allied Products	28–38	1,978.78	32.99	−98.33
VII	Plastics and Rubber and their Products	39–40	1,052.23	2,202.51	109.32
VIII	Raw Hides and Skin and their Products	41–43	-	23.49	
IX	Wood Articles	44–47	17.54	66.71	280.33
X	Wood Pulp and Paper	47–49	362.44	797.81	120.12
XI	Textiles and Textile Products	50–63	11,557.03	16,962.94	46.78
XII	Footwear, Feathers and Artificial Flowers	64–67	11.69	39.38	236.87
XIII	Articles of Stones, Glass Products	68–70	207.52	122.78	−40.83
XIV	Pearls and Precious Stones	71	38.00	13.31	−64.97
XV	Base Metals and Articles thereof	72–83	1,961.25	7,480.32	281.4
XVI	Machinery and Mechanical Appliances	84–85	-	4446.09	
XVII	Vehicles and Transport Equipment	86–89	1,294.83	3,545.23	173.80
XVIII	Optical and Photographic Articles	90–92	-	334.85	-
XIX	Arms and Ammunitions	93	-	-	-
XX	Miscellaneous Manufactures	94–96	52.61	234.63	345.98

XXI	Works of Art and Antiques	97–99	151.99	179.02	17.78
	Total		29,228.71	73,687.22	152.11

Note: Total may differ because of rounding off.
Source: Govt. of India, *Foreign Trade Statistics of India*, Calcutta: DGCIS, various issues.

Reduced Commodity Concentration

It is also very significant to analyse whether the grant of trade concessions has an impact of the commodity structure of trade. The impact is positive if the commodity concentration has reduced over the years. Measuring the commodity concentration based on the two-digit/section-wise commodity classification with the help of Gini coefficient of commodity concentration, it is found that during FYs 1997–2005, the commodity concentration of India's export to Bangladesh and also of India's import from Bangladesh has reduced respectively from 0.4487 to 0.3951 and from 0.5630 to 0.5292. It shows that the Indo-Bangladesh trade has diversified following preferential trading arrangement, but diversification in India's import from Bangladesh is only limited in view of not so broad-based economic activities there.

Thus, it is evident from the above analysis that the preferential trading arrangement under the aegis of SAARC has a definitive positive impact on the trade between India and Bangladesh.

QUESTIONS

1. What do you mean by preferential trading arrangement in a regional economic grouping?
2. What were the trade concessions under SAPTA?
3. Do you find a positive impact of SAPTA on Indo-Bangladesh trade? Explain.
4. Did SAPTA have an influence on the commodity concentration in Indo-Bangladesh trade?

References

Books

Balassa, B. (1962), *The Theory of Economic Integration* (London: George Allen & Unwin).

Dell, S. (1963), *Trade Blocs and Common Markets* (New York: Alfred A. Knopf).

Dosser, D. (1972), "Customs Unions, Tax Unions, Development Unions", in Bird, R. M. and J. G. Head (eds.), *Modern Fiscal Issues in Honour of Carl S. Shoup* (Toronto: Toronto University Press), pp. 86–104.

Edel, M. (1969), "Regional Integration and Income Redistribution: Complements and Substitutes" in Hilton, R. (*ed.*), *The Movement toward Latin American Unity* (New York: Praeger), pp. 185–202.

Meade, J. E. (1956), *The Theory of Customs Union* (Amsterdam: North Holland Publ. Co).

Mikesell, R.F. (1963),"The Theory of Common Market as applied to Regional Arrangements among Developing Countries" in Harrod, R.F. and D.C. Hague (*eds.*), *International Trade Theory in a Developing World* (London: Macmillan) pp. 205–29.

Scitovsky, T. (1958), *Economic Theory and Western European Integration* (London: George Allen & Unwin).

Shibata, H. (1967),"The Theory of Economic Unions, Free Trade Areas and Tax Unions" in Shoup G. (*ed.*), *Fiscal Harmonisation in Common Markets* (Columbia: Columbia University Press).

Strange, R. (1997),"Trading Blocs, Trade Liberalisation and Foreign Direct Investment", in Chryssochoidis, G. *et al* (*eds.*), *Internationalisation Strategies* (London: Macmillan) pp. 19–42.

Viner, J. (1950), *The Customs Union Issue* (London: Stevens).

Journals

Balassa, B. and A. Stoutjesdijk (1975),"Economic Integration among Developing Countries", *Journal of Common Market Studies*, XIV (1), 37–56.

Bhambri, R. S. (1962),"Customs Unions and Underdeveloped Countries", *Economia Internazionale*, XV (2), 235–58.

Bird, R. (1965),"The Need for Regional Policy in a Common Market", *Scottish Journal of Political Economy*, XII (2), 225–42.

Gehrels, F. (1956),"Customs Union from a Single Country Viewpoint", *Review of Economic Studies*, XXIV (1), 61–64.

Germanico Salgado Penaherrera (1980–81),"Viable Integration and Economic Co-operation Problems of the Developing World", *Journal of Common Market Studies*, XIX (2), 175–88.

Lipsey, R.G. (1960),"The Theory of Customs Union: A General Survey", *The Economic Journal*, LXX (2), 496–513.

Makower, H. and G. Morton (1953),"A Contribution towards a Theory of Customs Union", *The Economic Journal* LXIII (2), 33–39.

Samuelson, P. (1949),"International Factor Price Equalisation Once Again", *The Economic Journal*, LIX (233), 181–97.

Thorbecke, E. (1963),"European Economic Integration and the Pattern of World Trade", *American Economic Review*, LIII (Paper & Proceedings), 147–74.

Vaitsos, C.V. (1978),"Crisis in Regional Economic Co-operation (Integration) among Developing Countries: A Survey", *World Development*, VI (6), 719–69.

Select Further Readings

Robson, P. (1980), *The Economics of International Integration* (London: Allen & Unwin).

Tsoulakis, L. (1993), *The New European Economy* (Oxford: Oxford University Press).

Stoeckel, A. et al (1990), *Western Trade Blocs* (Canberra: Centre for International Economics).

* Indonesia is the world's largest LNG producer in 2005 and a leading LNG exporter. It had 97.8 trillion cubic feet (Tcf) of proven natural gas reserves as of January 2007. It produces LNG from it's Botang facility in Badak, East Kalimantan Indonesia. It's major exporters are Japan, South Korea and Taiwan.

Akihabara, Tokyo, Japan*

9

Political and Legal Environment

CHAPTER OBJECTIVES

The political and legal environment varies from one set of countries to the other. MNCs must be well acquainted with it for ensuring smooth operations. The present chapter attempts to:

- ✦ Explain the different forms of political and legal set-ups.
- ✦ Show how political and legal environment in the home country influences international business.
- ✦ Explain the nature of political risk MNCs often have to face in the host country.
- ✦ Describe how political risk is assessed.
- ✦ Explain how political risk is managed at the different stages of operation.
- ✦ Describe the move towards standardisation of legal issues across countries.

Besides the regulation of trade and investment at the national, regional and international levels, it is also the political and legal environment that plays a crucial role in international business. A firm cannot ignore the political situation and legal formalities existing either in the home country or in the host country if it has to operate successfully abroad. It is from this viewpoint that the present chapter discusses the various aspects of the politico-legal environment.

9.1 CONCEPT OF POLITICAL ENVIRONMENT

9.1.1 Political Diversity and Political Similarity

The political scenario in a country is the outcome of the interacting influence of various interest groups such as individual households, firms, politicians, bureaucrats, and many others. The stronger a particular interest group, the more prominent its ideology will manifest in the overall political scenario. In a country with federal character, where different interest groups are prominent at different levels, different ideologies exist side by side at the same juncture. The political scenario in different states may be different. Even at the centre, the political scenario may change with changes in the dominant interest group.

As opposed to diverse political environments in a particular country, a particular political ideology may be found in more than one country. It is because the ethnic background, language, religion, and so on bring many countries within the fold of one common political ideology. For example, it was the ethnic consideration that brought Serbs of the neighbouring regions into one political umbrella known as Greater Serbia. Thus, political environment is marked by, both, diversity and uniformity.

9.1.2 Democracy Versus Totalitarianism

A democratic political system involves citizens directly or indirectly, in the policy formulation of a country.

The political scenario often varies between the two extremes—democracy on the one hand and totalitarianism on the other. The purest form of democracy represents direct involvement of citizens in policy making. This is because, the democratic set-up is "of the people, for the people, and by the people". The Greeks experimented with pure democracy many centuries ago when all citizens participated freely in the political process. But with growing time and distance barriers over time, it did not remain feasible for all citizens to participate in the political process; and as a result, democracy turned into a representative democracy where only the elected representatives have a say in political decisions. Whatever may be the form of democracy, the people enjoy fundamental rights of various kinds of freedom and civil liberties. However, in parliamentary democracy, political decisions are influenced by widely varying interest groups. On the contrary, they are comparatively centralised in presidential democracy, although the head of the government is an elected representative.

Totalitarianism, at the other extreme, represents monopolisation of political power in the hands of an individual or a group of individuals with virtually no opposition. The policy is simply the dictates of the ruler. Constitutional guarantee are denied to the citizens. Germany under the rule of Adolf Hitler and Stalin's Soviet Union were historical examples of a totalitarian regime. Presently, Cambodia, China, Cuba, Democratic Republic of Congo, and Myanmar are examples of totalitarian governments.

Totalitarianism is a political system where political power lies in few hands with virtually no opposition.

Forms of Political Systems

- Democracy
  1. Parliamentary democracy
  2. Presidential democracy
- Totalitarian system
  1. Secular totalitarianism
  2. Theocratic totalitarianism
- Mixed political system with elements of both democracy and totalitarianism

Totalitarianism may represent either a theocratic government or a secular government. In the former, it is the religion that dictates the political philosophy. For example, Iran and a large part of Afghanistan controlled by pro-theocracy clergymen come under this group. On the contrary, in secular totalitarianism, political leaders rely either on military power or bureaucratic power. One form of secular totalitarianism is communism, which does not differentiate between the economic and the political bases of the government. It institutes a socialist economic system where the State owns and operates economic activities. East European countries set earlier an example of communism. The other form of secular totalitarianism is a tribal government when one ethnic group dominates the national identity. The other ethnic groups remain only silent spectators. Kenya, Burundi, Nigeria, and Rwanda are the examples of tribal totalitarianism.

In real life, neither the purest form of democracy nor the purest from of totalitarianism is found. In the United Kingdom and the United States of America which are emblems of democratic institutions, many restrictive political decisions are taken, while in China's communist regime, foreign investors play a free role in the special economic zones. It is, thus, the mixture of the two extremes in varying proportions that is found in different countries. Higher doses of democracy in the mixture make a country politically free. On the other hand, a higher proportion of totalitarian element in the mixture reduces freedom. Adrian Karatnycky (1995) surveys a large number of countries and groups and divides them into three categories, such as free, partly free and not free. The survey identifies

Australia, Bahamas, Belgium, Canada, Chile, and so on as free countries; Brazil, Burkina Faso, Cambodia, and so forth as partly free; and Algeria, China, North Korea, Nigeria, and some others as not free countries.

9.2 HOME COUNTRY PERSPECTIVE

It is true that firms move to a country with a stable political and less restrictive legal environment. So the political and legal environment prevailing in the host country is much more significant. But it does not mean that such an environment is not important in the home country. This is why the home-country perspective is dealt with first and then the host-country perspective will be discussed at greater length.

The political and legal environment in the home country may be encouraging. For example, the Indian government has announced incentives and has eased procedural formalities for the overseas operation of domestic firms. It has also encouraged export activities. If this is the home country environment, it will have a positive impact of the internationalisation of Indian firms.

Embargo is the complete prohibition of trade. Sanctions are not so broad in coverage but they also distort trade.

However, the political and legal environment in the home country is not always encouraging. It is often restrictive. The restrictions are manifest in various types of curbs on export and other forms of business. The extremely intense curb on export is manifest in the form of sanctions and embargo. Embargo is the complete prohibition of trade. Sanctions are not so broad in coverage as embargoes are, but they also distort trade in various ways, such as negation of trade financing or prohibition of high technology trade, and so on. Whatever the manifestation may be, the factor behind it is political and the purpose behind it is to compel the country in question to follow peace. Sanctions and embargoes are not very rare. There were as many as 46 between 1971 and 1983 (Hufbauer and Schott, 1984).

Sanctions and embargoes are not so frequent. More frequent are the *subtler forms of export restrictions*. A country puts certain items on the prohibited list of exports or the restricted list of exports. Such restrictions involve products that are important from the viewpoint of national security. However, the explanation of national security differs from one country to another. For example, German government feels that Patriot missile is made up of simple parts that can be exported (Czinkota, et al, 1999). Others may not think so.

It is not only trade. The home government, sometimes imposes restrictions on other forms of business too. In some countries, anti-trust laws are strictly implemented. The government does not allow national firms to move abroad if they lead to thwart competition. Again, some governments discourage their national firms from involving themselves in corruption and bribery in foreign countries. In some of the developing countries, foreign investment is approved in many cases where the bureaucrats or politicians demand some kind of benefit. If, in such cases, the home government does not allow the firms to be involved in bribery, international business is adversely affected (Elliot, 1997). Yet again, in some home countries, environmental protection is given the top priority, even if it is not so in the host country. In such cases, the home government does not allow the firms to move to such host countries. For example, the US government is against the cutting of forests for environmental reasons. But in Brazil, cutting of rain forest is allowed. In such cases, US firms cannot move to Brazil in this area of business. These are just some aspects of home country regulations. There are many more that affect international business.

9.3 HOST COUNTRY PERSPECTIVE

Firms moving abroad are well acquainted with the political and legal environment prevailing in the home country. But they are not necessarily in touch with those of the host country, particularly when different host countries have different environments. This is why there is always some risk involved in international business on account of differing political scenarios in host countries. This is known as political risk, which needs proper management for a successful international business operation. In other words, the study of political and legal environment in international business is essentially the study of political risk evaluation and management.

9.3.1 Meaning and Forms of Political Risk

> Political risk is unanticipated changes in political set-up in the host country leading to unexpected discontinuities that bring about changes in the very business environment.

Let us first explain what political risk is. There is no precise definition. However, in Thunell's view (1977), political risk is said to exist when sudden and unanticipated changes in political set-up in the host country lead to unexpected discontinuities that bring about changes in the very business environment and corporate performance. For example, if a rightist party wins election in the host country and the policy towards foreign investment turns liberal, it would create a positive impact on the operation of MNCs. On the other hand, if a left party comes to power in the host country, it will have a negative impact on the operation of MNCs. It is the negative impact that is normally the focus of attention of transnational investors.

For a long period, political risk was narrowly interpreted in terms of expropriation of assets. But for the past few decades, the coverage of political risk has come to be wider, also including risk from ethnic, racial, religious or civil strife, political corruption, and blackmail. Czinkota (1999) classifies political risk as (1) ownership risk, (2) operating risk and (3) transfer risk. Ownership risk exposes property and life. Operating risk includes interference of the host government with the ongoing operations of the firm. Transfer risk concerns the transfer of funds, either to home country or to any other country. Stephen Kobrin (1982) classifies political risk as:

1. Macro risk or country-specific risk, and
2. Micro risk or firm-specific risk.

The macro political risk affecting all foreign firms in a country emerges on account of expropriation, ethnic and other strife, currency inconvertibility, refusal of debt, and so on. The micro political risk affecting a particular industry or firm emerges on account of conflict between the bonafide objectives of the host government and the operation of the MNC or on account of corruption, which has become a way of life in many countries. Some of the forms of political risk are explained here.

Expropriation: Expropriation means seizure of private property by the government. Confiscation is similar to expropriation, but the difference between the two is that while expropriation involves payment of compensation, confiscation does not involve such payments. International law provides protection to foreigners' property. It provides for compensation in case of unavoidable seizure. But the process of compensation is often lengthy and cumbersome. The firm usually requires going-concern value tied to the present value of lost future cash flows. On the other hand, the government prefers depreciated historical book value, which is lower in the eyes of the firm.

Expropriation and Confiscation refer to seizure of private property by government. Expropriation involves payment of compensation while confiscation does not.

The reason behind expropriation has mainly been political turmoil or specific political ideology. In the post-war period, foreign and domestic firms were nationalised in China and Eastern Europe after the imposition of communist regime. The same factor was responsible for nationalisation of private sector firms in Cuba in 1960. However, it is sometimes economic compulsion motivating expropriation. The Swedish government nationalised the ship-building industry at a time when this industry was hit hard by worldwide recession (Walters and Monsen, 1981). An estimate reveals that around 12 per cent of all foreign investment made in 1967 was nationalised within less than a decade (Jodice, 1980).

There are still subtler forms of expropriation. For example, when Colonel Qadaffi headed Libya in 1969, wages were increased as well as taxes were revised upwards. Bank accounts of ESSO were seized and the government acquired majority interest in the foreign enterprise (Schnitzer, et al, 1985).

Host government enacts law prohibiting foreign companies from taking their money out of the country.

Currency Inconvertibility: Sometimes the host government enacts law prohibiting foreign companies from taking their money out of the country or from exchanging the host country currency for any other currency. This is a financial form of political risk. The reasons are both economic and political. Economic factors are concerned with the balance of payments problem. The political factor manifests in drastic changes in the internal politics of the country. The Government of Nigeria imposed such restrictions a couple of decades back in order to serve its economic and political objectives.

Refusal to honour a financial contract with a foreign company is credit risk.

Credit Risk: Refusal to honour a financial contract with a foreign company or to honour foreign debt comes under this form of political risk. The reason is sometimes economic, like when Mexico expressed its inability to repay its debt in the early 1980s. But sometimes the political reasons are more prominent. When Khomeini came to power in Iran, the Iranian government refused to pay its debt on grounds that loans were taken during Shah's regime (Micallef, 1981).

Risk from Ethnic, Religious, or Civil Strife: Macro political risk arises on account of war and violence and racial, ethnic, religious, or civil strife within a country. Recent examples of such risks are slaughter in Bosnia and Herzegovina, break-down of local authority in Somalia and Rwanda, the upsurge of Islamic fundamentalism in Algeria and Egypt, and many more. Such developments become major political risks for MNCs operating in these countries.

Conflict of Interest: The interest of MNCs is normally different from the interest of the host government. The former manifests in the maximisation of corporate wealth, while the latter is evident in the welfare of the economy, in general, and of the citizens of a constituency, in particular. It is the conflicting interest that gives rise to micro political risk. To elaborate on the nature of conflict, it may be said that the host government desires to have a sustainable growth rate, price stability, comfortable balance of payments, and so on, but the policy of MNCs operating there is sometimes found interfering with the smooth implementation of the policy. For example, transfer of funds by MNCs may influence the money supply and may cause inflation or deflation. MNCs may adopt transfer pricing techniques that may cause loss of tax revenue. Similarly, the payment of exorbitant amount of royalty, and other such dues by the subsidiary may worsen the balance of payments.

It is not simply the economic issues that are the source of conflict. There are also non-economic issues such as national security, and so on. The US government did not permit the Japanese purchase of Fairchild Industries on the grounds of national security.

Corruption: Corruption is endemic in many host countries, as a result of which MNCs have to face serious problems. McNulty (1994) gives an example of Cambodia, where greedy bureaucrats created problems for foreign firms. Foreign firms in Kenya had to sell a part of the equity to powerful politicians there (Eiteman, 1995). Transparency International has surveyed 85 countries and has brought out the Corruption Perception Index. Many countries rank high on this index. This is perhaps the reason that in February 1999, 34 countries, including the OECD members, and five others signed a convention to ban bribery of foreign public officials in international business transactions (The Economic Times, 1999).

> OECD members, and five others signed a convention to ban bribery of foreign public officials in international business transactions.

9.3.2 Evaluation of Political Risk

Assessment of political risk is an important step before a firm moves abroad. It is because if such risks are very high, the firm would not like to operate in that country. If the risk is moderate or low, the firm will operate in that country, but with a suitable political-risk management strategy.

But any such strategy cannot be formulated until one assesses the magnitude of political risk. The ways of assessment may be either qualitative or quantitative.

Qualitative approaches involve inter-personal contact. Persons may come from within the enterprise or may come from outside the firm.

Qualitative Approach: Qualitative approaches involve inter-personal contact. Persons are often available who are well acquainted with the political structure of a particular country or region. They may come from within the enterprise, particularly those who are posted in that area. They may come from outside the firm—from academic institutions or from foreign offices of the government or from the field of journalism, especially correspondents in that area. Despite the fact that different persons present different versions of the same fact, this approach has become common. Kraar (1980) has cited the example of Gulf Oil, which hired persons in government and from universities to find out whether investment in Angola would be safe. The experts said "yes" and the investment turned out to be a successful venture even in the Angolan Marxist regime.

Sometimes a company sends a team of experts for on-the-spot study of the political situation in a particular country. This step is taken only after a preparatory study yields a favourable feature. This method gives a more reliable picture but it is always subject to availability of correct information from the local people in the host country.

The qualitative approach also involves the examination and interpretation of diverse secondary facts and figures. Future trends are assessed based on the past trends of events (Kramer, 1981). For this purpose, companies maintain an exclusive risk analysis division. Exxon is a case in point that developed relation with specific influence groups such as politicians, labour unions, and the military that influence the political stability of the country (Schnitzer, 1985).

Quantitative Models of Political Risk: Quantitative tools are also used to estimate political risk. American Can uses a computer programme known as primary risk investment screening matrix involving about 200 variables and reducing them to two numbers. It represents an index of economic viability as also an index of political stability. The variables include, in general, frequency of changes in government, level of violence in the country, number of armed insurrections, conflicts with other nations, and economic factors such as inflation rate, external balance deficit, growth rate of the economy, and so on.

Robert Stobaugh (1969) uses a decision-tree approach to find out the probability of nationalisation. He begins his analysis from the very contention whether there will be change in the government. If there is change, the new government may or may not opt for nationalisation. If it does opt for nationalisation, the question of whether it will pay adequate compensation arises. Thus, in each possible event, there are many possible sub-events. Probabilities of the events occurring are indicated along the tree branches. Probabilities are multiplied along the branches and then they are summed up.

Example: There is 50 per cent probability of change in government and 50 per cent probability for no change in government. If the government changes, there is 40 per cent probability for nationalisation and 60 per cent probability for no nationalisation. Again, if there is nationalisation, there is 60 per cent probability for adequate compensation and 40 per cent probability for inadequate compensation. With these figures, the probability of nationalisation without adequate compensation would be:

$$0.5 \times 0.4 \times 0.4 = 0.08.$$

Harald Knudsen (1974) uses comparatively measurable variables and not very subjective ones. Notable among his variables are the: degree of urbanisation, literacy rate, degree of labour unionism, national resource endowment, infant survival rate, calorie intake, access to civic amenities, per capita GNP, and so on. Basing on these variables, he measures the national propensity to expropriate. It is found that Knudsen's measure successfully identified nationalisation in some Latin American countries.

Haner (1979) uses a scale beginning from zero to seven in order to rate political risk. He groups the factors leading to political risk into two parts—internal and external. Internal factors are: (1) fractionalisation of the political spectrum, (2) fractionalisation of the social spectrum, (3) restrictive measures required to retain power, (4) xenophobia, (5) socio-economic conditions, (6) strength of radical left government. Similarly, the external factors are: (1) dependence on a hostile major power, and (2) negative influence of regional political forces.

After adding up the rating points, if the total is 19 or below, Haner is of the view that the political risk is only minimal. If the total lies between 20 and 34, the risk may be acceptable. If the total lies between 35 and 44, the risk is suppose to be very high. Lastly, if the total exceeds 44 rating points, it is not advisable to invest in that country.

Again, Euromoney (1993) takes into account three types of indicators for rating. The first is the economic indicator, which comprises the debt service ratio, current account deficit/GNP ratio, and external debt/GNP ratio. This indicator has 40 per cent weight. The second indicator is known as the credit indicator, which embraces debt service record and ease of rescheduling. It has 20 per cent weight. The third is known as market indicator, which has a 40 per cent weight. It includes access to bond market, sell down of short term papers, and access to forfeiting market.

The Euromoney formula ranks countries from the highest risk to the lowest risk. The ranking is formulated as follows: the highest figure in each category receives full marks for weighting. On the other hand, the lowest receives zero. The scores for other figures are calculated proportionately, according to the following formula:

$$\text{Final score} = \frac{\text{Weighting}}{(\text{Maximum Figure} - \text{Minimum Figure})} \times (\text{Intermediate Figure} - \text{Minimum Figure})$$

Simon (1982) provides a predictive analysis, which he calls an early warning system. The technique involves the selection of lead indicators that would presage the emergence of a particular political risk. For example, continued demonstration and riots may lead to internal disorder and to overthrow of the government. The early warning may be country-specific or industry-specific. In both the cases, the lead indicators are monitored and the results are communicated to the management for evolving adequate strategy.

There are some other rating methods. However, MNCs should not rely heavily on these ratings. It is because the ratings do not include an in-depth analysis necessary for investment decision. Individual countries must be assessed in details.

9.3.3 Management of Political Risk

Primarily, as Gregory (1989) feels, there are two approaches to political risk management. While one is known as defensive approach, the other is known as integrative approach. The former aims to protect and preserve the firm's strength through reducing its dependence on a single subsidiary. Borrowing from the host country sources or obtaining guarantee from the host government, minimising the role of host country nationals in the management, concentrating on R&D in the home country, maintaining a single global trademark are some of the steps related to the defensive approach. On the contrary, the aim of the integrative approach is to make the foreign unit an integral part of the host country. Employment in large measure of local personnel, developing proximity with the political elite, use of local distributors and professionals are some of the steps of the integrative approach.

The experience shows that majority of the international companies adopt a mix of the two approaches in varying proportions. While a global firm emphasises on the defensive approach, a multi-domestic company adopts more of an integrative approach.

The political risk management strategy depends upon the type of risk and the degree of risk the investment carries. It also depends upon the timing of the steps taken. For example, the strategy will be different if it is adopted prior to investment from that adopted during the life of the project. Again, it will be different if it is adopted after expropriation of assets.

Management Prior to Investment: Investment will prove a viable venture if political risk is managed from the very beginning—even before the investment is made in a foreign land. At this stage, there are five ways to manage it.

1. In the first method, the factor of political risk is included in the very process of **capital budgeting**, and the discount rate is in-

creased. But the problem is that it penalises the flows in the earlier years of operation, whereas the risk is more pronounced in the later years.

2. The risk can be reduced through **reducing the investment flow** from the parent to the subsidiary and filling the gap through local borrowing in the host country. In this strategy, it is possible that the firm may not get the cheapest fund, but the risk will be reduced. The firm will have to make a trade-off between higher financing cost and lower political risk.
3. Can political risk also be reduced by negotiating **agreements with the host government?** If the investing company undergoes an agreement with the host government over different issues prior to making any investment, the latter shall be bound by that agreement. Ordinarily, it will not back out from the agreement.
4. **Planned divestment** is yet another method of reducing risk. If the company plans an orderly shifting of ownership and control of business to the local shareholders and it implements the plan, the risk of expropriation will be the minimal. In fact, the very plan is negotiated with the host government at the very beginning of investment.

Planned divestment refers to gradual shifting of ownership of company to local shareholders.

5. Political risk can also be reduced by the **insurance of risk.** The investing firm can be insured against political risk. Insurance can be purchased from governmental agencies, private financial service organisations, or from private property-centred insurers. The programmes for insurance are either multilateral or bilateral in character. The Foreign Credit Insurance Association and Overseas Private Insurance Corporation are bilateral agencies located in the United States of America.

At the multilateral level, it is the Multilateral Investment Guarantee Agency (MIGA), set up in 1988 as a sister unit of the World Bank that covers the non-commercial risk. MIGA insures *eligible projects* against losses relating to *currency transfer restrictions, expropriation, war and civil disturbance* and *breach of contract*. It resolves potential investment disputes before they reach claim status. Its guarantee helps investors to obtain project finance from banks.

Since 1997, MIGA has successfully used reinsurance to leverage its guarantee capacity, manage the risk profile of its portfolio and foster the growth of the private political risk insurance market. Whenever a project exceeds MIGA's own capacity, it reinsures itself, through a *syndication process*, with private and public sector (re)insurance companies in order to meet its clients' needs. MIGA's main programs are facultative reinsurance and the *cooperative underwriting program* (CUP). So far, MIGA has attracted more than $2 billion in capacity through facultative reinsurance and $0.6 billion in capacity through the CUP. Besides, MIGA provides technical assistance to projects to help them come up to the investors' requirements.

Beginning from 1990 to the end of June 2009, 952 guarantee contracts were signed by MIGA that covered 99 countries and that involved $20.9 billion. The trend in the recent years is shown in Table 9.1.

Table 9.1 Guarantee Contracts Issued by MIGA: 2005–2009

Year	*No. of Guarantees*	*Projects Covered*	*Amount of Guarantee ($ bill)*	*Gross Exposure ($ bill)*
2005	62	41	1.2	5.1
2006	46	41	1.3	5.4
2007	45	29	1.4	5.3
2008	38	21	2.1	6.5
2009	30	26	2.4	7.3

Source: Based on MIGA Annual Report: 2009

Risk Management during the Life Time of the Project: Management of risk during the pre-investment phase lessens the intensity of risk, but does not eliminate it. So the risk management process continues even when the project is in operation. There are four ways to handle the risk in this phase.

> In case of concession agreements, the government of the host country retains ownership of the property and grants lease to the producer.

1. The first method is the **joint venture and concession agreement.** In a joint venture agreement, the participant are local shareholders who have political power to pressurise the government to take a decision in their favour or in favour of the enterprise. In case of concession agreements that are found mainly in mineral exploration, the government of the host country retains ownership of the property and grants lease to the producer. The government is interested in earning from the venture and so it does not cancel the agreement. However, this is not a permanent solution. When the technology becomes standardised, the host government often cancels the agreement. Again, if a new government is formed, there is every possibility of the cancellation of agreements concluded under the previous regime.
2. Risk can also be managed with **political support.** International companies sometimes act as a medium through which the host government fulfils its political needs. As long as political support is provided by the home country government, the assets of the investing company are safe. However, such a relationship may change and the political alliance may be disturbed when a new government is formed.

> **Structured operating environment** creating a linkage of dependency between the operation of the firm in high risk country and the operation of other units of the same firm in other countries.

3. The third method is through a **structured operating environment.** Political risk can be reduced by creating a linkage of dependency between the operation of the firm in high risk country and the operation of other units of the same firm in other countries. If the unit in a high risk country is dependent on its sister units in other countries for the supply of technology or raw material or for marketing of its products, the former

is normally not nationalised so long as dependency is maintained. It is because the high risk unit will not be in a position to operate without the imported technology or raw material. In fact, this was an important reason for the fearless operation of international oil companies in the Middle East for a long time. But, when the host governments in the Middle East came to possess the necessary skill, many of the oil companies were nationalised.

4. **Anticipatory planning** is also useful tool in risk management. It is a fact that the investing company takes necessary precautions against the political risk prior to the investment or after the investment. But it is of utmost significance that it should plan the measures to be taken quite in advance. Gonzalez and Villanueva (1992) call it crisis planning. They give an example of the Philippines during the Marcos' regime. Years before the 1986 revolution, the foreign companies began to foresee the fall of Marcos regime. They began assessing every move of the opposition in the country and they took necessary measures well in advance.

Risk Management Following Nationalisation: Despite care taken by the international firms for minimising the impact of political risk, there are occasions when nationalisation takes place. In such cases, the investing company tries to minimise the effects of such a drastic measure. There are many ways to do it.

1. The investing company **negotiates** with the host government on various issues and shows its willingness to support the policy and programmes of the latter. Sometimes the investing company foregoes majority control in order to please the host government (Hoskins, 1970).
2. On failure of negotiation with the host government, the investing company tries to put **political and economic pressure.** Embargo on trade is one of the examples. But there are occasions when such pressures deepen the rift. Thus, firms should be cautious before taking such measures.
3. If nationalisation is not reversed through negotiation and politico-economic pressure, the firm goes for **arbitration**. It involves the help of a neutral third party who mediates and asks for the payment of compensation. But there are cases when the host government does not honour the verdict of the arbitrator.
4. When arbitration fails, the only way out is to **approach the court of law**. The international law suggests that the company has, first of all, to seek justice in the host country itself. If it is not satisfied with the judgement of the court, the company can go to the international court of justice for fixation of adequate compensation. However, there are occasions when the host government has failed to honour the verdict of the court. For example, the Cuban Government failed to pay compensation to US companies expropriated during 1959–1961 (Globerman, 1986).

9.4 LEGAL ENVIRONMENT

9.4.1 Legal System

A country's legal system, which embraces its law and regulations, is closely related to its political system. For example, in a totalitarian political set up, the laws favour state ownership of industries. In a free political set up, on the other hand, laws tend to encourage private initiatives. Again, in free countries, laws are quite independent of political control, while they are a part of the political policy in totalitarian or semi-totalitarian regimes. In other words, political environment shapes the legal environment and legal environment influences international business. The strategy of a firm will be different in a country with no restrictive regulations as compared to that in a country with too many restrictive regulations.

Civil Law is a system of law where rules and regulations are written in detail.

Common Law is a law based largely on interpretation, tradition and precedence.

Theocratic Law is a law based primarily on religious preaching.

On the global level, there are broadly three types of legal systems. The first is known as civil law, which had originated in Rome as far back as in the 5th century BC. It is marked with a detailed set of written rules and regulations, with the result that there is seldom any interpretation of the law by the court. Civil law is usually found in Central and South America, some West European countries and some Asian and African countries.

The second is known as the common law, which originated in England as back as in the 11th century. In this case, there is ample scope for the interpretation of law by the court. The interpretation is based on tradition and precedence. And so, a particular law can be interpreted in different ways in different cases. If the interpretation is novel, it can set precedence for subsequent similar cases. In this way, this legal system is more flexible than civil law. Common law is found usually in the United Kingdom, the United States of America, Australia, Canada, and in some parts of Asia and Africa.

The third is the theocratic legal system. In this case, law is based on religious teachings. The most important example of theocratic law is Islamic law, which is based on the Koran or the sayings of Prophet Mohammad. Islamic law was initially a guiding factor for ethical behaviour, but subsequently it was extended to commercial transactions. Under this law, a bank cannot demand interest on its loan, nor it can pay interest on deposits. So it will be difficult for international banks to operate in countries adopting Islamic law.

9.4.2 Principles of International Business Law

The international business law embraces the law of different countries as well as the bilateral and multilateral treaties and conventions. The principles governing international business law are as follows:

1. Rules of sovereignty and sovereign immunity
2. Rules related to international jurisdiction

3. Doctrine of comity
4. Rules related to aliens

Sovereignty of state means that every state has complete freedom and power to govern. Sovereign immunity means that the court of a particular country does not have the jurisdiction to settle dispute and impose punishment in any other country. If the government of a country expropriates the property of a foreign company, it cannot be questioned in the courts of the home country, although there can be negotiation between the company and the host government.

However, there are some exceptions under the concept of international jurisdiction. It involves the nationality principle as per which an Indian manager involved in corrupt practices abroad can be tried in India. Moreover, under the concept of protection, every country has jurisdiction over any kind of behaviour that entails upon national security, even if such conduct is committed abroad or by a foreign citizen.

The doctrine of comity states that each country should have respect for the other country's law. In fact, it is a normal custom that different countries and governments maintain. Again, a government can refuse to admit foreign citizens and can limit the area for their conduct. The government has the right to deport them. Thus, equality between a domestic citizen and a foreign citizen cannot be presumed under the international law.

9.4.3 Wide Variance in National Business Laws and the Issue of Legal Standardisation

There are many areas where the national business law differs widely and that causes irk to the international business managers. To mention a few of them, for example, the provisions of anti-trust law differ widely from one country to the other. Again, the financial laws vary widely. There are cases where the majority of the assets of a company lie in one country but a large share of the liabilities is related to some other country. If the law of the two countries differs, there will be a serious problem for the company while managing liquidation. Yet again, there may be trade disputes depending upon different rules followed in different countries. Similarly, MNCs find it difficult to protect intellectual property rights in a country where the laws are implemented loosely.

However, these problems can be controlled with the standardisation of legal issue across countries. Such efforts are afoot, although it is a very lengthy process and moreover, the political and the business environment in different countries are different with the result that many governments may not reach a consensus. Sometimes legal issues of global importance are dealt with differently in different countries, and they have an adverse impact on international business. This is why some international or the regional agencies are trying to bring about standardisation or uniformity with regard to such issues in respect of them. The WTO has made a move in this regard. The European Union too has brought about standardisation of some of the legal issues among member countries. Two of the more important of these legal issues are intellectual property rights and taxation.

Intellectual Property Rights: Intellectual property is a property that is the outcome of the people's intellectual talent and abilities, for example, specific designs, formula, and so forth. Since this type of property helps generate income, those developing the designs and formula need some sort of protection under the law so that they are able to generate income over a long period of time.

Intellectual property that embraces industrial property and copyrights, is protected through patents and trademark.

Intellectual property embraces industrial property and copyrights. Industrial property stands protected under the Paris Convention, to which around 100 countries are the signatories. It is normally protected through patents and trademarks. A patent is a sort of protection granted to the inventor of the product or the process that does not allow others to make use of such inventions. Trademark is a symbol that differentiates a product from similar products. So long as the symbol is there, the product continues to remain differentiated. Similarly, copyrights are related to published material and they protect the publication from being copied.

There are laws for patents and trademarks in many countries, but in most of the cases, they are very liberal and so ineffective. Wild et al (2000) have mentioned how these laws are broken in a number of countries. In their opinion, illegal copies of software accounted for 27 per cent of the US domestic market, for 96 per cent of the Chinese market, and for 99 per cent in Ukraine. Thus, in order to provide effective protection to intellectual property rights and to encourage international firms to operate overseas, the WTO has made an attempt to standardise such laws. Under the Agreement on Trade Related Aspects of Intellectual Property Rights (TRIPS), this international organisation has set minimum standards of protection that each member nation has to provide. It grants patents for a period of twenty years, which begins from the date of filing of patent application with the country's patent authorities.

Taxation: Taxation is another aspect where efforts are afoot to standardise rates. International firms move to a country where, among other things, the tax rate is low. In case the tax rate is high, these firms adopt transfer pricing in order to siphon off the before-tax profits to a country where tax rate is low. Alternatively, they transfer their dividends to be received from subsidiaries to tax haven countries. All this may be in the interest of the firm, but certainly has a negetive affect on the interests of the host country government or the home country government. Sometimes it becomes the bone of contention between the government and the firm, which has an adverse impact on foreign investment. Thus, in order to avoid these malpractices, the Organisation of Economic Cooperation and Development (OECD) has requested the government of the tax haven countries to equate the tax rate with that prevailing in the OECD countries.

SUMMARY

- The political and legal environment are important factors that influence international business, especially when they are different between the home country and the host country. Political set up vary widely between the two extremes—democracy on the one hand and totalitarianism on the other. The existence of civil rights and fundamental rights is seen in democracy, while totalitarianism represents monopolisation of political power. Normally, different countries are found blending the features of these two extremes.
- Again, the legal system is largely dependent on the political set up. In a free political set up, private initiatives are encouraged, while state ownership is common in totalitarian system. The legal system is based on civil law, common law, or on religious laws.
- When the home country has a liberal legal syatem, trade and investment find least restrictions. In a restrictive legal system there are curbs on trade and investment. There are different modes of restrictions, beginning from embargo and sanctions to less restrictive modes.
- The host's country legal and political system is normally not fully known to international investors and so there is always some amount of political risk prevailing in the host country. The risk may be of micro or macro nature, manifesting in expropriation of assets, currency inconvertibility, credit risk, risk of ethnic and religious strife, corruption, and so on. The first step is, therefore, to evaluate such risks either qualitatively or quantitatively or both.
- If political risk exists, it needs proper management. It can be managed even before making investment through its incorporation in the capital budgeting technique, negotiations, planned divestment, insurance, and so on. During the life time of the project, it can be managed through anticipatory planning, economic and political support, structured operating environment, and so forth. If the assets are expropriated even thereafter, various steps such as negotiation, arbitration, and in and out-of-court settlement may be taken.
- Again, for making the legal system smooth, standardisation of legal issues can be attempted. A few international institutions have taken up this matter.

REVIEW QUESTIONS

1. How is a totalitarian political set up different from a democratic political set up?
2. Explain the different types of legal system.
3. How does the home country government restrict international business?

4. What is political risk? How is it assessed? What are the different modes of its management?
5. Comment on the standardisation of legal issues.

Objective Type Questions

1. Mark True or False:
   (a) Political ideology may be the same among countries with a common ethnic background.
   (b) In a presidential democracy, widely varying interest groups influence the decision.
   (c) Totalitarian government may be theocratic government.
   (d) Secular totalitarianism may be likened with communism.
   (e) Laws are independent of political control in a totalitarian country.
   (f) Common Law originated in Rome has ample scope for interpretation.
   (g) Theocratic legal system, originated in England often encourages the operation of international banking system.
   (h) Political risk does not include political corruption and blackmail.
   (i) There may be qualitative and quantitative evaluation of political risk.
   (j) The WTO has moved towards standardisation of legal issues.
   (k) The laws regarding patents and trademark are ineffective in many countries.
   (l) There are cases when governments do not abide by the rulings of International Court of Justice.
2. Choose the Most Suitable Answer:
   (a) There is greater scope for the interpretation of law in the:
      (i) Theocratic legal system
      (ii) Civil law system
      (iii) Common law system
   (b) The management of political risk prior to investment means:
      (i) Inclusion of risk factor in capital budgeting
      (ii) Anticipatory planning
      (iii) Arbitration
   (c) Political risk following nationalisation means:
      (i) Planned divestment
      (ii) Insurance of risk
      (iii) Arbitration
   (d) Quantitative evaluation of political risk covers:
      (i) A team of experts for on-the-spot study
      (ii) Primary risk investment screening matrix
      (iii) None of the above
   (e) Monopolisation of political power is found in case of:
      (i) A democratic government
      (ii) A totalitarian government
      (iii) Both of the above

Study Topic

Corruption in International Business

Corruption is simply unethical. It is also treated as a form of political risk related to international business. There are thousands of corruption cases reported in the newspaper. As reported, the senior officials of a global giant automobile company had sought to profit through having undisclosed shareholding in an Angolan company. Similarly, money was reported to have flowed into the hands of some middlemen in India for a comfortable location of the plant of the same automobile company. Some fabulous parties were arranged costing $1.1 million and they were shown as the company's expenditure. These are the events related to a single company. Many such examples are found. Now, the question is how does bribing affect the home country or the host country. The host country does not get the best possible technology because bribing helps the inferior technology to flow to it. The competitors in the home country do not get the contract if they do not bribe. A survey has been made by Control Risks Group Limited alongwith Simmons and Simmons which reveals that over 40 per cent of the 350 multinational corporations in the sample did express such views. Again, bribe helps to raise the cost of the project, as it is found in the survey, the magnitude of the bribe varies from 5 per cent to 25 per cent of the project cost. In construction, it was estimated at 29 per cent.

The issue is not confined to a particular country/company or to a particular sector. Hong Kong companies, as reported in the survey, were on the top. Over three-fourths of the respondents expressed such views. Again, bribing is found common in construction, pharmaceuticals, financial services, etc. Even defence sector has not remained untouched.

Again, the question is whether the international companies are really concerned about such practices. On one extreme, there is a belief that corruption should thoroughly be investigated, authorities should be informed and appropriate punishment should be prescribed. Some of the Dutch companies were found pulling out of their proposed investment because bribe, they thought, would tarnish their image. But, on the other extreme, there are views that corruption is a part of business and there should be no problem, especially when the authorities themselves are involved in such practices.

If corruption is unethical, there should be enactment to control it. In almost all the countries, there are laws that deal with corruption cases and that prescribe punishment. But the problem is that majority of the senior officials of the companies are not fully aware of such laws. The governmental machinery in many countries is too weak to curb corruption. In many countries, the government does not review the legal mechanism and no effort is made to make it more stringent. In many cases, the law becomes ineffective because the bribing company proceeds through a middleman. The company simply denies the charges.

However, corruption can be curbed through effective management practices. Some of the companies maintain a code to avoid bribing. Such codes are common among the companies headquartered in the USA, the UK, the Netherlands and Germany.

Secondly, a large number of companies have initiated training programmes for the managers. They are trained about ethical behaviour. The US companies are very serious about the training programme.

Thirdly, a practice is followed among some companies that requires senior managers to sign periodically a formal statement that are not indulged in corruption and such other bad practices.

Fourthly, many companies verify the integrity of the middlemen through whom they proceed for a contract. Such practices are now common with the companies of the USA and the western world.

Nevertheless, the survey reveals that despite efforts limiting corruption, around one-third of the respondents in the sample believed that corruption cases would increase.

QUESTIONS

1. How does bribing affect the interest of the host country?
2. Why are laws not very effective in controlling corruption cases?
3. Describe some of the measures that are followed to curb corruption.

Source: Based on Deutsche Press Release, 11.11.2005 and International Business Attitudes to Corruption Survey: 2006.

REFERENCES

Books

Czinkota, M. R. *et al* (1999), *International Business* (New York: Harcourt Brace).

Eiteman, D. K., *et al* (1995), *Multinational Business Finance* (Readings Mass.:Addison-Wesley), Chap. 18.

Elliot, K. A. ed. (1997), *Corruption and the Global Economy,* Washington D.C.: Institute for International Economics.

Euromoney (1993), *The Euromoney Country Risk Method,* London, September.

Globerman, S. (1986), *Fundamentals of International Business Management* (Singapore: Prentice-Hall), p. 131.

Gregory, A. (1989), "Political Risk Management" in A. Rugman (ed.), International Business in Canada, pp. 301–29 (Scarborough: Prentice-Hall).

Hufbauer, G. C. and J. J. Schott (1984),"Economic Sanctions: An Often Used and Occasionally Effective Tool of Foreign Policy"in M. R. Czinkota (*ed.*), *Export Controls* (New York: Praeger), pp. 18–33.

Karatnycky, A. (1995), *Freedom in the World* (New York: Freedom House).

Schnitzer, M.C. *et al* (1985), *International Business* (Ohio: South Western Publishing Company).

Thunell, L. (1977), *Political Risks in International Business* (New York: Praeger).

Wild, J. J. *et al* (2000), *International Business: An Integrated Approach* (New Jersey: Prentice-Hall).

Journals

Gonzalez, M.V. and E. Villanueva (1992),"Steering a Subsidiary through a Political Crisis", *Risk Management,* October, 16–27.

Haner, F.T. (1979),"Rating Investment Risks Abroad", *Business Horizons,* XXII (1), 18–23.

Hoskins, W. R. (1970), "How to Counter Expropriation", *Harvard Business Review,* XLII (September–October), 110–12.

Jodice, D. A. (1980),"Sources of Change in Third World Regimes for Foreign Direct Investment: 1968–76", *International Organisation*, XXXIV (2), pp. 177–206.

Knudsen, H. (1974),"Explaining the National Propensity to Expropriate: An Ecological Approach", *Journal of International Business Studies*, V (1), 54.

Kobrin, S. J. (1980),"The Assessment and Evaluation of Non-economic Environments by American Firms: A Preliminary Report", *Journal of International Business Studies*, XI (1), 32–47.

Kraar, L. (1980),"The Multinationals Get Smarter about Political Risks", Fortune, March 24, 86–100.

Kramer, R. D. (1981),"Political Risk Assessment: A Brief Review of the State of the Art", *New International Realities*, VI (1), 23.

McNulty, S. (1994),"Welcome to Cambodia's Business Wilderness", *Asian Wall Street Journal*, January 13.

Micallef, J.V. (1981),"Political Risk Assessment", *Columbia Journal of World Business*, XVI (1), 47–52.

Pincus, L.B. *et al* (1991), "Legal Issues Involved in Corporate Globalisation", *Columbia Business Law Review*, (2), 269–85.

Simon, J. D. (1982), "Political Risk Assessment: Past Trends and Future Prospects", *Columbia Journal of World Business*, XVII (1), 62–70.

Stobaugh, R. (1969), "How to Analyse Foreign Investment Climates" Harvard Business Review, XLVII (September–October), 100–108.

The Economic Times (New Delhi Daily), February 16, 1999.

Walters, K. D. and R. J. Monsen (1981),"The Spreading Nationalisation of European Industry", *Columbia Journal of World Business*, XVI (1), 64–72.

SELECT FURTHER READINGS

Heidi Vernon-Wortzel and Lawrence H. Wortzel, eds. (1997), *Strategic Management in the Global Economy* (New York: John Wiley).

Rogers, J. ed. (1986), *Global Risk Assessments: Issues, Concepts and Applications* (California: Global Risk Assessments).

* During the 1950s and mid-1960s, Japan experienced what is widely described as the 'economic miracle', which transformed the nation from wartime devastation to the world's second-largest economy by 1966. As a result, Japan came to dominate a range of industries including steel, ship-building, semiconductors, automobiles and consumer electronics. Akihabra area (as shown) in the picture is considered to be the main centre for electronic goods in Tokyo. In recent years, it has also gained fame as a centre of gaming, manga and animation culture.

PETRONAS towers, Kuala Lampur, Malaysia*

10

Economic Environment

CHAPTER OBJECTIVES

The economic environment is no less important than the political and legal environment. The present chapter discusses the issues relating to economic environment from the viewpoint of international business. The objective is to:

- ✦ Describe different economic systems.
- ✦ Show how primary economic indicators influence international business.
- ✦ Show how the economic environment is analysed/evaluated.

Apart from the political and legal environment, the economic environment also influences international business decisions. This is because the decision to trade or to locate manufacturing operations varies from one host country to the other, depending on the form of the economic system existing there and on the various economic parameters prevailing there, for example level of income and inflation; health of industrial, financial and external sectors; fiscal and monetary policies; and many others. The present chapter discusses these issues at some length.

10.1 FORMS OF ECONOMIC SYSTEM

Centrally Planned Economy is an economy where production and distribution system is owned by the government.

Market based Economy is an economy where the market forces of demand and supply reign supreme.

Mixed Economy is a compromise between CPE and market-based economy where private and public sectors exist side by side.

There are primarily two forms of economic systems, that is, the centrally planned economy (CPE) and the market-based economy. The two forms lie on the two extremes and so the third form, known as the mixed economy, is a compromise between the two. In other words, the system of mixed economy possesses the features of the first two systems. It is a more common form of the economic system insofar as neither of the first two systems is found in the purest form.

A CPE is defined as an economy where decisions regarding production and distribution of goods is taken by a central authority, depending upon the fulfilment of a particular economic, social, and political objective. The government designs the investment and coordinates the activities of the different economic sectors. Ownership of the means of production and the whole process of production lies in the hands of the government. The former USSR and East European countries were apposite examples of this type of economic system.

At the other extreme, in the market based economic system, the decision to produce and distribute goods is taken by individual firms based on the forces of demand and supply. The means and factors of production are owned by individuals and firms and they behave according to the market forces. The firms are quite free to take economic decisions. They take such decisions for the purpose of maximising their profit or wealth. Consumers are sovereign, they are free to decide what they want to buy. This is nothing but economic freedom, which manifests normally in freedom from governmental restrictions on, or interference with, economic activities. The United States of America and West European countries are examples of the market based economic system.

Between the two extremes, there is the mixed economic system. As mentioned just above, there is no country that represents any of the two systems in its purest form. In China, which is a CPE, the government has demarcated an area, known as special economic zone where private initiatives are allowed. On the other hand, in the United States of America, which has been a staunch advocate of the free-market economy, some economic activities are owned and regulated by the government. Thus, mixed economy, which represents a mixture of state control on one hand and the economic freedom of entrepreneurs and consumers on the other is the natural outcome. In other words, one can say that it is a system that involves greater governmental intervention than found in a market based economy or that relies more on market forces than experienced in a centrally planned economy. To cite an example, the Indian economy represents a mixed economic system. Economic activities that are fraught with social considerations are owned and regulated by the government. The others are owned and performed in the private sector.

Again, the Commonwealth of Independent States (CIS)—representing 15 nations coming out of the former USSR-fold and some countries of central and eastern Europe, especially Albania, Bulgaria, the Czech and Slovak Republics, Hungary, Poland, and Romania—were one time representing a CPE but from the beginning of 1990s, they have converted to a market based economic system. In some cases, the process of transition is near completion, but in many of them, the transition is much delayed as a result of a number of economic problems.

The nature of doing business with these different sets of countries is naturally different. In case of a CPE, it is normally the state trading corporation that participates in international trade. On the other hand, in a market based economy, trade is handled by individual firms. In a mixed economy, both the trading systems are found. Thus, the trade process and the involved procedural formalities differ widely in these cases. The procedural formalities also differ in case of manufacturing of a product or providing services in these different sets of countries. For example, countertrade was more common in case of east-west trade than in intra-west trade. Even in the Indian case, trade with then Soviet Union was based on a different footing, as compared to its trade with market based countries. Again, the nature of doing business with the transition economies of central and eastern Europe is different insofar as their economic problems are different. Thus, in short, whenever a firm trades with any other country, or when it tries to locate its manufacturing operations there, it takes into account the existing economic system in the host country and accordingly shapes its trade and foreign operation policies.

> In case of a CPE, it is normally the state trading corporation that participates in international trade. In a market based economy, trade is handled by individual firms. In a mixed economy, both the trading systems are found.

10.2 PRELIMINARY ECONOMIC INDICATORS

Whenever a firm moves abroad for international business, it takes into account some preliminary economic indicators of the host country at a particular point of time, as well as over a particular period. These economic indicators help the firm know, among other things,

1. The size of demand for its product,
2. The expected cost of production and the net earning, so as to ascertain its competitive edge, and
3. Whether it will be able to smoothly repatriate its earnings back to its home country.

The size of demand depends inter alia upon the level of income and its distribution, the propensity to consume, and rate of inflation. The cost of production depends upon the availability of human and physical resources; development of infrastructure; and on the fiscal, monetary, and industrial policies. Similarly, smooth repatriation of income and profit depends upon the strength of the external sector. These economic variables need some explanation here (Figure 10.1).

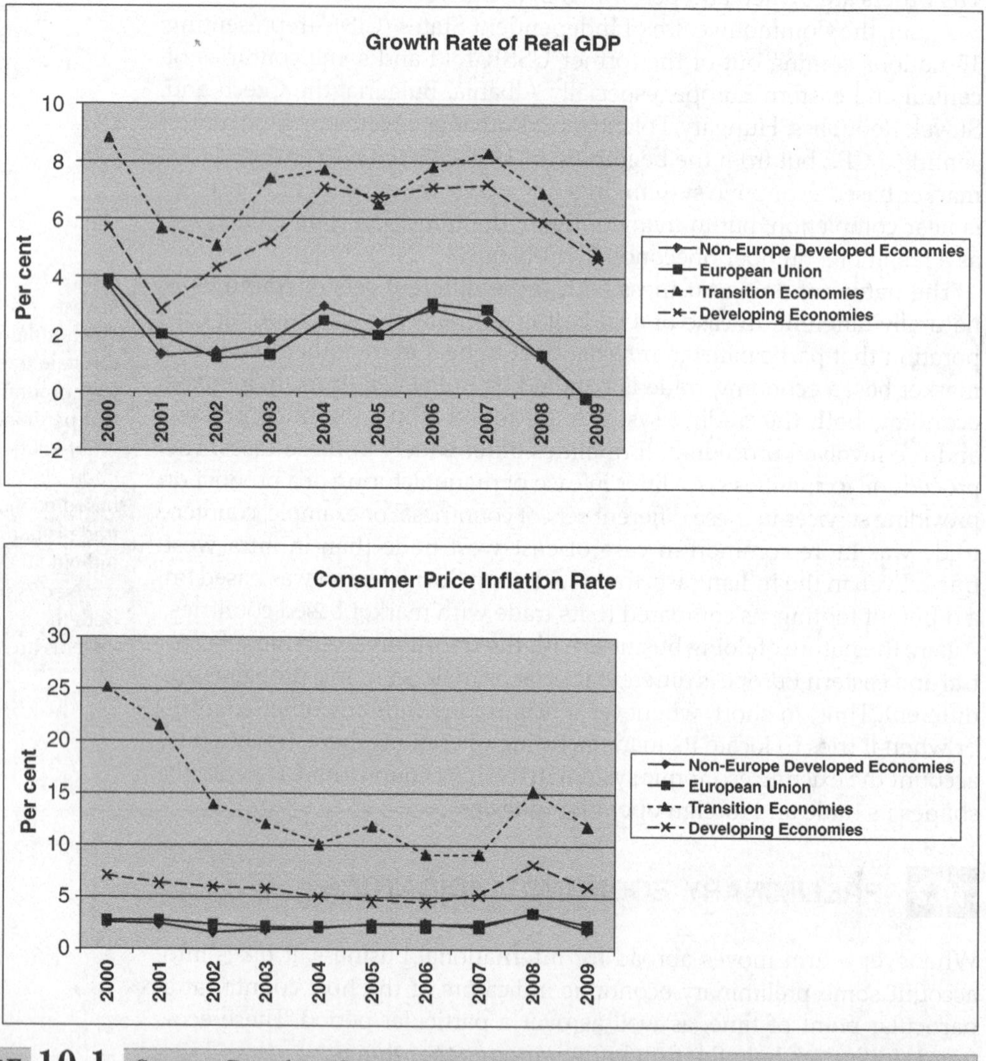

FIGURE 10.1 Source: Based on figures of World Development Indicators various issues.

10.2.1 Level of Income and Its Distribution

The size of demand for a product is dependent upon the size of income of its buyer. This is why a firm doing business with a foreign country evaluates the income level existing in that foreign country. The level of income is normally represented by the gross national product (GNP) or gross domestic product (GDP). GDP is the aggregate of the total output of goods and services provided during a year. If one adds to it the income from abroad, the sum is known as GNP. However, strictly speaking, GNP or GDP in absolute terms does not carry much meaning insofar as per capita income may be smaller and the per capita purchasing power may be lower if population in that country is very large, despite its large GDP. Thus the income level in a particular country should better be evaluated in terms of per capita income. It is on this basis that the World Bank (2008) has classified different countries as:

1. low income country
2. middle income country
3. high income country

The per capita income levels in these different groups of countries is as follows:

Country classification	*Per capita income based on 2007 dollar*
Low-income country	$ 935 or less
Lower middle-income country	$ 936–3705
Upper middle-income country	$ 3706–11455
High-income country	$ 11456 or more

Based on the level of income and some other economic and socio-economic indicators, one can group the countries into: (1) developed and (2) developing. The industrialised countries of North America, Western Europe, Asia, and the Australian continent are designated as developed countries. In the developing world, some of the countries have made fast strides towards industrialisation and have witnessed a high growth rate. They are known as newly industrialising countries (NICs) or emerging market economies. The others are the less developed countries in general. However, at the wrong end of the less developed countries are the least developed countries, presently numbering 50, that have very poor economic and socio-economic indicators.

Least developed countries are an economy with very weak economic and socioeconomic indicators that put them on the lowest rung of the less developed world.

Low income level means low purchasing power. Thus, multinational firms market or manufacture low price goods in such countries. The scope for a costly product in such countries is very limited. This is why a luxury car manufacturer will move to a country that is either a middle income country or a high income country.

However, on the basis of experience, it can be said that multinational firms also often move to low income countries for manufacturing high price goods. There are two reasons for this. First, when the population is quite large and the wage level in general is very low in view of the large supply of labour. In other words, MNCs move to such countries to take advantage of their cheap labour force, which has a positive impact on the cost of production. Secondly, high price items can have a market if the national income is not equally distributed. Suppose a country has a population of 500 million and 10 per cent of the population share 60 per cent of the national income. This means that there are 50 million persons that can buy even costlier goods. If this is the case, it is easy for multinational firms to market or to manufacture high-price goods in such countries. On the contrary, if the income is equally distributed, they will have the scope for marketing only low price goods. In brief, it is not simply the per capita income level that influences the international business decision, but more importantly, it is the distribution of the national income that is relevant in this context.

If national income is highly unequally distributed, MNCs go for market segmentation selling low cost good in low income segment and high cost goods in high income segment.

The distribution of income in the host country is important for multinational firms for attempting market segmentation. They can market a simple version of a particular product at low prices among low-income consumers. At the same time, they can market a sophisticated version of the same product at very high price among the wealthy people in the same country. This is possible if national income is highly unequally distributed. Seiko, a Japanese watch company manufactures low price watch, Seiko, for low income consumers and high price watch, Hittari, for affluent consumers in the same country.

As regards unequal distribution of income, the World Bank study (1996) finds that the widening gap between the rich and the poor has become a world wide phenomenon. The ratio between the national average of the per capita GNP and the average income of the poorest one-fifth of the population is 9:1 in the United States of America. It is almost similar in Brazil, although around 4:1 in the United Kingdom. But if the poorest section of the society has an income level that is sufficient for maintaining a good standard of living, income distribution does not matter much.

10.2.2 Inflation

It is a fact that the size of demand for a product depends not only on the level of income and its distribution, but it is also subject to the level of inflation in the country. It is because the purchasing power of the consumers depends on their real income. The higher the level of inflation, the lower is the real income and the purchasing power of the consumers. Thus, when a multinational firm decides to set up a manufacturing unit in a foreign country, it has to take into account the rate of inflation in the host country.

The rate of inflation is also important from the viewpoint of cost of production. If it is high in the host country, the production cost of the host country plant will be higher. The price may be competitive for the host country market because the other manufacturers in that country too face the same problem. But exports from the host country to markets with a lower rate of inflation will definitely be affected on account of higher cost. However, if the multinational firm exports its products to the high-inflation country instead of setting up of a manufacturing unit there, the exports may have a competitive edge in view of the lower rate of inflation at home. When one examines the impact of inflation on the foreign trade of the country, it should not be done in isolation of the changes in the exchange rate. It is because the changes in the exchange rate may nullify the effects of inflation rate changes.

Multinational firm exports its products to the high-inflation country instead of setting up of a manufacturing unit there.

Again, inflation has varying impact on different sections of the society. Fixed-wage earners are the worst hit. Inflation causes diminution in their purchasing power. But, on the other hand, the business community is well off. Profit is higher, which means nothing but rise in purchasing power. If the multinational firm pinpoints this particular consumer group and manufactures goods to meet its specific demand, it would be a profitable venture.

Besides the level of inflation, the way in which the monetary authorities tackle the growing inflation is also important. If they raise interest rates to bring down the rate of inflation, the rate of industrial growth would be adversely affected on account of availability of costly funds. Industrial stagnation may also be a factor inhibiting inflow of foreign investment.

10.2.3 Consumption Behaviour

Consumption behaviour or the pattern of consumption influences the demand for a particular product to a sizeable extent. In a low income country, where the consumers care more for price rather than for the quality of the goods, multinational firms find it very difficult to sell their improved quality, high price products, even if they are for the daily use of common people.

Again, in rural areas of less developed countries, people attach importance to saving or to real estate investment. As a result, their marginal propensity to consume is very low. This has a bearing on the demand for general consumption goods. Yet again, in less developed countries, it is found that a large segment of income is spent on food and housing, with the result that the demand for other goods languishes considerably.

Consumption behaviour depends on: 1. Preference for price/quality of the product, 2. Propensity to save, 3. Quality of population, 4. Existence of social security schemes.

In fact, the decision to save more or to consume more depends on the quality of population or on the social security schemes provided by the government. If the population is literate, it will have a different approach towards consumption. People will demand good quality products even if they are available at higher prices. On the contrary, uneducated people are price conscious and not quality conscious. Again, in absence of social security schemes, people prefer saving in order to meet exigencies, the propensity to consume is naturally very low. But where such schemes are ample, the propensity to consume is high. Thus, whenever a multinational firm selects a particular host country, it certainly takes into account the consumption pattern and the quality of the population.

10.2.4 Availability of Human and Physical Resources

Easy availability of human and physical resources makes the manufacturing process easier and at the same time lowers the cost of production so as to confer upon the firm a competitive edge. This is because if such resources are in abundance, they are available with no difficulty and at a lower cost.

A multinational firm looks at the availability of technical and managerial personnel whenever it analyses the economic environment in the host country.

It is not feasible for a multinational firm to transport the entire labour force from the home country. It normally employs its own men at the very senior positions and employs the rest of persons from the local manpower market. But this is possible only if skilled manpower is available locally. This is why a multinational firm looks at the availability of technical and managerial personnel whenever it analyses the economic environment in the host country.

Besides the issue of human resources, it is also necessary for multinational firm to assess the availability of physical resources. By physical resources, we mean various inputs necessary for manufacture. Moreover this fact lies at the core of the locational theory of foreign direct investment. Indian firms have moved to Sri Lanka for the manufacture of rubber products and to Nepal for the manufacture of herbal products. This is primarily because the required raw material is available in abundance in the host country.

10.2.5 Network of Infrastructure

In India, an important reason for the gap between the approval of foreign direct investment and its actual inflow is the lack of supportive infrastructure.

Building up of supportive infrastructure is a prerequisite for the development of industry. For successful operation, a firm needs uninterrupted power supply, good road/rail link, efficient communication system, and so on. This is why multinational firms must take into account the availability of infrastructure while analysing the economic environment in a host country. When US economic aid began flowing to developing countries for financing infrastructure projects as back as in the early 1950s, the primary objective was to pave the way for US investment in those countries (Ohlin, 1966). Presently, in India, an important reason for the gap between the approval of foreign direct investment and its actual inflow is the lack of supportive infrastructure.

10.2.6 Fiscal, Monetary, and Industrial Policies

Corporate income tax, excise duty and tariff on import in the host country do influence international trade and investment.

Various forms of economic policies pursued in the host country make the economic environment either congenial or act as a deterrent to the operation of a multinational firm. A firm never relishes a high rate of corporate income tax, as it lowers the net profit. Sometimes firms employ various techniques, for example transfer pricing devices, to lower the incidence of tax, but the management is not very easy. However, there are often tax treaties between the home government and the host government, which help reduce the burden of tax and so they act as a motivating factor for foreign direct investment. Similarly, in some countries, in order to attract foreign direct investment, tax holiday schemes are provided to the foreign investor for a specific period. This too lowers the burden of taxes.

The case of excise duties too is similar as such duties cause cost appreciation. In some countries, they are levied on the amount of output. In others, they are levied on the amount of value addition. So firms have to see which type of duties are less harmful to their interests.

Besides the corporate income tax and excise duties, there is tariff or import duty. As it is mentioned in Chapter 6, such duties are either ad valorem, based on the value of the import, or specific, based on the quantity of the specific import, or mixed, combining both of them. Whatever may be the form of import duty, it raises the price of the imported item in the hands of the consumers. Thus, whenever a firm exports goods to a foreign country, it has to assess the size of such duty. In case of foreign manufacturing too, this duty prevailing in the host country affects the cost of production if various inputs are imported either from the home country or from any other country. However, in case of a free trade area or a customs union, when tariff is abolished from the intra-region trade, the abolition encourages intra-region international business.

The fiscal policy does not deal simply with various taxes and duties, but it is more concerned with the budgetary deficit or fiscal deficit. If the fiscal policy in a host country is not effective in curbing high fiscal deficit, it will have a dampening impact on the monetary sector, external sector, and many other sectors and thereby will adversely influence the interest of the multinational firm.

With regard to the monetary policy, it is found that it has a definite influence on the money supply and the rate of inflation, rate of interest and the cost of credit, and on the general health of the financial sector. If the monetary policy is such that it keeps inflation within manageable limits, keeps the interest rate low, and strengthens the health of financial institutions and banks, credit availability for a firm will be easier and cheaper. All this will have a positive impact on the operational cost of the firm, which means greater competitive strength. A multinational firm may not be in a better position compared to other local firms as they too get easier and cheaper credit, but it will certainly be on a better footing compared to firms in other countries with not so effective monetary policies.

> If the monetary policy keeps inflation within manageable limits, keeps the interest rate low, and strengthens credit availability, all this will have a positive impact on the operational cost of a multinational firm.

Again, one of the aspects of the industrial policy is related to the area where foreign investors can invest. If the policy is restrictive on this count, it permits foreign investors only into a very limited area of the industrial economy. On the contrary, a liberal policy environment helps attract foreign investment. India's industrial policy was made more liberal in 1991, with the result that large number of foreign investors came to invest in this country during the period of liberalisation.

> Industrial policy if restrictive permits foreign investors only into a very limited area of the industrial economy.

10.2.7 Strength of External Sector

Multinational firms are greatly interested in repatriating profits to their parent unit. Repatriation is easier when the monetary authorities in the host country pursue a liberal policy in this respect. The policy is liberal only when the balance of payments position is strong enough and the size of foreign exchange reserves is comfortably large.

When a multinational firm has to select a host country, it analyses export-import ratio, current account balance/GDP ratio, or current receipt/ GDP ratio, import cover of foreign exchange reserves, external debt/GDP ratio, debt service ratio, and so forth.

It is a fact that the majority of the developing countries face deficit on current account balance in view of the fact that their import needs are large and they face both demand constraints and supply constraints on their exports. Their invisible trade is not big enough to cover the trade deficit. However, in some cases, the current account deficit is met by capital account flows. Such flows are so large that they not only make up the current account deficit but also, after meeting such deficit, add to the foreign exchange reserves. This is found in cases where ample incentives are given to foreign investors and the foreign investors find a safe place to invest on account of congenial economic and political environment. Thus, when a multinational firm has to select a host country, it analyses the health of the external sector of the host country. It relies on various ratios, such as export-import ratio, current account balance/GDP ratio, or current receipt/GDP ratio, import cover of foreign exchange reserves in terms of the number of months, external debt/GDP ratio, debt service ratio, and so forth. The stronger the health, the better the economic environment and the greater the foreign investment.

10.3 PROCESS OF ANALYSING ECONOMIC ENVIRONMENT

The preceding section incorporates some major economic indicators that are taken into consideration by a multinational firm. The firm judges these indicators prevailing at a particular point of time, mainly at the time of export or of setting up of a venture. But this is not enough. The firm has to analyse the trend of these variables over a specific period. For the past, there is no problem. This is because historical data is normally available. But for the future, the firm relies on the forecast that may be made on the basis of the past.

The first step in this process is to collect data. Collection of secondary data is easy and inexpensive. It may be collected from international publications. International organisations such as the IMF, the World Bank, the United Nations, and others as well as some private international agencies regularly publish the vital statistics of different countries. Country reports are exclusively published by some of them. However, the statistics published by governmental agencies of a particular country can also be relied upon as they are sometimes more informative.

Sometimes firms are interested in the collection of primary data, either through its own resources or through any agency or consultant. But this process is more expensive. Moreover, physical distance and cultural differences between the countries, language and comprehension problem, and other such obstacles make it difficult to conduct research.

The second step begins after the collection of data. In this process, the total market potential is evaluated. If necessary, a forecast is made for this purpose. The statistics concerning the existing consumption pattern and the growth rate of income are taken into account and on that basis the future demand for the product is determined. Sometimes an input-output table is constructed where output in one sector/country becomes the input for another sector/country. If this information is analysed in the light of the expected future economic trend, the demand can be predicted. If desired statistics for a particular country is not available, the statistics of another similar country can be used. In fact, the methodology varies from one firm to another. But the ultimate goal is to determine the size of the market in a desired host country.

SUMMARY

- Economic environment as a determinant of international business decisions is very significant in the sense that it normally differs between the home country and the host country and among different host countries. Broadly, there are two extremes: one being the free market economy and the other being the centrally planned economy. There are a number of countries that possess the features of both types of economics in varying proportions and they represent a mixed economic system. The transition economies fall, more or less, in this group until their transition to a market based economic system is complete. The nature of international business decision vary from one economic system to the other.
- Before making international business decisions, a firm makes an analysis of the broad economic indicators prevailing in the host country, such as the level of income and its distribution; inflation rate; consumption behaviour; availability of physical and human resources; network of infrastructure; fiscal, monetary, and industrial policy; and strength of the external sector.
- It gathers information based on primary and secondary data and evaluates them. Only then it takes a decision.

REVIEW QUESTIONS

1. What are the different forms of economic system? Do they influence international business decisions?
2. Briefly explain the major economic indicators that managers take into account before taking any international business decision.

Objective Type Questions

1. Mark True or False:
   (a) Economic information regarding the host country is collected from both published data and on-the-spot studies.
   (b) The health of the external sector in the host country is not very important for MNCs.
   (c) A restrictive policy in the host country attracts FDI.
   (d) Improved infrastructure in the host country eases the operation of MNCs.
   (e) GDP includes income from abroad.
2. Choose the Most Suitable Answer:
   (a) Mixed economy is a comprise between:
      (i) Two forms of centrally planned economies
      (ii) A centrally planned economy and a market based economy
      (iii) Two forms of market based economy
   (b) In a CPE, international trade is handled by the:
      (i) Individual exporter
      (ii) Star trading houses
      (iii) State trading agencies
   (c) GNP means:
      (i) Aggregate amount of goods and services produced during a year in a country
      (ii) Income from abroad
      (iii) The sum of the above two
   (d) Emerging market economies are:
      (i) A part of developed economies
      (ii) Newly industrialising countries
      (iii) None of the above
   (e) An equal distribution of income in the host country:
      (i) Matters greatly to an MNCs' market segmentation strategy
      (ii) Has nothing to do with the market segmentation strategy
      (iii) Has only little impact on the market segmentation strategy

Study Topic

Economic Environment Among Different Groups of Countries During 2008 and 2009

The US sub-prime crisis during 2008 had its impact not only on the entire US economy but also on different quarters of the world economy. The overall economic environment in the different countries or different groups of countries vitiated from that during 2007. Here, one can find such changes in very brief.

Developed Economies

As far as the developed countries outside Europe are concerned, they experienced recession during 2008–2009. The growth rate of real GDP fell from 2.5 per cent in 2007 to 1.2 per cent in 2008 and, as expected to −0.5 per cent during 2009. Let us take, first, the case of the USA. Following a slump in the housing sector and in the banking activities, the credit position was tight that led in turn to lower industrial activities, lower profits, falling equity prices and to lower business capital spending. The lower industrial activities led also to greater unemployment and thereby to lower household consumption spending. The real GDP growth rate plummeted from 2.0 per cent in 2007 to 1.2 per cent in 2008 and to an anticipated figure of −0.1 per cent during 2009. The government allocated a huge sum of $700 billion to recapitalise banks, but this measure was too late to revive the real economy. The federal funds rate was lowered and the tax rates were axed. But all this failed to hasten the revival of the economy.

As far as the euro area is concerned, the majority of the countries were found in recession. The consumption spending tended to shrink during the first half of 2008. High inflation was an important factor behind lower disposable income. Tightened credit limited the size of household lending. The investment spending too contracted in view of falling profitability and equity prices. Unemployment and wage prospects were diminished. The exports decelerated fast. Their growth rate was barely at 3.8 per cent and was expected to decline further in 2009. The imports were also low but not as low as the exports. This affected adversely the balance of trade. Some fiscal measures were taken up in majority of the countries in this area. State-backed guarantee of bank loans, greater deposit insurance and actual bail-out of financial firms were common. Similarly, monetary measures were apparent in lower interest rates. However, since euro remained volatile, especially against the US dollar and Japanese yen, exchange rate risk was high. When, during summer of 2008, euro had appreciated, the EU exporters were out of the key markets.

Japan too was sailing in the same boat. Slackened demand from abroad and the negative exchange rate effects coupled with rising input cost, especially on account of energy consumption were responsible for decreased economic activities. The real GDP growth rate was barely 0.4 per cent in 2008 which was expected to be lower at −0.3 per cent during 2009. The high rate of inflation eroded the purchasing power which was responsible for lower consumption spending that in turn influenced adversely the economic activities. The fiscal measures were not substantial in view of the already existing huge burden of public debt. However, monetary measures in the form of reduced interest rates were taken to revive the economic activities.

Transition Economies

The overall picture of the transition economies was different during 2008. The economic growth rate was high at 7.1 per cent in Commonwealth of Independent States (CIS) and 5.2 per cent in South-East Europe. The reason was that the domestic demand was high and also that these countries remained a bit aloof of the contagion effect of the world economic crisis. As far as CIS were concerned, Russia experienced a boom in agricultural production. The employment generation was normally sizeable but inflation rate remained higher. In some of the countries, such as Azerbaijan, Kazakhstan, Kyrgyzstan, Tazikistan and Ukraine, the rate of inflation was as high as 20 per cent. Russia and Ukraine followed liberal monetary policy. In early 2009, when there were some signs of the effects of international financial crisis, and particularly when real interest rates were negative in view of the high inflation rate in some countries, the government of those countries helped increase the liquidity position in the market. When the capital flow got reversed and when the trade deficit turned wider in 2009, there was found large-scale intervention by monetary authorities in the foreign exchange market in order to maintain stability in exchange rate.

In South-East Europe too, the growth rate of the economy slumped during 2009 despite the employment generation picture being buoyant. Fiscal deficit tended to widen during 2009 but it was expected to remain within limits. On the monetary policy front, of course, the rising rate of inflation led the government to raise the interest rate especially in Albania, Serbia and Macedonia. In Bosnia and Herzegovina and Croatia, the cash reserve requirements were increased.

Developing Economies

The growth rate of real GDP in the developing countries as a whole slumped from 7.1 per cent in 2007 to 5.9 per cent in 2008. In case of the African countries, the slump was recorded from 6.0 per cent in 2007 to 5.1 per cent in 2008 and to an expected level of 4.1 per cent in 2009. The reason was the slump in household spending consequent on high inflation and high interest rates, growing unemployment and the weakening of the commodity boom. Inflation rate climbed up by over 60 per cent in 2008 over the previous year in 90 per cent of 51 African countries. However, oil-exporting African countries were not so hard-hit. The monetary measures were focussed on the control of inflation and so it was basically a tight monetary policy.

In East Asia, the growth rate of real GDP dropped from 9.0 per cent in 2007 to 6.9 per cent in 2008 and to an expected level of 6.0 per cent in 2009 primarily in view of the fact that this region was more prone to the international financial crisis. With slowing growth rates, unemployment rate increased by one percentage point in 2009 over 2008. Again, the current account surplus of the countries in this region turned greatly eroded.

As regards monetary measures, interest rates were increased initially but with decreasing interest rates in the developed world, interest rates were cut. The fiscal policy remained expansionary. Some of the governments, such as those of Republic of Korea and China announced economic stimulus packages.

In South Asia, the growth rate of real GDP diminished from 7.9 per cent in 2007 to 7.0 per cent in 2008 and to an expected level of 6.4 per cent in 2009. In India and Pakistan, large outflow of foreign capital impinged upon the liquidity in financial market and on shrinking of foreign exchange reserves. In Bangladesh, Nepal and Sri Lanka, it was mainly the weaker performance in the commodity producing sector and in the services sector. Moreover, the inflation rate was high moving between 6.4 per cent and 20.0 per cent. In the sequel, the monetary measures were tight.

Remittances stood large among many countries of this region in so far as a large number of persons had have migrated to oil-exporting Gulf countries. So, with the rising oil prices, remittances tended to increase. In Bangladesh, the increase was over 20.0 per cent during 2008. But with slowdown of petroleum prices, the remittances were affected badly in 2009. Thus, on the whole, international economic shocks were the main reason for decelerating growth rate.

In Latin America and the Caribbean region, the growth rate of real GDP plummeted from 5.5 per cent in 2007 to 4.3 per cent in 2008 and to an expected level of 2.3 per cent in 2009. A majority of currencies depreciated against dollar and other major currencies. There was a decline in the household spending in 2009. Those South American countries being dependent on metal and mineral products were badly hit on account of lower commodity prices.

Again, in majority of Latin American and Caribbean countries, inflation rate remained high at 8.1 per cent during 2008, although it was expected to ease to some extent during 2009 on account of reduced commodity demand expectations. Unemployment rate, which was 7.5 per cent in 2008, was expected to move up to over 8.0 per cent in 2009. The current account deficit was expected to be higher during 2009. Public revenue was also expected to fall leading to fiscal crisis. Interest rates were increased in 2008 to help ease inflation but with changed economic environment in 2009, they were cut at least to some extent.

Thus, on the whole, the world economic environment during 2008 and 2009 was not in a good shape.

Source: Based on the figures available from: 1. World Development Indicators, 2009
2. World Development Report: 2009.

QUESTIONS

1. Comment on the economic scenario in developed market economies during 2008 and 2009.
2. In what way were the transition economies different from the developed economies during 2008 and 2009?
3. How did the developing countries fare during 2008? Was there any change in 2009?

REFERENCES

Books

Ohlin, G. (1966), *Foreign Aid Policies Reconsidered* (Paris : OECD).

Journals and Report

The Economist (1993), *Country Report,* Economic Intelligence Unit.
The Economist (1995), *Country Report,* Economic Intelligence Unit.
The World Bank (2008), World Development Indicators: 2008 (Washington, D.C.).

SELECT FURTHER READINGS

Garten, J. E. (1997), "Troubles Ahead in Emerging Markets", *Harvard Business Review,* LXXV (May–June), 38–50.
The World Bank (1996), *World Development Report: 1996* (NewYork: Oxford University Press).
Woo, W. T. *et al* (eds) (1997), *Economies in Transition; Comparing Asia and Europe* (Cambridge M. A.: MIT Press).

* PETRONAS, short for Petroliam Nasional Berhad, was incorporated on 17 August 1974 as the national oil company of Malaysia, vested with the entire ownership and control of the petroleum resources in the country. With a strategy of integration, adding value and globalisation, it continues to deliver excellence and has forayed into other domains like Exploration and Production, Oil, Gas, Petrochemicals, Logistics and Maritime, Research and Technology. It is ranked among the FORTUNE Global 500 largest corporations in the world.

Bombay Stock Exchange, Mumbai, India*

11

Socio-Cultural and Ethical Environment

CHAPTER OBJECTIVES

The socio-cultural and ethical environment varies among countries. Managers must be acquainted with the environment in order to enhance performance. The objective of the present chapter is to:

- ✦ Explain the concept of culture—its meaning and essential elements.
- ✦ Analyse the different bases of cultural diversity.
- ✦ Show how cultural diversity influences an international firm's competitive advantage.
- ✦ Explain how cultural diversity is managed.
- ✦ Explain the concept of ethics and social responsibility.
- ✦ Analyse the nature of normative and relative ethics, and their influence on international business.
- ✦ Mention some of the more important ethical issues, such as human rights, environmental safety, corruption, and transfer pricing.

The socio-cultural and ethical environment is an important factor that needs to be taken into account by an international manager. Since culture or human behaviour influences, to a great extent, international business decisions, while planning overseas operations, a multinational enterprise, takes into account the socio-cultural and ethical environment of the host country. If this environment is similar in both the home and host countries, the manager will try to take the maximum advantage of the similarity for strategy formulation. If it is different, the manager will try to understand the differences and shape the strategy according to the changed environment. For example, McDonald's do not sell beef products in India because a sizeable majority of the consumers being Hindu do not take beef. The BBC dismantled its Arabic Television Service in 1996 because of differences with the Islamic fundamentalists over the programme content.

11.1 CONCEPT OF CULTURE

11.1.1 Meaning of Culture

Culture is the entire set of social norms shaping human behaviour.

Culture represents the entire set of social norms and responses that dominate the behaviour of persons living in a particular geographic or political boundary. It is a fact that cultural boundaries may differ from national/political boundaries because individuals with varying cultural backgrounds may reside in a particular nation. For example, Canada has at least three cultures—an Anglo culture, a French-speaking "Quebecois" culture and a Native American culture. Alternatively, individuals with similar cultural background may represent different countries. For example, Islamic culture is shared by the citizens of many countries in the Middle East, Asia, and Africa. Yet cultural boundaries and national boundaries are often equated. Therefore, let us discuss what the socio-cultural environment means, what are the causes and impact of cultural differences, and how such differences can be managed.

Culture, as noted earlier, represents the whole set of social norms and responses that shape the knowledge, belief, morals, attitude, behaviour, and the very way of life of a person or a group of persons. Culture is not in-born. It is acquired and inculcated. The inculcation of culture begins at the very birth of a person and lies below the level of conscious thought. This means that an individual is unaware of the learning process because he or she learns through seeing how others behave. The learning persists throughout his or her life and does not escape him/her entirely. It may be mentioned that culture is not specific to a single individual, rather it is shared by a group of persons. In fact, it is culture that enables persons to communicate with others and to distinguish between what should be done and what should not be done (Dressler and Carns, 1969; Herskovits, 1963; Luthans, 1989).

11.1.2 Elements of Culture

Based on the definition of culture, there are a few basic elements of culture. These elements are universal; meaning that they form the cultural environment of all societies. But, what is important is that they perform differently in different societies, leading ultimately to cultural diversity across different societies. Czinkota et al (1999) list these elements as follows:

1. Language
2. Religion
3. Education
4. Attitudes and values
5. Customs
6. Aesthetics
7. Social institutions
8. Material elements

Language: Language is the medium through which message is conveyed. It may be verbal or non-verbal. The former includes the use of particular words or how the words are pronounced. The latter embraces the gestures through which feelings are expressed. When an international manager gives the instructions to his subordinates, who normally come from the host country, the instructions must be understood properly by the latter; or when the firm's salesmen tries to convince the consumers, the latter should follow the language of the former well. There is no problem if the language spoken in the home country and the host country is similar. But, normally, it is not.

> Language is the medium through which message is conveyed. It may be verbal or non-verbal.

Again, even if the language is the same in the two countries, it is possible that the same word or the same phrase carries different meanings in different countries. For example, the word, *homely* means friendly and comfortable in England but plain or even ugly in the United States. American brand names sometimes carry strange meanings when translated into other languages. American Motors' Matador became 'killer' in Spanish. Ford's low-cost truck Fiera meant 'ugly old woman' when translated into Spanish. The Pepsi Cola slogan, 'Come alive with Pepsi' was translated into German as 'come out of the grave'. DeVries (1969) feels that when legal contracts are formalised across national boundaries, they sometimes alter in character as well as language. It was the problem of language that compelled Close-up to change the name of its tooth paste as Klai-chid in Thailand so as to make the consumers aware of the product. Thus, multinational managers should be very careful of what their instructions really mean.

Even if the international managers make themselves acquainted with the principal language spoken in the host country, the problem is not over. There are many dialects spoken there and it would not be very convenient for the less educated employees to follow the instructions because they may be more well versed with a regional dialect rather than with the principal language. For example, only 60 per cent of the Malaysian population is Malay, the other 30 per cent is represented by Chinese, and the rest 10 per cent by Indians. Despite the fact that Malay is the official language, the ethnic groups use their own dialect and that creates problems for multinational corporations operating there.

As far as the non-verbal language is concerned, it is also different in different countries. For example, Latin Americans prefer standing close to a person with whom they are talking, but this is not liked by the Americans or by Britons. Thus, multinational managers must also be acquainted with the non-verbal language of the host country.

Religion sets the ideals of life and thereby the values and attitude of individuals living in a society.

Religion: Religion is another element of culture. Irrespective of forms, religion believes in a higher power. It sets the ideals of life and thereby the values and attitude of individuals living in a society. These values manifest in individuals' behaviour and performance. Since different forms of religion differ in details, the attitude towards entrepreneurship or consumption, and so on varies among different societies practising different forms of religion or among different schools of the same religion. For example, protestants and catholics, both represent Christianity, but the former give weightage to accumulation of wealth, while the latter oppose it. Similarly, in Islam, prayers five times a day and fasting during *Ramzan* are emphasised upon, which in turn, effects productivity. Moreover, the *purdah* system discourages women moving out for work. Income in form of interest is also prohibited in Islam, which restricts spread of banking.

In Hinduism, the caste system comes in the way of the mobility of the work force as certain types of works are to be performed only by a certain caste. It was very rigid a few decades ago, but this factor has softened considerably in recent years. Similarly, Buddhism believes in spiritual achievement and not in material achievement and this has a dampening effect on entrepreneurship and profit making.

Again Confucian thought believes in rigid organisational structure and unanswering reverence for authority. Most of the Koreans believe in this thought and they do not question strict chains of command. The application of this philosophy among Korean subsidiaries in Western countries has led to high-profile dispute. Yet again, Shinto, a native religion of many Japanese gives importance to ethics, patriotism and loyalty. This is one of the reasons behind the success of Japanese firms abroad.

Education has a close relationship with the availability of skilled manpower.

Education: The level of education in a particular culture depends primarily on the literacy rate and on enrolment in schools and colleges. This element has a close relationship with the availability of skilled manpower, availability of workers and managers who can be sent to the home country for training, production of sophisticated products, and with the adaptation of imported technology. If the level of education is high in a particular society, it is easy for multinational firms to operate there. It is because skilled manpower will be easily available, its training will be easy and the firm will be able to produce sophisticated goods. However, it is not only the level of education but also the pattern of education that is important. If the majority of persons in the host country are educated in the area of humanities or languages, they cannot be of as much use as those educated in the area of business studies or engineering.

Attitude and Values: Values are the belief and norms prevalent in a particular society. They determine largely the attitude and behaviour of individuals towards work, status, change, and so on. In some societies, where income and wealth are emphasised upon, people work for more hours in order to earn more. On the contrary, in societies where leisure is preferred, people work only for limited hours, just to meet their essential wants necessary for survival. However, the preference for leisure can change if people are influenced by the demonstration effects of higher living standards.

Values determine largely the attitude and behaviour of individuals towards work, status, change, and so on.

Again, the attitude towards social status is an important factor. Those who believe in higher social status spend even more; and to this end, they work more and earn more. For example, in Japan, youth pay a higher price for Levi's jeans because such jeans give them higher social status. It is the status that motivates individuals to opt for a particular branch of study. In less developed countries, bureaucracy is believed to the best profession. But in the United States of America and many other societies, business professionals have a higher social status. International managers will be able to reap larger benefits in the latter group of societies.

Yet again, in some societies, the attitude of the individuals does not favour change. To this end, they like to protect their own culture with elaborate sets of sanctions and laws. This means that individuals who deviate from their own culture are punished under the law. In such cases, the international manager tries to find out a way that does not deviate widely from the existing culture in the host country.

Customs: Customs and manners vary from one society to another. In the United States of America, silence is taken as negation, while it is not so in Japan. Similarly, Britons prefer instant coffee, while in the USA, ground coffee and instant coffee both are popular. Campbell's sells large cans of soup in Mexico in order to cater to the needs of large families, while in Britain, it is not so. In view of such differences, it is imperative for international managers to be aware of varying manners and customs.

Aesthetics: Aesthetics is concerned with the sense of beauty, good taste, and with the particular symbolism of colours. Colour symbolism, for example, is very important in international business. Black is the symbol of mourning in the United States of America and the United Kingdom, while it is white in Japan and some other Far Eastern countries. Green is popular in Islamic countries. Thus, while designing the advertisement programme or while packaging products, an international manager must take into account these facts so that the aesthetic sensibilities of the host country people are not marginalised and product marketing is smooth.

Social Institutions: Social institutions form an integral part of culture. They are concerned mainly with the size of the family and social stratification. In the United States of America and the United Kingdom and most other developed countries, the size of the family is small, comprising of a husband, wife, and children. But in many other countries, especially in developing ones, grand parents too are a part of the family. In yet another group of countries, the family is larger, comprising of cousins, aunts, and uncles. In India, the joint family system is still prevalent.

Similarly, in some societies, social stratification is very much apparent. Persons of different strata, may be in a single factory or in a single office, enjoy different facilities. For example, the more senior an officer, the more spacious his cabin is. On the other hand, there are countries where no such discrimination is practised. All the employees in a factory, irrespective of rank, eat lunch in the same dining hall.

Social stratification is also apparent in people's buying habits. Low income persons use low price products, while the same need of the affluent class is catered with a sophisticated variety of goods. Thus, when an international manager operates in a foreign land, he or she takes into account which segment of the society is the major buyer of the product or whether the persons employed in the firm believe in equality or unequal status.

Material Elements: Last but not least, this aspect of material culture cannot be ignored. Material culture is related to the economic, financial, and social infrastructure and to objects and things enjoyed by people. For example, Germans like beer, while the French like wine. So marketing of wine in Germany will be a bad proposal. In Japan, due to lack of space and the prevalence of small homes and apartments, marketing of lawn mowers will be a futile attempt. Similarly, in less developed countries, where power shortage is common, power generating machines can easily be marketed. But in developed countries, where the economic infrastructure is developed, marketing of time saving home appliances will turn out to be a good proposal. Social infrastructure manifests in form of housing, health and other facilities, and the level of education. If the consumers are uneducated, their consumption pattern will be different. In such cases, computer marketing will not be successful. Again, in cases where financial infrastructure is lacking, foreign companies will have to arrange funds, not from the host country financial market, but, from elsewhere. Thus, these varying elements of culture lead to cultural diversity among different societies, which need to be taken care of by international managers.

11.2 CULTURAL DIVERSITY

11.2.1 Basis of Cultural Diversity

In the preceding section, it has been mentioned how the various elements of culture vary in different societies. In some societies, individualism motivates personal accomplishment, while in others, the concept of the group is prominent. American culture comes under the former, while the Chinese and Japanese case conforms to the latter. In some societies, tradition, ceremony, and social rules do not figure, while they are maintained in other societies. Latin American managers, thus, differ from American managers who do not believe in traditions. Western culture encourages innovation in product and technology, while in some parts of the world where culture is highly rigid, people resist new products and technology. In some societies, decisions are taken only by top managers. In others, a greater number of officers take part in the decision making. The latter is found in Japan, while the former is found in the United States of America and some other western countries. It is the cultural diversity that shapes the managers as either risk averse or risk taking leaders. The former are conservative in their decisions, while the latter are aggressive. Some managers give priority to long-term goals, while the others are contended with achieving short term goals. It is the cultural background that makes the two different from each other (Reynolds, 1986).

But it is important to know that why such diversity exists. To explain the bases of diversity, a few of models have been developed. One is by Geert Hofstede (1980), the other is by Kluckhohn and Strodtbeck (1961), and the third and more recent one is by Fons Trompenaars (1994).

Hofstede's Study: Hofstede's study surveys 117,000 employees in 88 countries and suggests that cultural diversity among nations has four dimensions.

They are:

1. Individualism/collectivism,
2. Masculinity/femininity,
3. Power distance, and
4. Uncertainty avoidance.

Individualism is a culture where the individual cares for himself and not for the group.

Masculinity is a situation where success and money dominate the society.

Individualism exists when people look at themselves primarily as individuals and secondarily as members of a group. Hofstede measures this cultural difference on a bipolar continuum with individualism on one end of the continuum and collectivism on the other. Collectivism is related as loyalty to the group, where people care for one another. The survey reveals that wealthy countries have higher individualism scores, while poorer countries have represented collectivism.

Hofstede defines masculinity as a situation in which success, money, and material things dominate the society. On the contrary, femininity refers to a situation in which care for others and the quality of life dominates. Cultures with high masculinity index encourage large scale enterprises without caring for the conservation of environment. Higher level jobs are occupied by men. Women have a limited role to play. Job stress and industrial conflict are common. In a low masculinity index culture, small scale enterprises, conservation of the environment, women holding high level jobs, and so on are common. The survey finds a high masculinity index in case of Japan and a low index in case of Norway.

In cultures with high power distance index, power distribution is highly unequal, meaning that decisions are taken by high-ups and simply followed by the subordinates. In low power distance index countries, the

High power distance is the decision taken by senior managers to be followed by subordinates.

Uncertainty avoidance are beliefs that avoid uncertainty.

responsibility for decision making lies in a greater number of hands. The survey finds Mexico, South Korea, and India being high power distance countries.

Last but not least, uncertainty avoidance is related to the extent to which people have created beliefs and institutions to avoid uncertainty. Countries with a high uncertainty avoidance index maintain organisations with more written rules and regulations, risk averse management, and less ambitious employees. Organisations in low uncertainty avoidance societies have risk taking managers, less written rules, high labour turnover, and highly ambitious employees.

Hofstede has integrated all these four factors into two-dimensional plots and finds that they all do not move necessarily in the same direction and so there may be many combinations. All this shows the complexity of culture's effect on attitude and behaviour.

Kluckhohn and Strodtbeck's Study: Similarly, Kluckhohn and Strodtbeck identify five problems that tend to lead to cultural diversity. They are:

1. Human-Nature relationship,
2. Orientation towards time,
3. Beliefs about human nature,
4. Activity orientation of human being, and
5. Inter-human relationship.

Different individuals and societies have different views about nature. In Muslim countries, where nature is usually supposed to be supreme, guiding human fate, individuals being lethargic, making no attempt to innovate are common. On the contrary, in the United States of America, where individuals treat themselves as supreme, entrepreneural abilities and risk taking activities are common. In the United Kingdom, where people assign importance to themselves and at the same time try to accommodate nature, the pattern of human behaviour lies between the two.

Also culture varies because of varying orientation towards time. In China, past events matter more, while those in the United States of America are more concerned with the present. In Japan, the emphasis is normally on long-term planning. In cases where the present is emphasised upon, the reward for performance depends upon the actual performance.

It is a belief about human nature that shapes the behavioural pattern in a society. In societies where human nature is considered essentially evil, there are lot of rules and regulations so that an individual may not commit wrong acts. But where no doubt is cast on the purity of human nature, even verbal agreements are sufficient. Participative management is common in such societies.

In some societies, people are satisfied with what they have. They do not aspire to grow. But in other societies, people are "action-oriented" where they are constantly striving to achieves goals. This type of society is marked with a great deal of economic activity.

Lastly, in societies where individuals are treated as independent, they take the responsibility for their own actions. But in others, individuals do not feel themselves independent and they emphasise on lineage or organisational hierarchy. In yet other societies, the group, and not the individual, is given importance.

However, there may be changes in the social norms and the aptitude of people. The changes may be due to changes in the socio-economic environment or due to the availability of new alternatives. For example, in India, where rural people were normally averse to going to big cities for work half a century ago, rural to urban migration is very much common today.

Sometimes the cultural change takes place through imposition. This is found when a particular culture is imposed by outsiders on the local population, as in the case of many erstwhile colonies, the foreign trading companies or rulers introducted a new culture.

Fons Trompenaars' Study: Trompenaars' study covers 15,000 managers from 28 countries. It concludes that cultural diversity is found because of the existence of a few relationship orientations manifest in form of:

1. Universalism vis-à-vis particularism,
2. Neutralism vis-à-vis emotionalism, and
3. Achievement vis-à-vis ascription.

Societies believing in universalism feel that the same idea and belief can be applied all over the world. On the contrary, those believing in particularism feel that any idea or belief needs to be adapted for different societies. In the survey it was found that while American, British, and German managers subscribed to universalism, Chinese, Indonesian, and East European managers believed in particularism.

Neutralism means that the emotions are held in check and not expressed openly. On the other hand, emotionalism believes in the open expression of emotions. The Japanese and many Asian managers are found to be neutral. In contrast, Mexican, Dutch, and Swiss managers are emotional.

Again, those believing in the achievement culture rate the status of a manager on the basis of his/her performance or achievement. But those believing in ascription are of the view that status depends on who or what a person is. While American and British managers come in the former category, Venezuelan, Chinese, and Indonesian managers fall in the latter category.

Based on these attributes, host countries are clustered and, accordingly, the operational strategy is formulated by MNCs.

Universalism versus Particularism refers to universal application of ideas versus varying ideas for varying places.

Neutral and emotional culture differ as in emotions are checked in a neutral culture, while they are expressed openly in an emotional culture.

Achievement versus ascription differ as the status of a person depending on his achievement versus his status based on who and what he is.

Cultural Base in Japan and China as Different from the Western Culture

An analysis of cultural diversity focuses on the fact that one of the important factors behind the significant progress of the Japanese and Chinese economies is their specific cultural base which is very much different from the Western culture. Let us first discuss the cultural base of China.

Although there are large-sized firms in China, mostly run by the state, yet medium-and-small-sized firms dominate the industrial scene, especially in the south-eastern part of the country. Their management is based on the Confucian values that attach importance to the concept of family in the civic life. In other words, one can say that the concept of family relationship dominates the management of the industrial and business enterprises.

Confucianism is primarily based on a few cardinal values. They are as follows:

1. Filial piety which means respect for, and obedience to, the superiors and in turn due care for the juniors or subordinates by the superiors.
2. Complete loyalty of employees towards the organisation. They cannot question the policies of the organisation.
3. Sex discrimination in favour of men as far as allocation of power and duties is concerned.
4. Presence of mutual trust among the workers or between the employer and employees.

Confucianism believes in hard work and self-discipline. It also encourages frugality. It creates bondage among workers and between the employer and the employees. Every one in the enterprise feels that he or she is working in a family environment. The feeling adds to the growth of the enterprise.

In Japan, the cultural values are a bit different. The organisational structure is based on the "keiretsu". It denotes not simply the structure of the organisation, but broadly speaking, it represents a cultural value which is different from the Western culture. In keiretsu organisations, the chief executive officer is not very powerful; rather the power is exercised by a group of persons. Sometimes, the instructions move up from the bottom. The firms rely more on their retained earnings and less on external financing. As a result, retention of earnings is preferred to dividend payment. In-house development of production facilities and of technology is preferred to their outsourcing. Again, as regards human resource management, employees are regarded not as a factor of production but are treated as member of the organisation. Trade unions are not an independent union but they represent a company union. This way a sense of participation develops that is beneficial for the growth of the firm. The Japanese firms are thus found in a better position to achieve their strategic objectives and to possess competitive advantages.

11.2.2 Diverse Culture and Competitive Advantage

If an MNC moves to a country with a similar cultural environment, operational problems do not emerge on this count. But this is seldom a case. Generally, the culture in the parent company's country is found to be different from that in the country where its subsidiaries exist. This causes serious operational problems and effects the competitive advantage of the firm, which lies at the very root of every MNCs' success.

Cultural Diversity Impeding Competitive Advantage of an MNC

- Poor communication between top managers and subordinates
- Non-responsive attitude leading to inefficiency
- Lack of responsiveness towards innovated product/technology
- Buying pattern among consumers may not encourage large scale production
- Varying concept of human resource management may weaken employer-employee relationship
- Varying culture, limiting the scope for advertisement/sales promotion campaign

The operational problem is related to many aspects of culture.

1. First is the **problem of communication** or transmission of instructions from top managers to subordinates. If a company belonging to a high context culture moves to a low context culture country, the problem of communication will be immense. This is because the communication in a high context culture is indirect. The verbal part does not carry most part of the information, with the result that the message is often not understood in its right perspective.

High-context culture is the culture that lacks in direct communication.

2. It is the **attitude and temperament** that comes in the way of effective communication. It is found that Australian aboriginal workers are too slow in carrying out any instruction. This is because they think many times before doing any work. All this frustrates a manager from a western country who wants an immediate response from his subordinate employees, and at the same time, it impinges upon efficiency and productivity.
3. The operational problem is related to the **acceptance of the innovated product** in the host country. The organisational theory, explaining the fast growth of MNCs, believes that it is the firm-specific advantage arising out of innovated technology or product that provides MNCs with an edge over domestic firms in host countries. But this theory holds good only if the innovated technology or the new product is accepted in the host countries. The American company, Mattel innovated new dolls, known as Barbie dolls, and collaborated with a Japanese firm for their production and marketing. But these dolls were not accepted by Japanese children because their face, eyes, and the general appearance resembled American children and not their own. Again, when innovated technology is capital-intensive, it is opposed by trade unions in labour-surplus countries.
4. **Economies of scale** provide superiority to MNCs over domestic firms. But unfortunately, it is the cultural factor that sometimes negates this factor. This is because the size of production, price, and the quality of raw material may be influenced by cultural factors. For example, consumers living in smaller towns and villages in Japan and some European countries prefer to shop daily and so do not buy in bulk. This affects the prospect of large scale production.
5. The operational problem is concerned with the problem of **human resource management**. In the United States, promotion is based on merit-cum-seniority. In Japan, it is based on seniority and age. If an American company is operating in Japan and if it adopts the home-country policy of promotion, this will be resented in Japan. Again, the profit-sharing scheme is hardly found in the United States of America. If an American company is operating in Japan, Japanese employees will demand such scheme as it is common

in Japan. This will worsen the management-employee relationship and adversely effect productivity.

6. MNCs face a serious problem concerning advertisement due to the aesthetic and religious sentiments of certain host countries. In Islamic countries, showing a girl with far less clothes for advertisement purposes is not allowed, while it is common in western countries. Thus, if a western company is operating in these countries, it will have to narrow the scope of advertisement.

Only some of the major problems have been mentioned here that affect the competitive advantage of multinational firms while operating overseas. Infact, there are numerous problems connected with cultural diversity, as a result of which MNCs do not feel at home in a host country culture. There are many cases when they have not bagged operational success. All this, therefore, needs the management of cultural diversity, which is discussed in the following section.

11.3 MANAGEMENT OF CULTURAL DIVERSITY

11.3.1 Two Schools of Thought

Practical school of thought believes that a manager successful at home will be successful abroad. On the contrary, the cross-cultural school of thought argues for conditioning to accommodate cultural differences.

Since cultural diversity tends to impinge upon the performance of MNCs, it is essential to manage cultural diversity. Two different schools of thought are relevant in this context. One is known as the practical school of thought. Black and Porter (1991) contend that good management practices are effective everywhere. If a manager is successful in domestic operation, he or she will also be successful in foreign operations. What is important is that this contention has gained empirical support. Miller (1973) has found the practical school of thought to hold good in his survey. Black (1988) and Tung (1981) have found that over two-thirds of American managers posted on foreign assignments did not undergo special training.

On the other hand, the cross-cultural school of thought believes that the efficiency of managers operating abroad must be looked at in the context of the cultural environment prevailing in the host countries (Farmer and Richman, 1965). Ouchi (1982) examines the relationship between the companies' profitability and their Z-ness with respect to US-Japanese business and finds results in favour of the cross-cultural school of thought.

Compromising between the two schools of thought, we can say that there are some aspects of the communication process and some process related attitudes and behaviour that are no doubt universal, but the overall attitude and behaviour is diverse. The management process in general, thus, needs conditioning to accommodate cultural differences. If this is not done, it will be a blunder on the part of the MNCs.

11.3.2 Management Process

Lee (1966) outlines a procedure for decision making in different cultural setups. It is a four step model. The successive steps are:

1. To define the business goal from the home country perspective;
2. To define the same goal from host country perspective;
3. To compare the two and note the differences, and
4. To eliminate the difference and to find an optimal solution.

Elimination of differences normally means adaptation to the host country culture. However, sometimes, the management does not passively adapt to the ever changing pattern of cultural differences within which it is operating; rather it makes an effort to induce changes in, at least, some aspects of the host country culture. Let us now see how cultural differences are assessed, how the firm adapts to a local culture in the host country and how the home country culture is transfused in the host country.

Cultural Assessment: It never means that managers should be cultural anthropologists, but they should develop skills to assess basic cultural differences that have a bearing on their performance. The method differs according to the business decisions. However, broadly, there are two methods. One is partial assessment and the other is comprehensive assessment. When the differences are narrow and limited to only a few aspects, comprehensive assessment would be unnecessarily time consuming and costly.

In case of partial assessment, the aspects that are looked into are normally the attitude towards work and achievement, attitude towards the future, attitude towards authority, expression of disagreement, social structure, and so on. In a society, where wealth is not a significant motivation, employees do not care for work. They come to work only when they have exhausted their previous earnings. Those who are achievement motivated are serious regarding work. Again, when people have faith in the future, long term planning can be employed. Yet again, in an autocratic culture, decisions are centralised in the hands of top managers. In a democratic culture, it is distributed among different persons. Similarly, as regards expression of differences, some persons are straight forward, while others hesitate. Social status matters in some societies. In some cases, intra-class mobility is very low. So these aspects are carefully assessed.

In case of comprehensive assessment, all aspects of cultural diversity are taken into account. Farmer and Richman (1965) use a matrix approach, listing critical environmental constraints against which they set 77 critical elements in the managerial process.

Adaptation to Local Culture: Adaptation concerns many aspects of culture. However, according to Robock and Simmonds (1983), three classes of adaptation are important and relevant. The first is adaptation in **product policies**. This incorporates redesigning of market strategies that are in conformity with the host country market strategies. Here one can refer to the marketing strategy adopted by Singer Sewing Machine Company in some Islamic countries. Since the female population there maintains *purdah*, due to which women do not interact with strangers, the company first convinced the husbands about the utility of the machine, following which the women were automatically convinced.

The second type of adaptation relates to **individual adjustment**. This means that the managers should undergo personal changes. They should learn the local language, local manner of dealing with the people, and local behaviour. Only then will the managers be able to interact with the local employees, local consumers, and local suppliers.

The third type of adaptation is known as **institutional adaptation**. It incorporates changes in the very organisational structure and policies so as to resemble the local culture. In a host country, where caste system is very rigid, persons of different castes do not like to work together. In Lebanon, for example, Palestinian muslims hesitate to work with Lebanese Christians. If such is the case, the company has to bring about necessary changes in its recruitment policy.

An MNC is able to transplant the home. country culture if it:

1. assures large benefit,
2. protects the consumers and workers, and
3. works with opinion leaders who influence the workers and consumers.

Transfusion of Home Country Culture: It is a fact that there is ample evidence of cultural rigidity, but with the development of the visual media and of transport and communication, people living in one part of the globe have come in touch with the cultural environment prevailing in other parts of the globe. In some cases, they like the culture of others and they try to copy it. All this shows gradual diminution in the rigidity of attitude. MNCs take advantage of this fact and sometimes they try to transfuse their own culture into the cultural environment of the host country. The normal procedure is to discover the ways and incentive characteristics of the culture, which are likely to result in acceptance. The home country culture is easily transplanted if its benefits are exceptionally large. If a company supplies an innovated product that is not accepted by the local consumers, the common practice to be adopted is to promise and to ensure the after-sales service as well as to give a long term guarantee, in which case there is every possibility of the product being accepted by the local consumers. It has been found that if the company takes up measures to protect those adversely affected by the new product in terms of income, social status, dignity, and so on there will be no resentment towards the new product. Sometimes the company works through opinion leaders who influence others. In short, these techniques are normally adopted by MNCs to transfuse their own culture into host country operations.

11.4 ETHICS AND SOCIAL RESPONSIBILITY

When companies spread activities to foreign lands, managers are exposed to varying concepts of ethical behaviour and varying guidelines of social responsibility. Confronted by such unfamiliar elements, they sometimes adapt to the changed ethical behaviour and social responsibility. They change the product, follow a different production and marketing strategy, modify their human resource practices, and sometimes make changes in the very organisational structure. But there are cases when they stick to their own ethics and social behaviour, which is often a source of conflict with the host government.

11.4.1 Concept

Let us explain what ethics and social responsibility really mean. Ethical behaviour is primarily personal behaviour that should be in conformity with the rules or standards for right conduct or morality. On the contrary, social responsibility refers to the behaviour of the organisation, which should also be ethical and balance its commitments to investors, workers, customers and the societies in general. This means that shareholders should be given a fair and regular dividend and consumers should be asked to pay a fair price (Goyder, 1951). This is because the socially responsible behaviour of a company benefits every one related to it in the long run. Highlighting corporate social responsibility, the High-powered Expert Committee on Companies and the MRTP Act (1978) observes that a company must behave as a responsible member of society and it therefore, cannot shun moral values. Profit, although being an important consideration for business, is not the sole objective.

Ethics are standards for right conduct or morality.

Social responsibility is the ethical behaviour of an organisation towards different sections of the society.

Again, the nature of the ethical code of corporate behaviour is clear from the statement of R Kaku of Canon Inc., which is based on three value premises. They are:

1. **Human Dignity:** The dignity of an individual working in a corporation should not be violated even for the sake of fostering gains for the corporation.
2. **The Minnesota Principles:** A company should give due attention to the stakeholders, which includes not only the shareholders but also customers, employees, suppliers, competitors, and the local community.
3. **Philosophy of Co-existence:** A company should maintain a balance between healthy and fair competition on one hand, and mutual prosperity through co existence on the other (Suzumura, 1994).

11.4.2 Normative and Relative Ethics

When one talks about ethics or social responsibility in the context of international business, there is one view that the managers/companies should not bother about the varying norms of morality in the host country; they should implement their home country norms. The idea is based on Kantian normativism, which states that there are universal standards of human behaviour and every one, irrespective of their origin, personal preference, demands of the situation, and so on, should follow it. In fact, this type of normativism or universalism has come to be significant in the present-day world for matters such as civil rights, justice, fairness, equality of citizens, and employees.

On the other hand, the proponents of ethical relativism believe in the saying, "While being in Rome, do as the Romans do". It means that the managers/companies should follow the ethical norms prevalent in the host country. When the US company, Pizza Hut set up restaurants in Saudi Arabia, they built separate cabins for single men and for families in consonance with the Saudi value system. Similarly, McDonald's does not use beef in India as the majority of the Indian population are Hindus. Many oil companies operating in the United States of America profess that men and women should be treated equally and that bribery is wrong. But when they operate in the Middle East, women are regarded as subordinate to men and bribery is widely accepted. All this is nothing but representing the concept of relativism, which means that ethical truth is relative to groups holding it. Any action may be a right course of conduct in one country, but may be unethical in the other country.

Normativism states that there are universal standards of human behaviour. On the other hand, the proponents of ethical relativism believe in the saying, "While being in Rome, do as the Romans do".

Ethical relativism, despite being more suitable for a heterogeneous environment among widely dispersed host countries, is often refuted. It is said that it is based on non-sequitur. When two groups of persons have different beliefs, it is quite clear that one of the two beliefs is wrong. Again, there are specific norms that are a necessary condition for the very survival of the well being of any society. They cannot be different for different societies. Yet again, the apparent moral differences between societies often blur the fundamental moral similarities. Manuel Velasquez (1994) presents an example of an American manager making income disclosure to the income tax authorities in Italy. In Italy, since it was a usual practice to understate profits, the tax authorities overstated the profits and imposed a greater amount of tax. The American manager, who was not aware of this, presented the exact income with the result that the tax authorities overstated the income and imposed greater amount of tax, which was unjustified. This type of problem emerged because the American manager followed the ethics of his own country which was not fit for Italy. Velasquez is of the view that Italian tax practices were really not in conflict with American values. It looked different because Italian managers valued personal bargaining over rigid rules.

If one makes a survey of ethical behaviour among MNCs, it is evident that a number of them combine both normativism and relativism. They try to impose their home country ethics on the host country to the extent it does not entail upon their profitability or till it is not opposed by the host country government. In some other cases, it is neither the host country ethics in totality nor the home country ethics in totality, but a mix of the ethical standards prevalent in all the countries of the firm's operation that is followed. Infact, ethical behaviour and social responsibility depends upon whether an MNC is ethnocentric, polycentric, or geocentric in character.

MNCs, combine both normativism and relativism. They try to impose their home country ethics till it is not opposed by the host country government.

This analysis shows to what extent an international manager should stick to home country ethical norms and to what extent he should consider the local business ethics of the host country. Here we may mention the views of Donaldson (1996), which stress on respecting core human values that are basic to all business activities; on considering the local customs and tradition and on the manager's own judgement as to what is wrong and what is right in a particular situation.

11.4.3 Some Ethical Issues in International Business

It would be relevant to mention some ethical issues that have been a subject of debate among international managers in recent years. They are, for example, human rights, safety and environmental issues, corruption, and so on, which need some explanation here.

Ethics and Human Rights: It is often debated whether an international firm should move to a country, say, to China where human rights are found violated. One view is that trade with and investment in such countries hardly deter human rights abuses as it has been experienced in the case of western trade and investment relations with China. On the contrary, dismantling of apartheid in South Africa was possible through economic sanctions by some western countries.

The other view is that economic prosperity and political freedom go side by side. If foreign trade and investment bring about improvement in the living standards, human rights abuses would be contained. It is said that this was the philosophy behind President Clinton's decision to decouple human rights issues from foreign trade policy formulation.

> If foreign trade and investment bring about improvement in the living standards, human rights abuses would be contained.

Safety and Environmental Issues: It is often debated whether the multinational corporations should implement home country norms of safety and pollution measures in the host country. As one finds, the safety and environment protection rules are very strict in western countries. If those rules are followed in developing host countries, the cost of production will be higher and the competitive strength vis-à-vis the local manufacturers will be eroded. If they are not followed, it goes against the ethical norms of the multinational company. One such case is the employment of child labour, which is unethical according to western countries norms but very common in most developing countries. What then should the multinational corporation do? Here we may quote the views of Richard T De George (1993) that in such cases the company should adopt consistency. This does not mean that the company should act consistently everywhere its subsidiaries exist. It should abide by the local customs so long as it is tolerable by its own standards. If it is beyond tolerance, the company should stick to its own ethical norms.

> MNCs should abide by the local customs so long as they are tolerable by its own standards.

Issue of Corruption: In western countries, bribery is highly unethical. In the United States of America, there is a Foreign Corrupt Practices Act that prohibits companies from bribing any foreign official. The OECD countries do not allow their companies to enjoy tax deductions for bribing overseas. Sometimes it is said that making illegal payments speeds up

An international manager has to draw a line between what is ethical from the viewpoint of local custom and what is clearly unethical and then to take a decision.

the approval and the multinational corporations have not to wait longer for entry. But it cannot be denied that since money moves to bureaucrats/politicians that remains unproductive and that weakens the growth rate of the economy. In other words, bribery and corruption is counter productive (Mauro, 1995). On the contrary, there are many cases of illegal payment reported from different corners of the globe. In China reciprocal gifts are common and not unethical. In such cases, an international manager has to draw a line between what is ethical from the viewpoint of local custom and what is clearly unethical and then to take a decision.

A German engineering giant, Siemens is reported to have bribed potential customers at least in 10 countries to win business contracts. A sum of €1.3 billion has been found as a suspicious transaction. A German court has penalised such wrongdoings by Siemens. Many senior executives have left the company.

Again, a German automobile company, Volkswagen was found bribing labour representatives for their support. The chief executive was fined by a court.

Yet again, the petrochemical unit of a Swedish engineering company, ABB Ltd. bribed the local officials in Angola, Nigeria and Kazakhstan €1.0 billion in order to win contracts during 1997–2002. Its two officials were fined and the company agreed to return $5.9 million of profits without admitting/denying the allegations that it had violated the provisions of the Foreign Corrupt Practices Act.

—Based the reports published in *Mint*, 7.5.2008

Multinational companies market a number of medicinal products that are banned in their home country. They should care for social responsibility wherever they operate.

Issue of Consumerism: In developed countries, a lot of consumer protection activities take place. But in developing countries, they are lacking. It is reported that multinationals sell many harmful products in emerging economics. For example, companies market a number of medicinal products that are banned in their home country. They often perform human trials, especially on those who are uneducated. Companies manufacturing tobacco products sell them in developing countries without sufficient warning, whereas in the home market, they are sold under heavy marketing restrictions. Thus, it is advisable for multinational companies to care for social responsibility wherever they operate. They need apply home country norms in order to abide by ethical norms.

Transfer pricing lowers the tax burden of the firm as a whole and smoothens the firm's international cash management, but it is unethical as it brings about loss to the exchequer in both the home country and the host country.

Issue of Transfer Pricing: Transfer pricing is a means to encourage illegal transfer of funds among the different units of a company through over invoicing/under invoicing of export and imports. In many countries, there are strict rules restricting transfer pricing. Customs authorities are vigilant to check such practices. Even so, such practices are common. It is a fact that such practices lower the tax burden of the firm as a whole and smoothens the firm's international cash management, but it is unethical as it brings about loss to the exchequer in both the home country and the host country.

SUMMARY

- The performance of a firm depends largely on human behaviour. Human behaviour, in turn, depends on the socio-cultural and ethical environment. In other words, the socio-cultural and ethical environment influences international business decisions. If the environment is similar between the home country and the host country, the manager endeavours to reap maximum advantage from the similarity. If it is different, he or she tries to bridge the difference.
- Culture involves a whole set of social norms that shape human behaviour. The elements of culture are language, religion, education, attitudes and values, custom, aesthetics, social institution, and materialism. There is wide diversity among nations and regions as far as these elements are concerned. One study finds that there are four bases of cultural diversity. They are, for example, individualism/collectivism, masculinity/femininity, power distance, and uncertainty avoidance. An other study identifies five factors leading to cultural diversity. They are human-nature relationship, orientation towards time, beliefs about human nature, activity orientation of human being and inter-human relationship. Yet another theory emphasises on three factors, such as universalism/particularism, neutralism/emotionalism, and achievement/ascription.
- Cultural diversity influences competitive advantage. It effects communication between different levels of management, size of production, marketing of the product, and also upon employer-employee relationships.
- Cultural diversity should first be assessed and then managed. If diversity is only meagre, its partial assessment is sufficient. But if it is wide, comprehensive assessment is required. After an assessment is made, there is need for adaptation. Adaptation can be made to product policies. It can be done on an individual level or it can be institutional adaptation. Sometimes, when adaptation is not easy, the firm attempts to transfuse the home country culture into the host country operations.
- Ethics and social responsibility are very much related to culture. As far as international business is concerned, there is a long debate regarding whether MNCs should stick to their home country ethics or if they should adapt to the host country ethics.

REVIEW QUESTIONS

1. What is culture? What are its elements?
2. What are the factors that lead to cultural diversity? Does cultural diversity influence competitive advantage?
3. Explain how cultural diversity is managed.
4. What are ethics and social responsibility? Do you agree with the view that MNCs should stick to their home country ethics while operating in the host country.

OBJECTIVE TYPE QUESTIONS

1. Mark True or False:
   (a) Cultural boundaries may differ from political boundaries.
   (b) Culture is in-born.
   (c) Communication may be verbal only.
   (d) Social institutions form an integral part of culture.
   (e) Social stratification is apparent in buying habits.
   (f) Material culture is related to objects and things enjoyed by people.
   (g) Individualism, and not the group, motivates personal accomplishment.
   (h) Risk averse managers are conservative in taking decisions.
   (i) Communication between a high-context culture and a low-context culture is often very easy.
   (j) The cross-cultural school believes that the efficiency of managers depends upon the cultural environment in the host country.
   (k) Particularism suggests that the same idea and belief should be applied all over the world.
   (l) Ethical behaviour is primarily personal behaviour conforming to standards of morality.
   (m) Ethical relativism means that there are universal standards of human behaviour.
2. Choose the Most Suitable Answer:
   (a) Home country culture is transfused into host country operations by:
      (i) Providing after sales service to consumers
      (ii) Protecting adversely affected consumers in terms of income, dignity, and so on
      (iii) Both of the above
   (b) Adaptation in product policies incorporates:
      (i) Redesigning of market strategies in the light of host country market characteristics
      (ii) Changes in the manager's personal characteristics
      (iii) Changes in the organisation structure in line with the local culture in the host country
   (c) According to Black and Porter:
      (i) Managers successful at home are successful abroad
      (ii) Success of managers depends on the host country cultural environment
      (iii) Both of the above
   (d) Varying culture in the host country:
      (i) Often limits the scope for advertisement
      (ii) Encourages advertising campaigns
      (iii) Has no impact on advertising campaigns
   (e) Cultural diversity arises due to:
      (i) Human-nature relationship
      (ii) Orientation towards time
      (iii) Both of the above
   (f) The dimensions of cultural diversity among nations can be looked at in terms of:
      (i) Individualism/collectivism
      (ii) Power distance
      (iii) Both of the above

(g) Culture is:
  (i) In-born
  (ii) Acquired and inculcated
  (iii) None of the above

(h) Ascription denotes that:
  (i) Status depends on what or who a person is
  (ii) Status depends on the achievement of a person
  (iii) Both of the above

(i) A multinational manger should stick to his own ethical norms, if the:
  (i) Host country norms are beyond tolerance
  (ii) He feels that he will be meeting his social responsibility
  (iii) Both of the above

(j) Philosophy of coexistence means:
  (i) Maintaining a balance between fair competition and mutual prosperity
  (ii) Realising the dignity of an employee
  (iii) None of the above

(k) Ethical normativism means
  (i) While in Rome, do as the Romans do
  (ii) Human behaviour should be the same every where
  (iii) None of the above

CASE STUDY

McDonald' Success through Cross-Cultural Adaptation

McDonald's, one of the leading restaurant chains at the global level, began internationalising since 1980s and especially since 1990s. There are a host of factors behind its success (Mujtaba, 2004), yet the cross-cultural adaptability is the most important of them. It is natural that a customer, may be from any part of the world, does not relish that its own culture should be undermined by a foreign company. This is the reason that a company is successful abroad only when it helps preserve the culture, taste and belief of the host country customers. McDonald's policy-makers realised this fact well and they went largely for cross-cultural adaptation.

Some of the examples may be cited here. When this company entered India and when it found that the majority of the Indians are Hindus strictly not taking beef, it changed its strategy serving mutton burger in place of beef burger. In the state of Gujarat, where majority of the population is vegetarian, McDonald's introduced veggie burgers and other Indian traditional items, such as *samosa, vada, dosa*, etc. On the contrary, in Delhi, it sells meat burgers, popularly known as Maharajas McKababs to conform to the taste buds of the people of Delhi.

Again, in China, where McDonald's has more than 100 restaurants, this company emphasises more on beef burger, popularly known as Quarter Pounder, as it is supposed a luxury there.

Yet again, in Finland, it serves McRuis burger. Ruis is the Finnish word for rye which is very much liked by the Finns. On the contrary, in Spain, beer is served alongwith the meal. In Thailand, fast food consists of crunchy fried insects.

In the United States, McDonald's has named French fries as Freedom fries. In Canada, the company has modified the menu to suit the taste of the local population and provides cheese curd and hot gravy alongwith French fries which is popularly known as *poutine*.

In Israel, where the local population prefers that the food should be prepared according to Jewish dietary laws, McDonald's follows that norm. The Jewish culture does not permit the mixing of meat with dairy products, McDonald's does not serve kosher hamburgers, rather it serves cheese burgers and milkshake.

Source: Based on the reports published in The New York Times, 16.4.1993; Business Week, 1.1.1993; Wall Street Journal, 8.3.1990; www. McDonald's.com/corp/news/fnpr/2006; www. thunderbird.edu/about_thunderbird/caseseries/2005

QUESTIONS

1. Is it true to say that McDonald's has imposed the home-country culture on the consumers abroad?
2. How are India and China different from the viewpoint of McDonald's?

REFERENCES

Books

Czinkota, M.R. *et al* (1999), *International Business* (New York: Harcourt Brace).

De George, Richard T. (1993), *Competing with Integrity in International Business* (New York: Oxford University Press).

Donaldson, T. (1996),"Values in Tension: Ethics Away from Home" *Harvard Business Review*, XXIV (Sept.–Oct.), 26–34.

Dressler, David and Donald Carn (1969), *Sociology: The Study of Human Interactions* (New York: Knopf).

Dunning, J.F. (1993), *The Globalisation of Business* (London: Routledge).

Farmer, R.N. and B.M. Richman (1965), *Comparative Management and Economic Progress* (Illinois: Richard D. Irwin).

Goyder, G. (1951), *The Failure of Private Enterprise: A Study in Responsibility* (Oxford: Basil Blackwell).

Hofstede, G. (1980), *Culture's Consequences: International Differences in Work-related Values* (Beverly Hills: Sage Publishers).

Kluckhohn, C. and F. Strodtbeck (1961), *Variations in Value Orientations* (Westport, Conn., Greenwood Press).

Luthans, F. (1989), *Organisational Behaviour* (New York: McGraw Hill).

Robock, S.H. and Kenneth Simmonds (1983), *International Business and Multinational Enterprises* (Homewood: Richard D. Irwin).

Suzumura, K. (1994),"On the Social Responsibility of Corporations under Competition", in F. Neil Brady (ed.), *Ethical Universals in International Business,* (Berlin: Springer) pp.40–57.

Trompenaars, Fons (1994), *Riding the Waves of Culture* (New York: Irwin).

Velasquez, M. (1994), "Ethical Relativism and the International Business Manager" in Brady (ed.), *op.cit.,* pp. 15–26.

Journals

Black, J.S. (1988),"Work-role Transition: A Study of American Expatriate Managers in Japan", *Journal of International Business Studies,* XIX (2), 277–94.

Black, J.S. and L.W. Porter (1991), Managerial Behaviours and Job Performance: A Successful Manager in Los Angeles May Not Succeed in Hong Kong", *Journal of International Business Studies,* XXII (1), 99–113.

DeVries, H.P. (1969),"The Language Barriers", *Columbia Journal of World Business,* IV (1), 69

Government of India (1978), *Report on the High-powered Expert Committee on Companies and MRTP Acts* (New Delhi: Controller of Publications).

Lee, J.A. (1966),"Cultural Analysis in Overseas Operations", *Harvard Business Review,* XLIV (Mar–Apr.), 106–14.

Mauro, P. (1995),"Corruption and Growth". *Quarterly Journal of Economics,* no. 110, 681–712.

Miller, E.L. (1973),"The Selection Decision for an International Assignment: A Study of the Decision-maker's Behaviour", *Journal of International Business Studies,* IV (1), 49–65.

Mujtaba, B.G. (2004),"McDonald's Success Strategy and Global Expansion through Customer and Brand Loyalty", *Journal of Business Case Studies,* 3 (3), 17–23.

Reynolds, P.D. (1986),"Organisational Culture as Related to Industry, Position and Performance: A Preliminary Report", *Journal of Management Studies,* VII (3), 333–345.

Tung, R. (1981),"Selection and Training of Personnel for Overseas Assignments", *Columbia Journal of World Business,* XVI (Spring), 68–78.

SELECT FURTHER READINGS

Donaldson, T. (1989), *The Ethics of International Business* (New York: Oxford University Press).

Hofstede, G. (1997), *Culture and Organisations: Software of the Mind* (New York: McGraw-Hill).

Jamieson, I. (1982–83),"The Concept of Culture and its Relevance for an Analysis of Business Enterprise in Different Societies", *International Studies of Management and Organisation,* XII (1), 75–105.

Mead, R. (1994), *International Management: Cross-cultural Dimensions* (Oxford: Basil Blackwell).

Terpstra, V and K. David (1991), *The Cultural Environment of International Business* (Cincinnati: South-Western Publisher).

* What is now popularly known as the BSE was established as "The Native Share & Stock Brokers' Association" in 1875. It is the oldest stock exchange in Asia. Over the past 135 years, BSE has facilitated the growth of the Indian corporate sector by providing it with an efficient capital raising platform. The number of listed companies on BSE is 4900 and it is in the top ten of global exchanges in terms of the market capitalisation of its listed companies (as of December 31, 2009). The companies listed on BSE have total capitalisation of USD Trillion 1.28 (as of February, 2010)

12

International Financial Environment: Exchange Rate

NASDAQ, New York, America*

CHAPTER OBJECTIVES

International business operations are highly subjected to the international financial environment. The operations are conducted within the prevailing international monetary system, in which the exchange rate plays a very crucial role. The objective of the present chapter is to:

- ✦ Discuss the exchange rate regime beginning from the early days to the present one.
- ✦ Show how exchange rates are quoted.
- ✦ Explain how the exchange rate is determined in the spot market as well as in the forward market and the factors influencing exchange rate determination.
- ✦ Describe the theories of exchange rate behaviour.
- ✦ Show how exchange rate is forecast.

The international financial environment is an important factor in international business, influencing its size, pattern, and direction. For the convenience of the readers, the international financial environment is discussed in two chapters. The focus in the present chapter lies on the various aspects of the exchange rate, particularly regarding the evolution and development of the exchange rate system and exchange rate determination and forecasting. The following chapter will concentrate on the international financial and foreign exchange markets.

12.1 INTERNATIONAL MONETARY SYSTEM

12.1.1 Early System

The international monetary system discusses, among other things, the system of exchange rate or the relationship between the value of any two currencies. Centuries ago, when there was no established system and when the coins were made of valuable metal, the exchange rate was determined on the basis of the value of metal contained in the two currencies. The system was known as the commodity specie standard. The commodity specie standard was followed by the gold standard, which was considered of vital importance between 1870s and 1914. The gold standard was suspended during the Great War, after which it was readopted. But with substantial changes in the international economic scenario, it did not remain tenable; and by 1930s, it was finally abandoned.

> Gold Standard is a monetary system wherein the government holds gold coins in reserve against bank currency notes that are in circulation. The bank notes can be exchanged for gold on demand.

The form of gold standard was not essentially the same in the different countries adopting it. In the gold specie standard, gold coins were minted. Bank notes were exchanged for gold on demand. The price of gold was officially set, at which it was bought and sold. In the case of the gold bullion standard, however, there was no compulsion to maintain gold coinage. Individual bank notes were convertible into gold only through the purchase of gold bars at fixed rates, and not directly as in case of gold specie standard. The gold exchange standard was even more liberal as the currency was convertible into gold only through a currency being on gold specie standard. Russia had adopted the gold exchange standard and so the rouble was convertible into the British pound which was convertible into gold.

The gold standard possessed some inherent merits. Since the fixed weight of gold had formed the basis for a unit of the currency and since the free flow of gold was allowed among countries, the gold standard had provided for domestic price stability and for automatic adjustment in exchange rates and in the balance of payments. The supply of gold was fixed and so was the money supply. As a result, the domestic price level was stable. Again, any deficit in the balance of trade was made up through the price-specie flow mechanism. If a country experienced deficit on the trade account, the consequent outflow of gold led to shrinkage in money supply and to a lower price level. The lower price level made the exports competitive, which in turn wiped out the trade deficit. Yet again, any deviation from the mint parity could be avoided through the free flow of gold from one country to the other. During the pre-War period, one ounce of gold was equal to £4.24 or to \$20.67, meaning that \$4.87 was equal to one pound. If the value of dollar had depreciated to \$5.25 a pound, arbitrageurs bought one ounce of gold in the United State of America for \$20.67 and exchanged gold for £4.24 in the United Kingdom. They exchanged the pound for the dollar at the rate of \$5.25/£ getting \$22.26. This way they earned \$22.26−20.67 or \$1.59. The process continued till the deviated rate went back to mint parity.

12.1.2 Bretton Woods System of Exchange Rates

The demise of the gold standard led to large scale oscillation in the exchange rate. Three currency blocs were created, namely, Sterling Area, Dollar Area, and Gold Bloc. The exchange rates were fixed within a currency bloc, but oscillations in inter-bloc exchange rates could not be checked. All this required the creation of an international body that could help create an orderly exchange rate regime and could have surveillance over it. The Bretton Woods Conference of July 1944 resolved to create the International Monetary Fund (IMF) for this purpose. The IMF was established in 1945. A new system of exchange rate evolved. Since this new system was the aftermath of the Bretton Woods Conference, it was known as the Bretton Woods system of exchange rates.

Features of the Bretton Woods System of Exchange Rates

- The value of members' currency set in terms of gold or US dollar, meaning that the exchange rate was fixed.
- Provision for adjustable pegs, meaning that a country could devalue its currency to remedy its continued balance of payments problem
- Similarly, as in gold exchange standard, members' currencies were convertible into the US dollar and the US dollar was convertible into gold. This means the dollar was as strong as gold.

Fixed parity with adjustable pegs is a fixed exchange rate system along with provisions to devalue/revalue the currency vis-á-vis a foreign currency.

The Bretton Woods system of exchange rates represented a fixed parity system with adjustable pegs. Each member country was to set a fixed value, called the par value, of its currency in terms of gold or the US dollar. It was the par value that determined the exchange rate between any two currencies. Minor fluctuations, if any, within a band of ±1.0 were expected to be corrected through the active intervention of the monetary authorities. But if a country faced "fundamental disequilibrium" in its balance of payments, it could devalue its currency. It did not require approval of the IMF for the changes up to 5.0 per cent in the value of the currency, but beyond this percentage, the IMF's approval was necessary. Again, the Bretton Woods system was

Fundamental Disequilibrium is consistent balance of payments deficit reaching an unmanageable level.

like the gold exchange standard. The US dollar was convertible into gold at a fixed rate of $35 per troy ounce of gold. Other currencies were convertible into gold via the US dollar. In this system, the US dollar came to be the intervention currency, replacing the British pound that had played this role during the early decades of the twentieth century.

The Bretton Woods system did bring about stability in the exchange rate, but it could not go a long way. It was primarily the loss of confidence in the US dollar following deterioration in the US balance of payments since the late 1950s that hindered the smooth functioning of this system and led to its collapse by 1973. Since the US dollar was the strongest currency in the post-war years and since it was convertible into gold, a number of central banks held a large amount of dollar denominated securities as reserves. When the US balance of payments began deteriorating in the late 1950s and the real value of the dollar was expected to be lower, the central banks started converting these securities into gold. This caused a huge outflow of gold from the US Treasury, which in turn weakened the dollar. The weakening of the dollar led to further conversion of dollar denominated securities into gold. Barring US citizens from buying gold eroded their confidence further. Expectation of a record deficit in 1971 in the US balance of payments resulted in massive selling of dollar in the international financial market. The gold price in the free market rose, disturbing the relationship between the dollar and gold. There was a speculative run on the dollar. By August 1971, a full-blown crisis appeared against the dollar. Only during the first half of this month did the US government's reserves fall by $1.1 billion. The Nixon administration suspended the convertibility of the dollar into gold and this was a serious blow to the fixed parity system.

In December 1971, the Smithsonian Arrangement helped realign the par value of major currencies. For example, the US dollar was depreciated by 8.57 per cent. On the other hand, the currencies of the surplus countries were appreciated by percentages ranging from 7.4, for the Canadian dollar, to 16.9, for Japanese yen. Moreover, the fluctuation band of the par values was raised from +/−1.0 per cent to +/−2.25 per cent in order to provide greater room to member countries to manage their exchange rates. But this arrangement too could not go far. There was a tide of speculation against the dollar. The US Government devalued dollar further by 10.0 per cent in February 1973, but it failed to improve the situation. The foreign exchange markets were closed in 1973 to avert a crisis. But when they reopened, major currencies came on to float, thus delivering a death blow to the Bretton Woods system of exchange rates.

12.1.3 Exchange Rate Regime since 1973

In the wake of the collapse of the Bretton Woods exchange rate system, the IMF appointed the Committee of Twenty which suggested various options for the exchange rate arrangement. These suggestions were approved at Jamaica during February 1976 and were formally incorporated into the text of the Second Amendment to the Articles of Agreement, which came into force from April 1978. The options were broadly:

1. Floating—independent and managed
2. Pegging of currency
3. Crawling peg
4. Target zone arrangement

Floating Rate System: In a floating-rate system, it is the market forces that determine the exchange rate between two currencies. The following section of this chapter deals with how market forces help determine the exchange rate. The advocates of the floating rate system put forth two major arguments. One is that the exchange rate varies automatically according to the changes in the macroeconomic variables. As a result, there is no gap between the real exchange rate and the nominal exchange rate. The country does not need any adjustment, which is often required in a fixed rate regime and so it does not have to bear the cost of adjustment (Friedman, 1953). Secondly, in the long run, the exchange rate hovers around the equilibrium. In fact, it is the natural outcome of the market forces. The third argument is that this system possesses insulation properties, meaning that the currency remains isolated from the shocks emanating from other countries. It also means that the government can adopt an independent economic policy without impinging upon the external sector performance (Friedman, 1953). Last but not least, it provides for greater stimulus to trade and investment which is not possible is a fixed-rate system.

In a **floating-rate system**, it is the market forces that determine the exchange rate between two currencies. The merits of this system are:

1. Exchange rate is automatically adjusted according to the changes in macroeconomic variables.
2. Exchange rate is almost stable around the equilibrium in the long run.
3. It has insulation properties.
4. Trade and investment get greater stimulus.

However, empirical studies do not necessarily confirm these views. MacDonald (1988) finds that the exchange rates among countries on a floating rate system during 1973–85 were much more volatile than warranted by changes in the fundamental monetary variables. Dunn (1983) finds absence of insulation properties. During the early 1980s, when the United States of America was practising a tight monetary policy through raising interest rates, the European countries raised interest rates so as to prevent a large outflow of capital to the United States of America. Again, since the nominal exchange rate tended to adjust more rapidly than the market price of goods, the nominal exchange rate turbulence was closely related to real exchange rate turbulence (Frenkel and Mussa, 1980). Cushman (1983) feels that uncertainty in the real exchange rate did affect trade among several industrialised countries. Dunn (1983) gives an example of Canadian firms borrowing long term funds from the United States of America, which subsequently faced heavy losses due to 14 per cent real depreciation of Canadian dollar during 1976–79. He also finds that the large appreciation in the real value of pound in late 1970s had led to insolvency of many United Kingdom firms as their products turned uncompetitive in the world market.

Besides, developing countries in particular do not find floating rates suitable to their needs. Since their economy is not diversified and since their export is subject to frequent changes in demand and supply, they face frequent changes in exchange rates. This is more especially when foreign demand for their products is price-inelastic. When the value of

Clean floating represents no intervention by the monetary authorities in the foreign exchange market, while dirty floating involves frequent intervention.

their currency depreciates, export earnings usually sag in view of inelastic demand abroad. Again, greater flexibility in exchange rates between a developed and a developing country generates greater exchange risk in the latter. This is because of the low economic profile of developing countries and also because they have limited access to the forward market and to other risk reducing mechanisms.

The floating rate system may be either independent or managed. Theoretically speaking, the system of managed floating involves intervention by the monetary authorities of the country for the purpose of exchange rate stabilisation. The process of intervention interferes with the market forces and so it is known as "dirty" floating as against independent floating, which is known as "clean" floating. However, in practice, intervention is a global phenomenon. Keeping this fact in mind, the IMF is of the view that while the purpose of intervention in case of an independent floating system is to moderate the rate of change and to prevent undue fluctuation in the exchange rate, the purpose of the managed floating system is to establish a level for the exchange rate.

Leaning-against-the-wind Intervention refers to intervention meant to check the exchange rate from moving away from equilibrium.

Intervention is direct as well indirect. When the monetary authorities stabilise the exchange rate through changing interest rates, it is indirect intervention. On the other hand, in case of direct intervention, the monetary authorities purchase and sell foreign currency in the domestic market. When they sell foreign currency, its supply increases. The domestic currency appreciates against the foreign currency. When they purchase foreign currency, its demand increases. The domestic currency tends to depreciate vis-á-vis the foreign currency. The IMF permits such intervention. If intervention is adopted to prevent long term changes in the exchange rate, away from equilibrium, it is known as "leaning-against-the-wind" intervention. On the contrary, if the purpose is to support the current trend of exchange rate movement towards equilibrium, it is known as "leaning-with-the-wind" intervention.

Intervention also helps move the value of domestic currency up or move down through the expectations channel. When the monetary authorities begin supporting the foreign currency, speculators begin buying it forward in the expectation that it will appreciate. Its demand rises and, in turn, its value appreciates vis-á-vis the domestic currency.

Intervention may be stabilising or destabilising. Stabilising intervention helps move the exchange rate towards equilibrium, while destabilising intervention is found in cases where the rates are moving away from the equilibrium despite intervention. The former causes gains of foreign exchange, while the latter causes loss of foreign exchange. Suppose the rupee depreciates from 33 a dollar to 36 a dollar. The Reserve Bank of India sells US $1000 and rupee improves then to 33. The RBI will be able to replenish the lost reserves by buying the dollar at Rs. 33/US $. The gain will be US $(36000/33 − 1000) or US $91. But after intervention, if the rupee falls to 40 a dollar, the loss will be US $(36000/40 − 1000) or US $100. The monetary authorities do not normally opt for destabilising intervention, but it is very difficult to know in advance whether intervention would be really destabilising. Empirical studies show both stabilising and destabilising intervention. Longworth's study (1980) finds stabilising intervention in the case of the Canadian dollar, while Taylor (1982) finds destabilising intervention in case of some European countries and Japan during the 1970s.

Sterilised Intervention is intervention negating any increase in money supply.

Again, intervention may be sterilised or non-sterilised. When the monetary authorities purchase foreign currency through created money, the money supply in the country increases. It leads to inflation. This is an example of non-sterilised intervention. But if simultaneously, securities are sold in the market to mop up the excess supply of money, intervention does not lead to inflation. It takes the form of sterilised intervention. Obstfeld's (1983) study reveals that non-sterilised intervention is common, for sterilised intervention is not very effective in view of the fact that it does not change the ratio between the supply of domestic currency and that of the foreign currency very evidently. However, on the whole, Loopesko (1984) confirms the effect of intervention on the exchange rate stabilisation.

Last but not least, there has also been a case of coordinated intervention. As per the Plaza Agreement of 1985, G-5 nations had intervened in the foreign exchange market in order to bring the US dollar in consistence with the prevailing economic indicators.

Pegging involves fixed exchange rate. A currency can be pegged to: 1. a single currency, 2. basket of currencies, and 3. SDRs. In a currency-board arrangement, the currency is pegged to a foreign currency whose reserves are maintained to bring in exchange rate stability.

Pegging of Currency: Normally, a developing country pegs its currency to a strong currency or to a currency with which it conducts a very large part of its trade. Pegging involves fixed exchange rate with the result that trade payments are stable. But in case of trading with other countries, stability cannot be guaranteed. This is why pegging to a single currency is not advised if the country's trade is diversified. In such cases, pegging to a basket of currencies is advised. But if the basket is very large, multi-currency intervention may prove costly. Pegging to SDR is not different insofar as the value of the SDR itself is pegged to a basket of five currencies. Ugo Sacchetti (1979) observes that many countries did not relish pegging to the SDR in view of its declining value.

> The Russian Central Bank devalued rouble for the second time in the week by a total of 8.7 per cent. The rouble fell to a four-year low of 37.5481 per euro (the basket being composed of euro and US dollar). This decision was in view of a drain of 27 per cent of foreign exchange reserves and a 16 per cent fall in the value of the currency vis-à-vis US dollars consequent upon a 69 per cent fall in oil prices.
> —*Financial Express*, 16.12.2008

Sometimes, pegging is a legislative commitment that is often known as the **currency board arrangement.** The currency board pegs the domestic currency to the currency of another nation and buys and sells the foreign currency reserves in order to maintain the parity value. Again, it is a fact that the exchange rate is fixed in case of pegging, yet it fluctuates within a narrow margin of at most ± 1.0 per cent around the central rate. On the contrary, in some countries, the fluctuation band is wider and this arrangement is known as "pegged exchange rates within horizontal bands".

Crawling Peg allows the peg to change gradually over time to catch up with changes in the market determined rates.

Target-zone Arrangement is a sort of monetary union with fixed exchange rate within the union.

Crawling Peg: Again, a few countries have a system of a crawling peg. Under this system, they allow the peg to change gradually over time to cach up with changes in the market determined rates. It is a hybrid of fixed-rate and flexible rate systems. So this system avoids too much of instability and too much of rigidity. Edwards (1983) confirms this advantage in case of a sample of some developing countries. In some of the countries opting for the crawling peg, crawling bands are maintained within which the value of currency is maintained.

Target Zone Arrangement: In a target zone arrangement, the intra-zone exchange rates are fixed. An apposite example of such an arrangement was found in European Monetary Union (EMU) before coming in of Euro. However, there are cases where the member countries of a currency union do not have their own currency, rather they have a common currency. Under this group, come the member countries of the Eastern Caribbean Currency Union, the Western African Economic and Monetary Union, and the Central African Economic and Monetary Community. The member countries of the European Monetary Union too came under this group with the euro substituting their currency in 2002.

Global Scenario of Exchange Rate Arrangements: Firms engaged in international business must have an idea about the exchange rate arrangement prevailing in different countries as this will facilitate their financial decisions. In this context, it can be said that over a couple of decades, the choice of the member countries has been found shifting from one form of exchange rate arrangement to the other, but, on the whole, preference for the floating rate regime is quite evident. At present, as many as 25 of a total of 187 countries have an independent float, while the other 51 countries have managed floating system. The other 5 countries have a crawling peg, while 65 countries have pegs of different kinds. The EMU and other 20 countries of Africa and the Caribbean region come under some kind of economic and monetary integration scheme in which they have a common currency. Lastly, nine countries do not have their own currency as legal tender. The list is given here in Table 12.1.

Table 12.1 Exchange Rate Arrangements among Different Countries (As on July 31, 2006)

Sr. No.	*Exchange Rate Regime (Number of countries)*	*Countries*
1.	Exchange rate arrangements where the currency of another country circulates as sole legal tender (9)	Ecuador, El Salvador, Kiribati, Marshall Islands, Micronesia, Palau, Panama, San Marino, Timor-Leste
2.	Exchange rate arrangements where the members of the currency union share the same legal tender (32)	**Eastern Caribbean Currency Union:** Antigua and Barbuda, Dominica, Grenada, St. Kitts & Nevis, St. Lucia, St. Vincent and the Grenadines

	West African Economic and Monetary Union: Benin, Burkina Faso, Cote d'Ivoire, Guinea-Bissau, Mali, Niger, Senegal, Togo **Central African Economic and Monetary Community:** Cameroon, Central African Republic, Chad, Republic of Congo, Equatorial Guinea, Gabon **European Union:** Austria, Belgium, Finland, France, Germany, Greece, Ireland, Italy, Luxembourg, Netherlands, Portugal, Spain
3. Currency Board Arrangements (7)	Bosnia and Herzegovina, Brunei Daresalam, Bulgaria, China—Hong Kong SAR, Djibouti, Estonia, Lithuania
4. Conventional Fixed Peg Arrangements (52)	**Against a single currency (47)**: Aruba, Bahamas, Bahrain, Barbados, Belarus, Belize, Bhutan, Bolivia, Cape Verde, China, Comoros, Egypt, Eritrea, Ethiopia, Guyana, Honduras, Iraq, Jordon, Kuwait, Latvia, Lebanon, Lesotho, Macedonia FYR, Maldives, Malta, Mauritania, Namibia, Nepal, Netherlands Antilles, Oman, Qatar, Pakistan, Rwanda, Saudi Arabia, Seychelles, Sierra Leone, Solomon Islands, Suriname, Swaziland, Syrian Arab Republic, Trinidad & Tobago, Turkmenistan, Ukraine, United Arab Emirates, Venezuela, Vietnam, Zimbabwe. **Against a composite(5)**: Fiji, Libya, Morocco, Samoa, Vanuatu.
5. Pegged Exchange Rates within Horizontal Bands (6)	Cyprus, Denmark, Hungary, Slovak Rep., Slovenia, Tonga.
6. Crawling Pegs (5)	Azerbaijan, Botswana, Costa Rica, Iran, Nicaragua.
7. Managed Floating (51)	Afghanistan, Algeria, Angola, Argentina, Armenia, Bangladesh, Burundi, Cambodiá, Colombia, Croatiá, Czech Republic, Dominican Rep., Gambia, Ghana, Georgia, Guatemala, Guinea, Haiti, India, Jamaica, Kazakhstan, Kenya, Kyrgyz Rep., Lao PDR, Liberia, Madagascar, Malawi, Malaysia, Mauritius, Moldova, Mongolia, Mozambique, Myanmar, Nigeria, Papua New Guinea, Paraguay, Peru, Romania, Russia, Sao Tome and Principe, Serbia and Montenegro, Singapore, Sri Lanka, Sudan, Tajikistan, Thailand, Tunisia, Uruguay, Uzbekistan, Yemen, Zambia.
8. Independently Floating (25)	Albania, Australia, Brazil, Canada, Chile, Democratic Republic of Congo, Iceland, Indonesia, Israel, Japan, Korea, Mexico, New Zealand, Norway, Philippines, Poland, Somalia, South Africa, Sweden, Switzerland, Tanzania, Turkey, Uganda, United Kingdom, United States of America.

Source: *Based on IMF database.*

12.2 EXCHANGE RATE QUOTATION

12.2.1 Direct and Indirect Quotes

Exchange rates are quoted either directly or indirectly. A direct quote gives the home currency price of a certain quantity of foreign currency, usually one unit or 100 units. If India quotes the exchange rate between the rupee and US dollar directly, the quotation will be written as Rs. 45/US \$. On the other hand, in case of indirect quoting, the value of one unit of home currency is presented in terms of foreign currency. If India adopts indirect quote, the banks in India will quote the exchange rate as US \$0.022/Re.

12.2.2 Buying and Selling Rates

Normally, two rates are published—one being the buying rate and the other being the selling rate. Buying rate is also known as the bid rate. Selling rate is known as ask rate or offer rate. Bid rate is always given first, which is followed by the ask rate quote. Suppose the rupee-US dollar rate is Rs. 45.00−45.30/US \$, the former is the buying rate and the latter is the selling rate. The former is the rate at which the banks purchase a foreign currency from the customer. The selling rate is the rate at which the banks sell any foreign currency to their customers. Since the banks need some profit in these transactions, the selling quote is higher than the buying quote. The difference between these two quotes forms the banks' profit and it is known as spread. The bid-ask spread is often stated in percentage terms that can be computed as follows

$$\text{Spread} = \frac{\text{Ask price} - \text{Bid price}}{\text{Askprice}} \times 100 \qquad \text{...(12.1)}$$

12.2.3 Forward Rates

The quotes for the forward market are also published in the newspaper and periodicals. There are two ways of quoting forward rates. One is known as an outright quote, while the other is known as swap quote. The outright quote for the US dollar in terms of the rupee can be written for different periods of forward contract, as follows:

Spot	One month	Three months
Rs. 40.00−40.30	Rs. 39.80−40.40	Rs. 39.60−40.50

The swap quote, on the other hand, expresses only the difference between spot quote and forward quote. It can be written as follows:

Spot	One month	Three months
Rs. 40.00−30	(20)−10	(40)−20

It may be noted that decimals are not written in swap quotes.

In the above quotes, it is found that the longer the maturity, the greater the change in the forward rates. Again, with longer maturity, the spread too gets wider. This is because of uncertainty in the future, which increases with lengthening of maturity. The change in forward rates may be upwards or it may be downwards. With such movements, disparity arises between the spot and forward rates, which is known as forward rate differential.

If the forward rate is lower than the spot rate, it will be a case of forward discount. On the contrary, if the forward rate is higher than the spot rate, it would be known as the forward premium. Forward premium or discount is expressed as an annualised percentage deviation from the spot rate. It is computed as follows:

Forward premium (discount)

$$= \frac{n - \text{day forward rate} - \text{spot rate}}{\text{spot rate}} \times \frac{360}{n} \quad \text{...(12.2)}$$

where n is the length of forward contract expressed in number of days.

Applying the above example of one month forward quotation, we get:

$$\frac{39.80 - 40.00}{40.00} \times \frac{360}{30} = -\,0.06 \text{ or } 6\% \text{ forward discount}$$

12.2.4 Cross Rates

Sometimes the value of a currency in terms of another is not known directly. In such cases, one currency is sold for a common currency; and again, the common currency is exchanged for the desired currency. This is known as the cross rate trading and the rate established between the two currencies is known as cross rate. Suppose, a newspaper quotes Rs. 35.00 – 35.20/US $; and at the same time, it quotes C $0.76 – 0.78/US $, but does not quote the exchange rate between rupee and Canadian dollar. Thus, the rate of exchange between the rupee and the Canadian dollar will be found out through the common currency, the US dollar. The technique is similar for both the spot cross rates and the forward cross rates.

> One currency is sold for a common currency; and again, the common currency is exchanged for the desired currency. This is known as cross rate trading.

The selling rate of the Canadian dollar in India can be found out by selling the rupee to the bank for US dollars at Rs. 35.20/US $ and then buying the Canadian dollar with the help of the US dollar at C $0.76/US $. This means,

> Cross rate is exchange rate between two currencies determined via a common currency.

Rs. 35.20/US $1 × US $1/C $0.76 = Rs. 46.32/C$

The Buying rate of the Canadian dollar in India can be found out by buying the Indian rupee from the bank for the US dollar at Rs. 35.00/US $ and selling the Canadian dollar for the US dollar at C $0.78/US $. This means,

Rs. 35.00/US $1 × US $1/C $0.78 = Rs. 44.87/C$

Combining the two, one gets

Rs. 44.87–46.32/C$

12.3 DETERMINATION OF EXCHANGE RATE IN SPOT MARKET

12.3.1 Process of Determination

It is the interplay of demand and supply forces that determines the exchange rate between two currencies in a floating-rate regime. The exchange rate between, say, the rupee and the US dollar depends upon the demand for the US dollar and the supply of US dollar in the Indian foreign exchange market. The demand for foreign currency comes from individuals and firms who have to make payments to foreigners in foreign currency, mostly on account of import of goods and services and purchase of securities. The supply of foreign exchange results from the receipt of foreign currency, normally on account of export or sale of financial securities to foreigners.

In Figure 12.1, the exchange rate designated by the price of the US dollar (foreign currency) in terms of the rupee is shown on the vertical axis and the supply of, and demand for, the US dollar is shown on the horizontal axis. The demand curve slopes downward to the right because the higher the value of the US dollar, the costlier the imports and the importers curtail the demand for imports. Consequently, the demand for foreign currency falls. Similarly, a higher value of the US dollar makes exports cheaper and, thereby, stimulates the demand for export. The supply of the US dollar increases in the form of export earnings. This is why the supply curve of the US dollar moves upward to the right with a rise in its value. The equilibrium exchange rate arrives where the supply curve intersects the demand curve at Q_1. This rate, as shown in the figure 12.1, is Rs. 40/US $.

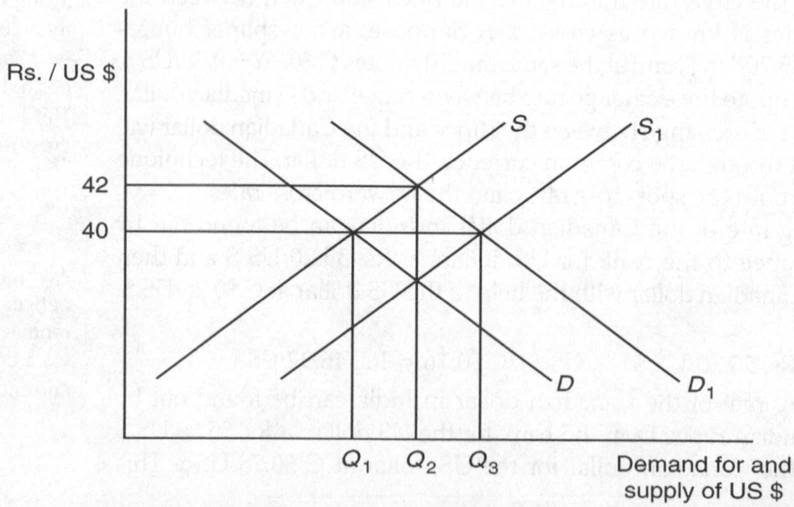

FIGURE 12.1 Exchange Rate Determination

If the demand for import rises owing to some factors at home, the demand for the US dollar will rise to D_1 and intersect the supply at Q_2. The exchange rate will be Rs. 42/US $. But if export rises as a sequel to decline in the value of rupee and the supply of dollar increases to S_1, the exchange rate will again be Rs. 40/US $. Quite evidently, frequent shifts in demand and supply conditions cause the exchange rate to adjust frequently to a new equilibrium.

12.3.2 Factors Influencing Exchange Rate

The most important factor influencing the exchange rate are

1. Flow of funds on the current and capital accounts
2. Rate of inflation
3. Rate of interest
4. Market intervention by the Central Bank
5. Psyche

The market intervention mechanism has already been discussed. So the other three factors will be discussed at some length.

Flow of Funds on the Current and Capital Accounts: A country with current account deficit experiences a depreciation of its currency. It is because there is a demand for foreign currency to make payment for imports. On the contrary, a current account surplus country possesses a large supply of foreign exchange with the result that the country experiences an appreciation of its currency. An apposite example of current account deficit country is the USA whose trade deficit was one of the more important causes for depreciation in dollar during post 2002 years. On the other hand, the currency of Japan and Switzerland appreciated in view of surplus current account. However, the current account alone is not responsible for this state of affairs. Sometimes, capital account flows help change the situation. There are countries, such as Australia, Britain, Iceland and New Zealand that experienced greater appreciation in their currency in the first half of 2008 even after having large deficit on their current account relatively to Japan and Switzerland that witnessed surpluses on their current account and, at the same time, smaller appreciation in their currency. In fact, this paradox is the result of carry trade that explains why trade flows are dwarfed by capital flows on account of interest rate differential.

Impact of Inflation: It is normally the inflation rate differential between two countries that influences the exchange rate between their currencies. The influence of inflation rate finds a suitable explanation in the Purchasing Power Parity (PPP) theory (Cassel, 1921; Officer, 1976). The theory suggests that at any point of time, the rate of exchange between two currencies is determined by their purchasing power. If e is the exchange rate and P_A and P_B are the purchasing power of

> Purchasing Power Parity Theory suggests that at any point of time, the rate of exchange between two currencies is determined by their purchasing power.

the currencies in the two countries, *A* and *B*, the equation can be written as:

$$e = \frac{P_A}{P_B} \quad ...(12.3)$$

In fact, this theory is based on the theory of one price in which the domestic price of any commodity equals its foreign price quoted in the same currency. To explain it, if the exchange rate is Rs. 2/US $, the price of a particular commodity must be US $50 in the United State of America if it is Rs. 100 in India. In other words,

US $ price of a commodity × price of US $
= Rupee price of the commodity ...(12.4)

If inflation in one country causes a temporary deviation from the equilibrium, arbitrageurs will begin operating, as a result of which equilibrium will be restored through changes in the exchange rate. Suppose, the price of the commodity soars up in India to Rs. 125, the arbitrageurs will buy that commodity in the United States of America and sell it in India earning a profit of Rs. 25. This will go on till the exchange rate moves to Rs. 2.5/US $ and the profit potential of arbitrage is eliminated.

The exchange rate adjustment resulting from inflation may be explained further. If the Indian commodity turns costlier, its export will fall. At the same time, its import from the United States of America will expand as the import gets cheaper. Higher import will raise the demand for the US dollar raising, in turn, its value vis-á-vis rupee.

However, this version of the theory, which is known as the absolute version, holds good if the same commodities are included in the same proportion in the domestic market basket and the world market basket. Since it is normally not so, the theory faces a serious limitation. Moreover, it does not cover non-traded goods and services, where the transaction cost is significant.

Relative version of the PPP theory states that the exchange rate between the currencies of the two countries should be a constant multiple of the general price indices prevailing in the two countries.

In view of the above limitation, another version of this theory has evolved, which is known as the **relative version of the PPP theory**. The relative version of PPP theory states that the exchange rate between the currencies of the two countries should be a constant multiple of the general price indices prevailing in the two countries. In other words, percentage change in the exchange rates should equal the percentage change in the ratio of price indices in the two countries. To put it in the form of an equation, where I_A and I_B are the rates of inflation in Country *A* and Country *B*, e_o is the *A*'s currency value for one unit of B's currency at the beginning of the period and e_t is the spot exchange rate in period *t*, then:

$$\frac{e_t}{e_0} = \frac{(1 + I_A)^t}{(1 + I_B)^t} \quad ...(12.5)$$

For example, if India has an inflation rate of 5 per cent and the United State of America has a 3 per cent rate of inflation and if the initial exchange rate is Rs. 40/US $, the value of the rupee in a two year period will be:

$$e_2 = 40\left(\frac{1.05}{1.03}\right)^2$$

or Rs. 41.57/US $.

Such an inflation-adjusted rate is known as the real exchange rate. When government sticks to a particular exchange rate without caring for inflation prevailing there, there emerges a gap between the real and the nominal exchange rates, which effects export competitiveness. This is why this theory suggests that a country with a high rate of inflation should devalue its currency relative to the currency of the countries with lower rates of inflation.

The theory holds good only if: (1) Changes in the economy originate from the monetary sector, (2) The relative price structure remains stable in different sectors in view of the fact that changes in the relative prices of various goods and services may lead differently constructed indices to deviate from each other, and (3) There is no structural change in the economy, such as changes in tariff, in technology, and in autonomous capital flow.

Again, if difference of the inflation rate between two countries is small, its effect on competitiveness may be offset by other factors, such as its balance of payments performance, development in real income, interest rate differential, and so on. As a result, comparison of inflation rates may not explain changes in exchange rates.

A number of studies have empirically tested the two versions of the PPP theory. The absolute version has been tested by Isard (1977) and McKinnon (1979). Both of them find violation of the theory in the short run, but in the long run, they find the theory holding good to some extent.

As regards the relative version, studies made till the early 1980s found that normally the rate of inflation and the exchange rate were related, especially in the long run (Aliber and Sickney, 1975; Dornbusch, 1976; Mussa, 1982). But subsequent studies also find clear-cut violation of the theory in the long run (Adler and Lehmann, 1983; Edison, 1985). Taylor (1988) finds very little evidence of PPP holding good. In a review of 14 cases, MacDonald (1988) finds that in 10 cases, the theory is not applicable even in the long run, but in four cases it holds good in the long run.

Primarily, there are three factors why the PPP theory does not hold good in real life. First, the assumptions of this theory do not necessarily hold good in real life. Secondly, there are other factors such as interest rates, governmental interference, and so on that influence the exchange rate. In early 1990s, some of the European countries experienced a higher inflation rate than in the United States of America, but their currency did not depreciate against dollar in view of high interest rate attracting capital from the United States of America. Thirdly, when no domestic substitute is available for import, goods are imported even after their prices rise in the exporting countries.

Interest Rate: Experts differ on how changes in interest rate influence the exchange rate. The flexible price version of monetary theory explains that any rise in domestic interest rate lowers the demand for money. Lower demand for money in relation to the supply of money causes depreciation in the value of domestic currency. On the contrary, the sticky price version of monetary theory has a different explanation. According to this version a rise in interest rate increases the supply of loanable funds, which means a greater supply of money and a depreciation in domestic currency. But at the same time, it shares the view of the balance of payments approach where a higher interest rate at home, than in a foreign country, attracts capital from abroad in anticipation of higher return. The inflow of foreign currency will increase the supply of foreign currency and raise the value of the domestic currency.

However, Fisher suggests, this proposition cannot be thought of in isolation of inflation, inasmuch as inflation negates the return on capital to be received. If the interest rate is 10 per cent and the rate of inflation is 10 per cent, the real return on capital would be zero. This is because the gain in the form of interest compensates the loss on account of inflation. In fact, it was Irving Fisher who decomposed nominal interest into two parts—real interest rate and the expected rate of inflation. And so, **the relationship between nominal interest rate and the expected rate of inflation is known as the Fisher Effect.**

Fisher effect states that a particular nominal interest rate, covers both the expected inflation and the required real interest rate.

The Fisher effect states that whenever an investor thinks of an investment, he is interested in a particular nominal interest rate, which covers both the expected inflation and the required real interest rate. In form of an equation, it can be shown as:

$$1 + r = (1 + a)\ (1 + I) \qquad ...(12.6)$$

Where r is the nominal interest rate;
a is the real interest rate; and
I is the expected rate of inflation.

Suppose, the required real interest rate is 4 per cent and the expected rate of inflation is 10 per cent, the required nominal interest rate will be:

$$1.04 - 1.10 - 1 = 14.4\%.$$

Suppose, the interest rate in the United States of America is 4 per cent and the inflation rate in India is 10 per cent higher than in the United States of America. A US investor will be tempted to invest in India only when the nominal interest in India is more than 14.4 per cent.

The concept of real interest rate applies to all investment—domestic and foreign. An investor invests in a foreign country if the real interest rate differential is in his favour. But when such a differential exists, arbitrage begins in form of international capital flow, which ultimately equals the real interest rate across countries. Suppose, the real interest rate is 5 per cent in India and 4 per cent in the United States of America, capital will begin flowing from the USA to India. In the USA, declining volume of capital will raise the real interest rate, while the increasing volume of capital in India will push down the interest rate. The capital flow will continue till the real interest rate in the two countries becomes equal. This means that the process of arbitrage helps equate the real interest

Since the real interest rate is equal in different countries, a country with higher nominal interest rate must be facing a higher rate of inflation.

rate across countries. And since the real interest rate is equal in different countries, a country with higher nominal interest rate must be facing a higher rate of inflation.

However, for this type of arbitrage, it is necessary that the capital market is homogeneous throughout the globe so that the investors do not differentiate between the domestic capital market and the foreign capital markets. In real life, a homogeneous capital market is not found in view of government restrictions and varying economic policies in different countries. As a result, interest rate varies among countries. Mishkin (1984) finds that investors have a strong liking for the domestic capital market in order to insulate themselves from foreign exchange risk. Arbitrage will not occur even if the real interest rate on foreign securities is higher. The Fisher effect is helpless on this count. Again, the Fisher effect normally holds good in case of short maturity government securities and very little in other cases (Abdullah, 1986).

International Fisher effect is a combination of the conditions of the PPP theory and Fisher's closed proposition.

Empirical tests present different results. Gibson (1970, 1972) and Fama and Schwert (1977) favour the Fisher effect; while the studies of Mishkin (1984) and Cumby and Obstfeld (1984) do not support the Fisher effect.

There is also Fisher's open proposition, known as the **International Fisher Effect** or the generalised version of the Fisher effect. It is a combination of the conditions of the PPP theory and Fisher's closed proposition. It may be recalled that the PPP theory suggests that exchange rate is determined by the inflation rate differentials, while the latter states that the nominal interest rate is higher in a country with a higher inflation rate. Combining these two propositions, the International Fisher effect states that the interest rate differential shall equal the inflation rate differential. In the form of an equation, it can be written as:

The International Fisher effect states that the interest rate differential shall equal the inflation rate differential.

$$\frac{1+r_A}{1+r_B}=\frac{1+I_A}{1+I_B} \qquad ...(12.7)$$

The rationale behind this proposition is that an investor likes to hold assets denominated in currencies expected to depreciate only when the interest rate on those assets is high enough to compensate the loss on account of depreciating exchange rate. As a corollary, an investor holds assets denominated in currencies expected to appreciate even at a lower rate of interest because the expected capital gain on account of exchange rate appreciation will make up the loss on yield on account of low interest.

The equality between interest rate differential and inflation rate differential can be explained with the help of the following example. Suppose, India is expecting 8 per cent inflation rate during the next one year as compared to 3 per cent inflation rate in the United States of America. If the exchange rate in the beginning of the year is Rs. 40/US \$, the value of rupee will fall vis-á-vis the US dollar at the end of the period to:

$$\text{Rs. } 40\left(\frac{1.08}{1.03}\right) = \text{Rs. } 41.94/\text{US } \$$$

Suppose that in the beginning of the period, interest rate in India is 7 per cent, as against 4 per cent in the USA. At the end of the period, interest rate in India will rise to an extent that will approximately equate the inflation rate differential. In order to find out change in interest rate, the following equation may be applied:

$$\frac{e_t}{e_0} = \frac{1 + r_{IND}}{1 + r_{USA}} \qquad ...(12.8)$$

Based on the above equation,

$$\frac{41.94}{40} = \frac{1 + r_{IND}}{1.04}$$

or

$$1 + r_{IND} = 1.09$$

$$r_{IND} = 1.09 \text{ or } 9\%$$

If rate of interest in India rises to 9 per cent, the interest rate differential between the two countries will be: $\frac{1.09}{1.04}$ or 4.81 per cent, which will be approximately equal to the inflation rate differential, which is $\frac{1.08}{1.03}$ or 4.85 per cent.

Bandwagon Effect: When a speculator being dominant in the market expects a drop in the value of a particular currency, he begins selling it forward. The other speculators follow the lead. As a result, the currency tends to depreciate despite favourable impact of inflation and interest rate. This factor played a crucial role in the depreciation of rupee during the closing months of 1997.

12.4 EXCHANGE RATE DETERMINATION IN FORWARD MARKET

Forward exchange rate is normally not equal to the spot rate. The size of forward premium or discount depends mainly on the current expectation of the future events. Such expectations determine the trend of the future spot rate towards appreciation or depreciation and, thereby, determine the forward rate that is equal to, or close to, the future spot rate. Suppose, the dollar is expected to depreciate, those holding the dollar will start selling it forward. These actions will help depress the forward rate of the dollar. On the contrary, when the dollar is expected to appreciate, the holders will buy it forward and the forward rate will improve.

> IRP theory states that equilibrium is achieved when the forward rate differential is approximately equal to the interest rate differential.

12.4.1 Interest Rate Parity Theory

The determination of exchange rate in a forward market finds an important place in the theory of Interest Rate Parity (IRP). The IRP theory states that equilibrium is achieved when the forward rate differential is approximately equal to the interest rate differential. In other words, the forward rate differs from the spot rate by an amount that represents the interest rate differential. In this process, the currency of a country with a lower interest rate should be at a forward premium in relation to the currency of a country with a higher interest rate. Equating forward rate differential with interest rate differential, we find:

$$A \times \frac{(n-\text{day}F - S)}{S} = \frac{1+r_A}{1+r_B} - 1 \qquad ...(12.9)$$

On the basis of the IRP theory, the forward exchange rate can easily be determined. One has simply to find out the value of the forward rate (*F*) in equation 12.9. The equation shall be rewritten as:

$$F = \frac{S}{A}\left(\frac{1+r_A}{1+r_B} - 1\right) + S \qquad ...(12.10)$$

Suppose interest rate in India and the United State of America is, respectively, 10 per cent and 7 per cent. The spot rate is Rs. 40/US \$. The 90-day forward rate can be calculated as follows:

$$F = \frac{40}{4}\left(\frac{1.10}{1.07} - 1\right) + 40$$

or $$F = \text{Rs. } 40.28/\text{US } \$.$$

This means that a higher interest rate in India will push down the forward value of the rupee from 40 a dollar to 40.28 a dollar.

12.4.2 Covered Interest Arbitrage

If forward rate differential is not equal to interest rate differential, covered interest arbitrage will begin and it will continue till the two differentials become equal. In other words, a positive interest rate differential in a country is offset by annualised forward discount. Negative interest rate differential is offset by annualised forward premium. Finally, the two differentials will be equal. In fact, this is the point where forward rate is determined.

> If interest rate differential is more than forward rate differential, covered interest arbitrage manifests in borrowing in a country with low interest rate and investing in a country with high interest rate so as to reduce the interest rate differential.

The process of covered interest arbitrage may be explained with the help of an example. Suppose, the spot rate is Rs. 40/US \$ and three-month forward rate is Rs. 40.28/US \$ involving a forward differential of 2.8 per cent. Interest rate is 18 per cent in India and it is 12 per cent in the United States of America, involving an interest rate differential of 5.37 per cent. Since the two differentials are not equal, covered interest arbitrage will begin. The successive steps shall be as follows:

1. Borrowing in the United States of America, say, US \$1,000 at 12 per cent interest rate.
2. Converting the US dollar into rupees at spot rate to get Rs. 40,000/-.

3. Investing Rs. 40,000 in India at 18 per cent interest rate.
4. Selling the rupee 90-day forward at Rs. 40.28/US $.
5. After three months, liquidating Rs. 40,000 investment, which would fetch Rs. 41,800.
6. Selling Rs. 41,800 for US dollars at the rate of Rs. 40.28/US $ to get US $1,038.
7. Repaying loan in the United States of America, which amounts to US $1,030.

   Reaping profit: US $1,038 − 1,030 = US $8.

So long as inequality continues between the forward rate differential and the interest rate differential, arbitrageurs will reap profit and the process of arbitrage will go on. However, with this process, the differential will be wiped out because:

1. Borrowing in the United States of America will raise the interest rate there.
2. Investing in India shall increase the invested funds and, thereby, lower the interest rate there;
3. Buying rupees at spot rate will increase the spot rate of the rupee;
4. Selling rupees forward will depress the forward rate of the rupee.

The first two narrow the interest rate differential, while the latter two widen the forward rate differential.

Now the question is whether the IRP theory holds good in real life or the arbitrageurs respond to interest rate differential. The study of Marston (1976) shows that the IRP theorem held good with greater accuracy in the Euro-currency market in view of the fact the there existed complete freedom from controls and restrictions. Similar findings emerge from the work of Giddy and Duffey (1975). However, there are studies that identify deviation from the theorem (Officer and Willet, 1970; Aliber, 1973; Frenkel and Levich, 1975). Since different rates prevail on bank deposits, loans, treasury bills, and so on, short term interest rate cannot be specific and the chosen rate can hardly be the definitive rate of the formula. Again, the marginal interest rate applicable to the borrowers and lenders differs from the average interest rate in view of the fact that the interest rate changes with successive amount of borrowing. Yet again, the investment in foreign assets is more risky than that in domestic assets. If greater diversification is applied to foreign investment in order to lower the risk element, diminishing return may apply; and as a result, arbitrageurs may not respond to interest rate differential as expected by the IRP theorem. Moreover, there are cases when interest rate parity is disturbed owing to the play of extraordinary forces. This leads to speculation. It is basically the market expectation of future spot rates that influences the forward rate. If market expectations are strong enough, they can push forward rates beyond the point that interest rate parity would dictate. Last but not least, the proponents of the modern theory feel that it is not only the role of the arbitrageurs but of all participants in the foreign exchange market, such as the traders and hedgers and speculators that influences the forward exchange rate. Since the action of the three different participants may not be similar in a given situation of the exchange rate, there is every possibility of the forward exchange rate differing from the no-profit forward exchange rate, as explained by the IRP theorem (Grubel, 1966; Stoll, 1968).

12.5 THEORIES OF EXCHANGE RATE BEHAVIOUR

The theories of exchange rate are compartmentalised into the balance of payments approach and the asset market model. The latter is again compartmentalised into two approaches on the basis of substitutability between domestic financial assets and foreign financial assets. Perfect substitutability between the two has led to the monetary approach, while the lack of perfect substitution has led to the portfolio balance approach. The monetary approach has two versions: one being the flexible price version and the other being the sticky price version.

Exchange Rate Theories

- **Balance of Payments Theory**
    1. Higher inflation rate differential at home → greater import and lower export → greater demand for foreign currency → depreciation of domestic currency
    2. Greater real income at home → greater import → depreciation of domestic currency
    3. Greater interest rate at home → inflow of foreign capital → greater supply of foreign currency → appreciation of domestic currency
- **Monetary Approach – Flexible Price Version**
    1. Increase in money supply → higher price level → depreciation of domestic currency
    2. Money supply being less than real domestic output → excess demand for money balances → lower domestic prices → appreciation of domestic currency
    3. Rise in interest rate → lower demand for money → domestic currency depreciates
- **Monetary Approach – Sticky Price Version**
    1. Increase in money supply → depreciation of domestic currency
    2. Increase in money supply → price rise → lower real interest rate → lower inflow of capital → depreciation of domestic currency
    3. Rise in interest rate → greater inflow of capital → appreciation of domestic currency
    4. Rise in interest rate → increase in money supply (loanable funds) → depreciation of domestic currency
- **Portfolio Balance Approach**
    1. Domestic income/wealth increase → greater demand for foreign financial assets → depreciation of domestic currency
    2. Foreign financial assets being more risky → demand for them decreases → appreciation of domestic currency

12.5.1 Balance of Payments Approach

Let us begin with the balance of payments approach (Allen and Kennen, 1978). It discusses the impact of inflation, growth in real national income, and interest rate on the exchange rate. An increase in the domestic price level over the foreign price level makes foreign goods cheaper. It lowers export earnings and boosts up the import bill. Lower export reduces the supply of foreign exchange; and at the same time, greater import increases the demand for foreign exchange. The domestic currency depreciates.

Similarly, growth in real national income causes larger imports if the marginal propensity to import is positive. Larger import will cause greater demand for foreign currency and thereby depreciation in the value of domestic currency.

On the contrary, increase in the domestic interest rate causes greater capital inflow that increases the supply of foreign exchange and, thereby, causes appreciation in the value of domestic currency. The first two factors influence the current account, while the third factor influences the capital account.

Pearce's (1983) empirical study shows that none of the above mentioned variables was very significant in case of exchange rate between the Canadian dollar and the US dollar. On these grounds, he has suggested an alternative theory.

12.5.2 Monetary Approach of Flexible Price Version

The monetary approach of the flexible price version emphasises the role of demand for money and the supply of money in determination of the exchange rate (Frenkel, 1976). The exchange rate between two currencies, according to this approach, is the ratio of the value of two currencies determined on the basis of the two countries' money supply and money demand positions. The demand for money—either in the domestic economy or in a foreign economy—is positively related to prices and real output and negatively related to the rate of interest. Any increase in money supply raises the domestic price level (based on the quantity theory of money) and the resultant increase in price level lowers the value of the domestic currency. But if the increase in money supply is lower than the increase in real domestic output, the excess of real domestic output over the money supply causes excess demand for money balances and leads to a lowering of domestic prices, which causes an improvement in the value of domestic currency. This way, this explanation is contrary to the balance of payment approach where increase in real output causes depreciation in the value of domestic currency through greater imports. Again, the monetary approach is different from the balance of payments approach in the sense that the former explains that a rise in domestic interest rate lowers the demand for money in the domestic economy relative to its supply and thereby causes depreciation in the value of domestic currency. However, critics of this theory argue that since the purchasing power parity theory is not applicable in the short run, this theory does not hold good in the short run.

12.5.3 Monetary Approach of Sticky-price Version

The monetary approach of the sticky price version rests on a couple of assumptions. The first is that the money supply in a country is endogenous, meaning that it is positively related to the market interest rate. The second is that the PPP theory applies in the long run and so the expected inflation differential changes have a role to play in the determination of the exchange rate. The argument in favour of this approach is that an increase in money supply (through changes in the real interest rate differential) leads to depreciation in the value of the domestic currency. On the other hand, like the flexible price version approach, an increase in the real output helps appreciate the value of the domestic currency.

The sticky price version makes a more detailed study of interest rate differential. The interest rate differential has three components. One denotes that when the interest rate rises, the money balances held by the public come to the money market in lure of high interest rate. Money supply increases leading to currency depreciation. The other denotes that if interest rate rises, financial institutions increase the funds to be supplied to the money market. Money supply increases and the value of domestic currency depreciates. The third is that a rise in interest rate stimulates the capital inflow into the country that, like the balance of payments approach, causes appreciation in the value of domestic currency.

Again, this approach specifically mentions the expected inflation rate differential. A rise in inflation rate compared to that in the foreign country leads to depreciation in the value of domestic currency. This is because a rise in inflation rate decreases the real interest rate and discourages the capital inflow (Dornbusch, 1976).

12.5.4 Portfolio Balance Approach

The portfolio balance approach (McKinnon, 1969) suggests that it is not only the monetary factor but also the holding of financial assets such as domestic and foreign bonds that influences the exchange rate. If foreign bonds and domestic bonds turn out to be perfect substitutes and if the conditions of interest arbitrage hold good, the portfolio balance approach will not be different from the monetary approach. But since these conditions do not hold good in real life, the portfolio balance approach maintains a distinction from the monetary approach.

This approach suggests that the exchange rate is determined by the interaction of real income, interest rates, risk, price level, and wealth. If a change takes place in these variables, the investor re-establishes a desired balance in its portfolio. The re-establishment of the portfolio balance needs some adjustments which, in turn, influence the demand for foreign assets. Any such change influences the exchange rate. For example, a rise in real domestic income or a rise in interest rate abroad leads to a greater demand for foreign bonds. Demand for foreign currency will rise, in turn, depreciating the domestic currency. Again, the legal, political, and economic conditions in a foreign country may be different from those at home. If foreign bonds turn out to be more risky on these grounds, the demand for foreign currency will decrease, in turn, appreciating the value of domestic currency. Similarly, rising inflation in a foreign country makes foreign bonds risky. The demand for foreign currency will drop and the domestic currency will appreciate.

When the exchange rate changes, the above mentioned variables change, which cause a shift in the desired balance in the investment portfolio. Thus two-way forces continue to act until equilibrium is reached. But the equilibrium is only short lived.

It may be asserted that although real income, interest rate, risk, and price level have an important role to play in exchange rate determination, the significance of wealth effect is quite large. When a country's wealth increases, holding of foreign assets increases. Demand for foreign currency goes up, which causes depreciation in the value of domestic currency. In this context, the possibility of substitution effect, which outweighs the impact of wealth effect, cannot be negated completely.

The portfolio balance approach is more comprehensive. But as Bisignano and Hoover (1982) find, data do not support the hypothesis of this approach.

12.6 EXCHANGE RATE FORECASTING

12.6.1 Relevance of Exchange Rate Forecast

Before taking any international business activity, the firm essentially takes into account the expected movement in the exchange rate. To this end, it should be able to make an accurate exchange rate forecast. There is, of course, one view that the foreign exchange market is efficient, meaning that the exchange rate reflects all available information. If it is so, there is no need for a forecast. There are reasons to believe that the content of "efficiency" is found in the foreign exchange market. But even then, this does not deny the need for exchange rate forecast. Forecasts of exchange rates are worthwhile for various reasons. It is more so in case of multinational corporations that have to shape their policy decision on the basis of expected exchange rate changes. Forecast is required in order to decide whether to go for hedging or not, while making short term investment of cash, for making long term investments, for raising funds in the international financial market, and for assessment of earnings from international operations.

> **Forecast** is required in order to decide whether to go for hedging or not, while making short term investment of cash, for making long term investments, for raising funds and for assessment of earnings.

12.6.2 Problems in Exchange Rate Forecast

There are, of course, some problems in exchange rate forecasting. First of all, the majority of forecasting techniques assume that past economic data would be a guide for the future. But it may be proven wrong, especially when the economy is prone to frequent structural shocks. In such cases, it is essential to recognise the structural changes and to modify the forecast model accordingly.

Secondly, the forecasts normally concern the nominal exchange rate changes. But if a country is consistently facing a high rate of inflation, the real rate of exchange moves far away from the nominal rate. Relying on the latter proves misleading.

Thirdly, forecasts of cases generally provide exposure management advice on a currency by currency basis. This way they are not so useful for evaluating risk in totality.

12.6.3 Techniques of Forecasting

The forecasting techniques can be grouped under four heads. They are:

1. Technical forecasting
2. Fundamental forecasting
3. Market-based forecasting
4. Mixed forecasting

In **technical forecasting**, movements in the past give an indication about movements in the future.

Technical Forecasting: In this technique, historical rates are used for estimating future rates. This is because in the majority of cases, movements in the past give an indication about movements in the future. There are two primary methods of technical analysis: charting and trend analysis. In the former, bar charts and sophisticated computer based extrapolation techniques are employed to find a recurring pattern of rates. The latter seeks to analyse trends through the use of various mathematical computations.

Technical forecasting techniques are used for short term forecasts. Their coverage is normally not very wide. If the value of a particular currency has moved up, the forecaster assumes that the demand for the currency has moved up; and without going deeper into details, he makes a prediction about its future value.

Technical forecasts are invariably used by speculators, although the technical forecasting models helping a particular speculator in reaping profits at a particular point of time may not be helpful at another point of time. Speculators depending upon the technical forecasts often incur losses. They also have to incur large transaction costs owing to frequent trading.

Companies do not benefit much from technical forecasts as these forecasts stress on the near future and not on the distant future. Moreover, since technical forecasts fail to estimate future exchange rates in precise terms, companies rely less on this technique.

Future rates are estimated on the basis of changes in the economic variables.

Fundamental Forecasting: In this technique, historical rates do not guide future rates. Rather it is various sets of macroeconomic variables. Future rates are estimated on the basis of changes in the economic variables. If the inflation differential is the cause for exchange rate changes and if the rate of inflation in Country *A* is higher than in Country *B* by 5.0 per cent, the value of Country *A*'s currency vis-á-vis Country *B*'s currency will decline by this percentage.

Similarly, many variables are taken into account and a forecast is made with the help of regression analysis. It may be that one variable is forcing down the value of a currency, while the an other is forcing it to move up.

Suppose, for estimating the Re/US $ rate, the forecaster takes into consideration the income growth rate and the rate of inflation in India as compared to those prevailing in the United State of America. He fits the quarterly percentage change in these two differentials, inflation (*I*) and income (*Y*) into a regression equation. The value of the rupee will be defined as:

$$\text{Rs.} = b_0 + b_1 I + b_2 Y + \mu \qquad ...(12.11)$$

Where b_0 is constant, b_1 and b_2 represent the sensitivity of Re to changes in *I* and *Y*, respectively, and μ represents an error term.

After the value of *b*s is generated, the movement in the value of rupee will be indicated. Suppose the value of b_0, b_1 and b_2 is, respectively, 0.002, 0.6, and 0.8 and if the inflation differential and income differential during the preceding quarter are, respectively, 4.0 per cent and 2.0 per cent, the value of rupee will tend to appreciate in the following quarter by:

$$= 0.002 + 0.6\,(4\%) + 0.8\,(2\%)$$
$$= 0.2\% + 2.4\% + 1.6\%$$
$$= 4.2\%$$

Some of the variables have immediate impact. In other cases, there may be a lag. In order to taken this problem, the forecaster uses sensitivity analysis. The more rigorous the technique, the greater it accuracy. In the age of computers, a host of factors can be taken into account. However, the probability of subjectivity cannot be completely ruled out.

It is a fact that this technique is simple and more reliable, yet it possesses a few limitations. First of all, the precise timing of impact of a particular variable is not known. There are factors that have a delayed impact and in those cases, the forecast will be fraught with error.

Secondly, there are some factors whose impact is instantaneous, although it is not very easy in all cases to know about those factors at very short notice. If they are not included, the forecast may be erroneous.

Thirdly, the coefficient derived from the regression model may change over the period. If, in our example, the US government imposes fresh trade barriers, the impact on the value of rupee will be different. However, there is always margin of error. The forecaster should take it into consideration.

Market-based Forecasting: In this technique, the estimation of future rates depends on the spot and forward rates prevailing in the market and on the expectation regarding the future. Suppose one US dollar is presently sold for Rs. 40, but due to some pressures—economic or non-economic—the dollar is expected to appreciate to Rs. 40.50 in the near future. If speculators have this kind of expectation, they will begin buying the dollar at the present point of time, so that in the near future, when the dollar become costlier, they will sell the dollar and, thereby, make profits equal to Rs. 40.50−40.00 or Rs. 0.50 per dollar. The moment the buying pressure starts, the value of the dollar rises due to greater demand and there is every possibility of reaping profits of this kind.

Estimation of future rates depends on the spot and forward rates prevailing in the market and on the expectation regarding the future.

This is not the case only with the spot rate. If the value of a currency is expected to be higher than its forward rate, of a given maturity, speculators will begin buying that currency in the forward market. At maturity, after taking the delivery of the currency, they will sell the currency at a higher rate in the open market and reap profits. The pressure of buying forward will raise the forward prices of the dollar.

Therefore, in both cases, expectation regarding the future influences the future rate. Thus, when the future value of a currency is estimated, expectation and present rates form the very basis of the forecast.

When the forecast concerns a long-run period, where the forward rate for such a long period is not available, the interest rate is taken into account. Consideration of interest rate is based on the interest rate parity theory where a country with a higher rate of interest faces a reduction in the value of its currency.

Mixed Forecasting: The techniques of forecasting explained above suffer from one limitation or the other. It usually happens that one technique is based on a particular type of information and the other technique relies on some other type of information. Relying on a particular technique may produce biased results. In order to avoid this problem, the forecaster uses a blend of different techniques. This is known as mixed forecasting. Each of the techniques is assigned a particular weight, the total weight being 1. The result of each technique is multiplied by the weight and they are finally summed up to derive the final forecast. Thus, the actual forecast of the currency would be a weighted average of the various forecasts that were developed.

In **mixed forecasting**, the forecaster uses a blend of different techniques assigning weight to each of them. They are summed up to get the final forecast.

12.6.4 Forecast Error

In the context of forecasting the exchange rate, it is not only the making of the forecast that is important, but monitoring the forecast is also very important. For this purpose, the forecaster compares the forecast with the actual value or the realised value and finds out the extent of difference between the two. The smaller the difference, the more accurate the forecast.

Forecast Error is disparity between actual and forecast exchange rate divided by actual exchange rate.

The difference between the actual value and the forecasted value is known as the forecast error. In percentage terms, forecast error is equal to:

$$= \frac{\text{Forecasted Value} - \text{Realised Value}}{\text{Realised Value}} \quad \text{...(12. 12)}$$

If forecasted value is Rs. 40.32/US $ and the realised value is Rs. 40.60, the forecast error will be:

$$= \frac{40.32 - 40.60}{40.60} = -0.69\%.$$

SUMMARY

- Developments in the international monetary system dates back to the commodity specie standard when metallic coins were used for international transaction.
- This was followed by the gold standard, which provided not only domestic price stability but also automatic adjustment in the exchange rate and the balance of payments. The gold standard failed to cope with the changes in international economic scenario and it was finally abandoned in 1930s. Its abandonment led to large fluctuations in exchange rates.
- A new system of exchange rate evolved in 1945 under the aegis of the Internation Monetary Funds, known as the "Bretton Woods' child". The system represented a fixed parity system with adjustable pegs. The currency of the member countries was convertible to the US dollar and the US dollar was convertible into gold. And so when the US economy turned into distress in late 1950s, the dollar failed to command confidence. Dollar denominated securities were converted into gold, in turn, depleting the stock of gold with the United States of America. The process weakened the dollar further and ultimately, the Bretton Woods system of exchange rate crumbled in early 1973.
- Post-1973, in the present system, various options are given to the member countries, such as independent and managed floating rate system, system of pegging currency, crawling peg, and target zone arrangement. The different systems no doubt have merits of their own, but they suffer from one limitation or the other.
- Exchange rates are quoted in different forms, namely, direct and indirect quote, buying and selling quote, spot and forward quote. Cross rates between two currencies are established through a common currency. They are found when the rates between any two currencies are not published.
- Exchange rate in a floating rate system is determined by the demand and supply forces. The higher the demand or the lower the supply, the greater the value of the currency in the spot foreign exchange market. The factors influencing the exchange rate are primarily the inflation rate and interest rate differentials. In the forward market it is the Interest Rate Parity theory that explains exchange rate determination.
- There are different theories explaining the exchange rate behaviour. While the balance of payments theory stresses on the current account and the capital account behaviour influencing the exchange rate, the monetary theories emphasise on the demand and

supply of money being the main force behind exchange rate behaviour. The portfolio balance approach also takes into account the behaviour of financial assets.

- Last but not least, the exchange rate is forecasted despite some problems involved in this process. The techniques are technical forecasting, fundamental forecasting, and market based forecasting. However, to get a better result, a weighted average of the results of all the three methods is computed.

SOME SOLVED NUMERICAL PROBLEMS

Problem 1 If direct quote is Rs. 45/US $, how can this exchange rate be presented under indirect quote ?

Solution
US $1/Rs. 45 = US $0.0222/Re.

Problem 2 If indirect quote is US $0.025/Re., how can this exchange rate be shown under direct quote?

Solution
Re. 1/US $0.025 = Rs. 40/US $

Problem 3 Consider the following bid-ask prices: Rs. 40 – 40.50/US $. Find the bid-ask spread.

Solution
(40.50 – 40.00)/40.50 = 0.0123 or 1.23%

Problem 4 Find out the bid rate if ask rate is Rs. 40.50/US $ and the bid-ask spread is 1.23%.

Solution
$(40.50 - x)/40.50 = 0.0123$
or $40.50 - x = 0.0123 \times 40.50$
or $40.50 - 0.50 = x$
or $x = 40.00$.

Problem 5 Find out the forward rate differential if spot rate of US $ is Rs. 45.00 and one-month forward rate is Rs. 45.80.

Solution
$360/30 \{(45.80 - 45.00)/45.00\} \times 100 = 21.33\%$. It will be known as a forward premium as the value of US dollar has increased.

Problem 6 Find the one-month forward rate of US dollar if the spot rate is Rs. 45.00 and the forward premium is 12%.

Solution
$360/30 \{(x - 45.00)/45.00\} = 0.12$
or $(x - 45) = 0.12 \times 45 \times 30/360$
or $x = 45 + 0.45$ or $x = 45.45$

Problem 7 Find Rs./Euro exchange rate if: the two exchange rates are: Rs. 43.93 – 43.95/US $ and Euro 0.83 – 0.84/US $

Solution
Bid rate = Rs. 43.93/0.84 = Rs. 52.30
Ask rate = Rs. 43.95/0.83 = Rs. 52.95
Cross rate = Rs. 52.30 – 52.95/Euro

Problem 8 If exchange rate at the end of 2004–2005 is Rs. 43.91/US $ and if the rate of inflation in India and the USA during 2005–2006 is 7% and 4%, respectively, then find the following:

i. Inflation rate differential between the two countries
ii. Exchange rate at the end of 2005–2006

Solution
Inflation rate differential between India and the USA: (1.07/1.04) – 1 = 0.0288 = 2.88%
Exchange rate at the end of 2005–2006: (1.07/1.04) × 43.91 = 45.18 Rs. 45.18/US $

Problem 9 If real interest rate is 5% and the inflation rate is 8%, what would be the nominal interest rate?

Solution
1.05 × 1.08 – 1 = 0.134 = 13.4%

Problem 10 If the rate of inflation in India and the USA is 7% and 4%, respectively and if the interest rate in the USA is 6%, find the interest rate in India.

Solution
$1.07/1.04 = 1 + x/1.06$
or $1 + x = 1.07//1.04 \times 1.06$
or $x = 0.0906 = 9.06\%$

Problem 11 If the interest rate in India and the USA is 9.06% and 6%, respectively and if the spot exchange rate is Rs. 43.91/US $, find the exchange rate during the next year.

Solution
1.906/1.06 × 43.91 = Rs. 45.18/US $

Problem 12 Find out the amount of profit out of covered interest arbitrage if the interest rate in India and the USA is 9% and 4.50%, respectively and the 6-month forward and spot exchange rates are Rs. 45.00 and Rs. 45.20, respectively.

Solution
There will be a covered interest arbitrage in so far as the interest rate and forward rate differentials are not equal.

To start with, borrowing $1,000 in the USA, converting it into rupee for 45,000 and investing the rupee for six months will fetch Rs. 47,025. Selling Rs. 47,025 forward will fetch $1,040. After repaying dollar loan alongwith interest for 1,022.50, the arbitrageur profits $1,040 – 1,022.50 = $17.50.

Problem 13 The value of rupee vis-à-vis US dollar for the first nine days of January 2005 is respectively as follows: Rs. 45.11, 45.10, 45.15, 45.15, 45.10, 45.30, 45.39, 45.50 and 45.41. Find a forecast of the exchange rate for the 10th day.

Solution
The average for the first four days is Rs. 45.13 and the average for the last four days is Rs. 45.40. On this basis, the actual value from the middle of 2nd and 3rd January to the middle of 7th and 8th January is Rs. 45.40 − 45.13 = Rs. 0.27. It means a daily increment in the value of dollar being Rs. 0.27/5. If the average trend value for the middle of 7th and 8th is Rs. 45.40, the exchange rate on the 10th of January will be:

$$\text{Rs. } 45.40 + 5/2 \times 0.27/5 = 45.40 + 0.1350 = \text{Rs. } 45.5350$$

Problem 14 If the average exchange rate in the first quarter of 2005 is 45.10/US $ with India having a positive interest rate differential of 2.30% and a positive inflation rate differential of 3.10% over that in the USA, and if the sensitivity of rupee to interest rate and inflation rate differential is 40%, find a forecast of the exchange rate during the second quarter assuming a constant term as 0.02.

Solution
Fitting these figures into a regression equation,

$$1 + 0.5 \times 0.023 + 0.5 \times 0.031 = 0.0470 = 4.70\%$$

Rupee will depreciate by 4.70%. The exchange rate forecast in the second quarter will be Rs. 47.22/US $.

Problem 15 The average spot rate during the first quarter of 2005 is Rs. 45.10/US $. But if there is pressure on dollars and its demand is expected to move up by 10 per cent, find out the forecast for the second quarter.

Solution
Assuming the supply of dollars being constant, the exchange rate in the second quarter should be:

$$\text{Rs. } 45.10 \times 1.10 = \text{Rs. } 49.61/\text{US }\$$$

Problem 16 The technical forecast, fundamental forecast and the market-based forecast of rupee vis-à-vis US dollar for the second quarter of 2005 are respectively as follows: Rs. 45.54, Rs. 47.22 and Rs. 49.61. If the forecaster assigns 30%, 30% and 40% weight respectively to the above forecast, what would be the weighted average of the forecasts, often known as mixed forecast?

Solution
Mixed forecast will be:

$$0.3 \times 45.54 + 0.3 \times 47.22 + 0.4 \times 49.61 = \text{Rs. } 47.67/\text{US }\$$$

REVIEW QUESTIONS

1. How far was the fixed parity system of exchange rate different from the gold standard? Explain the factors behind the collapse of the fixed parity system.
2. Do you agree that the floating exchange rate system is more beneficial than the system of fixed exchange rate?
3. Explain managed floating. Distinguish between sterilised and non-sterilised intervention.
4. How is the exchange rate determined in the spot market? What are the major factors influencing the exchange rate?

5. Explain Interest Rate Parity Theory. Is it sufficient to explain the behaviour of the exchange rate in a forward market?
6. Explain the monetary theory of exchange rate behaviour. How is it different from the Portfolio Balance Approach?
7. Discuss how movement in the balance of payments variables influences the exchange rate.
8. What are the different techniques of exchange rate forecasting? What is a forecast error?
9. Write short notes on:
   (i) Direct and Indirect quote
   (ii) Buying and selling quote
   (iii) Cross rate quote
   (iv) Crawling peg
   (v) Covered interest arbitrage

OBJECTIVE TYPE QUESTIONS

1. Mark True or False:
   (a) Gold coinage was essential under the gold exchange standard.
   (b) Gold standard was marked with a high degree of domestic price instability.
   (c) US balance of payments deficit was the main reason behind the collapse of the Bretton Woods system of exchange rate.
   (d) Wider discrepancy between the real and nominal exchange rates is a key feature of the floating rate regime.
   (e) Domestic currency is on the numerator in the case of a direct quote.
   (f) Bid rate and buying rate are synonyms.
   (g) Ask rate/offer rate and selling rate carry the same meaning.
   (h) Forward rate differential is greater in case of shorter maturity.
   (i) Cross rate is found out through a common currency.
   (j) Technical forecasting is usually applied to short term forecasts.
   (k) In fundamental forecasting, important macroeconomic variables are taken into account.
   (l) Mixed forecasting is the combination of different types of forecast.
   (m) Forecast error is the product of actual and forecasted values.
   (n) Market based forecast depends on spot and forward rates prevailing in the market and on the expectation about the future.

2. Choose the Most Suitable Answer.
   (a) Sterilised intervention by the monetary authorities is expected to:
      (i) Increase the money supply in the country
      (ii) Bear no ultimate effect on the money supply
      (iii) None of the above
   (b) "Fundamental disequilibrium" in the Bretton Woods system meant:
      (i) Consistent balance of payments deficit
      (ii) Consistent devaluation
      (iii) Rising inflation rate in the country

(c) Demand for foreign currency is influenced by:
   (i) Size of export
   (ii) Size of import
   (iii) None of the above
(d) The supply of foreign currency is influenced by the:
   (i) Size of export
   (ii) Size of import
   (iii) None of the above
(e) Domestic currency tends to depreciate owing to:
   (i) High inflation rate
   (ii) Lowering of inflation rate
   (iii) Constant inflation rate
(f) Nominal interest rate is the product of the:
   (i) Real interest rate and rate of inflation
   (ii) Real interest rate and exchange rate
   (iii) None of the above
(g) Covered interest arbitrage takes place when the:
   (i) Forward rate differential is equal to interest rate differential
   (ii) Forward rate differential is not equal to interest rate differential
   (iii) None of the above
(h) Forecast error is
   (i) The difference between the forecast value and the realised value
   (ii) The use of an inappropriate method of forecasting
   (iii) None of the above
(i) Technical analysis of forecast is based on:
   (i) Past trends
   (ii) Macroeconomic variables
   (iii) Behaviour of speculators

NUMERICAL PROBLEMS

1. If a direct quote is: Rs 50/US $, how can this exchange rate be presented in an indirect quote?
2. Consider the following bid-ask prices: Rs 40.00−41.00/US $. Find out the bid-ask spread.
3. Find the cross rate for SF/Euro, if: Euro 0.90−0.91/US $ and SF 65.00−65.20 / US $.
4. The exchange rate between the rupee and the US $ is Rs 47/US $ at the end of Period 1. The rate of inflation in India and the United States of America is 8 per cent and 3 per cent, respectively. What is the likely exchange rate at the end of Period 2 ?
5. If nominal rate of interest is 10% and rate of inflation is 6%, what would be the real interest rate?
6. Calculate the forward rate differential if spot rate is Rs. 46/US $ and 3-month forward rate is 45.50/US $.
7. Calculate the 3-month forward rate, if spot rate is Rs. 46/US $; interest rate in India and the USA is respectively 8% and 3%.
8. Find out the forecast error if the forecast value is Rs. 46.00/$, and the realised value is Rs. 46.50/$.

Case Study

Exchange Rate Scenario in India

The high level committee on balance of payments, commonly known as the Rangarajan Committee (1992), suggested a dual exchange rate system or a mix of official and market rates at least for a year before finally stepping into a managed floating exchange rate system in March 1993. The managed float involves essentially RBI's intervention in the foreign exchange market either directly through the purchase and sale of US dollars or indirectly through making changes in the repo rate and the resultant size of liquidity in the monetary and financial system. It is true that the new system of exchange rate alongwith reforms in trade and investment policies helped boost up trade and investment (Sharan and Mukherji, 2001), but the oscillations in exchange rate at times could not completely be ruled out.

Trend in the Exchange Rate

As regards the movements in the exchange rate, the following table shows that the annual average value of rupee vis-à-vis US dollar tended to depreciate all along from 31.37 in FY 1993–1994 to 48.40 in FY 2002–2003, although then appreciated moving in the range of 44.26 and 45.95 during FYs 2003–2007. In FY 2007–2008, rupee appreciated at a rapid pace making an average of 40.24 a dollar. But following the crisis in the Indian financial market, rupee depreciated to an annual average of 45.99 during FY 2008–09.

Rs./US $ Exchange Rate

FY	*Rs./US $ (Average)*	*FY*	*Rs./US (Average)*	*FY*	*Rs./US $ (Average)*
1993–1994	31.37	1998–1999	42.07	2003–2004	45.95
1994–1995	31.40	1999–2000	43.33	2004–2005	44.93
1995–1996	33.45	2000–2001	45.68	2005–2006	44.26
1996–1997	35.50	2001–2002	47.69	2006–2007	45.25
1997–1998	37.17	2002–2003	48.40	2007–2008	40.24
				2008–2009	45.99

Sources: 1. Govt. of India, *Economic Survey*, various issues.
2. RBI, *Reserve Bank of India Bulletin*, various issues.

For the appreciation of rupee during the FY 2007-2008, it was primarily the inflow of a large amount of foreign direct investment and foreign portfolio investment that helped to increase the supply of dollars in the foreign exchange market. It is because when the foreign institutional investors began making disinvestment in the wake of Subprime crisis, the rupee tended to depreciate fast during FY 2008-2009. By March 2009, rupee fell to 51.23 a dollar. Thus, it is primarily the demand and supply forces that help determine the exchange rate.

Probing still deeper, it is found that the standard deviation of daily spot rate remained confined to a level of 0.04 to 0.1 till FY 2001-2002. In fact, the exchange rate oscillations to such a low degree led some of the experts to analogise the managed floating regime in India with a fixed exchange rate regime for all practical purposes (Baig, 2001; Patnaik, 2003). Rakesh Mohan (rbi.org) has also presented the co-efficient of variation of daily spot rate beginning from March 1995 to March 2007 and is of the view that instability in the daily spot rate was confined between 0.1 and 0.3 except for March 1995, March 1996 and March 2004 when it was 2.5, 1.8 and 1.1, respectively.

Managed float, by its very nature, could not avoid exchange rate risk and the resultant forward trading to hedge the risk. Forward rates are expected rates in the future. The literature on the issue whether, or not, the forward rate is an unbiased indicator of future spot rate is vast (Kohlhagen,1975; Edwards, 1982; Hansen and Hodrick, 1983). Again, there are many studies to show that widening/narrowing of interest rate differential has influenced the forward exchange rate of Indian rupee (Chakrabarti, 2006; Patnaik, et al, 2003; Sharma and Mitra, 2006). Their discussion is not explained here; nevertheless, it can be said that the average discount on forward rate of rupee, both 3- and 6-month, was about 4.0 per cent per annum between late 1997 and mid 2004. To be more precise, it was 3.7 per cent for 3-month forward and 3.8 per cent for six-month forward (Chakrabarti, 2006). From June 2004 onward, forward premium was evident that was as high as 3.0 per cent by August 2004 but then it tended to decline to less than 2.0 per cent by June 2005 and further to less than 1.0 per cent by October 2005. At the close of FY 2005–2006, it ascended again to over 3.0 per cent but then shrank to less than one per cent by July 2006 (RBI, 2006). During FY 2006–2007, the forward premia increased reflecting growing interest rate differential in view of increased domestic interest rates. In March 2007, one-, three- and six-month premia were 7.30 per cent, 5.14 per cent and 4.40 per cent, respectively. In fact, it was because of the changes in the macro-economic variables that the spot rates and the forward rates tended to oscillate. In FY 2007–2008, because of continuous off-loading of forward position by the exporters, one-month, three-month and six-month tended to decline and reached to 3.45 per cent, 2.75 per cent and 2.50 per cent, respectively. During FY 2008–2009, forward premia showed larger volatility reflecting fast changes in supply and demand conditions and the relative interest rates.

Ensuring Stability in the Exchange Rate

The issue of financial stability attained significance in late 1990s in view of keeping at bay the spill-over effects of the turbulence in the South-East Asian financial markets and also the deepening of the financial crisis in Russia. The RBI announced a set of policy measures in June 1998. These measures emphasised on the RBI's role of meeting mismatches between the demand and supply of foreign currency through market intervention, allowing the foreign institutional investors (FIIs) to manage their exchange rate exposure through undertaking foreign exchange cover on their incremental investment, advising traders and banks to monitor their foreign currency position and allowing domestic financial institutions to buy back their debt from international financial market. Foreign Exchange Management Act (FEMA) replacing the Foreign Exchange Regulation Act came into force from June 1, 2000. It aimed at promoting an orderly development and maintenance of the foreign exchange market in India. The Act provides transparent norms relating to the RBI's approval for acquiring and holding of foreign exchange and the limits to which foreign exchange is admissible to current/capital account transactions from the viewpoint of full current account convertibility and growing convertibility on capital account.

In fact, it is the very macro-economic policy, especially the monetary measures and the administrative measures that have helped to ensure stability in the foreign exchange market through influencing the supply of, and demand for, the foreign currency. For example, when normal capital inflows faltered, the State Bank of India raised US $4.2 billion through the issue of Resurgent India Bonds during August 1998 and another US $5.5 billion through the issue of India Millennium Deposits during October–November 2000. However, the RBI's role in form of market intervention has been the most significant one. It has already been mentioned how RBI intervenes in the foreign exchange market but it needs some more details about the extent of intervention. Looking at the figures in the recent past in the following table, it is evident that the amount of the purchase of foreign currency ranged between US $15,239 million and US $55,418 million annually during FYs 2000–2006. Similarly, the sale of foreign currency varied between US $7,096 million and US $24,940 million during this period. The FY 2006–2007 was singular in the sense that the RBI bought US dollars and never sold them. The quantum of purchase was $26.824 billions that helped to check at least to some extent the rupee from appreciating. In 2007–2008, the purchases were much larger than the sale of dollar. But, on the contrary, in FY 2008–2009, the sales of dollar exceeded far the purchase in view of checking depreciation of rupee. Again, as a ratio of turnover in the foreign exchange market, the size of intervention varied between 3.9 per cent and 0.3 per cent. All this shows that the RBI has taken pains to avoid mismatches between demand and supply of foreign currency in the market and thereby to bring in stability in the exchange rate. Unnikrishnan and Mohan (2003) probe deeper into this issue and found that beginning from January 1996 to March 2002, the RBI adopted a "leaning against the wind" approach which is evident from a negative correlation between the exchange rate and net dollar purchases. It thereby stressed more on checking volatility in the foreign exchange market rather than simply checking appreciation/depreciation of the currency.

RBI's Purchase and Sale of Foreign Currency during 2000s

Millions of US $

Year	*Purchase*	*Sale*	*Net (Purchase – Sale)*	*RBI Intervention as % of Turnover in Foreign Exchange Market*
2000–2001	28,202	25,846	2,356	3.9
2001–2002	22,822	15,668	7,154	2.7
2002–2003	30,639	14,927	15,712	2.9
2003–2004	55,418	24,940	30,478	3.8
2004–2005	31,398	10,551	20,847	1.4
2005–2006	15,239	7,096	8,143	0.5
2006–2007	26,824	-	26,824	0.4
2007–2008	79,696	1,493	78,203	0.7
2008–2009	26,563	61,485	−34,922	0.3

Sources: 1. RBI, Annual Report, various issues.
2. RBI Bulletin, various issues.

QUESTIONS

1. What do you mean by managed floating of exchange rate regime? Why was it adopted in India?
2. Comment on the trend of the exchange rate of rupee during the managed floating regime.
3. How was fluctuation in the rupee/dollar exchange rate controlled?

REFERENCES

Books

Abdullah, F.A. (1986), *Financial Management for the Multinational Firm* (New Delhi: Prentice-Hall of India), p. 59.

Allen, P.R. and P.B. Kenen (1978), *The Balance of Payments, Exchange Rate and Economic Policy* (Athens: Centre for Planning and Economic Research).

Cassel, G. (1921), *The World's Monetary Problems* (London: Constable).

Chakrabarti, R. (2006), *The Financial Sector in India: Emerging Issues*, New Delhi: Oxford University Press.

Cumby, R.E. and M. Obstfeld (1984), "International Interest Rate and Price Level linkages under Flexible Exchange Rates: A Review of the Evidence" in J.F.O. Bilson and R.C. Marston (eds.), *Exchange Rate Theory and Practices* (Chicago: University of Chicago Press), pp. 121–52.

Dunn, R. M. (1983), "The Many Disappointments of Flexible Exchange Rates", *Essays in International Finance*, (Princeton: Princeton University Press), No. 154.

Grubel, H. G. (1966), *Forward Exchange, Speculation and International Flow of Capital*, Palo Alto: Stanford University Press.

Hansen, L.P. and R.J. Hodrick (1983), "Risk-averse Speculation in the Forward Foreign Exchange Markets: An Econometric Analysis of Linear Models" in J.A. Frenkel (eds.), *Exchange Rates and International Macroeconomics*, Chicago: University of Chicago Press.

MacDonald, R. (1988), *Floating Exchange Rates: Theories and Evidence* (London: Allen & Unwin).

McKinnon, R.I. (1969), "Portfolio Balance and International Payments Adjustment" in R.A. Mundell and A.K. Swoboda (eds.), *Monetary Problems in International Economy* (Chicago: University of Chicago Press), pp. 199–234.

——— (1979), *Money in International Exchange* (Oxford: Oxford University Press).

Sharan, V. and I.N. Mukherji (2001), *India's External Sector Reforms*, New Delhi Oxford University Press.

Journals and Report

Adler, M. and B. Lehmann (1983). "Deviations from Purchasing Power Parity in the Long Run", *Journal of Finance*, XXXVIII (5), 1471–87.

Aliber, R. Z. (1973),"Interest Rate Parity Theorem: A Reinterpretation", *Journal of Political Economy*, LXXXI (6), 1451–59.

_______ and C. P. Stickney (1975),"Accounting Measures of Foreign Exchange Exposure: The Long and Short of It", *The Accounting Review*, L (1), 4–57.

Baig, T. (2001), "Characterising Exchange Rate Regimes in Post-crisis East Asia", Technical Report, WP/01/152, *IMF*, Washington, DC.

Bisignano, J. and K. Hoover (1982),"Some Suggested Improvements to a Simple Portfolio Balance Model of Exchange Rate Determination with Special Reference to US Dollar/Canadian Dollar Rate", *Archiv Weltwirtschaftliches*, CXVIII (1), 19–37.

Cushman, D. (1983),"The Effects of Real Exchange Rate Risk on International Trade", *Journal of International Economics*, XV, 45–64.

Dornbusch, R. (1976),"Expectations and Exchange Rate Dynamics", *Journal of Political Economy*, LXXXIV (6), 1161–76.

Edison, H. (1985),"The Rise and and Fall of Sterling: Testing Alternative Models of Exchange Rate Determination", *Applied Economics*, XVII (6), 1003–21.

Edwards, S. (1982), "Exchange Rates and 'News': A Multicurrency Approach", *Journal of International Money and Finance*, 1, 211–24.

_________ (1983),"The Demand for International Reserves and the Exchange Rate Adjustments: The Case of LDCs, 1964–72", *Economica*, L (199), 269–80.

Fama, E.F. and and G.W. Schwert (1977),"Asset Returns and Inflation", *Journal of Financial Economics*,V (1), 115–46.

Frenkel, J.A. (1976),"A Monetary Approach to Exchange Rate: Doctrinal Aspects and Empirical Evidence", *Scandinavian Journal of Economics*, LXXXVIII (2), 200–24.

Frenkel, J.A. and R. M. Levich (1975), "Transaction Costs and Interest Arbitrage: Tranquil and Turbulent Periods", *Journal of Political Economy*, LXXXIII (2), 325–38.

Frenkel, J.A. and M. Mussa (1980), "The Efficiency of Foreign Exchange Markets and Measures of Turbulence", *American Economic Review*, LXX (3), 374–81.

Friedman. M. (1953), "The Case for Flexible Exchange Rates", *Essays in Positive Economics* (Chicago: University of Chicago Press), pp. 157–203.

Gibson, W. E. (1970),"Price Expectations Effects on Interest Rates", *Journal of Finance*, XXV (1), 19–34.

Gibson, W. E. (1972), "Interest Rates and Inflationary Expectations", *American Economic Review*, LXII (5), 854–65.

Giddy, I.H. and G. Dufey (1975),"The Random Behaviour of Flexible Exchange Rates", *Journal of International Business Studies*,VI (1), 1–32.

International Monetary Fund (2004), Annual Report 2003, Washington D.C.

Isard, P. (1977), "How Far We Can Push the Law of One Price", *American Economic Review*, LXVII (5), 942–48.

Kohlhagen, S.W. (1975),"The Performance of Foreign Exchange Markets: 1971–74","*Journal of International Business Studies*", 6, 33–39.

Longworth, D. (1980),"Canadian Intervention in the Foreign Exchange Market: A Note", *Review of Economics and Statistics*, LXII (2), 284–87.

Loopesko, B. (1984),"Relationship among Exchange Rates, Intervention and Interest Rates": An Empirical Investigation", *Journal of International Money and Finance*, III (2), 257–77.

Marston, R. C. (1976),"Interest Arbitrage in the Euro-currency Markets" *European Economic Review*,VII (1), 1–13.

Mishkin, F. (1984),"Are Real Interest Rates Equal Across Countries? An Empirical Investigation of International Parity Conditions", *Journal of Finance*, XXXIX (5), 1345–58.

Mussa, M (1982),"A Model of Exchange Rate Dynamics", *Journal of Political Economy*, XC (1), 74–104.

Obstfeld, M. (1983), "Exchange Rates, Inflation and the Sterilisation Problem: Germany 1975–81", *European Economic Review*, XXIII (2), 161–89.

Officer, L.H. (1976),"The Purchasing Power Parity Theory of Exchange Rates: A Review Article", *IMF Staff Papers*, XXVII (1), 1–60.

Officer, L.H. and T. D. Willet (1970),"The Covered Arbitrage Schedule: A Critical Survey of Recent Developments", *Journal of Money, Credit and Banking*, II (2), 247–57.

Patnaik, I. (2003), "The Consequences of Currency Intervention in India", Working Paper no. 114, *ICRIER*, New Delhi.

Patnaik, R.K. *et al* (2003), "Exchange Rate Policy and Management: The Indian Experience", *Economic and Political Weekly*, May 31.

Pearce, D. (1983), "Alternative Views of Exchange Rate determination", *Federal Reserve Bank of Kansas City Economic Review*, February Issue, 16–30.

Reserve Bank of India (1992), *Report of High Level Committee on Balance of Payments (Rangarajan Committee)*, Mumbai.

_________ (2006), *Annual Report: 2005–06*, Mumbai.

Sharma, A. K. and A. Mitra (2006), "What Drives Forward Premia in the Indian Foreign Exchange Market ?", *RBI Occasional Paper*, no. 27 (1&2).

Sacchetti, U. (1979), "The SDR: Ten Years of Experience", *Banca Nazionale del Lavoro Quarterly Review*, 395–405.

Stein, J.L. (1965),"The Forward Rate and Interest Parity", *Review of Economic Studies*, XXXII (1), 113–26.

Stoll, H. (1968),"An Empirical Study of the Forward Exchange Market under Fixed and Flexible Exchange Rate Systems", *Canadian Journal of Economics*, I (1), 56–78.

Taylor, D. (1982),"Official Intervention in the Foreign Exchange Market or Bet against the Central Bank", *Journal of Political Economy*, XC (2), 356–68.

Taylor, M.P. (1988),"An Empirical Examination of Long-run Purchasing Power Parity using Cointegration Techniques", *Applied Economics*, XX (10), 1369–81.

Unnikrishnan, N. K. and R. Mohan (2003), "Exchange Rate Dynamics: An Indian Perspective", *RBI Occasional Papers*, June.

SELECT FURTHER READINGS

Frankel, J. A. (1993), *On Exchange Rates* (Cambridge Mass.: MIT Press).

Krueger, A. O. (1983), *Exchange Rate Determination* (Cambridge: Cambridge University Press).

Tew, B. (1995), *Evolution of International Monetary System* (New York: Wiley).

* **NASDAQ**, which was founded in 1971, stands for National Association of Securities Dealers Automated Quotations. It is the largest electronic screen-based equity securities trading market in the United States. With approximately 3,700 companies and corporations, it has more trading volume than any other stock exchange in the world. Its total market value is estimated at around $4.5 trillion. It is owned and operated by the NASDAQ OMX Group.

Collins Street, Melbourne, Australia*

13

International Financial Markets

CHAPTER OBJECTIVES

Foreign currencies are bought and sold in the foreign exchange market and they are borrowed and lent in the international financial market. The present chapter deals with these markets. The objective is to:

- ✦ Analyse the distinctive features of the foreign exchange market and how transactions take place in the market.
- ✦ Delineate the features of the market for derivatives, such as the market for currency futures and currency options.
- ✦ Explain the multilateral sources of funds, especially international banks.
- ✦ Present a brief idea of how the international securities market works.

Continuing the discussion about the international financial environment in the preceding chapter, the present chapter discusses the international financial market. The term, international financial market has a broad meaning. It embraces, on the one hand, the foreign exchange market, where currencies are bought and sold, and on the other, international money and capital markets, where currencies are borrowed and lent. A firm needs to evaluate the state of the financial market and the procedures adopted therein before going international.

13.1 FOREIGN EXCHANGE MARKET

13.1.1 Distinctive Features

It has already been mentioned that different currencies are bought and sold in the foreign exchange market. The market does not denote a particular place where currencies are transacted. Rather it is an over-the-counter market. It consists of trading desks at major agencies dealing in foreign exchange throughout the world, which are connected by telephones, telex, and so on. Again, it is a round-the-clock market, meaning that the transactions can take place any time within 24 hours of the day. This is because different countries are located at different longitudes. If an Indian bank buys dollars at 12 am, it will be midnight in the United States of America. From this point of view, the foreign exchange market has to operate round the clock.

> It is the timing of the actual delivery of foreign exchange that differentiates between spot market and forward market transactions. In the spot market, currencies are traded for immediate delivery at the rate existing on the day of transaction. In forward market, currencies are delivered on a future date at a rate mentioned in the contract.

The foreign exchange market is classified either as a spot market or as a forward market. It is the timing of the actual delivery of foreign exchange that differentiates between spot market and forward market transactions. In the spot market, currencies are traded for immediate delivery at the rate existing on the day of transaction. For making book-keeping entries, delivery takes two working days after the transaction is complete. If a particular market is closed on Saturday and Sunday and if transaction takes place on Thursday, delivery of currency shall take place on Monday. Monday, in this case, is known as the value date or settlement date. Sometimes there are short-date contracts where time zones permit the delivery of the currency even earlier. If the currency is delivered the same day, it is known as the value-same-day contract. If it is done the next day, the contract is known as the value-next-day contract.

In view of the huge amount involved in the transactions, there is seldom any actual movement of currencies. Rather, debit and credit entries are made in the bank accounts of the seller and the purchaser. Most markets have an electronic system for transfer of funds, which saves time and energy. The system existing in New York is known as the Clearing House Inter-bank Payment System (CHIPS).

In the forward market, on the contrary, contracts are made to buy and sell currencies for a future delivery, say, after a fortnight, one month, two months, and so on. The rate of exchange for the transaction is agreed upon on the very day the deal is finalised. Forward rates with varying maturity are quoted in the newspaper and these rates form the basis of the contract. Both parties have to abide by the contract at the exchange rate mentioned therein, irrespective of the fact whether the spot rate on the maturity date resembles the forward rate. In other words, no party can back out of the deal even if changes in the future spot rate are not in his/her favour.

The value date in case of a forward contract lies definitely beyond the value date applicable to a spot contract. If it is a one month forward contract, the value date will be the date in the next month corresponding to the spot value date. Suppose a currency is purchased on the 1st of August; if it is a spot transaction, the currency will be delivered on the 3rd of August, but if it is a one-month forward contract, the value date will fall on the 3rd of September. If the value date falls on a holiday, the subsequent date will be the value date. If the value date does not exist in the calendar, such as the 29th February (if it is not a leap year), the value date will fall on the 28th of February.

Sometimes the value date is structured to enable one of the parties to the transaction to have the freedom to select a value date within the prescribed period. This happens when the party does not know in advance the precise date on which it would be able to deliver the currency.

Again, the maturity period of a forward contract is normally one month, two months, three months, and so on. But sometimes it is not for the whole month and represents a fraction of a month. A forward contract with a maturity period of 35 days is an apposite example. Naturally, in this case, the value date falls on a date between two whole months. Such a contract is known as a broken-date contract.

Broken-date contract is not a full-month forward contract.

13.1.2 Major Participants

The participants in the foreign exchange market are individuals, firms, banks, the government, and occasionally, international agencies. Individuals are normally tourists who exchange currencies. They are also migrants sending a part of their income to their family members living in their home country. Firms that participate are generally importers and exporters. Exporters prefer to get the payments in their own currency or in a strong convertible currency. Importers need foreign exchange for making payments for the import. When firms and individuals approach the local branch of a bank, the local branch, in turn, approaches the foreign exchange department in its regional office or head office. The latter deals in foreign exchange with other banks on behalf of the customers. Thus, there are two tiers in the foreign exchange market. One tier involves the transactions between the ultimate customers and the banks. The other tier consists of transactions between two banks. It is the second tier of the market that accounts for the largest segment of the total foreign exchange transactions in the market. The reason is that the purpose of inter-bank transactions is not only to meet the foreign exchange demand of the ultimate customers, but also to reap gains out of movement in foreign exchange rates. In some cases, inter-bank dealings take place directly, without any help from intermediaries, but generally banks operate through foreign exchange brokers.

It is either because of the length of transactions passing through two tiers of the market or because of the profit motive involved in the transactions that there is often a gap between the amount of purchase and the amount of sale of a currency by banks. If a bank buys less of a currency than it contracts to sell, the position is known as a short position in that currency. The reverse position, where a bank buys more of a currency than it contracts to sell, is known as a long position in that currency. When the quantum of sale and purchase is equal, it is a square position.

From the functional point of view, the major participants in the foreign exchange market are:
1. arbitrageurs
2. hedgers
3. speculators

It is a fact that commercial banks dominate the foreign exchange market, monetary authorities too participate in this market. However, the purpose of the latter is different. They help stabilise the value of the domestic currency. Sometimes international agencies purchase and sell foreign currencies in the foreign exchange market, but this is not a routine affair.

Again, the participants may be grouped also according to their behaviour and their motive behind foreign exchange transaction. They are:

1. Non-banking entities that simply exchange currencies in order to honour their obligation or to get the desired currency.
2. Non-banking entities, such as traders, that use the foreign exchange market for the purpose of hedging their foreign exchange exposure on account of changes in the exchange rate. They are known as hedgers. Hedging is discussed in chapter 20.
3. Banks that exchange currencies on behalf of their customers. In such cases, their profit is limited to the amount of spread between the bid and the ask rates.
4. Arbitrageurs who exchange currencies because of varying rates of exchange in different markets. The varying rates are the source of their profit.
5. Speculators who buy or sell currencies when they expect movement in the exchange rate in a particular direction. The movement of exchange rate in the desired direction gives them profit.

13.1.3 Currency Arbitrage in Spot Market

Currency arbitrage refers to making profit by buying a currency cheap in one market and selling it dear in the other market at a particular point of time.

With fast development in the telecommunication system, rates are expected to be uniform in different foreign exchange markets. Nevertheless, inconsistency exists at times. Arbitrageurs take advantage of the inconsistency and reap profit by buying and selling of currencies. They buy a particular currency at a cheaper rate in one market and sell it at a higher rate in the other. This process is known as currency arbitrage. The process influences the demand for, and supply of, the particular currency in the two markets, which ultimately leads to removal of inconsistency in the two markets. The value of the currency in the two markets becomes uniform.

Suppose,

In New York: $1.9800 – 10/£; and

In London: $1.9700–10/£.

Arbitrageurs will sell the pound in New York and buy it in London, making a profit of $1.9810–1.9700 = $0.0110 per pound sterling.

In the above example, two markets and two currencies are involved. This is why it is known as two-point arbitrage. There are also examples of three-point arbitrage or triangular arbitrage where three currencies and three markets are involved.

The above example does not include transaction cost. In the real world, transaction cost lowers the amount of gain. All this indicates that arbitrage will take place only when the burden of transaction cost is lower than the gain from exchange.

13.1.4 Speculation in Forward Market

If a speculator feels that the future spot rate of a currency will be higher than the forward rate, he will buy the currency forward. On the maturity date, he will get the currency cheaper at the forward rate and immediately thereafter, he will sell that currency in the open market at a higher rate, thereby, making a profit. On the contrary, if a currency is expected to depreciate more than the forward rate, the speculator will sell the currency forward. On the maturity date, he will make a profit equal to the difference between the forward rate and the spot rate. However, if the exchange rate moves the other way, the speculator will have to bear loss.

13.2 MARKET FOR DERIVATIVES

13.2.1 Market for Currency Futures

Currency Futures Market refers to organised foreign exchange market where a fixed amount of a currency is exchanged on a fixed maturity date in the pit.

Besides spot and forward markets, currencies are also traded in the market for currency futures and the market for currency options. These two markets are known as the market for derivatives insofar as the prices in these markets are driven by the spot market price. The market for currency futures came into being in 1972 in the United States. Presently, it is found at many important financial centres.

A currency futures contract is different from a forward contract. The size of a futures contract is standardised, involving a fixed amount of different currencies. The date of delivery is also fixed, whereas in a forward contract, neither the size of the contract nor the delivery date is fixed. The forward market is an over-the-counter market, while futures contracts are finalised in a pit by brokers. In every futures deal, the clearing house is necessarily involved as a party. If someone is a buyer of the currency, the clearing house is the seller of the currency. If someone is the seller of the currency the clearing house serves as a buyer of the currency.

Trading in currency futures is subject to specific margin and maintenance requirements. The margin is justified on the ground that traders represent a source of credit risk to the exchange or the clearing house. Long futures traders may not have sufficient funds to buy the underlying foreign currency. In order to cover the risk, they are required to deposit margin money with the clearing house. This is normally in the form of cash deposits, although liquid securities are also used. The initial margin amount varies from one exchange to the other. It is returned on the completion of the contract. If it is in the form of securities, the interest earned thereon is also paid to traders. In case of forward contracts, there is no question of margin and maintenance requirements (Table 13.1).

In case of forward contracts, the deal is settled on maturity. But in case of currency futures, the rates are matched everyday with the movements in the spot rates; and on this basis, gains and losses are settled everyday. This process is called 'marking to the market'.

Table 13.1 Distinction between Forward and Futures Contracts

Characteristics	*Forward Contract*	*Futures Contract*
Size of contract	Tailored to individual needs	Standardised
Maturity	Tailored to individual needs	Standardised
Method of transaction	Over-the-counter deal	Dealing on the floor of the exchange
Commission	Spread between the banks' buying and selling price	Brokerage fee
Security deposit	Not required except for compensating bank balances	Margin money to be deposited with the clearing house
Clearing operation	No clearing house	Clearing house for daily settlement
Access	Limited to very large customers who deal in foreign trade	Open to any one who needs hedging or speculation
Regulation	Self- regulating	Regulated by the rules of the stock exchange
Liquidation	Mostly settled by actual delivery; a few by offsetting contract	Mostly by offsetting contract, a few by actual delivery

Marking to Market refers to comparing today's exchange rate with yesterday's till maturity and transferring the profit/loss to a margin money account created for this purpose.

The process of marking to market can be explained with the help of an example. Suppose an investor buys Can. dollar futures (Can. $100,000) at US $0.75 on a Monday morning, which is to mature within two days. At the close of Tuesday, if the price moves up to US $0.755, the investor shall profit 100,000 × (US $0.755–0.750) or US $500. But if the price falls to US $0.749, the investor will have to bear the loss. The amount of loss will be deducted from the margin money. If the loss is big and as a result, the margin money falls below a certain level, which is known as the maintenance margin, the investor receives a margin call for depositing the margin money within a specified period. Again, on Wednesday, the prevailing price on that day will be compared with the price prevailing on Tuesday and the gain or loss will be determined. On the maturity day, the investor receives the amount of the contract, after the adjustment of profit/loss. However, it may be mentioned that in very few cases, the amount of the contract flows to the investor. In the majority of cases, there is a matching contract in the opposite direction. The investor gets only the difference.

The purpose of the daily settlement procedure is to create a safer futures market so that less creditworthy investors can participate. Contrary to it, forward contracts witness cash flow only on the date of maturity, which makes the contract more risky. Nevertheless, forward contracts are widely used. The reason is that:

1. They are available at many financial centres;
2. Forward contracts have no standard size and the amount can be tailored to individual needs; and
3. Maturity of thousands of transactions taking place daily is not necessarily compatible with the fixed maturity of the futures.

When a trader has to enter a currency futures contract, he informs his agent who in turn informs the commission broker at the stock exchange. The commission broker executes the deal in the pit for a commission/fee. After the deal is executed, the commission broker confirms the trade with the agent of the trader (client or principal). The agent informs the principal about the transaction and the futures price. The principal deposits the margin money with the clearing house at the very start of the next day. Settlement takes place every working day that is known as marking to the market. The final settlement is made on maturity.

Currency Futures Market in India

Rupee currency futures were started in Dubai in 2007 at the Dubai Gold and Commodity Exchange. In India, after a green signal from Raghuram Rajan Committee and the Expert Group at the RBI, three Indian exchanges, viz. BSE, NSE and MCX, applied for dealing in currency futures. RBI and SEBI released the guidelines in this respect on August 6, 2008. Finally, NSE started operating on August 29, 2008. MCX and BSE followed the suit.

The guidelines allowed only US dollar-rupee contracts with a size of $1,000 for a maturity not exceeding 12 months. The trading is done on Monday through Friday excluding public holidays between 9 AM and 5 PM and settlement is done on the last working day of the month, and not earlier. Thus, the standardised size is smaller than those at the international exchanges. The contracts are quoted and settled in rupee.

The membership of the currency futures market would be separate from the membership of derivatives/cash segment. Again, only a resident Indian, including banks, can participate in the deal. This means that the foreign institutional investors/non-resident Indians are not entitled to participate in the deal. A bank being a member must have reserves worth Rs. 5 billion, 10 per cent CRAR, an NPA of 3 per cent at the maximum and a profit record for least three years. The trading limit for an individual client is $5 million or 6.0 per cent of the total open interest, whichever is higher. For a trading member – bank or broker, it is $25 million or 15.0 per cent of the total open interest, whichever is higher.

The hedger or the client is first registered with the trading member who buys or sells the currency futures contract on behalf of the client. The marking to market is based on the daily settlement price which is arrived at after taking the weighted average of last half an hour's transactions. The loss or gain arising out of this process is settled on $t + 1$ basis. At the end of the day, net positions are reset with respect to the current day's daily settlement price and are carried forward to the next day. Finally, on the settlement day, the settlement is done in cash payable in rupee.

In the entire process, the clearing member has a crucial role to play. At the NSE, its wholly-owned subsidiary, National Securities Clearing Corporation Ltd. (NSCCL) carries out the entire clearing and settlement process. It acts as counter-party to all transactions and guarantees the final settlement. It also carries out novation which means that it helps the replacement of one obligation with another with the mutual consent of both the parties. The clearing banks help NDCCL in carrying out clearing and settlement.

The NSCCL monitors the members' operation online and asks for immediate halt of any transaction if the open position or the margin money requirements are violated. Here, it may be mentioned that the margin requirements are enforced by the NSCCL. It calculates the initial margin money requirements on the client's level using standard portfolio analysis of risk methodology and informs the trading members daily about the clients' margin liability. The trading members submit the compliance report. The extreme loss margin in case of the trading members is 1.0 per cent of the value of their gross open position.

Now the question is whether the currency futures are better than the forwards transacted in India. First of all, while in case of OTC forward contracts, the banks quote different bid-ask rates for different customers, the future rates are shown on the screen of the exchange. Thus, the price discovery is more transparent in case of futures.

Secondly, participants such as, exporters and importers can go for a forward contract only for their underlying transactions. Their purpose cannot be speculation. But in case of currency futures, no underlying securities are required.

Settlement of Transactions at the Currency Futures Market Rs. Million

	BSE		*NSE*		*MCX-SX*	
	MTM Settlement	*Final Settlement*	*MTM Settlement*	*Final Settlement*	*MTM Settlement*	*Final Settlement*
2008–2009 Aug.–Mar.	69.6	1.8	3,618.0	55.7	2,372.1	52.1
2009–2010 Apr.–Aug.	0	0	4,025.8	103.4	2,896.2	84.7

Source: SEBI Bulletin, various issues

13.2.2 Market for Currency Options

A currency options contract is similar as a forward contract or a futures contract in the sense that the buyer of currency options posseses the right to buy or sell foreign currency after the lapse of a specified period at a rate determined on the day the contract is made. But the currency options contract has a distinctive feature that is not found in a forward or a futures contract. It is that the buyer of a currency options has the freedom to exercise the options if the agreed upon rate turns in his favour. If it is not, he can let the options expire.

Currency Options Market refers to market for the exchange of currency where the option buyer enjoys the privilege of not exercising the option if the rate is not favuourable.

Types of Currency Options Market: The options market is of three types, namely, listed currency options market, over-the counter options market, and currency futures options market. Listed currency options market is found as a part of the stock exchanges. The size and the maturity of the contract are normally fixed. The option buyer or the seller makes the deal with the clearing house, of course, with the help of a broker. In case of the over-the-counter market, options deals are finalised with the banks. The size of the contract is normally bigger and the banks repackage the size of the contract according to the clients' needs. In the currency futures options market, the options are marked to market meaning that they undergo daily settlement, as in the case of a futures contract.

In **call options**, the option buyer contracts to buy the underlying currency. In **put options**, the option buyer contracts to sell the underlying currency.

Types of Options Contracts: Broadly speaking, there are two types of options. In a call option, the buyer of the option agrees to buy the underlying currency, while in a put option contract, the buyer of the option agrees to sell the underlying currency.

Again, the call and put options are of two types. One is known as the European option that is exercised only on maturity. The other is the American option, which may be exercised even before maturity. It is normally in the buyer's interest to exercise the option before maturity. This is why American options command a higher price than European options.

In recent years, some more variants of options have been available.

1. The first is known as a **forward reversing option**. In this case, the call option premium is paid only when the spot rate is below a specified level. The premium is quoted by the seller who charges the premium only when the options are not exercised. In this way the buyer gets a liberal term.
2. The second type is **preference options**. In this case, the buyer gets an additional privilege to designate the option either as a call option or as a put option. But this privilege is exercised only after the lapse of a specified period.
3. In case of **average rate options**, it is the arithmetic average of the spot rate during the life of the option that is taken into account, instead of the spot rate on the maturity. This type of option enables the buyer to hedge a series of daily cash inflows over a given period in one single contract.
4. A **look back option** provides the holder the right to purchase or sell foreign currency at the most favourable exchange rate realised over the life of the option. For example, the buyer of a call has the right to buy the underlying currency at the lowest exchange rate realised between the creation of the call and the expiry date. The buyer of a put option has the right to sell the underlying currency at the highest exchange rate during the life of the option. All this means that the strike rate in a look back option is not

known until the expiry date. Naturally, because of this speciality, the premium of a look back option is normally higher than the premium of the traditional option.

5. Buyers who are confronted with foreign exchange risk with respect to many currencies, buy a **basket option** where the underlying currency is not simply one but many.

Options Terminology: For a clear understanding of the currency options, readers must be acquainted with a few terms that are used in this context. They are as follows:

1. **Option buyer** is a person or a firm who holds the right to buy options. If the option buyer agrees to buy an underlying currency, he is the buyer of a call option. If he agrees to sell an underlying currency, he is known as the buyer of a put option. The option buyer is also known as the option holder.
2. **Option seller** is the party that is obliged to perform if the option is exercised. He is the party who charges a premium for granting such a privilege to the buyer. The option seller is also known as the option writer.
3. **Exercise price** is the price at which options are exercised. It is also known as the strike price.
4. **At-the-money** is the situation when the strike price is equal to the spot price on the maturity date.
5. If, in a call option, the strike price is lower than the spot rate, the situation is known as **in-the-money**. In case of the put option, an in-the-money situation warrants that the spot rate should be lower than the strike price. It is an in-the-money situation when the option buyer exercises the option. It is so because only then can the option- buyer gain. **Out-of-the-money** is the direct opposite of the in-the-money of situation. This means that the spot rate should be lower than the strike rate in case of a call option; and the spot rate should be higher than the strike rate in case of a put option.
6. **Premium** is the value or price of the option that the option-buyer pays to the option seller at the time of signing of the contract. So it is also known as the option value or the option price. It is not returned even when the option is not exercised. The amount of premium is the sum of the option's intrinsic value and the time value. Intrinsic value denotes the extent to which an option would currently be profitable to exercise. In other words, it represents the gains accruing to the holder on the exercise of the option. In case of a call option, it is the excess of the current spot rate over the strike price. The intrinsic value of a put option will naturally be represented by an excess of strike price over the current spot rate. Thus it can be said that when the option is in-the-money, it has some amount of intrinsic value. The intrinsic value of an option—put or call—may be positive. It may be zero. But it cannot be negative insofar as the option buyer will not exercise the option if the option is out-of-the-money.

In-the-money position occurs when the spot rate favours the option buyer. It is when spot rate > strike rate in a call and when spot rate < strike rate in a put.

Out-of-the-money is just the opposite of in-the-money.

The amount of **premium** is the sum of the option's intrinsic value and the time value. Intrinsic value denotes the extent to which an option would currently be profitable to exercise.

The time value of option, on the other hand, represents the sum of money that a buyer is willing to pay over and above the intrinsic value. Time value of an option exists because the spot rate of the underlying currency is expected to move towards an in-the-money position between the signing of the contract and the maturity date. On the maturity date, the time value of option is zero and the premium is entirely represented by the intrinsic value. Again, if there is an at-the-money position, it means that there is no intrinsic value and the option premium is represented entirely by the time value. Between these two positions, the premium is represented partly by the intrinsic value and partly by the time value. Suppose the strike price of a call option is Rs. 80.00/£. The premium is Rs. 0.05 per unit of British pound. The spot rate is Rs. 80.02/£.

$$\text{The amount of premium} = \text{Rs. } 0.05 \times 62{,}500 = \text{Rs. } 3{,}125$$
$$\text{Intrinsic value} = \text{Rs. } (80.02\text{–}80.00) \times 62{,}500 = \text{Rs. } 1{,}250$$
$$\text{Time value} = \text{Rs. } 3{,}125\text{–}1{,}250 = \text{Rs. } 1{,}875$$

Here the size of British pound options contract is £62,500.

Gains and Losses to Buyers and Sellers: The gains accruing to option buyers are unlimited, while the loss borne by them is limited to the amount of premium paid by them. On the other hand, the option-seller's risk of loss is unlimited. Gain is limited to the amount of premium it receives. This is why the market for currency options provides an asymmetry between income and risk of loss. In case of a call option, the buyer will gain if the spot price is greater than the sum of the strike price and the premium. For the seller of the call option, the profit profile is simply the mirror image of the loss profile of the option-buyer. If the buyer does not exercise the option, the gain accruing to the seller will be equal to the amount of the premium. But if the buyer exercises the call option, the seller will have to face a loss equal to the excess of the spot price over the strike price, which can be any amount.

The gains accruing to option buyers are unlimited, while the loss borne by them is limited to the amount of premium. For the seller, the profit profile is simply the mirror image of the loss profile of the option-buyer.

In case of a put option, the buyer will let the option expire if the spot rate is greater than the strike rate. The buyer will be put to a loss equivalent to the amount of premium. Profit will accrue to the buyer only if the spot price is lower than the sum of the strike price and the amount of the premium. As far as the seller is concerned, profit will be equal to the amount of premium. The amount of loss will be infinite, depending upon how much lower the spot price is.

13.3 INTERNATIONAL FINANCIAL MARKET

When a multinational enterprise finalises its foreign investment project, it needs to select a particular source, or a mix of the sources, of funds in order to finance the investment project. In this context, it may be asserted that international companies have easy access to the international financial market. Nevertheless, they should be acquainted with the different sources of funds and also with their comparative cost and benefit.

International Financial Market

A. Official Sources:
  1. Multilateral Agencies
    (i) International Development Banks such as the World Bank, IFC, and others
    (ii) Regional Development Banks such as Asian Development Bank, and others
  2. Bilateral Agencies or Different Governmental Agencies

B. Non-Governmental Agencies:
  1. Borrowing and Lending Market involving International Banks
  2. Securities Market
    (i) Debt Securities
    (ii) Equities

The international financial market can be compartmentalised into two segments. One is the international money market represented by the flow of short term funds. International banks or short term securities come under this segment. On the other hand, the international capital market forms the other segment where medium and long term funds flow. Irrespective of such a distinction between the two segments, there are a number of agencies and instruments through which funds move to resource needy institutions or firms. One can group the resource providing agencies under two heads. In one group come the official agencies; while in the other group come the non-official agencies. Among the official agencies, are, first, multilateral institutions such as international development banks and regional development banks, and, secondly, bilateral agencies such as different governmental agencies. The multilateral or bilateral funds can be concessional or they may be non-concessional. Those being highly concessional or, in other words, having large grant element, are known as official development assistance.

The non-official channel can be compartmentalised as the borrowing and the lending channel, on the one hand, in which international banks play a significant role; and on the other, the securities market in which the euro equities and debt instruments such as international bonds, medium term euro notes, short term euro notes and euro commercial papers are sold and purchased.

13.3.1 Multilateral Agencies

Up to the mid-1940s, there was no multilateral agency to provide funds. It was only in 1945 that the International Bank for Reconstruction and Development (IBRD) was established. It provided loans for reconstruction of the war ravaged economies of Western Europe and then also began providing development loans in 1948. The IBRD's function was limited to lending and so the provision of equity finance lay beyond its scope.

Moreover, it lent only after the guarantee by the borrowing government. Thus, in order to overcome these problems, the International Finance Corporation (IFC) was established in 1956 to provide loans even without government guarantee and also to provide equity finance. However, one problem remained to be solved. It was regarding the poorer countries of the developing world, which were not in a position to utilise the costly resources of the IBRD, because those funds were carrying the market rate of interest (Sharan, 1991). Another sister institution was created in 1960 for these countries and it was named the International Development Association (IDA). The two institutions—IBRD and IDA—together came to be known as the World Bank.

When IBRD was established, its main objective was not to distribute direct loans but to encourage private investment. It began lending on a large scale only when the desired amount of private investment failed to come up during the initial years. Lending naturally became the major function but the issue of encouragement to international investment remained to continue. And to this end, the Multilateral Investment Guarantee Agency (MIGA) was established in 1980s in order to cover the non-commercial risks of foreign investors. All these four institutions—IBRD, IDA, IFC, and MIGA—together are known as the World Bank Group. Talking liberally, the International Centre for Settlement of Investment Disputes (ICSID), that was set up in 1966, is also treated as a part of the World Bank Group.

> IBRD and IDA—together came to be known as the World Bank. IBRD, IDA, IFC, and MIGA—together are known as the World Bank Group.

When the World Bank Group emerged as a major funding agency, it was felt that its lending norms did not suit all member countries belonging to different regions equally. This is because the economic and political conditions as well as the requirements of the different regions of the globe were different. Thus, for tuning of the funding in line with varying requirements of the different regions, it was decided to set up regional development banks on the pattern of the international development banks. The 1960s were marked with the establishment of regional development banks in Latin America, Africa, and Asia. The Asian Development Bank, meant for the development of the Asian region, began operations from 1967.

13.3.2 Bilateral Agencies

The history of bilateral lending is not older than that of multilateral lending. During the first half of the twentieth century, funds flowed from the empire to its colonies for meeting a part of the budgetary deficit of the colonial government. But it was not a normal practice. Nor was it ever considered as external assistance, as it is in the present day context. Bilateral economic assistance was announced for the first time by the US President Truman in January 1951. In fact, the motivation behind the announcement was primarily political and economic. The cold war between the United States of America and the then Union of Soviet Socialist Republic (USSR) was at its peak during this period. The US government tried to befriend developing countries and bring them into its own camp in order to make itself politically more powerful. It could help the US economy to come closer to developing economies and also to get the desired raw material and food stuffs from them. The economic assistance could help build the infrastructural facilities in the developing countries, which could, in turn, help increase US private investment in those countries.

In the second half of 1950s, the then USSR bloc too announced its external assistance programme in order to counter the US move. By the late 1950s, many other governments of the Organisation of Economic Cooperation and Development (OECD) announced external assistance programmes. Thus, bilateral lending came to full bloom for the first time. In some cases, different governments joined hands with private agencies and the export credits came to form a sizeable part of the bilateral assistance programme.

13.3.3 International Banks

Among the non-official funding agencies, international banks occupy the top position. If one looks at their development since 1950s, distinct structural changes are evident. In the first half of the twentieth century and till the late 1950s, international banks were primarily domestic banks performing the functions of international banks. This means that they operated in foreign countries, accepting deposits from, and making loans to, the residents in the host countries. They dealt in the currency of the host countries, but at the same time, they dealt in foreign currency, making finance available for foreign trade transactions.

Euro banks deal with residents and non-residents, but not in the currency of the country where they are located.

Euro Banks: In the late 1950s and especially in the early 1960s, banks with a purely international character emerged on the global financial map. This new variety of banks came to be known as euro banks. The deposit with and the lending by the euro banks formed the euro currency market. The euro banks emerged on a footing quite different from the traditionally known international banks.

Euro banks deal with both residents and non-residents. They essentially, deal in any currency other than the currency of the host country. For example, if a euro bank is located in London, it will deal in any currency other than the British pound. The deposits and loans of the euro bank are remunerated at the interest rate set by the market forces operating in the euro currency market and not by the interest rate prevailing among the domestic banks in the host country. Again, the other difference between the traditional international bank and the euro bank is that the former is subjected to rules and regulations of the host country, but euro banks are free from the rules and regulations of the host government. The rationale behind the deregulation is that the activities of euro banks do not touch the domestic economy. This is because they are concerned normally with the movement of funds from one foreign market to another foreign market and so are neutral from the viewpoint of any direct impact on the balance of payments of the host country.

Factors behind the Emergence of the Euro Banks: There were a host of factors leading to the emergence and growth of euro banks.

1. It may be mentioned that after Stalin's death, the erstwhile USSR moved away from a closed economic policy. Its trade with the West and the South began to expand since the late 1950s and the early 1960s. During that time the US dollar was the most desired currency in international transactions. So the USSR earned US dollars through trade and tried to earn more of this currency in view of its great strength in international payments. But since the cold war between the two super powers was then at its peak, the United Soviet Socialist Republic preferred to keep its dollars in a bank outside the United States of America. London and a few other European financial centres were the best choice as they possessed the requisite infrastructure and stable political climate. The **dollar deposits in London and other European country based banks** came to be known as euro dollar. Banks accepting such deposits came to be known as euro banks.
2. The British government placed **restrictions on the use of the pound sterling for external transactions** in the wake of the foreign exchange crisis of 1955–57. Naturally, the dollar was in great demand in the United Kingdom for external transactions. In view of readily available supply of dollars, this currency was largely used in external transactions. Moreover, the emerging convertibility of some European currencies by the late 1950s led to the emergence of an active foreign exchange market in Europe linking, in turn, the US dollar with those European currencies. These links enhanced, in turn, the use of the US dollar by banks located in Europe.
3. The emergence of euro banks was supported by some **capital control measures by the US government** in the wake of its balance of payments crisis in the 1960s. In early 1965, the introduction of the Voluntary Foreign Credit Restraint Programme limited the ability of US based banks to lend directly to the non-residents, whereas this provision did not apply to the foreign branches of US banks. This shifted foreign operations of US banks from those located in the United States of America to their offices located in other countries, mainly in Europe. Data show that the number of US banks having foreign branches rose from 11 in 1964 to 125 in 1973 and the number of foreign branches of those banks moved up from 181 to 699 during the same period. The assets of those branches went up from US $7.0 billion to US $118 billion during the same period (Johnston, 1982).
4. Some of the European governments put **restrictions on holding of deposits** by non-residents in domestic currency and on paying of interest on non-resident deposits. It encouraged non-residents to hold deposits in Euro banks that were not subjected to such regulations.

5. The **interest rate ceiling** was imposed by the US government too. It means that when credit was tight and the market interest rate had risen, the US banks could not raise interest rate. On the contrary, euro banks that were not under the purview of such ceilings, raised their interest rate on deposits and lured depositors away from US based banks.
6. When **domestic credit was restricted**, companies borrowed from euro banks, normally at lower rates of interest. Increased lending and deposits contributed to the growth of euro banks. It was not only that the US banks came to be based in Europe. European banks too spread their branches overseas, perhaps as a defensive measure. Statistics reveal that the number of their overseas branches increased from 1,860 in 1961 to 3,764 in 1973. The number of foreign branches of UK based banks alone rose from 1,105 to 1,973 during the same period (Bhatt, 1991).

> Offshore banking centres are International banks dealing with non-residents only and not in the currency of the country where they are located.

Off shore Banking Centres: In the 1970s, a new type of international bank emerged which was different from traditional banks or from the Euro banks and these came to be known as off shore banking centres (OBCs). The distinctive feature of the OBCs was that they dealt with the non-residents only; although like the Euro banks, they did not deal in the currency of the host country. In fact, they channelled funds from one country to the other without influencing the domestic financial market.

OBCs came to cluster at places and in countries where the:

1. the Governmental control and regulations were the least interfering;
2. Tax rates were very low;
3. Necessary infrastructure for their smooth operation, such as an improved system of communication, supportive system, existence of an experienced financial community, and so on was available; and
4. political and economic stability was found.

Looking at specific cases, one finds that it was the non-flexibility of governmental restrictions that kept Germany, France, and Japan away from the growth of the OBCs. On the other hand, it was this flexibility that helped London, Luxembourg, Singapore, Hong Kong, and many others to attract OBCs. OBCs grew in Bahamas, Luxembourg, Cayman Islands, and in Panama in view of low rates of taxes. Better communication facilities and availability of experienced personnel were the additional factors for London based OBCs. The presence of exchange control measures grew with in the growth of OBCs in Latin American countries. On the contrary, Kuwait and Bahrain attracted OBCs on account of least governmental interference. Whatever might be the reasons for their growth, OBCs attracted a large number of borrowers and lenders. The foreign currency liabilities of OBCs in European reporting countries rose from US $79.3 billion in 1970 to US $801 billion in 1979 and the total liabilities of US banks' branches in the Bahamas and Cayman Islands alone grew from US $4.8 billion to US $121.8 billion during the same period (Johnston, 1982).

Syndicated Lending: Another structural change that took place in the international banking system during the 1970s was evident in form of syndicated lending. In the wake of international oil price rise, a number of oil importing countries experienced a huge deficit in their current account. Consequently, they went for bigger loans which were normally beyond the capacity of a single bank. The banks joined hands for providing large loans. It reduced their individual risk of lending. Besides, from the borrowers' point of view, the cost of the syndicated loans was smaller than the sum of the cost of individual loans borrowed from many banks. Whatever might be the reasons for the coming together of the banks, such lending came to be known as syndicated lending. Such loans served the interest of both the lenders and the borrowers and so they took a great leap forward. Born in the early 1970s, 'Syndication' crossed US $88 billion mark by 1980 and reached US $320 billion by 1995 (IMF, 1997).

Syndicated lending is found when banks join hands to provide large loans.

Syndicated loans are different from general loans. One of the lending banks is the lead manager who originates the transaction, structures it, selects the lending members, supervises the documentation, and in many cases, services the loan after the agreement is complete. It serves as a link between the borrower and the other banks of the syndicate. It collects interest and principal from the borrower and disburses the collected amount among the co-lenders. For its functions, the lead bank charges an additional fee.

Nature of Transactions in Euro-currency Market: Financial intermediation is the primary function of international banks. It has two aspects: one is to get deposits/borrowing, while the other is lending. A sizeable segment of financial intermediation, represented by inter-bank transactions, may be at a single financial centre or spread over different financial centres. Inter-bank deposits, borrowing and lending involve short term funds and, hence, they are very important from the viewpoint of smoothening of liquidity, transfer of liquidity, and equitable allocation of international liquidity. If a bank is short of liquidity, it can borrow immediately from other banks. If, on the other hand, it has surplus liquidity, it can lend or deposit the excess cash with other banks. Again, when banks borrow and lend in different currencies in different markets, the process influences the stock of a particular currency in a particular market. The allocation of liquidity in a particular market tends to move towards optimisation.

Inter-bank deposits, borrowing and lending, lead to smoothening of liquidity, transfer of liquidity, and equitable allocation of international liquidity.

Non-bank depositors/borrowers are mainly corporate bodies and governments. Deposits in Euro banks and off shore banking centres are not subject to national regulations such as cash reserves ratio. As a result, they are able to pay a higher interest rate on deposits compared to other banks. They normally accept time deposits with maturity varying between one day and several years, but usually between seven days and six months.

Non-bank depositors/borrowers are mainly corporate bodies and governments.

In case of lending, international banks do not insist on restrictive covenants such as ratio limit, dividend restrictions, interest coverage, and so on. The loans are short term, medium term, and long term. The interest rate applicable to deposits as well as lending depends on the movement of LIBOR. However, the lending rate of short term funds is usually greater than the deposit rate by one-eighth of one per cent so that the financial intermediation proves profitable for the banks. The greater the maturity, the higher the interest rate. This means that medium term and long term loans carry a higher rate of interest than short term loans. Nevertheless, the rate of interest charged by Euro banks and OBCs for lending is often lower than those charged by other banks. This is mainly because they lie outside the purview of local regulations.

> The credit creation ability of international banks is greater than the domestic banks' inasmuch as they do not have to abide by the host government's regulations.

It is not only the lending rate that is higher than the deposit rate, the amount of the loans given by the banks is often higher than their deposit base. This is because credit creation is common among international banks. It would not be an exaggeration to say that the credit creation ability of international banks is greater than the domestic banks' inasmuch as they also not have to abide by the host government's regulations (Lee, 1973; Bell, 1973; Klopstock, 1988). Fratianni and Savons (1971) estimated the credit creation multiplier among international banks between 3.0 and 7.0. Makin's estimate (1972) was higher, indicating between 10.31 and 18.45.

Besides financial intermediation, international banks are actively involved in the foreign exchange market. As mentioned earlier in this chapter, they play the role of middlemen in the foreign exchange market. They also function as arbitrageurs and speculators so they can play the role of a market maker by influencing the supply and demand of a particular currency.

13.3.4 International Securities Market

Shift towards Securities Market: There was a big leap in bank lending during the 1960s and more particularly during the 1970s, after international banks had acquired the surplus of oil exporting countries. But during the 1980s, a number of factors emerged on the map of international economy that led to a shift from bank lending to growing securitisation in the international financial market.

1. With stagnant oil prices, international banks could not sustain any sizeable increase in loans.
2. External debts of some of the borrowing countries turned unmanageable. The borrowers found themselves unable to repay loans. Mexico's refusal to repay loans added fuel to fire. The risk of repayment grew so large that banks hesitated in lending.
3. A drop in long term interest rates during the 1980s and the reappearance of positive real interest rates, and more importantly, a rising trend in the yield from long term bonds made investors invest in international bonds.
4. The rising intermediation cost associated with bank lending moved the borrowers away from banks and brought them closer to the securities market (Honeygold, 1989).

5. The securities proved highly liquid as the investors could sell them in the secondary market which had developed along with the growth in securitisation.
6. International banks liked to compensate lost income from the lending business through their active participation in off-the-balance sheet activities. The more commonly used securities came to be international bonds and euro equities for long term funds, medium term euro notes meant for medium term funds, and euro notes and Euro commercial papers that were meant for short term funds.

International Equities: Euro equities are not debts as holders are paid dividend. They do not represent FDI as the holders do not enjoy voting rights. They represent a mixture of the two and, hence, are in great demand. (1) They are issued when the domestic market is already flooded with shares and the issuing company would not like to add further stress to the domestic stock of shares since such additions may cause a fall in share prices; (2) companies issue such shares for gaining international recognition; (3) such issues bring in scarce foreign exchange; (4) capital is available at lower cost; and (5) funds raised this way do not add to foreign exchange exposure. From the viewpoint of investors, international equities bring in diversification benefits.

International Equity Issues by Different Groups of Countries in 2009

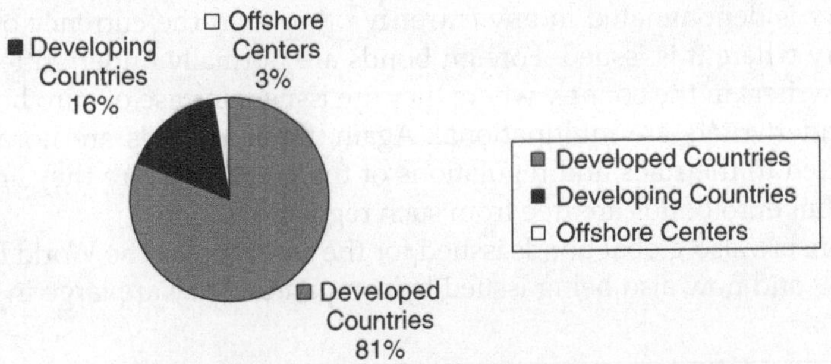

International Equity Issues by Developing Countries in 2009

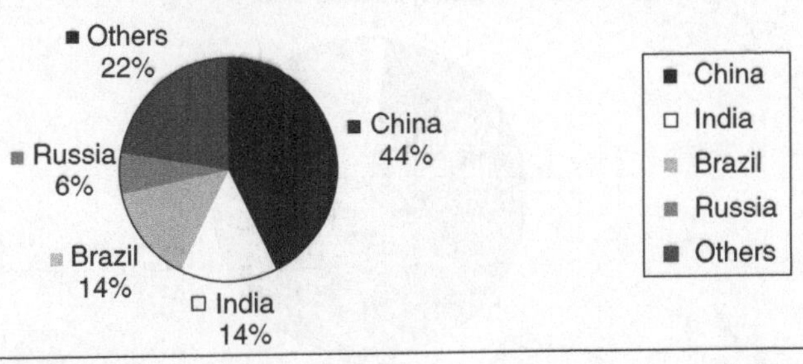

Source: Based on figure obtained from BIS

For the issue, the issuing company approaches a lead manager who advises the issuer on different aspects of the issue. On getting the advice, the issuer prepares a prospectus and other documents and takes permission from the regulatory authorities. It deposits the shares to be issued with a custodian bank located in the domestic country. The custodian bank is appointed by the depository in consultation with the issuing company. After the custodian holds the shares, the depository issues global depository receipts (GDRs). The ratio between the number of shares and the number of GDRs is decided before the issue is launched. The GDRs are sold to international investors and funds move from the investors to the depository, from the depository to the custodian bank, and from the custodian bank to the issuing company. The investor has right to surrender the GDR and to take back the investment. In this case, the GDR is submitted to the depository who informs the custodian who, in turn, will issue the share certificates in exchange for the GDR. The proceeds from the sale of shares are converted into foreign exchange and remitted to the investor through the depository.

> The GDRs are sold to international investors and funds move from the investors to the depository, from the depository to the custodian bank, and from the custodian bank to the issuing company.

In the process of the issue, the role of underwriting and listing is very important. The lead manager normally acts as the underwriter as well as the listing agent. After the listing formalities are over, the GDRs are traded on stock exchanges. International clearing houses facilitate the settlement of transactions.

> International bonds are of different kinds: foreign bonds, euro bonds, global bonds, cocktail bonds, straight bonds, floating-rate notes, convertible bonds, etc.

International Bonds: International bonds may take many forms. They may be foreign bonds or euro bonds. A bond issued in a foreign country's financial market and denominated in the currency of that country is known as a foreign bond. But a euro bond being issued in a foreign country is denominated in any currency other than the currency of the country where it is issued. Foreign bonds are normally underwritten by underwriters in the country where they are issued. In case of euro bonds, the underwriters are multinational. Again, foreign bonds are normally subjected to the rules and regulations of the country where they are issued, but euro bonds are free from such regulations.

There are also global bonds issued for the first time by the World Bank in 1989 and now also being issued by companies. They are large in size,

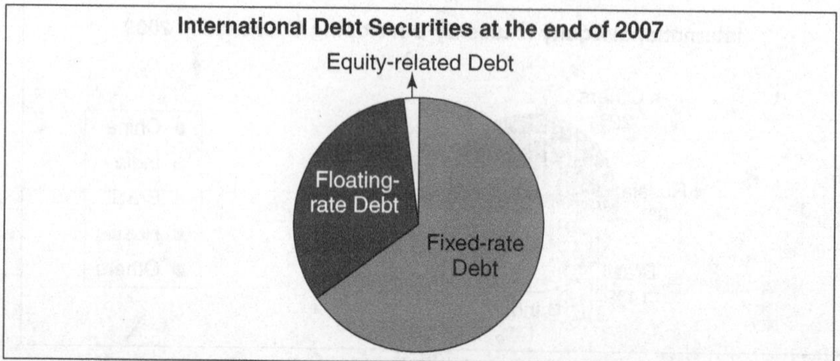

Source: Based on the figures available from *BIS Quarterly*, March 2008.

carry a high rating, and are offered for simultaneous placement in different countries. When bonds are denominated in SDRs, they are known as cocktail bonds as they represent more than one currency.

The bonds are either straight bonds carrying a fixed rate of interest; floating rate notes carrying a flexible interest rate based on the movement of the LIBOR; or they may be convertible bonds, meaning that they are convertible into equities after a specific period.

The procedure of issue is simple. The firm approaches a lead manager (a commercial bank or an investment bank) who advises the issuer on different aspects of the issue—such as timing, price, maturity, size, and the buyers' potential—for a fee. The lead manager may take the help of co-managers. After getting advice from the lead manager, the issuer prepares the prospectus and other legal documents and secures the approval of the regulatory authorities. After approval, it launches the issue. The documents accompanying the issue of bonds are normally: prospectus, subscription agreement, trust deed, listing agreement, paying agency agreement, underwriting agreement, and selling group agreement.

The lead manager underwrites the issue and charges an underwriting fee. After the underwriting is done, the bonds are sold. The lead manager functions as a selling group for a fee. There are also trustees appointed by the issuer, who protect the interest of the bondholders in case of default. In many cases, the lead manager functions as a trustee. Finally, there are listing institutions for listing the bonds for secondary marketing. The secondary market for international bonds is mainly an over-the-counter market, although the bonds are listed with stock exchanges. In case of foreign bonds, listing is limited to a particular country, but that in case of euro bonds involves many financial centres. Sometimes, before the secondary market starts functioning, the particular euro bond is in great demand and it is marketed. Such trading is known as grey trading, although such cases are rare.

Euro Notes: Euro notes are promissory notes issued by companies for raising short term funds. They are denominated in any currency other than the currency of the country where they are issued. Unlike euro bonds, documentation formalities are minimal. They can be easily tailored to suit the requirements of different kinds of borrowers. Investors too prefer them in view of their short maturities.

> Euro notes are promissory notes issued by companies for raising short term funds.

For the issue of euro notes, the company hires a facility agent or a lead manager who advises them on the different aspects of the issue, underwrites the issue, and sells the notes through placement agents.

The cost components of euro notes are underwriting fee; one-time management fee for structuring, pricing, and documentation; and the margin on the notes themselves. The margin is either in form of a spread above/below the LIBOR or built in to the note price itself.

> ECP is a promissory note like the euro note. It is not underwritten and also it is issued only by highly creditworthy borrowers.

Documents accompanying these notes are the underwriting agreement, paying agency agreement, and information memorandum showing, among other things, the financial position of the issuer. The notes are settled either through physical delivery or through clearing.

Euro Commercial Paper (ECP): This is also a promissory note like the euro note but it is different from euro notes in that it is not underwritten and also it is issued only by highly creditworthy borrowers. ECPs have evolved based on pattern of US and Canadian commercial papers that were issued as back as in 1960s. But they are different from the US CPs in the sense that ECPs have a longer maturity, going up to one year, and they are structured on the basis of all-in-costs, whereas in the case of the US CPs, various charges are collected separately.

ECPs vary in size from US $10 million to over US $1 billion and carry market based rates, normally the LIBOR. Non-interest-bearing ECPs are sold at discount. On maturity, they are settled through clearing houses. They are in great demand as they involve the least possible documentation.

Medium term Euro Notes: The euro notes met the requirements for medium term funds through rolling over. But the process of rolling over involved time and cost. This problem led to the issue of medium term euro notes that do not involve the rolling over process as they are issued for a medium term. They carry either a fixed rate of interest or a variable interest rate. Of late, the euro market has come up with global medium term notes where issues of different credit ratings are able to raise funds by accessing retail as well as institutional investors.

SUMMARY

- The foreign exchange market involves purchase and sale of foreign currencies. It is an over-the-counter, round-the-clock market. The participants are individuals, firms, banks, monetary authorities, and international bodies. The purpose is genuine transaction, hedging, arbitraging, and speculation. Transactions are spot and forward. In the forward market, transactions are made for the future delivery of currency.
- There are markets for derivatives such as the market for currency futures and the market for currency options. The market for currency futures has a particular place where transactions take place through brokers. The size and maturity of the contract is fixed. There is provision for margin money and marking to market is an essential feature. The transactions in the market for currency options differ in the sense that the buyers of options have the privilege of exercising the option or letting it expire. They have to pay a premium to the options seller. Options contracts could be in different forms, such as the call option, put option, European option, American option, and so on. Such markets are either over-the-counter or they have a fixed place, known as the'pit', where transactions are finalised.
- The international financial market witnesses the borrowing and lending of different currencies. There are different sources of funds. The multilateral sources are represented by the World Bank, the International Financial Corporation, and the regional development banks. There are also bilateral or governmental agencies involved in the lending business. Among

the non-official sources, there are international banks comprising of traditional international banks, Euro banks, and off-shore banking centres. Primarily, they are engaged in financial intermediation, but they also operate in the foreign exchange market.

- International banking had its hey days during 1960s and more so during the 1970s. But due to a host of factors, their activities reached the lowest ebb by the early 1980s. As a result, the international securities market turned to be the most important source of funds. The instruments used in this market are international equities, international bonds, medium term euro notes, euro notes and euro commercial papers.

REVIEW QUESTIONS

1. Distinguish between the spot and forward foreign exchange markets. Who are the participants in the foreign exchange market?
2. How is the market for currency futures different from the forward market?
3. What are the different types of currency options contracts? Distinguish between call options and put options.
4. Explain:
   (i) In-the-money position in an options contract
   (ii) Intrinsic value and time value of an options contract
   (iii) Syndication of lending
5. Distinguish between a Euro bank and an off-shore banking centre. What were the factors responsible for the emergence and growth of the Euro banking system?
6. What led to the growth of securitisation in the international financial market? Briefly explain some, common instruments used in the international securities market.

OBJECTIVE TYPE QUESTIONS

1. Mark True or False:
   (a) The purpose of arbitrage is to minimise/eliminate exchange rate risk.
   (b) Value date/settlement date is the date on which the currency is actually delivered.
   (c) In practice, exchange rate differs among markets.
   (d) Settlement date in spot market transaction falls after a week.
   (e) Exporters are in short position in respect of the currency they are to receive.
   (e) The size of futures contract can be tailored according to the needs of the client.
   (f) Options are exercised when they are in-the-money.
   (g) In a call option, the option buyer buys the underlying currency.
   (h) The intrinsic value cannot be negative.
   (i) Euro bonds are denominated in the currency of the country where they are issued.
   (j) Global bonds are large-size and have high rating.
   (k) The value of ECP issues varies normally between US $10 million and one billion.
   (l) ECP issues face nominal documentation.

2. Choose the Most Suitable Answer:
   (a) Currency arbitrage between two markets is encouraged because:
      (i) Exchange rates in the two markets are different
      (ii) exchange rates in the two markets are the same
      (iii) None of the above
   (b) Marking to the market is done:
      (i) Only on the date of maturity
      (ii) Everyday
      (iii) On the day the contract is signed
   (c) The size of a currency futures contract is:
      (i) Fixed in terms of the value of the currency
      (ii) Not fixed
      (iii) None of the above
   (d) Options are exercised when:
      (i) They are in-the-money
      (ii) They are out-of-the-money
      (iii) They are at-the-money
   (e) The time value of options on the date of maturity is:
      (i) Zero
      (ii) Negative
      (iii) More than the intrinsic value
   (f) Setting up a bank consortium means:
      (i) An organisation of two or more banks
      (ii) A single bank
      (iii) None of the above
   (g) Euro notes have a maturity of:
      (i) One year or less
      (ii) More than one year but less than five years
      (iii) More than five years
   (h) Euro commercial papers are:
      (i) Not underwritten
      (ii) Underwritten
      (iii) Borrower driven and not investor driven

NUMERICAL PROBLEMS

1. If the rate of exchange is:
   US $2.0010–2.0100/pound in New York
   US $1.9800–1.9810/pound in London
   Explain how the arbitrageurs will gain.
2. On the basis of the following figures:
   (i) Spot rate on maturity: US $1.58/British pound
   (ii) Strike rate: US $1.60/British pound
   (iii) Premium: US $0.05 per British pound
   Find out the:
   (a) intrinsic value of the British pound options contract, assuming (i) call option and (ii) put option

(b) Gain/loss to the option buyer assuming (i) call option and (ii) put option
(c) Gain/loss to the option seller assuming (i) call option and (ii) put option

CASE STUDY

Euro Issues of the Indian Firms

In 1992, the Indian Government allowed the resident firms to raise capital from the international capital market through the issue of foreign currency convertible bonds (FCCBs), American Depository Receipts (ADRs) and Global Depository Receipts (GDRs), collectively known as euro issues. FCCB is convertible into equity shares depending on the choice of the investors. If not converted, the interest payment and the repayment of the principal are made in foreign currency. But normally, the creditors convert these bonds into equity if the conversion price is higher because it brings in gain to them. FCCBs are issued through lead managers in the international financial market and often found listed on the Singapore Stock Exchange and Luxembourg Stock Exchange.

The Indian companies also raise funds through their ordinary shares converted into ADRs/GDRs. They deposit their shares with a custodian bank in India. The custodian bank makes contact with an American or global depository that in turn issues ADRs/GDRs in lieu of the shares deposited with the custodian bank.

Statutory Guidelines

The euro issues are guided initially by the Scheme for Issue of Foreign Currency Convertible Bonds and Ordinary Shares (Through Depository Receipt Mechanism) 1993 (GOI, 1993) alongwith the guidelines issued from time to time by the Ministry of Finance, SEBI and RBI. They have also to abide by the provisions of the Foreign Exchange Management Act.

The Government of India treats the euro issues a part of foreign direct investment for the purpose of sector-wise caps and some other purposes. The companies going for euro issues must have a consistent track record for good performance for a minimum period of three years, although relaxations can be made in case of infrastructural projects. Again, as per the SEBI regulations, the companies that are not eligible for accessing to domestic securities market cannot go for the euro issues. The company must be a listed one. If it is not listed, simultaneous listing must be made alongwith the euro issue. Similarly, those overseas corporate bodies which are not eligible for investing in India through the portfolio route cannot participate in such issues.

The issues are made either under automatic route or after the approval of the RBI. If they are related to the infrastructure sector or if they involve an amount up to US $500 million, they come under the automatic route. In other cases, RBI's approval is mandatory. As regards to maturity of the FCCBs, the minimum average should be three years if the issue amount is up to US $20 million. Beyond this amount, the maturity must be at last five years. There is no maximum limit for the maturity. Pre-payment of FCCBs is permitted up to US $200 million subject to the compliance of the minimum average maturity period.

The euro issues are priced at not less than the higher of the two averages—one being the average of the high and low weekly prices of the related shares at the stock exchange during the past six months and the other being the average of high and low prices during the past fortnight. Although the companies going for simultaneous issue for the domestic and foreign markets or going for the foreign issue within 30 days of the domestic issue may not abide by the price guidelines. They have simply to get approval of the market regulator.

The raised funds can be parked abroad till the actual use does not emerge. They can be used for the implementation of new projects or for the modernisation/expansion of the existing projects or for refinancing of an existing FCCB issue. But the proceeds cannot be used for investment in the capital market, real estate, working capital or for repayment of a rupee loan.

The guidelines have allowed for two-way fungibility since 2002. Prior to this provision, once a company issued ADR/GDR and if the ADR/GDR was converted into underlying equity shares of the Indian company, it was not possible to reconvert the equity shares into ADR/GDR. But now the reconversion is possible. The stock brokers in India are authorised to purchase shares of the Indian companies for reconversion. The reconversion is permitted to the extent the ADRs/GDRs are redeemed and the underlying shares are sold in the domestic market. The policy is liberal in the sense that no permission of the RBI is required for reconversion. The significant benefit of the two-way fungibility is that it leads to improvement in liquidity; and over and above, the scope for arbitrage is eliminated on account of similar price of the security in domestic and international market.

Annual Size of Euro issue

The policy facilitating euro issues paid rich dividends. Despite the fact that the annual size of mobilised funds in this way, as shown in Table 1, varied widely between Rs. 7 billion and Rs. 79 billion till FY 2004–2005, the amount grew fast subsequently touching Rs. 366 billion during FY 2007–2008. The number of issues too fluctuated over the years.

Table 1: Euro issues of Indian Companies

FYs	*Amount (Rs. in billion)*	*No. of issues*	*Average size of issue (Rs. in billion)*
1992–1993	7.023	2	3.512
1993–1994	78.978	27	2.925
1994–1995	67.432	31	2.175
1995–1996	12.966	5	2.593
1996–1997	55.943	16	3.496
1997–1998	40.095	7	5.728
1998–1999	11.478	3	3.826
1999–2000	34.872	6	5.812
2000–2001	41.971	13	3.229
2001–2002	23.848	5	4.770
2002–2003	34.264	11	3.115
2003–2004	30.975	18	1.721
2004–2005	33.532	15	2.235
2005–2006	113.575	49	2.318
2006–2007	170.051	40	4.251
2007–2008	366.060	26	14.077

Source: www.rbi.org.in

Secondary Market Trading of Euro issues

The ADRs/GDRs of Indian firms are listed on the American, London, Luxembourg, Dubai and Singapore-based stock exchanges and are traded there. The beginning was made in FY 1997–1998 when the MTNL securities got a room in the GDR secondary market followed by the ADRs of Infosys Technologies that were listed on NASDAQ in March 1999 and those of Satyam Infoway in October 1999. Since 1999–2000, the Ministry of Finance continued to liberalise the procedures and environment that had a positive impact on the listing trend. It is true that there were long legal formalities coming in the way of listing at foreign secondary market. One of such formalities was that the Indian firm had to make its financial books compatible with the US Generally Accepted Accounting Principles (GAAP). At the London Stock Exchange (LSE) too, the International Financial Reporting Standards (IFRS) were to be complied with. But with melting of such restrictions in 2005 and with the Indian Government permitting the unlisted companies to go for ADR/GDR issue, the secondary market activities of the ADRs/GDRs of Indian firms got a boost. The turnover at the LSE increased from $5.4 billion in 2005 and $5.2 billion in 2006 to as large as $11.9 billion in 2007 (Financial Express, 20.1.2008). The Indian firms began showing their presence in Dubai and Singapore stock markets.

The figures reveal that the ADRs/GDRs of Indian firms were transacted both at premium and at discount at the NYSE and the LSE. At the NYSE, on August 10, 2007, nine of the eleven ADRs were transacted at premium (*www.Indiamart.com*). Similarly, as reported by the India Report Astaire Research, London, only two of the 12 GDRs of Indian firms were transacted at premium on February 9, 2007. However, there was found a highly positive correlation between the price of a share at the Indian stock exchange and the price of ADR/GDR of the same share at the market abroad. The author's study deals with the price behaviour of nine ADRs and twelve GDRs at the international stock exchanges and that of the respective rupee shares at the BSE. The period covered is one month from February 15 to March 14, 2008 that has 20 working days. A correlation is found out between the price at which ADRs/GDRs were traded and the respective rupee shares were traded on a particular day. The correlation is found to be highly significant over 0.8 in majority of the cases (Sharan, 2009).

QUESTIONS

1. What do you mean by euro issues? Are the governmental guidelines encouraging to such issues?
2. Comment on the trend of the funds raised by the Indian firms through euro issues.
3. Do you feel that the Indian capital market has come to be integrated with the international financial market based on the trend of the secondary market trading of securities?

REFERENCES

Books

Bell, G. (1973), *The Euro-Dollar Market and the International Financial System* (New York: Wiley).

Bhatt, P. R. (1991), *International Banking* (New Delhi: Commonwealth Publishers).

Honeygold, D. (1989), *International Financial Markets*, New York: Woodhead-Faulkner.
International Monetary Fund (1997), *International Capital Markets*, Washington, D.C.
Johnston, R. B. (1982), *The Economics of Euro-market: History, Theory and Policy* (New York: St. Martin's Press).
Klopstock, F. H. (1988), "The Euro-dollar Market: Some Unresolved Issues", *Princeton Essays in International Finance* (Princeton: Princeton University Press).
Sharan, V. (1991), *The World Bank Group and the SAARC Nations* (New Delhi: Anmol Prakashan).
_______ (2009), *India's Financial Market: An Era of Reforms*, New Delhi: Sage Publishers, p. 176.

Journals

Fratianni, M. and P. Savons (1971), "Euro-dollar Creation: Comments on Professor Machlup's Propositions and Developments", *Banca Nazionale del Lavoro Quarterly Review* 103, 13–22.
Lee, B. E. (1973), "The Euro-dollar Multiplier", *Journal of Finance*, XXVIII (4), 867–74.
Makin, J. H. (1972), "Demand and Supply Functions for Stocks of Euro-dollar Deposits: An Empirical Study", *Review of Economics and Statistics*, LIV (4), 381–91.

SELECT FURTHER READINGS

Giddy, I. H. (1994), *Global Financial Markets* (Lexington: D. C. Heath).
Joshi, P. R. (1996), *Global Capital Markets* (New Delhi: Tata-McGraw Hill).
Park, Y. S. and J. Zwick (1985), *International Banking in Theory and Practice* (Reading Mass.: Addison-Wesley Publishers).

* **Melbourne** is the capital and most populous city in the state of Victoria, and also the second most populous city in Australia. As of late 2009, the greater geographical area had an approximate population of 4 million. Today, it is a centre for the arts, commerce, education, entertainment, sport and tourism. Melbourne is less than 200 years old and never sits still with industries like foundries works, oil refineries, textile mills, food processing and large printing establishments.

The Collins Street (as shown in the picture) is city's premier commercial streetscape and home to big corporations and the stock exchange. It is major financial hub and a boulevard of chic designer shopping, five-star hotels, exclusive jewelers, grand heritage buildings and private clubs. It boasts of the brands like Chanel, Giorgio Armani, Tiffany & Co and Louis Vuitton.

PART

PART 3

Strategy of International Business

Seoul, South Korea*

14

Strategy, Planning, Organisation and Control

CHAPTER OBJECTIVES

International business operations are not at random. A proper strategy is formulated, planning follows to define the means to attain the goal, organisational structure provides a route for decision-making and the control assesses the extent to which the goals have been achieved. The present chapter deals with these issues and aims to:

- ✦ Explain the different approaches to strategy formulation.
- ✦ Delineate the areas for strategy formulation.
- ✦ Indicate the different levels at which strategy is formulated.
- ✦ Explain the nature of the different steps in the process of strategic planning.
- ✦ Distinguish between centralised and decentralised planning.
- ✦ Explain the different types of organisatonal set up.
- ✦ Describe the features and the design of an effective control system.

After a firm decides to involve itself in international business through any of the entry modes, it begins devising a strategy to achieve the goal of maximising corporate wealth. There are different approaches to devising strategies. The international manager relies on any one, or a combination, of strategies. Moreover, the strategy varies from case to case. In some cases, the parent unit likes to have a greater say in the functioning of the entire organisation, which means a great deal of centralised decision making. In others, the parent unit does not interfere much with the subsidiaries' performance, which means the subsidiaries have reasonable amount of freedom. Irrespective of the approach, the strategy is set by the process of planning. Planning shapes the strategy as well as defines the means to attain the goal. Thus, there is a close link between the goals of the firm, strategy, and the process of planning.

Again, it is the control process that measures how far the goals have been achieved; and if there are deviations, it tries to find out the factors behind the deviations and helps acquaint the management with the corrective measures. Thus, the mechanism of control too has a close relationship with strategy and planning.

Yet again, it is the structure of an organisation that provides the framework for planning and control. It helps identify the works to be performed and ensures the desired communication between the different functionaries of the enterprise, so that the accomplishment of the chosen strategies is facilitated.

The formulation of strategies, the process of planning and control, and the organisational structure are much more complex in international business than in a domestic business. It is because international firms operate in a heterogeneous environment. In some cases they enjoy some privileges, while in others, they have to face tough challenges. This is why any discussion regarding these issues is of much concern for international business.

14.1 STRATEGIES

14.1.1 Different Approaches to Strategy Formulation

Strategy is a managerial action to attain specific goals of a firm.

The strategy of a firm is of course to achieve superior performance (competitive advantage) on a sustainable basis. There is no single answer as to how this can be achieved. Experts on international business differ on this issue. A couple of views need reference here.

Porter (1985) is of the view that a firm's competitive advantage depends on the selection of the most appropriate generic strategy, which incorporates three elements, namely, cost leadership, differentiation, and focus. If the cost of a product is lower than the competitors', the firm can maximise its sale/profit. Similarly, if the product is unique, differentiated from the rivals' product, and it meets consumers' preference, the firm will be able to maintain an edge over its rivals. Again, if the firm has focus on a particular segment of the market, either with a low-cost product or a differentiated product, the concentrated effort will definitely confer a competitive advantage upon it.

Approaches to Strategy Formulation

- Porter (1985, 1986, 1990)
  (a) Selection of an appropriate generic strategy
    - Cost leadership
    - Product differentiation
    - Focus on a specific segment of a market
  (b) Application of the generic strategy for international business
    - Configuration
    - Coordination
- Prahlad and Hamel (1990); Kay (1993)
  Development of core competence
    - Unhindered availability of least-cost resources
    - Better network of relationship within and outside the firm
    - Improved features of product
    - Improved communication links with the consumers
    - Improvement in the market position
- Yip (1992)
  Adoption of total global strategy
    - Development of core business strategy
    - Internationalisation of core business strategy
    - Coordinating activities of the firm in different countries

Porter (1986, 1990) developed the generic strategy theory for international business through the incorporation of the concept of configuration and coordination. The concept of configuration is based on the value chain concept. It shows whether it is better to concentrate the manufacturing activities in one or two nations and cater to the outside demand through export, or to disperse the manufacturing activities over a number of countries. However, Porter is of the view that configuration alone does not assure competitive advantage unless and until the activities in different countries are properly coordinated. Prahalad and Doz (1987) support this view and are of the opinion that a sound global management requires (1) centralised management of the dispersed activities, (2) coordination of R&D, pricing and intra-firm technology transfer, and (3) the subsidiaries' ability to make decisions with respect to local issues.

The concept of **configuration** shows whether it is better to concentrate the manufacturing activities in one or two nations or to disperse the manufacturing activities over a number of countries.

The other approach, which has been developed by Prahalad and Hamel (1990) and Kay (1993) is known as competence-based strategy. It is the core competence or the distinctive capability of the firm that puts it in a superior position. Core competence can be possessed if the resources—physical, financial, technological, and human—are available at the least cost, conveniently and, without interruption. Again, the existing core competence can be strengthened and new core competence can be built up.

Kay is of the view that core competence can be improved through (1) better network of relationship within and outside the firm, (2) improvement in the quality and features of the product and in communication links with the consumers, and (3) improvement in the market position.

While Porter emphasises on generic strategies and Prahalad and Hamel on the competence-based strategy, Yip (1992) talks about the total global strategy. He suggests a three-stage move towards total global strategy. In the first stage the core business strategy is developed, which includes decisions on type and pricing of product, customers, markets, and so on. In the second stage, the core strategy is internationalised, which involves, inter alia, adaptation of the product for the global market. Lastly, in the third stage, all the activities of the firm, in different countries, are integrated. This way Yip supports the two views mentioned above but places greater stress on the global aspect.

The above views boil down to the simple fact that the international business strategy of a firm manifests in, first, the development of core competency, which helps the firm either to market an innovated/differentiated product or to reduce the cost of the existing product so as to earn large profits; and, second, adaptation of the technology and product, which is known as local customisation, to suit the local consumers in different markets, leading to large profits. Normally, an international firm combines both these strategies. However, either of the two strategies varies from one case to the other. In one case, development of the core competency gets greater emphasis; in the other, local customisation gets greater emphasis; in yet another case, both are given equal importance.

14.1.2 Spectrum of Strategy Formulation

The **spectrum** of IB strategy deals with: 1. Sources of funds, 2. Location of manufacturing, and 3. Market and product diversification.

The spectrum of strategies in international business covers financial, production, marketing, human resource and other related aspects. In view of the varied sources of funds, an international manager has to decide from where he can raise funds. He compares not only the cost of the funds among different sources, but also considers the fluctuation in the exchange rate of different currencies that are borrowed. This is because large fluctuation in the exchange rate raises the effective cost of funds to be raised. Therefore, it is the least effective cost of funds that shapes, among other things, the financial strategy.

Production strategy is also complex as the firm has to select the most suitable location for the manufacture of the product or for the purchase of inputs. The selection is quite difficult as the economic and political scenarios of different locations vary widely.

Marketing strategy is even more complex in view of varied background of consumers in different markets. A firm likes to move abroad to reap benefits from the firm-specific advantage possessed by it. It also moves abroad when its business at home is consistently unprofitable. Its move is successful when the market characteristics abroad are different from those in the home market. It may be that the foreign market is still in a "new product" stage, while the domestic market is already saturated with the product. In such cases the market diversification will tend to reduce risk and to offer ample returns.

It is not only market diversification but also product diversification that is often a crucial strategy of an international firm. If the firm's strategy is to go for product diversification or to enter a new product line, its success depends on whether the revenue stream in case of the new product is negatively correlated with that of the existing product. Because, only then would the risk be lower with a given return. However, the diversification should preferably be in related, upstream or downstream, businesses. Most of the leading international oil firms have varieties of related items on their selling list, such as gasoline, petrochemicals, and so on, besides oil exploration and refining. Diversification helps achieve physical and financial economies of scale. But its success depends on the strength of the rival firms in the market.

If a firm relies on a single product, it possesses the advantage of a single brand name. A single brand name is more familiar with the consumers of different markets and this ultimately pushes up sales. But what is often needed is to adapt the features of the product to the varying features of different markets. We know that the international market is segmented on account of the varying economic and socio-cultural environment. A particular product that is in great demand in a particular market may not be in demand in other market. So the product with the same brand name needs adaptation to the local requirements.

As regards human resource, the strategy varies from one country to the other. As McGregor (1960) believes, it is a choice between Theory *X* and Theory *Y*. Theory *X* holds that the workers are generally irresponsible and more often are unwilling to work. They need persuasion by the employer to work. On the contrary, Theory *Y* explains that the workers are themselves well-motivated to perform their task, barring very exceptional circumstances. It is found that the strategy of the American and European management is normally Theory *X*-oriented. The Japanese management strategy, on the other hand, is normally Theory *Y*-oriented. On comparing the American and the European management, the strategy is found somewhat different. While in America, the lower-level employee does not participate in the management, the European management involves such employees in decision-making at least to some extent.

In short, the strategy of international firms—its product strategy, or market strategy or its financial strategy—differs from one case to another depending upon the varying environment and the varying secondary goals.

14.1.3 Various Levels of Strategy Formulation

Strategy at the international level depends on whether the structure of the international firm is ethnocentric, or polycentric or geocentric.

Strategy at the International Level: It was Perlmutter (1967) who suggested that three broad and distinct types of strategies—ethnocentric, polycentric and geocentric—shaped the structure of international firms. In his view, ethnocentrism is compatible with dominance of the parent company over the entire network of the firm. The products are standardised and designed primarily for the home country market. But they are sold without any virtual change by different subsidiaries in different markets. It is not necessary that the products are manufactured in the home country itself. They may be manufactured by any of the subsidiaries where the cost is the lowest, either on account of cheap labour or cheap raw material. It may also be that a part of the manufacturing process is located in one country and the other part in any other country with a view to minimising the cost of production. Again, since the product characteristics are the same, the pricing is global and not different for different markets. The financing, marketing, and other decisions are centralised, at the parent unit.

Since products are uniform throughout the world, bulk production is possible, which reaps economies of scale, which in turn fosters the competitive power of the firm. But the greatest demerit of this strategy is that markets requiring adaptation of the product in order to suit the consumption pattern of the local consumers is out of reach for the firm. Moreover, ethnocentrism can lead to problems connected with industrial relations, and can hamper the firm's relations with the host government.

Polycentrism is opposite to ethnocentrism and so it is opposed to centralised control. It means that polycentric international firms have free standing subsidiaries that do not have much operational linkage among themselves or with the parent unit. Their products are not standardised. They are adapted freely to suit the local demand in different countries, with the result that the price decision is taken by the subsidiaries, which are often more aggressive while taking such decisions.

The relative freedom enjoyed by the subsidiaries does not mean that this strategy is not going to confer benefits on the parent unit. The parent unit does reap benefit from geographic diversification. Since economic conditions in different countries often vary, the revenue stream of different subsidiaries are often negatively correlated and, as a result, there is stability in the revenue stream, which reduces risk with a given return. Besides geographic diversification, there is also product diversification in the form of a more dispersed production structure, which reduces the risk with a given return.

All this does not mean that revenue does not rise. Because of freedom in pricing, according to what is suitable to individual markets, revenue can be maximised and huge profits can be generated. An ethnocentric firm cannot generate profits in this manner. However, the greatest demerit polycentric organisations suffer from is that the communication medium among the subsidiaries or with the parent units gets weaker and, as a result, potential synergies are not realised. Moreover, the products of a particular subsidiary are not accepted universally. The firm is not known throughout the world by its brand name.

Geocentricism lies between the two—ethnocentrism and polycentrism. It means that this strategy, like ethnocentric strategy, has a global perspective aiming at maximising the global profit, but at the same time, like a polycentric strategy, it has a multi-product production system. This strategy reaps the benefits of both the strategies discussed above and so it is more proximate to real life.

Corporate level Strategy: Companies having more than one line of business formulate a corporate level strategy that coordinates the different business level strategies. Since business level strategies may differ among themselves, it is necessary to formulate a corporate level strategy so that none of the business level strategies go against the corporate level strategy. The corporate level strategy may stress growth, retrenchment, or stability, or a combination of the three. The growth strategy is common as companies usually aim at gradual expansion of their operations. But sometimes they adopt a retrenchment strategy, when they have to curtail their operations in view of tough competition or macroeconomic downtrends. Rarely do companies adopt the strategy of stability, in which they are satisfied with what they have. However, a combination of strategies can also be formulated when the corporate strategy allows successful business lines to grow, unsuccessful business lines to cut short their activities, and allows still others to maintain stability.

Corporate level strategy allows successful business lines to grow, unsuccessful business lines to cut short their activities, and allows still others to maintain stability.

Business level Strategy: If the company has only one line of business, a business level strategy is not formulated. But it becomes essential in cases where there is more than one line of business. Although the purpose is served by the corporate level strategy, the business level strategy is formulated for either minimising costs or for differentiating the product by adding special features therein. The cost minimising strategy, normally possible either through the achievement of economies of scale or through the use of cost-reducing technology, may help grab a larger share of market and enhance the total profit. This strategy is more useful when the demand for the product is highly price elastic.

Business level strategy is formulated for either minimising costs or for differentiating the product by adding special features therein.

The product differentiation strategy, either by creating a brand image or by creating a unique design, helps establish an oligopolistic status for the firm which may lead to market leadership and maximisation of revenue. Consumers of the differentiated product do not mind paying high prices if it is superior quality. But differentiation is useful only when consumers are loyal to the product and the revenue is large enough to compensate the high cost of producing and marketing the unique product.

Sometimes the two strategies—cost-economising and the product differentiation—are simultaneously adopted by the firm at the business level. Dave Barry gives an example of this strategy, narrating how coffee beans are taken out of the waste of animals eating coffee berries and how they are processed into coffee and sold at a much lower price than the coffee processed out of original beans. The new variety of coffee has lower cost and at the same time carries a distinctive taste liked by its consumers (Wild, et al, 2000).

Department level Strategy: The efficacy of the department level strategy is a prerequisite for sound corporate level/business level strategy. This is because, at the department level, customer value is created through low cost and differentiated products. Primary activities—consisting of manufacturing activities, logistics, and marketing activities—have a crucial role to play in lowering the cost or in making a differentiated product. However, this does not mean that supportive activities are less important. Strengthening of R and D activities, human resource, and accounting and financial activities does support cutting of cost and making the product unique. Thus, if the department level strategy is sound, the corporate level and business level strategy gets valuable support.

14.2 PLANNING

14.2.1 Nature of Planning Process

The **process of planning** seeks to answer question regarding what the firm expects to achieve and what method the firm is going to use to this end.

It has already been mentioned that planning shapes strategy and defines the means to achieve goals. It is rather the matching of markets with products and other corporate resources so that the long term competitive advantage of the firm gets strengthened. In other words, the process of planning seeks to answer question regarding what the firm expects to achieve and what method the firm is going to use to this end. It decomposes problems and issues, applies rational tools on the basis of available information, and finalises action to achieve the goal. In a small firm, planning may be ad hoc. But in large firms, especially in multinational corporations that operate in varying environments, the process of planning is more systematic and comprehensive.

The process of planning may be short term or long term. The former is known as operating planning and is concerned with day-to-day operations. On the contrary, long term planning, called strategic planning, precedes the operating planning. Moreover, strategic plans are broader and more comprehensive. Inputs for the process come from all parts of the organisation and only senior executives involved in the firm's worldwide activities participate in strategic planning.

14.2.2 Steps in the Process of Strategic Planning

There are different steps in the process of strategic planning, which are adopted in sequence, although sometimes they occur simultaneously. The steps are:

1. Assessment of the external environment and internal resources

2. Formulation of global strategy
3. Development of global programme

Assessment of the external environment and the internal resources: The assessment of the external environment has a greater relevance in case of an international company as host countries present varying environments. The assessment takes into consideration the present position and the future trends in relation to the size of the market, consumption pattern in different markets, the intensity of competition, and the business linkages in different markets. Only then can the firm's share of the market and the amount of its output be known. It is also decided as to whether the firm has to adapt its products to local requirements in the host countries and what benefits it can derive from the backward and forward linkages in the host countries. A number of executives coming from different functional areas and from different geographic regions participate in the discussion and make the assessment. The usual practice is to begin with broad groups of regions and to come down to specific countries. Data used for the assessment comes from the publications of the different countries. The experience of executives working in those regions or countries is also valuable. If additional information is required, the firm approaches international or national information agencies.

When the assessment of external factors is complete, the firm assesses how far the resources available at its disposal are able to meet the desired objectives. If the resources fall short of the requirements, the firm plans for supplementing them. The assessment of resources includes that of financial resources, human resources, and product resources. For the assessment of financial resources, the firm evaluates the present and future cash flows, availability of capital, ability to transfer funds from one unit to the other, and the profits and dividend target.

When the assessment of external factors is complete, the firm assesses financial resources, human resources, and product resources.

Similarly, human resource assessment is concerned with the availability of skilled persons and their attitude towards employment in a foreign country. It is not very difficult to get persons having general skills but it is difficult to get persons with specific skills, and still more so to get persons suitable for foreign country postings. A person to be posted in a foreign country should be acquainted with language, socio-cultural and political environment, and other factors prevalent in that country.

Apart from the financial and human resources, the firm has to assess whether its product can be adapted to the requirements of the host country's consumption pattern. The assessment takes into consideration some other factors too, such as the capacity utilisation, monopolistic characteristics of the product, economies of scale, transportation facilities, and so on. This is because these factors are very important from the viewpoint of establishing competitive advantage.

A market is selected that represents large demand, least competition and that resembles with the existing market.

Formulation of global strategy: This strategy involves the market as well as the product. As far as the market strategy is concerned, a suitable market representing a sufficiently large demand for the product or having the least competition is selected. The ease with which the parent company can allocate resources is yet another factor that influences market selection. Also, a foreign market that has some kind of resemblance with its existing markets is preferred, as in this case, it will be easier for the firm to cope with the market demand.

Sometimes, the strategy involves market segmentation. This means creation of various groups in a particular market in order to address the unique needs and expectations of specific sections of consumers. Segmentation is based on the principle that a particular society possesses persons of varying tastes. The wealthier and better-educated people refuse consumer stereotypes and appreciate exclusive products. This might be the reason that the Seiko Watch Company makes a costlier watch under the brand name of Hittari in order to meet the demand of affluent-class consumers in different markets. However, the segmentation strategy suffers from certain limitations. The first is that the number of consumers in the segmented group should be fairly large. Secondly, segmentation of the market does not allow achieving the economies of scale that is easily achieved in case of standardised production. It is often said that segmentation is not usually required because the same standardised product can be demanded by different classes of consumers, based on different considerations (Baalbaki and Malhotra, 1993). Thus, when market strategy is formulated, the firm weighs the merits of segmentation or non-segmentation based on several considerations.

Product strategy normally combines differentiation with cost containment strategy.

Apart from the market strategy, product strategy also needs formulation. In case of product strategy, the emphasis lies on a single product vis-à-vis a multiple product strategy. Single product theory is advocated on the grounds of economies of scale, awareness of the consumers, and market leadership. Product differentiation, on the other hand, helps the firm reap oligopolistic advantages, although the process of differentiation may lead to cost escalation. Thus, it is evident that combining product differentiation with cost containment and, thereby, in expanding the market share is the best strategy.

Development of global programme: This step includes planning, mainly with the respect to the degree of product standardisation, marketing programme, and location for production. Both standardisation of product and adaptation of product have merits and demerits. Therefore, the firm needs to asses how much adaptation/standardisation of the product can be recommended so as to achieve economies of scale and at the same time attract the consumers abroad. Similarly, planning is done with respect to marketing and advertising techniques—whether they should be uniform in different countries or different for different countries. It of course takes into account the disparity in the taste of the consumers in different markets. Again, the firm plans the location of the plant and the service centre based on a couple of factors. The first factor is the cost consideration, while the second is consumer convenience. Infact, it is because of the cost consideration that international concerns have started manufacturing in the developing countries where labour or raw material is cheap. Planning offshore production is a case in point. However, the cost of transport to

The firm plans the location of the plant on cost consideration and consumer convenience.

carry the manufactured goods to the market centre and making the products easily available to the consumers cannot be overlooked.

14.2.3 Centralised versus Decentralised Planning

When decisions related to the process of planning are taken at the parent office it is known as centralised planning. On the contrary, when the planning process evolves at the subsidiary level, it is called decentralised planning. In real life, neither of the two exists in its purest form. There is usually a combination of the two.

Planning decision taken at the parent unit is known as centralised planning, but those taken at subsidiary level are decenteralised planning.

When a product involves intricate technology developed at home, it is often globally standardised. And, in this case, the planning is carried on at the parent unit, the subsidiaries have virtually no say in the decision. Again, when different units of a firm are closely interlinked and when host governments do not impose control over the cross-border mobility of funds and other factors of production, it is often due to centralised planning. Yet again, when pricing and product decisions in one country are expected to influence the demand in other countries, centralised planning is often evident. This is because executives at the parent unit have a better idea of pricing and demand in all the host countries.

On the contrary, when products need adaptation on account of widely differing economic and socio-cultural environments, planning needs more local inputs and it is decentralised. Executives at the subsidiary level have a better idea of the local issues and so decentralised planning in this case is closer to reality. However, in most of the cases, it is the hybrid of centralised and decentralised planning that is often called transnational planning.

14.3 ORGANISATIONAL STRUCTURE

Organisational structure provides a route and locus for decision making. It also provides a system, or a basis, for reporting and communication networks. The basics of an organisation chart, which can be found in any book on management concepts, are similar for both domestic firms and international firms. But since international firms have to face complex problems, the form of the organisational structure is specific to them. The structure of an organisation becomes complex with the growing degree of internationalisation.

Organisational structure is a structure of linkages among organs of a firm establishing the route and locus of decision-making

14.3.1 Absence of Formal Organisational Structure

In the beginning, when a firm has just begun international transactions, and that too on an ad hoc basis, meaning that the export is only fortuitous, it is the domestic division that handles export. The organisational structure is not different from that of a domestic company despite occasional involvement in international business. The structure is either a functional structure or a product structure. In a functional structure, below the chief executive officer, the organisation is divided into different functional divisions,

Functional structure is organisational structure based on the nature of functions.

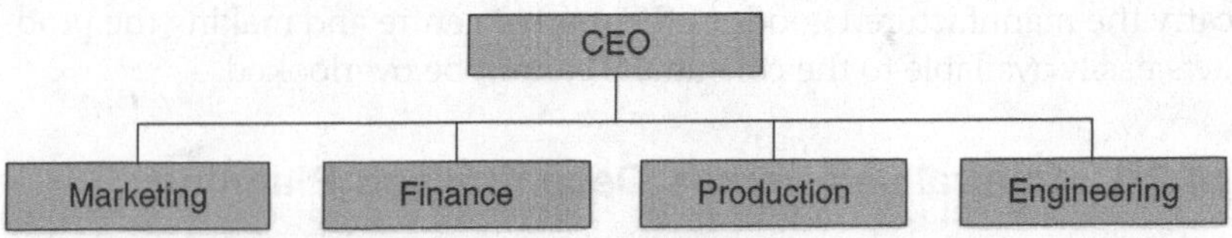

FIGURE 14.1 Functional Structure

such as marketing, finance, production, and so on and power centres are located in these different divisions. Figure 14.1 shows a functional structure.

Product structure is organisational structure based on the nature of products.

On the other hand, in a product structure, below the chief executive officer, the organisation is divided into different product groups that allows the firm to segment internal operations in order to comply with product and market variations. Figure 14.2 shows a product structure.

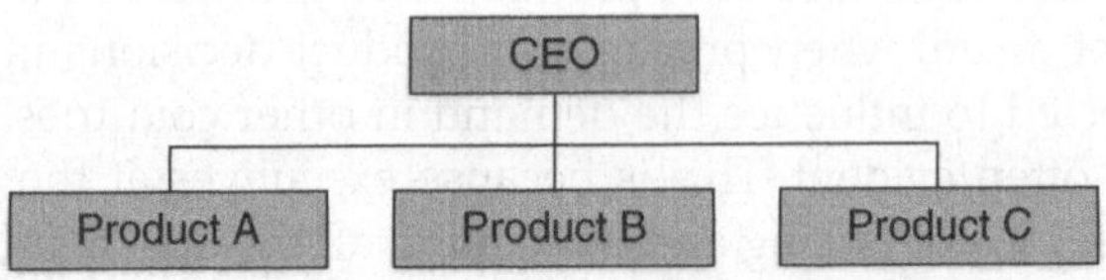

FIGURE 14.2 Product Structure

14.3.2 Creation of Export Department

With export activities being deliberate, the firm sets up an export department as a sub-department of marketing.

The organisational structure changes the moment the firm begins exporting on a continuous basis. Export activities do not remain fortuitous, rather they are deliberate. In such cases, the firm may set up an export department as a sub-department of marketing, manned by experts in the field of international business. If the international business becomes a permanent phenomenon, the export department will have some freedom to operate and an international organisational structure will begin to emerge. Nevertheless, priority in this type of organisation is mainly the domestic market, rather than on the foreign market, with the result that the domestic marketing department maintains an overall control over the export department. Figure 14.3 presents a clear picture of this type of structure.

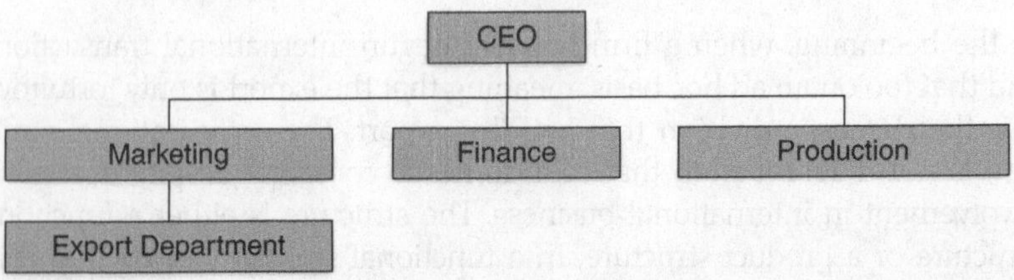

FIGURE 14.3 Creation of Export Department

14.3.3 International Division

With exports moving on to a stronger footing and sometimes with growing competition for the same market, the firm's attitude towards the organisational structure changes and it sets up an independent functional division, that is, an international division that assumes the entire responsibility for international business. It may be a part of the firm; or it may be incorporated as a separate entity, depending upon how the objectives of the firm are accomplished more easily.

With exports moving on to a stronger footing the firm sets up an independent international division that assumes the entire responsibility for international business.

There are often cases when the domestic market is preferred despite a clear focus on the international market. It is found in cases when the firm believes that better domestic opportunities still exist. In such cases, though the domestic division concentrates on manufacturing and on other domestic activities, the international division performs its function freely under the supervision of a separate vice-presidency. Proper coordination is of course maintained between the two divisions—the domestic division, on the one hand, and the international division, on the other. However, the international division fails to cope with the multiplicity of products and with greater international diversity. This was perhaps the reason that in the 1970s many US based firms changed their organisational structure from a traditional international division based one to more sophisticated structures (Davidson and Haspeslagh, 1982). Figure 14.4 presents this type of organisational structure, particularly when the international division is a part of the firm.

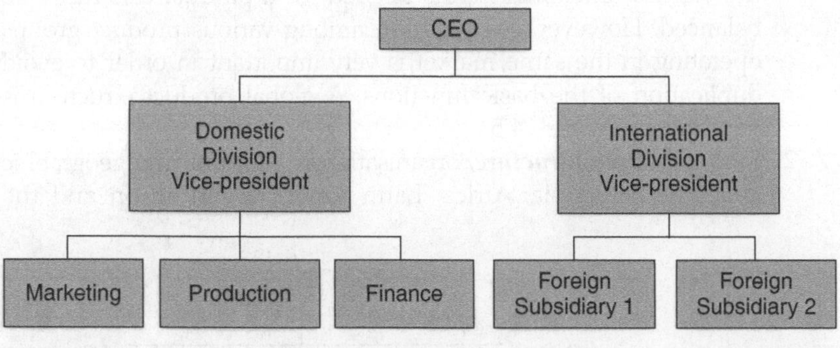

FIGURE 14.4 International Division

14.3.4 Global Division

The international division is successful only when the domestic purpose dominates the firm's activities and the international activities are simply an extension or a part of the domestic activities. But when a firm starts its foreign operation, the foreign subsidiary may need transfer of technology or certain components, which means considerable attention to the foreign

> With foreign operation being more complex and being the prime motive, the firm sets up a global division. The global structure may be product structure, area structure, functional structure, and customer-oriented structure.

operation by lower-level management and technical staff. Consequently, the organisational structure needs a change in favour of a global division. In this structure, global operation is the prime motive; domestic operation is simply a part of the firm's global operation.

The global structure may vary from case to case. If it emphasises on the product, the product division performs the job of manufacturing and world wide marketing. Alternatively, the global structure may be area oriented, where the geographic divisions are responsible for manufacturing and marketing in their respective areas. Yet again, the global structure may be based on the functional areas where the different divisions, such as manufacturing, marketing, finance, and personnel are responsible for global operation of their own functional area. Last but not least, the global structure is sometimes customer oriented, where worldwide customers are segmented into different classes and the firm's operations are structured accordingly.

1. ***Product structure*** is more common in international business and more suitable in case of a multiple brand system (Franko, 1977). In this case, there are different product divisions. In each division, there are sub-divisions—one sub-division looking after the manufacturing and sales at home and the other sub-divisions looking after the sales of foreign subsidiaries. The centralisation of manufacturing leads to economies of scale, while decentralisation of marketing is often more effective. In this structure, product-specific attention is possible, which is significant for competing in different markets. This structure is useful also in the sense that the various functional inputs needed for a product can easily be balanced. However, coordination among various product groups operating in the same market is very important in order to avoid duplication of the basic functions. A global product structure is depicted in Figure 14.5.

> **Area structure** is organisational structure based on geographic area.

2. In case of ***area structure***, organisation is based on the geographic areas, namely, Asia, Africa, Latin America, and so on and the

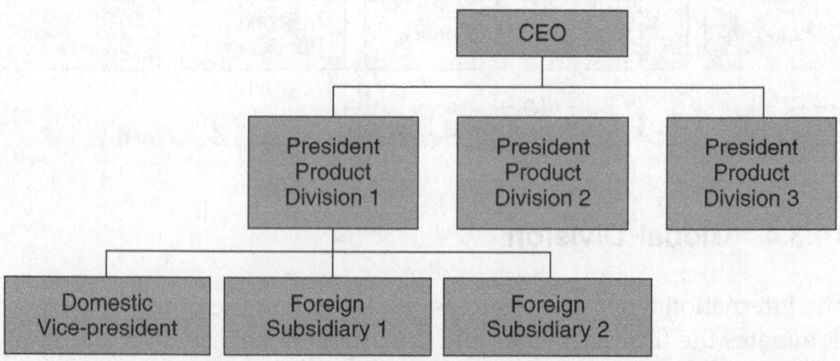

FIGURE 14.5 Global Product Structure

operation is divided accordingly. The parent unit, however, provides coordination support for worldwide planning. Similarly, as in product structure where product-specific attention is possible, area/market-specific attention is possible in area structure. When a particular region requires greater attention in view of its own problems it is given the attention. This structure is more suitable where brands are few but disparity in host country market is quite large. However, it is necessary that experts for each product group are appointed in each of the regions so that any duplication in product management is avoided. Figure 14.6 gives a clear picture of global area structure.

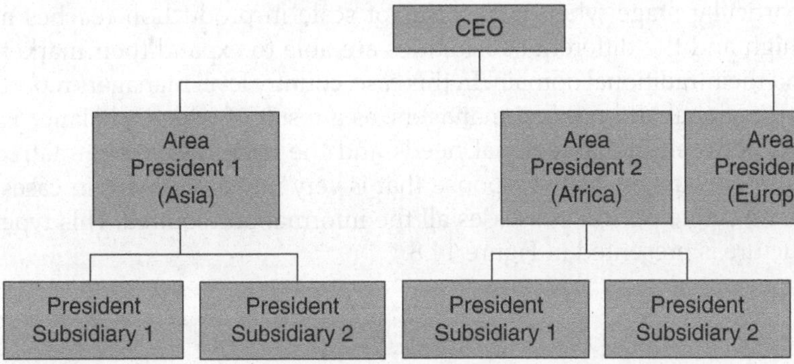

FIGURE 14.6 Global Area Structure

3. The ***functional structure*** emphasises on specific functions such as manufacturing, marketing, finance, and so on. It is more suitable where the products and customers are few and homogeneous. The only problem is that of coordinating personnel of different functional groups. Figure 14.7 gives a clear view of this structure.

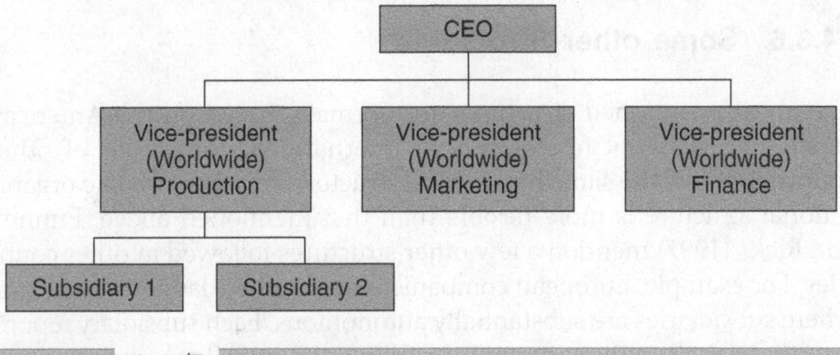

FIGURE 14.7 Global Functional Structure

4. The ***customer-oriented structure*** is more relevant where customers are widely heterogeneous and their consumption pattern differs widely. This structure helps emphasise all the different classes of customers.

14.3.5 Multidimensional/Matrix Structure

Matrix structure is a combination of product, area, and functional structures.

The global matrix structure is more complex when it combines all the three aspects — product, area, and function. This is found in multi-product firms where one group of products needs area structure of organisation, while the other group of products needs functional structure, and for yet another group, product structure is found more appropriate. A firm reaches this particular stage when economies of scale in production reaches a new high and the different subsidiaries are able to expand their market beyond their traditional domain. In this case, country level managers report to both regional and product managers, as a result of which a balance is created between global/regional needs and the local needs. The matrix structure encourages team response that is very much pertinent in cases where no single person possesses all the information required. This type of structure is presented in Figure 14.8.

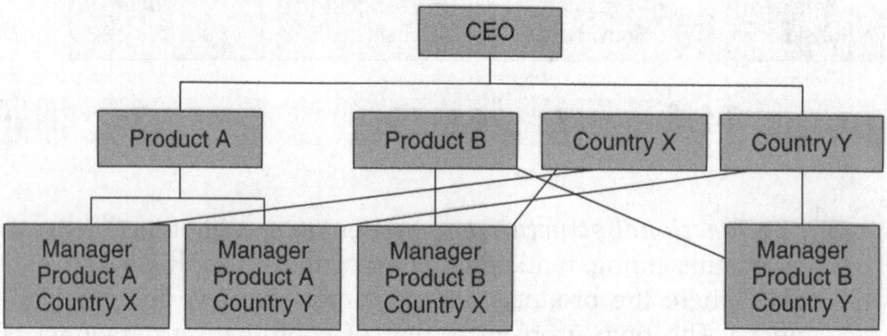

FIGURE 14.8 Matrix Structure

14.3.6 Some other Structures

The above mentioned structures are normally based on the American experience. It is not necessary that international companies of other countries follow the same hierarchical structure. In this sense, the organisational structure is more flexible than that mentioned above. Punnett and Ricks (1997) mention a few other structures followed in other countries. For example, European companies use "mother-daughter" structure where subsidiaries are substantially autonomous. Each subsidiary reports directly to the top management. In China, the industrial organisational structure interweaves various levels of the governmental functionaries.

In some developing countries, a matrix of government structure is used where various ministries and central agencies come between the highest body of the government and the industrial organisation.

14.3.7 Coordination among the Sub-units

It is quite evident from different organisational structures that the units/ sub-units are widely dispersed. The dispersion is product based, functional, or geographic. Whatever may be the form of dispersion, the different units/sub-units need to be well coordinated in order to make the organisational structure effective. Proper coordination smoothens communication between one unit and another. It is true that there are impediments to effective coordination. Managers at different units may have varying orientation. The geographic distance may be too much to ensure effective coordination. But these problem can be sorted out.

Proper co-ordination—formal or informal—smoothens communication between different units.

The coordinating mechanism can be either formal or informal. Formal coordination can be ensured through direct contact among the managers of different sub-units. It can also be ensured by giving a manager of a unit the responsibility for coordinating with his counterpart in another unit. A number of international firms have adopted the practice of direct reporting to headquarters by managers.

In a system of informal coordination, a management network is established through which information is disseminated throughout the organisation. The managers of different units know one another either directly or throughanother manager. The use of intra-firm communication devices helps in this respect. Managerial development programmes too fosters proximity among the managers of different units. However, the success of coordination efforts depends on how far the organisational culture is developed, meaning that how far the team spirit prevails among the managers.

14.4 PROCESS OF CONTROL

The process of control had been discussed earlier in this chapter. Infact, it involves examination of the facts to verify whether the set goals have been achieved. To this end, it identifies deviation, if any, from the set goals and suggests measures to do away with the factors behind the deviation. The process of control, as it has been said, is more crucial for a multinational enterprise in view of its complex operation, especially on account of large physical and cultural distances and in view of a substantial degree of delegation of authority. Thus, it is very significant to know what the shape of an effective control system should be.

14.4.1 Features of an Effective Control System

An effective control system must be based on accurate information and the information regarding performance should be compared with a set standard. If the parent unit and the subsidiary maintain their accounts in the same currency, there is normally no problem in getting accurate information. But if the currency of the accounts differs, the changes in the exchange rate may blur the reliability of information. Similarly, the standard for performance may differ from one set of business environment to another. A particular data, which may be standard for a subsidiary operating in one particular country, may not be standard for the same firm operating in some other country. Thus, the firm must set a particular standard incorporating the local variations on the one hand and at the same time reflecting an overall view of the company on the other; and only then the performance may be judged against the set standard.

> The firm must set a particular standard incorporating the local variations, reflecting an overall view of the company and then the performance may be judged against the set standard.

Secondly, the control system should be cost-effective. It is a fact that refinements brought in the setting of the standard should be preferred. But incorporation of too many refinements raises the cost of the control system. A very costly control system may prove counter-productive. Thus, there should be frequent appraisal of the control system from the viewpoint of its cost effectiveness. It would maintain the costs within manageable limits.

> An effective control system must be: (1) based on accurate information, (2) based on timely information, (3) cost-effective and (4) based on objectivity.

Thirdly, whatever information is available, should be available in time. It is because only then can any strategy of control be applied effectively. Untimely or delayed information loses its relevance. However, in international business it is the geographic distance that often causes delay. Sometimes, it is the cultural attitude that is the reason behind delayed information. For example, Latin Americans do not generally attach importance to timeliness. On the contrary, in the United States of America and the United Kingdom, accurate timing is maintained.

Last but not least, the information should be objective, which means possessing the least possible subjectivity. This is because it is easier to interpret objective information. At the same time, objective decisions lead to unbiased decision, which is essential for initiating a correct control strategy.

14.4.2 Design of Control

Control mechanisms can be designed in many ways. They vary from one location to the other or from one firm to the other. However, some of the techniques are common. Some of the common techniques are discussed here.

Accounting and audit control: Accounting and auditing control is normally designed for measuring financial results. Accounting control analyses past financial data, such as cash inflow, cash outflow, profits, assets, liabilities, and so on with the help of various accounting techniques, such as ratio analysis, funds/cash flow analysis, and so forth and reaches a particular conclusion. The analysis may show whether the firm is operating up to the set standard or the performance is below the mark. The technique known as standard costing and variance analysis is very common. It shows whether the material used, labour used, or the overhead cost incurred is compatible to the set standard or whether there is any variance. On the contrary, audit control verifies the information provided by financial statements. In other words, it ensures reliability and validity of the reported financial statements.

Accounting control analyses past financial data and compares them with the set standard. Audit control verifies the available financial information.

However, the problem is that accounting procedures and practices vary widely in different countries (Rathore, 1996). It is beyond the scope of this book to discuss the various practices followed in different countries. Nevertheless, it needs to be stressed that it is very difficult to set the standard against which performance is judged in view of the varying practices.

Control through Plans, Policies and Procedures: This is also known as bureaucratic control or formalised control. It has already been stated that planning and control are closely interrelated. Plans are both long term and short term. They may be for whole of the firm or for different units located in different geographic regions. The short term plans are often accompanied by annual budgets and the annual budgets serve the purpose of a control mechanism as they refer to short term guidelines regarding production, marketing, personnel, and other aspects. Again, at frequent intervals, the actual performance is evaluated against the set plans. If the actual performance differs from the set plans, which is often the case, measures are taken to correct the deviations. The long term plans are more qualitative in nature and they stress long-term goals.

Similarly, as plans are formulated, the policies and procedures are also formalised for the whole of the firm and for each and every unit. Sometimes, the same policy and procedures are formulated for all the units located in different countries. It no doubt brings in similarity of operation among different units and facilitates coordination of activities and transfer of personnel from one unit to another, but leads to confrontation with the host country regulations and practices. So, the normal practice is to maintain a balance between the global procedures and policies and the procedures adopted in different host countries.

Actual performance is evaluated against the set plans and measures are taken to correct the deviations. Policies and procedures are also formalised to maintain a balance between the global procedures and policies and the procedures adopted in different host countries.

Cultural Control: Since bureaucratic control is too rigid, emphasis is given on corporate values and culture. Cultural control is based on the concept of socialisation where informal personal interaction is very significant. A considerable amount of resources is used for training individuals so that they can share a homogenised corporate culture. Training brings improvement to their performance. It is nothing but the process of acculturation that promotes better performance among the firms (Czinkota and Ronkainen, 1997).

Cultural control is acquainting personnel with corporate culture.

Centralised and Decentralised Control: Control may be centralised, meaning that the parent unit maintains control over the operations of the entire firm and the subsidiaries get the least freedom. In a decentralised system, the subsidiaries get greater freedom to control their operation. Both systems have their merits. Decentralisation is preferred because the management of the subsidiary is normally better acquainted with the market behaviour and it can react quickly to changes in the market. Drake and Caudill (1981) are of the view that decentralisation should be the design of control when the subsidiary has only marginal involvement in overall international business, when product is a consumer product and when the human resource of the subsidiary is capable of taking important decisions. On the contrary, centralisation of control is favoured when the firm is faced with a global competitive threat, when a large amount of research and development (R&D) is involved in the manufacturing of product, or when cultural similarity is found between the home country and the host country. However, centralisation of control is normally not feasible when the subsidiary is marked with host country dominance.

In real life, subsidiaries are given independence to take control measures, but essentially within the framework designed by the parent unit.

In real life, the two extremes are rarely found. It is usually a mix of the two—often termed as coordinated decentralisation—where subsidiaries are given independence to take control measures, but essentially within the framework designed by the parent unit. Proper coordination between the parent unit and the subsidiaries or among the different subsidiaries is maintained through frequent meetings of personnel representing different units or through intranet or internet services that are quite popular today.

SUMMARY

- Strategy involves setting of goals. The ultimate goal is the maximisation of corporate wealth, which can be achieved through superior performance (compared to the rivals) on a sustainable basis. There are different strategies to put the firm in a superior position. Some of the more important are the strategy of competitive positioning, competence-based strategy, and total global strategy. The spectrum of strategy may be broad, covering production, financial, marketing, and other vital aspects.
- Strategy is formulated at different levels. At the international level, it may be ethnocentric, polycentric, or geocentric strategy. At the corporate level, it may be a growth strategy, retrenchment strategy, stability strategy, or a combination of any two of these or more. At the business level, it may be a cost-minimisation strategy or product differentiation strategy, or both. At the department level, the strategy concerns both primary and supportive activities.
- Planning shapes strategy and defines the means to achieve goals. The process of planning has three sequential steps. The first is the assessment of the external environment and internal resources. The second is the formulation of global strategy, which involves identification of the market and matching of the products with market-specific needs. The third step is to develop a global programme that includes planning with respect to the degree of product standardisation, marketing programme, and the location for manufacturing. The planning may be centralised. Alternatively, it may be decentralised, leaving it to different strategic business units (SBUs). The choice depends, among other

things, upon the level of technology used, mobility of funds and other factors of production, and the heterogeneity of host country environment.

- The organisational structure facilitates the implementation of measures designed through the planning process. When the involvement of a firm in international business is only ad hoc and fortuitous, the domestic division looks after the international business too, and as a result, the organisational structure of the international firm is not different from that of a domestic company. But with growing export of a permanent character, an export department is added to the marketing department.
- With massive growth in export, when the export department proves incapable of handling export, an international division is created independent of the domestic marketing department, although proper coordination is maintained between the domestic division and the international division. However, when the firm begins international operation, the challenges appear far greater. The organisational structure becomes global. The emphasis is the on product structure, area structure, or still on the functional structure.
- The growing complexities in the organisational structure do not end here. If, with growing international involvement, all the three structures—product, area, and the function—need to be combined, the structure turns to be a global matrix structure that permits different types of inter-linking between products and areas. However, the organisational structure has also come to evolve in different shapes in different sets of countries.
- Lastly, the process of control involves examination of whether the set goals have been achieved and also corrective measures in case of deviations from the set standards, if any. An effective control system is based on correct and timely information, which is judged against the set standards. It is difficult to set standards in view of wide heterogeneity in the international environment. Nevertheless, the standard maintains a proper balance between the firm's overall view and host country variations.
- There are various techniques for control. One is accounting and audit control, used mainly for judging the financial performance. The other is control through plans, policies, and procedures, where performance is compared with the actual plans and policies. Procedures differ from one country to another and so they come in the way of process of control. Cultural control is based on the concept of socialisation where informal personal interaction is very significant. Again, the process of control may be centralised or decentralised, or a mixture of the two known as a coordinated decentralisation approach.

Review Questions

1. What are the different approaches to strategy formulation? Explain its broad spectrum.
2. "The characteristics of strategy formulation at different levels are different." Comment.
3. What are the different steps in the process of strategic planning? Distinguish between centralised planning and decentralised planning.
4. "The nature of organisational structure depends on the extent of the firm's involvement in international business." Discuss.
5. What are the features of an effective control mechanism in international business? Explain the techniques of control.

OBJECTIVE TYPE QUESTIONS

1. Mark True or False:
   (a) Planning shapes strategy and defines the means to achieve the goal.
   (b) The process of control has no business to suggest corrective measures to minimise deviation from the goal.
   (c) The organisational set-up provides communication between different functionaries.
   (d) Porter formulates the concept of total global strategy.
   (e) Market diversification strategy works if the foreign market is still in new-product stage.
   (f) The strategy of an MNC is homogeneous among different host countries.
   (g) Geocentric strategy is a compromise between ethnocentric and polycentric strategies.
   (h) Corporate level strategy is found normally in case where a company has more than one line of business.
   (i) Export department needs to be set up if exporting becomes a major and continuous affair.
   (j) In a global division structure of organisation, domestic purpose dominates and international activity is simply an extension of domestic activity.

2. Choose the most suitable answer:
   (a) Porter's generic strategy incorporates:
      (i) Cost leadership, differentiation, and focus
      (ii) Cost, profit, and monopolising trend
      (iii) Cost, profit, and coordination
      (iv) All of the above
   (b) Core competence can be improved by:
      (i) Improving the quality of the product
      (ii) Building better network of the relationship inside and outside the firm
      (iii) Improvement in the marketing position
      (iv) All of the above
   (c) International business strategy covers the aspects of:
      (i) Production and finance
      (ii) Marketing and finance
      (iii) Production, marketing, and finance
      (iv) None of these
   (d) Ethnocentric strategy is reflected in:
      (i) Freedom of subsidiary
      (ii) Dominance of the parent
      (iii) No specific branding of the product
      (iv) None of the above
   (e) Polycentric strategy is reflected in:
      (i) Free standing subsidiaries
      (ii) A single brand all over the world
      (iii) Dominance of the parent
      (iv) None of the above

(f) A global division is created when:
  (i) Export becomes more or less a continuous affair
  (ii) Domestic purpose dominates the total activity
  (iii) The activity involves not only trade but also transfer of technology
  (iv) None of the above

(g) Multidimensional strategy in an organisation is appropriate when:
  (i) A firm is a multi-product firm
  (ii) A firm is a single-product, single-market firm
  (iii) A firm is a multi-product, multi-market firm
  (iv) All of the above

CASE STUDY

Daiichi Sankyo's Strategy to buy out 34.8 per cent Stake in Ranbaxy of India

Daiichi Sankyo of Japan was established in 2005 following the merger of two leading century-old Japanese pharmaceutical companies. Being Japan's second largest drug maker, it focuses on therapeutic areas, such as cardio-vascular disease, cancer, etc. and maintains a robust R&D set-up.

On the Indian side, Ranbaxy was founded in 1937. Since 1952, it has been one of the India's leading generic drug makers. Despite the fact that it focuses least on drug discovery, it has its presence in more than 100 countries. In 2007, its sales touched $1.6 billion.

On June 11, 2008, an agreement between the above two companies was signed as per which Daiichi decided to buy out Ranbaxy's promotor's 34.8 per cent stake and to make an open offer for acquiring another 20 per cent of the public shareholdings of the company at a rate of Rs. 737 per share in Ranbaxy.

Is this deal gainful for Ranbaxy?

Now, a very pertinent question arises as to what motivated the two companies to agree for this type of acquisition. Experts believe that, first, Ranbaxy, through this deal, will be able to tap the Japanese market where the rate of generic drug use is barely 17 per cent of the volume compare to 63 per cent in the USA. In absence of such a deal, it is difficult to enter the Japanese market in view of strict regulatory environment.

Secondly, in the pharmaceutical sector, giant MNCs are operating. The level of competition is very high. It is difficult for a single firm to compete. But if two or more firms merge, the competitive strength will naturally be greater. The survival in a keenly competitive environment would be easy.

Thirdly, based on the present scenario, it is not possible for the generic business firms to survive for a longer period without making huge investment in R&D. From this point of view, Ranbaxy would benefit from the strong R&D base of Daiichi.

Fourthly, the consideration value of Rs. 737 is lucrative. If one looks at the Ranbaxy's share price in the market, it is found moving to and fro between Rs. 506.80 and Rs. 560.70 during preceding 10 days. Thus, if the consideration value is Rs. 737, it would be a gain of around one-third of the prevailing price in the market. The gain is still more significant in view of the fact that the company has not experienced an encouraging trend in the return on equity in the recent past.

Fifthly, in view of the emerging synergies, it is expected that Ranbaxy will reach its 2015 sales target three years earlier.

Gains to Daiichi Sankyo

After this deal, Daiichi will have an added share in the market for generic drugs. The quality of these drugs will certainly improve with its own strong R&D. This will add further to its market share. Moreover, Daiichi's presence in the international market will improve. So far, it has its presence in only seven overseas markets. With Ranbaxy's greater spread in the overseas market, it will improve its position definitely.

The earning per share in the combined firm will improve. With greater consideration value, a shareholder owning 100 share in Ranbaxy will own around 76 shares in the combined firm. The number of shares in the combined firm will be lower and the earnings will tend to swell due to the reaping of synergies. The earning per share may lead to higher market price of the shares in the combined firm.

Last but not least, Daiichi is expected to hit the 1.5 trillion yen target earlier, by 2012, as around one-third of the revenue should come from Ranbaxy's Soda.

Source: Based on the reports published in *Financial Express*, June 12/13, 2008 and *Mint*, June 12/13, 2008.

QUESTIONS

1. What kind of strategy does the present deal represent?
2. Is it beneficial for both the parties?
3. Does this deal have a financial strategy?

REFERENCES

Books

Davidson, W. H. (1982), *Global Strategic Management* (New York: John Wiley and Sons).

Franko, L. G. (1977), "Organisational Structures and Multinational Strategies of Continental European Enterprises" in Ghertman, M. and J. Leontiades (eds.), *European Research in International Business* (Amsterdam: North Holland Publishing Company).

Kay, J. (1993), *Foundations of Corporate Success* (Oxford: Oxford University Press).

McGregor, D. (1960), *The Human Side of Enterprise* (New York: McGraw Hill).

Porter, M. E. (1985), *Competitive Advantage* (New York: Free Press).

——— (1990), *The Competitive Advantage of Nations*, New York: Free Press.

——— and Y. L. Doz (1987), *The Multinational Mission: Balancing Local and Global Visions* (New York: Free Press).

Punnett, B.J. and D.A. Ricks (1997), *International Business* (Oxford: Basil Blackwell).
Rathore, S. (1996), *International Accounting* (New Delhi: Prentice-Hall of India).
Wild, J. J. *et al.* (2000), *International Business: An Integrated Approach* (New Jersey: Prentice Hall).
Yip, G. S. (1992), *Total Global Strategy: Managing for World-wide Competitive Advantage* (Englewood Cliffs: Prentice-Hall).

Journals

Baalbaki, I.B. and N. K. Malhotra (1993), " Marketing Management Bases for International Market Segmentation: An Alternate Look at the Standardisation/ Customisation Debate", *International Marketing Review*, 10 (1), 19–44.
Czinkota, M. R. and I. A.Ronkainen (1997),"International Business and Trade in the Next Decade: Report from a Delphi Study", *Journal of International Business Studies*, XXVIII (4), 676–94.
_______ and P. Haspeslagh (1982),"Shaping a Global Product Organisation", *Harvard Business Review*, LIX (Mar.–Apr.), 69–76.
Drake, R. and L. M. Caudill (1981), "Management of the Large Multinational: Trends and Future Challenges", *Business Horizons*, XXIV (May–June), 83–91.
Perlmutter, H.V. (1967),"L'Entreprise internationale trois conceptions", *Quarterly Journal of AISEC International* (translated form), August Issue.
_______ (1986),"Changing Patterns of International Competition", *California Management Review*, XXVIII (2), 9–40.
Prahalad C. K. and G. Hamel (1990), "The Competence of the Corporation", *Harvard Business Review*, LXVIII (May–June), 79–91.

SELECT FURTHER READINGS

Davidson, W.H. and Jose de la Torre (1989), *Managing the Global Corporation* (New York: McGraw-Hill).
Garland, J. *et al* (1990), *International Dimensions of Business Policy and Strategy* (Boston: Kent Publishing).
Higgins, J.M. (1983), *Organisational Policy and Strategic Management* (Hinsdale: Dryden Press).
Prahalad C. K. and Y. L. Doz (1987), *The Multinational Mission: Balancing Local and Global Visions* (New York: Free Press).

* **South Korea**, officially the **Republic of Korea (ROK),** is a developed country in East Asia and classified as a high-income economy by the World Bank, an advanced economy by the IMF and CIA. The South Korean economy is led by large conglomerates known as Chaebol. These include global multinational brands such as Samsung, LG and Hyundai-Kia. Samsung and LG are among the top three manufacturers of televisions and mobile phones. Samsung is currently the world's most valued consumer electronics brand.

Its capital, Seoul, is consistently placed among the world's top ten financial and commercial cities and was named the world's sixth most economically powerful city by Forbes with a GDP per capita of $32,171 in 2008. Almost half of South Korea's population lives in the Seoul National Capital Area, and nearly a quarter in Seoul itself, making it the country's foremost economic, political, and cultural centre.

Shanghai, China*

15

Global Technology Management

CHAPTER OBJECTIVES

It is often technological superiority that enables an international firm to operate abroad successfully. This is why the present chapter deals with various aspects of technological development and the transfer of technology by an MNC. The objective is to:

- ✦ Show what technology really means and how it is an strategic asset.
- ✦ Explain what the development of technology means.
- ✦ Explain the merits of inter-firm versus intra-firm transfer of technology and the problems involved therein.
- ✦ Explain modification and protection of technology.
- ✦ Focus on the role of information technology in international business.

As already mentioned in Chapter 4, multinational corporations possess, among other things, some kind of firm-specific advantage in order to maintain a competitive edge over other firms. Such advantage is mostly in the form of innovated technology, which is put into operation either for manufacturing a product or for providing services. If a proper technology strategy is adopted, the attainment of competitive advantage becomes easy. The present chapter, therefore, discusses different aspects of technological strategy in international business.

15.1 TECHNOLOGY AND INTERNATIONAL BUSINESS

15.1.1 Meaning of Technology

Technology is a sort of knowledge or skill used for employing and controlling factors of production that, in turn, could lead to the output of products and services. Baranson (1978) mentions three types of technology. They are:

1. Product technology
2. Process technology
3. Management technology

Product technology is the information that specifies a product's features and uses. Process technology is the knowledge used in the processing or manufacturing of a product. Management technology is the managerial skills required for running a business. It helps the firm in optimal utilisation of its resources. A firm possessing superiority in any, or all, of these three types of technology maintains an edge over other firms.

In the literature available on the subject, some other terms are also used to denote different types of technology. The term *hard technology* is used to denote blue-prints, specifications, capital goods, and so on which are used for the purpose of production. Soft technology is concerned with management and administrative techniques. Similarly, proprietary technology is controlled as a trade secret. Bundled technology is also a controlled technology and is transferred by the owner as a part of the package.

Here proprietary technology needs some more explanation. It is that innovated technology which is unavailable to other firms in the market place. It is analogous to Magee's (1977) appropriability approach where the innovator of the technology does not pass it on to other firms with a view to enjoying a monopolistic position in the market. It does not mean that proprietary technology is not diffused or transferred. It is diffused, but among different units of the same firm. The intra-firm diffusion of technology is often known as internalisation of technology.

> **Product technology** is technology concerned with features of a product.
>
> **Process technology** is technology related to the processing of a product.
>
> Blueprints and specifications are **hard technology** while management technique denotes **soft technology**.
>
> **Bundled Technology** is technology controlled and transferred as a part of the whole package.
>
> **Proprietary technology** is technology that is neither diffused nor transferred outside the firm.

15.1.2 Technology as a Strategic Asset

Technology is a strategic asset. It enhances the firm's product portfolio. It helps produce items with new features. New features attract consumers who are ready to pay a higher price for the novel product. When the technology matures, the consumers do not like to pay a high price. But since the process of innovation is often a continuous phenomenon a new technology is innovated and takes the place of the mature one. A product's performance picks up fast; and consequently, the firm is able to charge a high price for the product. It is because of this fact that Abernathy and Utterback (1978) analogise the product performance (in the wake of technological innovation) with a "S" shaped curve. The curve shows that product performance rises fast with the use of new technology. It slows down with the ageing of the technology, but picks up pace again with the introduction of new technology.

It is not only the product innovation that helps a firm to earn large profits. The process innovation also acts in the same way. The reason is that such an innovation leads to lowering of the cost of production. The product cost is normally reduced on account of shortening of lead time and a shorter manufacturing cycle. The use of computers in designing a component is a major factor in cutting of the manufacturing cycle.

On the basis of the above discussion, one can say that technology has much to do with international business. There are studies to confirm that the major factor behind the growth of US exports has been the higher technological intensity in its products. Similarly, technology has been a major factor behind large growth of multinationalism among US firms (Gruber, et al., 1967).

15.2 TECHNOLOGICAL STRATEGY

The preceding section mentions the benefits of innovated technology in the form of new features of products and the reduced production cost. The present section discusses how proper management of technology could enhance the firm's competitive advantage.

The technological strategy or the proper management of technology has various aspects that need adequate consideration. Some more important of these are:

1. Technology audit
2. Development of technology
3. Acquisition/transfer of technology
4. Modification of technology
5. Protection of technology

These aspects are explained here at some length.

15.2.1 Technology Audit

Technology audit is the process of identifying a particular technology, the firm's capabilities to develop it, and the funds required to develop it.

At the very first step, prior to the development or acquisition of technology, it is essential to identify the specific technological competence and its relevance to the business opportunities lying ahead. It is also essential to identify the existing technological gap that needs to be filled up. Goodman and Lawless (1994) term this process as technology audit.

The process of technology audit has three aspects. The first is identifying the risk involved in the use of technology: whether the new product will be liked by the consumers or the life span of the technology is too short to get ample returns. Secondly, it is identifying the firm's capabilities to develop the required technology. The capabilities include the level of expertise among the R&D staff, the cost that is borne by the firm, and their ability to commercialise the developed technology. The third aspect concerns identifying the amount of investment that should be put into R&D. Goodman and Lawless are very specific on this issue. If the technological foundation of business is not the exclusive asset of the firm, large investment is not suggested. But if the new technology is significant for the building of competitive advantage, liberal investment may be made. Again, if the technology has the potential to alter the very basis of competition, even in the long run, selective investment is suggested with continuous monitoring.

15.2.2 Development of Technology

> Technology can be developed through R&D activities that should be:
> 1. cost-effective
> 2. properly located
> 3. ensuring lower cost of production
> 4. ensuring better quality product in tune with the consumers' preferences.

The aspect of the technology development is an extension of technology audit. Product or process technology can be developed through research and development (R&D) activities. Most of the large MNCs, especially the technology-intensive ones, rely on internally generated technology that is derived through R&D. But as far as R&D is concerned, it is sometimes very expensive and may not be justified on the grounds of cost efficiency. Thus, a firm, as mentioned above, must evaluate the cost aspect before setting up its R&D activities. However, the cost can be axed through joint R&D programmes. For example, IBM, AT&T, and MIT formed a research consortium to explore new possibilities in the area of high temperature super-conductivity. Nevertheless, in such cases, the possibility of competition among the partners themselves for access to the market cannot be ruled out completely.

It is not only the cost involved in R&D, but also it is how far the cost of the product diminishes, and how far the quality of the product improves that should be considered. If a new product is designed not keeping in mind the capabilities of the production department, the attempt will be a failure. It will require redesigning, which will involve additional cost. All this means that there should be close integration between the R&D and production departments.

Again, R&D activities involve great uncertainties. It may be that the product innovated on the basis of R&D is not successful in the market and is not accepted by the consumers. If it is so, there would be huge wastage. But if the new product succeeds, the firm would be able to reap unusually large profits. We can quote the experiences of Hoffman la Rosch, a Swiss pharmaceutical company that earned huge profits by developing sedative drugs. The reason is that the development of a new technology confers on the firm technological superiority and market leadership that is not found in case of the technology bought that is unless and until the purchased technology undergoes substantial modification in the hands of the purchaser. However, it cannot be easily predicted whether the new technology would really succeed in the market. So there should be effective integration between the R&D department and the marketing department. In order to reduce uncertainty, many firms have started bringing refinements on the already proven technology through the process of continuous R&D instead of initiating fundamental research.

Another issue that concerns R&D is the place where such activities are located. Normally, R&D activities are centralised at the firm's headquarters. But it can easily be decentralised if the situation warrants. Stonehouse et al. (2000) feel that if R&D activities are decentralised at some key subsidiaries, the transnationals' competitive position will be enhanced greatly as the developed technology is greatly in consonance with the consumption pattern of that region. Hewlett-Packard (HP) is an apposite example here. HP maintains four basic research centres. They are located at Palo Alto in California, Bristol in England, Haifa in Israel, and Tokyo in Japan. These centres work on different aspects of technology and they are complementary in nature. It was the Palo Alto centre that pioneered the thermal ink-jet technology. The headquarter at San Diego designs, develops, and manufactures various products based on this technology for the world market. The subsidiaries customise the product to suit the consumers in their own geographic area. For example, the Singapore subsidiary of HP designs and manufactures thermal ink-jet printers for Japan and other Asian countries.

Many international firms have created cross-functional teams composed of the representatives of the three departments – R&D, production, and marketing. Because these functions are located in different countries, the team normally has international representation. The team facilitates the communication of the information about the market and the production possibilities to the R&D department, making R&D more effective.

Thus, in view of the problems involved in R&D activities, the firm has to take vital decisions with regard to the cost involved in R&D, focus of the R&D effort, its location, and the nature of R&D at the subsidiary level.

15.2.3 Acquisition of Technology through Purchase

Purchase of already developed technology is found to be a good substitute for the R&D activities. In the developing countries, where funds are too limited to undertake R&D, import of technology is more frequent, although firms located in industrialised countries too purchase technology. There are two ways to transfer technology. While one is point-to-point transfer, the other is the diffusion. In case of point-to-point transfer, technology passes on from one firm to the other along with a strict guard on its secrecy. On the contrary, in case of diffusion, the recipients are many and all have access to the same technology. So in case of diffusion, secrecy is not assured.

Point-to-point technology transfer is transferring of technology while maintaining complete secrecy.

Diffusion of technology means transfer of technology without much care to maintain secrecy.

Policy of the Host-Country Government: The policy of the host-country government towards the acquisition of technology varies from one case to the other. If the strategy is to allow continuous flow of technology, the policy involves minimum of restriction. It rather provides a number of incentives to this end. On the contrary, if the strategy is to reduce gradually reliance on the imported technology, the policy puts conditions on its import and encourages R&D within the country. Yet again, if the strategy is to have a full grip over the import of technology, the host-country government targets specific MNCs and provides them incentives for upgrading technology. However, in majority of the cases, it is a mix of all the three strategies stated above. Table 15.1 summarises the technology import strategies, policies and conditions.

Table 15.1 Objectives and Strategy relating to Technology Import

Objectives	*Strategy*
Development of domestic technological base	• Imposing restrictive conditions on FDI, such as restrictions on equity participation by foreign investors • Support to domestic R&D through licensing and hiring of foreign experts
Focusing on technology transfer with pro-active government intervention	• Targeting select FDI • Providing incentives to foreign firms to upgrade technology, such as improved infrastructure and friendly IPR regime
Liberal import of technology	• Providing incentives to foreign investors • Minimising restrictions on FDI inflow • Ensuring macroeconomic stability • Strengthening backward linkages

Source: Based on *World Investment Report, 2003*

Inter-firm and Intra-firm Transfer: Transfer of technology may be either inter-firm or intra-firm. Inter-firm transfer normally takes place when:

1. The price of technology is within the reach of the buying firm.
2. It is difficult to protect the innovated technology with the help of patents, trademarks, and so on, and there is every possibility of its being copied by others.
3. Technology does not lie at the very root of the competitive advantage of the innovating firm.
4. The technology supplying firm lags with respect to marketing the final product.
5. The cost of technology is exorbitant and technology innovating firm likes that a substantial part of the cost is recovered through sale of the technology to some other firm.

In case of intra-firm transfer, the price of the technology is not a crucial factor as it can be manoeuvred in tandem with the firm's objective. However, there are factors that encourage the intra-firm transfer of technology. They are when:

1. The firm is sure that the technology cannot be copied easily.
2. Technology forms the very backbone of the firm's competitiveness. The firm fears that if technology is available to rival firms, it will lose its competitive strength.
3. The firm relies more on the sale of the product using the innovated technology.
4. The firm considers the technology more valuable than the potential buyers of the technology.
5. The technology is too costly to be purchased by other firms in normal circumstances.

Problems in Technology Transfer

Foreign companies have set up their own captive R&D projects in India in order to improve quality and cut the cost of the product. According to a study, there are presently 594 foreign firms which have their captive development centres in India, of which 390 are software development firms, 120 relate to engineering services and 84 are embeded service companies. But the latest trend shows that these foreign companies now prefer to rely on independent third party service providers to setting up their own R&D unit. The number of MNCs setting up their own captives in India which was 82 in 2004 fell continuously to 16 in 2007. The potential captives are expected to grow at 20 per cent compared to vendors that are growing at 28 per cent. The primary reason for the slow growth of captives is the increase in operational cost, insufficient hardware talent pool and the lack of infrastructure. M/S Zinnov Management Consulting Pvt. Ltd has estimated the cost per employee is to grow at 14.3 per cent over the next 5-year period. It is owing to cost escalation that the firms are now shifting the location of their captives. For example, Dell India Pvt. Ltd. shifted its captive's location from Bangalore to Taiwan. Others are expected to wind up their Indian location of their captives.

Source: Based on report published in *Mint*, 11.4.2008.

- Difficulty in maintenance of secrecy of the technology
- Exorbitant price of the technology
- Inappropriateness of technology
- Governmental restrictions on the transfer

Problems in Technology Transfer: Transfer of technology—whether it is between a developed country and a developing country, between two developed countries or between two developing countries—is fraught with problems.

1. The developer of the technology does not generally like to transfer the latest technology to some other firm because it does not want its market leadership to be shared by others. Baranson (1970) has observed that international firms are not even willing to part with technology under joint-venture agreements because it comes in the way of maintaining secrecy. The sale to an independent firm is even more of a remote possibility. However, inter-firm transfer of technology is often found; and in large number of cases, the traded technology is obsolete.
2. The developer of the technology charges an exorbitant price for the technology. Infact, it likes that a substantial part of the

The developer does not generally like to transfer the latest technology.

The developer charges an exorbitant price for the technology.

expenses on R&D is recovered. Sometimes the selling firm ties unnecessary technology to a contract for one desired item so that it covers payment for all instead of just one product (Sauvant and Lavipour, 1976). The high price of technology entails upon the cost of production and, thereby, the very competitive edge of the technology buying firm. Statistics reveal that technology payments by developing countries have grown steadily since the 1980s. In 1981–1985 they grew by 4 per cent a year, despite a fall in FDI inflows of 12 per cent a year and in 1991–1995 by 13 per cent, growth that continued in the second half of the 1990s. FDI grew by 15 per cent in developing countries in the latter half of the 1990s. (WIR 2003)

Technology is often inappropriate.

3. It is often necessary to ascertain whether the purchased technology is appropriate. In case of transfer of technology between two developed countries or between two developing countries, the problem is not great on this count because the consumption pattern, the size of market, capital-labour ratio, and other factors are almost similar. But when the technology is transferred from a developed country to a developing country, it is often inappropriate. R&D department in developed countries designs technology from the viewpoint of a large market, which is more capital intensive. But the size of the market in the developing countries is small. Moreover, the capital-labour ratio is low. Therefore, the technology is often inappropriate. However, this problem is more often redressed through modification of technology, which is explained in the subsequent section.

   Intra-firm transfer of technology is more common than inter-firm transfer. As stated above, it does not infringe upon the secrecy of the technology. Rather, it works behind the internationalisation of firms. But in this case, the price of the technology is arbitrarily fixed. When the demand for the final product is expected to be price-elastic, the parent company charges a very low price from its subsidiary for the use of the technology. It is because the cost of production will remain confined within the lower limits, leading to greater demand for the product. On the other hand, if the demand for the final product is price-inelastic, the parent unit will try to recover the cost of R&D as far as possible and inflate the price of technology, without impairing the revenue of the subsidiary.

   Again, the appropriateness of the technology even in case of intra-firm transfer cannot be guaranteed. The problem in this respect is the same as in the case of inter-firm transfer. However, the subsidiaries can modify the technology if it is not suitable. Thus, modification of technology is crucial to the process of technology diffusion.

Government restricts the size of royalty to be paid.

4. There are a lot of governmental restrictions on the transfer of technology from one country to another. In industrialised

countries, the restrictions are not as many as in the developing countries. Yet they exist. They are mainly regarding the size of royalty to be paid. Immigration laws are sometimes restrictive as they do not permit the technical personnel to accompany the technology.

Developing countries place greater restrictions on the transfer of technology and demand greater participation in the process of technology creation and diffusion. However, they offer lower patent protection. This is so despite the fact that these countries need a greater amount of new technology.

15.2.4 Modification of Technology

There are studies to show that the modification or adaptation of technology is only negligible. Yoeman found in a cross-sectional study of foreign subsidiaries of 13 US firms that most firms transferred their production process intact (Morley and Smith, 1977). Louis Wells (1973) supported this view in his case study of Indonesia. In Reuber's study (1973), it was found that 57 out of 78 investing firms did not attempt modification. In India, the study of the Reserve Bank of India (RBI, 1974) reveals that out of 111 financial collaborations, there were only 26 cases where an R&D wing was set up for modification of technology. Infact, there are a few factors that come in the way of modification. The nature of industry is one of them. In some industries, the production process requires sophisticated capital intensive techniques with the result that there is virtually no room for the behavioural elasticity of substitution between labour and capital. Morley and Smith (1977) find that international firms in Brazil rarely used labour intensive techniques as they were engaged in the production of consumer durables like automobiles and process products like chemicals. Apart from the nature of the industry, it is the attitude of the host country governments that prefer newest and latest production techniques even though they are not very suitable.

> Firms in the newly industrialising countries imported technology, modified it, and manufactured goods in order to suit to their own market.

On the contrary, there are the cases where substantial modification in the imported technology is reported. Infact, this is one of the factors behind the success story of the multinationals headquartered in the developing countries (Sharan, 1985). Firms in the newly industrialising countries imported technology from the industrialised world, modified it, and manufactured goods in order to suit to their own market and to the market of fellow developing countries. After their export became mature, they exported the technology to those markets or they set up manufacturing units in those foreign markets. The modified technology was happily accepted by the firms in the developing countries because it was more useful for them than the technology imported from the developed world. However, in many cases, developing countries brought about scale-up modifications and exported the modified technology to the industrialised countries too.

Winlee Ting (1982) mentions the case of Tatung Company of Taiwan, which imported technology from the United States and Japan for the manufacture of household appliances and after its successful modification, they set up affiliates in these two countries. Here it may be mentioned that since the income level is low in developing countries where consumers pay more attention to price rather than to quality, the modification in the technology is scaled down. On the other hand, the consumption pattern in developed countries is dented to quality and it is the scale-up modification that is adopted for exporting technology to them.

15.2.5 Protection of Technology

Innovated technology can be protected through and Patent Trademark. **Patent** rewards the innovator with temporary monopoly rights. **Trademark** is a unique mark on the product that differentiates it from similar products of rival firms.

Every international firm likes to protect its innovated technology in order to maintain its competitive strength. There are different ways through which it can be protected. They patent and trademark are two such methods. The patent rewards the innovator with temporary monopoly rights. However, there are some disadvantages in gaining a patent. (1) As per the laws prevailing in some countries, the firm getting the patent has to publish a detailed explanation of the technology and its application. Rivals may take advantage of this. (2) A patent is granted only for a limited period, after which no protection is possible. (3) Sometimes a patent is contested by rivals, leading to huge litigation costs. (4) Some governments do not offer patent facilities with the result that technology is not protected.

Again, trademark is a unique mark on the product that differentiates it from similar products of rival firms. The trademark may be in the form of a design, a picture, or in written words. However, no form is foolproof. The Wall Street Journal (December 5, 1989) gives an account of how branded products are imitated by some East Asian countries. Moreover, in cases of industrial espionage technological secrets are collected through bribing the officials of the innovating firm. Again, it is the mobility of labour force from the technology innovating firm to other firms that often leads to leakage of the protected technology.

In less developed countries, the protection measures are often weak due to ineffective laws. Grosse and Kujawa (1995) mention the example of some Latin American countries where the law does not protect the patented technology brought in by multinational corporations.

Thus, whenever a firm plans to operate abroad, it needs to consider these aspects of technological strategy and adopting safeguards to do away with the problems that come in the way of proper technology management.

15.3 INFORMATION TECHNOLOGY IN INTERNATIONAL BUSINESS

Information technology (IT) plays a significant role in IB beginning from the pre-negotiation stage to the finalisation of the deal and also in respect of the performance and control of the subsidiary in the host country.

Whenever a firm plans to set up a subsidiary or an affiliate abroad, it evaluates the economic, political, socio-cultural and regulatory environment prevailing in the host country. When IT was not developed, the evaluation process was time-consuming. There was no guarantee of cent per cent reliability of information and moreover, the entire process was a costly affair. But with the development of IT, this process has become quite reliable and easy and also with the minimum of time consumed and the least possible cost in so far as the entire information is available on the internet.

When the pre-negotiation stage is complete and the actual negotiation starts, IT makes this process quite convenient as the travelling cost and the time spent in negotiation are axed considerably. Samii (2004) discusses this aspect at greater length. According to him, the process of IT is in conformity with the "O-L-I" concept of foreign direct investment. The concept of "O" or the organisational theory of foreign direct investment explains that it is the firm-specific advantage that motivates a firm to go international. IT being more transparent and with very high speed of communication helps globalise the innovation and technical know-how. Again, the concept of "L" or the location-specific theory of foreign direct investment explains that easy availability of an input, such as cheap labour or cheap raw material attracts foreign direct investment. It may be noted that IT has strengthened the "L" factor. It is because of outsourcing, which is found on a substantial scale from India, Korea, Taiwan, the Philippines and Argentina that top global multinationals have been able to maintain a competitive edge. Their competitive advantage has shifted from value addition to cost advantage and as a result, there is relocation of the international activities. Last but not least, IT provides impetus to "I" factor or to the process of internalisation that is an important motive behind internationalisation of firms. The reasons are many, some more important are as follows:

1. IT helps reduce the transaction cost of negotiations with buyers/sellers. The explanation is that with IT, information is easily available and the market information is transparent. Naturally, there is greater competition. Greater competition reduces the transaction cost.
2. The procurement process becomes simpler and the time consumed is the least.
3. The transaction risk turns lower. It is because accurate and reliable information is available.

In fact, it is because of IT that even the small and medium-size enterprises are going international and investing even in the remotest corners of the globe. Thus, IT has provided strength of the process of internationalisation. The magnitude of international business has thus attained new heights which was not possible in absence of IT.

Again, when the negotiation is complete and the firm's subsidiary begins operation, it is the IT that helps in enhancing performance and control. It is easier to co-ordinate the activities of different units of a firm located in different countries. For example, if two or more airlines merge, it is easier to prepare flight schedules without duplication. It is also easier to design the product in accordance with the preference of the consumers living in different parts of the world. As far as control of subsidiaries is concerned, it has turned easier and smoother. The variety of systems available in different countries can easily be made identical or they can be integrated with the result that the control is not a problem. With the help of IT, the controlling unit keeps itself in constant touch with the units being controlled.

Furthermore, it is the IT that has brought revolution in the international financial market. There are numerous structural changes, such as cross-border internet banking, electronic equity and bond trading, electronic foreign exchange trading, etc. Foreign exchange trading platform, multi-banking portals, and project finance portals are among the new and emerging tools in the global financial system. In all, easy recourse to finance on account of the development of IT has encouraged international business.

It is not only the easy availability of finds but also the marketing facilities that have been created by IT. The development of intranet and extranet alongwith business to business (B2B) and business to consumers (B2C) has well complied to the marketing challenges. For many customers and suppliers, a web page is sufficient. Online commerce is a new area in domestic and international marketing (Karimi and Konsynski, 1991).

Thus, it is the significance of the IT that the world spent on it exceeded three trillions of dollars in 2006 and it is estimated at four trillion dollars during 2009. However, there is a great deal of complexity in building and maintaining of the IT infra-structure that could support a required level of global business activities. There are a few limitations to the functioning of internet, such as lack of bandwidth, development of language, equality of service in different parts of the world, etc. But they can be improved.

SUMMARY

- Technology—product, process, and management—is a strategic asset in the sense that it confers upon the firm a sort of competitive advantage through the creation of new product features or through cutting of costs. This is why it is essential for to have a sound technology strategy.
- Technology strategy incorporates, among other things, technology audit, development and acquisition of technology, its modification, and its protection. Technology audit is concerned with the identification of the technological gap and of technological competence, and its relevance to business opportunities.
- Technology can be developed through R&D, but it involves huge costs and high risk of probable failure. It can be acquired through transfer. The transfer can be either inter-firm or intra-firm, depending upon the circumstances. However, there are some problems involved in the transfer of technology, such as high cost, outdated quality, inappropriateness, and so on. Moreover, there are often restrictions imposed by the

home country and host country governments. In case the technology is not appropriate, it is often modified by the recipient.

- Technology can be protected through patents and trademarks, but both of the techniques are not foolproof. Again, with the fast growth in information technology and its use in international business, decision making, configuration and coordination of different units located in remote geographical locations have become very smooth.

Review Questions

1. What are the different types of technology?
2. What are the problems involved in the development of technology through R&D?
3. Distinguish between inter-firm and intra-firm transfer of technology and explain the problems involved in it.
4. Write short notes on:
   (i) Modification of technology
   (ii) Protection of technology
   (iii) IT and international business

Objective Type Questions

1. Marks True or False:
   (a) Soft technology is concerned with blueprints, specifications, and so on.
   (b) Proprietary technology is an innovated technology that is not available to other firms in the market.
   (c) Technology is a strategic asset that helps produce new products having price-inelastic demand in the early phases.
   (d) Technology audit involves identification of technology and the firm's ability to develop R&D.
   (e) Inter-firm transfer of technology takes place when technology lies at the very root of competitive advantage of an MNC.
   (f) Intra-firm transfer of technology normaly takes place when the technology is too costly to be bought by other firms.
   (g) The scale-up modification of technology is meant for low-income consumers.
   (h) Patent rewards the innovator with temporary monopoly rights.
   (i) Industrial espionage involves the leakage of protected technology.
   (j) IT can ensure full control of the parent over its subsidiary.

2. Choose the Most Suitable Answer:
   (a) Technology is protected through:
      (i) Patents and not trademark

(ii) Trademark and not patent
(iii) Both trademark and patent

(b) In less developed countries, laws protecting technology are:
(i) Often very effective
(ii) Not very liberal
(iii) Not very effective

(c) Process technology:
(i) Specifies product features
(ii) Involves managerial skills for running business
(iii) Is the knowledge used in manufacturing a product

(d) Proprietary technology:
(i) Helps a firm enjoy a monopolistic position
(ii) Is easily available to other firms in the market
(iii) Is diffused inter-firm

(e) Intra-firm transfer of technology is found when:
(i) The price of technology development is very low
(ii) It is difficult to protect the technology through patents
(iii) The price of developed technology is very high

(f) A low-income developing country modifying technology for its own market goes for:
(i) Scale-up modification
(ii) Scale-down modification
(iii) Both of the above

CASE STUDY

Technological Intensity and Technology Export of Indian Firms

The exporters of manufactures vary in export performance based on the intensity of technology they have. The manufactures have either high-intensity technology or medium-intensity technology or still low-intensity technology. Experience shows that the more advanced is the level of technology, the faster is the growth of export, irrespective of the fact whether the exporter is a developed country or a developing one. It is also found that the developing countries are growing faster than the developed countries in the export of more technology-intensive products (World Investment Report, 2002). Table 1 shows the top five export winners by technology category during 1985–2000.

Table 1: Top five exporters of varied technological intensity

Rank	*Exporters of high-technology manufactures*	*Exporters of medium-technology manufactures*	*Exporters of low-technology manufactures*
1	China	China	China
2	Malaysia	Mexico	USA

3	Taiwan	USA	Mexico
4	Korea	Korea	Indonesia
5	Singapore	Spain	Thailand

India was not a big exporter of technology-intensive products But in the recent years, it has improved its position. The Indian Institute of Foreign Trade has made a survey of 303 firms, of which 56 are low-technology ones, 153 are medium-technology ones and 94 are high-technology firms. Table 2 shows their export performance during FY 2002–2007.

Table 2: Export Performance of 303 Technology-intensity Firms

Technology Intensity	*Export (Rs. in billion)*				
	2002–2003	2003–2004	2004–2005	2005–2006	2006–2007
Low Technolgy	180.287	256.011	395.524	487.293	872.959
Medium Technology	82.265	114.359	151.563	199.138	284.005
High Technology	266.191	333.118	362.272	497.438	648.220
Total	528.743	703489	909.359	1,183.870	1,805.185

It is revealed from the figures that over the years, the share of low-intensity technology export has risen; on the contrary, that of high-intensity technology export has dwindled. The share of medium-intensity technology export has been stationary.

Again, the form of technology export of the firms under survey has been quite broad. Table 3 shows how far the different forms of technology export have performed.

Table 3: R&D Expenditure and Export Performance of Different Forms of Technology Export: FY 2004–2007

(Rs. in billion)

Sector	*No. of Firms*	*R&D Expenditure*			*Export*		
		2004–2005	2005–2006	2006–2007	2004–2005	2005–2006	2006–2007
Consultancy Services	8	0.126	0.197	240.624	1.160	1.582	2.285
Turn-Key Project	19	2.040	2.181	732.987	68.623	90.199	120.435
Capital Goods	36	3.163	3.749	205.905	13.496	13.074	17.802
Computer Hardware and Software Services	9	1.716	1.903	98.579	82.710	123.718	166.897

Technology know-how	4	0.015	0.011	11.778	1.890	2.502	5.060
Technology-Intensive Products	227	43.241	50.309	5,328.919	741.612	952.883	1,492.836
Total	303	50.300	58.349	6,618.791	909.491	1,183.959	1,805.315

It is evident from Table 3 that technology-intensive products have the largest share. Computer software and hardware service exports and turn-key project exports too share large. But India is still lagging in case of the export of consultancy services and the export of know-how. However, in all the forms of technology export, rising trend is evident.

Again, there is some relationship between R&D expenditure and the export volume. But it is different in different forms of technology export.

Source: Based on: IIFT, Compemdium of Technology Exports, New Delhi, 2008.

QUESTIONS

1. What do you mean by technology intensity? Is it true that the developing countries have fared well in technology export compared to developed countries?
2. Do you find any relationship between technological intensity and the performance of technology export in the Indian case?
3. What are the different forms of technology exports India is making? In which category, this country has excelled during recent past?

REFERENCES

Books

Baranson, G. (1978), *Technology and the Multinationals* (Lexington, M.A.: D.C. Heath).

Goodman, R. A. and M. W. Lawless (1994), *Technology and Strategy* (Oxford: Oxford University Press).

Grosse, R. and D. Kujawa (1995), *International Business* (Chicago: Irwin).

Magee, S. (1977), "Information and Multinational Corporations: An Appropriability Theory of Foreign Direct Investment", in J. Bhagwati (ed.), *The New International Economic Order* (Cambridge M. A.: MIT Press), 317–40.

Reuber, G. L. *et al* (1973), *Private Foreign Investment in Development* (Oxford: Clarendon Press).

Samii, M. (2004),"Globalisation and IT"in Samii, M. and G. Karush, *eds., International Business and Information Technology*, New York: Routledge, pp. 10–23.

Sauvant, K. P. and F. G. Lavipour (1976), *Controlling Multinational Enterprises* (Colorado: Westview Press).

Stonehouse, G. *et al* (2000), *Global and Transnational Business: Strategy and Management*, Chichester: John

Wiley & Sons Limited.

Journals and Report

Abernathy, W. J. and J. M. Utterback (1978),"Patterns of Industrial Innovation", *Technology Review*, June/ July, 40–47.

Baranson, J. (1970),"Technology Transfer through the International Firm", *American Economic Review*, LX (Papers and Proceedings), 935–37.

Gruber, W. H. *et al* (1967),"The R&D Factor in International Investment of US Industries", *Journal of Political Economy*, LXXV (1), 20–37.

Karimi, J. and B.R. Konsynski (1991), "Globalisation and Information Management Strategies", *Journal Management Information System*, 7 (4), 26.

Morley, S. A. and G. W. Smith (1977),"The Choice of Technology: Multinational Firms in Brazil", *Economic Development and Cultural Change*, XXV (2), 239–64.

Reserve Bank of India Bulletin, June 1974.

Sharan, V. (1985),"Internationalism of Third World Firms: An Indian Case Study", *International Marketing Review*, II (Summer), 63–71.

Ting, Wenlee (1982),"The Product Development Process in NIC Multinational", *Columbia Journal of World Business*, XVII (1), 76–81.

UN, (2003), World Investment Report 2003

Wells, L. T. (1973),"Economic Man and Engineering Man: Choice of Technology in a Low-Wage Country", *Public Policy*, XXI (3), 319–42.

SELECT FURTHER READINGS

Davidson, W. H. (1983), *Experience Effects in International Investment and Technology Transfer* (NewYork: UMI Research Press).

Rosenberg, N. ed. (1984), *International Technology Transfer* (London: John Wiley & Sons).

Teece, D. J. (1977), *Technology Transfer by Multinational Firms* (Cambridge M. A.: Ballinger).

* **Shanghai** is a metropolis in eastern China and a direct-controlled municipality of the People's Republic of China. It is often regarded as the centre of finance and trade in mainland China. Shanghai has recorded a double-digit growth for 15 consecutive years since 1992 and has increased its role in finance, banking, and as a major destination for corporate headquarters, fueling demand for a highly educated and modernised workforce. In 2008, it's nominal GDP posted a 9.7 per cent growth to 1.37 trillion Yuan.

Port of Singapore*

16 Management of International Operations

CHAPTER OBJECTIVES

The present chapter discusses the operational aspect of MNCs. The objective of the discussion is to:

- ✦ Explain the different options for locating the manufacturing operations, the factors behind the selection of a particular location, and the process of selecting a particular location.
- ✦ Show how inventory is managed and whether there is any deviation either from the EOQ or from the normal re-ordering point.
- ✦ Identify the sources from where the inputs can be procured and also the mode of procurement.
- ✦ Explain whether the inputs can be bought from another firm or they should be manufactured within the firm.
- ✦ Focus on international logistics—the relative merits of different modes of transport, the packaging of products, and the storage facility.
- ✦ Show how international services are different from manufacturing.
- ✦ Explain how services are internationalised and what problems arise during the process of internationalisation.
- ✦ Delineate the management aspect of international services including also the off-shoring of corporate service functions.

When an international firm possesses any specific technology and decides to begin operation, it needs to follow a sound operation strategy so as to enjoy competitive advantage. The operations strategy in a manufacturing firm involves many decisions. The most important among them are concerned with location for production; management of inventory; sourcing of inputs; and international logistics, including transport, packaging, and storage. The purpose of these decisions is to minimise the cost of production and to ensure production flexibility and market responsiveness. However, if a firm provides services, the strategy would be slightly different.

16.1 LOCATION FOR PRODUCTION

16.1.1 Options for Location

The traditional theory of location suggests that if the inputs account for a large share in the value of the final product or if the raw material carries heavy weight but loses its weight during the manufacturing process, the manufacturing unit should be located near the source of inputs. On the other hand, if input does not matter very much, from the viewpoint of cost or transportation, the manufacturing unit should be located near the market. However, the decision regarding the location of an international firm is complex insofar as, firstly, these firms are spread over a far wider geographic area; secondly, they source the inputs globally; and thirdly, their market is spread over different countries.

An international firm may have various alternatives regarding the location of manufacturing activities. Dicken (1998) describes these options as:

1. Centralisation of the manufacturing operations at the parent unit or any one of the subsidiaries. It will help reap either the economies of scale or the location specific advantage in the form of climatic, cultural, governmental, and other factors.
2. Decentralisation of manufacturing operations at different subsidiaries and distribution of the product in the respective areas.
3. Location of the different parts of the manufacturing process at different subsidiaries under a vertically integrated framework. Vertical integration may be of two types. They are:
   (i) The different units are linked in a chain-like sequence.
   (ii) Different units manufacturing spares and components export the output to a particular unit engaged in assembling them. It is common that the spare parts of a product are produced in a country with abundance of capital and the assembly part is located in a labour surplus country.

16.1.2 Factors behind Selection of Location

Dunning (1980) mentions five factors behind the selection of a location. They are:

1. Size and growth of market and the degree of competition in the market
2. Availability of raw material and labour force of required skill
3. State of logistics and the degree of currency fluctuation
4. Political and legal environment
5. Cultural and linguistic environment

Not a single factor determines the location decision. It is rather a combination of all factors that really works. For example, if a market is large and promising, the plant may be located close to the market. But if raw material or labour is cheap in a particular country, the plant may be located there without considering proximity to the market. Again, if both of the above factors are favourable, but the logistics are not well developed, the firm may not be attracted by the availability of raw material or manpower. Scully and Fawcett (1993) have found in their empirical study that despite finding cost advantageous locations, US companies did not locate their plant there. This is because the state of logistics there was not supportive. Similarly the plant is located only in countries that are marked with political stability and where socio-cultural and language problems do not exist as a major barrier.

Logistics is a process involving movement of inputs from supplier to the firm and of the finished product from the firm to the market.

In fact, the purpose of considering these factors is to:

1. Minimise cost
2. Maintain quality
3. Have flexibility in designing the product and in the volume of production

The centralisation of plant at a particular unit leads to economies of scale, which tends to reduce the cost of production. But the benefit on this account needs to be weighed against the cost of transportation that is involved in carrying the product from the plant to different markets. However, cost can be reduced by locating a part of the manufacturing activities at a low-cost site. A number of US companies ship components necessary for the assembly of a product to Mexican maquiladora (a synonym for the export processing zones). The components are assembled there and the final product is shipped back to United States of America and other markets. The offshore assembly of many products of US companies is done in East Asian countries such as Taiwan, South Korea, and so on. All this is done to reap the benefits of low wage cost in Mexico or in the East Asian countries. This is especially so in cases where the assembly cost accounts for a very large share in the total production cost (Stobaugh and Telesio, 1992).

Again, quality control is a significant aspect. An international company locates its manufacturing activities only at a place where it feels trained manpower is available to make the best use of the technology and where the quality of the product is maintained. Maintenance of quality in international business means either zero-level defect or an acceptable level of defect. The former is in use among Japanese multinationals, whereas the latter is used by Western companies. It is because of this view that international companies stress on ISO 9000. Products maintaining ISO 9000 standards are widely accepted among the consumers, irrespective of geographical differences.

As regards flexibility in designing and volume of production, it is suggested to locate the manufacturing plant at different subsidiaries. This is because the subsidiaries can easily make relevant changes in the design of the product to suit the local consumption pattern or in the volume of production in the wake of fluctuating demand.

16.1.3 Selecting a Location

It is evident from the preceding section that some factors are favourable attracting a firm to locate its manufacturing activities in a particular place/country. At the same time, there are unfavourable factors, especially various types of risks that detract firms from locating their manufacturing unit. From this viewpoint, managers should first assign weightage to different factors depending upon the firm's requirements and then use a matrix showing favourable factors/locations on the Y-axis and unfavourable factors/locations on the X axis. Finally, they should plot the locations depending upon the favourable and unfavourable factors. The most suitable location would be the one that has the highest ratio of favourable points/unfavourable points. This is the easiest way to select a location.

The most suitable location would be the one that has the highest ratio of favourable points/unfavourable points.

16.2 MANAGEMENT OF INVENTORY

Inventory accounts for the biggest share of current assets. At the same time, it is the least liquid among the current assets. This is why its management deserves sufficient care. In an international firm, compared to a domestic firm, its management is complex in view of international sourcing of inventory, maintaining of inventory simultaneously in different countries, longer transit time, lengthy customs procedures, and political risk as well as exchange rate risk. Consequently, there are some deviations from the simple norm of inventory management of a domestic firm. These deviations are explained here at some length.

16.2.1 Deviation from the Economic Order Quantity

The **economic order quantity** (EOQ) is the optimal size of inventory that a firm orders at a particular point of time.

The economic order quantity (EOQ) is the optimal size of inventory that a firm orders at a particular point of time. Books on production management or corporate finance explain EOQ and the details about its calculation. However, it may be pointed out here that EOQ refers to a particular quantity of order, where the sum of the ordering cost and the carrying cost of inventory is the minimum. With the growth in the size of order, the number of orders in a particular period of time gets fewer and the ordering cost reduces. But, on the other hand, the carrying cost increases. Thus, to arrive at the EOQ, the firm has to trade-off between the carrying cost and the ordering cost. The trade-off is complete where the sum of these two costs is the minimum.

Domestic firms adhere to this norm strictly. But international firms normally possess a bigger stock than the EOQ, which is often known as stockpiling. A particular unit of a firm gets a significant part of its input from sister units located in other countries, especially in case of vertical integration; alternatively, it may get its input from other firms—local or international. In case of international sourcing, political risk and the exchange rate risk cannot be denied completely. If there is political disturbance, there will be obstruction in the import. If the currency of the importing country depreciates, imports turn costlier. Thus, in order to avoid these problems, stockpiling is favoured.

Stockpiling is carrying more inventory than the EOQ.

However, stockpiling cannot be done indefinitely. The firm will have to decide against stockpiling if the cumulative carrying cost exceeds the expected increase in the price of the input on account of changes in the exchange rate. Nevertheless, if the probability of interruption in supply is very high, the firm may go for stockpiling even if it is not justified on the grounds of higher cost.

If the probability of interruption in supply is very high, the firm may go for stockpiling even if it is not justified on the grounds of higher cost.

16.2.2 Shifting of Re-order Point

The general principle is that the next lot of inventory is to be ordered when the existing stock comes down to the sum of safety level of stock and the lead time—both expressed in terms of number of days. Suppose the existing stock, based on the present usage rate, can go for 30 days. If the firm maintains a safety level of stock for five days and if the lead time—time elapsed between placing an order and the arrival of input—is six days, the firm will place an order for the next lot only after nineteen days of the arrival of the existing stock. However, in case of the international firms, the lead time is larger as the different units are located far apart in different parts of the globe. Even after goods reach the port, there are a lot of customs formalities. Because of all these factors, the reorder point in case of international firms lies much earlier.

Re-order point lies much earlier in view of larger lead time and lengthy customs formalities.

Nevertheless, decisions regarding stockpiling or re-order point depends on how much of the goods are to be imported and how much of them are locally available. Dependence on imports varies from one case to another, but it is definitely large in case of international sourcing.

16.2.3 Just-in-time System

Initially Japanese firms and now many Western firms too have opted for the just-in-time (JIT) system of inventory management. The very rationale of this system is that the input—raw material, spare parts, and components—should reach the production process just in time so that the carrying cost or holding cost is reduced to the minimum. However,

In **JIT system** inputs reach the manufacturing location just when they are required.

in view of the complexity of the international production that is manifest in longer transit time, Vickery (1989) suggests a few measures such as air transportation, adjustment in the expected lead time, and so on. Nevertheless, the risk of not getting the desired input in time is always there. The firm should be very careful while adopting this method.

16.3 SOURCING OF INPUTS

The broad objectives of the input-sourcing decision are cost minimisation, regular and uninterrupted supply, quality advantage, enhancement of service, and fast adjustment with the requirements. Risk minimisation is another factor influencing the input sourcing policy. While developing an international sourcing strategy, the firm has to consider not only the cost but also the exchange rate fluctuations, industrial and cultural environment, the ease of working with foreign governments, and so on. Hickman and Hickman (1992) consider political stability, developed infrastructure, and an educated urban work force as attributes of low risk procurement success.

16.3.1 Modes of Procurement

Procurement may be centralised at the parent unit. Alternatively, it may be decentralised at the subsidiary level. When the input is standardised, centralised procurement is common. On the contrary, if host government policies prefer local sourcing or if the inputs are of specialised nature, available in a particular locality, procurement is often decentralised. Between the two extremes, procurement may be quasi-centralised, meaning that the firm sets up regional purchasing organisations.

Irrespective of the fact whether the procurement is centralised or decentralised, there are broadly three modes for this purpose. They are:

1. Importation
2. Establishment of international procurement offices (IPOs)
3. Sourcing through direct investment

Import may be made directly by the firm itself. It may be indirect, through agents or distributors. In this mode, cost is low and the room for manoeuvrability is big. However, there is often the problem of timely delivery schedule and assured product quality.

Many companies have set up IPOs for procurement. Qua and Thian (1991) have found that many original equipment manufacturers have set up IPOs in Asia to buy components for their master. In Singapore, in 1993, there were more than 100 IPOs of different international companies.

Sometimes international firms make direct investment in foreign subsidiaries just to supply raw material and components. In this case, the availability of inputs is assured. The input supplying unit exports its output to different sister units as well as to the parent unit. This is intra-firm supply of inputs and in this case, transfer pricing is very common.

It is the assured supply of raw material that has led at least some of the Indian companies to go for international acquisitions. To mention one such case, Tata Steel Ltd. acquired stake in Brazilian miner Companhia Vale do Rio Doce and South African Kumba Resources Ltyd. in order to assure supply of iron ore for its Anglo-Dutch plant, Corus Group Plc.

Tata Steel Ltd. signs two joint-venture agreements for sourcing raw material. The first is with Australia's Riversdale Mining Limited to set up a hard coking and thermal coal project in Mozambique in South-East Africa where it will have the right to source 40% of the total coal production from the mines there. Tata Steel has invested $88.5 million and has 35% stake in the equity.

The second is its joint-venture agreement with Ivory Coast's state-owned company, Sodemi to mine iron ore from Mount Nimba deposits. It will have 75% stake in the equity. The iron ore so procured will be supplied to Tata Steel Group located in the UK and the Netherlands. All these efforts are aiming at ensuring raw material supply at lower cost and thereby widening the profit margin of the Group.
Source: Based on *Financial Express*, 13.12.2007.

16.3.2 Make or Buy Decision

In the manufacturing process, it is of utmost importance to obtain inputs from the cheapest source as well as of the best quality. Sometimes, the manufacturing unit of the firm obtains inputs from sister units, particularly when there is some sort of vertical integration among the different units of a firm. Alternatively, it tries to obtain inputs from other firms. Thus, whether there should be intra-firm transfer of inputs or they should be obtained from outside sources is an important decision. In other words, it is a "make-or-buy" decision.

Make-or-buy decision refers to procurement of inputs: from within the firm/from outside sources.

If the firm makes its own inputs, it may have full control over the supply from the viewpoint of quality and timing. Apart from getting the desired inputs well in time, it is easy for the firm to maintain their quality. This is because the firm has full control over the raw material, product design, and the production process. Minor or major modification in the design can easily be made, which is not easy in case of buying inputs from the outside supplier. If the manufacturing of inputs requires sophisticated technology, which the firm does not like to part with, in-house production is the only way out.

Make versus Buy Decision

- Advantages of making inputs within the firm:
  - Full control over the quality and timing of supply
  - Availability of input at lower cost
  - Easy modification in design
  - Maintenance of secrecy of technology
  - Generation of profit through arbitrary pricing of inputs

- Advantages of buying inputs from outside
  - No additional investment for input manufacturing
  - No need for acquiring technology required for input manufacturing, which may be inappropriate/obsolete
  - Freedom to get inputs from the cheapest source
  - Diversification of the sources of inputs leading to lower political and exchange rate risk
  - Operational flexibility in face of changing demand

Again, the in-house production of spares sometimes leads to lowering of costs. Levin (1994) found that Compaq manufactured motherboards at a lower cost than it paid to outside suppliers. This way it saved money and also lead time. Moreover, a firm can generate profits through arbitrary pricing of the inputs.

But the problem is that it has to make additional investment for this purpose; and over and above, it needs to acquire specific know-how, technicians, and managerial skills for this purpose, which may prove to be an additional financial burden on the firm. At the same time, even after additional investment and acquiring necessary technical and managerial skills, the quality of inputs may not be up to the mark and the cost may be high.

On the contrary, if inputs are obtained from other firms—local and international—there may not be effective control over the cost, quality, and timeliness of supply, but the firm may enjoy wide choice and can select the cheapest/best quality supplier. It has to neither make additional investment nor worry about the acquisition of technical and managerial skills. Exchange rate risk and political risk are also lower if the firm obtains its inputs from many sources. This is the benefit of diversifying the outsourcing process. The firm can also enjoy operational flexibility. If it has to reduce the size of the output of the final product abruptly in view of changes in demand, it can easily lower the size of input import. This is not so easy when the firm itself produces the desired inputs. Birou and Fawcett (1993), based on their empirical findings, mention the benefits from international sourcing such as availability of cheaper/higher quality inputs, access to world class technology, better delivery performance, and better customer services.

Thus, the firm needs to balance the benefits and costs of both of the alternatives and develop a procurement model. However, the model must be in conformity with the basic strategy of the firm.

16.4 INTERNATIONAL LOGISTICS

Logistics are concerned with the movement of raw material, spares, and components from the supplier to the user (the manufacturing firm) and of the final product from the manufacturing firm to the consumer. Since the logistics cost is around 10 to 30 per cent of the landed cost of an international order (Czinkota, 1999), its management is really significant with a view to increasing efficiency as well as minimising cost. Moreover, in case of an international firm, where different units are widely spread over different countries with unfamiliar environments, and where sourcing of raw material as well as marketing of the final product is normally international, logistics management becomes more complex.

The formulation of an international logistics strategy is significant also in view of the fact that there are major problems confronting it. The problems are either of general nature or of specific nature. Among the general problems are the long distances that require more time and greater cost, changes in the exchange rate leading to foreign exchange exposure, and a poor transport network. Similarly, the specific problems vary from one country to the other. Mode of transport, warehousing facilities, packaging and labelling requirements, and so on differ from one country to the other. International firm should be aware of these specific problems of the countries where its units are located or from where the supplies of inputs are to be made or where the market exists.

16.4.1 Transportation Issue

Among the various issues connected with logistics management, the transportation issue is the most important. In this respect, it is not only the transport network that attracts attention, but it is also the mode of transport that is available and the choice of a particular mode that is to be taken care of.

In developed countries, the transportation network—land, sea or air—is normally well built. But in developing countries, it is often not up to the mark. While in the developed countries, roads are 41.7 km per 100 km of territory, the low-income developing countries have barely 17.7 km per 100 km of territory. These figures for rail lines are 2.5 and 0.7 for the developed and the low-income developing countries, respectively (World Trade Report, 2004). So, whenever an international firm starts operations in a developing host country, it has to see whether the transport network is really supportive. If it is not, it will be difficult to get the supplies of inputs and to reach the market. Ricks (1993) mentions the case of a pineapple cannery at the delta of a Mexican river where ripe fruit upstream were floated downstream for processing. But, during the following harvest season, it was found that the river current shifted far away from the factory. In the absence of an alternative mode of transport, the factory could not transport its raw material and ultimately it had to be closed.

With regard to the mode of transport, it may be said that in international business, it is normally ocean and air transport that matter, although land transport is also important for carrying goods between the factory and the port or airport. Air transport is a costlier mode, but more supportive when the weight-volume ratio of the goods is high or where the commodity is

Air transport is a costlier mode, but more supportive when the commodity is perishable.

With regard to **ocean transport**, the first is the liner service, which provides a regular service on a fixed route and the second is the bulk service, which provides contractual service.

perishable. But the question is how far this mode is developed in a developing host country. In many poor developing countries, the air transport system could not be developed for want of resources.

With regard to ocean transport, two types of vessels are available. The first is the liner service, which provides a regular service on a fixed route. The second is the bulk service, which has neither a fixed timing nor a fixed route. It simply provides contractual service. Similarly, ships are of different types. Container ships carry standard size containers, while conventional cargo vessels can carry even large size goods. There are also

Poor Road Infrastructure: Who Pays the Cost? The Case of Beer Distribution in Cameroon

Cameroonian transport infrastructure is very poor. In 1995, there were 2.6 kilometres of road per 1,000 people. Of these, less than a tenth are paved, and most are badly cracked or potholed which rainstorms make much worse. Road repairs are undertaken occasionally by amateur workers or street boys who fill holes with sand. In these conditions, a trip of 500 kilometres can take up to 4 days and a rainstorm may render roads impassable.

Guinness has a local subsidiary in Cameroon, the fifth biggest market by volume for the company. The company performance is good. Returns to capital are about 16 per cent and sales of the main brands have gone up by 14 per cent over the past five years.

However, bad infrastructure is estimated to add an average of 15 per cent to the production costs of beer in Cameroon. Bad infrastructure makes "just-in-time delivery" impossible. Factories and wholesalers need to keep large stocks and this increases costs. Guinness Cameroon keeps a 40-day inventory in the factory, while some European factories keep only a few hours of inventories. At the start of the rainy season, a wholesaler might need up to five months of inventory, as the rain renders the road impossible to travel.

Who loses? The big losers are ordinary Cameroonians, who pay higher prices or are paid lower wages. A Guinness that cost 350 CFA in Douala may cost up to 30 per cent more in an eastern village that can be reached only on foot.

Source: Adapted from *World Trade Report*, 2004.

roll-on-roll-off ships into which fully loaded trucks can be accommodated, which saves the cost and time of unloading goods from the trucks and loading them on to the ship.

An appropriate mode of transport should be cost effective, reliable, and speedy.

The logistics manager has to select an appropriate mode of transport that would be cost effective, reliable, and speedy. If these are the criteria for the selection of the modes of transport, air transport is costlier. But air transport assures timely delivery of goods and significantly cuts the lead time. If the input usage rate turns abnormally high at a specific point of time, it is only air transport that can make the input available to the firm in time. Again, if the goods are perishable or the transport cost/value of goods ratio is only negligible, air transport is preferable. Air transport is more predictable than ocean transport and it can be more useful for customers. The logistics manager has to weigh the benefits and costs of a particular mode and only then can any decision be made. However, such a decision is influenced by factors beyond the control of the manager as most of governments prefer that their own shippers are used so that scarce foreign exchange can be saved. The UNCTAD has a clear resolution on this issue. It says that 40 per cent of traffic between any two nations should be allocated to the vessels of the exporting country, 40 per cent to the importing country, and the remaining 20 per cent should go to a third country.

16.4.2 Packaging of Products

The purpose of packaging is to make the product maintainable and presentable. This factor is very important in international business as the goods are carried through different modes—by land route to the port and then by ship to distant locations with climatic differences. If the climate is highly humid or cold, special precautions have to be taken while packaging. Again, the packaging of perishable products, such as fruits, vegetables, needs special care. But the packaging material should not be heavy, as it creates problems in transportation. Where duty is imposed on the basis of weight, the amount of duty will be unnecessarily high. Fortunately, packaging has come to be a special branch of study at technical institutes, as the industry is now aware that suitable and efficient packaging is also capable of solving many related problems.

16.4.3 Storage Facility

Storage plays an important role in logistics management. When the inputs arrive at the firm, they have to be stored for at least some time. This is because the entire delivery cannot be used immediately. Again, before the final product reaches the market, it has to be stored for some time. So, how large warehouses should be, where they should be located or what kind of facilities they should possess are important aspects that need to be addressed. The size of the warehouses should be based on the demand for, and the frequency of the arrival of, the products. If the size is unusually large, the cost of storage will be too large to be justified. Moreover, warehouses should provide all the facilities required by the product in question. Normally, the space is compartmentalised according to the requirements of the products and the products are stored accordingly in different compartments.

> The size of the warehouses should be based on the demand for, and the frequency of the arrival of, the products.

Besides the above, the location of the warehouse is also important. If it is for storing the final product, it should be located near the market. This is because the presence of warehousing facilities assures the customers or retailers that the supply of the product is a continuous phenomenon. All this has a positive impact on the marketability of products.

16.4.4 Centralised and Decentralised Logistics management

Logistics issue may be looked after either by the parent unit or by different subsidiaries or the entire management is outsourced.

Whatever the logistics issue may be, it has to be looked after either by the parent unit or by different subsidiaries at their own level or, still, the entire management is outsourced. In other words, there is a choice among centralised management, decentralised management and outsourcing.

The centralised approach may be more decisive. It may be well co-ordinated. But the staff at headquarter may suffer from lack of desired information. Moreover, the same decision cannot hold good equally in different host countries. On the contrary, the decentralised management does solve effectively the local problems. But it lacks proper co-ordination. Moreover, the individual subsidiaries may not be having desired bargaining power with the result that the transport cost may turn high. Thus, both of the practices suffer from some limitations. A better course of action may be that the local managers acquaint headquarter with the local issues and the headquarter adjust its logistics policy after considering those local issues.

When the firm does not like to look after the logistics issue itself on various grounds, it can outsource this function. There are independent logistics firms that can manage the transportation, warehousing and packaging more efficiently. They do charge for these services but they enjoy the economies of scale and their efficiency may lower the entire logistics cost. Presently, one-step logistics firms are available to whom this function can be outsourced. They ensure more efficient movement of goods and perform greater number of functions, such as handling of customs clearance, warehousing, packaging, etc.

16.4.5 Present State of Logistics in India

The logistic sector in India has turned out as a growth driver for the economy. As per an Associated Chambers of Commerce report, logistics sector in the country is expected to grow from the 2007 level of Rs. 4 lakh crores to Rs. 7.5 lakh crores by 2012. This sector employs directly and indirectly around 40 million persons. It employs new technology like GPS tracking, radio frequency identification, online supply-chain tools, etc. The global companies are supporting the domestic companies to bench-mark with global standards.

The logistic space in the country is multi-tier. The first is the surface transport that includes companies, viz. Blue Dart, Gati and Transport Corporation of India. During the present decade, there has been growth in all kinds of transport. The road transport, in terms of millions of tonnes of cargo transported, has witnessed the biggest growth from 1075 to 1560 during 2001–2007. The railways accounted for a jump up from 475 to 667 million tonnes and the sea transport moved up from 364 to 578 million tonnes. The air transport still occupies the smallest share but it too recorded an upward move from 0.9 million tonnes to 1.4 million tonnes.

The multi-modal logistics and warehousing companies are Allcargo Global, Container Corporation of India, Aegis Logistics, etc. However, small transporters are reigning the market. Those with a fleet of five trucks or less have captured around four-fifths of the market. Again, there are thousands of small customs brokers and clearing and forwarding agents. The warehousing service segment too employs thousands of service operators.

As far as the logistics costs are concerned, they are higher in India than in many developed countries. As per the report, they are 15 per cent of GDP in India compared to 11 per cent in Japan, 10 per cent in Europe and as low as 9 per cent in the USA. The major reason for it is the lack of basic infrastructure. The governmental policy is not very encouraging and there exists extensive industry fragmentation.

16.5 INTERNATIONAL SERVICES

Goods and services are sometimes complementary to each other. But they have different identities. Hence, the strategy of operations is more often different in these two cases. The speciality of services needs some explanation in view of the phenomenal growth in, and fast-changing character of, the inter-nationalisation of services in the recent past.

16.5.1 Goods and Services

Services complement goods in the sense that goods sold can be maintained in order with the help of after sales services. Sometimes services follow the transaction of goods so that consumers can be trained regarding how to use the goods. Again, the goods complement the services. Services cannot be provided efficiently if the quality of the goods transacted is not up to the mark.

> Despite goods and services being complementary, services, in normal course cannot normally be stored, have the same time of production, cannot be standardised, and are not tied to specific location.

Nevertheless, the goods are different from services. Services are intangible; they are consumed but they are not stored. Goods, on the other hand, can be stored. Again, since services cannot be stored, they perish if not used. For example, an unused seat in a bus cannot be retained for the next trip. However, with the development of information communication technology, it is possible to store some of the services through digitisation.

In case of services, the time of production and consumption normally coincides. This leads to a situation where the provider of services is physically present when services are provided. The customer-producer relation matter more in case of services. On the other hand, goods begin the journey from the producer-point and reach the consumers through wholesalers and retailers.

Services cannot normally be standardised and have a greater element of heterogeneity. This means the quality of services varies with each delivery. For example, the quality of the services rendered by a physician usually varies from one patient to the other.

Services are not necessarily tied to a specific location. The location can shift from one place to the other. Again, since labour is mobile, it can be geared up for a specific location. Moreover, with the development of internet services, consumers can avail of services from any part of the world. Infact, the distance education system is based on this principle.

16.5.2 Some Flourishing International Services

There are many areas where services have gone international. Banking is one of them. The US, European, and Japanese banks have done well in this respect. Even the banks from developing countries have spread their branches throughout the globe. Insurance services are other such services where internationalisation has increased. Tourism represents an important service export. Many companies have constructed hotels and tourist resorts in different countries. Consultancy and engineering services represent yet another area where internationalisation is frequent. However, in this case, the host countries are largely developing countries where technical skill is still lagging behind. Again, teaching services too flourish. Many educational institutions of world repute are collaborating with teaching institutions of the developing world. Communication services are one of the latest in this area. These services have made the world a global village.

Major Groups of Services	
Business services	Environmental services
Communication services	Financial services
Construction and related engineering services	Tourism- and travel-related services
Distribution services	Health-related social services
Educational services	Transport services
Recreational and cultural services	

16.5.3 Internationalisation of Service Firms

Motives: Motives behind the internationalisation of firms, in general, have already been explained in Chapter 4. Most of them apply to the internationalisation of service firms. Over and above, there are some additional factors applicable in case of service firms. They are:

1. **Lowering of cost on account of economies of scale.** As the cost gets lower, the competitiveness of the firm improves.
2. **Lowering of cost on account of economies of scope.** It is because a firm uses its experience gained from one specific country for some other ventures.
3. **Internationalised activities of clients.** Across-the-border mobility of clients has aroused among them a taste for services that conform to international standards.

Phases: There is no specific route through which service firms spread internationally. Nevertheless, in normal course, they move in three consecutive phases. First, they perform project type, customer-oriented studies on a temporary basis by sending their employees abroad. Second, they open offices abroad to be operated by their own employees as well by locally recruited employees. Third, they set up a foreign subsidiary and operate on a large scale.

Mode: Service firms operate through three distinct modes. The first is through the export of final services. For example, banks sell financial solutions to clients abroad. The second is that the firms undergo a contractual agreement normally for intermediate services such as management consultancy. Yet another is the provision of services through a foreign establishment.

Rising India's Services Export

India's services export in value terms rose from $17.1 billion in FY 2001–2002 to $103.2 billion in FY 2007–2008. The annual figures show a compound annual growth rate of over 35 per cent. The import, on the other hand, swelled from $13.8 billion to $56.9 billion. In fact, the surplus on this account lowered the deficit on account of merchandise trade. Despite the fact that the software exports dominated the scene, their share slipped from 46 per cent in FY 2002–2003 to 41 per cent in FY 2006–2007. On the contrary, the share of non-software miscellaneous services export moved up from 22 per cent to 35 per cent during this period.
Source: Based on the reports published in *Mint*, 29.5.2008 and *RBI Bulletin*, July 2008.

16.5.4 Barriers to Internationalisation of Services

Ban on entry of, and discrimination against, foreign service providing firms present barriers to their internationalisation.

Barriers to international trade manifests primarily in two ways. One is that many host governments impose bans on the entry of service-providing firms. For example, in 1973, the Indian government imposed a ban on the fresh entry of foreign banks. It is only during the period of economic reforms in 1990s that the banking sector was opened to foreign investors and with the turn of the century, the insurance sector has also been opened, of course, with limited equity participation by foreign investors. Again, in some countries, international accountants have to appear at a written examination before working in that particular host country. The form of ban on the entry varies from one country to another and from one case to another. However, the rationale behind the ban is to preserve the economic security or the national security.

The other form of the barrier, besides the ban on the entry, manifests in the very environment in which the service providing firms operate. They have to face restrictive national rules and regulations. The reason for such a restrictive environment is to foster social justice through economic policies. To this end, many governments discriminate between local firms and foreign firms. Local firms get incentives, while foreign firms have to abide by restrictive regulations.

Hufbauer and Warren (1999) calculated the tariff-equivalent size of restrictions on trade in services in some countries and found that it was over 100 per cent in the USA and Canada, 143 per cent in Brazil and as high as 182 per cent in Mexico.

However, the Uruguay Round resolutions tried to equalise both trade in goods and trade in services. The General Agreement on Trade in Services (GATS) is an essential segment of the functioning of the WTO. As stated earlier in Chapter 7, it provides for most-favoured-nations treatment, transparency in the formulation of rules and regulations, and free flow of payments and transfers with respect to trade in services. With the negotiations in this area at the WTO, it is expected that a time will come when trade in services will be substantially free.

16.5.5 Management Aspect

The strategy of operations may be different in a service providing firm that is tagged to an international manufacturing firm from that of a service firm that is independent. The operational activities of the former category of firms are largely designed to cope with the needs of the firms with which they are associated. For example, US based banks operating in India do have US firms operating in this country as their clients, and especially those with whom they are associated in the United States of America, on their preference list. On the other hand, service firms of the second category do not possess a bias of this kind. They are more concerned with the area in which they are specialised. They are more concerned with developing customer relationships and with image building among the customers in general.

How to Manage Services

- To find out whether the services are aimed at people or they are aimed at things and design the strategy accordingly
- To develop close relationships with consumers
- To respond to changing demand

Berry (1996) provides some guidelines for the operations of an international service firm. In his view, the manager must find out whether the services are aimed at people or they are aimed at things. Health care, passenger transportation, restaurants, broadcasting and information services, and so on are concerned with people. On the contrary, freight transportation, repair of industrial machinery, drycleaning services, banking, legal services, accounting, and so on are examples of services aimed at things. Again, services are grouped between tangible actions and intangible actions. For example, restaurant services are tangible services, while broadcasting and information services are intangible ones. Freight transportation is a tangible action, while banking services are intangible. The strategy of providing services varies from one group to the other.

Whatever the form of services may be, the firm has to develop a close relationship with its consumers and convince them that it is the most capable firm for the provision of the particular services. In international business, consumers have varied tastes and so the firm must have the necessary feedback from the market. Again, in services, personnel providing services must be present at the time of delivery in order to convince consumers. This requires them to be well trained in design and in the delivery of the services. Johanson and Sharma (1987) are of the view that a successful manager of a service firm should map his/her initial network, should analyse how the present relationship has emerged, and should see how the present relationship could be used for future clients. This is primarily networking, on which a number of experts have emphasised (Johanson and Mattsson, 1988).

Networking of services refers to design and delivery of services including maintenance of present and future customer-relationship.

Since a number of services cannot be stored, the study of their demand is more meaningful than in the case of products. There should be flexibility in pricing and the structure of operations so as to respond to changes in demand.

16.5.6 Off-shoring of Corporate Service Functions

Off-shoring of manufacturing activities is nothing new insofar as a large number of multinational firms have long been locating a part of their operations in different countries under a vertically integrated set-up. But off-shoring of service functions has a recent origin. In fact, with the developments in information communication technology, it is now possible to codify, standardize and digitise knowledge and thereby to fragment information in smaller components that can be located within the country as well as outside the country. Off-shoring of a variety of services is the aftermath of this development. According to an estimate, the total market for all off-shore service exports involved $32 billion in 2001. Around 30 per cent of the world's largest companies have off-shored business processes that should involve $24 billion by 2007. Companies in the USA and the UK account for around 70 per cent of the business process off-shoring. The major destinations are India, China, Malaysia, Philippines, Brazil, South Africa and may others (United Nations, 2004).

In view of a very fast growth in off-shoring of a variety of service functions in recent years, it is befitting to throw light on its features, modes, motivating factors and impact on the economy of home and host countries.

Features: Off-shoring occurs when a multinational firm removes a particular service function previously undertaken in-house at home and entrusts to a provider that is either its own foreign affiliate or a third party located abroad. The off-shored service functions can be grouped broadly in four categories. They are:

1. Call/contact centre services or the front-office functions including help desk, technical support/advice, after-sales, employee enquiries, claims enquiries, customer support/advice, market research,

answering services, prospecting, information services, customer relationship management, etc.

2. Back-office services, such as claims processing, accounts processing, transaction processing, query management processing, customer administration processing, HR/payroll processing, data processing, logistics processing, quality assurance, supplier invoices, etc.
3. IT services, such as software development, application testing, content development, engineering and design, product optimisation, etc.
4. Regional headquarters services.

Off-shoring of services is related mainly to white-collar workers, whereas off-shoring of manufacturing activities is related mainly to the blue-collar workers. Secondly, off-shoring of services may be more footloose than that of manufacturing. Thirdly, it is simpler to offshore services in terms of resources, space and equipment requirements. While services off-shored to own affiliate abroad is captive off-shoring, that to a third party is outsourcing.

Taking into account the variety of the service functions that are off-shored, it is evident that off-shoring of service functions is different form off-shoring of manufacturing activities. First of all, off-shoring of services is related mainly to white-collar workers, whereas off-shoring of manufacturing activities is related mainly to the blue-collar workers. Secondly, off-shoring of services may be more footloose than that of manufacturing insofar as capital intensity and sunk cost are lower. Thirdly, it is simpler to offshore services in terms of resources, space and equipment requirements.

However, not all services can be off-shored. Only those services can be off-shored that do not possess face-to-face servicing requirements, have high information content, encounter low set-up barriers, have high wage differential vis-á-vis the destination country and have low social networking requirements (Bardhan and Kroll, 2003).

Mode: As already mentioned, service functions are off-shored either to firm's own foreign affiliate or to a third party abroad. While the former is known as captive off-shoring, the latter is commonly known as outsourcing. As per an estimate, 45 per cent of the largest firms in Europe off-shored services to their own affiliates, whereas 48 per cent of the companies outsourced service functions to independent firms abroad (United Nations, 2004). In fact, which of the two modes will be adopted depends on a few factors. First, when secrecy of information is vital to maintain competitive edge, captive off shoring is preferred. This is why financial service industry relies more on this mode. Texas Instruments and GE have their own design and development centres in Bangalore.

Second, when there is close interaction among different segments of the service functions, own foreign affiliates are preferred. On the contrary, when back-office operations are greatly compartmentalized and standardized, outsourcing to a third party is more frequent.

Third, when skilled manpower is not available in the host country, captive off-shoring is common. But when it is available, outsourcing is favoured. It is perhaps because of this fact that British Airways in 1996 and General Electric in 1998 set up their own affiliate in India. But when local expertise was available during the subsequent period, American Airlines and Sabena outsourced revenue and traffic accounting to AFS, a wholly-owned affiliate of Tata Consultancy Services.

Fourth, when the quantum of services to be off-shored is quite large, captive off-shoring is common in order to enjoy the economies of scale. But if it is small, affiliate need not to be set up, rather outsourcing to a third party can be a better alternative.

Motivations behind Off-shoring: Cutting cost is the primary consideration behind off-shoring, especially to labour-cheap countries. Labour cost account for 50–70 per cent of the cost in call centres in the developed countries. In India, such costs are 80–90 per cent lower.

Off-shoring of services to developing countries helps a firm reap low wage cost advantages, low infra-structure cost advantages, improvement in quality of services, and time-zone advantages leading to round-the-clock operation.

Apart from cheap labour, it is the consolidation of operations and low cost of infra-structure, training and management that has beneficial effect on the cost. Any major international bank having 50–60 data centres can consolidate operations into 5 to 10 off-shore centres. Consequently, the cost of infra-structure and maintenance will be lower.

Again, it is not only the cost cut, off-shoring improves the quality of services. In developed countries, call centres employ majority of school drop-outs, but in India, they employ graduates. This is perhaps the reason that one British bank's call centre agents in India process 20 per cent more transaction with a three percent more accuracy than their counterpart do in the UK (Agrawal, 2003).

Yet again, in case of specific services where round-the-clock operation is required, companies try to locate their offices in different time-zones in order to ease the operations.

Home-country Perspective: It is true that off-shoring of services has led to job cut in the home country. According to one estimate, 2.8 per cent of all IT software and service jobs were lost in the United States during 2002 and 2003 (United Nations, 2004). But more importantly, there are benefits the home country reaps and that outweights the loss of jobs. The benefits are manifest in form of reduced cost and improved quality, as discussed above, of services that enhance the competitiveness of the firm. With greater competitive edge, profits rise. A study shows that the USA gains twice as much as India from off-shoring. For every dollar spent on off-shoring to India, the firms in the United States reap $ 1.12–1.14 in benefits (NASSCOM, 2004).

Host-country Perspective: The impact of off-shoring on the host-country economy manifests, first of all, in increasing jobs. It is estimated that a quarter of a million of jobs have been created in IT-enabled services in India.

Again, it is also the quality of job that improves. The upgrading of skill leads to the creation of a competitive human resource base. The ICT infra-structure broadens. All this benefits the whole economy through the spill-over effects.

Last but not least, the host country earns substantial foreign exchange through the export of services. The balance of payments improves. As NASSCOM (2004) reveals, the value of India's software and other service exports soared up from $0.5 billion in mid-1990s to $12 billion during 2003–04.

SUMMARY

- The operations strategy of an international firm is concerned primarily with the location of the manufacturing activities, inventory management, sourcing of the inputs, and supportive logistics.
- Location may be centralised, reaping economies of scale and some other benefits. It may be decentralised at the subsidiaries level, keeping in view the specific demand of consumers. Again, the firm may have a vertical set up, locating different activities of production in different countries. The decision depends on the size of the market; availability of inputs; state of logistics; and political, legal, and socio-cultural environment. The strategy aims at minimising cost, maintenance of quality, and at production flexibility.
- As regards inventory management, an international firm normally places orders for a greater amount of stock than warranted by the economic order quantity. This is known as stockpiling, and is done in order to avoid various risks in international transactions. Similarly, the re-order point lies much earlier, keeping in view the distance between the user and the supplier and the obstructions coming in the way. The JIT system of inventory management is often applied. It saves carrying cost, but the risk of delayed transit of goods cannot be easily avoided.
- Inputs are either sourced from another independent firm or manufactured by the firm itself. The international manager takes the "make or buy" decision only after weighing the cost and benefits of the two alternatives. The procurement may be made through imports, through procurement offices abroad, or through direct investment.
- International logistics are concerned with the movement of inventory. However, there are a couple of problems associated with logistics. One is of general nature, and is common to all host countries. The other is specific, and varies from one host country to another. The transportation issue dominates logistics management. The transportation network should be well developed. The mode of transport should be chosen based on the cost, availability, and actual need. Packaging and storage are other important elements of international logistics. Packaging should consider cost and quality. Similarly, when warehouses are created, their location, size, and the availability of necessary facilities are the main points for consideration.
- Although goods and services are more often complementary to each other, they have different identities. So the operations management in an international service providing firm is to some extent different. It is also different between a service firm that is closely tagged with some manufacturing firms and an independent service firm. There has been phenomenal growth in international services such as banking and insurance, tourism related services, consultancy and engineering services, and communication services. Factors responsible for growth are mostly the same as those applicable to manufacturing firms; however, there are some additional factors.
- Service providing firms have to face restrictive regulations in a number of developing host countries; but the WTO has eased the problem by assuring most-favoured-nations treatment for trade in services, by providing for transparency in rules and regulations and by the free flow of payments in this context.

- The operations management of service providing firm's should stress, among other things, a close relationship with consumers and flexibility in prices as well as in the structure of operations.
- With the developments in information communication technology, it is now possible to offshore a part of service functions. It avails cost advantage and is beneficial for both the home country and the host country.

REVIEW QUESTIONS

1. What are the different options for the location of an international firm? What are the factors influencing location?
2. Is inventory management in an international firm different from that in a domestic firm? Explain.
3. Comment on the "make or buy" decision as far as sourcing of input is concerned in an international firm. What are the modes for the procurement of input?
4. What are the considerations that influence the selection of the transport mode?
5. Explain the difference in the management of the operations of a service providing firm from that in a manufacturing firm.
6. What are the barriers to the internationalisation of service firms?
7. What are the different modes of off-shoring of services ? Is it beneficial from the viewpoint of home and host countries ?

OBJECTIVE TYPE QUESTIONS

1. Mark True or False:
   - (a) Plant using weight loosing raw material should be located near the market.
   - (b) Centralisation of manufacturing operations helps achieve economies of scale.
   - (c) Minimisation of cost and maintenance of quality are the key guiding factors behind the decision to locate a plant.
   - (d) Lead time in case of an MNC's inventory management is often shorter than that in case of a domestic firm.
   - (e) Stockpiling is common among MNCs.
   - (f) Inputs are also obtained by making foreign direct investment in the source country.
   - (g) Cost is the only consideration while deciding the mode of transport.
   - (h) Warehousing of the final product should be located near the port.
   - (i) Management of international services needs a closer link with consumers.
   - (j) One of the advantages of purchase of inputs from a third party is that the firm can maintain flexibility in their use.
   - (k) Off-shoring to a third party is known as captive off-shoring.
   - (l) Off-shoring leads to job cuts in the host country.
   - (m) It is not only the cost cut but also improved quality of services that motivates off-shoring.

2. Choose the Most Suitable Answer.
   (a) Manufacturing of spares, rather buying them from other firms, is advocated on the grounds that:
      (i) It involves huge investment
      (ii) The firm has full control over the price, time, and quantity of supply
      (iii) The supply can be the cheapest
   (b) Logistics are more important in the case of MNCs' operation because:
      (i) Different units are widely spread over different countries
      (ii) Logistics account for 80–90 per cent of the landed cost of the international order
      (iii) None of the above
   (c) Inputs are procured through:
      (i) Importation only
      (ii) Importation and setting up of IPOs
      (iii) Importation, setting up of IPOs, and FDI
   (d) Location of warehousing of the final product should be:
      (i) Near the port
      (ii) Near the market
      (iii) In between the port and the market
   (e) Services are normally:
      (i) Standardised
      (ii) Not standardised
      (iii) Represented by an element of homogeneity
   (f) The GATS:
      (i) Has limited the scope for trade in international services
      (ii) Has accorded most-favoured-nations treatment to trade in services
      (iii) None of the above
   (g) Services may be aimed at:
      (i) People only
      (ii) Things only
      (iii) Both people and things

CASE STUDY

Suzuki-Maruti's Policy of Local Procurement of Inputs

Suzuki-Maruti has a long history in the Indian automobiles arena. It was the 16th November 1970 when Maruti Technical Services was formed as a private limited company. It was supplying the passenger cars manufactured in Japan. With growing market for the passenger car in India, a joint-venture agreement was signed between the Indian Government and Suzuki where the latter was to be satisfied with only 26 per cent share in the equity. The company was transformed into a government company. The joint venture was a better option. The share of the company in the Indian car market increased. Moreover, by the end of 1980s, there was demand from abroad too. But there was often clash of interest between Suzuki and the Indian Government. And in 1992, Suzuki's share in the equity was raised to 50 per cent. The company did not remain a government company. Finally, in 2002, after a long controversy, Suzuki's share in the equity was raised to 54.21 per cent.

The changes in the ownership pattern did have an influence on the production policy, labour relations, procurement and sales policy. It was for the first time in 1984 that an assembly plant was created with a production capacity of 20,000 cars. The components like tires, batteries, electric wiring, wheel rims, seat and glass were procured from the local suppliers. To be precise, indigenisation was estimated at 23 per cent. In 1985–1986, key components like clutches, brakes, filters, shock absorbers, air cleaner, engine valves, alternators, etc were indigenised. In fact, there were three factors behind indigenisation. One was the Suzuki's policy of low vertical integration and outsourcing. The second was the Indian Government's quest for buy-local inputs. And the third was to make available low-cost vehicles to price-sensitive, entry-level customers. In view of the JV agreement and then Indian Government's foreign direct investment policy, Maruti-Suzuki had to observe high local content requirements. It was agreed that out of the 70 per cent of the non-company value addition, at least 60 per cent had to be procured locally. Moreover, existence of high import tariffs, high transport cost and higher value of yen led the company to rely on the local supply. But the problem was that the local supply infrastructure was not at all developed either in terms of the magnitude of supply or in terms of quality. Indian suppliers were unable to cope with Maruti-Suzuki's demands. Tierisation and JIT supply logistics were unheard of. Under these conditions, Maruti-Suzuki embarked on a comprehensive supplier development program—to build up suppliers that could deliver parts and components in the right quantity and quality. Initial efforts were focussed primarily on developing close and trustful relations with suppliers and providing a wide range of support—financial and technical. In order to win the trust of the suppliers, the annual tender system was replaced by long-term contracts, assurance for volumes, guaranteed prices and fixed dates of payment. Then, as a second step, Maruti-Suzuki got involved in establishing suppliers through joint-venture agreements and asked Japanese suppliers to do the same. Many of these suppliers were located on the company compound in Gurgaon. Although Maruti-Suzuki held a minority equity positions in these companies, it was strongly involved in quality and productivity assurance in these companies.

Since 1992, the procurement policy got still diversified. Besides stress on establishing reliable supplier relationship, it was thought to emphasise upon upgrading the quality of the supply and on bringing down the high inventory levels. The company pushed its suppliers to acquire ISO certifications. A cluster approach was adopted in 1995 that grouped vendors together, trained them in quality management and assisted them in obtaining the ISO 9000 certification. One of the reasons behind this approach was that the component defect rate was as high as 30,000 parts per million (PPM) as compared to 200 (PPM) for the developed countries. The company developed a failure monitor mechanism for each of the 2,000 types of components which went in the manufacture of each car. Internal and external audit of the vendors were started and the company's executives checked the sources of raw material the suppliers had. Maruti-Suzuki set up a vendor consultancy cell which looked into problems of vendors and advised them on modernisation and upgradation.

As far as high inventory levels were concerned, the total value of inventories as a percentage of sales revenue improved from a high of 20 per cent in 1992 to 10 per cent in 1997. Maruti-Suzuki sought to reduce its inventory levels by locating majority of the suppliers within a radius of 80 kms. By 1996–1997, about 70 per cent of Maruti's domestically sourced components and materials came from within 80 kms. The company created industrial park in the nearby areas and it provided incentives to attract the suppliers. In fact, the objective was to get a JIT supply. Finally, in the late 1990s Maruti-Suzuki started streamlining its supplier base—reducing the number of suppliers making same components from then four or five to three and encouraging tiersation among them.

In 2000s, the role of the component suppliers turned gradually from a tactical one to a strategic one where they went hand in hand with the company to achieve the long-term goal of maintenance of international quality and cost control. Suzuki conducted cost reduction workshops with key suppliers and set targets for cost reduction. To help suppliers reach the targets, Maruti-Suzuki sent its engineers to the supplier sites and supported the development of action plans. It consolidated the raw material requirements of suppliers, mainly for steal and aluminum, and negotiated competitive prices for them. It also supported them to build up their own R&D facilities. Maruti-Suzuki also extended its cluster approach for small and medium suppliers to adopt QS 9000 and TS 16949 certifications. As a result of these measures, Maruti-Suzuki was able to substantially reduce supplier warranty costs per vehicle. In 2003 Maruti-Suzuki started efforts to integrate its suppliers into Suzuki's worldwide purchasing system. This provided suppliers the opportunity to become the sole supplier for a Suzuki product in several countries.

Thus, over the years, Suzuki's relationship with its component suppliers went stronger in terms of quality, cost, efficiency and reliability of supply. This is not a singular case with India. In other countries too, Suzuki has followed similar plans to get the required components. However, the objective has not been exactly the same. For example, in Hungary, where Suzuki started its production in 1992, the most important reason behind the local procurement was to meet the "rules-of-origin" requirements. Since over three-fifths of the output was exported to the European Union countries, Hungarian inputs worth 60 per cent of the value of the car were an essential criterion for the export. By 2000, Japan supplied only 30 per cent of the inputs; 29 per cent of the input represented in-house production; 26 per cent of the inputs were supplied by the Hungarian suppliers and the rest 15 per cent of them were imported from the EU members.

Source: Based on 1. Becker-Ritterspach, F.A.A., (2006), *The Hybridization of Local MNE Production Systems: The Case of Subsidiaries in India* (Ridderkerk: Ridderprint).

2. Chatterjee, B. (1990), Japanese Management: Maruti in the Indian Experience (New Delhi: Sterling Publishers).
3. D'Costa, A.P. (2003), "Institutions and industrial governance in India: Learning to cooperate the Japanese way", Asian Business and Management, 2, 63–89.
4. Joseph, A. (1990), "Japan's FDI in India's industrial development: A case study of Maruti Udyog Ltd.", The CTC Reporter, No. 30, 26.05.2003.
5. Maruti Udyog Ltd (Annual), Annual Report, Various Issues.
6. Maruti-Suzuki website, 2007. http://www.marutiudyog.com. (13.05.2007).

7. Nayak, A.K.J.R (2005), "FDI Model in Emerging Economies: Case of Suzuki Motor Corporation in India", *The Journal of American Academy of Business*, March, 238–45.
8. Parul, M. and S. Manish, S.(1997), Maruti Udyog to reduce number of vendors, *Indian Express*, 26.05.2003.
9. UNIDO (1999), *In-depth Evaluation of Selected UNIDO Activities on Development and Transfer of Technology*, Component 4 Transfer of Technology in Subcontracting, http://www.unido.org/userfiles/PuffK/dtt-com499.pdf (23.03.2006).

QUESTIONS

1. What were the objectives of Suzuki behind local procurement of the components? Do the objectives fit into normal behaviour of the MNCs?
2. What steps did Suzuki take to improve the quality and timely supply of the inputs from the suppliers? Were the steps taken during 2000s different from those in 1990s?
3. Comment on the statement that maintenance of lower cost of Maruti cars was an important factor behind the local procurement?
4. Do the objectives behind Suzuki's local procurement in India resemble those in Hungary?

STUDY TOPIC

Outsourcing in Drug Development Industry: India at Advantage

According to recent estimates, the global drug development and discovery market is booming up. The market for outsourcing in this area was expected to touch $48 billion by the end of 2008 and still higher at $89.6 billion by 2013. The reason for fast growth in outsourcing is that it is cost-effective. It is estimated that the cost saving of outsourcing should be around 80 per cent on labour and 50–75 per cent on facilities and equipment.

Presently, the experience shows that almost every part of the R&D process is being outsourced. Outsourcing covers almost the entire spectrum of pharmaceutical and biotech value chain—from drug discovery services to manufacture of intermediates, active pharmaceutical ingredients and doses, besides the traditional areas of accounting and human resource functions. There is, of course, difference between big companies and small companies. While the former go for selective outsourcing, the latter outsource almost all critical functions.

It is true that Japanese and South Korean firms are capable of taking up high-tech research and are at par with the American and European firms. Singapore too possesses quite developed infrastructure. But they cannot ensure cost saving. On the other hand, Thailand, Philippines and Vietnam may ensure cost-effectiveness, but they utterly lack the required infrastructure. China, of course, presents a tough competition in view of the fact that it possesses the infrastructure and it can ensure cost saving. It is building up fast the science parks where different types of facilities are available. But these facilities are confined to Beijing and Shanghai periphery. The government there provides fiscal incentives but they are more focussed on export-oriented pharmaceutical and biotech firms.

Taking the above facts into consideration, the Indian firms are posited with comparative advantage. Here, the incentives are broad based. They combine pilot facilities and other project incubator functions. They include tax holidays in many cases.

Presently, the Indian drug discovery outsourcing market involves less than 500 millions of dollar which was expected to grow to over $900-million market by 2008-end. Moreover, this country has good experience in the field of outsourcing of clinical trials, process R&D, medicinal chemistry, formulation development and contract manufacturing and so this country has potential for far bigger outsourcing.

Moreover, outsourcing to India may ensure cost advantage ranging from one-sixth to one-third of the total cost. Capital cost can also be reduced to three-fourths on account of good quality of material and skills. Good quality of compliance controls and business processes and sound clinical practices may help this country to take advantage of the growing market of pharmaceutical and biotech outsourcing.

The Indian firms are already in tie-up with educational institutions to boost up R&D. The centres of excellence are being set up. Training of doctors and improvement of the facilities in the hospitals have already been taken up to ensure clinical trials. Over and above, the Indian Government has announced to set up National Biotechnology Regulatory Authority which should foster these activities in a more regulated and planned way.

Source: Based on the reports published in *Mint*, 2.6.2008.

QUESTIONS

1. What do you mean by outsourcing ?
2. What are the factors working behind pharmaceutical outsourcing to a developing country?
3. Do you support the view that India will bag a big chunk of outsourcing of pharmaceutical and biotech product and processes?

References

Books

Berry, L. L. (1996), "Services Marketing is Different" in Lovelock, C. H. (ed.), *Services Marketing* (New Jersey: Prentice-Hall).

Czinkota, M. R. et al (1999), *International Business* (New York: Harcourt Brace).

Dicken, P. (1998), *Global Shift: Transforming the World Economy* (London: Paul Chapman).

Hickman, J. and S. C. Hickman (1992), *Global Procurement* (Homewood, Illinois: Irwin).

Hufbauer, G. and T. Warren (1999), The Globalisation of Services: What has Happened? What are the Implications?" in G. Fels (ed.), *The Service Economy: An Engine for Growth and Employment* (Dresden: IDWK).

Johanson, J. and L. G. Mattsson (1988), "Internationalisation in Industrial Systems: A Network Approach" in Hood, N. and J. E. Vahne (eds.), *Strategies in Global Competition*, New York: Croom Helm, pp. 287–314.

Qua, C. F. and T. C. Thian (1991),"Procurement from Asia: Emerging Sources in S.E. Asia" referred by Rajagopal S. and K. N. Bernard (1997),"Global Procurement: A Strategy for Improving Business Competitiveness" in Chryssochoidis, G. *et al (eds.)*, *International Strategies* (Houndmills: Macmillan Press).

Ricks, D. A. (1993), *Blunders in International Business* (Cambridge: Blackwell Publishers).

Stobaugh, R. and P. Telesio (1992),"Match Manufacturing Policies and Product Strategy" in Bartlett, C. A. and S. G Ghoshal (eds.), *Transnational Management* (Homewood, third.: Richard D. Irwin) pp.760–68.

Journals

Agrawal, V. et al (2003),"Off-shoring and Beyond", *The McKinsey Quarterly,* special edition.

Bardhan, A. D. and C. Kroll (2003), "The New Wave of Outsourcing", *Fisher Centre Research Report,* http//repositories.edlib.org/iberfcreue/reports/1103.

Birou, I. M. and S. E. Fawcett (1993),"International Purchasing, Benefits, Requirements and Challenges," *International Journal of Operations and Production Management,* XXIX (1), 27–37.

______ and D. D. Sharma (1987),"Technical Consultancy in Internationalisation", *International Marketing Review,* IV (Summer), 87–97.

Levin, D. P. (1994), "Compaq Storms the PC Heights from Its Factory Floor", *New York Times,* Nov. 13, sec.3, p.5.

NASSCOM (2004), *Indian IT Software and Services Directory: 2003,* New Delhi.

Scully, J. and S. Fawcett (1993),"Comparative Logistics and Production Costs for Global Manufacturing Strategy", *International Journal of Operations and Production Management,* XXIX (1), 62–78.

United Nations (2004), *World Investment Report: 2004,* New York and Geneva.

Vickery, S. K. (1989), "International Sourcing: Implications for Just-in-Time Manufacturing", *Production and Inventory Management Journal* (3), 67–70.

Wells, L. T. (1973),"Economic Man and Engineering Man: Choice of Technology in a Low-Wage Country", *Public Policy,* XXI (3) 319–42.

SELECT FURTHER READINGS

Ferdows, K. (1989), *Managing International Manufacturing* (Amsterdam: North-Holland Publishing Company).

Lovelock, C. H. (1996), *Services Marketing* (New Jersey: Prentice-Hall).

Wood, D. E. (1995), *International Logistics* (New York: Chapman & Hall).

Li, J. and S. Guisinger (1992),"The Globalisation of Service Multinationals in the Triad Regions: Japan, Western Europe and North America", *Journal of International Business Studies,* XXIII (4), 675–96.

* The port of Singapore is the world's busiest port in terms of total shipping tonnage, it also transships a fifth of the world's shipping containers as the world's busiest container port/transshipment port and half of the world's annual supply of crude oil. It is not a mere economic boon, but an economic necessity due to the fact that Singapore is lacking in land and natural resources. It is now recognised as a principal centre for shopping activities. The port is the world's busiest port in terms of shipping tonnage handled with 1.15 billion gross tons (GT) handled in 2005.

South Africa*

17

International Market Strategy

CHAPTER OBJECTIVES

An MNC has to compete not only with other MNCs but also with the domestic units in a host country as far as the marketing its products is concerned. So it follows that an appropriate marketing strategy is crucial. The present chapter deals with this aspect and aims to:

- ✦ Explain the process of identifying the market and of estimating the demand potential.
- ✦ Delineate the product strategy—whether to go for a standard product for all the markets or to adapt the product for different markets.
- ✦ Explain the pricing strategy—the basis of pricing strategy and various kinds of pricing techniques.
- ✦ Show the comparative merits of the direct and indirect channels, the suitability of a channel and whether the distribution channel should be adapted for different markets.
- ✦ Describe the modes of sales promotion programme and to discuss whether the advertising strategy should be adapted for different markets.
- ✦ Explain the objectives of foreign trade documentation and the various documents used in international trade.

The ultimate aim of production of goods and services is to market them. It is marketing that brings in revenue and compensates any expenditure incurred during production. An excess of revenue over the cost leads to the emergence of profit.

The strategy of marketing deserves far greater attention in international business than in the case of domestic business. This is because consumers are widely spread over a number of countries. Their social and cultural background, taste, consumption pattern, income, and so on differ widely. The political and legal environment in different markets is considerably heterogeneous, and geographic distance is yet another problem.

The marketing strategy in international business begins with the identification of the market and estimation of the demand potential. The decision concerning market concentration versus market diversification forms an essential part of the market identification process.

After the market is identified and the demand is estimated, the next step is to reach the market with appropriate products, at appropriate prices, and through effective channels of distribution. If actual sales tend to lag behind potential sales, the firm adopts a variety of promotional activities.

Again, for effective marketing of the product, the firm should have knowledge of various documents and procedural formalities related to marketing, in general, and those prevalent in the host country, in particular.

17.1 MARKET IDENTIFICATION AND DEMAND ESTIMATION

17.1.1 Selection of Market

The first step in the marketing strategy is to identify the potential market on which the firm has to emphasise. It is because particular product cannot necessarily be demanded in all markets. If the firm is manufacturing snowboards, they will not be demanded in a country with no snowfall. Similarly, many Islamic countries have imposed a ban on the import of liquor. In many developing countries, establishing retail outlets requires prior approval from the host government. In short, markets are not homogeneous. They differ chiefly on three dimensions. One is the geographic distance. The other is the varying socio-cultural and legal environment. Yet other dimension is the varying economic environment such as disparity in per capita income, income elasticity of demand, degree of concentration of income and wealth in the country, and so on. Thus, in the very beginning, the firm has to identify the countries where the product can be marketed. Rugman and Hodgetts (2002) talk about six successive steps in the process of market selection.

> Market differs on account of: 1. geographic distance, 2. varying socio-cultural and legal environment, and 3. varying economic environment.

1. The first step tries to find an answer to who will be interested in buying the company's product. The answer is largely based on the import structure and import policy of different countries and

the demographic changes that have a bearing on the consumption pattern.

2. The second step is to screen the market on the basis of some economic variables, such as level of income, interest rates, inflation rates, expected rate of return on investment, availability of credit, and so on. The purpose is to establish whether the market is financially feasible.
3. The third step is to examine the market on the basis of the political and legal environment prevailing there so that political risk and too many legal formalities should not come in the way.
4. The fourth step is to screen socio-cultural environment. The purpose is to know whether the product is socially and culturally acceptable and to know whether the operations can be located there.
5. The fifth level of screening aims at knowing the level of competition existing in a particular market. This is because some companies prefer to operate in markets where they can enjoy monopolistic status and may not have to face stiff competition.
6. The sixth and final step means on-the-spot study after the first five screenings clear a particular market.

When markets are identified, the firm needs to pinpoint a particular segment of the selected market. This is because some products are meant for a specific segment of the market. A luxury product, is normally meant for the high-income segment of that market. The firm has to then focus on this particular segment of the market. In other words, segmentation follows market identification. In the process of segmentation, the firm comes to know how far the structure of market segments is similar in different markets. If the market segments across borders are similar, the firm can earn large revenues by selling a standard product using the same market mix. But it is not necessary that the consumption pattern of a particular segment in a foreign market is similar to that in the home country market. If it is not similar, the firm will have to adopt a unique market mix to attract a uniquely composed market segment.

When markets are identified, the process of segmentation starts and the firm will have to adopt a unique market mix to attract a uniquely composed market segment.

17.1.2 Estimation of Demand

After the identification of the markets, it is necessary to estimate the size of the total demand in a particular market and the possible share of the firm's own product. If the firm is in a monopolistic position, it need not bother about estimating its own share. But normally there are many firms marketing similar products and then it is necessary for the firm to estimate its own share. Infact, its share depends inter alia upon the features of its own product compared with those of other suppliers, the brand of its product differentiating it from similar products, its price and promotional efforts in relation to other suppliers, potential threat from the substitutes, potential entry of competing firms, and so on. If the product has greater number of features conferring upon the consumers greater satisfaction or utility, its share will naturally be large. Sometimes it is the brand that appeals to the consumers' psychology. They buy branded goods even if their price is higher. However, in case of unbranded products, price is an important consideration. If the price is competitive, the product will enjoy a large share in the market, although consumers can be motivated to buy a particular product through appropriate promotional measures even if the product is not very competitive on account of features or price. However, the market share of a product may shrink if consumers begin using substitutes or if a new competitor enters the market. All these facts need to be considered while estimating the market share of the product.

The variables taken into account for market-potential analysis are:

1. market size
2. market intensity
3. market consumption capacity and
4. commercial infrastructure

For the estimation of demand at a particular point of time, the firm analyses different economic and non-economic variables obtained from a particular market. Cavusgil (1997) refers to some important variables commonly included in the market-potential analysis. They are, for example, market size, normally dependent upon the size of the population; market intensity, depending upon the level of per capita income; market consumption capacity, depending upon income elasticity of demand for the product and the degree of concentration of income and wealth in the country; and commercial infrastructure, including communication facilities, economic freedom, and so on. The firm's own officials gather necessary information about different markets, based either on secondary sources or primary survey. They utilise the input-output table that is published regularly in many countries, which provides a summary of economic structure by showing the impact of the changes in the demand for one industry's goods on other industry's goods. However, the input-output table is more reliable in case of demand estimation of industrial goods.

The estimation of demand by a firm's own officials is a cumbersome process and is sometimes more expensive and time consuming. So, alternatively, a firm hires the services of some specialised agencies meant for this purpose. For example, Euromonitor is a company that undertakes country specific studies for many international companies.

Again, demand for the product may change over time. One of the important factors in this regard is the growth in per capita income. It is expected that a rise in income should lead to greater consumption. The Korean example is clear. Schuman (1996) finds that with a rise in per capita income in South Korea, the demand for apparel, cosmetics, and automobiles has grown there. Thus, the marketing manager relies on time-series data of per capita income and estimates the potential demand for the product over a period of time. However, the relationship between rising per capita income and the rising demand for the product depends on: (1) income elasticity of demand, and (2) the degree of concentration of income in the country. If the income elasticity of demand in a particular market is lower than unity, the rise in income will not be matched by a proportionate rise in the demand for the products. Similarly, if the income is concentrated in a few hands, the majority of persons will not be able to raise their demand.

If a firm does not have the necessary figures of per capita income growth for a particular country, those found in other markets can be used. This process is commonly known as estimation by analogy. But in this case, the figures should be interpreted with much caution insofar as the tastes and habits of the consumers and the income elasticity of demand applicable to one market may not necessarily be applicable to the other. Weber (1979) gives an example of how the consumption pattern differs between countries despite similar levels of per capita income. He finds that Denmark and Switzerland have similar levels of per capita income, but the demand for frozen food is larger in Denmark than in Switzerland.

Markets are listed in order of preference so that greater emphasis may be placed on markets where potential demand is greater.

Last but not least, when the size of potential demand is estimated for the selected markets, these markets are listed in order of preference so that greater emphasis may be placed on markets where potential demand is greater.

17.1.3 Market Concentration versus Market Diversification

Market concentration strategy means that the focus of marketing activities is confined to a smaller area. On the contrary, the marketing activities spread over a large area is a market diversification strategy. Again, in a market concentration strategy, there may be segment diversification, which means opting for very wide coverage in a limited number of markets. On the contrary, in a market diversification strategy, segment concentration strategy may be followed, focussing upon limited segments over a wide range of markets.

Market concentration strategy is based on focussing on a particular market.

Market diversification strategy involves wider coverage of markets.

Ayal and Zif (1979) explain the various aspects of these strategies and are of the view that both of them have merits and demerits. However, there are certain situations wherein a particular strategy is adopted. The firm adopts a market concentration strategy if the demand for its product is growing and fluctuating only in a limited number of markets. Similarly, when the geographic distance between the firm and the market is great, the firm adopts a market concentration strategy. Again, when the different markets are not homogeneous and the marketing of a product in different markets needs substantial adaptation, a market concentration strategy is preferred. This is because substantial product adaptation is often a costly affair. As a natural corollary, it means that where the product is standardised or where the different markets experience stable growth in demand, market diversification strategy is the suitable option.

Where the product is standardised or where the different markets experience stable growth in demand, market diversification strategy is the suitable option.

17.2 PRODUCT STRATEGY

17.2.1 Standardisation versus Adaptation

At the very core of the product strategy lies a crucial decision regarding whether the product to be marketed should be a standard product or it

Product standardisation refers to homogeneous features of a product for all markets. On the contrary, **adaptation** means that the product undergoes modification for different markets.

should be an adapted product. Standardisation means that the features of the product should be homogeneous for all markets. On the contrary, adaptation means that the product undergoes modification for different markets, depending on the taste of the consumers in those markets. A standardised product has some advantages. They are:

1. It is easier to achieve economies of scale, which may in turn lead to greater profits.
2. When consistency in product image is required, standardisation is useful. The success of McDonald's lies in consistent product quality and services.
3. In case of some high-technology products, both the manufacturers and the users prefer to encourage compatibility through industry specifications and, to this end, standardisation is desirable.
4. Some products have universal demand. For example, watches are universally demanded for time keeping and so they should be standardised.

All this might be the reason behind the fact that in 81 per cent of samples, products exported by US firms did not undergo any modification (Koh, 1991).

On the contrary, there are other studies that show results in favour of adaptation. Hill and Still (1984) found that in their sample only 10 per cent of the products made by US firms were exported to the less developed world without modification. The majority of the products were modified to suit the consumers' choice. Modification—which is either liked by the consumers or suits the economic, legal, and other conditions prevalent in different markets—leads to greater demand for the product, which is the very purpose of product strategy. Sprite turned out to be the largest selling soft drink in Japan when the lime flavour was done away with for consumption in this country. There are thousands of such examples justifying modification.

17.2.2 Factors behind Adaptation

There are a host of factors leading to the adaptation of products. Some of the factors are mandatory, while the others are optional. A particular factor is treated as mandatory if it does not allow a product to enter a market. Government regulations prohibiting the entry of a product come under this group. To quote a few examples, Demark bans aluminium cans; the United States of America bans automobiles without proper safety and pollution standards. Managers must consider the legal requirements and redesign the product accordingly. On the contrary, local use conditions, space constraints, environmental characteristics, income level of the consumers, and so on are the optional factors. However, here these factors are grouped as those:

1. Related to the features of the product
2. Related to the features of a particular market
3. Related to firm's own decision

Product Features: Branding, which creates identification for the product and helps ensure a minimum level of quality, is one of the most important factors related to product characteristics. It is a fact that a single brand throughout different markets boosts up the image of the product in question, reduces the advertising cost, and provides convenient identification. Bata shoes are marketed in over 90 countries under a single brand name. But when a firm is unable to ensure uniform product quality across countries, it prefers multiple branding—different brands for different markets. A local brand is more easily understood by consumers. Close up toothpaste did well in Thailand when the brand name was translated as Klai chid.

Renault, a French automobile company, has started producing passenger cars in India in collaboration with Mahindra & Mahindra. In French-speaking countries or in countries where Renault has already a strong presence, the cars will be sold under the brand name of Renault, but in other countries, the brand name will be different as Mahindra-Renault.
Source: Based on the report published in the *Financial Express*, 24 July, 2008.

Apart from the brand, the technical features of the product must be consistent with the product specifications in different markets. For example, electrical appliances to be used in the United States of America should conform to 110 volts, while they should conform to 220 volts in Europe and many other countries.

Again, packaging and labelling requirements differ among different products. Owing to longer channels of distribution in international business, especially for a distantly located market, there is special packaging for food and other easily perishable products.

Market Features: It is the market feature that varies from one country to another. The most important factor influencing market features is governmental regulations. The European Union countries have spelled out specific standards for more than 10,000 products. If international firms have to market their products in this area, they have to modify their product according to the set standard. Many countries differ on the proportion of ingredients put in a number of food products. International firms have to take into account this factor while marketing their products.

Secondly, it is the attitude, taste, social behaviour, and educational level of the consumers in a particular market that influences the demand for a particular product. Brazilians seldom eat breakfast at home. In order to suit their taste, Dunkin' Donuts sells doughnuts as snacks, and that too with local fruit fillings. Again, computers and other electronic items are less in demand in markets where the educational level is low.

Thirdly, the income level in different markets is normally different and so is the consumption pattern. In a low-income developing country, consumers go for the price and not necessarily for the quality of the goods. Thus, a firm producing sophisticated and costly product may not be able to sell it in such a market. Singer sells simple and hand powered sewing machines in Africa, while it sells electrical sewing machines in high income countries.

Firm's Own Decisions: Even if the features of the product or the markets are in favour of modification, the modification strategy is adopted only when it adds up to the profitability of the firm. Thus, before any modification is attempted, the firm analyses its impact on its profitability; it compares the cost of modification with the cost of lost sales on account of no modification. It is because of the cost involved in modification that firms make a compromise between complete modification and no modification and often go for partial modification. For example, Whirlpool uses the same basic compressor for refrigerators for all markets, but make changes in doors/shelves for different markets.

17.3 PRICING STRATEGY

17.3.1 Basis of Pricing in the International Market

Pricing is an important strategy to achieve the desired sales target. It is basically a function of cost and demand. This means that the price of a product should cover the cost. There is one view that international pricing of products should cover all costs, meaning that the price should be equal to the sum of domestic price and the overseas cost. The process is simple but in the international market the price is often very high, effecting the demand for the product (Figure 17.1).

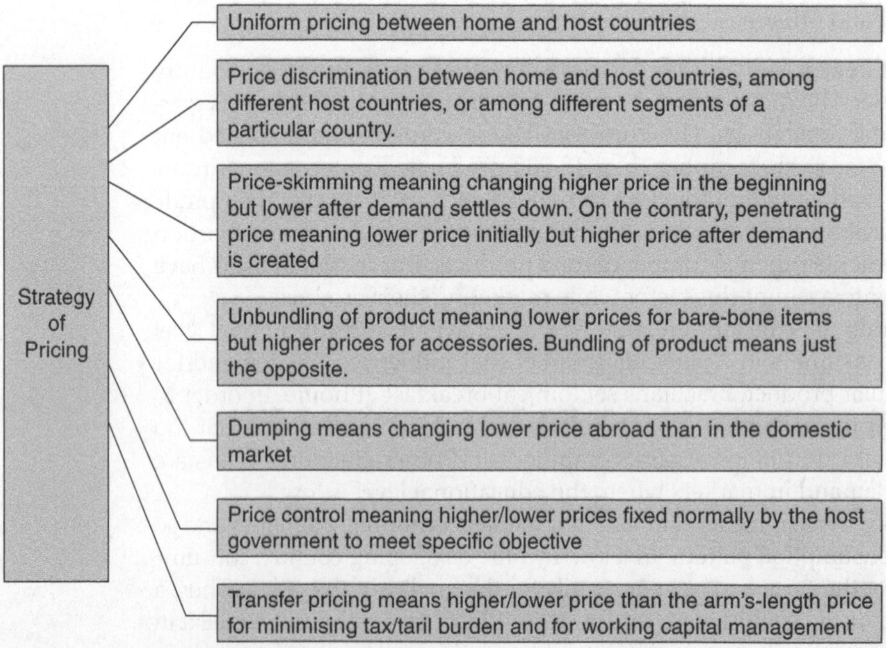

FIGURE 17.1 Pricing Strategy

On the contrary, the other view favours the inclusion of incremental cost in international pricing. It is supposed that research and development cost and the cost of running operations at headquarters are already included in the domestic market price and so they should not be included in the price for international markets. The actual cost of production along with foreign marketing cost only should form the basis for international market pricing. Based on these two different approaches, the international price may be higher than the domestic price or it may be lower.

Besides these two approaches, there is also one view that prices should be uniform both in the domestic market and the international market. Uniform price is possible when the demand conditions in different markets are uniform and the product features are identical along different markets (Piercy, 1982).

However, it is not simply the cost structure that influences the pricing of a product. If the demand for a product is very high on account of high product image, the firm may charge a greater price than warranted by the cost. US beef sells at a higher price in Japan than Australian beef insofar as the former is the product of grain-fed cattle and not grass-fed cattle. Moreover, if the demand is price-inelastic, the firm may charge a higher price for the product.

17.3.2 Price Discrimination

It is because demand conditions vary among countries and among different segments of consumers in a particular country, a multinational firm charges different prices for the same product in different markets or in different segments of a particular market. The practice, known as price discrimination, helps firms maximise profits. For example, the firm can charge a higher price from consumers who come under the high income category and whose demand for the product is price inelastic. On the contrary, it can charge a lower price, just to cover the cost of the product, from the other consumers who come under the low income category and care more for the price. The sale of the product will be large in both market segments. In the first segment profit per unit will be large. In the other, profit per unit will be small but total profit will be large.

> **Price discrimination** refers to different prices for different markets or for different segments of the same market.

17.3.3 Skimming Price versus Penetration Price

Sometimes a firm charges a higher price in the beginning in view of the fact that the product is new to consumers and they will pay a high price for the new product. But with the maturing of demand, sales turn slow and the firm lowers the price. This is the price skimming strategy. On the contrary, when a lower price is charged in the beginning in order to attract the consumers followed by a higher price, when the consumers settle down to the product, it is known as the penetration price strategy. When

> **Skimming and Penetration Price:** Charging a higher price in the beginning followed by lower prices later is price skimming. Penetration pricing is just the reverse.

Dell launched its personal computer in the market, it adopted a penetration price strategy to compete with Compaq.

17.3.4 Bundling/Unbundling of Product

Bundling/Unbundling of Product: Higher price for bare-bone items and lower prices for accessories is bundling of a product. Unbundling is just the reverse.

If the prices based on cost are very high in the international market, they can be moderated at least to some extent through different devices. Unbundling of a product is one of such device. It means that the manufacturer charges a very low price for a bare-bones product. So it seems very lucrative for the buyer. But the accessories are priced very high, so as to compensate any loss on pricing of the bare-bones product. In India, when Suzuki launched Maruti 800, the price of the car was low, but the accessories were very expensive. On the other hand, bundling of the product carries greater price for the product. But since the accessories add only a little value to the product, this strategy is also used sometimes to attract consumers.

17.3.5 Dumping

Dumping: Lower international prices than the domestic market prices either to clear distressed stock or to throw the competitors out of market.

Dumping, as explained in Chapter 6, means selling the product in international market at a lower price than in the domestic market. There are normally three types of dumping. They are: (1) Sporadic dumping, (2) Predatory dumping, (3) Persistent dumping.

In sporadic dumping, the manufacturer, in order to eliminate the distressed stock of goods, sells the product at a throwaway price in the international market. The purpose is to reduce the loss as far as possible.

In predatory dumping, the objective is to penetrate a new market and throw the competitors out of the market so as to establish a monopolistic position in that market and charge high prices when monopoly is established.

Persistent dumping is a permanent type of dumping. When the product is highly price-elastic abroad, the firm adopts full-cost pricing covering the fixed cost for the domestic market and adopts marginal cost pricing abroad. It is a fact that domestic consumers have to pay a greater price, but the firm is able to generate large sales and revenue in the international market and get large foreign exchange. Again, if the price elasticity is the basis of persistent dumping, there may be reverse dumping when the product is price inelastic in markets abroad. In this case, domestic consumers are charged lower prices and the loss is recovered from foreign markets.

Despite dumping being not allowed by the WTO, it has been a widespread practice. There are many firms that resort to dumping and conceal their dumping activities through several means. However, in many countries, the imposition of anti-dumping duties mars the adverse effect of dumping by foreign firms.

17.3.6 Price Control

In many cases, the government arbitrarily sets the price of imported goods so as to discourage their consumption in the domestic market. US wheat was sold in Japan at a higher price than its landing price in Japan. Sometimes the government fixes lower prices for imported goods in the interest of the community as a whole. Whatever may be the purpose behind price control by the importing government, the manufacturer/exporter has a very limited role in the pricing of its exports under these circumstances.

17.3.7 Transfer Pricing

Meaning: Transfer pricing is arbitrary pricing of exports and imports that may be greater than or less than the arm's-length prices. It is basically the pricing of intra-corporate transactions. Different units of an MNC operate in different countries on the basis of vertical and horizontal linkages. Varieties of goods, especially intermediate goods, move among different units. Prices in such cases are often arbitrary through under-invoicing and over-invoicing of transactions. It is a fact that transfer prices are set in reference to the arm's-length price prevailing in transactions between unrelated parties engaged in similar or the same trade under similar conditions in the open market, but deviation from the arm's-length prices is quite arbitrary, depending upon the subservience of the objectives of the firm.

Forms: There are many forms of transfer prices. When pre-tax profit of a unit located in a high tax country is shifted through transfer pricing to another unit of the same firm located in a low tax country, it is called money transfer pricing. Again, if the objective is to maximise the aggregate net output of the firm in terms of a constant reference price (excluding the intermediate goods), the price of intermediate goods is designed to boost up the production multiplier so as to facilitate production in different units. Such designing of prices, quite different from the arm's length prices, is known as efficient transfer pricing. Thus, the difference between the income (or money) transfer prices and the efficient transfer prices is that the former aims at maximising centralised profit, while the latter focuses on the maximum net output (Diewert, 1985).

Money transfer pricing causes intra-firm fund transfer to minimise tax burden and, thereby, maximise global profit.

Efficient transfer pricing encourages intra-firm input movement to maximise global output.

The Diewertian income transfer prices are in some ways similar to the fiscal transfer prices explained by Horst (1971), Copithorne (1971), and Elam and Henaidy (1980). They are meant to minimise the tax-cum-tariff burden and to mitigate the effects of barriers to capital flows. But, on the contrary, Hirschleifer (1956) sees transfer price as a shadow price aimed at optimum allocation of resources among various units of a firm, which leads to optimum liquidity adjustment. It emphasises on liquidity rather than on profitability. Funds are transferred from cash-surplus units to cash-deficient units of a firm through transfer pricing devices.

Setting of Transfer Prices: Since transfer prices are set on the basis of arm's-length prices, the process embraces two elements. These elements are:

1. the arm's-length price determined by:
   (i) market price, or/and
   (ii) cost of production
2. the element of arbitrariness, which is influenced by the desire to achieve a particular corporate objective

Arm's-length price is normally equal to the uncontrolled market price and the resale price. It is ascertained also using cost-plus method especially when the sale of semi-finished goods is involved.

When an open market exists, the arm's-length price is normally equal to the market price. Here one must distinguish between the uncontrolled market price and the resale price. The comparable uncontrolled market price method offers the most direct way of determining the arm's-length price. Uncontrolled sales are sales made to an unrelated party outside the firm's own network. For the prices of goods to be comparable, it is essential to look at the prices of goods sold in markets that are economically comparable. It is an important condition in view of the fact that market conditions differ from one country to another. Economic and social structures, geographical situations, consumers' habits, and so on are different in different countries. Again, for prices to be comparable, it is necessary to compare goods sold at the same point of the distribution channel. It is because there is a difference between the wholesale and the retail price of a commodity. If the retailer's mark-up of prices is easily ascertainable, there will be no problem in making the necessary adjustments. But if goods are non-standardised or if they are not completely processed or are differentiated on account of trademark, quality, monopoly element, and other such factors, it will not be easy to find the comparable uncontrolled prices.

The resale price, on the other hand, is the price at which a product is purchased from a related seller, is resold to an independent purchaser. From this price, the margin (cost and profit) of the reseller is deducted to arrive at the arm's-length price. This method is useful where the margin of the reseller is not substantial or where the evidence of comparable uncontrolled sales does not exist. But this method is not suitable where the original product undergoes substantial transformation at the hands of the reseller. It is not suitable also where the time elapsing between the original sale and resale is significantly large so as to be exposed to changes in the exchange rate, in the market conditions, or in the cost structure.

Another method for ascertaining arm's-length price is the cost-plus method, which is more useful when semi-finished products are sold between related parties, although it is not often easy to determine the cost as well as the profit. The cost accounting concepts and practices vary from one set of countries to another and from one set of businesses to another. It is often the vendor's cost that is calculated. Purchasers too incur some expenses that need to be considered. As regards profit, any specific amount cannot be guaranteed. The cost-plus method generally overemphasises historical cost. If the cost is unnecessarily high due to inefficiency at the seller's point, the inefficiency may be transmitted to the buyer.

The two methods—market price and cost-plus—do not necessarily arrive at the same result in view of their specific limitations. In such cases, therefore, it is necessary to make additional calculations to cross check the results with the cost/profit structure of similar firms in the same industry. These two methods find further limitations if the transfer of intangible property, such as technical knowhow, has to be priced. In such cases, the usual practice is to base the price on the prices that are related to transfer of similar technology or on the cost incurred on research and development.

Despite limitations, the two methods are normally used. In this respect, Hirschleifer (1956) believes that market price should form the basis when the market for traded items is perfectly competitive. If not, the marginal manufacturing cost should form the basis. From a survey conducted by Business International (1982) it is clear that both these methods are employed. The cost-plus method was employed mostly by US MNCs, whereas the market price method was adopted generally by non-US MNCs. Large size firms preferred market based transfer prices, probably because of the greater visibility of different governments, tax, and other systems. Similarly, market based price was adopted mainly by decentralised units of MNCs, while more centralised units adopted cost-plus methods (Benvignati, 1985). Arpan (1972) has found that the US, French, British, and Japanese MNCs preferred cost-oriented methods, while Canadian, Italian, and Scandinavian firms opted for market based methods. Lecraw (1985) finds that the non-market based factor accounted for 58 per cent of the transfer pricing decisions. It was as low as 32 per cent in case of US MNCs and as high as 75 per cent in case of Japanese firms.

After the arm's-length price is set, the element of arbitrariness follows as to how much of deviation—plus or minus—from the arm's-length price should be brought in. This decision depends upon the firm's objectives that need to be achieved. The degree of arbitrariness is high in cases where market does not exist. For example, when an MNC gathers a particular knowledge on account of experience or research and development, which it does not like to part with any other firm, there is no open market for transfer of knowledge. If such knowledge is transferred within the firm, prices can either be very high or very low when compared to the arm's-length price. Richman and Copen (1972) have found a price mark-up of imports in India's drugs and chemical sector to the extent of 400 per cent in general, and in special cases, as high as 1,000 per cent.

Motivations behind Transfer Pricing: Minimisation of income-tax liability for the maximisation of overall profit is a pressing factor behind transfer pricing (Kim and Miller, 1979). The MNC transfers pre-tax profit from a unit facing a higher rate of tax to a unit subjected to a lower rate of tax. This is done through over invoicing of import of the former unit from the latter or under-invoicing of export to the latter.

Suppose an MNC has its subsidiary in Country *A* and Country *B*. Corporate tax in Country *A* is 10 per cent and 25 per cent in Country *B*. The unit in Country *A* produces intermediate goods that are exported to the Country *B* unit. In the absence of transfer pricing, the unit in Country *A* exports 50,000 units of the component at the rate of $10 per unit. But owing to a higher tax rate in Country *B*, the MNC likes to siphon before tax profit from the unit in Country *B* to the unit in Country *A*. This export is over priced, say, by 20 per cent. As a result of transfer pricing, the total profit of both the units taken together increases as the total tax liability of the two units taken together decreases. Assuming a fixed ratio between operating expenses and revenue, one finds:

Table 17.1 Income Statement (in the Absence of Transfer Pricing)

	Unit A $	*Unit* B $
Revenue	5,00,000	8,00,000
Cost of material	3,00,000	5,00,000
Gross margin	2,00,000	3,00,000
Operating expenses	50,000	80,000
Before tax profit	1,50,000	2,20,000
Tax	15,000	55,000
Net profit	1,35,000	1,65,000

Total Net Profit (*A* + *B*) = $3,00,000
Total Tax Liability (*A* + *B*) = $70,000

Transfer pricing by 20 per cent leads to an increase in profit by $15,000 as the tax liability shrinks by $15,000.

Table 17.2 Income Statement (After Transfer Pricing)

	Unit A $	*Unit* B $
Revenue	6,00,000	8,00,000
Cost of material	3,00,000	6,00,000
Gross margin	3,00,000	2,00,000
Operating expenses	50,000	80,000
Before-tax profit	2,50,000	1,20,000
Tax	25,000	30,000
Net profit	2,25,000	90,00

Total Net profit (*A* + *B*) = $3,15,000
Total Tax Liability (*A* + *B*) = $55,000

However, if there is a tax avoidance treaty between the two countries or if the administrative machinery is slack in evaluating taxes, the need for transfer pricing loses its significance.

Lowering of tariff burden is another factor motivating for transfer pricing. A survey made by Kim and Miller (1979) reveals that this factor is more significant than reducing tax burden. However, it is only ad valorem tariff burden that can be reduced. Quantitative restrictions do not lend themselves to transfer pricing gambits because their impact falls upon the quantities and not on the price of import. Similarly, if there are specific duties on import, structured according to physical characteristics of imports, transfer pricing would not be of much use.

In order to illustrate the impact of transfer pricing on the tariff, in the above example, we can add a tariff rate of 30 per cent and at the same time equalise the corporate tax rate at 10 per cent in the two countries.

Table 17.3 Income Statement (Without Transfer Pricing)

	Unit A $	*Unit* B $
Revenue	5,00,000	8,00,000
Cost of material	3,00,000	6,50,000
Gross margin	2,00,000	1,50,000
Operating expenses	50,000	80,000
Pre-tax profit	1,50,000	70,000
Tax	15,000	7,000
Net profit	1,35,000	63,000

Duty paid = $1,50,000
Tax paid = $22,000
Net profit = $1,98,000

Table 17.4 Income Statement (After Transfer Pricing)

	Unit A $	*Unit* B $
Revenue	4,00,000	8,00,000
Cost of material	3,00,000	5,20,000
Gross margin	1,00,000	2,80,000
Operating expenses	50,000	80,000
Pre-tax profit	50,000	2,00,000
Tax	5,000	20,000
Net profit	45,000	1,80,000

Duty paid = $1,20,000
Tax paid = $25,000
Net profit = $2,25,000

Since the transfer price is less than the arm's-length price, the size of duty paid plummets by $30,000, the amount of tax increases marginally by $3,000, and profit increases by $27,000. Profit increases because the company has to pay lower duty. However, one has to take care of the fact that the issue of reducing tariff burden cannot be thought of in isolation of other factors such as the tax liability. In the above example, tax burden has risen marginally, but since the tariff burden has diminished substantially, the net profit has increased considerably. But it may be that the tax burden increases significantly to eat away the benefits from tariff reduction. In that case, transfer pricing will lose its significance. Suppose that the tax rate in Country *A* and Country *B* is respectively 10 per cent and 25 per cent. In the absence of transfer pricing, the tariff burden will be $1,50,000; the tax burden will be $32,500; and the net profit will be $187,500. After under invoicing of export to Unit *B*, the amount of duty will shrink to $1,20,000 but the tax burden will increase to $55,000 and the profit will increase only marginally by $7,500. A greater tax differential between the two countries will lead to a reduction in total profit. This means, while adopting transfer pricing devices, a balance has to be maintained between reducing tariff burden and reducing tax burden.

> While adopting transfer pricing devices, a balance has to be maintained between reducing tariff burden and reducing tax burden.

Transfer pricing cannot prevent changes in the exchange rate between currencies but it can minimise the adverse impact of such changes by reshuffling cash balances and profits among the different units of a firm located in weak and strong currency countries. If large cash balances of the firm are held with the unit located in a strong currency country, any weakening of the currency in other countries will not matter much. Rather it is possible that the firm could gain from such changes. This is the reason that an MNC prefers to shift surplus cash from units situated in a weak currency country to units located in a strong currency country. For such shifting of cash balances, the firm uses transfer pricing. The goods exported by the weak currency unit to a strong-currency country will be under invoiced.

Similarly, when the host government imposes restrictions on the remittances of dividend and other payments, the parent company uses transfer pricing so as to effect such remittances.

When different units of a firm are well knit, the parent unit maintains a centralised control on the management of cash. Surplus cash of one unit is either sent to the cash deficit unit or to a centralised pool for the purpose of its investment in near-cash assets. When the government of the cash surplus unit imposes restrictions on such movement of cash, the parent company uses the transfer pricing technique.

The parent unit likes its subsidiary to possess an edge over the local firms and, to this end, it supplies the intermediate products at much lower than the arm's-length price or without any charge. This enables the subsidiary to sell the final product at a lower price and compete with local firms.

Regulation: One school of thought favours complete deregulation where government shall apply no exchange control. Naturally, no MNC will be compelled to adopt the transfer pricing technique. The play of market forces will foster optimal allocation of resources. But complete deregulation is utopian and hence transfer pricing is quite prevalent. Because of its prevalence, there is need for its regulation. The regulation may be direct or indirect. Direct regulation includes measures that directly replace a particular transfer price by another set of prices determined by the host government. There are cases when the government has set a particular price at which intra-firm transactions take place. For the first time, a legislation was enacted to this end in the United States of America in 1973. The United Nations published a similar report in 1978. However, there are problems in following such a move. Kyrouz (1975) found that out of the 900 cases reviewed by the US Internal Revenue Service, the arm's-length standards were completely unsuitable in over 40 per cent of the cases. In many cases, comparable uncontrolled prices were not available. In many other cases, the cost-plus method was not feasible. In many developing countries, the government has fixed a ceiling on royalty payment, but this irks MNCs. Nevertheless, direct regulation is possible. In many cases, intermediate products are standardised; expert arbitration is also available.

On the contrary, indirect measures may be manifest in different forms. First, harmonisation of tax and tariff differential between home country and host country may be thought of. Kim and Miller (1979) found that profit tax consideration is comparatively less relevant than what is popularly believed. Yet this factor needs harmonisation. The system of tax holiday may be encouraged. Treaties for avoidance of double taxation may also be helpful.

The second form of indirect regulation is to tax royalty and other intra-firm transfer payments that compensates the loss of corporate tax revenue on account of transfer pricing. A few countries are found to disallow deduction of intra-firm royalty altogether as a business expense for the purpose of taxation. This is because they treat royalty payment as the remittance of profit. This measure checks transfer pricing through a higher rate of royalty payment. But other forms of transfer pricing remain unchecked.

The third form of indirect regulation is to apportion the consolidated profit of the MNC among the relevant jurisdictions, usually on the basis of total assets, sales, and labour and capital employed. But this measure goes against the very fundamental notion that the MNC is interested is maximising global profits. Moreover, when different subsidiaries are interdependent, especially in a vertical set up, any such apportionment is difficult to be justified on the grounds of the contribution of different subsidiaries to the total profit. If the apportionment is based on the amount of labour employed, differences in the productivity of labour in different countries cannot justify it.

The regulatory measures—direct and indirect—are not foolproof. Host governments need to take a mix of measures supplemented by a series of negotiations with the parent companies of units operating in their country.

Transfer Pricing and Indian Tax Provisions: For the first time, it was the Indian Finance Act, 2001 that incorporated the detailed provisions relating to transfer pricing by the multinational companies. The rules are based on the OECD guidelines, but the Indian rules stress on the computation of arm's-length price rather than considering an arm's-length range. The Central Board of direct taxes prescribes five methods to compute arm's-length price. They are as follows:

1. Comparable uncontrolled price method
2. Resale price method
3. Cost-plus method
4. Profit-split method
5. Transactional net margin method

The adoption of a particular method depends on the nature of transaction.

Again, it is the tax payer that has to prove that the transactions have taken place in accordance with the norms of arm's-length pricing. It has to obtain the accountant's certificate in respect of the international transactions. Any violation of the norms is subject to stiff penalty. The penalty goes up to 100–300 per cent of tax in addition to income on account of concealment of details. Again, it may be 2.0 per cent of the value of international transactions if proper documents are not furnished with the tax authorities. The penalty can be equal to Rs. 1,00,000 if the accountant's certificate is not obtained.

After the submission of the documents, the tax officer forwards them to the specially appointed transfer pricing officer to review the entire matter. The latter finalises the assessment proceedings.

17.4 SELECTING CHANNEL OF DISTRIBUTION

17.4.1 Direct and Indirect Channels

The marketing strategy also involves the selection of a suitable channel of distribution that proves most effective and involves the least cost. The channel of distribution may be either direct or indirect. In a direct channel, the firm deals directly with a foreign firm without going through any domestic intermediary and exports goods through its own internal organisation. The manufacturer may appoint a foreign distributor which is usually known as an importer or a foreign wholesaler. It may use a foreign retailer or it may export directly to a state owned trading company. In India, certain products are imported only by the State Trading Company. Sometimes the manufacturer exports the product directly to the ultimate consumer or the end user, but it is often faced by customs clearance problems. This way, the firm has full control over overseas sale and is able to implement its marketing policy uniformly in all the markets. But at the same time, direct channel is often expensive and time-consuming. It is fraught with problems insofar as the manufacturer is normally not familiar with the foreign market.

> In a direct channel, the firm deals directly with a foreign buyer. But an indirect channel involves an intermediary, such as export broker, export agent, export vendor, export merchant, etc.

In indirect channel, on the other hand, the manufacturer need not correspond with the foreign party abroad. It involves rather intermediary that may be either domestic agent or domestic merchant. The marketing through this channel is least cumbrous as the intermediary takes the entire responsibility. But it is unreliable as the intermediary may refuse handling of sales at any point of time.

In case of the indirect channel, the intermediaries can be classified as:

(i) those who do not take title to the goods and simply charge commission for their job, such as export broker, export agent, export vendor, and so on; and
(ii) those who take title to the goods, such as export merchants.

An **export broker**, who possesses wide knowledge about the potential market, brings the seller and buyer together. It negotiates with the buyer on behalf of the seller and concludes the agreement only after approval from the buyer. **Export agents** are also independent business persons who contact potential buyers for a specific commission. An **export management company** manages the entire export programme of a manufacturer under a contract. It works simultaneously for several non-competing manufacturers. An **export vendor** is normally a manufacturer who sells the products of other manufacturers along with its own products.

Export merchants estimate the potential buyers abroad, take title to the goods to be exported and then they supply the goods to the buyers. They make profit out of it rather than charging commission for their activities. An **export drop shipper**, also known as a desk jobber or cable merchant, is a special kind of export merchant. It finds out the buyer and asks the manufacturer to supply the goods directly to the buyer. A drop shipper normally handles bulk products with low unit value. The other type of export merchant is the export distributor who deals with the manufacturer on a continuous basis. The export merchant buys goods from the manufacturer and sells them abroad, bearing all risks involved in foreign trade.

17.4.2 Suitability of Channel

Direct and indirect channels—both of them have their merits and demerits. The firm needs to select a particular channel or a mix of channels. Infact, the decision depends upon the product, features of the channels, various factors operating in different markets, and the firm's overall strategy of market penetration and market control.

For big-ticket items such as automobiles or for high volume products, it is better for the manufacturer to sell its product directly to a foreign retailer under the direct channel. Low price, high turnover products need a wider channel, where the number of middlemen at a particular point is large. On the other hand, high image products, and high price, low turnover goods are better distributed through narrow channels. Clinique's products are sold only at a few shops in Japan. On the contrary, ice-cream is sold through a wide distribution channel.

When the importing government has greater control on the imports and the imports are canalised through a state agency, the firm has no option but to export its products to the government agency. In India, many items are canalised only through the State Trading Corporation (STC). In those cases, foreign suppliers have to export these products only to the STC. In some importing countries there are other legal constraints. The supplier has to abide by the regulations. For example, foreigners cannot own trading and marketing agencies in Bahrain. Similar laws are found in Indonesia. When regulations are changed, the channel of distribution also changes.

Different channels have different features. A particular channel is adapted by a firm when its features suit its own interest. For example, export agents are preferable where the market is widely spread, a particular market is quite thin, demand is uncertain, the manufacturer is unfamiliar with the market and it wants to lower its selling burden. Taking help from export management companies is preferred when they are specialised in their product type or when they devote a lot of their money and managerial efforts for launching their client's products.

A manufacturer wants to maintain greater control over the distribution of his products. To this end, it selects either a wide distribution channel or a narrow distribution channel. In England, three-quarters of beer sales are conducted by pubs where top brewers manage to push their own brand.

17.4.3 Adaptability of the Distribution Channel

Related to the question of suitability of distribution channel, is the issue of adaptability of the channel. It is important to decide whether the firm should adapt a single channel throughout its entire market or it should adapt channels according to the needs of the different markets. It is often argued that since different markets differ in their approach, a universal policy regarding distribution channel may not be effective. Grosse and Zinn (1990) found a highly adapted distribution channel in the case of US based multinationals doing business with Latin American countries. Litvak and Banting (1968) classified markets depending upon political stability, market opportunity, economic development, cultural factors, and legal and psychological factors. They are of the opinion that the shape of the distribution channel should vary in different markets based on these factors.

17.4.4 Costs Involved in Overseas Distribution Channel

It is true that a firm adopts either a direct channel or an indirect channel for distribution and sometimes adapts the channel depending on the conditions prevalent in the overseas market. But, at the same time, it is also true that it tries to identify the hidden cost in the distribution process and tries to minimise it. It would be worthwhile to mention these costs here.

First, in some cases there are a greater number of chains or middlemen in the channel of distribution, such as national wholesalers, regional wholesalers, retailers, and so on. The larger the number, the greater is the cost/margin added to the price of the product. According to an estimate, the margin added is three times greater in Japan than in France. Thus, an MNC needs to lower the number of middlemen.

Second, in some of the countries, there is paucity of an efficient transport system; roads are bad; warehousing facilities are poor; and the law and order problem is acute. All these problems add to the cost involved in the distribution of the product. According to a report, Nestle had to build warehouses in Nigeria and had to post armed guards on the trucks carrying their products (Daniels, *et al*, 2002).

Distribution cost may be curtailed through:
1. curtailing the number of middlemen
2. improving distributional infra-structure, and
3. adapting to the market rules in the host countries.

Thirdly, in many countries, the retailers' shop is open only for a limited number of hours, say, from late forenoon to early evening. As a result, fixed cost is stretched only over a few hours. It adds to the price of the product.

Thus, a firm's strategy should be to limit the cost related to the overseas distribution system within a manageable range. To this end, the number of middlemen between the producer and the consumer should be minimal. The firm should have an idea of the distributional infrastructure of the overseas market as well as the general market rules prevailing there before it launches its product there.

17.5 SALES PROMOTION

When actual demand for the product lags behind its potential demand, it simply means that the firm is not able to communicate the consumers effectively about the features and usefulness of the product. It is then necessary to ensure effective communication through right media suiting consumers' attitude and belief structure.

17.5.1 Modes of Sales Promotion

The mode of promotion is normally a mix of personal selling, publicity, and advertising. Personal selling is an example of push strategy. On the contrary, publicity and advertising is a pull strategy.

Personal selling is an example of push strategy. On the contrary, publicity and advertising is a pull strategy.

Personal Selling: In case of personal selling, the sales representatives come closer to the consumers and are able to develop a sense of confidence in the minds of the latter. This mode is more effective when the sale and purchase is infrequent and when the market is concentrated where the product carries a high unit value. It is also preferable to advertising in the sense that there is a two-way communication process. If the consumer has any doubt, it is cleared by the seller. However, there is often a question of whether the sales representatives should come from the home country or they should be appointed from the host country. In the former case, the sales representatives are better acquainted with the features of the product and the company's overall objectives. In the latter case, they are more acquainted with the market conditions. So a balance must be maintained between the two.

Publicity is not paid for by the sponsors, while advertising is paid for.

Publicity: Publicity, another mode of communication, is effected through media, but unlike advertisement, it is not paid for by the sponsors. In order to illustrate, one can quote Nike distributing shoes to professional athletes and thereby gaining additional exposure when the teams appeared on television. Pepsi arranged for Michael Jackson's shows in Japan, which helped double its sales during summer.

Advertising: Last but not least, advertisement occupies the most significant place in sales promotion strategy. The superiority of a product over similar products is displayed through newspaper, television, and many other means such as radio, magazines, cinema, directories, and so on. All this involves sizeable cost but is often rewarding. However, the success of advertising depends upon when and how much media time and space is available. This is because in many countries the scope for advertisement is limited by governmental regulations or by other local regulations. In Canada and Mexico, advertisement for health-related products needs prior clearance from the government. In over three dozen countries, there is complete/partial ban on advertising for cigarette.

17.5.2 Adaptability of Advertising

Irrespective of media, there is an important question that, whether advertising should be standardised or individualised, varying from one market to the other. Standardised advertising is based on the belief that the basic physiological and psychological needs of consumers living in different countries are similar. It is normally favoured on the grounds of simplification, low cost, and efficiency (Elinder, 1965; Strouse, 1966). Jain (1989) mentioned the conditions in which standardised advertising seemed to be more appropriate. Some of the more important of those conditions are: economically uniform markets; similar customers' behaviour and life style across countries; cultural compatibility of the product across countries; uniformity in the firm's competitive position in different markets; high-tech industrial products; similar physical, political, and legal environment in different markets; existence of strategic consensus among parent-subsidiary managers; and so on.

However, standardised advertising may not be feasible on account of (1) local regulations, (2) media and agency availability, and (3) level of literacy. It has already been mentioned that many governments impose restrictions on the nature and content of advertisements. Similarly, there is hardly any agency that has control over local agencies in importing countries. Moreover, if the level of literacy is very low, consumers will not be able to appreciate the theme of advertisement.

Again, standardised advertising may not be desirable in the sense that consumers across countries are practically not homogeneous. This is why the very approach towards advertising differs from one market to the other. The Western advertisement is normally more verbal, direct, and logical, while the Japanese one is more emotional, indirect, and suggestive (Lazer, *et al*, 1985).

It is evident that both the standardised and individualised advertisement have their merits. Thus, it would be better if both are mixed in different proportions, depending upon the conditions prevailing in different cases.

17.6 FOREIGN TRADE DOCUMENTATION

17.6.1 Objectives of Foreign Trade Documents

The basic objective behind foreign trade documentation is to assure the exporter of getting the export proceeds and to the importer getting the shipment in order. Since exporters and importers are located at quite a distance from each other, they do not know much about each other. There is every possibility of either non-payment of export proceeds or non-receipt of goods according to specifications. But documents such as letter of credit, draft, bill of lading, and so on overcome these problems. The exporter is confident about the receipt of export proceeds. The importer too is confident of receiving the goods in order. All this means that proper documentation helps eliminate the non-completion risk.

Foreign trade documents help the exporter and the importer to hedge the foreign exchange risk in a better way because they assure the amount and the time of payments. In the absence of necessary documents, when the time and amount of the flow of funds are not known with certainty, it becomes difficult to practise any hedging technique.

Foreign trade documents facilitate payments from the importer to the exporter. Infact, they are the media through which payments are made. They are more significant when the importer's creditworthiness is not well known.

Foreign trade documentation eliminates various types of risks trading firms are exposed to, and at the same time, it facilitates payments.

Thus, in short, foreign trade documentation is significant in the sense that it eliminates various types of risks trading firms are exposed to, and at the same time, it facilitates payments. It is still more significant when foreign trade is episodic with no sustained relationship between the exporter and the importer.

17.6.2 Letter of Credit

A letter of credit (L/C) is an instrument signed by the importer's banker promising the exporter to make payments if the exporter abides by the conditions mentioned in the L/C and if the specifications of the export tally with those mentioned in the L/C. It is a letter of promise, but not a letter of guarantee, of the underlying commercial transaction. The bank receives a fee for issuing it. The document incorporates a specified expiration date and a specified amount of money. The bank's responsibility of making payments arises only after the presentation of specific documents. The importer's obligation to reimburse the bank is based on the same conditions on which the bank has paid the amount.

This instrument serves the interest of the exporter as well as of the importer. The exporter gets assurance for the payment even if credit risk or political risk is involved in the trade. Similarly, the importer has to make payments only of the goods of the shipment are in a good condition and the terms set in the L/C are met. However, the advantage accruing to the importer must be judged against the fee charged by the bank for issuing the L/C. Sometimes the L/C reduces the importer's borrowing line of credit from its bank. This is another factor to be judged while estimating the benefits of an L/C.

How Does L/C Operate? When an importer places a purchase order with the exporter, he (importer) requests his own banker to issue an L/C. The banker writes an L/C and delivers it to the exporter's bank. The latter confirms it and passes it on to the exporter. The exporter ships the goods and deposits the L/C, draft and other export documents with his banker. The exporter's bank delivers the L/C and other documents to the importer's bank. The latter accepts the draft and remits money or export proceeds to the exporter's bank if the contents of the shipment tally with those mentioned in the L/C. The exporter's bank credits the exporter's account. The exporter can get the money even earlier if he discounts the bill under L/C with his bank or if he raises loans on the strength of the L/C.

L/C refers to an instrument signed by importer's bank, assuring exporter of the payment.

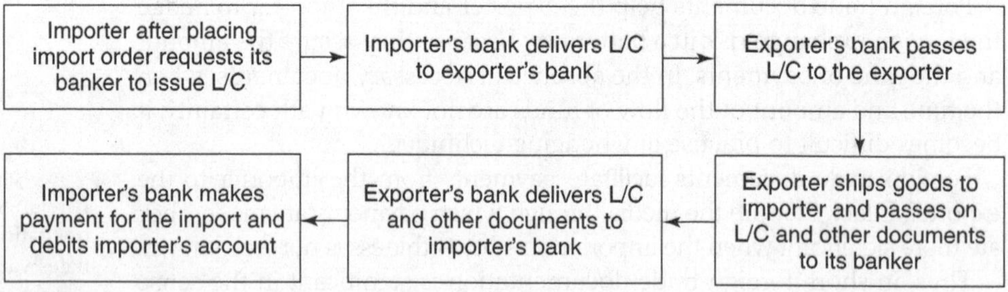

Variants of L/C: There are many variants of L/C. A **clean L/C** does not require the documents of title to goods or other documents to accompany the bills drawn under the L/C, while a **documentary L/C** does require them. In case of a clean L/C, the exporter sends the documents directly to the importer. After sending the documents, it does not retain control over the goods under transaction. As a result, it may have to face the risk of default. This is why a clean L/C is used only when the importer is highly creditworthy. On the contrary, a documentary L/C is normally used because it minimises such risk.

Again, an L/C may be **revocable** or it may be **irrevocable**. The former may be cancelled or amended by the issuing bank at any time without prior notice to the beneficiary. An irrevocable one cannot be cancelled or amended. Thus, revocable credit does not provide guarantee for the payment of export proceeds. Exporters naturally prefer an irrevocable L/C.

When an L/C is advised to the exporter through a bank in the exporter's country, the exporter may request another bank to add its (the latter's) confirmation. With the added confirmation, the L/C becomes a **confirmed L/C**.

In the absence of any such confirmation, the L/C remains an unconfirmed L/C. All this means that a confirmed L/C is always an irrevocable L/C because then only bank dares to confirm it. A confirmed L/C gives an added guarantee of payment of export proceeds.

An L/C may be a **fixed** or **a revolving.** The former limits the amount of bill to be drawn under the L/C. On the contrary, under the revolving L/C, the limit of the bill amount is renewed automatically after the amount of the bill is paid. Indian laws prohibit the opening of a revolving L/C against import of goods into the country.

Similarly, a **transferable L/C** is one where the exporter has the right to transfer the L/C to third parties. It normally happens where the exporter is simply an intermediary procuring goods from the producers or suppliers and exporting them. Normally, the entire amount involved is transferred. But, sometimes only a reduced amount is transferred as the exporter deducts its own commission. Here it may be mentioned that the L/C can be transferred only if the transfer clause is present in it. If it is not, another L/C may be opened in favour of the supplier. This ancillary L/C is known as a back-to-back L/C or a countervailing L/C.

Last but not least, there is also a **red-clause L/C** that authorises the negotiating bank to extend advances to the exporter in the form of preshipment credit. The amount of the advance is recovered from the bill tendered under the L/C.

17.6.3 Draft

A draft, also known as the bill of exchange, is an instrument through which an exporter instructs the importer or its agent to pay a specified amount of money at a specified time. In this case, the exporter, who initiates the draft, is known as the maker, originator or drawer. The importer, on the other hand, is known as the drawee. The amount mentioned in the draft may not necessarily be paid to the drawer. Sometimes it is paid to its agent, normally the bank. In this case, the drawer is not the payee, rather the payee is the bank.

Draft is an instrument through which an importer makes payment to the exporter.

A draft is normally a negotiable instrument if it is properly drawn. A properly drawn draft means that:

(i) it should be in writing and signed by the drawer,
(ii) it should incorporate an unconditional promise or order to pay a specified amount of money,
(iii) it should be payable either at sight or at a specified time, and
(iv) it must be payable to order or to bearer. When it is payable to order, the payment is made to the person specified. When it is a bearer draft, the amount can be paid to any person presenting the draft.

Types of Draft: When a draft is a **sight or demand draft**, payment is made immediately on presentation of the draft. In case of non-payment, it is treated as dishonour of the draft. On the other hand, in a **time draft**

payment is made after the lapse of a specified time. The specified time is known as *tenor or usance*. When a draft is drawn on, and accepted by, a bank, it becomes a bankers' acceptance. It is now the duty of the bank to honour the draft on maturity. The holder of such a draft, which is normally an exporter in international trade, may enjoy various options. It can hold it till maturity and get the specified amount of money minus the bank's acceptance commission. Alternatively, it can sell it or get it discounted in the money market where it immediately receives the face value of the draft minus the sum of acceptance commission and discount.

Again, draft is classified also as a **clean draft and a documentary draft**. In case of a clean draft, no other document accompanies it. Other documents are sent directly by the exporter to the importer. A clean draft is normally in use in case intra-firm trade where trust and credit are not involved. It is also used in case of non-trade remittances where the collection of an outstanding amount is sought. On the contrary, shipping documents are enclosed with the documentary draft. In such cases, these documents are obtained by the importer only after making payments or on acceptance of the draft. In the former, that is, when documents are delivered to the importer only after payment, the documentary draft is known as D/P. When it is delivered after the acceptance, the documentary draft is known as D/A.

Bill of Lading is a shipping document issued by the carrier.

17.6.4 Bill of Lading

A bill of lading is a shipping document issued by a carrier to the exporter or its banker. It can be treated simultaneously as a receipt, a contract, and a document of title. It is a receipt because it shows that the carrier has received a certain amount of goods for transportation. It is a contract because the carrier has to deliver the goods to the importer for a fee. It is a document of title because it establishes the ownership of goods. All this means that this document ensures payment before the goods are delivered.

Bill of lading may be **straight**. It may be **to order**. The former stipulates that the carrier shall deliver the goods to the designated consignee, but shall not provide it the title to the goods. So it is not a suitable collateral for loans. However, it is used when the goods have been paid for in advance or when it is an intra-firm transaction.

The order bill of lading, on the other hand, grants title to the goods only to the person to whom the document is addressed. The title of the goods remains with the exporter until payment is made. On payment, the exporter endorses the order bill of lading to the payment making party, which is normally the importer. The endorsed document can be used as a collateral for loans.

The bill of lading may be a **clean bill of lading** or **a foul bill of lading**. The former assumes that the goods have been received by the carrier in good condition and the carrier is not obliged to check the goods. On the contrary, a foul bill of lading allows the carrier to check the goods.

17.6.5 Additional Documents

Besides the above three important documents, there are other documents too that are used in foreign trade. To mention some of them, the first is the commercial invoice incorporating the description of the goods and terms of sale. The second is the insurance document that gives the details of the insurance and the risk covered. The third is the consular invoice which is issued by the consulate of the importing country and which provides customs information. The fourth is the packing list showing the contents of the container. Last but not least, is the export declaration that is prepared by the exporter. It helps the government to prepare export statistics.

SUMMARY

- The first step in an international marketing strategy is to identify the potential market and the specific market segments for the product, as market characteristics differ widely. After the selection of a market, its demand is estimated. In this context, the issue of concentration on specific segments vis-a-vis market diversification is important.
- Product strategy is also important. A firm may have a standard product. Alternatively, it may adapt its product to conditions prevailing in different markets. The decision depends upon a host of factors.
- Pricing strategy is no less important. The firm may go for bundling/unbundling of the product, price discrimination, skimming price/penetration price, or it may also adopt dumping. It may also adopt transfer pricing, especially in case of intra-firm sale of products.
- Selection of channels of distribution is another element in the marketing strategy. Channels may be direct/indirect, based upon a host of factors. A firm may adopt a single channel for all market segments. Alternatively, channels may vary from market to market.
- When actual demand lags behind potential demand, the firm adopts different sales promotion schemes, such as personal selling, publicity, and advertising.
- Last but not least, a firm should have knowledge of foreign trade documentation, especially letter of credit, draft , bill of lading, and so on, the use of which reduces/eliminates non-completion risk and facilitates trade.

REVIEW QUESTIONS

1. How is demand estimated? Do you think that a firm should concentrate on a specific segment of the market?

2. "Standardisation and adaptation of products have their own merits". Discuss its implication in international marketing and explain the factors behind adaptation of the product.
3. What do you mean by bundling and unbundling of product as far as pricing strategy is concerned?
4. What is transfer pricing? What are the motivations behind it? How can it be regulated?
5. Comment on the suitability of a channel of distribution in international marketing.
6. What are the different techniques of sales promotion in an international market?
7. Write a short notes on:
   (i) Letter of credit
   (ii) Draft
   (iii) Bill of lading
   (iv) Skimming price and penetration price

OBJECTIVE TYPE QUESTIONS

1. Mark True or False:
   (a) Market diversification policy is favoured where market features are widely varied.
   (b) Products are standardised throughout the globe if they involve highly sophisticated technology.
   (c) Transfer prices are used in case of intra-firm transfer of goods, services, and intermediate products.
   (d) A draft is an instrument wherein the exporter instructs the importer to make payments.
   (e) A bill of lading is a shipping document issued by the exporter to the carrier.
   (f) Advertisement is paid for by the sponsors, while publicity is not.
   (g) The distribution channel is usually indirect in case of big-ticket items.
   (h) Transfer prices are equal to arm's length prices.
   (i) Persistent dumping is a permanent type of dumping.
   (j) Unbundling of a product means high price for bare-bone items and low price for accessories.
2. Choose the Most Suitable Answer.
   (a) Selection of market depends on:
      (i) Geographic distance
      (ii) Socio-cultural and economic environment
      (iii) Both of the above
   (b) Demand is estimated by analogy in cases when:
      (i) Economic and socio-economic indicators are not available
      (ii) Geographic distance is large
      (iii) None of the above
   (c) Market concentration policy is adopted where:
      (i) Demand in a particular market is least fluctuating
      (ii) Product needs substantial adaptation
      (iii) Both of the above
   (d) Bundling of product means:
      (i) Charging high prices for bare-bone items and lower prices for accessories

(ii) Charging lower prices for bare-bone items and higher prices for accessories
(iii) None of the above

(e) The purpose of predatory dumping is to:
(i) Sell distressed stock
(ii) Eliminate rivals
(iii) Both of the above

(f) An L/C is issued by the:
(i) Exporter's bank
(ii) Importer's bank
(iii) Exporter

CASE STUDY

Mahindra & Mahindra Entering the US Sport Utility Vehicle Market

M/S Mahindra & Mahindra (M&M), the Indian automobile manufacturer has diversified its production structure. It has started manufacturing sport utility vehicles (SUV) not only for the domestic market but more importantly for the overseas market where the demand for such vehicles is quite large. In 2006, it launched SUV in the UK market. It was a well-conceived plan based on its experiences of selling SUV in France, Italy, Spain and South Africa. After catering the British market, it planned to enter the US market by 2009. However, for the US market, M&M had to modify its technology in order to cope up with the safety and emissions standard. Compliance to safety norms delayed the entry into the USA at least for some months. Presently, M&M have started assembly operation in Brazil as they intend to widen the market in Latin America.

It may be noted that M&M is not the only SUV supplier to the US market; General Motors is one of the largest suppliers of SUV in the US market. But the competitive strength of M&M depends upon the cost advantage it possesses. The SUVs of M&M are price cheaper than the comparable SUVs supplied by the General Motors. The reason is that M&M is able to get cheaper components in the wake of the establishment of an automobile hub in India. Moreover, the cost of design, etc. meant for the US market is expected to be around $120 million, less than one-fourth of the amount a US car maker might spend.

Again, M&M does not have to face many competitors like Italian Fiat and French Renault which do not cater to the US market for strategic considerations.

The competitive strength that M&M possesses is also due to the fact that it has long been selling tractors to the US market and thus has knowledge of the economic and other variables influencing the demand in this market.

Source: Based on the news published in *Financial Times*, 6.6.2006, Financial Express, Jan. 24, 2010.

QUESTIONS

1. Do you find that the product strategy of M&M is the same in the UK and the US markets?
2. What are the factors behind M&M's success in the US market?
3. What should be the nature of pricing strategy for the US market?

REFERENCES

Books

Benvignati, A. M. (1985),"An Empirical Investigation of International Transfer Pricing by US Manufacturing Firms", in Rugman, A. M. and L. Eden (eds.), *Multinationals and Transfer Pricing* (New York: St. Martin's Press), pp. 193–211.

Diewert, W. E. (1985),"Transfer Pricing and Economic Efficiency"in Rugman and Eden, *op.cit.*, pp.47–81.

Lecraw, D. J. (1985),"Some Evidence on Transfer Pricing by Multinational Corporations" in Rugman and Eden, *op.cit.*, pp. 223–246.

Litvak, I. A. and P.M. Banting (1968),"A Conceptual Framework for International Business Arrangements" in R. L. King (ed.), *Marketing and the New Science of Planning* (Chicago: American Marketing Association), pp. 460–67.

Piercy, N. (1982), *Export Strategy: Markets and Competition* (London: George Allen & Unwin).

Richman, B. M. and M. Copen (1972), *International Management and Economic Development* (New York: McGraw-Hill), p. 603.

Journals and Reports

Arpan, J. S. (1972),"International Intra-corporate Pricing: Non-American Systems and Views", *Journal of International Business Studies*, III (Spring), 1–18.

Ayal, I. and J. Zif (1979),"Marketing Expansion Strategies in Multinational Marketing", *Journal of Marketing*, XLIII (1) 84–94.

Business International (1982), *Assessing Foreign Subsidiary Performance; Systems and Practices of Leading Multinational Corporations*, New York, p. 59.

Cavusgil, S. T. (1997),"Measuring the Potential of Emerging Markets: An Indexing Approach", *Business Horizons*, Jan.–Feb., 87–91.

Copithorne, L. W. (1971), "International Corporate Transfer Prices and Government Policy", *Canadian Journal of Economics*, IV, (August), 321–341.

Elam, R. and H. Henaidy (1980),"Transfer Pricing for the Multinational Enterprise", *International Journal of Accounting*, Spring, 49–65.

Elinder, E. (1965),"How International can European Advertising be", *Journal of Marketing*, XXIX (1) 7–11.

Grosse, R and W. Zinn (1990),"Standardisation in International Marketing: The Latin American Case", *Journal of Global Marketing*, IV (1), 53–78.

Hill, J. S. and R. R. Still (1984),"Adapting Products to LDC Tastes", *Harvard Business Review*, LXII (Mar.–Apr.), 92–101.

Hirschleifer, J. (1956),"On the Economics of Transfer Pricing", *Journal of Business*, XXIX (2), 172–184.

Horst, T. (1971),"Theory of Multinational Firm: Optimal Behaviour under Differing Tariff and Tax Rates", *Journal of Political Economy*, LXXIX (Sept.–Oct.), 1059–1072.

Jain, S. C. (1989), "Standardisation of International Marketing Strategy: Some Research Hypothesis", *Journal of Marketing*, LIII (1), 70–79.

Kim, S. H. and S. W. Miller (1979), "Constituents of International Transfer Pricing Decisions", *Columbia Journal of World Business*, XIV (Spring), 65–77.

Koh, A. C. (1991), "An Evaluation of International Marketing Research Planning in United States Export Firms", *Journal of Global Marketing*, IV (2), 7–25.

Kyrouz, M. E. (1975), "Foreign Tax Rates And Tax Bases", *National Tax Journal* (March) 61–80.

Lazer, W., *et al* (1985), "Japanese Marketing: Towards a Better Understanding", *Journal of Marketing*, IL (1) 69–81.

Schuman, M. (1996), "US Companies Crack South Korean Market", *Wall Street Journal*, Sept. 11, p. A 14.

Strouse, N. H. (1966), "The Internationalisation of the Ad Man", *Columbia Journal of World Business*, I (2) 115–20.

SELECT FURTHER READINGS

Cateora, P. R. (1990), *International Marketing*, (Homewood third.: Richard D. Irwin).

Czinkota, M. R. and I. A. Ronkainen (1995), *Global Marketing Imperative: Positioning Your Company for the New World of Business*, (Lincolnwood, third.: NTC).

Thorelli, H. and H. Becker ed. (1980), *International Marketing Strategy* (New York: Pergamon Press).

Daniels, J. D. *et al* (2002), *Globalisation and Business* (New Delhi: Prentice-Hall of India).

Rugman, A. M. and R. M. Hodgetts (2003), *International Business* (Delhi: Pearson Education).

* **South Africa** is a country located at the southern tip of Africa, with a 2,798 km coastline on the Atlantic and Indian Oceans. By UN classification, South Africa is a middle-income country with an abundant supply of resources, well-developed financial, legal, communications, energy and transport sectors. It is a popular tourist destination, and a substantial amount of revenue comes from tourism.

Principal international trading partners of South Africa—besides other African countries—include Germany, the United States, China, Japan, the United Kingdom and Spain. Chief exports include corn, diamonds, fruits, gold, metals and minerals, sugar and wool. Machinery and transportation equipment make up more than one-third of the value of the country's imports.

OPEC headquarters, Vienna, Austria*

18

Global Human Resource Management

CHAPTER OBJECTIVES

Human resource management is a great challenge for an MNC operating in a complex environment. The present chapter discusses its various aspects. In particular, it attempts to:

- ✦ Analyse the complexities faced by MNCs in managing human resources.
- ✦ Discuss various staffing policies and the factors influencing them.
- ✦ Examine whether expatriates have an edge over the locals.
- ✦ Discuss the process of recruitment and training of expatriates.
- ✦ Explain how industrial relations are managed—how far the industrial relations issue is relevant, how employees participate in the management, and what role trade unions play.

Human resource management is a process concerned broadly with recruiting of persons, training them, and putting them to the most productive use. It is also concerned with maintaining congenial industrial relations. It is the proper human resource management that lies behind effective planning, organisation, and control, and also behind cost effective operations and marketing. Therefore, it is an essential prerequisite for the success of a firm. It is true that the process of human resource management is crucial for both domestic and international firms, but it is far more crucial for an international firm in view of its complexities. The present chapter discusses the distinction of international firms in this context and also the various aspects of human resource management.

18.1 COMPLEXITIES OF INTERNATIONAL FIRMS

The management of international human resource is highly complex.

1. Different countries have different **labour-mixes**. This means that while in one country, more skilled workers are available, the others may not have sufficient availability of skilled personnel. If in one country, cheap labour is available, the others may have costly labour resource. It is this variance that poses a major problem while recruiting personnel from international sources.
2. The legal, economic, social and, cultural environment varies from one country to another. It is thus difficult for a person to move to any other country and work in a different environment. Any difficulty in mobility hampers the global productivity and efficiency of a firm. In this context, therefore, it is crucial decision whether to adopt a uniform staffing policy or to adapt to the staffing policy of the host country's environment.
3. **Employer-employee relations** may be strained if the firm emphasises on global productivity and efficiency.
4. Senior managers in a subsidiary normally have broader duties than in a domestic firm. This is because they have to deal with the consumers, with the general public, and more importantly, with top governmental officials and the politicians in power in the host country. This is because foreign operation is highly dependent upon the **political relationship between the home country and the host country**.
5. Managers of an international company often face **communication problems** in a host country. Because of language problem and the cultural diversity, senior managers coming from the home country often feel isolated and do not interact much with lower level workers.

However, these complexities may be softened with proper human resource management that takes care of the diversity between the home country's and different host countries' environment.

18.2 STAFFING POLICY

18.2.1 Ethnocentric, Polycentric, and Geocentric Policies

There is no disagreement on the issue of recruiting additional manpower in the wake of the growing involvement of a firm in international business. But at the same time, there is no unanimity on the issue whether the personnel should be recruited from the home country, from the host country, or from a third country. Different firms adhere to different policies in this regard, depending upon whether they have an ethnocentric approach, polycentric approach, or geocentric approach.

The ethnocentric staffing policy means manning of senior management cadre for overseas operations by home country individuals. The basic purpose of adhering to this policy is that the managers are fully aware of the company's policies and programmes and they can implement these policies and programmes more efficiently. Japanese managers have proved successful in implementing their home country policy. This is perhaps the reason for two-thirds of Japanese foreign subsidiaries having Japanese presidents (Reitman and Schuman, 1996). But, on the other hand, home country managers often find it difficult to assimilate with the local environment, with the result that this system entails upon efficiency.

The **ethnocentric staffing policy** means manning of senior management cadre for overseas operations by home country individuals.

Polycentric staffing policy is just the reverse of ethnocentric policy, meaning that overseas operations are managed by host country individuals. A US based express delivery company, FedEx employs less than one-half of one per cent home country personnel in overseas operations. Their rationale is that local managers are aware of local problems and so they can handle the problems more efficiently. However, the question is how loyal are locals towards the parent company.

Polycentric staffing policy means that overseas operations are managed by host country individuals.

In a geocentric staffing policy, senior managers are recruited irrespective of their nationality; from the home country, host country, or from a third country. Gillette, J P Morgan, and many others follow a geocentric policy. The merit of this policy is that the company can avail the services of best-proven managers from wherever they are recruited.

In a **geocentric staffing policy**, senior managers are recruited irrespective of their nationality; from the home country, host country, or from a third country.

In practice, the different staffing policies boil down to the issue of whether senior managers working in foreign subsidiaries should be locals coming from the host country itself or if they should be expatriates representing either home country or any third country. Readers should note that expatriates are persons moving from one country to the other for jobs. So a home country official or an official from a third country, working in a foreign subsidiary of an MNC is known as an expatriate.

Expatriate is a person employed in a foreign country.

Expatriates versus Locals: The employment of expatriates is advocated on different grounds. First, it helps the parent unit to infuse new methods of management at the subsidiary level and to maintain a full grip over the overseas operation. Secondly, it is useful when qualified managers are not available in the host country. This happens more often when a developed country firm begins operation in a developing country where managerial and technical expertise is in acute shortage. Thirdly, it provides a firm with an opportunity to train the home-country officials for overseas operation, which in turn helps develop the integrative competence of the managers.

But, on the other hand, employment of expatriates has some limitations. First, the remuneration of expatriates is often large or much larger than the locals'. Secondly, it is often difficult for expatriates to adjust themselves to the local socio-cultural environment prevailing in the host country. Thirdly, the local employees resent their managers coming from a foreign country. Fourthly, the families of the expatriates resent any transfer. It is because the very way of living is quite different in a foreign country. The shopping habits, school system, unfamiliar business practices, and so on are quite different in different countries.

The employment of locals is found in international firms where the subsidiaries enjoy a certain level of autonomy. It is also found where the host-country government restricts the use of expatriates. The merit of this policy is that the human resource management cost is lower. Moreover, managers are well acquainted with the local environment. The host country managers acquaint themselves with the firm's overall strategy in due course of time as the company arranges for training programmes for global managers. However, a polycentric staffing policy is not suitable for firms that emphasise on uniform global image.

Home-country managers move to subsidiaries when:

1. Technology secrecy is to be maintained.
2. Parent's investment in equity is large.
3. It is early phase of the product cycle.
4. Host-country environment is not widely different.

Factor Influencing Staffing Policy: A particular type of policy is adopted, depending upon the very strategy of the firm going international, the modes of operation, the stage of the product cycle, and on the extent of disparity between the home country environment and the host country environment. If the very existence of a firm rests on the firm specific advantage it possesses, it will like to maintain secrecy of its superior technology or superior product in order to preserve its superiority in the market. In such cases, it will employ home-country managers in the key posts. If, on the other hand, reaping of locational advantage lies behind internationalisation, the firm will not mind employing locals at the top managerial positions.

If the mode of operation overseas is the branch form of organisation or a wholly-owned subsidiary, normally expatriates are employed. But if foreign collaboration represents a sizeable share of the host country investors in the equity, there are often locals occupying top managerial positions.

Sometimes, the issue of expatriates versus locals depends upon the stage of the product cycle. Franko (1973) finds that during the initial stages of foreign operations, the proportion of expatriates is often large.

This is with a view to accomplishing successful technology transfers. But with growing assimilation of technical and managerial knowledge by the local managers during the subsequent phases of the product cycle, the proportion of expatriates drops. But again, the proportion of the expatriates increases when operations in the host country gradually become an integral part of the global operational framework.

Last but not least, if the disparity between the home country and the host country environment is very wide, expatriates find it very difficult to function. In such a situation, locals have to be employed in managerial posts even if the firm does not favour this.

There are many empirical studies to show the adoption of different staffing policies by the international firms. We mention here a couple of them. Kujawa (1986) found extensive use of Japanese expatriates among Japanese firms operating in the United States of America. The purpose was to implement and monitor the home country management practices. In another study by Tung and Miller (1990), it is found that the European and Japanese multinationals use more of the expatriates than the US firms do. Again, Tung (1982) has found that around three-fourths of US MNCs have experienced expatriate failure rates of 10 per cent or more. The reasons were manifold, such as the inability of managers to adjust into a new environment and to cope with large overseas responsibilities, inability of the spouse to adjust to a new location, and so on.

18.2.2 Culture Shock, Reverse Culture Shock, and Compensation

The difficulty in adjusting to a foreign country by managers often leads to "culture shock", which means that the expatriates feel uncomfortable in a foreign country environment that changes their psychological orientation and makes them irritable, home sick, and low performing. In other words, culture shock has an adverse impact on the managers' capability and performance. Again in cases where expatriates are able to adapt themselves to the local environment in the host country and find themselves unsuitable for the home country environment after working abroad for some time, they prefer to stay abroad. If the company compels them to return home, they suffer from "reverse culture shock". In such cases, they leave the company and join another company because of difficulty in blending back with the home country culture. Adler (1990) finds in his study that around one-fifth of employees coming back to their home country after foreign assignments leave their job and join some other firms.

> **Culture shock** refers to problems faced while working in a foreign country.
>
> **Reverse culture shock** refers to problems faced at home after returning from a foreign country job.

In order to manage the culture and reverse culture shock, international firms provide different types of compensations. The compensation is a premium over and above the basic salary. In case of a foreign assignment, the compensation helps maintain the real income of the expatriates at least equal to that in the home country. Sometimes compensation helps raise the overseas real income more than the home-country real income

Salary of the Expatriate =

Basic salary at par with the home country level	+	Allowances for higher cost of living index in the host country	+	Compensation to meet loss on account of exchange rate changes	+	Compensation to cover the higher tax rate in the host country	+	Non-pecuriary benefits, such as medical and schooling facilities for children

FIGURE 18.1 Compensation Related to Culture Shock

so as to provide a sort of incentive for taking up a foreign assignment. On the contrary, in case of the managers' re-entry into the home country, the compensation helps maintain the same status or perks that the manager was enjoying abroad.

Compensation related to Culture Shock: The compensation that encourages a manager to go on a foreign assignment falls into two categories:

1. allowances related to the basic salary
2. non-salary-related allowances

As far as the salary related allowances are concerned, some amount is added to the basic salary. This additional amount is determined on the basis of a higher cost of living index abroad, changes in the exchange rate between the host country currency and the home country currency, higher tax rate in the host country, and so on (Figure 18.1). The added cost of living arises not only from geographic relocation and the higher price index in the host country, but also from changed lifestyle. There is every possibility that housing, education facilities, medical facilities, recreation, security, and other such facilities may be very costly in the host country. Suppose the cost of living in the United States of America is double that in India. If an Indian manager gets Rs. 20,000 in India and his disposable income is Rs. 15,000, his salary in the United States will be fixed as:

$$\text{Rs. } 15{,}000 \times 2 = \text{Rs. } 30{,}000.$$

Tung and Miller (1990) find that the cost of expatriates is often two-to-three-fold higher than their base salary level.

Again, if the Indian rupee is going to depreciate vis-á-vis US dollar by 5.0 per cent, the salary to be paid to the Indian expatriate in the United States of America will be:

$$\text{Rs. } 30{,}000 \times 1.05 = \text{Rs. } 31{,}500.$$

It is because, if adjustments for exchange rate changes are not made, the salary of the manager will be lower and effect his decision to serve in a foreign country.

The salary needs also to be adjusted for taxes in the host country. It does not matter if the tax rates in the host country are lower than in the home country of the expatriate. But if it is higher, it needs to be compensated. Fortunately, most of international firms have tax equalisation plans where the firm pays the tax differential.

Last but not least, there are certain locations where the environment is highly unfriendly, for example, climate is greatly adverse, facilities for children's education do not exist, and housing facilities and the facilities for shopping and recreation are utterly lacking. In such cases, adaptation to the local environment is extremely difficult. In such cases, the company provides hardship allowances that are added to the salary.

Besides salary related allowances, there are non-salary-related allowances. For example, if there is no public school for children, the company provides for expensive private schooling. In many cases, the firm bears the expenses of the children's schooling in a foreign country. Similarly, if there is no proper medical care for serious ailments, managers can avail of the facilities for treatment in a foreign country. If suitable accommodation is not available, managers stay in hotels for which the entire cost is borne by the company. These are some examples of non-salary-related allowances.

Compensation for Reverse Culture Shock: In this case, the compensation is often non-pecuniary. Some companies provide each manager returning home from overseas assignment with a letter promising a job at least on par in terms of responsibility. Harvey (1981) suggests that managers to be sent on foreign assignment must be told in advance when they have to come back home. Moreover, while they are on foreign assignments, they must be in constant touch with the developments at the headquarters and their future career path in the firm. Finally, when they come back home, they need to undergo intensive organisational reorientation and counselling. It is better if the entire family gets counselling. All this means that the compensation for reverse culture shock includes the benefit of status; psychological input, leading to readiness to serve at home; and some other non-pecuniary benefits for the family.

Compensation for reverse culture shock includes the benefit of status; psychological input, leading to readiness to serve at home; and some other non-pecuniary benefits for the family.

18.3 THE PROCESS OF RECRUITMENT AND TRAINING

18.3.1 Estimation of Human Resource Requirements

Irrespective of the staffing policy followed by the firm, it is of utmost necessity to recruit persons for overseas operations. However, prior to recruitment, it is essential to estimate the manpower requirements at different levels. The requirements depend upon many factors. If the international business is at its earlier stages and is restricted to trade only, only few persons need to be recruited. But if the firm sets up an operational unit abroad, a larger number of persons will have to be recruited. Similarly, if the operation abroad is concerned with marketing, it can be manned by a few persons. On the contrary, in a manufacturing operation, a large number of persons will be required. But, if the manufacturing process involves a good amount of subcontracting, recruitment of personnel will be only limited. Thus, keeping in view of all these factors, the firm estimates how many persons need to be recruited at different levels.

18.3.2 Sources of Recruitment

After the human resource requirements for the overseas operation are estimated, it is necessary to determine whether these vacancies need to be filled up through transfer of the existing manpower; or alternatively, fresh recruitment is required. The existing manpower is normally not in a surplus position, with the result that the transfer is only minimal. The vacancy is filled up through fresh recruitment.

Business management colleges are an important source of human resources. Reputed colleges of the host country are listed and companies recruit from among recent college graduates. If a company pursues an ethnocentric policy, managers are selected from home country colleges. But, in such cases, preference is given to graduates who do not belong to the home country, but come there for education from countries where the company has to operate. It is because these graduates are well versed in both the home country and the host country culture.

This does not mean that colleges are the only source of manpower. Recruitment can be made from the general market. In such cases, these persons selected are normally working in some other firm. They take up the new assignment lured by higher remuneration. The recruiting officer prefers them because they possess the necessary work experience and do not have to be trained from the scratch.

However, as far as the recruitment of the non-managerial workers is concerned, they are taken from the host country market. This is because they are available in ample number. Moreover, in order to promote employment, the host country government imposes restrictions on the employment of expatriates especially at this level. In cases, where manpower is in short supply, non-managerial jobs are taken up by expatriates. For example, in Kuwait such jobs have been taken up mostly by workers coming from Egypt, India, Lebanon, and Pakistan.

18.3.3 Process of Selection

Selection means choosing the best performers out of the available supply of manpower. Selection, or the process of screening, is essential for finding suitable managers. Thus, all persons duly qualified are not necessarily suitable for an international job or for a particular job in an international company. The suitability of a person assigned for a particular job is very significant for achieving efficiency. This aspect is no doubt relevant while selecting host country personnel, but is far more relevant while selecting a person for overseas assignment. Heller (1980) points out a few specific qualities that are taken into account while selecting managers, especially for an overseas assignment. They are: flexible personality, attitudinal values of cultural empathy, friendliness, patience and prudence, excellent educational and professional credentials, and so on. The Tung study (1981) revealed that the criteria vary widely among different levels of management positions; nevertheless the more important are managerial talent, maturity and emotional stability, adaptability in a new environment, initiative and technical knowledge, and so on. At present, it is increasingly believed that it is basically the personal traits that make an international manager more successful. According to Czinkota, *et al* (1999), these traits incorporate:

1. Competence
2. Adaptability
3. Personal characteristics

Competence means, among other things, technical and managerial competence and area expertise. Technical and managerial competence means the manager's ability to perform the job and successfully dealing with the employees. Area expertise means full knowledge of the local conditions. To be more precise, the person should be aware of the political and legal systems, economic and socio-cultural environment, and so on in the host country. Of all these, knowledge of local language is very important as it is the most significant medium of communication.

Competence means technical and managerial competence and area expertise.

Adaptability means that managers must possess flexibility and a positive attitude towards change. They should be able to mould themselves according to the circumstances prevalent in the country where they are posted. On the basis of experience, it has been found that with growing age, there is more rigidity rather than flexibility in attitude. Thus, younger managers are often preferred from this point of view. Again, adaptability depends upon the family situation of the manager. It is because the entire family accompanying the manager on a foreign assignment has to face a new environment that is often not very congenial. Czinkota, *et al* (1999) gives an example of how US managers were replaced in Italy when their family members were not ready to cope with the Italian environment. So whenever the managers are selected, the firm looks into the family cohesiveness. It checks the marital status of the person to be selected and also the behaviour of the children. Sometimes, when the spouse of a manager is employed at home, she or he does not like to leave the job in favour of the foreign assignment. In such cases, the firm also interviews the spouses and tries to provide them employment.

Adaptability means that managers must possess flexibility and a positive attitude towards change.

As far as personal characteristics are concerned, the selection process should consider the health, age, religion, race, and so on of the person to be selected. Aged persons or persons with some ailment are normally not fit for a foreign assignment. Similarly, religion and race often come in the way. For example, the managers of Arab origin are not liked in Israel and managers of Israeli origin are not liked in Arab countries.

Personal characteristics consider health, age, religion, race, and so on of the person.

18.3.4 Training

It is a fact that a firm takes maximum care while selecting a person for a foreign assignment. Yet there is possibility for deviations from an optimal selection. The persons selected may not be completely fit for serving overseas. So, to make them suitable, the firm provides training programmes or orientation programmes. These programmes differ among firms with respect to their content and the involvement of trainees, yet their basic objectives of fostering flexibility or adaptability among the managers is the same. The programmes provide specific area studies and prepare managers to respond to different situations arising in a particular geographic area. To be specific, the training programme concentrates on cultural training, language training, and practical training (Dowling and Schuler, 1990). Cultural training acquaints the manager regarding the host country culture, which adds to his ability to deal with the persons there. Sometimes managers are sent to the host country on a familiarisation trip prior to the final posting.

Training programme concentrates on cultural training, language training, and practical training.

Despite the fact that English is a language of international business, managers are taught about the language of the host country. Lastly, practical training provides the management ease in day-to-day activities in the host country.

It is not that all the international firms maintain international career-orientation programmes; but many of them do. Tung (1981) is firm on the view that rigorously designed orientation programme is an important factor behind expatriates' success.

Reasons for Public Support for Having Foreign Trainees Learn the Local Language (Japanese)

Professor H. Shimada argues that "the Japanese Government—in other words the taxpayers—should foot the bill for the language education of foreign workers, as part of the nation's educational ODA, for several reasons. First, there is the humane reason that the ability to speak Japanese will make living and working in Japan safer and more pleasant for foreign workers. Second, it will be of economic benefit, by helping to increase their work capacity and efficiency. Third, there is a public merit in that acquiring the ability to speak Japanese can be considered an investment in public goods. Clearly Japanese language ability does have the character of private goods, in being of benefit to both the individual trainees and their employers. But, in contrast to visiting foreign students, whose chief objective in coming to Japan is study and research, foreign workers come mainly to work, and therefore lack the freedom, ability, or inclination to master Japanese on their own time and at their own expense. Again, there is very little economic incentive for employers to help trainees acquire more than the most basic working knowledge of the language. But if the government, through foreign aid, were to support an overall improvement in the ability of foreign workers to speak Japanese, this would bring significant social benefits by increasing the effectiveness and improving the results of the Work-and-Learn Programme. Hence, any investment in improving foreign workers' standard of Japanese could be seen as a public investment. Finally, an overall improvement in the ability of foreign workers to speak the language would have significant social and economic utility in the sense of raising the profile and usefulness of Japanese in international business and in workplaces."

Source: *World Labour Report*, 1997.

18.4 MANAGEMENT OF INDUSTRIAL RELATIONS

18.4.1 Relevance of Industrial Relations Issue

Industrial relations are concerned with collective employee-employer relationships. Such relationships vary from one country to the other or from one industry to the other. It means industrial relations are a location-specific issue. There is one view that being location-specific, the industrial relations issue is not very relevant to multinational corporations as their operation is not limited to any particular location. But this is not true. Multinational corporations view industrial relations with a lot of interest as amicable relationships between employees and the employer leads to rise in productivity and cost reduction. It is a fact that the formation of trade unions strengthens the bargaining power of the employees, aims more at upward revision in wages, and betters working and living conditions for the employees. But since the employees participate in the management, they strive hard to promote the interest of the firm as a whole. This is why even ethnocentric firms do have a global industrial relations policy. However, multinational corporations allow their subsidiary considerable autonomy in managing industrial relations insofar as the subsidiaries are more capable of solving the local problems. Many international firms maintain industrial relations staff at the parent unit or sometimes at the subsidiary. It is an advisory body taking care of industrial relations. Sometimes the body negotiates with the host country unions on work rules even before setting up operations there. For instance, when Nissan had decided to make an investment in Northern England, it got a commitment from the unions there to agree to a change in work norms. It also participated in the selection of personnel. In the event of strike or lock-out, it provides necessary advice regarding the firm-level production, logistics, finance, and marketing. At the subsidiary level, the industrial relations staff monitors various aspects of industrial relations and participates in bargaining with the employees' union.

18.4.2 Employees' Participation in Management

Self-management is where all the major issues are decided by the workers' representatives. Co-determination process is where employees' representatives are appointed on supervisory boards. Work council is that consists entirely of workers or of both managers and workers.

Whenever one talks about industrial relations in a multinational firm, a couple of questions appear. One is whether the participation of the employees in the management helps improve the firm's overall performance. The other is whether trade unions have a significant impact on collective bargaining. As regards workers' participation in management, various techniques have evolved. One is self-management, which is supposed to be the highest level of participation strategy. All the major issues are decided by the workers' representatives. And so, the policies are definitely pro-employees.

The other is the co-determination process where employees' representatives are appointed on supervisory boards. With this process, management problems are more effectively communicated to the workers, to the satisfaction of the latter. The co-determination process is practised in Germany and many other countries.

Yet another method is the creation of a work council that consist entirely of workers or of both managers and workers. The council participates in all decisions concerning the workers. These councils are found in Britain and some other countries.

What is important to note is that the participation of workers in management helps generate a feeling of satisfaction among the workers. They feel themselves as a part of the organisation, which motivates them to work more sincerely for the firm. They are able to monitor their own interest as a result of which the quality of work life improves significantly. They feel responsible for any action taken. In a Honda unit in Ohio, USA, workers react favourably to the responsibilities they were assigned. They inspected their own workers and instructed the fellow workers to perform better (Rice, 1985). This is not all. The process of workers' participation helps generate a team spirit. The team spirit is bound to improve the performance of the firm.

18.4.3 Role of Trade Unions

It is true that workers' participation in management is conducive to a firm's overall performance. But the impact of the trade unions on collective bargaining or the industrial relations in a multinational firm depends upon the structure of the trade union as well as on the extent of manoeuvrability by these firms. The structure of trade unions varies from one country to the other. Some trade unions are company based, while the others are industry based. Still the others encompass many companies and many industries. The single company based union normally has lesser influence on industrial relations than multi-company or multi-industry unions have. In Japan, trade unions are single company based; and as a result, there is seldom any strike. If at all there is a strike, workers do not stop working; they simply wear arm bands to show their displeasure. On the other hand, trade unions in the United States of America are generally industry based. They have a greater influence on the industrial relations. In Germany, the employers form an association and then negotiate with the trade unions. In this way the bargaining strength of the employers matches the bargaining strength of the trade unions.

However, the trade unions are often not very effective in a multinational firm in view of the greater manoeuvrability of such firms. Even if the trade union goes on strike, its impact on the output is not large. This is because other units of the firm make up the loss of the output. Moreover, since the output in a particular country represents only a small fraction of the total output of the firm, a strike in that particular host country does not have a sizeable impact on the firm's total output. Naturally, an international firm can hold out against a strike for a longer period than a domestic firm can.

But this argument holds good if the same product is manufactured in all units. Again, if the strike affected unit is producing essential spares to be supplied to other units, the supply will be affected and the impact of the strike will permeate to other units too.

It is also argued that an international firm can shift the location of the production to any other country if it faces labour trouble in a particular country. The impact of the strike will be minimal. But in such cases, the firm may not capitalise the benefits of the least cost location, especially when the location is shifted not necessarily to a cost effective country. It may, in turn, effect upon the firm's competitiveness.

Last but not least, top officials in a multinational firm are often posted at the headquarters. Because of larger geographic distance, workers find it difficult to convey their demands directly to the chief of the firm. Some of the demands are no doubt met by the chief of the subsidiary. But there are some demands that can be met only by the parent company and in those cases, trade unions are not very effective. It is a fact that subsidiaries have the autonomy for settling industrial disputes, but they too have some limitations in this regard. Nevertheless, if trade unions spread across the country maintain relations with trade unions in other countries, their impact on the industrial relations may be large.

SUMMARY

- Human resource management in an international firm is highly complex in view of the different labour-mix in different countries, varying objectives of the employees, and more importantly, of the communication problem.
- The staffing policy may be ethnocentric, polycentric, or geocentric. The employment of expatriates may be advantageous in some respects but at the same time, it may not be effective in others. In specific cases, the employment of locals, is more suitable. Infact, there are different factors influencing the staffing policy.
- Expatriates face problems in adjusting themselves to the local environment in host countries, and suffer from cultural shock. But when they come back home after staying abroad for some time, they do not find themselves comfortable at home. This is a reverse cultural shock. A firm provides compensation—pecuniary and non-pecuniary—to do away with these shocks.
- Irrespective of the staffing policy, a firm, first of all, estimates the human resource requirements at different levels of operation, recruits persons from different backgrounds based on competence, adaptability, and personal characteristics; and finally, provides them training.
- Again, the industrial relations scenario differs from country to country. Workers' participation in management in any form is pro-employee. However, it is normally found that trade unions are not very effective in international firms.

Review Questions

1. "Human resource management is highly complex in an international firm". Explain.
2. What are the merits and demerits of employing expatriates? What are the factors influencing the employment of the expatriates?
3. What do you mean by culture shock and reverse culture shock? How are they dealt with?
4. Name different sources of recruitment. Explain the process of selection and training.
5. Do you feel that the issue of industrial relations is relevant to an international firm?

Objective Type Questions

1. Mark True or False:
   (a) Trade unions are effective in MNCs.
   (b) International firms organise international career orientation programmes.
   (c) MNC managers should not only be competent, but also be adaptable to different conditions.
   (d) Local people are often preferred for non-managerial posts.
   (e) Organisational reorientation and counselling are not necessarily required to overcome reverse culture shock.
   (f) Expatriates get the same salary that they get at home.
   (g) Senior managers in a subsidiary normally have broader duties than those in a domestic firm.
   (h) Culture shock means an uncomfortable feeling by expatriates when they come back home after a foreign assignment.
   (i) Language is never a major problem in international human resource management.
2. Choose the Most Suitable Answer.
   (a) Global human resource management is complex because:
      (i) Different countries have different labour mixes
      (ii) Communication problems comes in the way
      (iii) Both of the above
   (b) The expatriates in a host country:
      (i) Come from the local population
      (ii) Come from home country
      (iii) Come from home country or a third country
   (c) Culture shock occurs when:
      (i) Expatriates feel uncomfortable on a foreign assignment
      (ii) Expatriates feel uncomfortable after coming back home from a foreign assignment
      (iii) None of the above
   (d) Reverse culture shock means:
      (i) Expatriates feel uncomfortable on a foreign assignment
      (ii) Expatriates feel uncomfortable after coming back home from a foreign assignment
      (iii) None of the above

(e) Compensation related to culture shock includes:
   (i) Only allowances related to basic salary
   (ii) Non-salary related allowances only
   (iii) Both of the above

(f) Compensation related to reverse culture shock is:
   (i) Often pecuniary
   (ii) Often not pecuniary
   (iii) None of the above

(g) Selection of managers depends upon:
   (i) Competence only
   (ii) Personal characteristics only
   (iii) Both of the above

CASE STUDY

International Industrial Relations of Chinese Multinational Corporations

In view of cultural diversity and geographical dispersion between home country and the host country, it is normally crucial for a multinational corporation (MNC) to adopt a right type of international industrial relations (IIR) policy. In cases where the MNC dominates, it is the home country policy that finds a way into the host country subsidiaries. In the opposite case, the MNC adapts its IRR policy to local conditions in the host country. Both of these options are found on a wide scale. The US firms in Germany are found adapting to German norms. On the other hand, Wall Mart refused to adopt the Chinese norms and threatened to dismantle its operations in China. However, in many cases, an integrative approach is adopted by the MNCs. This approach combines both the home country and host country norms in varying proportions.

The liberal policy regimes in China led to the emergence of a number of MNCs. As per the available figures, by the end of 2003, Chinese firms had established more than 7,470 non-financial enterprises in over 160 countries and made an investment over $33.2 billion. It is true that till 2001, as it was evident from the interviews of the senior officials of the Chinese MNCs, there were no major IIR-related troubles in their overseas subsidiaries, and as a result, there was no formal policy either at corporate or at subsidiary levels concerning unionism, collective bargaining, labour standards and labour dispute resolution. But by 2006, as evident from the second round of interview, the employees at the host country locations were difficult to deal with. Naturally, the IIR became crucial. There is news that one steel company and one mineral-related company of Chinese origin had to abandon the Indian operation in so far as the Indian unions organised strikes quite frequently. The HR managers from these two companies experienced great difficulties in settling these disputes. The executive managers in BankCo and PlantCo were in trouble on account of labour disputes and had to review their choices of host nations and be more careful when dealing with labour issues in the future.

Again, the 2001 interviews revealed that the HR managers at the parent office had allowed subsidiary managers substantial autonomy to manage IIR. But the 2006 interviews revealed that there had been a move towards centralisation of decision making on IIR. All the respondents except Instrument Trade Co, Ocean Shipping Co and Plant Co had instructed subsidiaries to report any new development in dealing with local unions, particularly with collective labour contracts. The managers at the parent office of five firms—Bank Co, Minmetals Co, Steel Co, Electronics Co1 and Electronics Co2—were directly involved in negotiations with host unions over wages and labour dispute resolution.

Yet again, none of the managers in the 2001 interviews were opposed to unionism in their overseas subsidiaries because the local firms did do the same as they were doing. Unionisation rates were generally high in the case of Chinese MNCs' overseas subsidiaries: 185 out of 293 subsidiaries (63 per cent) were unionised in September 2001. But in 2006, the HR managers saw host country unions as troublemakers. Unionisation rates dropped from 63 per cent to 59 per cent between 2001 and 2005, during which 33 new subsidiaries had been established, 12 in manufacturing, of which nine had recognised trade unions. While the parent country nationals working overseas joined the Chinese workers' congresses, the host-country nationals were found joining the local unions. By June 2006, ElectronicsCo1, BankCo, MinmetalsCo, ElectronicsCo2, SteelCo and PlantCo had all signed collective contracts on wages in their overseas manufactories. The contracts in resource-based MinmetalsCo and SteelCo were mainly between the sub-contractors and trade unions, and modified twice during 2004 and 2006. The collective contract in SteelCo's South American copper refinery was modified for the third time by increasing wages. It is true that successful collective bargaining improved industrial relations in the subsidiaries, but a failure to reach collective agreements often became a cause of labour disputes.

Thus, the IIR policy of the Chinese MNCs took a major shift during mid-2000s. However, on the whole, it is found that the Chinese MNCs have come to follow an integrative approach. The attitude of the top-level managers toward the activities of the host-country unions is greatly influenced by the home IR system meaning that they are not against unionism, but, at the same time, they do not like to involve host-country unions in settling labour terms in their overseas subsidiaries. The collective bargaining and labour dispute settlement are, of course, mainly host-based—influenced primarily by the observation of local practices, compliance with host IR legislation, labour traditions and political compromise with the host authorities. While the growing incidence of labour disputes is commensurate with the rapid expansion of the Chinese MNCs, it is also influenced by the local IR policies. The Chinese MNCs tend to localise employment conditions, particularly wages, working conditions and labour disputes settlement. The process has, of course, led to higher wages and better working conditions in developed countries but lower labour standards in the developing economies. Such an IIR approach had caused problems in South America and Africa, where better wages and working conditions are expected from the MNCs.

One of the views suggests that aligning with the local IR norms among the Chinese MNCs is mainly because of the fact that these MNCs are found to rely greatly on the host markets and also they are not very efficient in the transfer knowledge and technology to host enterprises.

Source: Based on 1. Shen, J., *et al* (2005): "Developing an integrative HRM model: The contribution of Chinese MNEs", *Asia Pacific Business Review*, 11(3), 365–84.
2. Shen, J. (2006) "Analysis of changing industrial relations in China", *The International Journal of Comparative Labor Law and Industrial Relations*, 26(3), 347–68.
3. Shen, J. and R. Darby (2006) "International training and management development in Chinese multinational enterprises", *Employee Relations*, 28(4), 342–62.

QUESTIONS

1. Comment on the IIR policy of the Chinese MNCs prior to 2001.
2. Do you find any change in the IIR policy of the Chinese MNCs during 2002–2006?
3. How do you characterise the present IIR policy of the Chinese MNCs?

REFERENCES

Books

Adler, N. J. (1990), *International Dimensions of Organisational Behaviour* (Boston: PWS-Kent).

Czinkota, M. R. *et al* (1999), *International Business*, New York: Harcourt Brace.

Dowling, P. J. and R. S. Schuler (1990), *International Dimensions of Human Resource Management* (Boston: PSW-Kent).

Kujawa, D. (1986), *Japanese Multinationals in the United States: Case Studies* (New York: Praeger).

Journals

Franko, L. G. (1973), "Who Manages Multinational Enterprise?", *Columbia Journal of World Business*, VIII (Summer), 30ff.

Harvey, M. G. (1981), "The Other Side of Foreign Assignments: Dealing with the Repatriation Dilemma", *Columbia Journal of World Business*, XVI (Summer), 79–85.

Heller, J. F. (1980), "Criteria for Selecting an International Manager', *Personnel Management* (May–June), 18–22.

Reitman, V. and M. Schuman (1996), "Men's Club: Japanese and Korean Companies Rarely Look Outside for People to Run their Overseas Operations", *Wall Street Journal*, Sept. 26, p.17.

Rice, F. (1985), "America's New No. 4 Automaker—Honda", *Fortune*, Oct. 28, 26–29.

Tung, R. L. (1982), "Selection and Training Procedures of US, European and Japanese Multinationals", California Management Review, XXV (1), 57–71.

Tung, R. I. (1981), "Selection and Training of Personnel for Overseas Assignments", *Columbia Journal of World Business*, XVI (Spring), 68–78.

_______ and E. I. Miller (1990), "Managing in the Twenty-first Century: The Need for Global Orientation", *Management International Review*, XXX (1), 5–18.

SELECT FURTHER READINGS

Dowling, P. J. and R. S. Schuler (1990), *International Dimensions of Human Resource Development* (Boston: PWS-Kent).

Hays, R. D. (1974), "Expatriate Selection: Insuring Success and Avoiding Failure", *Journal of International Business Studies*, V (Summer), 25–37.

Mendenhall, M. and G. Oddou (1991), *International Human Resource Management*, (Boston: PWS-Kent).

* The Organization of the Petroleum Exporting Countries (OPEC) is a permanent intergovernmental organisation of 12 oil-exporting developing nations that coordinates and unifies the petroleum policies of its member countries. These countries are Algeria, Angola, Iran, Iraq, Ecuador, Kuwait, Libya, Nigeria, Qatar, Saudi Arabia, United Arab Emirates and Venezuela. The mission of OPEC is to coordinate and unify the petroleum policies of its member countries, and ensures the stabilisation of oil markets in order to secure an efficient, economic and regular supply of petroleum to consumers, a steady income to producers and a fair return on capital for those investing in the petroleum industry.

Rome, Italy*

19

International Investment and Financing Strategy

CHAPTER OBJECTIVES

Financial strategy is yet another significant aspect of an MNC. It incorporates a number of issues that are discussed in the present chapter. The objectives are to:

- ✦ Discuss the process of international capital budgeting, which primarily includes the calculation of cash flows and the cost of capital.
- ✦ Show how a particular source/form of fund is selected.
- ✦ Acquaint readers with the nature of financial swap, especially the interest-rate swap and currency swap.
- ✦ Analyse international cash management, which includes the assessment of cash requirements, optimisation of cash needs, and the investment of surplus cash.

Financial strategy in international business begins from the very investment decision. This is because investment is believed to be fruitful only when it represents a net cash inflow into the firm. The technique of evaluation, known as international capital budgeting, is an essential aspect of financial strategy.

When an investment decision is made, the sources of the funds should be determined. Selection of the sources or the types of funds is important. If the desired type of funds is not available, the firm often opts for a swap. Thus, the swap is a meaningful strategy in the context of raising of funds.

Besides, maintenance of sufficient liquidity among the different units of a firm, without impairing profitability, is no less significant and so international cash management is yet another important aspect in this respect. The present chapter deals with all these aspects of the financial strategy.

19.1 INTERNATIONAL CAPITAL BUDGETING

> Net present value (NPV) is present value of future cash flow minus initial investment.
>
> Internal rate of return (IRR) is the discount rate equating future cash flow with initial investment.
>
> Profitability ratio is present value of future cash flow divided by initial investment.
>
> Salvage value refers to sale proceeds of assets at the end of the life of the project.

There are different methods of capital budgeting, such as accounting rate of return, pay back period, net present value, internal rate of return, profitability ratio, and so on. The purpose of these techniques is to find out whether the cash inflow is greater than the cash outflow. Some of the techniques are discounting techniques where future cash flows are discounted to the present value and then they are compared with the initial investment. Nevertheless, the discounting and non-discounting techniques apply to both, domestic capital budgeting and international capital budgeting. Books on corporate financial management would contain a more elaborate discussion regarding the evaluation criteria, which is beyond the scope of this book.

19.1.1 Computation of the Cash Flow

Any investment for a new project demands a part of the firm's current wealth, but, in return, it brings in funds and adds to the firm's stock of wealth in the future. The former results in cash outflow from the firm, while the latter is represented by cash inflows into the firm. Cash outflow occurs on account of capital expenditure; other expenses, excluding depreciation; and the payment of tax. Cash inflow includes revenue on account of additional sale or cash from eventually selling off an asset, which is known as salvage value. Thus, cash flows are grouped under three heads. One is the initial investment during the period, t_0; the other is the operating cash flow during the period, t_1 to t_n; and yet another is the terminal cash flow or the salvage value that emerges at the end of the period, t_n.

Complexities in Cash Flow Computation: The computation of cash flow is complex in international firms. At the very onset of multinational capital budgeting, a decision needs to be taken regarding whether the cash flow should be computed from the viewpoint of the parent company or from the viewpoint of the subsidiary. This is because the cash flow accruing to the subsidiary may not be represented entirely by the cash flow accruing to the parent company. In some cases the cash outflow of the subsidiary is treated as the cash inflow of the parent company. It is also possible that the cash inflow accruing to the subsidiary may be large enough to justify the investment proposal, but its size accruing to the parent company may be too small to justify the investment proposal. In such cases, it seems difficult to take a decision regarding acceptance or rejection of the investment proposal.

Infact, there may be many situations when disparity in the cash flow between the parent and its subsidiary arises.

1. If the tax rates in the home country and the host country are different, disparity will arise in the cash flow. It is possible that on account of lower tax rates in the host country, after tax cash inflow is large enough to justify the investment proposal. On the other hand, owing to high tax rates in the home country, the investment proposal may not be feasible from the viewpoint of the parent company.
2. The parent company may not accept the investment proposal due to low inflow of cash on account of exchange control applied by the host government, despite the fact that the cash flow of the project in question is sufficient for implementation.
3. When the parent company charges an exorbitant price for technology and management, the cash inflow accruing to the parent company will be larger, justifying the investment proposal. But such exorbitant payments may lower the cash flow of the subsidiary and the subsidiary may not like the investment proposal.
4. Changes in the exchange rate may change the cash flow of the parent company. When the currency of the host country appreciates, the parent company gets a larger flow of cash in terms of its own currency. This may change its accept-reject decision.

However, the ethics of the corporate financial management is very clear on this issue; that is, the value of the project is determined by the net present value of the future cash flows available to the investor. Since the parent company is the investor, it is the cash flow of the parent company that is primarily taken into account in the context of international capital budgeting. This is why cash flowing from the subsidiary to the parent company, either in the form of royalty and technical service fees or in any other mode, is treated as cash inflow. On the contrary, any flow of cash flowing from the parent company to the subsidiary is treated as cash outflow. The parent company will agree to invest in a foreign project only if the net present value of the cash flow is positive from its own point of view.

Parent's Perspective: The computation of cash flow in the context of international capital budgeting incorporates factors that influence the very size of the cash flow at different stages. These factors operating at different stages of cash flow need to be analysed here.

Initial Investment: If the entire project cost is met by the parent company, the entire amount of initial investment is treated as the cash outflow (Figure 19.1). In some cases, the project is partly financed by the subsidiary itself through local borrowing. But such borrowings of the subsidiary do not form a part of the initial cash outflow.

Again, in some cases, the subsidiary makes additional investment for expansion out of the retained earnings. At the first instance, there is apparently no flow of cash from the parent company to the subsidiary. But it should be treated as an opportunity cost insofar as in the absence of retention of earnings, these funds could have been remitted to the parent company rather than invested in the project in question. Thus, investment out of retained earnings should be treated as cash outflow from the parent's perspective.

Initial Investment = Fresh Investment Made by Parent + Use of Retained Earning, if any + Use of Blocked Funds, if any

FIGURE 19.1 Initial Investment

Blocked Funds: Profit of subsidiary not repatriated to parent due to exchange control.

Yet again, the issue of blocked funds is very pertinent in this respect. Sometimes the host government imposes exchange control and does not allow any cash to flow to the parent company. These funds are known as blocked funds. Thus, this part of the cash inflow of the subsidiary, which is represented by blocked funds, is not treated as cash inflow from the parent's perspective. Suppose the incremental cash inflow of the project is $20 million, out of which only $15 million is allowed to flow to the parent company by the host government. In this case, a sum of $15 million will be treated as the cash inflow. But if the blocked funds are invested in some new project, that amount is treated as an investment by the parent company and is recorded as a cash outflow.

Last but not least, if the host government provides subsidised initial establishment for the subsidiary, the gain on this account should not be included in the initial investment of the parent company.

Operating Cash Flow: The operating cash flow is computed on an after tax basis as well as on an incremental basis. It does not consider depreciation as it is a non-cash expense. Depreciation, however, helps arrive at the pre-tax profit. Financing cost is also not included despite the fact that capital has a cost. The reason is that such costs are considered elsewhere while determining the project's required rate of return.

As a normal practice, the revenue generated through the sale of subsidiary's product in the local market as well as in other countries is shown as the operating cash inflow from the parent's perspective. But it is subject to downward adjustment by the lost income on sales previously realised through the parent company's export to these markets. On the contrary, if the operation in the subsidiary leads to import of components and raw material from the parent company, the value of such imports will be added to the revenue.

The operating cash flow is influenced by some other factors too.

1. If the subsidiary pays royalty to the parent company, the operating cash inflow will rise. But if the parent company faces loss on account of lack of economies of scale, due to shifting of production to the host country, the operating revenue will come down.
2. The operating cash flow is influenced by **transfer pricing** when the parent company or any other unit of the firm charges

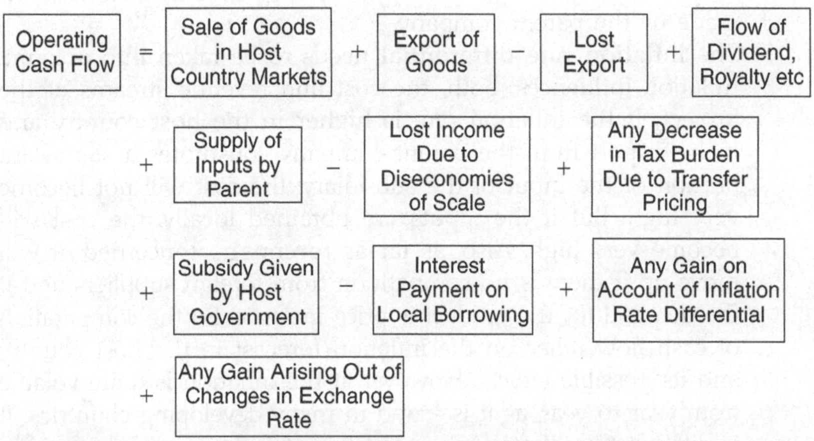

FIGURE 19.2 Factors that Influence Operating Cash Flow

arbitrary prices for intra-firm movement of intermediate goods (Figure 19.2). It may be noted here that transfer pricing is adopted either for better working capital management or for reducing the overall burden of taxes of the company through shifting of the before tax profit to a country with lower tax rates. If transfer pricing lowers the overall tax burden of the company and thereby increases the revenue of the parent company, the additional revenue or saving should be treated as cash inflow. However, it may be noted that such inflows are discounted at a higher rate because they involve greater risk.
3. If the host government offers **incentives**, they should be included in the capital budgeting decision. For example, if the host

government offers tax incentives or provides loans at subsidised rates, the amount of gain on this account should be added to the operating cash inflow.

4. When the subsidiary avails of **local borrowing** for meeting a part of the initial investment and pays interest on such borrowings, the amount of interest payment is deducted from the operating cash inflow. Had it been domestic capital budgeting, the interest payment on such borrowing would not have formed a part of cash flow insofar as financing cost is included in the discount rate. But in case of international capital budgeting, the cash remitted to the parent company will stand overstated if interest payments are not treated as cash outflows for the subsidiary. This is why it is very much necessary that the investment made by the subsidiary out of local borrowings is separated from the investment made by the parent. The present value of cash flow received by the parent company should take into consideration the interest paid by the subsidiary on the local borrowing and only then should it be compared with the initial investment made by the parent company.
5. The **inflation rate differential** needs to be taken into account. Inflation influences, both, the cost and revenue streams of the project. If the inflation rate is higher in the host country and if the import from the parent company constitutes a significant portion of the input of the subsidiary, the cost will not become very high. But if the inputs are obtained locally, the cost will become very high. Also, as far as revenue is concerned, it will move up if there is no competition from foreign suppliers and if the demand for the product is price inelastic. So the computation of cash flow relies on the inflation forecast in the host country and its possible effects. However, if the inflation is quite volatile from year to year, as it is found in many developing countries, it is difficult to make an accurate forecast.
6. **Exchange rate fluctuation** influences the size of the cash flow. It is a fact that changes in the exchange rate are tagged to changes in the rate of inflation. But there are other factors too that shape exchange rate fluctuations. It is difficult to predict the behaviour of all those factors. Nevertheless, the cash flow computation process incorporates different scenarios of exchange rate movements. From the parent company's point of view, appreciation in the currency of the host country will be favourable and will increase the size of the cash inflow in terms of the home country currency. A joint effect of inflation and exchange rate changes may produce a partial offsetting effect on the net cash flows of the subsidiary. But if the rate of inflation is expected to be lower in the future, appreciating the value of the host country's currency, the subsidiary may locally invest the amount of its payments to the parent company till the currency

strengthens. The accumulated earning of the parent company will be larger after the appreciation of the host country's currency.

Terminal Cash Flow: Besides adjustments in the initial investment and in the operating cash flow, some adjustments have to be made for the salvage value that influences the terminal cash flow.

1. If there is a provision in the foreign collaboration agreement for the reversion of the project to the host government after a certain period of time on the payment of a specific amount, the specific amount is treated as the terminal cash inflow.
2. If the first condition is not present, the net cash flow generated in the terminal year is multiplied by the specific number of years and the product is treated as the terminal cash inflow.
3. If the project is dismantled in the terminal year, the scrap value is treated as the terminal cash inflow.
4. When the salvage value is uncertain, the parent company makes various estimates of the salvage value or terminal cash flow and computes the NPV based on each possible outcome of the terminal cash flow. Alternatively, it computes the **break-even salvage value**, which is the terminal cash flow necessary to achieve a zero NPV for the project. The break-even salvage value or the break-even terminal cash flow is then compared with the estimated terminal cash flow. If the estimated terminal cash flow is less than the break-even salvage value, the investment proposal will be rejected. This is because in this case, the NPV will be negative. On the contrary, if the parent company assesses that the subsidiary would sell for more than the break-even salvage value, it will incorporate this assessment into its accept-reject decision.

For computing the break-even salvage value, the cash flow beginning from the first year to the *n* th year is segregated into the operating cash flow, OCF_t, and the terminal cash flow, TCF_n. The break-even salvage value is derived as follows:

$$NPV = \sum_{t=1}^{n}\left[\frac{OCF_t}{(1+k)^t}\right] + \left[\frac{TCF_n}{(1+k)^n}\right] - I_0$$

$$0 = \sum_{t=1}^{n}\left[\frac{OCF_t}{(1+k)^t}\right] + \left[\frac{TCF_n}{(1+k)^n}\right] - I_0$$

$$I_0 - \sum_{t=1}^{n}\left[\frac{OCF_t}{(1+k)^t}\right] = \frac{TCF_n}{(1+k)^n}$$

$$TCF_n = \left[I_0 - \sum_{t=1}^{n}\left\{\frac{OCF_t}{(1+k)^t}\right\}\right] \times (1+k)^n \qquad 19.1$$

Suppose the net cash inflow in a three-year period, which is the life span of the project, is respectively $10,000, $12,000 and $13,000. The initial investment is $20,000 and the discount rate is 10 per cent. The break-even salvage value will be:

$$\$\left[20{,}000-\left\{\frac{10{,}000}{1.10}+\frac{12{,}000}{1.10^2}-\frac{13{,}000}{1.10^3}\right\}\right]\times(1.10)^3=\$-11{,}680$$

Parent-Subsidiary Perspective: An Alternative Approach: The analysis of project appraisal so far takes into account the parent unit's perspective, of course, based on valid reasons. Even in this case, the parent unit takes into account the subsidiary's perspective, at least to some extent, and makes adjustment in the cash flow and the discount rate under the NPV framework. But it is often argued that for a more transparent appraisal of the investment project, the project appraisal needs to be made in greater detail—both from the parent's point of view and from the viewpoint of the subsidiary. It is for this reason that in a survey of 121 US MNCs operating in early 1980s, 48 per cent of the decisions were made on the basis of the project's cash flow, 36 per cent were taken on the basis of the parent's cash flow, and 16 per cent of the decisions considered both viewpoints (Stanley and Block, 1983).

The very rationale of this argument is that if a project's NPV is positive, it is bound to add to the corporate wealth of the firm as a whole. Under this approach, two NPV_S are computed. One is the NPV from the parent's perspective (NPV_P) and the other is the NPV from the viewpoint of the project itself, which is known as the subsidiary's perspective (NPV_S). Finally, the acceptance/rejection decision of the project is based on the NPV of both of them.

In order to find out the NPV_P, the following successive steps are taken:

1. Estimate the cash flow in the host country currency
2. Estimate the future spot exchange rate on the basis of available forward rates
3. Convert the host currency cash flow into the home country currency
4. Find NPV in home country currency using the home country discount rate

Here the cash inflow represents all cash flowing towards the parent unit in a manner similar to what has been explained earlier. Cash outflow will represent cash flowing out of the parent unit.

Similarly, to find out the NPV_S, the following steps are taken:

1. Estimate the cash flow in host country currency
2. Identify the host country discount rate
3. Discount the host currency cash flow at the host country discount rate
4. Convert the resultant NPV into the home country currency at the spot exchange rate

In this case, the cash inflow represents the earnings of the project in the host country currency irrespective of the fact whether cash moves towards, or away from, the parent unit.

These two methods assume an all-equity capital structure and so, if the parity conditions existed in the real world, the result of the two approaches would be the same. But in the real world, debt is normally included in the capital structure in order to lower the cost of capital; and, moreover, parity conditions do not exist. Naturally, the result of the two approaches will differ. The possible results will be:

1. NPV_P and NPV_S are, both, negative. In such a case, the project cannot be accepted.
2. NPV_P and NPV_S are, both, positive. In such a case, the project is accepted.
3. $NPV_P > 0 > NPV_S$. The project is attractive from the viewpoint of the parent unit but not attractive from the subsidiary's viewpoint. In such a case, the project may be accepted but there will be chances of loss in value, in terms of the host country currency.
4. $NPV_P < 0 < NPV_S$. The project is attractive from the subsidiary's perspective but unattractive from the parent's perspective and though it may be accepted, it is doubtful how far the project will be useful to the parent unit.

19.1.2 Cost of Capital

In discounting methods of capital budgeting, the future cash flow is discounted to the present value. The discounting factor is nothing but the cost of capital, incorporating the risk factor.

The cost of capital is simply the weighted average of the cost of equity and the cost of debt. The debt-equity ratio has a definite bearing on the average cost of capital. An elaborate discussion on the cost of capital and effects of the debt-equity ratio lies beyond the scope of this book. Any book on corporate financial management would be suitable for this purpose. At present moment, the focus of discussion lies on how far the computation of the cost of capital in an international firm is different from that in domestic business finance.

> The cost of capital is simply the weighted average of the cost of equity and the cost of debt.

1. In case of domestic investment, the cost of retained earnings is not calculated separately because the market price of shares, which determines the cost of equity, also embodies the influence of retained earnings. But in case of international investment, the cost of retained earning is calculated separately because the earnings repatriated by the subsidiary to the parent company are subject to tax. The after-tax cost of retained earnings is,

$$K_s = k_e(1-t) \tag{19.2}$$

2. The large size of an MNC ensures it to get preferential treatment from creditors. The size of its issue is quite large, involving lower floatation cost per share or bond.
3. The firm has easy access to the international capital market and so it gets funds from the least-cost source. The subsidiary too borrows from the domestic capital market if it finds the cost of capital low there.
4. An MNC can internationally diversify its sources of funds and so the inflow of funds is more stable. It reduces the probability of bankruptcy and lowers the cost of capital.

On the contrary, the cost of capital in case of an MNC's operation is higher insofar as the flow of funds in a multinational operation is highly exposed to exchange rate exposure. It raises the bankruptcy cost and compels creditors and shareholders to require a higher rate of return on the capital. Again, the international operation is subject to political risk, which too deserves a higher rate of return on capital.

Thus, computation of the cost of capital in the context of multinational investment needs to incorporate these facts. In other words, the MNC needs to adjust its own (parent unit's) cost of capital to some more important variables while evaluating its foreign investment projects. However, those who believe in an efficient capital market suggest that the cost of capital in different countries is analogous and hence the parent company's cost of capital may be used for discounting the cash flow from foreign operations. But, in practice, the international capital market is segmented, requiring adjustments to the parent unit's cost of capital.

1. The cost of capital should be adjusted for **variations in capital structure norms**, which are very much evident in international investment. Normally, MNCs, whose operation is well diversified across countries, have a comparatively stable cash flow and can handle more debt. They have a large share of debt also because they have easy access to credit as well as they are exposed to lower credit risk. On the other hand, MNCs, whose profit is relatively large, use more retained earnings and not debt.

   Capital structure norms depend also on the rules and regulations in the host country. In host countries where foreign equity participation is restricted to lower limits, the debt-equity ratio is generally high. Again, when the subsidiary is more exposed to exchange rate risk, a higher debt-equity ratio is desirable. Yet again, when political risk is very high in the host country, the MNC relies more on loans from the host country creditors. It is because the creditors will put pressure on the local government to maintain good relations with the MNC. But, if the interest rate is high in the host country, as it is often found in many developing countries, the MNC uses more of equity capital. Thus, the capital structure norms vary from one host country to another and from one MNC to another. If the same MNC invests in different countries, its target capital structure in each host country will differ from its global target capital structure. In order to minimise this difference, the MNC adopts different norms in different host countries. If it relies more on debt in one host country, it tries to rely more on equity in some other host country. If the debt-equity mix in all the subsidiaries taken together does not match its own (parent unit's) capital structure norms, the MNC tries to adjust its (parent unit's) norms to the global target capital structure norms by adding a premium to, or making a discount from, the parent unit's cost of capital.

2. The parent unit's cost of capital is adjusted according to how far the subsidiary is able to get funds at a lower cost, either from the **domestic financial market** or from international financial market. If the cost is lower than the cost of capital of the parent unit, the discount rate needs to be reduced.
3. The discount rate needs **adjustment for inflation**. There are two ways of doing this. If the cash flow is adjusted for inflation, it should be discounted by the real discount rate or the inflation adjusted discount rate. But, if the cash flow is not adjusted for inflation, it should be discounted by nominal discount rate.
4. The discount rate is adjusted for various types of **risks prevalent in the host country**. Such risks may be political, may be economic, or both. If these risks are expected to be present in the host country, the discount rate needs an upward revision. The extent of upward revision depends upon the severity of the risk.

19.1.3 Adjusted Present Value Approach

Lessard (1985) has developed a technique that is known as the adjusted present value (APV) technique (Figure 19.3). It incorporates most of the complexities emerging in the computation of cash flow and in the determination of the discount rates that have been explained in the preceding sections.

Adjusted present value (APV) refers to a capital budgeting technique for evaluating international projects.

Under the APV technique, the initial cash flow consists of the capital cost of the project minus blocked funds, if any, activated by the project, in the host country. This amount is converted into the home country currency at the spot exchange rate.

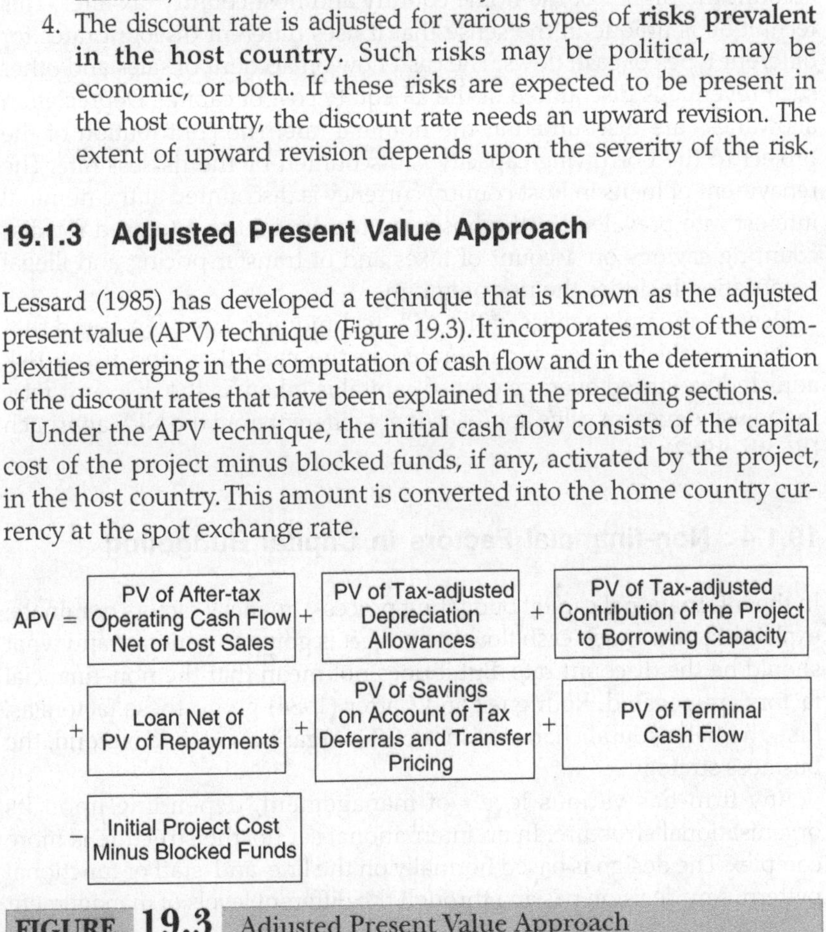

FIGURE 19.3 Adjusted Present Value Approach

Similarly, the operating cash flow under the APV technique consists of:

1. Present value of after tax cash flow from the subsidiary to the parent, converted into the home country currency at the expected spot rate minus the profits on the lost sales of the parent company;
2. Present value of tax adjusted depreciation allowances in terms of the home country currency;
3. Present value of the contribution of the project to the borrowing capacity in terms of home country currency, subject to adjustment for taxes;
4. Face value of loan in the host country currency minus the present value of repayments converted into the home country currency;
5. Present value of the expected savings on account of tax deferrals and transfer pricing; and
6. Present value of expected illegal repatriation of income.

Terminal cash flow consists of the present value of the residual plant and equipment.

It may be noted that for tax adjustment, the APV technique takes into account the higher of the home country and host country tax rates. This technique is unique in the sense that it uses different discount rates for different types of cash flows. The cash flow on account of sales and other such revenue is discounted at the all equity cost of capital. Depreciation allowances are discounted at the nominal rate. The contribution of the project to the borrowing capacity is discounted by the riskless rate. The repayment of loans in host country currency is discounted at the nominal interest rate prevalent in the host country. Again, the rate used for discounting savings on account of taxes and of transfer pricing and illegal repatriation includes the risk premium.

Despite the uniqueness of the APV technique, it has been found that if the complexities are incorporated in the cash flow and if the risk adjusted weighted average cost of capital is taken as the discount rate, the adjusted present value approach is not different from the NPV approach (Booth, 1982).

19.1.4 Non-financial Factors in Capital Budgeting

The international capital budgeting is influenced also by: 1. views of the managers with disparate backgrounds, and 2. business strategy of the firm.

In the international capital budgeting process, financial factors dominate, explaining how much cash flow the project is going to generate and what should be the discount rate. But it does not mean that the non-financial factors are negated. Rodriguez and Carter (1984) group these factors as, first, the behavioural characteristics of the organisation, and, second, the business strategy.

Any firm has various levels of management, depending upon its organisational structure. In an international set up, the structure is more complex. The design is based normally on the line-and-staff or functional pattern. Any decision passing through the different levels of management is influenced by the attitude of the managers. The view of one manager is normally different from that of another as they come from disparate socio-cultural backgrounds. Naturally, the final decision is the result of bargaining among the different levels of management.

Apart from the organisational behaviour that influences the capital budgeting decision, proposals meeting the financial norms must fit into the corporate strategy. The management frames the combinations of strategies depending upon its preferences and capabilities and then fits the financially viable projects into the strategy framework.

19.2 SELECTION OF THE SOURCES AND FORMS OF FUNDS

Selection of a particular source or form of funds is done to suit the corporate objectives, such as minimisation of the effective cost of funds, matching of the raised funds with its target debt-equity ratios, matching the raised funds with its target current liability-long-term liability ratio, avoidance of lengthy legal and procedural formalities, and so on.

19.2.1 Minimisation of Cost of Funds

The effective cost of funds depends *inter alia* on the rate of interest and the changes in the exchange rate or in the value of the borrowed currency. In the form of an equation, the effective cost of borrowing from a foreign market is,

$$k_{bf} = (1 + r_f)\,(1 + E_f) - 1 \qquad (19.3)$$

Where r_f is the rate of interest in the foreign market, and
E_f is the change in the exchange rate.

Suppose the interest rate in the London money market is 12 per cent compared to 14 per cent in New York and the pound sterling is expected to appreciate by 4 per cent. The effective cost of borrowing in pound would be:

$$(1.12 \times 1.04) - 1 = 16.48\%$$

In this case, the multinational enterprise will borrow from the New York money market despite the fact that the rate of interest is lower in the London money market. This is because the effective cost of borrowing pounds is greater than that of borrowing dollars.

The effective cost of total borrowing will be lower if there is negative correlation in the movement of the value of different currencies.

In cases where the firm borrows from more than one financial market, the weighted average of the effective cost of borrowing in different currencies is computed. Again, the effective cost of total borrowing will be lower if there is negative correlation in the movement of the value of different currencies. The cost may move up if the correlation coefficient is positive. So the firm takes into account not only the expected change in the value of the currencies but also the correlation coefficient of the expected change in the value of different currencies so as to lower the effective cost of total borrowing.

19.2.2 Borrowing to Conform to Capital Structure Norms

There are different capital structure theories each suggesting a different point of optimal capital structure. These can be found in any book on corporate financial management. However, as noted earlier, the capital structure norms in a multinational company set up are complex. The study of Sekely and Collins (1988) examines the capital structure norms among 677 firms in 9 industries in 23 countries and finds that the debt ratio may be large or small, depending upon economic, social, cultural, and political factors. Since these factors vary among countries, capital structure norms also vary widely among countries. On the whole, debt ratio is found to be large in the Scandinavian, Mediterranean, and some Asian countries. It is low in case of some of the South Asian, Latin American, and Anglo-American countries.

In this context, an important question arises regarding whether the affiliates of multinational corporations should follow host country norms or they should be guided by the parent company norms. If the norms in the home country and the host country are similar, there is no problem. But if they are different, it becomes an important decision. If the capital structure norms conform to the local norms in the host country, they are well in line with the monetary and financial policy of the host government. They help evaluate return on equity investment relative to local competitors in a particular industry. On the other hand, when the norms conform to the parent company's global target debt ratio, they are, first of all, more suited to maximising the global profit; secondly, there is every possibility that they have a comparative advantage over the local firms in the host country; and thirdly, a high debt ratio in one country may offset the low debt ratio in another country; and on the whole, it is best suited for the firm as a whole.

> Long-term capital is more liquid but lowers profitability. Short term capital may push up profitability but it is less liquid. The finance manager uses perfect trade off between short term capital and long term capital.

19.2.3 Selection of an Optimal Maturity

While raising funds from the international financial market, a multinational firm likes to maintain a proper balance between short term liabilities and the long-term liabilities. There is no confusion in case of financing fixed assets because they are financed with long term capital. But in case of financing of current assets, a decision needs to be made regarding the ratio between the long term capital and the short term capital. The normal view is that permanent current assets should be financed with long term capital and the fluctuating part of the current assets should be financed with short term capital. This is nothing but a tradeoff between liquidity and profitability. Long-term capital is more liquid but lowers profitability. Short term capital may push up profitability but it is less liquid.

However, if the finance manager is conservative, he uses more of long term capital. If he is aggressive, short term capital is greatly used. Thus, whenever a multinational enterprise raises funds, it has in mind a perfect tradeoff between short term capital and long term capital.

19.2.4 Avoidance of Legal and Procedural Formalities

Any firm raising funds does not like to undergo too many procedural formalities. From this viewpoint, the issue of international bonds is complex; much more so than in the case of euro notes. Again, the borrowing programme can be designed only within the framework of local laws. If the government prohibits the issue of a particular instrument, the borrower cannot issue it despite its cost efficiency. For example, prior to 1992, the Indian government had not allowed the Indian companies to issue euro equities or euro convertible bonds. Sometimes these considerations become really significant.

19.3 FINANCIAL SWAP

Very often a borrowing firm may not have easy access to a segment of its own choice in the financial market. For example, a firm needs fixed-rate funds, but has an easy access to floating-rate funds. Similarly, a firm needs borrowing from the US dollar market, but has an easy access to the euro market. In this case, it can borrow the funds from easily available sources and then can exchange its liability into another form of liability of its own choice. This exchange is called a swap. The swap may be either a interest-rate swap or currency swap. These two forms are discussed here.

19.3.1 Interest-rate Swap

Interest rate swap involves the exchange of interest payments. It usually occurs when a person or a firm needs fixed rate funds but is only able to get floating rate funds. It finds another party who needs ony floating rate loan but is able to get fixed rate funds. The two, known as counter parties, exchange the interest payments and the loans according to their own choice. It is the swap dealer, usually a bank, that brings together the two counter-parties for the swap. The essential condition for the interest-rate swap is that the amount of loan is identical in the two cases and the periodic payment of interest takes place in the same currency. At the same time, there must be coincidence between the two parties—one getting cheaper fixed rate funds and the other getting cheaper floating rate funds.

Interest-rate swap refers to exchange of interest payments through a swap dealer, normally between fixed-rate loans and floating-rate loans.

Since the principals are identical in size, they are not exchanged. They are only notional. It is the interest payment that is exchanged on periodic payment dates. The interest payments are called the legs of the swap and the fixed rate is called the swap coupon. The process of interest rate swap will be clear from the following example.

Example: Suppose Firm *A* needs fixed rate funds, which is available to him at the rate of 10.50 per cent to be computed half yearly, but it has access to cheaper floating-rate funds available to it at LIBOR + 0.3 per cent.

Firm *B* needs floating rate funds, available to it at 6-month LIBOR flat, but has access to cheaper fixed rate funds available to it at the rate of 9.50 per cent to be computed half yearly.

Both the principals are identical in size and maturity and are in the same currency.

The interest rate swap will take place in the following stages (Figure 19.4):

Stage 1: If Firm *A* has access to the floating rate loan market, it will borrow from the floating rate loan market. Similarly, Firm *B* having access to the fixed rate loan market, will borrow a fixed rate loan.

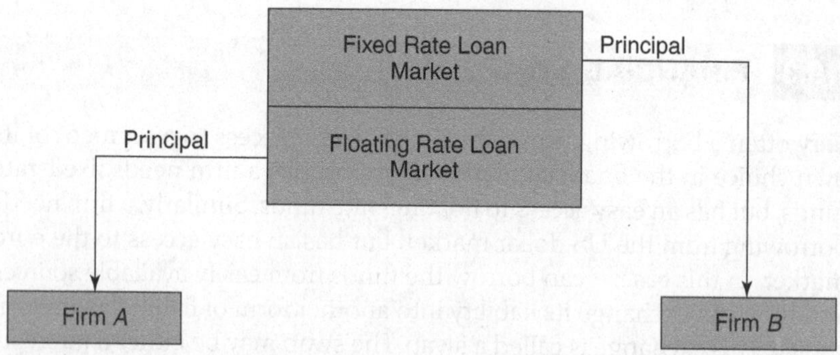

FIGURE 19.4 Stage 1 of Interest Rate Swap

Stage 2: Both the counterparties approach a swap dealer. Since Firm *A* needs a fixed rate loan, the swap dealer asks firm *A* to pay fixed rate interest to it (swap dealer) as if it has borrowed fixed rate loan. The fixed rate of interest payable through the swap dealer is higher than what firm *B* has to pay to the lender in the fixed rate loan market but lower than what firm *A* has to pay to the lender if it had borrowed from the fixed rate loan market. It is, say, 9.75 per cent. In exchange, the swap dealer pays firm *A* the interest at 6-month LIBOR. Firm *A* pays LIBOR + 0.3 per cent to the lender on its floating rate borrowing.

On the other hand, the swap dealer asks firm *B* to pay 6 month LIBOR as if it has borrowed a floating rate loan. In exchange, the swap dealer pays firm *B* fixed rate interest, which is higher than what Firm *B* has to pay to the ultimate lender. This is the interest rate that the swap dealer has received from firm *A* minus its (swap dealer's) own commission. It is, say, 9.65 per cent. Here firm *B* gets interest from the swap dealer at 9.65 per cent and pays interest to the fixed rate lender at 9.50 per cent (Figure 19.5).

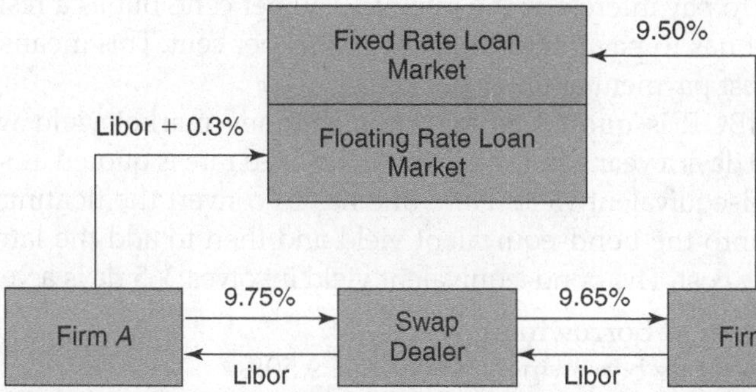

FIGURE 19.5 Stage 2 of Interest Rate Swap

Firm *A* is attracted to the swap deal as it uses the loan according to its own choice and also because the fixed rate of interest payable by it is lower than what it had to pay in case it borrowed from the fixed rate loan market. Firm *B* is attracted to the swap deal not only because it is using the loan according to its own choice but also because the swap dealer gives an interest rate that is higher than what it has to pay to the ultimate lender. The swap dealer is attracted to the swap deal because it earns from such a deal.

Stage 3: At maturity, the two firms repay the loan. Firm *A* repays the floating rate loan and Firm *B* repays fixed rate loan (Figure 19.6).

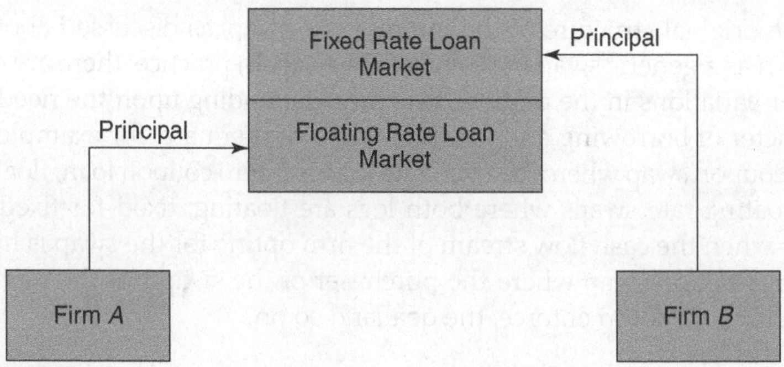

FIGURE 19.6 Stage 3 of Interest Rate Swap

Firm *A*'s cost of borrowing:

Cost of floating-rate loan	... LIBOR + 0.3%
Less floating interest rate received	... LIBOR
Net cost differential	... 0.3 %
Converting the cost differential from money-market yield to bond equivalent yield	... $0.3\ \% \times \frac{365}{360} = 0.304\%$

Add swap coupon	... 9.75%
Total cost of borrowing	... 10.054%

Had firm *A* borrowed the fixed rate loan that it actually needed, it would have to pay interest at the rate of 10.50 per cent. But as a result of swap deal, it has to pay interest only at 10.054 per cent. This means, it is saving interest payment at 0.446 per cent.

LIBOR refers to interest rate at which major banks in London offer deposit to the others among them.

(**Note:** LIBOR is quoted as an annual money-market yield which involves 360 days a year. On the contrary, the fixed rate is quoted as semi-annual bond-equivalent yield. Here one has to convert the floating-rate differential into the bond-equivalent yield and then to add the latter to the fixed rate cost. The bond-equivalent yield involves 365 days a year.)

Firm *B*'s cost of borrowing:

Cost of fixed rate borrowing	... 9.50%	
Less fixed rate received	... 9.65	
Net cost differential	... –0.15%	
Converting the net cost differential from *BEY* to *MMY*	.... $0.15\ \% \times \frac{360}{365}$	... –0.148%
Total cost of borrowing	... LIBOR – 0.148%	

Had firm *B* taken the floating rate loan, it would have to pay LIBOR. But as a result of the swap deal, it has to pay LIBOR –0.148 per cent. This means, it has saved interest payment equivalent to 0.148 per cent.

Gain to Swap dealer:

Interest rate received	... 9.75%
Interest rate paid	... 9.65%
Net gain	... 0.10%

The original structure of the interest rate swap, as discussed above, is known as a generic swap or plain vanilla swap. In practice, there are often minor variations in the original structure, depending upon the need and character of borrowing and lending. Some of them are, for example, the zero coupon swap where the fixed rate loan is a zero coupon loan; floating-for-floating rate swaps where both legs are floating; fixed-for-fixed rate swap when the cash flow stream of the firm opting for the swap is highly volatile; option swap where the purchaser of the swap has the privilege to enforce, or not to enforce, the deal and so on.

19.3.2 Currency Swap

Currency Swap is exchange of one borrowed currency for the other borrowed currency through a swap dealer.

A currency swap is different from the interest-rate swap insofar as it (currency swap) involves two different currencies. This is the reason that the two currencies are exchanged in the beginning; and again at maturity they are re-exchanged. The exchange of currencies is necessitated by the fact that one counter-party is able to borrow a particular currency at a lower interest rate than the other counter-party. Suppose firm *A* can borrow the euro at a fixed rate of 8.0 per cent or the US dollar at a floating rate of one-year LIBOR. Firm *B* can borrow euro the at a fixed rate of 9.2 per cent and can borrow the US dollar at one-year LIBOR. If firm *B* needs the fixed rate euro, it will approach the swap dealer, provided that firm *A* needs the floating rate US dollar. The swap deal will be conducted in different stages, as follows:

Stage 1: In the first stage, firm *A* borrows euro at 8.0 per cent interest rate. Firm *B* borrows US dollar at LIBOR.

Stage 2: The two firms exchange the borrowed currencies with the help of the swap dealer. After the exchange, firm *A* will possess US dollars. Firm *B* will possess euros (Figure 19.7).

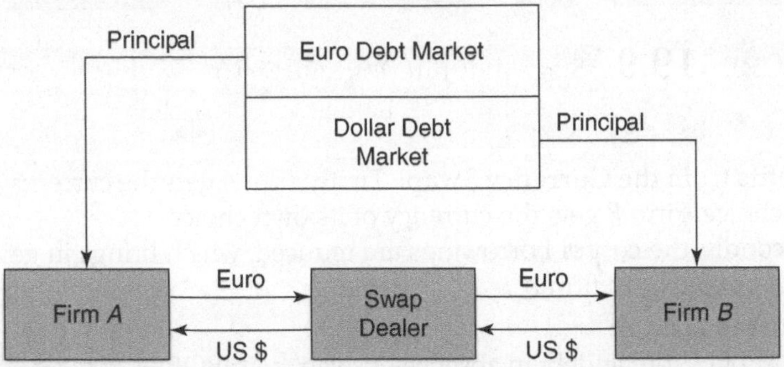

FIGURE 19.7 Stage 1 and 2 of Interest Rate Swap

Stage 3: Interest payment will flow. Firm *A* will pay LIBOR on the US dollar that will reach the US dollar market first, through, the swap dealer and then through Firm *B*. Similarly, firm *B* will pay a fixed rate interest that will flow to the fixed rate DM market through the swap dealer and through firm *A*. Firm *B* will pay a fixed rate of interest to the swap dealer, which will be more than 8.0 per cent but less than 9.20 per cent. It will be, say, 8.60 per cent. The swap dealer will take its own commission and shall pay to firm *A* in this case only, say, 8.40 per cent.

Stage 4: The two principals are again exchanged between the two counter-parties. Firm *A* gets back euro and repays them to the lender. Firm *B* gets back US dollars and repays it to the lender (Figure 19.8).

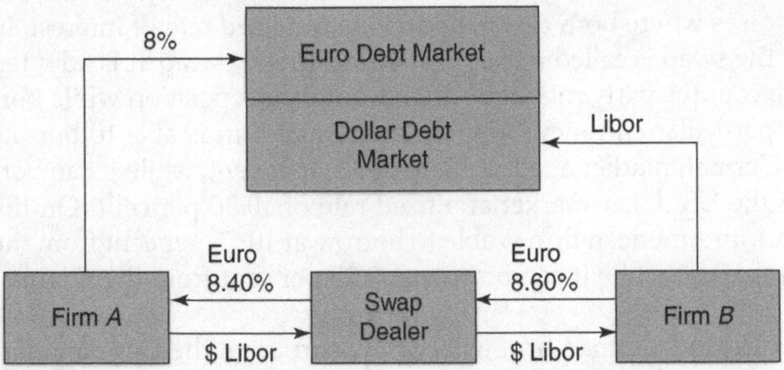

FIGURE 19.8 Stage 3 of Interest Rate Swap

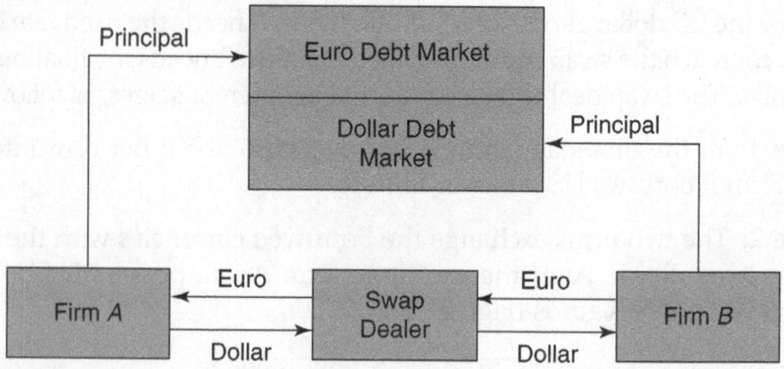

FIGURE 19.9 Stage 4 of Interest Rate Swap

Benefits from the Currency Swap: Firstly, firm *A* gets the currency of its own choice. Firm *B* gets the currency of its own choice.

Secondly, the cost of borrowings are reduced, which brings in gains to firm *A* as well as to firm *B*.

Cost to Firm *A*:

Cost of US dollar debt in absence of swap ...LIBOR

Cost of US dollar debt after swap:

Interest paid minus interest received ... 8.0% + LIBOR – 8.40%
= LIBOR – 0.40%

This means that the cost of the dollar debt used by firm *A* is 0.40 per cent less under the swap arrangement. This is the gain accruing to firm *A*.

Cost to Firm *B*:

Cost of DM debt without swap ...9.2%

Cost of DM debt after swap:

Interest paid minus interest received ... 8.60% + LIBOR – LIBOR
= 8.60%

This means that the cost of DM loan used by firm *B* is 9.20 per cent – 8.60 per cent = 0.60 per cent less under the swap arrangement. This is the gain accruing to firm *B*.

Normally, a currency swap is a fixed-for-floating currency swap. But there are cases where both counter parties pay a fixed rate of interest. In this case, the swap is called a fixed-for-fixed currency swap. It is adopted when one counter-party maintains an advantageous position while borrowing a particular currency. Suppose a German firm is able to borrow from the German market at a fixed rate of 8.50 per cent, while it can borrow from the US dollar market at a fixed rate of 10.50 per cent. On the other hand, an American firm is able to borrow at 10.75 per cent from the US dollar market, while it can borrow at 9.25 per cent from the German market.

In this case, the German firm will borrow euro from the German market. The American firm will borrow US dollars from the dollar market. The two will exchange the currency through a swap dealer. After the exchange of the principal amount, the German firm possesses US dollars and the American firm possesses euro. The German firm pays interest on the dollar loan to the American firm at 10.50 per cent. The American firm adds to it 0.25 per cent interest and pays 10.75 per cent interest rate to the lender. At the same time, the American firm pays to the swap dealer an interest at 8.80 per cent on the euro loans. The swap dealer deducts its commission at 0.05 per cent and passes on the remaining interest at 8.75 per cent to the German firm. The German firm pays interest to the German lender at 8.50 per cent and saves 0.25 per cent. This means that the German firm uses dollar loan only at 10.50 per cent – 0.25 per cent = 10.25 per cent. Had it not swapped the currency, it would have to pay 10.50 per cent for the dollar loan. There is a distinct gain of 0.25 per cent.

Similarly, the American firm is paying 0.25 per cent more to the dollar market lender than what it receives from the German firm, but since it is saving 9.25 per cent – 8.80 per cent = 0.45 per cent on the euro loan, its net gain on the borrowing is 0.45 per cent – 0.25 per cent = 0.20 per cent. Both the counter parties gain on account of fixed-for-fixed currency swap.

This second form of currency swap is known as the floating-for-floating currency swap. In this case, both counter parties pay a floating rate of interest. This type of swap can be achieved through a single swap agreement or through a double agreement. In the latter, it is a combination of one fixed-for-floating currency swap and one fixed-for-floating interest-rate swap. The combination is usually known as a circus swap. The currency swap is used for the initial transaction, while the interest rate swap is used for converting fixed rate side to floating rate. If the two fixed rate payments are equal, the net result is manifest in the flow of floating rate interest.

19.4 INTERNATIONAL CASH MANAGEMENT

After raising funds, the firm begins operation. During operations, an optimum cash balance is maintained so as to ensure adequate liquidity without impinging upon profitability. In an international firm, management of cash is a complex task in view of intra-firm transfers of cash and the restrictions imposed on them by the home and the host governments.

The management of cash basically involves four steps. They are:

(i) Assessment of the cash requirements
(ii) Optimisation of cash need, by restructuring inflows and outflows
(iii) Selection of sources from where cash could be brought in
(iv) Investment of surplus cash, if any, into near-cash assets

Selection of the sources of funds has already been discussed in the present chapter; the other issues are discussed here.

19.4.1 Assessment of Cash Requirements

The first step in international cash management is to establish the need for cash during a specific period, which may be a week, a fortnight, or a month. It is computed on the basis of the expected amount of cash disbursements vis-à-vis expected inflow of cash during a particular period. The outflow and inflow of cash occurs mainly on account of various transactions. The firm holds cash also to meet precautionary and speculative needs, but such needs are fixed and the amount of cash for these purposes is determined on the basis of experience and the general trend of the business environment.

For the assessment of cash needs, a cash budget is prepared for each subsidiary. The figures are consolidated in order to assess the cash need of the firm as a whole.

For the assessment of cash needs, a cash budget is prepared for each subsidiary. Any book on corporate financial management would contain a detailed discussion regarding the preparation of cash budget. After assessing the cash need of each of the subsidiaries, the figures are consolidated in order to assess the cash need of the firm as a whole. It is because in a multinational enterprise, it is the cash flow of the firm as a whole that is taken into account and which needs to be managed.

19.4.2 Optimisation of Cash Needs

After the preparation of the cash budget and the estimation of the cash requirements, the firm needs optimisation of cash level at different units. It can be done in three ways. First, it is through cash flow from a cash-surplus unit to a cash-deficit unit. Second, the required cash level is minimised during a particular period through restructuring of inflows and outflows. The inflows are accelerated; and at the same time, outflows are delayed, so as to lower the cash needs at a particular point of time. Third, netting of payments is adopted especially with respect to intra-firm transfers, which reduces the cash needs.

Intra-firm Transfer of Cash: When a particular unit faces a shortage of cash, it gets it from a cash surplus unit, may it be the parent unit or any other sister subsidiary. It may raise funds from outside the firm if outside funds are cheaper and easier than the intra-firm flow of cash in view of governmental restrictions on such flows. However, the unit often prefers intra-firm transfer of cash in view of the fact that the surpluses of the other units are utilised. This is perhaps why funds are transferred from one unit to the other, circumventing the restrictions. The modes are: transfer pricing, leads and lags, parallel loans, changes in the rates of royalty, dividend, and so on. Transfer pricing is discussed in Chapter 17. Leads and lags and parallel loans are explained in Chapter 20.

Accelerating Inflows and Delaying Outflows: There are two types of delays in the collection of cash. One is the mailing delay and the other is the processing delay. In collection from across the border, long procedural formalities and governmental restrictions too come in the way.

As regards curbing of mailing delay, the use of cable remittances is often suggested. In this respect, the Society for Worldwide Inter-bank Financial Telecommunications (SWIFT) is doing a commendable job. It has brought into its fold around one thousand banks among which funds are transferred electronically with ease. Again, the firm opens up regional mobilisation centres and instructs customers to make their payments to the centres falling in their respective vicinity. Sometimes, a postal box are set up in post-offices within customers' vicinity. The postal box is operated by the local offices of the bank authorised by the firm. This method is commonly known as the lock-box system.

Mailing delay is cut through:
1. electronic transfer of funds
2. opening of regional mobilisation centres
3. operating of lock-box system.

As far as processing delay is concerned, there are some multinational banks that provide "same-day-value" facilities. Under this facility, the amount deposited in any branch of the bank in any country is credited to the firm's account on the same day. This is done through electronic devices. Thus, it is suggested that the firm should take help from such banks to cut short processing delays. Again, some firms adopt a pre-authorised payment system in which they are authorised to charge a customer's bank account up to a specific limit.

Besides, disbursements are delayed in order to conserve cash, at least for some time. But the firm should be careful that making such delays does not effect its creditworthiness. Again, when disbursements are delayed, there are chances for retaliatory measures. Thus, the process of disbursements demands extra care.

Since accelerating cash inflow and decelerating disbursements involve additional cost, it is advisable for the company to follow them as long as their marginal returns exceed their marginal cost.

Netting of Intra-firm Payments: Another step towards lessening the requirements for cash at a particular point of time is to encourage netting of intra-firm payments. There is usually a large volume of intra-firm payments. Such payments require not only a huge amount of cash, but also transaction cost, inter-currency conversion cost, and opportunity cost of float. The different units of a firm require cash not only for making payments but also for meeting such costs. Netting is a solution to this problem.

Netting is in fact the elimination of counter payments. This means that only the net amount is paid. For example, if the parent company is to receive US \$3.0 million from its subsidiary and if the same subsidiary is to get US \$1.0 million from the parent company, these two transactions can be netted to one transaction, where the subsidiary will transfer US \$2.0 million to the parent company. The cost of transfer too will be lower.

Netting is in fact the elimination of counter payments. This means that only the net amount is paid.

Netting can be bilateral, involving two units. It may be multilateral, involving more than two units. Suppose *A*, *B*, and *C* are the three units of a firm. *A* has to receive US \$15.0 million from *B* and US \$12.0 million from *C*. *B* has to receive US \$20.0 million from *C* and US \$20.0 million from *A*. *C* has to receive US \$30.0 million from *A* and US \$6.0 million from *B*. In

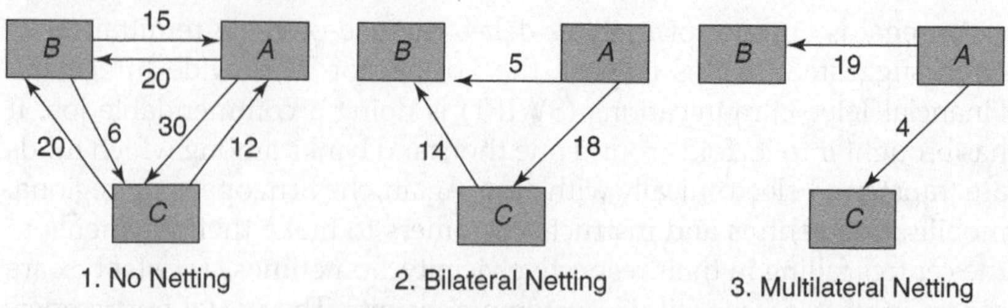

FIGURE 19.10 Netting of Payments

the absence of netting, there will be 6 transactions involving US $103 million. If it is bilateral netting, there will be three transactions involving US $37.0 million. If it is a multilateral netting, there will be only two transactions involving only US $23.0 million.

Problems with the Cash Optimisation Process: The problems coming in the way of accelerating and decelerating of cash flows or the netting process may be grouped as:

(i) Firm-related problems
(ii) Governmental restrictions
(iii) Deficiency in the banking system
(iv) Opposition by subsidiaries

(i) When a multinational enterprise has a large number of subsidiaries and there is large fluctuation in host country currencies, the acceleration or deceleration of cash flows or netting of payments will turn out to be too complicated. It is a fact that owing to computers, the problem can be solved to a great extent. But in view of complications, the parent company finds it difficult to take a correct decision.

(ii) There are many host governments that practise exchange control mechanisms in view of their weak balance of payments. The parent company's decision to accelerate or decelerate cash flows of a subsidiary or to net the payments cannot be carried out unless the government of the host country permits such actions.

(iii) There are still a number of international banks that have not developed sophisticated system of collections and payments. In these cases, acceleration of collection and netting of payments cannot be effective.

(iv) The acceleration or deceleration of cash flows may be beneficial for one unit or one firm, but it may not be beneficial for the other unit or another firm. In such cases, the subsidiaries or firms that are at loss resent such a move. Affected firms may take retaliatory measures. Subsidiaries, over which the parent company has only meagre control, may come in the way of such moves.

19.4.3 Investment of Surplus Cash

The cash balance for precautionary and speculative purposes is fixed and so it is held in the form of near-cash assets. Surplus cash in excess of transaction purposes too is held in the form of near-cash assets or short-term marketable securities. The reason is that near-cash assets earn for the firm and are definitely preferable to an idle cash balance. In this context, a few questions need to be probed. They are:

1. Should the surplus cash balance of the entire firm centralised and only then invested?
2. How much of the surplus cash balance should be invested in near-cash assets?
3. Which currency should be preferred for investment?

Centralisation of Surplus Cash: The process of centralisation of surplus cash can take two forms. One is the centralised control of the parent company over the surplus cash of different units. In this case, cash does not actually move to a centralised pool, but its movement to a cash-deficit unit or for investment in near-cash assets is strictly guided by the parent company. The other form manifests in the actual movement of cash to a centralised pool. Any investment in near-cash assets takes place only out of the centralised pool.

Centralisation is preferred as the funds of the firm are invested in the most desirable way so as to avoid the weaknesses of some of the host country currencies. Whenever any unit falls into liquidity distress, funds are immediately rushed to it. It also reaps economies of scale. There are many investment avenues that need large sums of money. The centralised pool with a large amount of cash can tap such avenues of investment. However, the success of the centralisation approach depends on how the intra-firm transfer of cash is restriction free and how efficient the intra-firm information system is.

> The success of the centralisation approach depends on how the intra-firm transfer of cash is restriction-free and how efficient the intra-firm information system is.

Again, the centralised pool may be located either in the host country or in the home country or in a third country. A particular location is preferred where the local currency is strong, the money market is developed, tax rates are low, the political climate is stable, and the attitude of the government is congenial.

How Much of the Surplus to be Invested: Surplus cash should not lie idle. It should be invested. The larger the investment, the greater the interest earned, but at the same time the great risk is of illiquidty. Lower the investment, liquidity will improve but earning on the investment will be lower. Thus, an optimal division of funds between cash and near-cash assets requires a tradeoff between liquidity and profitability.

The optimal ratio between cash and near-cash assets is also influenced by the transaction cost or the cost of conversion from cash to securities and back in the form of brokerage, and so on. The larger the near-cash assets, the greater the transaction cost. On the contrary, a larger cash balance does involve large opportunity cost in the form of interest foregone

Surplus cash should be invested to a point where the sum of transaction cost and opportunity cost is the minimum.

that the near-cash assets could have earned. The optimal level, therefore, represents a point where the sum of transaction cost and opportunity cost is the minimum.

While making an investment in near-cash assets, the international finance manager has to take care of a number of facts, of which the following are important.

1. Portfolio should be diversified so as to maximise yield for a given level of risk.
2. The portfolio should be reviewed daily so as to decide which particular investment has to be liquidated or which particular securities should remain undisturbed.
3. Investment should only be made in assets where liquidity prevails.
4. The maturity structure of investment should coincide with the need for cash so that securities can be easily converted back into cash whenever the need for fresh cash arises.

Currency of Investment: Normally, the surplus cash is invested in a country where the interest rate is higher. However, the answer is not so simple. In fact, the firm has to take into account the effective yield/return that depends not simply on the rate of interest but also on the changes in the exchange rate. If the currency of the country where the funds are invested depreciates vis-á-vis the home-country currency, the return in terms of home country currency will be lower. More often, a firm makes multiple-currency investments and reaps the benefit of diversification. Uncertainty in exchange rate changes is greatly reduced if there is negative correlation in the changes in the exchange rate of different currencies.

Thus, whenever a firm has surplus cash, it is better to have a centralised pool located in the most suitable place. The centralised funds should be translated into a multiple-currency investment. However, care should be taken that the cost of investment does not exceed the benefits from it.

SUMMARY

- International financial strategy is multi-pronged. It begins with capital budgeting, where only those foreign operations, that represent excess of cash inflow over the cash outflow over a specific time period, are accepted. The computation of cash flow is complex in international operations. This is because the same cash flow may be cash outflow for the subsidiary and cash inflow for the parent unit. This is why cash flow and NPV are calculated from the viewpoint of both the parent and the subsidiary. Similarly, the computation of discount rate or the risk-adjusted cost of capital in international investment is complex in view of varying debt-equity norms, inflation rate differential, exchange rate risk, political risk, and many other factors. The adjusted present value approach uses different discount rates for different types of cash flow. However, it is not only the financial factors but also the non-financial factors, such as the behavioural pattern of the organisation and the corporate business strategy, that influence the capital budgeting decision.

- The funds raising strategy involves the selection of the least cost source on the basis of interest rates and exchange rate changes, matching with the company's global debt-equity norms as well as with such norms in the host country, matching with maturity norms and the avoidance of lengthy procedural formalities.
- If the desired type of funds are not available, the firm goes for swap where fixed rates are exchanged for floating rates and vice versa, and where the currency of borrowing is exchanged for the desired currency through a swap dealer.
- When the firm begins operation, the strategy is to ensure optimal level of cash among the different units. This involves, (1) estimation of cash needs; (2) optimisation of the cash level through transfer of funds to cash deficit units, accelerating inflows, delaying disbursements and through netting of payments; and (3) determination of investment in near-cash assets.

Review Questions

1. What are the distinctive features of the cash flow calculation in international capital budgeting? Explain.
2. What are the factors influencing the discount rate in the context of international capital budgeting?
3. Write a short note on Adjusted Present Value Approach of international capital budgeting.
4. Explain the factors taken into account while funds are raised by an international firm.
5. Write short notes on:
   (a) interest-rate swap
   (b) currency swap
6. Describe the different steps involved in international cash management.

Objective Type Questions

1. Mark True or False:
   (a) Depreciation is included in the cash flow.
   (b) Cash flow is considered only on an after tax basis.
   (c) The average cost of capital is the weighted sum of the cost of equity, cost of debt and cost of retained earnings.

(d) Cost of retained earnings is included in the cost of equity in the context of international business.
(e) Mailing delay lessens the need for cash.
(f) Netting increases the transaction cost.
(g) Investment of surplus cash depends upon a trade-off between liquidity and profitability.
(h) Effective return from investment of cash includes changes in the exchange rate.
(i) The APV technique of capital budgeting involves the same discount rate for different types of cash flows.
(j) Interest rate swap and currency swap are similar.

2. Choose the Most Suitable Answer.
   (a) International capital budgeting incorporates:
      (i) Only financial factors
      (ii) Financial and non-financial factors
      (iii) Only non-financial factors
   (b) Free land and building given by the host country government:
      (i) Is not included in the initial cash flow
      (ii) Is included in the initial cash flow
      (iii) Is added to the initial cash flow
   (c) Higher exchange rate/political risk:
      (i) Adds to the cost of capital
      (ii) Lessens the cost of capital
      (iii) Bears no influence on the cost of capital
   (d) An investment proposal is accepted if:
      (i) Break-even salvage value is greater than the actual salvage value
      (ii) Break-even salvage value is lower than the actual salvage value
      (iii) None of above
   (e) The centralised cash pool is located in a country where:
      (i) The tax rate is very high
      (ii) The tax rate is very low
      (iii) Political instability is a big problem

NUMERICAL PROBLEMS

1. The cost of the subsidiary's project is $25 million. It is financed through different modes of funds. The parent unit makes an investment for $15 million. A sum of $5 million is drawn out of retained earnings and sum of $2 million is drawn out of blocked funds. The subsidiary borrows $2 million from the host country market. The remaining $1 million is in form of free land and building supplied by the host country government. Find out the amount of initial investment from the viewpoint of the parent unit.
2. Calculate the operating cash flow on the basis of the following data:
   (a) Sales in the domestic market = $14 million
   (b) Export = $4 million
   (c) Replacement of parent's export = $3 million
   (d) Parent's export of components to subsidiary = $6 million

(e) Royalty payment by subsidiary = $1.5 million
(f) Dividend flow to the parent = $1.5 million

3. Find the break-even salvage value if:
   (a) Initial investment = $30 million
   (b) The net cash inflow during the first and the second year, respectively = $25 million and $16 million
   (c) Discount rate = 10 per cent
4. Unit A has to pay $20 million to Unit B and $15 million to Unit C. Unit B has to pay $15 million to Unit A and $10 million to Unit C. Unit C has to pay $5 million to Unit B and $9 million to Unit A. Find out the amount of funds movement after multilateral netting.

STUDY TOPIC

HSBC Payments and Cash Management in the Asian Region

In view of the regulatory environment following the recession of 1997–1998 and the subsequent slow growth of the economy, many Asian governments tightened their regulatory measures so as to control money supply and help improve the balance of payments. Consequently, a number of banks withdrew from the local market. Liquidity went down. The market for derivatives squeezed; margins had widened; and pricing transparency had reduced. In countries where the pegged exchange rate regime had been followed, the rates were oscillated widely. The hedging strategy had become the order of the day. But the problem was that hedging was not risk free in the face of wide disparity in interest rate among countries and its unhealthy impact on forward transactions. Even forward and swap markets were not found in many countries. Options were still rare. Thus, there was a need for a well designed hedging policy.

This is not all. Disparity in interpretation and application of taxation was another problem. Corporation tax varied from being based on all income sourced within a particular jurisdiction to being residence based, with the interpretation of residents differing in each jurisdiction. Tax was an important issue while establishing new liquidity arrangements. In some countries, notional pooling was treated as an inter-company loan even when there was no physical movement of funds. Yet another issue was the requirement to prove the transaction between a regional treasury and a local entity taking place at the arm's-length rate. This was of particular concern to cross country liquidity arrangements.

Again, except for Hong Kong, Singapore, and Japan, there was an acute dearth of regional clearing houses. In China, the clearing of cheques took around a fortnight's time. Similarly too with Malaysia. However, efforts were on in many countries to change over to automated clearing.

The MNCs were increasingly looking for centralising the payables and receivables for easing regional liquidity problems. But the question was whether this will be feasible. The establishment of in-country pooling or the cash concentration arrangements followed by reliable cash flow forecasting precedes such a decision. To sum up, cash management among an MNCs' units was very difficult in the Asian region.

Source: Based on "The Guide to Cash Management". *Euromoney*, January 2000.

QUESTIONS

1. Explain reasons why MNCs find it difficult to manage cash in Asian region?
2. Does processing delay loom large in the management of cash in the Asian region?
3. What suggestions would you like to make for improving the cash management by MNCs in the Asian region?

REFERENCES

Books

Lessard, D. R. (1979), "Evaluating International Projects: An Adjusted Present Value Approach" in D. R. Lessard (ed.), *International Financial Management: Theory and Application* (Boston Mass.: Warren Gorham & Lamont) pp. 577–92.

Rodriguez, R. M. and E. E. Carter (1984), *International Financial Management* (Englewood Cliffs: Prentice-Hall), Chap. 17.

Journals

Booth, L. D. (1982), "Capital Budgeting Frameworks for the Multinational Corporation", *Journal of International Business Studies*, XIII (1), 113–23.

Sekely, W. S. and J. M. Collins (1988), "Cultural Influences on International Capital Structure" *Journal of International Business Studies*, XIX (1), 87–100.

Stanley, M. T. and S. B. Block (1983), "An Empirical Study of Management and Financial Variables influencing Capital Budgeting Decisions for Multinational Companies in the 1980s", *Management International Review*, XXIII (3), 61–72.

SELECT FURTHER READINGS

Marshall, J. F. and K. R. Kapner (1993), *The Swap Market* (Miami: Kolb Publishers).

Smith, K.V. *ed.* (1980), *Readings in Management of Working Capital* (St Paul, Minnesota: West Publisher).

Stonehill, A. I. and L. Nathanson (1968), "Capital Budgeting and Multinational Corporation", *California Management Review*, XI (Summer), 39–54.

* Rome is the capital of Italy. The economy of Rome is largely dominated by services, high-technology companies (IT, aerospace, defense, telecommunications), research, construction and commercial activities (especially banking). The huge development of tourism is very dynamic and extremely important to its economy. With a 2005 GDP of €94.376 billion (US$121.5 billion), the city produces 6.7% of the national GDP.

Hong Kong*

20

Management of Exchange Rate and Interest Rate Risk

CHAPTER OBJECTIVES

A study of financial strategy is not complete without the study of the risks involved in this type of strategy. The present chapter acquaints readers with such risks. The objective is to:

- ✦ Explain the nature of different forms of exchange rate risk and how they are measured.
- ✦ Describe the contractual, natural, and other hedging techniques to manage exchange rate risk.
- ✦ Explain the nature of interest rate risk and the techniques to manage such risks.

While the preceding chapter discusses important financial strategies aimed at maximising corporate wealth and putting the firm in a competitive position, the present chapter, continuing of the preceding discussion, focuses especially on the risk/exposure management strategy. The gain or loss arising on account of unanticipated exchange rate changes is known as exchange rate exposure. Similarly, the gain or loss arising in the sequel of interest rate changes is the interest rate exposure. The purpose of exchange rate and interest rate risk management is to minimise/eliminate the loss accruing on account of exchange rate and interest rate changes.

20.1 NATURE AND MEASUREMENT OF EXCHANGE RATE EXPOSURE

20.1.1 Translation Exposure

Translation exposure refers to exchange rate risk arising out of the translation of the functional currency into the reporting currency.

Exchange rate exposure is classified as translation exposure, transaction exposure, and real operating exposure. Translation exposure, which is also known as accounting exposure, does not involve cash flow. It emerges on account of consolidation of the financial statements of different units of a multinational firm for the purpose of ascertaining overall profitability and evaluation of the comparative performance of different subsidiaries. When the currency of any of the host countries changes its value, its translated value in the domestic currency of the parent company (home-country currency) changes and the picture of the consolidated statement changes. The extent of this change represents the magnitude of translation exposure. It is a fact that if the subsidiary maintains its account in the reporting currency (domestic currency of the parent company), as it is sometimes done by the extended departments of a firm abroad, translation exposure does not emerge. But since the subsidiaries normally maintain their accounts in a functional currency, which is normally the currency of the host country, there is every possibility of the translation exposure emerging in subsequent exchange rate changes. The larger the fluctuation in the value of host country currency, the greater the size of accounting exposure.

The size of exposure also depends on the methods of translation. There are different methods of translation. In the current method, all the items of the financial statements are translated at current or post-change rates. In the current/non-current method, current liabilities and current assets are translated at post-change rates. Long term liabilities and fixed assets are translated at pre-change or historical rates. In monetary/non-monetary method, current assets except inventroy and all the liabilities are translated at current rates. Fixed assets and inventory are translated at historical rates. The temporal method is different from the monetary/non-monetary method insofar as inventory is translated at pre-change rate only if it is not shown at market rate. Different methods are adopted in different countries and hence the size of translation exposure has to vary from one case to the other (Sharan, 2003).

20.1.2 Transaction Exposure

Transaction exposure refers to changes in the exchange rate causing changes in the present cash flow.

Transaction exposure involves changes in the present cash flows, on account of:

1. Export and import of commodities on open account
2. Borrowing and lending in a foreign currency or
3. Intra-firm flows.

If a firm has to make payments for imports in a foreign currency and the foreign currency appreciates, the firm will have to incur loss in terms of its own currency. Similarly, if an exporter has to receive foreign currency for its export and the foreign currency depreciates, the exporter will have to face loss in terms of its own currency. Similarly, the borrower of a foreign currency is put to loss if that particular foreign currency appreciates. Again, changes in exchange rate alters the value of the intra-firm cash flow. The extent of change in the value of cash flow as a sequel to exchange rate changes denotes the amount of transaction exposure.

When transaction exposure of a multinational corporation is referred, it should be considered in terms of **consolidated net exposure**. The word, "net" means that both the inflows and outflows of funds have to be considered and it is the net amount that determines the size of transaction exposure. If the Indian subsidiary of a US company is repatriating dividend to the parent company, any depreciation of the rupee will lower the value of dividend to be received by the parent company in dollar terms. But if the Indian subsidiary exports goods to its parent company invoiced in rupees, the parent company will have to pay a lesser amount in terms of dollars for this transaction due to the rupee's depreciation. So the loss on account of dividend has to be adjusted with the gain on account of trade transaction and it is only the net amount that will determine the size of transaction exposure.

Again, the term consolidated is used when the subsidiaries of a firm are located in different countries. The currency of two or more host countries may change. The change in the value of different currencies may push the transaction exposure in different directions. This means that change in the value of a particular currency may cause gain to the parent company, while change in the value of other currencies may cause loss to the parent company. Thus, it is the consolidated net figure of cash flow with which the parent company is concerned. The severity of exposure, thus, depends upon the correlation between the changes in the value of different currencies. If it is a positive correlation, the magnitude of transaction exposure will be large. But if it is a negative correlation, the loss in one case is compensated by gain in the other. The result is that the size of transaction exposure will be small.

Again, if the transaction exposure manifests in terms of gain, it has to be treated for tax. This is because the gain adds to the profitability and it is the net profit (after taxes) that really matters.

> **Real operating exposure** refers to changes in the exchange rate together with rates of inflation that cause change in the future cash flow.

20.1.3 Real Operating Exposure

Real operating exposure arises when changes in exchange rate, together with rates of inflation, alters the amount and risk element of a company's future revenue and cost stream. The extent of the change in the present value of future cash flows denotes the real operating exposure. There may be different scenarios for such changes and so the different results are put to sensitivity analysis to find out the exact size of exposure.

The word "real" denotes the concept of real exchange rate, which means nominal exchange rate adjusted for inflation. The word "operating" is used because it considers the operating cash flow, a change which causes change in the value of the firm. The measurement of real operating exposure is not very easy, insofar as the measurement of inflation rate differential in the years to come is not easy, especially when the countries are experiencing a highly volatile rate of inflation. However, if the inflation rate differential is forecasted correctly, real operating exposure can be estimated. To mention a very simple example, if the rupee depreciates by 10 per cent, Indian exports will turn competitive as well as imports will be costlier. This will have an impact on the cash flows. But if the inflation differential in India is higher by 10 per cent, the ultimate result may manifest in zero real operating exposure.

Again, changes in the exchange rate will tend to influence the value of imported inputs as well as the value of export. This will, in turn, change the revenue and cost stream in the years to come.

20.2 MANAGEMENT OF EXCHANGE RATE EXPOSURE

20.2.1 Transaction Exposure

The techniques for hedging transaction exposure are sometimes grouped under internal and external techniques (Figure 20.1). The former form a part of the firm's regulatory financial management and do not involve any contractual relationship with any party outside the firm. The latter involve

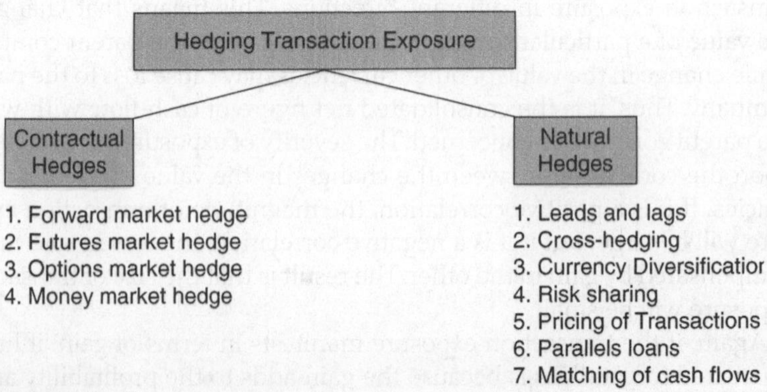

FIGURE 20.1 Techniques for Hedging Transaction Exposure

contractual relationships with parties outside the firm for ensuring that potential foreign exchange loss do not occur (Buckley, 1996).

However, we group the hedging techniques as:

1. Contractual hedge
2. Natural hedge

Hedging refers to minimising the exchange rate risk through buying and selling of currency in the foreign exchange market or in the market for derivatives.

Contractual Hedges: They include the forward market hedge, money market hedge, futures market hedge, and the options market hedge. In the forward market hedge, the exporter sells forward, and the importer buys forward, the foreign currency in which the trade is invoiced. Suppose an Indian exporter signs a contract for leather export to USA for US $1,000. The export proceeds are to be received within three months. The exporter fears a drop in the value of the US dollar, which may diminish the export earnings. To avoid this diminution, the exporter goes for a three-month forward contract and sells US $1,000 forward. The spot as well as the forward rate is Rs. 40/US $. If the dollar depreciates to Rs. 39 after three months, the export earnings in the absence of any forward contract would have diminished to Rs. 39,000. But since the exporter has already sold forward a similar amount of dollars, the loss occurred due to depreciation of the dollar will be met through the forward contract. Selling the dollars on maturity, would fetch him Rs. 40,000, which will be equal to the original export value.

RBI Guidelines for Forward Contracts

Forward Contracts in India—Residents

- Residents were allowed to book forward contracts and participate in hedging instruments for managing risk in the foreign exchange market. Authorised Dealers (ADs) were allowed to offer foreign currency-rupee options on a back-to-back basis or run an option book as per specified terms and conditions.
- Residents were permitted to book forward contracts for hedging transactions denominated in foreign currency but settled in rupees.
- Resident entities were also allowed to hedge their overseas direct investment exposure against exchange risk.
- The eligible limit for booking of forward contracts by exporters/importers was increased to 50 per cent (from 25 per cent earlier) of the average of the previous three financial years' actual import/export turnover or the previous year's turnover, whichever is higher, (from only average of past three years' turnover earlier) without any limit (US $100 million, earlier). Importers/exporters desirous of availing limits higher than the overall ceiling of 50 per cent were allowed to approach the Reserve Bank for permission.
- ADs were permitted to enter into forward/option contracts with residents who wish to hedge their overseas direct investment in equity and debt. These contracts could be completed by delivery or rollover up to the extent of market value on the due date.

Forward Contracts in India—Non-residents

- Non-residents were permitted to enter into forward sale contracts with ADs in India to hedge the currency risk arising out of their proposed FDI in India.
- Holders of FCNR(B) accounts were permitted to book cross-currency forward contracts to convert the balances in one currency into another currency in which FCNR(B) deposits are permitted.
- FIIs were permitted to trade in exchange traded derivative contracts approved by the SEBI subject to the limits prescribed by it.
- NRIs were allowed to invest in exchange traded derivative contracts approved by the SEBI out of rupee funds held in India on a non-repatriable basis.

Source: *RBI Annual Report,* 2003–04

Similarly, an Indian importer buys goods from United States of America for US $1,000. If the importer fears an appreciation in the value of US dollar, he will buy the same amount of dollars forward. If the dollar appreciates to Rs. 41 after the three-month period, the importer, in the absence of any forward deal, would have to pay Rs. 1,000 more. But if he has gone for a forward deal for buying a similar amount of dollars, he will purchase US $1,000 with Rs. 40,000 in the forward market and pay US $1,000 to the US exporter. This way the importer saves himself from a loss of Rs. 1,000.

Hedging in a futures market is similar. The only difference is of the procedure, with a view to the varying characteristics of the futures market, which have been explained in Chapter 13 of this book.

The importer buys a call option or sells a put option or performs both functions at the same time. The exporter buys a put option and sells a call option or performs both functions simultaneously.

For hedging in the currency options market, the importer buys a call option or sells a put option or performs both the functions at the same time. The exporter buys a put option and sells a call option or performs both the functions simultaneously. Suppose an Indian firm is importing goods for £62,500. The amount is to be paid after two months, which coincides with the maturity in the options market. If an appreciation is expected in the value of the pound, the importer will buy a call option on pounds with maturity coinciding with the payment for import. If the strike price is Rs. 84.00/£, the premium is Rs. 0.05 per sterling pound and the spot price at maturity is Rs. 84.20/£, the importer will exercise the option. It will have to pay Rs. 84.00 × 62,500 + 3,125 = Rs. 52,53,125. If the importer does not go for buying an option, it will have to pay Rs. 62,500 × 84.20 = Rs. 52,62,500. Buying the call option reduces the importer's obligation by Rs. 52,62,500 − 52,53,125 = 9,375. If, on the other hand, the pound falls to Rs. 83.80, the importer will not exercise the option. His obligation will be reduced even after paying of the premium.

Suppose an Indian exporter exports goods for £62,500. He fears a depreciation of the pound within two months, when payments are to be made. In order to avoid the risk, he will buy a put option for selling pounds for a two-month maturity. Suppose the strike rate is Rs. 84.00, the premium is Rs. 0.05, and the spot rate at maturity is Rs. 83.80. In case of a hedge, he will receive Rs. 62,500 × 84.00 − 3,125 = 52,46,875. In the absence of a hedge, he will receive only Rs. 52,37,500. This means, buying of a put option helps increase the exporter's earnings, or reduces his exposure, by Rs. 52,46,875 − 52,37,500 = 9,375.

Hedging through selling of options is advised when the volatility in the exchange rate is expected to be only marginal. Suppose the Indian importer imports for £62,500. He fears an appreciation in the pound and so he sells a put option on pounds at a strike price of Rs. 84.00/£ and at a premium of Rs. 0.15 per pound. If the spot price at maturity goes up to Rs. 84.05, the buyer of the option will not exercise the option. The importer, as a seller of the put option, will receive premium of Rs. 9,375 which will be a relief for him while making payments for import as compared to no relief in case of no option.

Exporters sell a call option. An Indian exporter exports goods worth £62,500. He fears that the pound will depreciate and sells a call option on pounds at a strike price of Rs. 84.00 and at a premium of Rs. 0.15 per pound. If the spot rate at maturity really falls to Rs. 83.95, the buyer of the call option will not exercise the option. The exporter being the seller of the call option will get Rs. 9,375 as premium.

Foreign exchange exposure can also be hedged through the use of tunnels or, in other words, through simultaneous sale and purchase of options. It depends upon the degree of exchange rate changes, whether the two options will be out-of-money or one of the options will be in-the-money.

Money market hedge is just taking a money market position to cover future payables or receivables position. An importer, who is to cover future payables, firstly, borrows local currency; secondly, converts the borrowed local currency into the currency of payables; and finally, invests the converted amount for a period matching with the payments to be made for imports. On the contrary, an exporter hedging receivables, firstly, borrows the currency in which the receivables are denominated; secondly, converts the borrowed currency into local currency; and finally, invests the converted amount for a maturity coinciding with the receipt of export proceeds. The money market hedge may be covered or uncovered. If the firm makes sufficient money out of business operations to buy the foreign currency or to repay the foreign currency loan, it is called a covered hedge. However, purchasing foreign currency out of borrowed funds or repaying foreign currency loan by purchasing foreign currency in the spot market is known as an uncovered money market hedge.

Money market hedge is just taking a money market position to cover future payables or receivables position.

A simple example will make the process clear. Suppose an Indian importer has to make payments for imports worth US $1,000 after 90 days. If it is a covered hedge, it creates a 90−day investment in the foreign currency in which the import is invoiced. The amount of initial investment will be such that the principal plus interest after 90 days equals the payments for import. If the rate of interest on investment is 12 per cent per annum and if the amount of import is US $1,000, the sum of initial investment will be:

$$\text{US \$}\,\frac{1{,}000}{1.03} = \text{US \$970.87}$$

On the day imports will be paid, the importer will receive US $1,000 from investment and there will be no problem even if the exchange rate changes.

If it is an uncovered hedge, the importer borrows Rs. 970.87 × 40 (assuming a spot rate of Rs. 40/US $) = Rs. 38,834.80, it will convert the rupee amount into US dollar to get US $970.87 and invest it at 12 per cent per annum interest rate. On the day the imports are paid, the importer will get US $1,000 and there will be no problem in paying for the imports. The only cost it has to bear is the interest payment on borrowing.

In case of 90−day receivables, if it amounts to US $1,000, the exporter will borrow US $970.87, convert this amount into Rs. 38,834.80 and invest this amount at 12% p.a. interest rate. On the day the export proceeds are received, the investment (principal + interest) will amount to Rs. 40,000. The exporter will not be exposed to exchange rate changes, if any. The cost of hedging borne by it is the payment of interest on borrowing.

Natural Hedge: Firms go for natural hedges because contractual hedge provides only temporary protection against exchange rate movement and sometimes the market for contractual hedge is not well developed. Some important natural hedge techniques need to be mentioned here.

Lead means accelerating or advancing the timing of receipt or payment of the foreign currency. Lag is just the reverse.

Leads and Lags: Lead means accelerating or advancing the timing of receipt or payment of the foreign currency. Lag is just the reverse, which means decelerating or postponing the timing of receipt or payment of foreign currency. Suppose a firm is located in a weak currency country and it has to pay debt denominated in hard currency. There is every possibility of the hard currency appreciating against the weak currency. In such a situation, the debtor firm will like to lead the payments. On the contrary, if a firm located in hard currency country has to pay debt denominated in weak currency, it would like to lag the payment. In both the cases, the purpose is to lower the debt burden.

Leading and lagging is practised between two independent firms or in intra-firm transactions. In case of inter-firm transactions, practising of this technique is normally opposed. It is because if one firm reaps the gain, it will cause loss to the other firm. But within a firm, it is a common strategy.

Cross hedging refers to hedging in some other currency correlated with the desired one.

Cross-hedging: It is adopted when the desired currency cannot be hedged. In this case, the firm has to identify a foreign currency that can be hedged, the volatility of which is highly correlated with that of the desired currency. The hedging of the identified currency in the forward market will be a substitute for the forward market hedging of the desired currency.

Currency Diversification: If transactions are diversified over a number of currencies and if there is negative correlation in the change of their values, the exchange rate risk is automatically minimised. The greater the diversification, the lesser is the risk.

Risk sharing: Risk sharing is a contractual arrangement through which the buyer and the seller agree to share the exposure. Both parties normally agree to such a proposal if their business relationship is a long term one. Under this arrangement, a base rate is fixed with mutual consent, which is generally the current spot rate. A neutral zone is also agreed upon, which is a few points minus and plus the base rate. When the exchange rate changes within the neutral zone, the transaction takes place at the base rate. But if the exchange rate crosses the neutral zone, the risk is shared equally by the two parties.

Pricing of Transactions: Pricing policy is adopted in two ways. One is price variation and the other is currency of invoicing. Price variation involves marking up/marking down of sale price in order to counter the adverse effects of exchange rate changes. The normal rule is to charge the price in foreign currency on the basis of the forward rate and not the spot rate. In case of sequential payments to be made or received at different time points, a weighted average of forward rates of different dates is computed. Charging of a different price from the arm's-length price is a usual practice in case of intra-firm transactions. But for the purpose of exposure management, this practice is also adopted in inter-firm transactions.

As far as invoicing of transaction is concerned, the exporter is willing to invoice the bill in its own currency or in the currency in which it incurs the cost so that the transaction exposure is avoided. But, if the importer is dominant, the bill is normally invoiced in the importer's currency. In other cases, the exporter follows the market leader or its major competitors.

It may be noted here that in intra-firm transactions, this technique does not figure large as the gain accruing to one unit is offset by the loss incurred by the other unit of the firm. Nevertheless, the advantages appearing on account of tax differential between two countries encourage intra-firm transactions to be invoiced in either the appreciating or depreciating currency. Suppose there are two subsidiaries of a firm located in Country *A* and Country *B*. The marginal tax in Country *A* is higher than in Country *B*. In such a case, other factors remaining the same, the subsidiary in Country *A* shall invoice the transaction with *B* in a weak currency. The subsidiary in Country *B* shall invoice the transaction in a strong currency. This way, the before-tax profit of the subsidiary in Country *A* can be passed on to that in Country *B*, if the currency depreciates further. Ultimately, the tax burden of both the subsidiaries taken together will be lower.

Parallel Loans: A parallel loan is often known as back-to-back loan or a credit swap loan. Under this arrangement, the amount of the loan moves within the country but it serves the purpose of a cross-border loan. At the same time, such loans are not exposed to changes in exchange rate because the funds do not move across the national border. Suppose a US company (parent company) has a subsidiary in India. At the same time, an Indian company (parent company) has a subsidiary in United States of America. Suppose further that the US parent company has to lend US $1,000 to its subsidiary in India for a specific period. The Indian parent company too has to lend a similar amount for the same maturity to its

> **Parallel loan** is the simultaneous borrowing and lending involving four parties in two countries.

subsidiary in United States of America. If the funds move between the two countries and if the exchange rate changes, transaction exposure will be caused. Thus, in order to avoid the exposure, the Indian parent company will lend the above amount converted into the rupee at the spot exchange rate to the US subsidiary. Simultaneously, the US parent company will lend a similar amount, in terms of US dollars, to the Indian subsidiary. At the expiry of the specified period, the two loans will be repaid to the respective lenders. Figure 20.2 shows how the transactions take place in a back-to-back loan arrangement.

This is no doubt an efficacious technique of hedging the transaction exposure, but it is difficult to find a firm that has to lend a similar amount for similar maturity. If such a firm, known as a counter-party, is located, it cannot be guaranteed that the counter-party repays the loan within the specified period. If it fails to make repayments, counter-party risk will emerge. It is this particular limitation with the parallel loan that has made the currency swap popular.

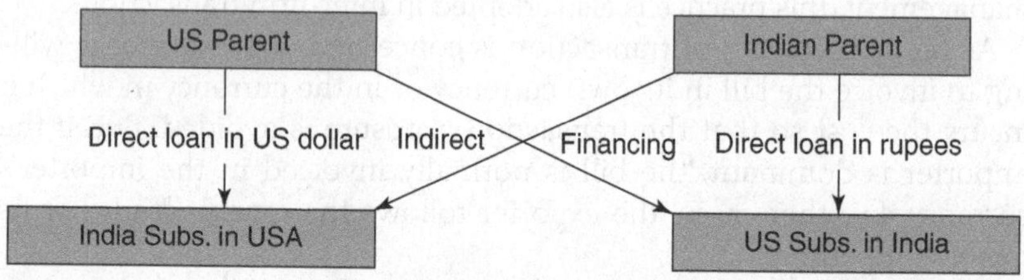

FIGURE 20.2 Creation of Back-to-back Loan

Matching of Cash Flows: Under this mechanism, a firm matches its foreign currency inflow with the outflow in that currency not only in respect of size but also in respect of timing. But, for this purpose, it is necessary that the firm has both inflows and outflows in the same currency.

20.2.2 Hedging of Real Operating Exposure

Since the area of real operating exposure extends to future cost and revenue streams, the steps taken to manage such exposure must consider the management of future cost and revenue. So it is not only the domain of the finance manager, but also of the production and marketing managers. In other words, the management of real operating exposure includes strategy concerning finance, production, and marketing (Figure 20.3).

Financial Strategy: The hedging techniques used for transaction exposure, especially those that are used for long term transaction exposure, are also used for managing real operating exposure. However, they are of little use in this case because the effects of currency changes on the expected cash flows are hard to predict. It is, therefore, better to use sophisticated computerised tools for this purpose.

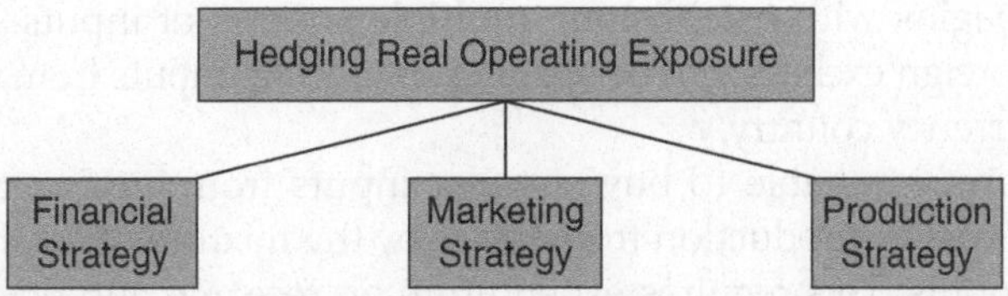

FIGURE 20.3 Strategies for Management of Real Operating Exposure

Nevertheless, while developing a financial strategy, the finance manager has to ensure that the firm's liabilities during the application of marketing and production strategies are so structured that they could match a reduction in assets' earnings during that period. This means that if assets' earnings drop, the servicing burden of liabilities too should be lower. To this end, assets and liabilities are restructured.

> The finance manager has to ensure that the firm's liabilities are so structured that they could match a reduction in assets' earnings during that period. The marketing strategy includes, among other things, selection of market, product planning, and pricing policy.

Marketing Strategy: The marketing strategy includes, among other things, selection of market, product planning, and pricing policy. The policy in this respect is influenced by the geography of the market, dominance of the firm in the international market, and the elasticity of demand for the product.

If the domestic currency appreciates, export would turn uncompetitive on account of price. The strategy in this case should be to pull out of the existing market and to develop new markets. The market segmentation approach within a particular importing country may be adopted. If the product is demanded more by an affluent class of consumers, appreciation of domestic currency may not matter much. The strategy of market segmentation should, therefore, be to concentrate on this class of consumers. Again, if the firm is a dominant supplier of the product or if the price-elasticity of demand for the product is low, the firm can stick to the existing market without making changes in the price.

The firm can respond to changes in the exchange rate by modifying the product strategy. It can innovate and introduce a new product or can make the product differentiated and, thereby, charge a higher price for the product to compensate the loss on account of exchange rate changes.

Similarly, it may adopt a different pricing policy. It may raise or lower the price of the product due to exchange rate changes, depending upon the price elasticity of demand, availability of the substitutes, and so on.

> Production strategy concentrates primarily on product sources, input mixing, and plant location.

Production Strategy: Production strategy concentrates primarily on product sources, input mixing, and plant location. If the currency of a country supplying inputs appreciates, the input buying firm has to find out some other sources of supply that may be cheaper. If the home currency appreciates, it would be in the interest of the input buying firm not to change the source of supply, and preferably buy inputs from the countries to which it exports its final product. This is to ensure that its terms of trade will improve. This step would be highly beneficial if the imported inputs account for a lion's share of the total inputs. Sometimes the strategy begins with establishing multiple sources of inputs. This is to save the foreign exchange to be spent on importing inputs from an appreciating currency country.

If the firm is unable to buy cheaper inputs from any source, it can arrest the cost of production from rising by the mixture of local inputs or cheaper inputs. This requires expenditure on research and development so that a new technology using cheaper inputs in a greater proportion could be evolved. For such a decision, it is required to weigh the benefit of input mixing against the cost of research and development.

Alternatively, the firm can locate the plant in a country whose currency has depreciated, provided that the inputs are available there. In cases where inputs are available only in a particular country, the firm will have to import them even if the currency of the input supplying country appreciates.

There are, thus, different options open for improving the future cost-revenue streams. The firm chooses any one of them or combines more than one of them, depending upon their suitability in a particular case.

20.2.3 Managing Translation Exposure

There is one view that there is no need for hedging translation exposure as it does not affect the cash flow. But firms try to hedge it in view of its potential impact on the reported consolidated earnings.

Balance sheet means if the liabilities are lower than the assets, fresh borrowings are made. If the liabilities exceed assets, fresh investments are made to eliminate the mismatch. Borrowings are made in weaker currencies and investment is made in stronger currencies.

The commonly used technique with respect to hedging of translation exposure is known as the balance sheet hedge. Since translation exposure arises out of mismatch between the size of assets and the size of liabilities resulting from the convertion of figures in the functional currency to those in the reporting currency using different methods of conversion, balance sheet hedge eliminates such mismatches. If the liabilities are lower than the assets, fresh borrowings are made. If the liabilities exceed assets, fresh investments are made to eliminate the mismatch. But it may be noted that borrowings are made in weaker currencies and investment is made in stronger currencies. This is because weaker currencies tend to depreciate vis-à-vis strong currencies. So the exposure can be hedged if strong currency assets substitute weak currency assets and weak-currency liabilities substitute the strong currency liabilities.

If borrowings/investments are made under the process of balance sheet hedge, there is every possibility of the emergence of transaction exposure in face of changing exchanges rates. If this is the case, contractual and natural hedges may be adopted.

20.3 NATURE OF INTEREST RATE RISK

With growing preference for a floating interest rate since the 1980s, the interest rate risk or exposure has become more significant. When it moves in favour of the lender, the debt burden of the borrower gets bigger. When it moves in favour of the borrower, the lender has to suffer loss on account of interest. It is not only the size of interest payment that causes exposure. Changes in interest rate influence the market price of the bond and the changes in the price of the bond are often the source of exposure.

The nature of interest rate exposure varies between a financial and a non-financial firm. For a non-financial firm, changes in interest rate lead to changes in financial cost and, thereby, to changes in earnings before tax and returns from investment. But for a financial firm, changes in the interest rate affect the very assets and liabilities and, thereby, the very net worth of the firm.

Interest rate risk may be grouped under three heads:

1. Credit risk
2. Liquidity risk
3. Basis risk

Credit risk is concerned with default risk when the borrower fails to make payments of interest and principal. In order to minimise this type of risk, the lender makes loans to only borrowers who are financially sound and who have no record of default. The risk can also be minimised through diversification of lending among large number of borrowers.

> **Credit risk** is loss on account of default of repayment of loan.

Liquidity risk, which is also known as the gap risk, is more typical of a non-financial firm. Such risk is related to the timing mismatches between cash inflows and cash outflows on account of interest payment. A non-financial firm usually possesses a comparatively small amount of interest sensitive asset, while interest sensitive debt may account for a large segment of the total liabilities. In such a situation, if long duration interest sensitive assets are financed by short duration interest sensitive liabilities, liquidity risk is bound to arise. In order to ascertain the magnitude of gap risk, the firm divides the entire planning horizon into sub-periods. For each sub-period, the difference between the assets and the liabilities is assessed.

> **Liquidity risk** is risk on account of mismatches of cash inflow and outflow in a non-financial firm.

On the other hand, basis risk is related primarily to financial companies. It arises when the interest rate exposure on one instrument is offset by the interest rate exposure on another instrument. It also happens when floating-rate financial assets tied to one index are funded by floating rate liabilities tied to some other index. Financial companies, whose revenues and costs consist primarily of interest rate payment flows, are more prone to such risks. This is because the net interest income, that is, the difference between receipt of interest on assets and interest payment on liabilities, is of great importance for such firms.

> **Basis risk** is risk in a financial firm owing to differences in the index to which financial assets and liabilities are tied.

Whatever the type of risk, its magnitude depends also upon how the interest is calculated. This is because the practices differ from one country to another. In Switzerland, for example, 360 days make a year for calculating interest. On the contrary, the British practice involves 365 days. With the same amount of principal, the interest will vary in these two cases.

20.4 TECHNIQUES OF MANAGING INTEREST RATE EXPOSURE

There are different techniques to hedge the interest rate risk. A particular technique is practised depending on the circumstances and the cost involved. Broadly speaking, the techniques can be grouped under three heads:

1. Yield curve based techniques, such as mismatched borrowings and forward rate agreement.
2. Derivative based techniques, such as interest rate futures and interest-rate swap.
3. Option based techniques, such as options on forward rate agreements, swaptions, caps, floors, and collars.

One can group the various techniques of interest rate management also on the basis of whether they are practised in over-the-counter markets or through organised stock exchanges. In the first category come the mismatched borrowings, forward rate agreements, interest rate and currency swaps, caps, floors, and collars; while interest rate futures come under the second category.

20.4.1 Mismatched Borrowings

The yield curve is normally supposed to be a forecast of future spot interest rates. Thus, if the yield curve is upward sloping, the future rate of interest will be more attractive for the investor. In this case, it is better to borrow short and invest long. The short term borrowing will bring funds for long term investment. At the same time, the cash inflow in the medium term on account of investment will cover the repayment of the short term borrowing.

If, on the other hand, the yield curve is sloping downward, the firm can borrow long and invest short. The long term borrowing will provide funds for making short term investments. At the same time, the inflow from short term investment will enable the firm to service the long term borrowing.

20.4.2 Forward Rate Agreements

Forward Rate Agreements is a contract through which a borrower/lender locks the interest rate and protects itself from loss on account of change in interest rate.

Forward rate agreements (FRAs) are contracts through which a borrower or a lender/investor locks the interest rate on his future borrowings or lending/investment and protects himself from unfavourable changes in the interest rate. A simple example will illustrate this. Suppose a firm needs to borrow in the near future when it expects the interest rate to move up. This means that with rising interest rate, it will have to make a larger interest payment. To protect itself from a larger interest payment, it goes for an FRA deal with its banker for an amount equivalent to its borrowing amount. The principal amount under the FRA deal will just be a notional amount and the bank will pay the firm the present value of the difference of the interest payment between the pre-change rate or the locked interest rate and at the post-change rate prevailing at the time of maturity. The interest payment differential is discounted because FRA is settled in the beginning of the period and not at the end when interest is normally paid. The discount factor is the actual (post-change) interest rate. This payment would be rather a compensation that eliminates the interest rate exposure faced by the firm.

Forward Rate Agreements (FRAs)/Interest Rate Swaps (IRS) in India: 2003–05

There was a sharp increase in the volume in FRAs/IRS market during 2003–04, both in terms of number of contracts and outstanding notional principal amounts. The number of contracts rose from 9,363 to 19,867, while the outstanding amount rose from Rs. 2,42,983 crore to Rs. 5,18,260 crore during the period April 4, 2003 to March 19, 2004. The participation in the market was broad based and included public sector banks, PDs, foreign banks and private sector banks.

In a majority of these contracts, the National Stock Exchange-Mumbai Inter-bank offered Rate (NSE-MIBOR) and Mumbai Inter-bank Forward Offered Rate (MIFOR) were used as the benchmarks. Other benchmark rates used were secondary market yields of the Government securities with residual maturity of one-year and primary cut-off yield on 364-day Treasury Bills. Activity in FRAs/IRS is expected to pick up after the regulatory and prudential norms for over-the-counter (OTC) and exchange traded derivatives are harmonised by the Reserve Bank. During 2004–05, the number of contracts rose further to 23,331 and the outstanding amount moved up to Rs. 6,11,595 crore as on May 28, 2004.

Source: *RBI Annual Report*, 2003–04.

Example: Suppose the present interest rate is 6 per cent per annum, the amount of future borrowing is \$100,000; the maturity is three months; and the risen interest rate is 7 per cent per annum. This means that at the risen rate, the borrowing firm will have to make interest payment equivalent to \$1,769.44 or \$252.77 more than that at the pre-change rate. The interest rate exposure the borrowing firm has to face is \$252.77. If it purchases FRA for an equivalent principal, it will get the following amount as compensation from its banker (seller of the FRA):

$$\frac{\left[100{,}000 \times \left\{(0.07 - 0.06) \times \left(\frac{91}{360}\right)\right\}\right]}{\left\{1 + \left(\frac{0.07 \times 91}{360}\right)\right\}} = \$248.39$$

Thus, when an interest rate rise is expected, the borrower purchases FRA. But when interest rate is expected to fall, the borrower does not go for an FRA deal. As far as lender is concerned, it will buy FRA if the interest rate is expected to fall.

20.4.3 Interest-rate Swap

When borrowers expect a rise in interest rates, they swap a floating-rate loan for a fixed rate loan. On the contrary, when they expect a fall in the interest rate, they swap a fixed rate loan for floating rate loan.

Interest rate swap has already been discussed in the preceding chapter. However, it may be pointed out that when borrowers expect a rise in interest rates, they swap a floating-rate loan for a fixed rate loan. On the contrary, when they expect a fall in the interest rate, they swap a fixed rate loan for floating rate loan.

The use of interest rate swap for hedging risk may be explained through the help of an example. Suppose a television manufacturing firm provides a loan to its customers for financing the purchase of television sets at a fixed rate of 12 per cent. Such loans are financed by medium term notes that the firm issues at LIBOR + 25 basis points. LIBOR is 7 per cent and the administrative and other costs involved in borrowing and lending come to 2 per cent. If LIBOR does not fluctuate, the firm will enjoy a margin of 12.0 − (7.25 + 2.0) = 2.75 per cent. But if LIBOR moves up, the margin will squeeze and the firm will face a loss. In order to check this squeeze, the firm will go for interest rate swap with a swap dealer. It will pay a fixed rate of interest at 7 per cent to the swap dealer; and in return, will get a floating rate of interest from the swap dealer. The receipt of floating interest rate from the swap dealer will neutralise to a great extent/eliminate the loss on account of increase in LIBOR.

After the swap, the interest margin of the firm will be equal to the difference between the interest received from the consumers as well as from the swap dealer and the interest paid to the swap dealer and to the purchasers of medium term notes. If LIBOR is 7 per cent, the margin, assuming zero administrative cost, would be:

$$(12.0 + 7.0) - (7.0 + 7.0 + 0.25) = 4.75\%$$

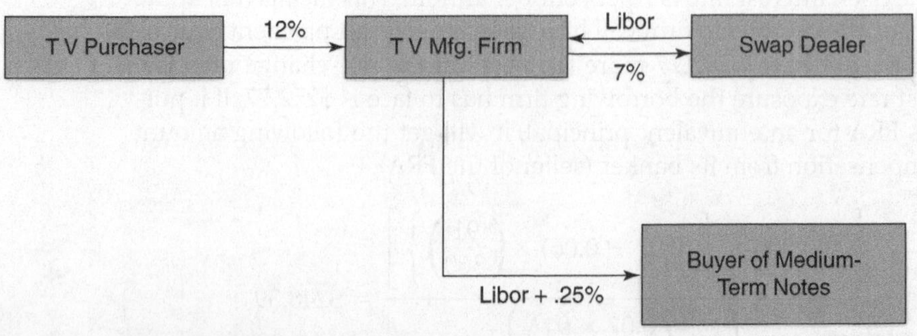

FIGURE 20.4 Hedging with Interest Rate Swap

If LIBOR goes up to 8 per cent, the interest margin will be:

$$(12.0 + 8.0) - (7.0 + 8.0 + 0.25) = 4.75\%$$

Had there been no swap, the margin would have squeezed to 3.75 per cent after an increase in LIBOR. But after the swap, the margin remains the same. This means the interest rate swap hedges the risk (Figure 20.4).

20.4.4 Interest Rate Futures

Interest rate futures refer to a contract to hedge interest rate risk made through an authorised broker.

Interest rate futures (IRFs) were meant to hedge interest rate risk evolved in mid-1970s in the US financial market. Presently, they are available in many other markets and in many other currencies. The IRFs market is like the currency futures market where deals are contracted in the pit of the organised exchange through an authorised broker. A nominal amount of the contract is standardised. Maturity falls in March, June, September and December. There is usually a clearing house to record the transactions and to function as a counterparty. Margin money and margin call mechanisms are found. On maturity, the contract is reversed.

IRFs are used, both, in case of rising interest rate and falling interest rate. The value of a bond diminishes with a rise in the interest rate, and vice versa. Firms in long position, that is, firms holding bonds incur loss with a rise in interest rates inasmuch as the value of the bond diminishes. When they suspect loss, they go for IRFs. Suppose a company is having 10-year French government bond for € 1,000,000. The interest rate, which is 10 per cent in July, is expected to move up to 1 by December, as a result of which a fall in the price of the bond is expected. The company would like to go for interest rate futures for protecting itself from this loss. It will instruct its broker to sell interest rate futures for the equivalent amount, which is a notional amount. Since the standard size of FF futures is € 500,000, two futures will be sold.

In December interest rate rises to 11 per cent and as a result, the value of the bond drops to € 991,000 (€ 941,000 as the price of the bond plus € 50,000, as the interest accrued). The broker will then go for a reverse contract, that is, for buying December delivery futures at a price of € 941,000. By doing so, the broker will gain:

Price sold − price bought

or

$$€\ 1{,}000{,}000 - €\ 941{,}000 = €\ 59{,}000$$

Now,

1. After the future deals, the value of the company's portfolio at the end of December will be equal to:

$$€\ 941{,}000 + 50{,}000 + 59{,}000 = €\ 1{,}050{,}000$$

2. If the bondholder does not opt for IRFs, the value of the investment portfolio will be equal to:

$$€\ 941{,}000 + 50{,}000 = €\ 991{,}000$$

3. If there is no interest rate change and no futures deal, the value of the investment portfolio will be equal to:

$$€\ 1{,}000{,}000 \text{ as principal} + €\ 50{,}000 \text{ as the interest} = €\ 1{,}050{,}000$$

Thus, it is clear that with a rise in interest rate, the value of the investment portfolio diminishes and it puts the investors to loss. But if the investor goes for interest rate futures, the loss is hedged.

So far we have discussed that the interest rate rises as per expectation. But it may be that the rate of interest falls contrary to expectation. In that case, there will be loss on future contracts, but the loss would be compensated by an increase in the value of the bonds.

Again, if the bond holder expects a fall in the interest rate, he will buy interest rate futures for an equivalent notional amount that will be reversed on the maturity date.

20.4.5 Interest Rate Caps

Interest rate caps refer to a contract through which a borrower caps the interest rate and avoids loss owing to any rise in the interest rate.

Interest rate cap (IRC) is an option based technique practised in over-the-counter market. This technique evolved in the mid-1980s in the euro-dollar market and now it is more frequently used.

When a firm borrowing a floating rate loan fears a rise in LIBOR, it may buy an IRC for the loan equivalent amount that will help reduce the interest rate exposure. This is because the seller of the IRC, normally a bank, reimburses the buyer's loss in the event LIBOR exceeds the cap's interest rate level. In order to arrive at the net gain accruing to the buyer of the cap, the amount of premium paid by the buyer of the cap must be deducted from the amount of the reimbursement. The principal amount of the cap is notional. The total maturity is divided into a number of reset periods.

Example: Suppose a firm borrows $100,000 for four years at 6−month LIBOR + 25 basis points. If the firm fears a rise in LIBOR, it buys IRC for an equivalent amount with the same maturity at a strike price of 7.0 per cent, which is equal to the prevailing rate. The premium is 0.5 per cent for the reset period. If, at the end of the first reset, LIBOR rises to 10.0 per cent, the amount of interest paid by the borrower will be equal to:

$$\$100{,}000 \times 10.25\% \times \frac{180}{360} = \$5{,}125$$

Moreover, the borrower will have to pay premium equivalent to:

$$\$100{,}000 \times 0.005 = \$500$$

On the other hand, the borrowing firm will receive from the bank, that is, from the cap seller an amount equivalent to:

$$\$100{,}000 \times (0.10 - 0.07) \times \frac{180}{360} = \$1500$$

As a result of the cap deal, the entire interest rate exposure of the borrower is eliminated. The only thing is that it has to pay premium for the cap. But even after taking into the amount of premium, we find that the interest rate exposure is greatly reduced.

However, if, contrary to the expectation, LIBOR diminishes at the end of the first reset period or the other reset periods, the borrowing firm will have to pay a lower amount of interest but it will have to pay the premium. The net gain depends upon the extent of changes in LIBOR and the amount of premium.

20.4.6 Interest Rate Floors

Interest rate floor is a contract through which a lender avoids loss on account of decrease in interest rate.

Interest rate floor (IRF) is different from IRC inasmuch as the IRF protects against a fall in the interest rates. So it is the investor or the depositor who buys IRF, whereas IRC, as we know, is bought by a borrower. However, many features of the two instruments are similar. IRF is also an over-the-counter market instrument. The seller of IRF compensates the loss of the buyer on account of change (fall) in interest rates. For this privilege, the buyer pays premium to the seller.

Suppose a firm makes Euro deposits for \$100,000 at 6–month LIBOR minus 25 basis points for one year. It fears a fall in LIBOR and so buys an IRF with a strike price of 6.0 per cent per annum, which is equivalent to the prevailing LIBOR. It pays a lump sum premium at 0.5 per cent for the whole of the year. As expected, LIBOR moves down to 4.0 per cent after the six month period.

If the depositor does not go for IRF, it will receive \$1875 as interest for the six-month period, which will be lower by \$1,000 than that during the beginning of the deposit period. But if it goes for IRF, the bank will compensate this loss. The compensation is computed as:

$$\$100{,}000 \times (0.06 - 0.04) \times \frac{180}{360} = 1{,}000$$

However, the net gain accruing to the depositor will be lower by the amount of the premium.

20.4.7 Interest Rate Collars

Interest rate collars are a combination of interest rate caps and floors. A borrower buys a cap and sells a floor simultaneously or an investor or a depositor buys a floor and sells a cap simultaneously.

Interest rate collar is a combination of caps and floors. It is just like a tunnel where an importer buys a call option and sells a put option simultaneously or an exporter buys a put option and sells a call option. Similarly, a borrower buys a cap and sells a floor simultaneously or an investor or a depositor buys a floor and sells a cap simultaneously. In this way the collar fixes a maximum and a minimum interest rate. A borrower limits risk owing to a rise in the interest rate, but it also limits the opportunities of benefiting from a fall in the interest rate. An investor limits the risk owing to a fall in interest rate and also limits the gains owing to rise in interest rates. The premium in both the cases is calculated in such a way that the premium received normally equals the premium paid.

Example: A simple example will make clear the distinctive characteristics of a collar. Suppose a firm borrows $100,000 for two years at LIBOR plus 0.25 per cent. It purchases cap with a strike price of 7.0 per cent and sells a floor at a strike price of 5.0 per cent. If LIBOR varies between 5.0 per cent and 7.0 per cent, no payment is made on the collar. The borrower pays interest at LIBOR + 0.25 per cent. If the interest rate exceeds 7.0 per cent, the bank (seller of the cap) pays the difference. If the interest rate falls below 5.0 per cent, the borrowing firm pays the difference to the bank. In the former case, the cost of the loan is 7.25 per cent; in the latter it 5.25 per cent.

20.4.8 Interest Rate Corridors

While interest rate collars present a combination of cap and floor, interest rate corridors present a combination of two or more caps. A borrower buys one cap with a specific strike rate and simultaneously sells another cap with a higher strike rate with a view to offsetting at least a part of the cost of the cap purchased. The purchased cap protects from rising interest rate; on the contrary, the sold cap obligates the borrower to pay only when it (the sold cap) is activated.

20.4.9 Options on FRAs

Options on the FRAs are normally used for short term borrowing. A borrowing firm, when it is not sure of the direction of the interest rate changes, buys a call option on the FRA. If interest rate moves up, it exercises the call option and locks itself to the lower rate. If interest rate moves down, it prefers to let the call option expire and pays interest at the lower rate. But in both the cases it has to pay the premium. On the contrary, a lending firm buys a put option on the FRA. If the interest rate moves up, it lets the option expire and receives interest at a higher rate. But if the interest rate moves down, the option is exercised as a result of which the lending firm locks itself to the higher rate. In both the cases, the interest inflow gets reduced by the amount of premium.

20.4.10 Options on Swaps

Swaption is option on swap in medium term and long term borrowing.

An option on swap is also called a swaption. It is used in case of medium-term and long term borrowing. This instrument confers the right to enter into an interest rate swap either as the payer or as the recipient of the fixed side of the swap. When it is a payer swaption, it confers the right to pay the fixed rate in the swap. If the interest rate exceeds the swaption strike rate, the buyer exercises the option and locks itself to a lower interest rate. The seller gets the fixed rate equal to the strike price and pays the floating rate. If the interest rate does not exceed the strike rate, swaption is not exercised.

In case of receiver swaption, the buyer exercises the option and locks itself to a higher rate when the interest rate falls below the swaption strike rate. If it is not so, swaption is not exercised.

SUMMARY

- Exchange rate exposure is the loss or gain caused by changes beyond anticipation in exchange rate. Foreign exchange exposure is of different types. One is known as accounting exposure, leaving no impact on the cash flows. The other is transaction exposure, involving changes in the present cash flows. Yet another is real operating exposure, altering the future cash flows.
- Transaction exposure is often concerned with changes in trade receipt/payments, changes in external debt burden or changes in the amount of intra-firm flows. In case of MNCs, it is the consolidated net figure of cash flows that determines the size of transaction exposure.
- Real operating exposure is concerned with, both, changes in inflation rate and the exchange rate, causing changes in the future revenue and cost stream of the firm.
- Translation exposure emerges on account of consolidation of financial statements of foreign subsidiaries by the parent company. With changes in the exchange rate, and particularly on account of varying methods of translation, the picture of the consolidated statement changes. This change represents the size of the translation exposure.
- Transaction exposure is managed by both contractual hedges and natural hedges. There are different techniques of contractual hedges such as hedging in the forward, futures, and options market, and the money market hedge. In the natural hedge, the usually adopted techniques are leads and lags, price variation and currency of invoicing, matching of currency flows, currency swaps, currency diversification, risk sharing, cross hedging, parallel loans, and so on.
- While managing real operating exposure, some of the natural hedging techniques are applied, which are especially meant for hedging long term transaction exposure. But in this case, the firm applies a combination of financial, marketing, and production strategies so that the future net cash inflow improves significantly to offset the adverse effects of exchange rate changes.
- In case of translation exposure management, the balance-sheet hedge is the most common technique, followed by some financial hedging techniques.
- Again, borrowers and lenders have to face interest rate exposure on account of changes in the interest rate. Such a change influences the earning position of a non-financial firm, while it affects the very asset-liability position of a financial firm. Interest rate risk is grouped as credit risk, liquidity risk, and basis risk.
- There are different techniques for management of interest rate exposure. Most of them are found in the over-the-counter market. Only few of them are practised through the organised exchanges. They are grouped as yield-curve-based techniques, such as mismatched borrowing and forward rate agreement; derivative based techniques such

as interest rate swap and interest rate futures; and yet again, option-based techniques, such as interest rate caps, floors, collars, options on FRA and swaption.

REVIEW QUESTIONS

1. Describe the different forms of exchange rate exposure. How do they differ among themselves?
2. Explain, with suitable examples, the different forms of contractual hedge.
3. Explain the techniques adopted for natural hedge.
4. What are the different types of interest-rate risk? Do they affect financial and non-financial firms in the same way?
5. Discuss some more common techniques of interest rate risk management.

OBJECTIVE TYPE QUESTIONS

1. Mark True or False:
   (a) A borrower not sure of the direction of changes in the interest rate buys a call option on FRA.
   (b) A lender buys a put option on FRA.
   (c) Investors buy a cap.
   (d) Investors buy a floor.
   (e) Basis risk is caused when two indices are used for calculating interest rate.
   (f) Money market hedge is a natural hedge technique.
   (g) Options market hedge is a natural hedge technique.
   (h) Leads and lags are a natural hedge technique.
   (i) Balance-sheet hedge is adopted for hedging real operating exposure.
   (j) Currency diversification normally increases the exchange rate risk.
   (k) Translation exposure involves cash flow.
   (l) Transaction exposure involves present cash flow.
   (m) Real operating exposure does not consider changes in the price level.
   (n) Functional currency is the currency in which subsidiaries convert their financial statement figures for the purpose of reporting to the parent unit.
2. Choose the Most Suitable Answer.
   (a) An investor expecting a fall in interest rate:
      (i) Buys a cap and sells a floor
      (ii) Buys a floor and sells a cap
      (iii) Buys a floor and also a cap
   (b) A borrower apprehensive of rise in interest rate:
      (i) Buys a cap and sells a floor
      (ii) Buys a floor and sells a cap
      (iii) Buys a floor and also a cap

(c) In a receiver swaption, the buyer exercises the option and locks itself to:
  (i) Higher rate of interest
  (ii) Lower rate of interest
  (iii) None of the above

(d) Credit risk is concerned with:
  (i) Liquidity risk
  (ii) Default risk
  (iii) None of the above

(e) Real operating exposure takes into account:
  (i) Only changes in cash flow
  (ii) Only changes in price level
  (iii) Both, changes in price level and exchange rate

(f) Real operating exposure includes:
  (i) Only the present cash flows
  (ii) Future cash flows
  (iii) Both, present and future cash flows

(g) Translation exposure takes into account:
  (i) Present cash flows
  (ii) Future cash flows
  (iii) None of the above

(h) Transaction exposure arises on account of:
  (i) Borrowing and lending
  (ii) Consolidation of financial statements by the parent unit
  (iii) None of the above

(i) Translation exposure arises:
  (i) When reporting and functional currencies are the same
  (ii) When reporting and functional currencies are not the same
  (iii) None of the above

(j) Lag means:
  (i) Postponing the payment of foreign currency
  (ii) Accelerating the payment of foreign currency
  (iii) None of these

(k) Lead:
  (i) Is the same as lag
  (ii) Is opposite to lag
  (iii) None of the above

(l) Matching of cash flows means:
  (i) matching of cash inflows and outflows
  (ii) matching of cash inflow from two different sources
  (iii) none of the above

NUMERICAL PROBLEMS

1. A borrower borrows $2.0 million for three months, six months from now at LIBOR flat. LIBOR is 7.5 per cent at present but is expected to rise to 9 per cent after three months.

In order to hedge the rise in interest rate, the borrower buys an FRA. How much will the borrower receive from the seller of the FRA?

2. A firm borrows \$2.0 million at six-month LIBOR + 25 basis points for a period of 2 years. It anticipates a rise in LIBOR and so it goes for (a) buying a cap/collar from a bank with a strike rate of 7 per cent. The premium is 1 per cent for the whole of the maturity period and the fixed rate of interest is 6 per cent. LIBOR increases during the reset periods, respectively, to 8.00 per cent, 8.50 per cent, and 9.00 per cent. Find out whether the interest rate risk is hedged through (a) cap and (b) collar.

STUDY TOPIC

Interest Rate Futures Contracts and the Indian Banks

Interest rate futures (IRFs) contracts are the tools used by banks, primary dealers, corporate houses, financial institutions, foreign institutional investors and retailers in order to hedge interest rate risk. In fact, they are now an important instrument to manage interest rate volatility. That is why they have become popular at the global level as well as in India. At the global level, based on the database of the Bank of International Settlements (BIS), IRFs involved over 74 million outstanding contracts for the value of over \$17.8 trillion at the end of March 2009.

Features

IRFs contracts are of a definite lot size which is Rs. 0.2 million. The underlying securities are normally a 10-year notional coupon bearing Government of India security. The notional coupon is normally 7.0 per cent with semi-annual compounding. The maximum maturity is one year and the maturity falls in the month of March, June, September and December.

The contract is settled through physical delivery of securities. The electronic book-keeping entry system of NSDL/CDSL/PDO of RBI is used for this purpose. The delivery of deliverable securities can take place from the very first to the last working day of the settlement month. The working day lies between Monday and Friday and the working hours lie between 9.00 a.m. and 5 p.m. It is the owner of the short position that initiates the delivery. The clearing house needs to be informed at least two working days in advance. The conversion factor for the security to be delivered is equal to the price of the security on the first day of the delivery month and is to yield 7.0 per cent, which is to be compounded semi-annually.

The settlement price is the closing price of 10-year notional coupon-bearing Government of India security futures contract on the trading day, whereas the closing price is the weighted average price of the futures for last 30 minutes on the working day. If there is no transaction in IRFs during the last half an hour on that day, it is the stock exchange that determines the settlement price.

Why do banks go for IRFs

Banks are one of the major participants in the IRFs market. The reason is that the IRFs help alleviate different kinds of risk, such as basis risk, re-pricing risk, risk arising on account of SLR/non-SLR securities, options risk, etc. It may be noted that basis risk arises when the cost of liabilities and the yield on assets are based on different benchmarks. Re-pricing risk arises on account of fluctuation of cash flow due to revaluation of assets and liabilities over a period of time. Risk arising on account of Statutory Liquid Ratio (SLR)/non-SLR securities is manifested when such assets get devalued. Similarly, option risk arises in case of optionality provisions in lending and borrowing.

Besides hedging of the risk, IRFs help to increase the yield on fund advances ratios that increases in turn the net interest income. Any such increase means improved financial performance. There is also improvement in the capital adequacy ratio. It is because that the clearing house performs the clearing and settlement functions which help to lower the capital allocation risk for the hedged assets.

Again, IRFs help to minimise the portfolio volatility. They also decrease the sensitivity of returns on banks' assets and liabilities on account of interest rate fluctuations.

Case Example

A bank in India has SLR investment for some amount, a part of which is classified as "available for sale" and also "held for trade". The bank is expecting an increase in interest rate which may increase the yield rates manifesting in decreased value of these assets. The bank prefers to go for an IRF contract.

The position on November 10, 2008 is as follows:

(a) The yield on a 10-year Government of India security (priced at Rs. 102.40) is 6.09 per cent and it is trading at 5.76 per cent.
(b) March 2009 futures contracts on 10-year, 7.0 per cent GOI security is trading at Rs. 108.34 indicating a yield-rate of 5.85 per cent.
(c) The bank takes a short position based on March 2009 IRFs.

The position on January 1, 2009 is as follows:

(a) The yield rate of 6.09 per cent goes up to 7.56 per cent. As a result, the price of the security falls to Rs. 90.10.
(b) March 2009 futures contract on a 10-year, 7% GOI security is trading at Rs. 96.03 indicating a yield rate of 7.59 per cent.
(c) The bank unwinds a short position through buying the futures contract.
(d) This way the long position in the cash market is hedged through taking a short position in the IRF market.

QUESTIONS

1. What are the essential features of IRFs contracts?
2. Why do the banks go for such contracts?
3. Present a hypothetical example showing how such contracts are used for hedging interest rate risk.

REFERENCES

Books

Buckley, A. (1996), *Multinational Finance* (New Delhi: Prentice Hall of India).

Sharan, V. (2003), *International Financial Management*, Second Edition (New Delhi: Prentice-Hall of India).

SELECT FURTHER READINGS

Antl, B. (1988), *Management of Interest Rate Risk* (London: Euromoney Publication).

DeRosa, David F. (1991), *Managing Foreign Exchange Risk* (Chicago: Probus).

Moffett, Michael H. and Jan Karl Karlsen (1994),"Managing Foreign Exchange Rate Economic Exposure", *Journal of International Financial Management and Accounting,* V (2), 157–75.

*Hong Kong is one of the two special administrative regions of the People's Republic of China and the world's leading financial centres and a highly developed capitalist economy. The Hong Kong Stock Exchange is the sixth largest in the world, with a market capitalisation of US$2.97 trillion as at October 2007. Hong Kong is the world's largest re-export centre and its economy is dominated by the service sector, which accounts for over 90 per cent of its GDP.

Brazil*

21 International Taxation and Accounting

CHAPTER OBJECTIVES

Accounting is an important aspect in international business that tells us how far an international operation has been successful. Taxation with varying rates and systems among countries is another aspect that influences international business and its profitability. The present chapter discusses these issues. The objective is to:

- Delineate the basis of the international tax system and the types of taxes.
- Give an idea about tax havens.
- Present the shape of international tax strategy.
- Describe the modes of double taxation relief.
- Outline the Indian tax system and its influence on international business.
- Show how financial statements of different units in a firm are consolidated and how the functional currencies are translated into the reporting currency for this purpose.
- Show how the inflation factor is dealt with for the purpose of accounting.

The discussion of the different forms of strategies aiming at maximising the global profit of a multinational firm is not complete in the absence of any discussion of international taxation. This is because the rate of tax a firm has to pay in different tax jurisdictions has direct bearing on the size of the global profit. Moreover, there is also another important question as to how to arrive at global profit. Keeping in view these two facts, the present chapter deals with some important aspects of international taxation and accounting.

21.1 INTERNATIONAL TAXATION

21.1.1 Tax Complexity in International Firms

Tax management by MNCs is complex. The reasons are:
1. Multiplicity of tax jurisdictions
2. Varying definitions of tax base in different countries
3. Varying tax treatment in different countries
4. Presence of arbitrage opportunities.

Taxation lies at the core of various financial decisions such as international investment decisions, international working capital decisions, funds raising decisions, and decisions concerning dividend and other payments. It is true that the tax issue is relevant to such decisions also with respect to domestic firms. But the management of taxation is highly complex with respect to international corporations. The reasons are very much evident. Firstly, these firms have to operate in many tax jurisdictions where tax rates are different and also the administration of tax system is not uniform.

Secondly, the ultimate burden of tax in the context of international firms is determined by a more complicated interplay of varying definitions of the tax base.

Thirdly, the varying tax treatment in different countries can lead to distortions in international trade and investment. Firms located in a low tax country can have an edge over other firms in the international market. Similarly, investment can be diverted to countries having lower tax rates.

Lastly, international firms often straddle different tax jurisdictions, exploit the arbitrage opportunities, and maintain an edge over domestic firms. The present section, therefore, discusses some of the more significant issues related to the international tax environment and some of the provisions of the Indian tax laws in this respect.

21.1.2 Basis of International Tax System

It is expected that the international tax system should be neutral, meaning that it should not entail upon economic efficiency. At the same time, it should be equitable, ensuring equal sacrifice by different tax payers. And also, a firm should not be taxed twice for the same income. These three concepts are further elucidated here.

Tax neutrality refers to tax encouraging optimal allocation of capital among countries.

Tax Neutrality: Neutrality of international taxation is based on the concept of economic efficiency. This means that tax should not come in the way of optimal allocation of capital among different countries. If tax is neutral, capital will move from a country with lower returns to a country with higher returns. Consequently, the gross world output will be maximised. On the contrary, if international taxation does not possess this objective, the after-tax return from investment will stand distorted. As a result, resources may not be allocated efficiently. Gross world output, in turn, will be lower.

Tax neutrality may be explained in terms of capital-export neutrality and capital-import neutrality (Horst, 1980). Capital-export neutrality means that the rates of taxes should be the same between domestic investment and foreign investment. This means that investors are indifferent to the choice between domestic investment and foreign investment. It is possible when pre-tax and post-tax return on capital is the same between a capital exporting country and the capital importing country. But uniformity of this kind is difficult to be achieved in practice. This is because accounting norms are different in different countries. The tax policy of different governments is also heterogeneous.

Capital-export neutrality means that the rates of taxes should be the same between domestic investment and foreign investment.

Capital-import neutrality, on the other hand, occurs when the same tax is applied to the income of all firms competing in the same capital-importing country so that no firm—domestic or foreign—enjoys any competitive advantage. But since tax bases are different, it is not easy to achieve capital-import neutrality. Some of the capital-exporting companies reconcile the two forms of neutrality and they follow a mix of the two. For example, the taxes on their subsidiaries' earnings are credited against their own taxes.

Capital-import neutrality occurs when the same tax is applied to the income of all firms competing in the same capital-importing country.

Tax Equity: The principle of tax equity rests on the belief that all similarly situated taxpayers should participate in the cost of operating the government according to the same rules. The concept of equity can be interpreted in two ways. One is that the contribution of each taxpayer should be in conformity with the amount of public services he or she receives. The other is that each taxpayer should pay taxes according to his or her ability to pay. The ability to pay means a person with greater ability has to pay a greater amount of tax. However, it is difficult to define the concept of equity when the tax jurisdiction is more than one. Let us consider a simple example. There are two Indian residents. The first one is deriving entire income from domestic sources. The second one has the same amount of income, but a part of income is derived from foreign sources. Now, the second has to pay a greater amount of taxes as he or she also pays taxes in the foreign country where the income is generated. The same income from the foreign source is taxed twice. Thus, if the principle of equity has to be ensured, something needs to be done in this respect.

Tax equity means tax that the payer pays according to his/her ability to pay or according to the amount of public services he/she receives.

Avoidance of Double Taxation: Corporate income tax is levied when a firm earns income. But if the post-tax income is remitted to foreign countries, the recipient of such income is taxed again. This means the same income is subject to double taxation. Double taxation dampens the incentive to invest. And so, it needs to be avoided. For this purpose, the entire income from foreign sources may be exempted from tax. Alternatively, provisions of foreign tax credits may be created in the domestic tax system. In a subsequent section these relief provisions are discussed at some length. Additionally, there may also be treaties for the avoidance of double taxation between the home government and the host government. For the

Double taxation refers to the same income taxed twice in two countries.

first time, it was the League of Nations that had drafted a model for double tax avoidance treaty in 1929. The OECD developed its own model in 1963 and revised it in 1974. In 1967, the United Nations set up a Group of Tax Experts on Tax Treaties; and on its recommendations, issued "Guidelines on Tax Treaties", between developed and developing countries, in 1974. India has signed such treaties with a number of countries. Such treaties provide, among other things, exemption from tax in the country in which minor activities are carried on.

21.1.3 Types of Taxes

The international operation of a firm is subjected broadly to three kinds of taxes. They are:

1. Income tax
2. Withholding tax
3. Value added tax

Income Tax: A significant part of the tax revenue in a country is represented by tax on personal income as well as on corporate income. The tax is levied on income arising out of a firm's operation—whether the operation is a manufacturing one or it is concerning the provision of services. However, the rate of the tax varies widely among different countries or different tax jurisdictions with the result that the concept of neutrality or equity is hard to be adhered to.

Withholding tax is tax levied on the passive income of an individual/ company.

Withholding Tax: Withholding tax is a tax levied on the passive income earned by an individual or a corporate body. The word, "passive" is used because the income arises, or is generated, in another country. Suppose a corporate body in India earns dividend from its subsidiary operating in another country and pays tax on the dividend income to the Indian government. The dividend income is a passive income as it is generated abroad. The tax on such income is known as withholding tax because the corporate body receiving the dividend withholds the tax borne by the taxpayer (shareholder) and passes on the tax amount to the tax authorities.

The passive income takes many forms such as dividend income, income from royalty and technical service fees, income from interest, and so on. It has been observed that the rate of taxes varies from one form of passive income to the other and from one country to the other. For example, the United States of America withholds 5 per cent of interest income from taxpayers residing in a large number of countries, but the rate moves up to 30 per cent in case of those residing in Pakistan. Similarly, in the United States of America, the withholding tax rate, with respect to portfolio investment, is higher than that in case of direct investment (Eun and Resnick, 1998).

Value added tax is tax levied on the value added at different stages of production.

Value added Tax: A value added tax (VAT) is a tax levied on the value added at different stages of production of a commodity or services. VAT is an indirect tax and it is often preferred to direct income tax insofar as it (VAT) discourages unnecessary consumption, fosters national savings, and is easier to be collected. However, this tax too faces the same problem of having different rates in different tax jurisdictions.

21.1.4 Tax Havens

Tax havens are where a country imposes no tax/ lower rates of tax on the profits routed through that country.

A tax haven country is one that has zero rate, or a very low rate, of income tax and withholding tax. Additionally, there are some non-tax factors that make a country a tax haven. Gordon (1981) mentions them as (1) strict rules on secrecy and confidentiality with respect to business transactions, (2) relative importance of banking and other financial activities, (3) lack of currency controls, and (4) governmental measures promoting tax haven status. Alworth (1988) groups the tax havens into four types:

1. Those having no income or capital gains tax
2. Those having a very low rate of tax
3. Those exempting all income from foreign sources from taxation
4. Those allowing special tax privileges in specific cases

In the first group are the Bahamas, Bermuda, the Cayman Islands, Nauru, the New Hebrides, and the Turks and Caicos Islands. In these countries, their government does not have any specific rate of taxes, but has fixed a small amount of tax. Manufacturing companies get a long term guarantee against taxes.

In the second group of countries, are the British Virgin Islands, the Netherlands, the Antilles, Montserrat, Jersey, Guernsey, and the Isle of Man, where tax rates are very low and special tax privileges are provided to shipping, aviation, and to holding companies.

Costa Rica, Hong Kong, Liberia, and Panama represent the third group. Their governments tax only locally generated income and not any income flowing from foreign sources.

In the fourth group are Luxembourg, the Netherlands, Switzerland, Liechtenstein, Gibraltar, Barbados, and Grenada. In the first four countries, special tax privileges are provided to qualified holding companies; while in the latter three countries, low rates of taxes are applicable to special status companies or to international business companies.

The 38 Jurisdictions below have made Commitments to the OECD to Implement *Transparency and Effective Exchange of Information for Tax Purposes*

1. Andorra	5. Bahamas	9. British Virgin Islands (1)
2. Anguilla (1)	6. Bahrain	10. Cayman Islands (1)
3. Antigua and Barbuda	7. Bermuda (1)	11. Cook Islands (4)
4. Aruba (2) (3)	8. Belize	12. Cyprus

13. Dominica
14. Gibraltar (1)
15. Grenada
16. Guernsey (5)
17. Isle of Man (5)
18. Jersey (5)
19. Liberia
20. Liechtenstein
21. Malta
22. Marshall Islands
23. Mauritius
24. Monaco
25. Montserrat (1)
26. Nauru
27. Netherlands Antilles (2)
28. Niue (4)
29. Panama (Spanish), (English)
30. Samoa
31. San Marino
32. Seychelles
33. St. Lucia
34. St. Kitts & Nevis
35. St. Vincent and the Grenadines
36. Turks & Caicos Islands (1)
37. US Virgin Islands (6)
38. Vanuatu

Source: 'Jurisdictions Committed to Improving Transparency and Establishing Effective Exchange of Information in Tax Matters' http://www.oecd.org/document/19/0,3343,en_2649_33745_1903251_1_1_1_37427,00.html

21.1.5 International Tax Management Strategy

International tax management strategy includes primarily:
1. Trade-off between dividend repatriation and retention of earnings.
2. Higher cost allocation in higher tax country.
3. Selecting mode of operation-branch or subsidiary-so as to get a room for tax manouevrability.
4. Constant eye on tax rate differential between home and host country.

The minimisation of the overall tax burden so as to maximise the overall profit is the strategy of an international firm. A number of activities are directed to this end. First of all, a firm has to take a decision whether the profits of the subsidiaries should lie with them and their repatriation to the parent unit should be delayed in order to evade taxes at home. In this case, the profits would be reinvested in profitable channels and the corporate wealth of the subsidiary will increase. But if repatriation is delayed, the parent unit will not witness a net cash inflow and the basic purpose of investment in a subsidiary is marred. Thus, there should be a tradeoff between the repatriation of dividend and retention of earning with the subsidiary.

Secondly, the objective of minimisation of tax burden depends on the cost allocation between the different units of the firm. If a firm allocates higher cost in a high tax country and shows greater profits in a low tax country, the total tax burden would be greatly reduced. However, there are limits to cost allocation. And so, to overcome these limits, a firm adopts transfer pricing devices. Chapter 17 of this book discusses how funds are moved through intra-firm transfer pricing. Profits shift from one subsidiary to the other through the movement of funds, which, in turn, depends on the successful operation of transfer pricing. However, there are limits to transfer pricing. When tariff is imposed on the imports, transfer pricing can be used only to a limited extent. It is because tariff influences the profits and, thereby, the taxes.

Thirdly, the tax management strategy incorporates the decision whether the foreign operation should take the form of either a branch or a subsidiary. If foreign operation is expected to incur huge losses in some of the years, it is better to operate through branches. Branches do not represent an independent entity and so the loss incurred by one branch will be absorbed by the profits earned by other units and the total tax burden will be lower.

Whatever the strategy, a firm needs to consider the tax provisions in the home country as well as in the host country. It is only then that any strategy should be implemented.

21.1.6 Tax Treaties and Double Taxation Relief

Besides firms adopting different strategies to reduce tax burden so as to facilitate FDI flow, the home and host country governments too undergo tax treaty to facilitate FDI. The treaty reduces barriers to FDI in three ways. First, it harmonises tax definitions and jurisdictions of the host and home governments and helps avoid double taxation (Hamada, 1966; Janeba, 1996). Second, it influences the statutory taxation of the firms through changes in rules concerning double taxation and withholding taxes levied on repatriation by investors (Altshuler and Newlon, 1991; Hines, 1992). Third, it facilitates improved information exchange between the partner governments. Pointing at double taxation which is basic to such treaties, it would be useful to explain its modes. The modes are

1. Credit system without deferral
2. Credit system with deferral
3. Exemption
4. Deduction of tax paid abroad as expenditure
5. Investment credit

Credit System without Deferral: Taxes paid in the host country are allowed as a credit against the tax liability in the home country. Suppose the tax rate in India is 35 per cent and a foreign subsidiary of an Indian company pays taxes on its profit, at the rate of 40 per cent, in the host country. The Indian government will allow the excess tax paid within foreign tax jurisdiction as an offset against the amount of tax paid within its own jurisdiction.

The tax credit without deferral is based on the principle of capital-export neutrality, which means that the income generated domestically or in a foreign country should both be taxed at the same rate. Bearing this principle in mind, the profits earned by a foreign branch or subsidiary are clubbed with those of the parent company and all eligible taxes levied in the host country are allowed as credits. It means that the foreign investment is taxed at the rate prevalent in the home country. However, in practice, consolidation is not common in most countries as it is expected to raise a host of administrative problems. In case of losses, the credit system operates as if double taxation relief were provided as an exemption.

Tax Credit with Deferral: In this case, taxation in the home country is deferred until earnings are repatriated by the subsidiary to the parent company. It is similar as in case of a holding company whose subsidiaries are located within the national boundary or the same tax jurisdiction. Profits of the subsidiary are taxed at the rate prevalent in the host country. They are subject to home-country taxes only when they are repatriated.

Tax Exemptions: In this case, if the profits of the subsidiary are taxed in the host country, they are exempted from any taxation in the home country. In some cases, where the host country government provides a tax holiday for a specific number of years, dividend distribution by the parent company is normally taxed in the home country. This type of relief is, thus, based on the principle of territoriality, where profits of the multinational corporation are taxed only in one tax jurisdiction. This type of provision is found in France and the Netherlands.

Deduction of Tax Paid Abroad as Expenditure: In this case, the amount of tax paid in a foreign country is treated as expenditure and is therefore deducted from the total income earned in the country. It is similar to exemption, although the procedure is different.

Investment Credit: In this method, the amount of capital invested abroad is deducted from the income earned in the country of residence. The purpose is to encourage capital export by reducing the burden of taxes.

21.2 INDIAN TAX SCENARIO

The foreign investors operating in India are subject to Indian tax rules and regulation. The taxes are both direct and indirect. Some of the major provisions relating to taxes on corporate income, taxes on the income of the expatriates working in India and also the customs duty are discussed here.

From the viewpoint of taxes, it is necessary to identify the assessee company whether:

1. it is a domestic company or a foreign company,
2. it is resident assessee or a non-resident assessee and
3. the income is Indian or foreign.

Similarly, foreign income is an income that accrues/arises outside India and is received/deemed to be received outside India.

A resident assessee is taxed on both its Indian income and foreign income. But a non-resident/foreign company is not taxed on its foreign income. There are, of course, some foreign incomes which are treated as Indian income. Income of a business process out-sourcing (BPO) units in India, even if they are a permanent establishment of a non-resident foreign company, specific cases of interest, dividend, technical fees, royalty, etc. are apposite example. However, many of them are exempted from tax.

As far as the rate of corporate income tax is concerned, it varies between a domestic company and a foreign company. The Budget proposals for 2005–06 have brought down the tax rate from 35 per cent to 30 per cent alongwith a surcharge of 10 per cent and education cess of 2 per cent in case of a domestic company. But in case of a foreign company, it is 40 per cent alongwith a surcharge of 2.5 per cent and education cess for 2 per cent. The surcharge is applicable only after deducting rebate under Section 88E which deals with taxes on the transaction of corporate securities.

In case the tax liability of a company—domestic or foreign—is less than 7.15 per cent (plus surcharge) of the book projects, the book profits are deemed to be the total income chargeable to tax at the rate of 7.5 per cent plus surcharge, which is known as Minimum Alternate Tax (MAT). Presently, a credit is allowed for MAT that will be available in the next five years.

21.2.1 Taxes on Corporate Income

The rate of corporate income tax is 33.99 per cent for an Indian company. The rate is inclusive of a surcharge of 10.0 per cent (for income over Rs. 10 million) and an education cess of 3.0 per cent. The rate applicable to a foreign company is 42.23 per cent, inclusive of a surcharge of 2.5 per cent and education cess of 3.0 per cent. The income is computed after adding certain disallowances, depreciation, loss on sale of assets, etc. to the declared profit and after deducting certain allowances and the fringe benefit accorded to the employees.

Again, it is true that the dividend income in the hands of shareholders is exempt from tax, yet the companies have to pay dividend distribution tax on declared dividend at 16.995 per cent, inclusive of surcharge and education cess.

Yet again, with a view to bringing zero-tax companies into the tax net, minimum alternate tax (MAT) is levied at 11.33 per cent of the book profits in case the amount of tax is less than 10 per cent of the book profits. In case of payment of MAT, the company does not pay normal corporate income tax. It means that a company pays higher of the MAT and normal corporate income tax.

Moreover, the company has to pay capital gains tax. If it is a short-term capital gain, normal income tax rate is applicable. But on long-term capital gains, the tax rate is 22.66 per cent for a domestic company and 21.16 per cent for a foreign company.

21.2.2 Taxes on the Income of the Expatriates

The income of expatriates is taxable similarly as the income of an individual. However, the expatriates are grouped as resident, ordinarily resident and non-resident. A resident expatriate has to be physically present in the country for 60 days or more during the tax year or 365 days or more during the preceding four tax years. An ordinarily resident expatriate should be a resident in India for at least two out of ten years preceding the relevant tax year or he/she should have been in India for 730 days or more during seven years preceding the relevant tax year. If the expatiate does not fulfil the above-mentioned conditions, he/she is treated as a non-resident.

The expatriates of the first two categories pay taxes on the income earned in India as well as outside. But the non-resident expatriate is taxed on his/her income earned and received only in India.

21.2.3 Indirect Taxes

Customs duty is the most important among the indirect taxes. It is imposed on the imports. It is either ad valorem or specific. The rate is amended from time to time. In the past one and half decades, the rate has been slashed significantly.

Besides the basic customs duty, there is countervailing duty. The purpose is to ensure that the protection provided by the basic customs duty to the domestic manufacturers is not eroded.

Again, additional duty is levied at 4.0 per cent in order to counter the local sales tax/vat, etc.

The manufacturers of goods in India have also to pay excise duty normally at 16.0 per cent. However, the foreign investors operating in India get some credit in specific cases.

Assuming the basic customs duty at 10.0 per cent, countervailing duty at 16.48 per cent, education cess at 3.0 per cent, additional duty at 4.0 per cent and allowing for credit at 10.84 per cent, the impact of these indirect taxes comes to around 23.29 per cent.

21.2.4 Tax Incentives

The Indian tax system provides incentives to attract FDI as also to encourage exports. Some more important of these are:

1. A unit in Special Economic Zone set up after March 2002 is allowed 100 per cent tax deduction of export profit for a period of 5 years and 50 per cent for the next two years followed by 50 per cent deduction of export profit credited to a special reserve account for the next three years.
2. The initial depreciation rate has been increased from 15 per cent to 20 per cent that will in effect lower the amount of tax. Moreover, the requirement of a 10 per cent increase in the installed capacity for availing the benefit of the initial depreciation has been removed so as to make easier the application of this scheme.
3. Credit in respect of MAT will be available for the next five years.
4. With a view to promote scientific research, capital and revenue expenditure in this respect is allowed as deduction while computing taxable income. This would enhance the capability of Indian firms to modify the imported technology.
5. Specific deductions are allowed if FDI moves to backward regions of the economy.
6. Similarly, deductions are allowed in specific conditions if FDI moves to infra-structure sector.
7. Profits of a resident company are exempted from taxes if they are related to the development of computer software.
8. Profit from export, if export proceeds are received in convertible currencies within a specified period, is exempted from tax to a maximum of 30 per cent.

21.2.5 Double Tax Avoidance Agreements in India

Section 90 of the Income Tax Act empowers the Indian government to enter into an agreement with a foreign government for the purpose of avoidance of double taxation. The Indian government signed such a treaty for the first time in 1965 with the Austrian government. Presently, there are such treaties with 70 governments. The treaties are either comprehensive, partial or specific. Comprehensive treaties cover all items of income, while partial treaties cover income only from specific sources, such as air transport, shipping and so on.

> Comprehensive treaties cover all items of income, while partial treaties cover income only from specific sources.

However, this does not mean that in cases where any treaty is absent, there is no relief. An Indian resident will get tax relief under Section 91 and shall be entitled to deductions under the Indian Income Tax Act. The income is subjected to Indian tax rate as well as to the tax rate of a specific foreign country. The lower of the two amounts is considered for relief. If both are equal, any of the two may be considered.

These agreements are based on the UN model of double tax avoidance agreements allocating jurisdiction between the source and residence country and prescribing maximum rate of taxation in the source country which is generally lower than the rate of tax under the domestic laws of that country. The double taxation in such cases are avoided by the residence country agreeing to give credit for tax paid in the source country. These agreements cover normally the gross income of the nature of interest, dividend, royalty and fees for technical services to the country of residence. Recently, there were some modifications made in the Indo-Cyprus Double Taxation Avoidance Agreement. The agreement is all set to lose the capital gains tax exemption benefit, meaning that the residents, both individuals and companies of Cyprus, would have to pay capital gains tax at the rate of 10 per cent. The agreement with the Grand Duchy of Luxembourg is also of the same nature.

Treaties Signed with Countries for Avoidance of Double Taxation

S. No.	Name of the country	Effective from assessment year	
1.	Australia	1993–94	
2.	Austria	1963–64	
3.	Bangladesh	1993–94	
4.	Belgium	1989–90; 1999–2000	(Revised)
5.	Brazil	1994–95	
6.	Belarus	1999–2000	
7.	Bulgaria	1997–98	
8.	Canada	1987–88; 1999–2000	(Revised)
9.	China	1996–97	
10.	Cyprus	1994–95	
11.	Czechoslovakia	1986–87; 2001–2002	(Revised)
12.	Denmark	1991–92	
13.	Finland	1985–86; 2000–2001	Amending protocol
14.	France	1996–97	(Revised)

15.	F.R.G	1958–59	(Original)
	F.R.G.	1984–85	(Protocol)
	D.G.R.	1985–86	
	F.R.G.	1998–99	(Revised)
16.	Greece	1964–65	
17.	Hungary	1989–90	
18.	Indonesia	1989–90	
19.	Israel	1995–96	
20.	Italy	1997–98	(Revised)
21.	Japan	1991–92	(Revised)
22.	Jordan	2001–2002	
23.	Kazakistan	1999–2000	
24.	Kenya	1985–86	
25.	Libya	1983–84	
26.	Malta	1997–98	
27.	Malaysia	1973–74	
28.	Mauritius	1983–84	
29.	Mongolia	1995–96	
30.	Myanmar	2008–09	
30.	Namibia	2000–2001	
31.	Nepal	1990–91	
32.	Netherlands	1990–91	
33.	New Zealand	1988–89	
	(1999–2000 amending notification)	(2001–2002 Supp. Protocol)	
34.	Norway	1988–89	
35.	Oman	1999–2000	
36.	Philippines	1996–97	
37.	Poland	1991–92	
38.	Qatar	2001–2002	
39.	Romania	1989–90	
40.	Singapore	1995–96	
41.	South Africa	1999–2000	
42.	South Korea	1985–86	
43.	Spain	1997–98	
44.	Sri Lanka	1981–82	
45.	Sweden	1990–91; 1999–2000	(Revised)
46.	Switzerland	1996–97	
47.	Syria	1983–84	
48.	Tanzania	1983–84	

49.	Thailand	1988–89	
50.	Trinidad & Tobago	2001–2002	
51.	Turkmenistan	1999–2000	
52.	Turkey	1995–96	
53.	U.A.E.	1995–96	
54.	U.A.R.	1970–71	
55.	U.K.	1995–96	(Revised)
56.	U.S.A.	1992–93	
57.	Russian Federation	2000–2001	
58.	Uzbekistan	1994–95	
59.	Vietnam	1997–98	
60.	Zambia	1979–80	

Source: Government of India, Ministry of Finance website

21.3 INTERNATIONAL ACCOUNTING

The concept of international accounting is interpreted in different ways. First of all, international accounting refers to the principles and practices of accounting followed in different countries. Secondly, it refers to a globally accepted set of accounting principles that could eliminate the hurdles coming in the way of international transactions on account of varying accounting practices followed in different countries. For example, the European Union has issued directives and framed regulations for intra-Union payment accounting. The United Nations Commission on Transnational Corporations has established guidelines for accounting standards and disclosure of financial information. Thirdly, international accounting embraces the principles of accounting that are practised for studying and evaluating the financial relationship between a parent company and a subsidiary company, or between two or more subsidiaries of a single multinational firm. This an important aspect of international accounting which will be discussed presently at greater length. The focus of explanation is on:

(a) How a parent company consolidates the financial statements of subsidiaries with those of its own,
(b) How the figures of financial statements shown in different currencies are translated into those of the home country currency,
(c) How the inflation factor is taken into account, and more importantly,
(d) How the transfer pricing is practised for maximising profitability or net aggregate output.

The fourth aspect has already been dealt with in Chapter 17; the other three will be explained here.

21.3.1 Consolidation of Financial Statements

Consolidation of financial statement refers to parent unit combining the financial statement of its subsidiaries in order to arrive at global profit.

If a firm sets up its network abroad by opening subsidiaries, it would like to evaluate its overall performance by combining the financial statements of subsidiaries along with its own. The process of combining financial statements is known as consolidation.

Techniques of Consolidation: There are two ways for consolidating financial statements. One is known as **gross consolidation**. The other is known as **net consolidation**. Under the process of gross consolidation, the assets and liabilities of the subsidiary are added to the respective values of the balance sheet of the parent company irrespective of the share of the parent company in the equity of the subsidiary. However, the value of the minority interest is shown on the liabilities side of the consolidated balance sheet. Suppose the minority interest accounts for 20 per cent of the subsidiary's equity. The subsidiary's equity amounts to $80,000. The minority interest, which is $16,000 in this case, will be entered on the liabilities side of the consolidated balance sheet. The minority interest in reserves will be similarly indicated on the liabilities side. The entire profit of the subsidiary is added to the profit of the parent company, but the profit accruing to the minority interest is identified and adjusted against the consolidated profit.

Under the net consolidation method, the long procedure of adding up of the whole of the subsidiary's value and then making adjustments for the minority interest is avoided. Instead, the net figures are added depending upon the parent company's share in the subsidiary's equity. This means that the minority interest is excluded from the very beginning.

Whatever may be the method of consolidation of financial statements, the profits of intra-firm transactions are excluded.

When the date of financial year closing differs between the parent and the subsidiary, adjustments are made for significant transactions that occur between the two reporting dates.

Whatever may be the method of consolidation of financial statements, the profits of intra-firm transactions are excluded. If this is not done, profits will remain overstated. Again, if the entire amount of intermediate goods supplied by the parent company to the subsidiary is sold by the latter, there is no accounting problem. But if only a part of it is sold, the proportionate share of intra-firm profit is eliminated.

One problem often arises in this context when the date of financial year closing differs between the parent and the subsidiary. In such cases, the span of the period is taken into account and adjustments are made for significant transactions that occur between the two reporting dates.

A simple example will illustrate how consolidation is done. Suppose a parent company has 80 per cent share in the equity capital of the subsidiary. At the year-end, the balance sheet items of the parent and the subsidiary are as follows:

	Parent company	*Subsidiary*
Assets	$	$
Investment in subsidiary	48,000	-
Plant and machinery	3,00,000	25,000
Current assets	1,75,000	30,000

Total	5,23,000	55,000
Liabilities		
Equity shares	2,00,000	40,000
Reserves	3,23,000	15,000
Total	5,23,000	55,000

In the consolidated balance sheet, the fixed and the current assets of the two units will be clubbed together. The fixed assets will be valued at $3,25,000 and the current assets will amount to $2,05,000. The amount of goodwill will be equal to investment in subsidiary minus the parent company's share in subsidiary's equity, that is, $48,000 – 80 per cent of 40,000 = 16,000.

On the liabilities side, the share capital will be $2,00,000. The reserves will be equal to $3,23,000 + 80 per cent of $15,000 or $3,35,000. The minority interest will be shown as 20 per cent of $40,000 + 20 per cent of $15,000 or $11,000.

Consolidated Balance sheet (Gross consolidation method)

Assets	$
Plant and machinery	3,25,000
Current assets	2,05,000
Goodwill	16,000
Total	5,46,000
Liabilities	
Equity capital	2,00,000
Reserves	3,35,000
Minority interest	11,000
Total	5,46,000

The above is an example of the gross consolidation method. If the balance sheet is prepared on the basis of the net consolidation method, the fixed assets and the current assets of the consolidated balance sheet will embrace only those of the parent company. The amount of investment will be equal to the sum of investment and the proportionate share in the reserves of the subsidiary. This proportionate share will be clubbed with the reserves of the parent company. There will be no mention of the minority interest. The consolidated balance sheet under the net consolidation method will be as follows:

Consolidated Balance sheet (Net consolidation method)

Assets	$
Fixed assets	3,00,000
Current assets	1,75,000
Investments ($48,000 + 80 per cent of $15,000)	60,000
Total	5,35,000
Liabilities	
Share capital	2,00,000
Reserves ($3,23,000 + 80 per cent of $15,000)	3,35,000
Total	5,35,000

Treatment of the Consolidation Differences: In many cases, the date of acquisition of the subsidiary by the parent company does not coincide with the closing date of the financial year. Again, in many cases, profit and loss prior to acquisition is taken over. In these cases, consolidation differences arise. This means that in such cases, there may be disparity between the purchase cost and the amount of capital to be consolidated. If disparity arises, it needs adjustment.

The difference may be positive, meaning that the purchase price is greater than the amount of capital to be consolidated. This is normally found on account of taking over of undisclosed reserves or goodwill. In such cases, the difference is added to the respective assets and is gradually adjusted through raising the value of depreciation or writing off the goodwill. On the contrary, there may be a negative difference when the purchase price is lower than the amount of capital to be consolidated. Such a possibility is rare, but it arises when a firm acquires another firm with overvalued assets or with consistently low earnings. In such cases, the difference is adjusted by providing a spread of depreciation on the assets or through opening a subsidy account which is gradually written back over a specified period.

Consolidation Provisions in Different Countries: In the United States of America, all parent companies have to consolidate accounts, except where their control over subsidiaries is only temporary or where the control does not rest with the majority owners. In the United Kingdom, the Companies Act of 1989 makes consolidation compulsory, except in some cases where consolidation is not practical and where it involves undue expense and time. Exemptions are also allowed in cases where consolidated figures are misleading. The German law makes consolidation compulsory, especially where the parent company has a major stake in the subsidiary. In Japan too, consolidated financial statements are compulsory, although exemptions are allowed where the sales of the subsidiary account for less than 10 per cent of that of the parent company or where the total assets of the subsidiary are less than 10 per cent of those of the parent company.

In India, Section 212 of the Companies Act provides that the balance sheet of the subsidiary has to be attached with that of the parent company if the financial year closing of both coincide. In other cases, the holding company has to submit a copy of the profit and loss account, the Director's report, and the Auditor's report of the subsidiary along with its own. Indian Accounting Standard 21 shows how the financial statements of parent and subsidiary are consolidated. Similarly, Indian Accounting Standard 13 procedures are followed in case of joint-ventures.

21.3.2 Accounting of Foreign Currency Translation

Consolidation of financial statements is a step in the direction of evaluating the overall financial performance of an MNC. But the problem is that the figures of the financial statements of subsidiaries are expressed in different currencies. The problem would not be serious, if there is fixed exchange rate between different currencies. But in a floating rate regime, volatility of rates creates a problem for translation of figures in different currencies into those of the domestic currency of the parent company.

In a volatile exchange rate regime, the procedure of translation takes into account three types of exchange rates. One is the pre-change or historical rate. The other is post-change or current rate. The last is the average of the historical and current rates. Use of different rates gives different results. There is every possibility of loss or gain with changes in the exchange rate. In such a situation, two important questions arise. One is, regarding which rate should be used for a particular type of transaction. The other is regarding how the translation loss or gain should be treated. The first one is dealt with in Chapter 20.

Treatment of Translation Gains or Losses: There are broadly three approaches for the treatment of translation losses or gains. They are:

1. Deferral approach
2. Immediate recognition approach
3. Deferral and amortisation approach

The deferral approach suggests that since translation gains or losses are "unrealised", having no effect on the cash flow between the parent and the subsidiary, they are not shown in the consolidated income statement. Rather, they accumulate separately as a part of consolidated equity.

The immediate recognition approach suggests that translation gains or losses should immediately be shown in the income statement. The rationale is that their immediate inclusion will enable the financial statement to show the impact of changes in exchange rate.

The deferral and amortisation approach is a mixture of the above two approaches. Under this approach, the gain or loss is amortised over the life of the related balance sheet items.

Which of the three approaches should be used depends upon the objective of translation. If it is viewed from the parent company's point of view, the gain or loss is adjusted in the income statement. But if the subsidiary's interest prevails, gain or loss is reflected through increase or decrease in equity, in terms of the domestic currency of the parent company.

Translation Practices in Different Countries: In the United States of America, Financial Accounting Standards–8 (FAS–8) was implemented in 1975, which suggested the use of the temporal method. FAS–8 was subsequently substituted by FAS–52, which suggested the use of the temporal method only in cases where the US dollar happened to be the primary currency. But in cases where foreign currencies were the functional currency, FAS–52 suggested the use of the current method. Similarly, in Canada, the temporal method is used where subsidiaries are an integral part of the firm. In other cases, the current method is used. The Swedish

Companies Act permits the use of the current rate method in normal cases, but the monetary/non-monetary method is used in case of high inflation country subsidiaries. In France, the current rate is used on a wide scale. In the United Kingdom, the current method and the temporal method are widely used.

In India, it was for the first time in 1976 that the Institute of Chartered Accountants of India (ICAI) presented a guideline. It was primarily in favour of the use of the current/non-current method. In 1988, the practice became mandatory, although the compliance rate was very low. Again, a revised guideline came into force from April 1995. But it is restricted to accounting for transactions in foreign currencies and to the translation of financial statements of foreign branches. For the purpose of translation:

(a) Revenue and cost, other than the depreciation, are translated at average rates. Inventory is translated at rates prevalent at the time of acquisition. Depreciation is translated at historical rates.
(b) current rate is applied to monetary items, while historical rate is applied to non-monetary items and fixed assets, and
(c) contingent liabilities are translated at current rates.

21.3.3 Accounting for Inflationary Trends

Restate-translate method involves first the adjustment for inflation and then the translation of the adjusted figures. **Translate-restate** method is just the opposite.

Consolidation of accounts faces not only translation problems but also inflation prevalent in the host country. If the inflation factor is not taken into account, the profits of the subsidiary will stand overstated and the consolidated picture will be different. This is why adjustment for inflation differential is essential.

The accounting for foreign inflation is required when the subsidiary is operating in an inflationary environment. There are two methods in this respect. One is known as the **restate-translate** method. The other is the **translate-restate** method. In the former case, the figures of the financial statement of the subsidiary are first adjusted for inflation and then translated into the currency of the parent company. On the other hand, in the latter method, the figures are first translated into the currency of the parent company and then adjusted for inflation.

There are different techniques for the adjustment of inflation. They are usually:

1. Creation of reserves
2. Devaluation of assets
3. Last In-First Out method of inventory valuation
4. Historical cost accounting
5. Current value accounting

1. A part of the profit is transferred to reserves that may be used for meeting the increased cost of asset replacement. This eliminates the problem of asset replacement as well as reduces overstated

profits. The technique is very simple and so it is used in many countries. However, how much of the profit should be transferred to reserves is often an arbitrary decision. The transfer may not help completely adjust the inflation factor.

2. The book value of assets is revised, which helps the cost of fixed assets to conform to the current price and, thereby, provide a realistic measure of capitalisation. Depreciation is charged on the revised value, which is able to meet the replacement cost of the assets. Overstatement of profits is also checked. This is a common method used in many countries.
3. The inventory is valued in a way that helps in the matching of current revenue with current cost of goods. The income statement shows a collection of most recent purchase cost. However, this method is useful in cases where raw material is purchased at frequent intervals and where all the goods produced are sold during the same period. In many countries, this method of inventory valuation is not allowed as it understates the profit and, thereby, the tax liability.
4. Various items of the income statement and the balance sheet are adjusted for inflation. In this context, the items are bifurcated under monetary and non-monetary heads. This is because monetary items such as cash, bills receivable, fixed earnings on investment, bills payable, fixed rate long term obligations, and so on are not adjusted for inflation. Adjustment is made for non-monetary items only, such as inventory, fixed assets, share capital, and so on. The rationale is that the monetary items are fixed by contract, regardless of changes in the purchasing power of the involved currency. Even in case of non-monetary items, where adjustment is made, the index for adjustment varies. For example, if sales spread over the whole year, the revenue is adjusted for inflation by the average of the index. If inventory is purchased in the beginning of the year, it is adjusted by the year end index/initial price index. Suppose an inventory for \$100 is put into operation and the output is sold for \$150. If price level is stable, the income will amount to \$50. But if the price index moves up from 100 at the beginning of the year to 121 at the end of the year, the revenue will be adjusted as:

   $$\$150 \times \frac{121}{110} = 165$$

   The cost of inventory will be adjusted as:

   $$\$100 \times \frac{121}{110} = 121$$

   Naturally, the inflation-adjusted operating income will be:

   $$\$165 - 121 = 44$$

5. The current value accounting method is applied in case of price rise of specific commodities. Since a firm is continually replacing

its assets, it is the replacement cost, and not the historical cost, that should be taken into account while preparing the income statement or the balance sheet. If the value of inventory rises by 40 per cent, the equity needs upward revaluation by the same percentage so that the risen cost of inventory is met by increased liabilities.

SUMMARY

- Taxes play an important role in international financial decisions. An international tax system has three bases: neutrality, equity, and avoidance of double taxation. Neutrality may be viewed as capital-export neutrality and capital-import neutrality. The principle of equity is based on the principle of equal sacrifice. It is convergent with the principle of neutrality. Double taxation is avoided through relief either under treaty or even without any treaty.
- An international firm is usually subjected to income tax, withholding tax, and VAT. There are tax-haven countries that have zero/very low rate of taxes. In some cases, they exempt foreign income from tax; or alternatively, they provide specific tax privileges.
- There are different relief measures provided for the avoidance of double taxation. They are tax credit with or without deferral, tax exemptions, treating foreign paid tax as expenditure, and investment credit.
- Under Indian tax laws, various kinds of deductions/exemptions are provided to residents on their income from foreign sources. Specific forms of income of foreign enterprises in India are also exempted from tax. Last but not least, the Indian government has signed treaties for the avoidance of double taxation. Even in cases where the treaty has not been signed, relief is provided to the assessee.
- As far as international accounting is concerned, consolidation of the financial statements of the parent and subsidiaries is done through gross/net methods. When the currency of the subsidiary is translated, translation gain/loss occurs. International accounting deals with their treatment. Again, for the consolidation of accounts, the inflation differential is taken into account. There are different techniques to make adjustments for inflation.

REVIEW QUESTIONS

1. Explain the different bases of the international tax system.
2. What are the major forms of taxes an international firm is subjected to?
3. Describe the different modes of double taxation relief.
4. Explain the various tax incentives given to foreign investors under Indian tax laws.
5. Distinguish between gross and net consolidation methods.
6. How is currency translation loss/gain treated?

7. Explain different techniques for the adjustment of inflation for the purpose of international accounting.

Objective Type Questions

1. Mark True or False:
   (a) Capital-import neutrality means the same rate of tax for residents as well as non-residents.
   (b) Ability-to-pay principle means the same amount of tax for taxpayers of varying income-groups.
   (c) Income from foreign sources may be exempted from tax for avoidance of double taxation.
   (d) VAT is a direct tax.
   (e) Tax havens vary among themselves with respect to taxe rates.
   (f) Differing dates of the financial year come in the way of consolidation of financial statements of the parent and the subsidiary.
   (g) Foreign currency translation gains/losses under the deferral approach are shown in the consolidated income statement.
   (h) The current value accounting method of accounting inflation is more appropriate in cases where the price of only specific commodities tends to rise.
   (i) In France, the current-rate method of currency translation is widely used.
   (j) As per the Indian Companies Act, the balance sheet of the subsidiary is attached with that of the parent company.
2. Choose the Most Suitable Answer.
   (a) High inflation in the host country:
      (i) Overstates the profit of the firm as a whole
      (ii) Understates the profit of the firm as a whole
      (iii) None of the above
   (b) Under the deferral approach to treat translation gains/losses:
      (i) Such gains/losses are shown in the income statement
      (ii) Such gains/losses are not shown in the income statement
      (iii) Such gains/losses are amortised over the life of related balance sheet items
   (c) Comprehensive treaties for double tax avoidance include:
      (i) All aspects of income
      (ii) Specific income
      (iii) None of the above
   (d) Section 90 of the Indian Income Tax Act provides for:
      (i) Double taxation relief under the framework of treaties
      (ii) Double taxation relief even without any tax treaty
      (iii) None of the above
   (e) Any new EPZ unit gets tax deductions if its export accounts for:
      (i) 50 per cent of total sales
      (ii) 75 per cent of total sales
      (iii) None of the above

REFERENCES

Books

Alworth, J. S.(1988), *The Finance, Investment and Taxation Decisions of Multinationals* (Oxford: Basil Blackwell).

Eun, C. S. and B. G. Resnick (1998), *International Financial Management* (Boston: Irwin-McGraw-Hill), p. 509.

Gordon, R. 1981, *Tax Havens and Their Use by United States Taxpayers: An Overview*, (Washington D.C.: US Department of the Treasury), pp. 15–19.

Journals

Horst, T. (1980),"A Note on the Optimal Taxation of International Investment Income", *Quarterly Journal of Economics*, XCIV (Sep.–Oct.), 793–99.

Altshuler, R. *et al* (1991), *The Effects of US Tax Policy on the Income Repatriation of US Multinational Enterprises*, NBER Discussion Paper, no. 571.

Hamada, K. (1966),"Strategic Aspects of Taxation on Foreign Investment Income", *Quarterly Journal of Economics*, 80 (2), 361–75.

Hines, J. R. (1992), *Credit and Deferral as International Investment Incentives*, NBER Working Paper, no. 4191.

Janeba, E. (1996),"Foreign Direct Investment under Oligopoly: Profit Shifting or Profit Capturing ?" *Journal of Public Economics*, 60 (3), 423–25.

SELECT FURTHER READINGS

Bhargave, U. K. and R. Bhargave (2000), *Income Tax Act* (New Delhi: Taxmann Publications).

Grundy, M. (1984), *The World of International Tax Planning* (Cambridge: Cambridge University Press).

Rathore, S. (1996), *International Accounting* (New Delhi: Prentice-Hall of India).

* Brazil is the largest national economy in Latin America and the world's eighth largest economy at market exchange rates. Its current GDP (PPP) per capita is $10, 200. It has large and developed agricultural, mining, manufacturing and service sectors, as well as a large labor pool. Major export products include aircraft, electrical equipment, automobiles, ethanol, textiles, footwear, iron ore, steel, coffee, orange juice, soybeans and corned beef and is one of a group of four emerging economies called the BRIC countries.

Zurich, Switzerland*

22

Host Country Heterogeneity and International Business Strategy

CHAPTER OBJECTIVES

Host countries vary on account of varying economic, political and legal, socio-cultural, and other environmental characteristics. Naturally, MNCs have to adopt different entry and operating strategies for different sets of host countries. The present chapter discusses this issue. The objective is to:

- Analyse the economic indicators of developed market economies and the entry and operating strategy, of the MNCs, meant for these countries in general and the European Union in particular.
- Show the broad compartments of the less developed world and to indicate the environment in a less developed country.
- Discuss the entry and operating strategy of MNCs in the less developed world.
- Present the features of the emerging market economies, especially the Asian Tigers and the People's Republic of China.
- Discuss the entry and operating strategy of MNCs in case of emerging market economies.
- Explain the features of transition economies and the process of reforms that had started in the 1990s.
- Analyse the entry and operating strategy of MNCs, with respect to transition economies.

The earlier chapters discuss various strategies related to international business. These strategies need at least some modification when they are applied to different sets of the host country environment. Some of the strategies may be more important for a particular type of host country, whereas other strategies may be more relevant for other sets of countries. It is from this point of view that the present chapter discusses the basic features of the different sets of countries and the entry and operating strategies related to conducting business there. For purposes of the discussion, host countries are grouped broadly as developed market economies or industrialised countries; less developed countries, in general; and emerging market economies and transition economies of the developing world, in particular.

22.1 DEVELOPED MARKET ECONOMIES

22.1.1 Basic Economic Indicators

Table 22.1 shows that the per capita income level in 2006 in select industrialised countries was very high varying from $36,170 to $44,970. The growth rate in GDP during 2005–06 varied between 1.7 and 2.9 per cent. The share of industry in GDP stood at between 21.0 and 30.0 per cent. Their share in the world trade was high as their trade figure (export + import) varied in the range of $745 and $2,957 billion. Some of them experienced deficit on the current account. The size of FDI varied between $132.851 billion in Japan and $2,093.049 billion in the USA. The size of FDI stock as percentage of GDP too varied in a wide range. Despite variation, the industrialised countries accounted for a lion's share in the world trade and investment.

In four newly industrialised countries, as Table 22.2 shows, per capita income varied between $17,690 and $29,320. The growth rate varied between 4.7 and 6.9 per cent and so it was higher than in the industrialised world. The current account balance/GDP ratio varied widely. The FDI stock/GDP ratio was as high as 573.0 per cent in Hong Kong and 154.7 per cent in Singapore and as low as 12.3 per cent in Korea.

However, when one looks at them individually, some more differences appear among them, especially the way in which they regulate international business and also the basic environment pertaining to international business. For example, the cultural environment is different in Japan from that in the United States of America. The traditionally inward-looking business culture in Japan presents a sort of barrier for international business entrants (The Economist, 1990). Language is another problem in non-English speaking countries such as Japan, France, and Germany. Again, in the countries coming under the fold of European Union, international business entrants have to take into consideration not only the rules and regulations of the individual country but also those of the European Union. Yet again, in European Union countries, imports from outside the Union have to face a common external tariff. On the contrary, in case of the countries in the European Free Trade Area, goods normally make their entry through a country with lower tariff.

Table 22.1 Economic Indicators in Select Industrialised Countries

Country	*Per capita income ($) in 2006*	*Growth rate % in 2005–06*	*Share of industry in GDP %*	*Export in 2006 $ billion*	*Import in 2006 $ billion*	*Current Account balance in 2006 $ billion*	*FDI stock in 2007 $ billion*	*FDI stock as % of GDP in 2007*
Canada	36,170	2.0	n.a.	387.551	357.274	21.441	520.737	36.5
France	36,550	1.7	21	490.145	533.407	–27.667	1,026.081	40.1
Germany	36,620	2.9	30	1,112.320	910.160	146.874	629.711	19.0
Italy	32,070	2.0	27	409.572	436.083	–27.724	364.839	17.3
Japan	38,410	2.4	30	647.137	577.472	170.517	132.851	3.0
Netherlands	42,670	2.6	24	462.083	416.121	57.448	673.430	87.9
UK	40,180	2.6	26	443.358	600.833	–79.966	1,347.688	48.6
USA	44,970	2.4	22	1,037.320	1,919.574	–856.669	2,093.049	15.1

Source: *World Development Report, 2008*

Table 22.2 Economic indicators in four newly industrialised countries

Country	*Per capita income $ in 2006*	*Growth rate % in GDP in 2005–06*	*Current account balance/GDP ratio in 2006 %*	*FDI stock/GDP ratio % in 2007*
Hong Kong	28,460	5.9	12.0	573.0
Korea	17,690	4.7	1.0	12.3
Singapore	29,320	6.6	32.0	154.7
Taiwan*	n.a.	4.0	5.8	n.a.

* Relates to 2005.
Source: 1. *World Development Report, 2008*
2. *World Investment Report, 2008*

22.1.2 Entry and Operating Strategy for the MNCs

Sequential Entry refers to the strategy acquired to enter a new market. MNCs first adopt the contractual mode and only then make an investment.

As far as the entry strategy is concerned, it is the kind and the extent of competition that really matters. The government of these countries does not normally differentiate between a domestic firm and a foreign firm, with the result that the competition is very strong. In such a situation, an MNC operating there looks for the ways to maintain an edge over its competitors. It opts for transferring the latest technology that the competitors do not possess. If this is the case, technical collaboration would be an appropriate mode of entry. But if tariff and transportation cost are a greater hurdle in the way of competing with rivals, setting up its subsidiary would be a more feasible proposition for the MNC. Again, if the cultural barriers are more prominent in the host country, joint ventures with the host country producers may be suggested. It is a fact that cultural barriers are not very significant in industrialised countries, but in Japan, the problem of language persists even today and also consumers maintain preference for domestically produced goods. In such cases, joint ventures with host country firms are preferred. Mostly American MNCs have entered Japan in this way. The sequential entry strategy is yet another strategy often adopted by MNCs. In this they opt for licensing in the first stage and after making themselves well acquainted with the host country market, they proceed to set up a manufacturing unit.

An MNC can operate successfully if it launches a differentiated product.

Apart from the entry strategy, the operating strategy is also worth considering in face of severe competition from rival firms. The operating strategy is normally based on a combination of three factors, namely, cost, product differentiation, and market segmentation. Infact, it is the cost factor that has motivated MNCs to locate their assembly units in countries with cheap labour force and not in industrialised countries. Again, the strategy of product differentiation is very significant in conducting business with industrialised countries because consumers in these countries have large amounts of discretionary income to spend on both necessities and luxury items. An MNC can operate successfully in such countries to bag a large part of the consumers' disposable income if it launches a differentiated product. In the United States of America, McDonald's, Burger King, and so on were already operating, but Wimpy's and Kentucky's Chicken operated successfully with their differentiated products.

Furthermore, since the market in an industrialised country is quite large and the consumers choices vary, market segmentation strategy can prove more successful than in a less developed country. Even if an MNC caters to the need of a single segment or only a few segments of the market, it can easily survive.

22.1.3 International Business Strategy for EU

Since a large part of the industrialised world is represented by the European Union member countries, it is worthwhile to discuss international business strategy with respect to these counties. Chapter 8 discusses the various aspects of economic integration schemes along with the EU at some length. So at the present moment, only strategy is taken into account.

The strategy is no doubt similar to that of other industrialised countries. Nevertheless, the EU is distinguished by some special characteristics. Over the decades, this integration scheme has moved ahead from a mere customs union to a common market and an economic community, and also to some extent towards a political union. The result is that the integration is now quite strong; intra-union trade is greatly free; factors of production move freely; and the monetary union too is in a mature stage with the adoption of a common currency, the euro. From the viewpoint of an international business entrant, the size of the market has grown considerably large and so has the size of the demand.

The adoption of the euro has a definite impact on international business. Let us assume that an MNC sets up its plant in France, gets its supplies from Germany, raises funds from Belgium, and caters to the Dutch market. Had there been different currencies in these four countries and had these currencies been fluctuating greatly, the MNC's performance would have been jeopardised considerably. The euro has solved this problem. Moreover, the euro has, to a great extent, eased the accounting procedures, pricing policy, and the management of administration. Prices will now be more transparent, in the interest of the consumers.

The EU is moving towards a political union, as it is evident from the Common Foreign and Security policy. With this move, there will be greater consistency in the policy across the EU. The greater the consistency and stability in policy, the lower the political risk and more smooth the operation. However, in certain quarters, there is a fear that stronger political unification will lead to the emergence of a 'United States of Europe', in turn, weakening the bargaining power of MNCs.

There is also fear in some quarters that the EU has erected high trade barriers under the provisions of customs union and by devising a common agricultural policy. It is a fact that "trade diversion and trade creation" is the motive behind the economic integration scheme. But as far as the EU is concerned, it has gone along with the GATT/WTO provisions and its tariff is one of the lowest in the world. Its common agricultural policy does have the element of subsidies and import control measures, but over the years, the restrictive provisions have eased considerably. Moreover, it has pioneered the introduction of a Generalised System of Preferences that facilitates the import of manufactured goods from the developing world duty free into the EU. Under the Lome Convention, imports from erstwhile colonies are given preferential treatment. Imports from East European countries have become freer through various agreements with these countries and now with the enlargement of the EU. The EU has turned out to be a major export market for Mediterranean countries after it took a decision to maintain closer ties with these countries in 1994. There is a possibility that a free trade area will be created between the EU and these countries by 2010.

It is of course true that the labour cost is very high in Germany and MNCs would not like to set up their operations there. But considering it in totality, the EU definitely represents a fertile ground for international business.

22.2 BUSINESS WITH A LESS DEVELOPED COUNTRY

22.2.1 Income-based Classification of Developing Countries and their Broad Features

A less developed country, often termed as a developing country, is different from industrialised countries in the sense that it is posited on a lower ladder of economic development with lower per capita income and lower socio-economic indicators. The World Bank (2008) groups developing countries on the basis of per capita income valued at the rate of the US $ 2007. They are:

Country classification	*Per capita income based on 2007 Dollar*
Low-income country	$935 or less
Lower middle-income country	$936–3,705
Upper middle-income country	$3,706–11,455
High-income country	$11,456 or more

There is wide gap in the per capita income between the industrialised countries and the developing countries, in general, and also among different sets of developing countries. Similarly, their involvement in international business too varies widely. Table 22.3 presents a few important indicators regarding the different types of developing countries.

The growth rate of GDP during 2005–06 was higher in low-income countries than in the upper middle-income and high-income countries. The current account balance/GDP ratio in low-income countries during 2006 was negative compared to a positive ratio in the middle-income countries. As regards FDI stock/GDP ratio in 2006, the low-income countries lagged behind compared to the lower and upper middle-income countries but fared slightly better than the high-income developing countries.

Table 22.3 Some major economic indicators of the developing world

Group of countries	*Growth rate in GDP in 2005–06 %*	*Current account balance/GDP ratio % in 2006*	*FDI stock as % of GDP in 2006*
Low-income	6.5	–0.4	1.5
Lower middle-income	7.6	1.0	2.9
Upper middle-income	3.9	3.0	2.8
Middle-income as a whole	5.6	2.0	2.8
High-income	2.3	0	1.4

Source: 1. *World Development Report, 2008*
2. *World Investment Report, 2008*

Note:

Low-income countries: Burundi, Comoros, Congo, Ethiopia, Kenya, Madagascar, Malawi, Mozambique, Rwanda, Somalia, Sudan, Tanzania, Uganda, Zambia, Zimbabwe, Benin, Burkina Faso, Central African Republic, Chad, Cote d'Ivoire, Gambia, Ghana, Guinea, Guinea-Bissau, Liberia, Mali, Mauritania, Niger, Nigeria, Sao Tome & Principe, Senegal, Sierra Leone, Togo, Cambodia, Laos, Mongolia, Myanmar, Solomon Islands, Vietnam, Afghanistan, Bangladesh, India, Nepal, Pakistan, Kyrgyzistan, Moldova, Tajikistan, Uzbekistan, Yemen Rep., Haiti, Papua New Guinea, Timor-Leste, Eritrea.

Lower middle-income countries: Lesotho, Congo Rep., Cameroon, Angola, Bhutan, Egypt, Nicaragua, Namibia, Swaziland, Cape Verde, China, Fiji, Kiribati, Marshall Islands, Micronesia Fed. Sts., Philippines, Samoa, Thailand, Tonga, Vanuatu, Maldives, Sri Lanka, Albania, Belarus, Bosnia and Herzegovina, Latvia, Lithuania, Macedonia, Federation, Yugoslavia, Iran, Iraq, Jordan, Syria, West Bank and Gaza, Algeria, Djibouti, Morocco, Tunisia, Bolivia, Colombia, Cuba, Dominican Republic, Ecuador, El Salvador, Guatemala, Guyana, Honduras, Jamaica, Paraguay, Peru, Surinam, Georgia, Azerbaijan, Armenia, Indonesia, South Africa, Ukraine, Turkmenistan.

Upper middle-income countries: Botswana, Mauritius, Seychelles, Gabon, American Samoa, Malaysia, Croatia, Czech Republic, Hungary, Poland, Slovak Republic, Lebanon, Oman, Libya, Argentina, Barbados, Chile, Dominica, Grenada, Mexico, Panama, St. Kitts & Nevis, St. Lucia, Uruguay, Venezuela, Palau, Coasta Rica, Belize, Lithuania, Lativa, Mayotte, St. Vincent and Grenadines, Northern Mariana Islands, Bulgaria, Kazakhstan, Montenegro, Romania, Russia, Serbia, Turkey, Brazil, Equatorial Guinea.

High-income countries: Brunei, French Polynesia, Guam, Macao, New Caledonia, Slovenia, Channel Islands, Cyprus, Greenland, Liechtenstein, Monaco, Israel, Kuwait, Qatar, United Arab Emirates, Bahamas, Bermuda, Cayman Islands, Netherlands Antilles, Virgin Islands, Andorra, Aruka, Isle of Mau, Malta, Puerto Rico, San Marino, Antigua and Barbuda, Bahrain, Brunei Darussalam, Estonia, Faeroe Islands, Hong Kong, Saudi Arabia, Singapore, Taiwan, Trinidad & Tobago.

—Based on *World Development Report: 2008*

Source: The World Bank (2008), *Global Development Indicators: 2008*, Washington, D.C.

Apart from the economic indicators presented in Table 22.3, developing countries, in general, present a greater regulatory environment than the industrialised countries as a whole. It is a fact that some of the Asian and Latin American countries maintain substantial freedom of economic activities and it is also that many others have been limiting regulations under the aegis of structural adjustment and macroeconomic reforms, yet regulatory environment is prominent in these countries in the form of limitations on the activities of the private sector and still large participation of the government in their economic activities.

Again, the socio-cultural environment in developing countries is more rigid than in the industrialised countries. At the core of the problem lies a low literacy rate and low level of socio-economic development. The result is that consumers do not prefer using new varieties of goods; producers are often not innovative; superstitions reign the social customs and beliefs; and workers have only limited mobility.

Moreover, the existence of a dual economy is found in these countries. A large part of the economy is represented by the traditional sector, which experiences either little or no development. On the other hand, only a small part of the economy is developed, representing a greater amount of manufacturing activities and higher level of income and consumption. It is only this sector that attracts international business. In other words, the scope for foreign investors is limited to the developed part of the economy.

> Developing countries present:
> 1. a greater regulatory environment
> 2. rigid socio-cultural environment
> 3. a dual economic structure
> 4. immature political system
> 5. lack of finance and improved technology.

The political system in developing economies is not matured with the result that they present far greater political risk from the viewpoint of international business. Naturally, the number of cases of expropriation, nationalisation, and ethnic crisis has been much larger in developing countries than in industrialised countries. Many of the developing countries enforce restrictions on the outgoing foreign exchange in view of their ailing balance of payments. Many of them impose restrictions on the participation of foreign investors in the equity of national enterprises. There are many other such cases found in developing countries.

Lack of finance and improved technology is a common feature of the developing countries. Since their income level is low, savings are low, and the necessary funds are not available for achieving the desired rate of investment. It is not only the question of domestic savings, but also the availability of foreign exchange on account of bleak export performance that poses a serious problem for desired investment. In order to conserve foreign exchange, the government imposes control on the outflow of funds. But it leads to the emergence of a black market, worsening the problem further. Similarly, the R&D activities in these countries are minimal, with the result that the level of technology used is low. They have to depend mostly on the import of technology.

The need for funds is met by the inflow of foreign investment. But the inflow of foreign investment is constrained by the poor level of infrastructure, such as absence of good roads, accessible power supply, improved communication network, technically skilled manpower, good public utility services, and so on. Since returns from investment in infrastructure are not quick, this sector hardly attracts any investment.

22.2.2 Entry and Operating Strategies

The mode of entry MNCs adopt for developing countries in general may not be the same as those adopted in case of industrialised countries. The

MNCs have to be very wary of the political and exchange rate risks that are high in the developing world. The host government may nationalise the assets of MNCs, and fair compensation may or may not be given. Moreover, because of constraints on the external balance position, the government can impose restrictions on the imports of MNCs and encourage local procurement. It may impose curbs on the repatriation of profits and other transfers. The host country currency may depreciate and may cause shrinkage of profits in terms of the home country currency. This does not mean that these risks are absent in industrialised countries, but they are more common in developing countries. So, any entry strategy with respect to a developing country must take into account all these facts. In fact, it is the bargaining power of the MNC vis-á-vis the host government that matters. Sometimes the conditions are favourable at the time of entry but after some time they turn restrictive putting the MNC in a tight spot. If this is the case, it is only the bargaining strength of the MNC that counts. It is because of such risks that MNCs first opt for technical collaborations and when they find the host country environment suitable for making any investment, they commit financial resources.

> MNCs first opt for technical collaborations and when they find the host country environment suitable for making any investment, they commit financial resources.

Again, it is the bargaining power of the MNC that is crucial for the operating strategy. In order to maintain the bargaining power, MNCs prefer to provide proprietary technology to the affiliate and try to strengthen the intra-firm information, production, and distribution linkages. If the affiliate in a particular host country is largely dependent on its sister concerns in other host countries or on the parent company, the host government will deliberate at length before attempting nationalisation. This is perhaps the reason that the offshore assembly projects of American and other MNCs in some East Asian countries have been immune to the changing political scenario in these countries. The government cannot achieve any purpose by nationalising them as they obtain their supply from the parent unit or any of the other sister units located elsewhere, and their market lies mostly in other countries.

It is true that the operating strategy in a developing country is influenced by cost minimisation, product differentiation, and market segmentation similar to that of an industrialised country. But in developing countries, market segmentation plays a crucial role. This is because some sectors get government protection and they become sheltered markets. MNCs can gain from such protection through market segmentation.

Financial strategy is more important in the case of a developing country than in the case of a developed market economy. This is because the currency of developing countries is often weak and tends to depreciate frequently vis-á-vis convertible currencies. Moreover, the financial market is not developed with the result that the interest rate structure is rigid and procurement of funds within the host country is not so easy. The financial strategies discussed in Chapter 19 and 20 of the book should be used very carefully.

Last but not least, the government of a developing host country often sees an MNC as a "foreign" company and maintains a strict vigil in order to protect its own economic and political interests. It is very particular regarding the issues of repatriation of dividend and other remittances, employment of foreign personnel, tax evasion, use of appropriate technology, and so on. If an MNC operates with the motive of maximising its global profit it is bound to develop a relationship full of tensions with the host government. So, the appropriate operating strategy for MNC should be to maintain cordial relations with the host government and within this limit, it has to meet its objective of maximising global profit.

22.3 LESS DEVELOPED COUNTRIES: A FUNCTIONAL CLASSIFICATION

The less developed countries or the developing countries can be grouped not necessarily on the basis of per capita income but on the basis of a number of macro-economic and socio-economic indicators. From this point of view, the different groups may be as follows:

1. Tax havens
2. Least developed countries
3. Emerging market economies
4. Transition economies

The classification is not water-tight. A particular developing country can be placed under two groups. For example, Czech Republic and China can be grouped both as emerging market economies (EMEs) and as transition economies. The readers need to be acquainted with the broad features of the different groups and also with their significance for international business.

22.3.1 Tax Havens

The features of a tax haven or a low tax-rate country have already been discussed in the preceding chapter. It does not need repetition. However, from the viewpoint of international business, the tax havens are very significant in the sense that the MNCs are found directing their profits and other incomes to these countries in order to lessen their tax burden. And then, these funds are again directed to different host countries in the form of foreign direct investment. In other words, the tax havens act neither as a host country nor as a home country but as a financial entrepot encouraging in turn the operation of the MNCs. Quoting one of such cases, Mauritius stands as the biggest source of FDI to India. It is not because many of the MNCs are headquartered there, but this country is a tax haven where the US and European MNCs channel their profits and from there itself, they make FDI in India.

22.3.2 Least Developed Countries

Among the less developed countries, there are presently 50 countries designated as the least developed country (LDCs). They share around 11 per cent of the world population but only 0.6 per cent of the world GDP. Many of them are land-locked countries meaning that they are far

> The various LDCs are: Afghanistan, Angola, Bangladesh, Benin, Bhutan, Burkina Faso, Burundi, Cambodia, Cape Verde, Central African Republic, Chad, Comoros, Democratic Republic of Congo, Djibouti, Equatorial Guinea, Eritrea, Ethiopia, Gambia, Guinea, Guinea-Bissau, Haiti, Kiribati, People's Democratic Republic of Lao, Lesotho, Liberia, Madagascar, Malawi, Maldives, Mali, Mauritania, Mozambique, Myanmar, Nepal, Niger, Rwanda, Samoa, Sao Tome and Principe, Senegal, Sierra Leone, Solomon Islands, Somalia, Sudan, Timor-Leste, Togo, Tuvalu, Uganda, United Republic of Tanzania, Vanuatu, Yemen, and Zambia.
> —Based on the criteria developed by UNCTAD

away from any sea port. It is not convenient for them to make export or import. The transport cost is high as well the time consumed in trade is large. Consequently, their foreign trade does not expand smoothly. Again, many others are small-island countries where the size of domestic market is small and the foreign markets are quite remote. Moreover, some of them are highly prone to natural calamities that do entail upon the output. All of them are the LDCs because of the following reasons:

1. The level of income is very low. The "vicious circle of poverty" does exist meaning that low level of income limits domestic savings; low rate of savings means low rate of investment and thereby low level of income. Among African LDCs, over one-half of the population has less than 1 US dollar per capita income per day. The statistics reveal that in 18 out of 46 LDCs, the per capita income grew by 1 per cent between 2000 and 2004. Again, in 17 out of 41 countries, the growth rate in per capita income was negative during the same period (UNCTAD, 2006). The domestic-savings-investment gap is, to some extent, bridged up by foreign economic aid but that has created huge external debt burden.
2. The human asset is very weak. This is natural in view of the fact that the educational and health facilities are still very poor in these countries. The lack of healthy and skilled persons affects productivity adversely.
3. A very high degree of economic vulnerability exits in these countries. Their export list is highly concentrated among only a few agricultural and primary items. With high fluctuations in their demand, their export earnings fluctuate that creates vulnerability. According to a study, the economic vulnerability index in these countries is 34 per cent higher than in developing countries in general (UNCTAD, 2006). It is because of all these factors that

the share of LDCs in global trade fell from 0.4 per cent in 1980 to 0.2 per cent in 2003.

From the viewpoint of international business, the LDCs are not significant as the size of domestic market is small and the physical and financial infrastructure is inadequate. There are, of course, few evidences of FDI but it is primarily confined to extractive sectors. The statistics reveal that 10 of the LDCs absorbed 84 per cent of FDI flow meant for this group of countries during 2004 (UNCTAD, 2006).

22.3.3 Emerging Market Economies

The EMEs are those with high saving, investment and economic growth rate. To be precise, there are 38 EMEs spread over different continents and comprising of:

1. The newly industrialising countries, such as South Africa, Brazil, China, India, Malaysia, Mexico, Thailand, etc.
2. The countries having potential to become the newly industrialising country, such as Argentina, Chile, Indonesia, Philippines, Brunei, Czech Republic, Hungary, Poland, Russia, Slovakia, Turkey, Vietnam, etc.

As per a World Bank study, the 38 EMEs are: Argentina, Bolivia, Brazil, Bulgaria, Chile, China Mainland, Columbia, Costa Rica, Croatia, the Czech Republic, the Dominican Republic, Ecuador, Egypt, El Salvador, Hungary, India, Indonesia, Jordon, Malaysia, Mexico, Morocco, Panama, Pakistan, Paraguay, Peru, the Philippines, Poland, Romania, the Russian Federation, the Slovak Republic, South Africa, Thailand, Tunisia, Turkey, Ukraine, Uruguay, Venezuela, and Vietnam.

—Based on the criteria developed by the World Bank Working Group of the Capital Markets

One of the reasons behind high investment and growth rate is that they have adopted an outward-looking policy of foreign trade and investment. As a result, they are a very fertile ground for international business, especially FDI. The statistics show that the quantum of FDI inflow into these 38 EMEs went on increasing from US $19.7 billion in 1990 to US $149.5 billion in 2000 and to US $217.5 billion in 2005 despite a fall in the world FDI inflow during 2000s. Consequently, their share in world FDI inflow moved up during this period from 9.4 to 10.7 per cent and to 23.7 per cent, respectively. The Asian EMEs accounted for the largest share in 2005 which stood at 10.6 per cent, followed by the Latin American ones sharing the other 7.1 per cent. The Eastern and Central European EMEs and those of the Middle East and Africa shared, respectively, 3.6 and 2.3 per cent of the world FDI inflow during 2005 (WIR, 2006). It is because of the significance of the EMEs in the area of international business that a few select cases will be discussed in the subsequent Section 22.4.

22.3.4 Transition Economies

There is another group of the developing world represented by the transition economies that were earlier under a communist regime but now they are on the transition from socialist ownership and centralised planning to a market-based economy with private ownership. They are spread mainly in the central and eastern Europe and Baltics, but they are also in Asia. In some of them, where the process of transition has been successful, the volume of trade and the FDI inflow has increased in recent years as the MNCs have shown interest in them. A detailed discussion in respect of them from the viewpoint of international business is presented in Section 22.5.

22.4 THE FIVE EMERGING MARKET ECONOMIES

Table 22.4 enlists five countries—two from Asia, two from Latin America and one from Eastern Europe. It shows that per capita income varies from $720 in India to $7,310 in Mexico. The growth rate is the highest at 9.1 per cent in China. It is slightly lower in India and Russia but far lower in Brazil and Mexico. The export/GDP ratio is about one-third in China and Russia but lower at 13–16 per cent in other countries of the list. In case of import as percentage of GDP, the figure stands at 30 in case of China but lower at 10–19 per cent in others. The figures show that except for India and Mexico, the other countries experience surplus balance of current account. The FDI stock/GDP ratio stands around a quarter in all except for India where it is barely 6.0 per cent. The apparent reason is that India adopted liberal policy late in 1991. The inflation rate is, of course, disturbing as it is as high as 9.7 per cent in Russia and 5.6 per cent in India. In all, the EMEs present heterogeneous macroeconomic indicators, despite the fact that they are very important from the viewpoint of international business.

Table 22.4 Select Macroeconomic indicators in select EMEs: 2005

Country	*Per capita income US $*	*Growth rate of GDP % during 1998–2006*	*Export/ GDP ratio %*	*Import/ GDP ratio %*	*FDI stock/ GDP ratio %*	*Inflation rate in 2006*
China	1,740	9.1	34	30	27	105
India	720	6.6	13	19	6	5.6
Russia	4,460	5.4	32	18	22	9.7
Brazil	3,460	2.4	15	10	25	4.5
Mexico	7,310	3.2	16	19	27	3.5

Source: 1. *World Development Report: 2008.*
2. *World Investment Report: 2008.*

22.4.1 FDI in China and India

As mentioned earlier, Asian EMEs have attracted the largest segment of the world FDI inflows. In Asia, China and India are the major host, although there is wide difference in the quantum of the FDI inflow between these two countries. During 1992–1995, the size of FDI inflow in China was US $109 billion compared to US $4 billion in India. During 1996–2000, it was US $209 billion in China vis-à-vis US $15 billion in India. Again, during 2001–2005, it was US $286 billion in China as against US $24 billion in India. The difference in the two sets of figures is natural in view of the fact that China adopted a liberal FDI policy as back as in 1979, whereas in India the liberal policy dates back to 1991. In India too, in the recent past, there has been a fast increase in the size of the FDI inflow. In FY 2006–07, it was US $17.7 billion compared to US $7.7 billion in FY 2004–05 and US $9.3 billion in FY 2005–06. It is expected that over the years, this difference will be narrow.

Rising FDI in Asian R&D and Real Estate

In 2005, 315 new FDI projects in R&D were recorded in South, East and South-East Asia, four-fifths of them being located in China and India. The number of foreign-owned R&D centres rose to 750 in China by the end of 2005. Similarly, the Asian real estate sector has attracted large FDI. Foreign investors have entered this sector through different ways including establishing new real estate developers, acquiring local ones, investing via financial institutions and buying properties directly. According to an estimate, foreign investment now accounts for 15 per cent of China's real estate market. Again, FDI in India's real estate sector was $120 million in 2005 despite the fact that this sector is not formally open to FDI. After the SEBI allowed foreign funds to invest in the local real estate sector in April 2004, there are over 30 foreign funds that have applied to conduct business in Indian real estate.
Source: *World Investment Report, 2006*

Again, the development of infrastructure supporting FDI inflow in China is quite large compared to that in India. The Indian Government is, of course, giving emphasis on infrastructure development. The policy towards the setting up of special economic zones (SEZs) is being fine-tuned. But all this will take at least some time. In China, the amount of electric power available to the SEZs is large being comparable to electricity generated in England and Thailand taken together. In India, the availability of electric power is still a problem area. Thus, it is also a question of time. Over the years, India may emerge as a big host for the MNCs.

Last but not least, it is observed in some quarters that the figures of FDI inflow in respect of China stand exaggerated in view of large-scale round-tripping. Intra-MNCs funds move from Mailand China to Hong Kong and again back from Hong Kong to Mainland China in the form of FDI. Xiao (2004) believes that the extent of round-tripping in the Chinese case is as high as 50 per cent. Thus, if it is true, the difference between India and China attracting FDI flow is not so big as it appears from the figures.

> *Round-tripping* is channelling of local funds by direct investors to special purpose entities (SPEs) abroad and the subsequent return of the funds to local economy in the form of direct investment. Round-tripping is represented by another nomenclature, 'trans-shipping', the amount of which was US $113.226 billion or 96.6 per cent of total FDI inflow into Luxembourg during 2002.
> — *World Investment Report, 2006*

22.4.2 Strategy of MNCs

It has already been narrated that despite being a part of the developing world, emerging market economies have many similarities with developed market economies. It is also a fact that they vary widely amongst themselves. But in a few of them the income level is high; the saving rate, investment rate and the resultant growth rate is high; and there are the least restrictions on the trade and the flow of capital. This means that MNCs do not face any significant entry hurdle. Nor do they face significant operating hurdles. The mode of entry may be through simple technical collaboration, a greenfield investment, or mergers and acquisitions. It is found that MNCs have moved into them through the export of technology in a sizeable way. The reason is that these countries have the capability of modifying the imported technology in order to suit the market requirements of the developing world. Sometimes the modified technology is exported back to the home country because it enjoys a competitive advantage (Sharan, 1985). Modification of technology is an important reason behind the entry of MNCs through the export of technology. But, at the same time, it is also that MNCs have started setting up R&D centres in these countries in collaboration with research institutes to benefit not only the host country but also the home country.

> MNCs export technology to emerging market economies and modify it through setting up R&D centres, although green field investment and M&As are also common. But in view of competition from rival firms, just as in case of developed economies, they adopt product differentiation and market segmentation strategy in a big way.

This does not mean that MNCs do not involve equity investment. Since the financial sector is strong as well as the return from the investment is handsome, the entry mode with equity investment is also significant. Moreover, in recent years, mergers and acquisitions have become a more common mode of entry.

As far as operating strategy is concerned, MNCs find ample freedom. There are a large number of offshore assembly units in at least some of the emerging market economies. It is because these countries enjoy the advantage of cheap labour and at the same time have the developed infrastructure required for industrial activities. But MNCs face tough competition from rival firms, just as they do in case of developed economies. This is why they adopt product differentiation and market segmentation strategy in a big way, as they have been adopting in case of a developed host country.

22.5 TRANSITION ECONOMIES

Transition economies are countries shifting from a centrally planned economic system to a market based economic system.

Transition economies are mainly the economies of central and eastern Europe and the Baltic countries and the countries, carved out of the former Soviet Union, now known as the Commonwealth of Independent States (CIS). Some of them are also in Asia, the most important among them being China, Vietnam, and Cambodia. In some cases, the transition began earlier, in the 1970s and the 1980s, but in majority of them, the move towards transition began in the 1990s. While some of the countries have witnessed consistent growth, others had to face growth reversal. In many, the economy is too weak to have a successful transition and to involve itself greatly in international business.

22.5.1 Early Experiences

Glasnost refers to reforms in the erstwhile Soviet Union for freedom of expression.

Perestroika refers to economic reforms in the erstwhile Soviet Union.

The former Soviet Union and its allies continued to remain under the influence of communism for decades and remained practically isolated from the growing magnitude of international business. With excessive dependence on the public sector and with huge expenditure on defence, the rate of economic development and standard of living was low in many cases. The centralised planning mechanism failed to bear desired fruits. A couple of countries, namely. Poland and Hungary, began reforming the economic system as back as in the 1970s and the 1980s. In the former Soviet Union, it was President Gorbachev who initiated reforms in the mid and late 1980s. **Glasnost** encouraged open political discussion and freedom of expression, while **perestroika** implied major economic reforms. Beginning from 1988, individuals were allowed to set up enterprises, although in the service sector only. The economic reforms did not face much resistance as the communist party was not against it. The year 1989 was probably the last year representing the old system for the entire region. This was the year when the officially measured output had peaked in the former Soviet Union and in many other countries of this group.

22.5.2 Reforms during 1990s

The reform process in CIS and other east European countries was characterised by wide ranging political reforms. Western governments too participated in a big way. However, the success rate varied from one country to the other. In Poland, Hungary, and the Czech Republic, the success rate was comparatively high in view of the fact that they had allowed foreign investment during the final years of communist regime. The bureaucracy was honest and efficient and the general public supported the reforms. On the contrary, CIS member countries had to face serious economic problems. Most of them did not have supportive infrastructure for making the reform a success.

Whatever might be the rate of success, the process of reform mainly incorporated:

1. Price liberalisation measures
2. Monetary and fiscal stabilisation
3. Liberalisation of the external sector
4. Creation of the private sector

The price stabilisation schemes embraced, among other things, withdrawal of subsidies that could ensure competition. But it led to inflation, especially in Russia and other CIS countries, where shortages had prevailed.

The monetary and fiscal stabilisation programme included mainly tax reforms and reduction in the level of government expenditure so as to limit the fiscal deficit within a reasonable range. In Russia, budgetary deficit was met through central bank lending, but this caused inflation. In Hungary and Poland, it was met through the issue of government securities to the public. The government got the funds as well as excess money supply was mopped up.

The reforms in the external sector was brought about through import liberalisation, through exchange rate rationalisation and through conclusion of Bilateral Investment Treaties (BITs) and Double Taxation Treaties (DTTs). In the Czech Republic, currency convertibility was introduced in 1995, but in other countries overvalued currency and scanty foreign exchange reserves came in the way.

Last but not least, the private sector was encouraged and restrictions on FDI inflow were lifted. However, the approach to privatisation differed in different countries. In Hungary, the sale of an enterprise to foreign investors was common and at the same time, private sector investment was encouraged through the provision of incentives. In the Czech Republic, the pace of privatisation was faster than in Hungary. Joint ventures were more common and not the outright sale of the enterprise to foreign investors. In Poland, public sector units were converted into limited liability companies and then these companies represented the interest of domestic/foreign investors. In the beginning, the pace of privatisation was slow because private sector entrepreneurs did not have enough money to invest. But in 1995, with the creation of privately managed national investment funds, the pace turned rapid. In Russia, the process was not very successful in view of retention of control by the government. Moreover, as Harrison *et al* (1999) point out, privatisation process was overshadowed by corruption at the bureaucratic level.

The figures in Table 22.5 confirm wide variation in four transition economies. The per capita income varied from $5,780 in Russia to 21,470 in Czech Republic in 2006. The growth rate varied during 2005–06 from 4.2 per cent to 7.3 per cent. The trade figures during 2006 (export + import) was the

Table 22.5 Economic Indicators in Select Transition Countries

Country	*Per capita income in 2006 $*	*Growth rate % in GDP in 2005–06*	*Export in 2006 $ billion*	*Import in 2006 $ billion*	*FDI stock/ GDP ratio %*
Czech Republic	21,470	6.2	95.106	93.198	57.7
Hungary	18,290	4.2	73.719	76.514	70.6
Poland	14,830	5.9	109.731	124.178	33.8
Russia	5,780	7.3	304.520	163.867	25.1

Source: *1. World Development Report, 2008*
2. World Investment Report, 2008

lowest at $188 billion in Czech Republic compared to $468 billion in Russia. Similarly, FDI/GDP ratio in 2007 too varied from 25.1 per cent in Russia to as large as 70.6 per cent in Hungary. All this shows that the features and pace of transition has been different in different countries of this region.

22.5.3 International Business Strategy in Transition Economies

The entry and operating strategy of MNCs in these countries depends on how far the process of transition has been successful. MNCs are not normally interested in countries where the supportive infrastructure is still not developed and where sufficient income has not been generated to give boost to the demand. MNCs are interested in others that have shown consistent growth. Statistics show that these countries have been capable of generating a large volume of trade and also that they have attracted a good amount of FDI. However, the early phases of transition carried high business risk. As a result, MNCs moved to these countries with the minimum possible equity capital (Rivoli and Salorio, 1996).

MNCs have normally gone for joint ventures and free play of MNCs is still remote.

As far as entry strategy is concerned, MNCs have normally gone for joint ventures. The reason is that despite the move towards privatisation, the government is still in favour of maintaining control over private enterprises and free play of MNCs is still remote. In case of joint ventures, both technical and financial collaborations are common. The former is common because these countries only have an obsolete technological base and they are eager to have new and updated technology. Financial collaborations are common because they lack the required foreign exchange. They get it through financial collaboration, which involves transfer of capital.

The entry of MNCs are largely found in the consumer goods segment as there is still shortage of consumer goods. The purpose is primarily to cater to the domestic consumers in the host country. Moreover, the domestic market is more profitable than exports.

The entry of MNCs are largely found in the consumer goods segment as there is still shortage of consumer goods.

However, there are still many challenges facing MNCs. The rules and regulations are still cumbersome. MNCs have to go through a number of procedural formalities for entry as well as for operation. Trade restrictions are common and it is still the governmental organisations that control a large part of foreign trade. Restrictions in respect of the convertibility of the domestic currency exist. Consumers enjoying subsidies for decades are not in favour of the market determined price, which is usually higher. The bureaucratic set up has not kept abreast of the changing scenario. The supply of managerial expertise has not picked up. These are some of the challenges that MNCs have to take into account while entering these countries and beginning their operation. However, there is a large area that can be explored for the purpose of international business, especially in case of transition economies that have joined the European Union recently.

SUMMARY

- Since economic and socio-economic indicators differ widely between the developed market economies and the developing countries, and also among the different groups of developing countries, the same international business strategy cannot be applied to all host countries.
- Developed countries are characterised by a high income level, quality oriented consumption pattern, rich financial and technological resources, and the minimum of regulations and restrictions. MNCs rate them high as they find their environment congenial for entry and operation. But, at the same time, MNCs have to face strong competition from rivals. In order to maintain an edge over their rivals, they adopt, among other things, cost minimisation, product differentiation, and a market segmentation strategy. If the host country is a member of any regional grouping, such as the EU, MNCs have to consider additionally the rules and regulations of the regional grouping.
- The developing world has various sets of countries ranging from low-income to middle-income and high income countries. There are 48 least developed countries where economic and socio-economic indicators are very poor. MNCs do not prefer them for operation, unless these countries offer an abundance of natural resources for exploitation. Again, tax haven countries have attracted MNCs to pool their funds and to enjoy the benefit of a very low rate of taxes.
- There is also other group of countries that are known as emerging market economies. They are in many respects similar to developed market economies, providing unrestricted entry to MNCs. Transnational companies get an additional benefit of cheap labour and so they have gone for offshore assembly operations on a large scale in these countries.

- Last but not least, there are also transition economies making a shift from centralised planning to a market-based system. In cases where the transition process has been successful, MNCs have moved in a big way. However, they do not commit too much financial resources in the earlier phase of operation in view of the large business risk there. The operating strategy is greatly focussed on meeting the demand of domestic consumers rather than on exporting goods.

REVIEW QUESTIONS

1. Explain what distinguishes a developed market economy from a developing economy.
2. What are the challenges faced by MNCs in a developed market economy? What strategy do they follow while operating there?
3. How do MNCs operate in a tax haven country?
4. In what way are the emerging market economies similar to developed market economies? What type of strategy do MNCs follow in an emerging market economy?
5. What do you mean by transition economy? Discuss the entry and operating strategy of MNCs moving to these countries.

OBJECTIVE TYPE QUESTIONS

1. Mark True or False:
   (a) Per capita income alone may be the dividing line between a developed and a developing country.
   (b) Public sector accounts for less than one-third of the economic activities in developed countries.
   (c) Developed countries experience normally surplus balance on current account.
   (d) Japan traditionally possesses an inward-looking business culture.
   (e) Cost factor is an important factor behind doing business in an industrialised country.
   (f) LDCs are also from among the lower middle income countries.
   (g) Emerging market economies have experienced a high growth rate over the past few decades.
   (h) Transition economies are mostly from Eastern Europe and the Baltic countries.
   (i) Tax havens are not good hosts of offshore banking centres.
   (j) Developing countries present a smooth regulatory environment compared to that found in developed countries.

2. Choose the Most Suitable Answer.
   (a) US firms have entered Japan mostly by:
      (i) Opening branches
      (ii) Joint ventures
      (iii) Setting up of wholly owned subsidiaries

(b) The operating strategy in an industrialised country is based on:
   (i) Cost reduction
   (ii) Product differentiation
   (iii) Both product differentiation and market segmentation

(c) EU is a fertile ground for international business, because:
   (i) Labour is costly
   (ii) There is common external tariff
   (iii) The euro provides transparency in operation

(d) Developing countries present an:
   (i) Immature political system
   (ii) Dual economy
   (iii) Both of the above

(e) MNCs enter a developing country:
   (i) First through investment and then by providing technology
   (ii) First through technical collaboration and then through investment
   (iii) None of the above

(f) Financial strategy is crucial while doing business in a developing country, because its:
   (i) Currency is weak
   (ii) Financial sector is underdeveloped
   (iii) Both of the above

(g) Emerging market economies include:
   (i) NICs
   (ii) Countries having the potential to become NICs
   (iii) Both of the above

(h) MNCs have moved to transition economies mostly in the area of:
   (i) Consumer goods
   (ii) Capital goods
   (iii) Services

STUDY TOPIC

The 2008 International Financial Crisis and its Impact on International Business of Different Sets of Countries

The international financial crisis of 2008 was primarily the outgrowth of the sub-prime mortgage crisis in the USA. A continued escalation in the real estate prices for a decade or so and then a sudden and drastic drop in those prices during 2007 made the collateral of the home loans sub-prime. There were large defaults that in turn led to huge bank losses and put abnormal pressure on the functioning of the banks. The losses on this account were expected for over $400 billion, over one-half of which was to be borne by banks and other highly leveraged financial institutions. For each dollar of loss, these institutions had to shrink their balance sheet by $10 to $25 with the result that their lending was to be squeezed for over $2 trillion (*www.livemint.com*). All this had a spill-over effect in the form of dwindling currency, an economic recession and subdued activities in the financial market of the USA.

It is true that the immediate impact fell on the financial markets, but the impact spilled over gradually to the different sectors of the economy. In the beginning, the foreign institutional investors pulled back their funds from the financial market in order to salvage the banks in which they had a stake. The pull-back had a demonstration effect. The other investors turned hesitant to make any investment that led in turn to the emergence of the liquidity crisis. The economic activities remained starved of the required funds. As a result, the performance of different sectors fell far down. The growth rate in the economy plummeted. The fall in income and thereby in demand for spending was a natural corollary. In such a situation, it was not possible for the international business to remain aloof of these trends. Those economies that had maintained an open economic policy were hit hard. Thus, the crisis emerging in the USA spread over to different parts of the globe.

Shrinking World Trade

The shrunk income led to lower demand for imports. At the same time, lower availability of funds entailed on the capacity to export. Both the exports and imports slackened during 2008. The annual growth in the world trade (at constant prices) plummeted from 6.0 per cent in 2007 to 2.0 per cent in 2008. The respective figures for the US exports were 7.0 in 2007 and 5.5 in 2008. For its import, they were 1.0 in 2007 and (−)4.0 in 2008. The fall was recorded also in the growth rate of EU's export and import. For the export, the fall was recorded from 3.5 per cent to zero per cent. For the import, it was from 3.5 to (−)1.0 per cent. The downtrend was not limited to the industrialised countries. In EMEs also, the situation was not different. The growth rate in Chinese export and import dropped from 19.5 per cent to 8.5 per cent and from 13.5 per cent to 4.0 per cent, respectively. In case of India, the respective figures for export were 13.0 and 7.0 per cent and they were 16.0 and 12.5 per cent for imports. This is not all. Based on the trends, the growth rate in the world trade was to drop by 9.0 per cent in 2009.

Table 1 Annual change in merchandise trade at constant prices

Per cent

Country	*Export*		*Import*	
	2007	2008	2007	2008
World	6.0	2.0	6.0	2.0
USA	7.0	5.5	1.0	−4.0
EU	3.5	0.0	3.5	−1.0
China	19.5	8.5	13.5	4.0
India	13.0	7.0	16.0	12.5

Source: *WTO, Press Release, 24.3.2009*

The impact of the international financial turbulence was not limited to trade in merchandise. The trade in services too was the victim. The annual growth rate of world trade in services fell from

19.0 per cent in 2007 to 11.0 per cent in 2008. The growth rate of export of services in case of the USA fell from 16.0 per cent in 2007 to 10.0 per cent in 2008. In imports, the drop was recorded from 9.0 to 7.0 per cent. In case of the EU, the respective figures were 21.0 and 0.0 per cent, and 19.0 and 10.0 per cent.

Table 2 Annual change in services trade at constant prices

Per cent

	Export		*Import*	
	2007	2008	2007	2008
World	19.0	11.0	19.0	11.0
USA	16.0	10.0	9.0	7.0
EU	21.0	10.0	19.0	10.0

Source: *WTO, Press Release*, 24.3.2009

Squeezing FDI

Besides trade, FDI too suffered a blow from the international financial crisis. The global inflow of FDI shrank by 21.0 per cent—from $1,833.3 billion in 2007 to $1,449.1 billion in 2008. The developed countries experienced a greater squeeze of 32.7 per cent—from $1,247.6 billion to $840.1 billion during the above period. In case of the EU, it was a drop of 30.7 per cent—from $804.3 billion to $557.4 billion. In other developed countries, the percentage fall was lower.

The FDI flow into developing countries, on the other hand, increased by 3.6 per cent—from $499.7 billion to $517.7 billion. However, the rate of increase was lower than in 2007. The geographic pattern was heterogeneous. Except for West Asia where the inflow plummeted by 21.3 per cent, there was an increase in all other regions varying between 3.3 and 12.7 per cent. As far as India is concerned, there was an increase of 59.9 per cent—from $23.0 billion in 2007 to $36.7 billion in 2008.

Table 3 Changes in FDI inflow during 2008 over 2007

Billions of US Dollar

Region/ Country	*FDI Inflow*			*Cross-border M&As*		
	2007	2008	% change	2007	2008	% change
World	1,833.3	1,449.1	–21.0	1,637.1	1,183.7	–27.7
Developed countries	1,247.6	840.1	–32.7	1,454.1	981.8	–32.5
EU	804.3	557.4	–30.7	782.0	506.4	–35.2
US	232.8	220.0	–5.5	379.4	314.9	–17.0
Japan	22.5	17.4	–22.6	21.4	19.1	–10.8

Billions of US Dollar

Region/ Country	FDI Inflow			Cross-border M&As		
	2007	2008	% change	2007	2008	% change
Developing countries	499.7	517.7	3.6	152.9	177.0	15.7
Latin America & Caribbean	126.3	142.3	12.7	30.7	29.5	–3.8
West Asia	71.5	56.3	–21.3	30.3	31.5	4.0
South, East & South-east Asia	247.8	256.1	3.3	81.5	89.4	9.7
South-east Europe & CIS	85.9	91.3	6.2	30.1	25.0	–17.0
India	23.0	36.7	59.9	5.6	11.2	100.8

Source: *Compiled from UNCTAD Press Release*, 19.1.2009

When one analyses the cross-border M&As exclusively, it is evident that the international financial crisis affected them adversely. On the global level, there was a downturn of 27.7 per cent in 2008 over 2007. In this case too, the developed countries suffered a greater shock as the fall was recorded at 32.5 per cent. In case of EU, it was still greater at 35.2 per cent. On the contrary, the developing countries as a whole experienced a rise in cross-border deal in value terms of 15.7 per cent in 2008 over 2007. In India, this percentage was as big as 100.8. However, the Caribbean and Latin American countries and the South-east Europe and CIS witnessed a fall in such deals in value terms.

QUESTIONS

1. What led to the international financial crisis?
2. In what way was the international financial crisis related to the international business?
3. Comment on the extent of the influence of international financial crisis on the world trade and investment.

REFERENCES

Book

Harrison, A. L. *et al* (2001), *International Business: Global Competition from a European Perspective* (Oxford: Oxford University Press).

Journals and Report

Ramamurti, R. (2001), "The Obsolescing Bargaining Model? MNC-Host Developing Country Relations Revisited", *Journal of International Business Studies,* XXXII (1), 23–40.

Rivoli, P. and E. Salorio (1996), "Foreign Direct Investment and Investment under Uncertainty", *Journal of International Business Studies,* XXVI (2), 335–58.

Sharan, V. (1985), "Internationalisation of Third World Firms: An Indian Case Study", *International Marketing Review,* II (Summer), 63–72.

The Economist (1990), "America and Japan: The Unhappy Alliance", February 17, 21–24.

The World Bank (2006), *World Development Report: 2007* (New York: Oxford University Press).

UNCTAD (2006), *The Least Development Countries: 2006,* Geneva.

—— (2006), *World Investment Report: 2006,* Geneva.

Xiao, G. (2004), "Peoples Republic of Chine's Round tripping FDI: Scale, Causes and Implications", ADB Institute Discussion Paper No. 7, Manila.

SELECT FURTHER READINGS

Behrman, J. and R. Grosse (1990), *International Business and Governments* (Columbia SC: University of South Carolina Press).

Blanchard, O. (1997), *The Economics of Post-communist Transition* (Oxford: Clarendon Press).

Child, J. and D. K. Tse (2001), "China's Transition and Its Implications for International Business", *Journal of International Business Studies,* XXXII (1), 5–21.

Roy, H. and K. Calder (1984), *The Eastasia Edge* (New York: Basic Books).

* Zürich is the largest city in Switzerland and the capital of the canton of Zürich. It is a leading financial centre and global city. The high quality of life has been cited as a reason for economic growth and the most important sector in the economy of Zürich is the service industry, which employs nearly four fifths of workers. Other important industries include light industry, machine and textile industries and tourism.

GLOSSARY

Absolute Advantage: It is a theory of international trade propounded by Adam Smith. It states that a country produces those goods in which it possesses greater efficiency and exports them for other things it needs.

Absorption Approach: It explains that consumption/investment/governmental expenditure needs to be curtailed in order to help improve the trade balance

Acquired Advantage: It is a sort of trade advantage that arises on account of technology rather than the availability of natural resources.

Acquisition: It is purchase of a company by another company.

Ad Valorem Duty: It is tariff levied on the basis of the value of the item.

American Depository Receipt (ADR): It is a certificate issued by a US bank (depository) in the USA in lieu of the shares of foreign companies.

Andean Group: It is an economic integration scheme embracing five countries, viz. Bolivia, Colombia, Ecuador, Peru and Venezuela.

Antidumping Duty: Additional tariff levied on imported product on the notion that it is sold intentionally at a price below cost.

Arbitrage: Buying and selling foreign currency in different markets in order to reap profit out of varying exchange rates.

Arm's-length Price: A market price charged for a product by unrelated parties. It does not involve any over/under-invoicing.

Association of South East Asian Nations (ASEAN): It is a free trade area involving six Asian countries, viz. Brunei, Indonesia, Malaysia, the Philippines, Singapore and Thailand.

Back-to-back Loan: A loan that involves a company in Country X with a subsidiary in Country Y and a bank in Country Y with a branch in Country X.

Balance of Payments: It is a statement showing inflow and outflow of foreign exchange in a country. It has different compartments. If the value of imports is greater than the value of exports, the balance of trade is deficit. In the reverse case, the balance of trade is surplus. If one includes also the invisible trade, the difference between the inflow and outflow is known as the balance of current account. After taking into account also the capital account transactions, the difference between the inflow and the outflow is known as the balance of payments.

Bank for International Settlements: A bank located in Switzerland that facilitates transactions among the central banks.

Barter: Goods are exchanged for goods and not for money.

Basis Risk: It arises when the interest rate exposure on one instrument is not completely offset by interest rate exposure on other instrument.

Berne Convention: An international treaty that protects copyrights.

Bid Rate: It is the buying rate of foreign currency.

Bond: A debt instrument

Bonded Warehouse: A storehouse for imported goods for the purpose of deferring payment of custom duties.

Branch (foreign): Foreign office of a company that does not have a separate entity from the parent unit.

Brand: It is a name or logo of a company usually protected by trademark registration.

Brown-field Investment: This form of foreign direct investment is a mix of green field investment and merger & acquisition.

Buyback: Export of industrial equipment in return for products manufactured by that equipment.

Capacity Planning: It is a process to assess company's ability to maximise production for meeting market demand.

Capital Structure: It shows the mix of different forms of capital, such as equity and debt.

Capitalism: It is a form of economic system where resources are owned, allocated and used by private initiatives.

Caste System: It is a system of social stratification. A person born in a particular caste is expected to perform the economic functions meant for that caste. It impinges upon labour mobility.

Centrally Planned Economy: An economic system in which the government has full control over the allocation and use of resources.

Certificate of Origin: A shipping document showing the origin of product for the purpose of imposition of tariff.

Civil Law System: A form of legal system where detailed set of laws is found.

Common Agricultural Policy (CAP): The policy is found in European Union in the area of trade and development of agriculture.

Common Law System: A form of legal system based largely on precedence, customs and tradition.

Common Market: A form of regional economic integration that does not have any tariff on intra- group trade, maintains common external tariff like customs union, and over and above, allows free movement of factors of production.

Comparative Advantage: It is Ricardo's theory of foreign trade. A country should produce and export those goods in which it has comparative efficiency, even if it does not have absolute efficiency.

Compound Duty: It is tariff imposed on the basis of both the value and quantity.

Confiscation: Forced acquisition of a company's assets by the government without paying compensation.

Consolidation: It is a process through which a multinational corporation combines the financial statements of its different units just to have an overall picture of its financial performance.

Copyrights: Property rights conferring upon the creator of the original work the freedom to publish or dispose of them.

Corporate Culture: It is sharing of the common values by the employees in a company. It helps enforce control mechanism.

Countertrade: It is a sort of bilateral trade on barter terms.

Countervailing Duty: Additional tariff levied on a product to counteract subsidy given by the exporting country.

Country Similarity Theory: It explains that trade occurs between countries with similar macro-economic conditions.

Credit Risk: It is concerned with default risk.

Creolization: It is a process through which the elements of outside culture are introduced.

Cross Licensing: When technology is exchanged by different countries.

Cross Rate: Exchange rate between two currencies established through a common currency.

Culture: The norms of a society based on attitude, values and belief.

Cultural Diffusion: It is a process through which a particular culture is transmitted from one country to another.

Cultural Trait: It is a way of life including belief, attitudes, tradition, etc.

Culture Shock: When an employee of a company experiences some kind of trauma while working in a different cultural environment abroad.

Currency Futures Market: It is a market for currency derivatives. The purpose is hedging or speculation. But the features of transactions are different from those in a forward market.

Currency Hedging: Currencies are bought or sold forward in order to minimise the risk arising on account of changes in the exchange rate.

Currency Options Market: A market where currencies are bought and sold for their delivery on a future date. Here the options buyer has the privilege of exercising, or not exercising, the options contract on the maturity date.

Currency Swap: Simultaneous purchase and sale of foreign currency for two different dates. It is done in a forward market.

Customs Union: It is a form of regional economic integration where intra-union trade is duty-free and every member has a common external tariff.

Depreciation of Currency: It is a state of affairs when the external value of a currency falls.

Derivative: Financial instruments whose value is derived from other financial instruments.

Dumping: When the goods are exported at a price below the cost of production or those prevailing in the domestic market.

Direct Quote: Quoting of exchange rate where the amount of domestic currency is shown per unit of foreign currency.

Economic Community: It is a higher level of economic integration where free intra-union trade, common external tariff, free mobility of factors of production are found. Over and above, common economic policy among the member states is also found.

Economic Exposure: It is that form of exchange rate risk which influences the cash flow and revenue and cost stream of a firm.

Economic Integration: Coming of the countries of a region under one economic umbrella for the purpose of trade creation among themselves and for their economic development as a whole.

Economic Order Quantity: It is the optimal size of inventory that a firm orders at a particular point of time.

Economies of Scale: Benefits of larger production as a certain amount of fixed costs per unit of output tends to lower.

Effective Tariff: Effective tariff is different from the nominal tariff depending on the value addition to the imported input and the tariff on the imported input.

Elasticity Approach: It explains that the devaluation of the currency leads to greater exports and lowering of imports so as to improve the balance of trade.

Embargo: Complete ban of export and import of one or more products with a particular country.

Entente Council: A regional economic scheme among the African countries, viz. Benin, Burkina Faso, Cote d'Ivoire, Niger and Togo.

Entrepot: A country being export/import intermediary between two sets of countries. For example, Hong Kong is an entrepot between China and the rest of the world.

Ethnocentrism: It is found in those multinational companies that apply home-country policies among the foreign subsidiaries. It is based on the belief that what works well at home must work well abroad.

Euro: The currency of the European Union.

Eurobond: A bond denominated in any currency other than the currency of the country where it is issued.

Eurocredit: A loan in Eurocurrency market having a maturity of more than one year.

Eurocurrency: A currency banked outside the country of its origin.

Euro-currency Market: A market dealing with Eurocurrencies.

Euro-dollars: Dollars banked outside the USA.

European Free Trade Association: It is a free trade area among four West European nations, viz. Iceland, Liechtenstein, Norway and Switzerland.

European Monetary Union: The plan of the European Union to go for monetary union setting up its central bank and its own currency.

European Union: It represents the highest level of economic integration among 25 European countries.

Exclusive Channel: It is found when the manufacturer grants the right to sell its product to only one reseller or only limited number of resellers.

Exotic Currencies: The currencies of developing countries.

Expatriates: Citizens of a country living and working in another country.

Export Management Company: Companies exporting products on behalf of indirect exporters.

Export Packing List: A shipping document that provides the details of the goods shipped.

Export Trading Company: Companies providing services to indirect exporters as well as providing services directly related to the client's direct export activities.

Expropriation: When the government takes over the assets of a company and gives compensation.

Externalities: External economic costs in respect of the business activity.

Extraterritoriality: The extension of the home-country laws for their application among overseas subsidiaries.

Factor Proportions Theory: A theory explaining that a country exports those goods for the production of which it has abundant resources. It imports those goods for which it possesses resources in short supply.

First-in-advantage: The benefit gained in terms of brand recognition. It arises because the firm enters the market prior to the entry of its competitors.

First World Countries: The non-socialist industrialised countries.

Fisher Effect: A theory explaining relationship between inflation rate and interest rate.

Fixed Exchange Rate: The exchange rate between two currencies determined through some sort of agreement.

Flexible Exchange Rate: Exchange rate which is determined by the forces of demand and supply.

Foreign Trade Zone: An area designated by the government where goods are manufactured with the help of duty-free inputs and are exported to foreign markets. It is also known as export-processing zone.

Forward Contract: Sale and purchase of currency on the condition of future delivery of currency. It is different from spot contract where delivery of currency is made within two working days.

Forward Rate Agreements: They represent a contract through which a borrow/lender locks the interest rate on future borrowing/lending in order to protect itself from unfavourable changes in interest rate.

Franchising: When a franchiser, usually a firm, supplies another firm known as franchisee intangible property rights, such as patent, trademark, etc. for a given payment, known as royalty.

Fringe Benefit: The benefits given to an employee other than salary/wages and cash bonus.

Functional Currency: The currency in which subsidiary operates. It is usually the currency of the host country.

Gap Analysis: The process to find out why the actual demand for a product is lower than its potential demand.

General Agreement on Tariffs and Trade (GATT): An institutional arrangement established in 1947 to regulate multilateral trade.

Generalised System of Preferences (GSP): Preferential treatment by the industrialised countries to the imports of manufactures and semi-manufactures from the developing countries.

Generally Accepted Accounting Principles (GAAP): Accounting standard adopted for preparing financial statements for external users.

Generic: A non-branded product.

Geocentric: Operations or the management decisions taking into account the environment prevailing in both the home country and the host country.

Global Matrix Structure: Organisational structure splitting the chain of command between area and product divisions.

Global Product Structure: Organisational structure dividing the worldwide operations according to company's product.

Globalisation: It is a move towards open economic policies lifting up the restrictions on international economic flows with the result that the different countries get closely inter-woven and become indispensable part of the world economy.

Gold Standard: A form of international monetary system where the value of currency is linked to gold.

Grandchild Subsidiary: Operation of a firm in tax-haven country.

Grantback Provisions: A situation in which the licensee provides the licensor with the use of modified technology.

Green-field Investment: It is a form of foreign direct investment where the foreign investor invests in the equity capital of a new company.

Grey Market: Distribution of goods through unofficial channels.

Gross Barter Terms Trade: It is the ratio between export quantity index and import quantity index.

Gross Domestic Product: Value of goods produced and services rendered in the country during one-year period.

Gross National Product: Gross domestic product plus income from abroad.

Hard Currency: It is a freely convertible currency.

Hedge: Use of various techniques to minimise exchange rate risk.

Heterarchy: Organisational structure in which partners of an alliance operate on an equal footing rather than on superior-subordinate footing.

High-context Culture: A form of culture where it is believed that peripheral culture influences the decision-making.

Hofstede Framework: Study of cultural differences based on individualism versus collectivism, power distance, etc.

Home Country: A country in which an international company is headquartered.

Host Country: A country in which subsidiary is located.

Imitation Lag: Strategy of a firm to move to a country to develop local production and thereby to exploit monopoly advantage at least for a short period.

In-bond Industry: Industry using duty-free inputs for the sole purpose of exporting the output.

Income Terms of Trade: It is the product of net barter terms of trade index and the size of export index. It assumes that the lowering of export prices leads to greater demand for export.

Indigenisation: The process of introducing elements of an outside culture.

Indirect Export: When a firm exports its output through an intermediary.

Indirect Quote: Quoting of exchange rate in a way when the units of foreign currency are shown per unit of domestic currency.

Inefficient Market View: It represents a condition when financial instruments do not reflect publicly available information.

Infant-industry Argument: When duty is imposed on imports for making newly born domestic industry capable of competing with similar foreign products.

Intensive Channel: A channel of distribution where a number of retailers exist to sell a producer's product.

Intellectual Property Rights: Ownership rights to intangible assets, such as patents, copyrights, trademark, etc.

Inter-bank Market: A market representing sale and purchase of currencies among banks.

Interest Rate Cap: A borrower buys it in order to protect itself from rising interest rate.

Interest Rate Collar: It is a combination of interest rate cap and floor.

Interest Rate Corridor: It is a combination of two or more interest rate caps.

Interest Rate Floor: A lender buys it for protecting it from a falling interest rate.

Intra-industry Trade: The goods produced in the same industry are both exported and imported. The goods may be either homogeneous or differentiated on account of brand, etc.

Interest Arbitrage: Sale and purchase of interest-paying securities denominated in different currencies for the purpose of making profit.

Internalisation: Intra-firm transfer of intermediate products and centralised control of the subsidiaries with a view to reduce the cost.

International Area Structure: An organisational structure dealing with a company's global operation based on geographic areas.

International Bond Market: Sale and purchase of bonds outside the country of the issuing company.

International Capital Market: Borrowing and lending activities by financial institutions and other bodies throughout the globe.

International Division Structure: Organisational structure separating its external operation from its domestic operation through the creation of an international division.

International Equity Market: When equities are bought and sold outside the country of the issuing company.

International Fisher Effect: The principle explaining equality of interest-rate differential with inflation rate differential between two countries.

International Monetary Fund: It is an international institution created by the Bretton Woods resolutions for guiding international monetary system, especially the exchange rate regime and international liquidity.

Intervention Currencies: The currencies in which a large part of trade is invoiced.

Invisibles: They include non-merchandise trade, such as services, investment income, unilateral transfers, etc.

Inward-looking Policy: It represents a situation when a country establishes its domestic market for its own product through discriminating against imports. It is also known as Import Substitution Policy.

Jamaica Agreement: The present system of exchange rate (after the collapse of the fixed parity system) was finally approved by the IMF members in Jamaica in 1976.

Joint-venture: Process through which separately created companies are jointly owned under an agreement.

Just-in-time System: The raw material arrives at the factory only at the time when it is needed. This helps in minimising the size of inventory and thereby the handling cost.

Kluckhohn-Strodtbeck Framework: It is a framework for the study of cultural differences.

Lag Strategy: A financial strategy delaying collection of foreign currency when foreign currency is going to appreciate or delaying payment when the foreign currency is going to depreciate.

Latin American Free Trade Association: A free trade area created in 1960 by Mexico and some other Latin American countries and replaced by ALADI in 1980.

Law of One Price: Theory explaining that identical product commands identical price in all countries at the current exchange rate.

Lead Country Strategy: A strategy to introduce a product on test basis in a small market prior to its sale in a bigger market.

Lead Strategy: It is just the opposite of the lag strategy. *See lag strategy*.

Learning Curve: It is a theory explaining that cost tends to decrease with the workers and managers getting more experience.

Leontief Paradox: It is a critique of Factor Proportions theory of international trade. It shows that the USA having abundant capital exported more of labour-intensive goods.

Letter of Credit: A document issued by the importer's bank wherein the bank assures the exporter to pay the export value if the terms and conditions are fulfilled.

Licensing Agreement: An agreement through which a licensor permits the licensee to use its intellectual property rights for a specific period of time.

Logistics: Management of the flow of inputs to the factory and of the final products from the factory to the users.

London Inter-bank Offer Rate (LIBOR): It is the interest rate applicable to inter-bank loans of Euro-currencies in London financial market.

Liquidity Risk: It is also known as gap risk which means mismatched timings between cash inflows and cash outflows on account of interest payment.

Louvre Accord: An agreement among the G-7 nations reached in 1987 to maintain the value of US dollar through market intervention.

Low-context Culture: A culture where only that particular information is considered for decision-making which is received first-hand.

Maastricht Treaty: A treaty bringing European Union to a higher level of economic integration was signed at Maastricht in December 1991.

Make-or-buy Decision: Decision of a firm whether to manufacture a component or to import it from some other firm.

Managed Floating: It is that type of floating exchange rate regime where the central bank of the country sells and buys foreign currency in order to stabilise the exchange rate.

Management Contracts: An agreement where one company provides specialised management services to another company for a fee.

Management Technology: It is the managerial skill required to run a business.

Maquiladora: The export-processing zones of Mexico.

Marginal Rate of Transformation: It is the amount of one product that a country must forego to produce each additional unit of the other product.

Market Capitalisation: The product of total number of shares and the market price per share.

Market Economy: An economic system where resources are allocated depending upon the market forces.

Matrix Structure: An organisation structure where foreign units report to more than one group in terms of area, function and product.

MERCOSUR: A group of four countries, viz. Argentina, Brazil, Paraguay and Uruguay that got out of ALADI in 1991for creating a customs union.

Merger & Acquisition: A company buys another running company, which is known as a target company, for a consideration value.

Mixed Economy: An economic system where both public sector and the private sector enterprises exist side by side.

Monetary Approach to the BOP: It is the supply of and, demand for, money that may be changed in order to make improvement in the balance of payments.

Monochronic Culture: A culture representing sequential behaviour of individuals meaning that an individual deals with different persons in sequence.

Most-favoured-nations Treatment: It is a GATT/WTO principle meaning that any trade concession availed by an individual member country is essentially available to all member countries.

Multi-domestic Company: Less integrated international companies where foreign subsidiaries enjoy ample freedom.

Multifibre Agreement: An agreement establishing rules concerning trade in textiles.

Multilateral Investment Guarantee Agency (MIGA): A World Bank Group institution providing insurance to international investors against non-commercial risk.

National Competitive Advantage: An edge maintained by a particular country in a specific industry. The factors are explained by Porter.

Natural Advantage: Advantages available in form of natural resources, climatic conditions, etc.

Neomercantilism: A theory suggesting for achieving a favourable balance of trade.

Net Barter Terms of Trade: It is the ratio of export price index and import price index.

Net Export Effect: Export stimulus minus export reduction.

Net Present Value: An amount showing the present value of future net cash flows.

Netting: Flow of funds, often intra-firm, on a net basis.

Non-tariff Barriers: Import barriers that are not tariff. They are manifest in form of quota, etc.

North American Free Trade Agreement (NAFTA): A free trade agreement among the USA, Canada and Mexico.

Offset: A barter trade on a bilateral basis.

Off-shore Banking Centre: Those international banks that deal only with non-residents and only in foreign currencies.

Off-shoring: Intra-firm outsourcing is known as off-shoring.

Offer Rate: The rate of exchange at which a foreign currency is sold. It is also known as selling rate or ask rate.

Official Reserves: It is a country's foreign exchange reserves comprising of monetary gold, special drawing rights and foreign currency assets.

Oligopoly: A situation where sellers are only a few.

Open Account: Credit sale.

Optimal Import Tariff: It is a position where the excess of terms of trade gains over the deadweight loss on account of tariff imposition is the highest. It means that at this point the net increase in welfare is the maximum.

Optimum Tariff Theory: A theory explaining that with the imposition of tariff, foreign sellers reduce the price of their product.

Options: A derivative used for hedging or speculation in the foreign exchange market. The distinctive feature is that the options buyer has the privilege of exercising the options or letting them expire.

Organisation for Economic Co-operation and Development (OECD): A multilateral organisation participated by industrialised and semi-industrialised first world countries.

Organisation of African Unity (OAU): A political integration among some of the African nations.

Organisation of Petroleum Exporting Countries (OPEC): An alliance among twelve petroleum-exporting countries for the supply and pricing of petroleum products.

Organisational Structure: The reporting relationship within an organisation.

Outsourcing: Sourcing of inputs from abroad.

Outward-looking Policy: It represents a policy where imports are liberalised and exports are promoted through various incentives.

Over-the-counter: Absence of a particular place for trading in currencies or in securities.

Par Value: The value of a currency quoted earlier in terms of US dollar or gold, now in terms of SDRs.

Patents: A right granted by the government for the protection of an invention.

Peg: Fixing relationship of a currency with another currency in terms of value.

Penetration Price: It means charging lower price in the beginning but higher price when demand settles down.

Pluralistic Society: Society in which different ideologies are followed by its different segments at a particular point of time.

Polycentrism: A strategy of international firms where subsidiaries have the freedom of designing their own operational policies.

Porter's Diamond: Porter has delineated four conditions for attaining and sustaining the national competitive advantage. They are: demand, factor endowment, supporting industries and the firm's own strategy and structure.

Portfolio Investment: Investment in securities without having voting power in the company's management.

Power Distance: A measurement of preference for consultative or autocratic styles of management.

Price Discrimination: It is a method under which different prices are charged from different groups of customers.

Price Skimming: It means charging higher price in the beginning but lower price when demands settle down.

Process Technology: It is the knowledge used in the processing or manufacturing of a product.

Product Life Cycle Theory: A theory explaining that manufacturing location shifts internationally with varying stages of the product.

Product Technology: It is the information that specifies a product's features and uses.

Production Possibilities Frontier: It represents various combinations of two goods produced in a country with fully employed factors of production.

Purchasing Power Parity Theory: Ability of any two currencies to buy the same basket of commodities in respective countries influencing in turn the exchange rate.

Pull: Marketing strategy to create buyer demand. In the sequel, the channel members will demand for greater stock of the product.

Push: A marketing strategy to put pressure on the channel members to augment sale of the product.

Quota: Restrictions on the quantity of import. They may be in terms of a particular country or there may be a global quota.

Quoted Currency: The quoted value of a currency through which another currency is to be bought.

Rationalised Production: It represents specialisation of production in different countries based on varying cost of labour, capital and raw material.

Regional Economic Integration: It is a process through which countries of a particular region co-operate with one another in order to eliminate trade barriers and to foster movement of factors among themselves.

Relationship Enterprises: They represent a network of inter-country/inter-industry strategic alliances among big companies.

Re-negotiation: It denotes a process through which the international companies go for changing the terms of operation.

Repatriation: Movement of expatriates to their home country or flow of profit to the home country.

Resource-based View of the Firm: It is a concept which means that each company has a unique combination of competencies.

Return on Investment: It represents a product of profit margin and asset turnover.

Reverse Culture Shock: The cultural shock encountered by an expatriate while returning to the home country. It tends to appear when the person develops familiarity with the host country environment.

Royalty: Payments received from abroad for the use of intangible assets.

Sales Response Function: The amount of sales created at different levels of marketing.

Second-tier Subsidiaries: Subsidiaries reporting to a subsidiary located in a tax-haven country.

Second-world Countries: Centrally planned economies or the communist countries.

Securitization: Rebundling of difficult-to-sell financial assets into more liquid and easily negotiable financial assets.

Service Export and Import: Earnings received from abroad and earnings paid abroad on account of trade in intangible goods.

Sight Draft: A commercial bill of exchange where payment is made just on presenting the bill.

Smithsonian Arrangement: It was an arrangement initiated in 1971 to restore faith in the international monetary system. The fluctuation band of currencies was widened and different currencies were realigned.

Social Structure: A fundamental organisation in a culture that embraces its groups and institutions, its system of social position and the relationship among them.

Socialism: It is an economic system where means of production and distribution are owned by the State.

Southern African Development Community: It is a regional co-operation scheme in the south African region. It was formed to counter the economic influence of South Africa in that region.

Special Drawing Rights: International reserves created by International Monetary Fund for the purpose of improving world liquidity.

Specific Duty: Tariff levied on the basis of units.

Speculation: Buying and selling of foreign currencies for the purpose of reaping profit.

Spot Market: A market where transacted currencies are delivered immediately within two working days.

Spread: It denotes the difference between the buying and the selling rates of a currency.

Strategic Alliance: It is a financial joint-venture or equity alliance with a pre-defined purpose, such as development of technology or increase in the size of the market.

Subsidiary: A foreign company being legally separate from the parent company despite the fact that the parent company owns the entire/majority equity of the subsidiary.

Subsidies: Direct or indirect financial assistance given by the government to companies in order to make them more competitive.

Super 301: It is a provision in the US tax laws that allows the US traders to adopt rigorous trade restrictions when other countries practise restrictions on the import of US goods and services.

Swap: A simultaneous spot and forward foreign exchange transactions. It may be also exchange between loans in different currencies or between a fixed interest-rate loan and a floating interest-rate loan.

Switch Trading: It is a process through which one company sells its obligation to import to another company.

Syndication: When two or more banks join hands for providing big loans or the loans beyond the capacity of one individual bank.

Tariff: A governmental tax levied on the imports.

Tax Neutrality: It means that tax should not come in the way of optimal allocation of capital among different countries.

Tax Treaty: A treaty between two countries for reciprocal reduction of taxes on dividend, etc.

Tax-haven Countries: Countries where tax rate on income from abroad is either zero or very low.

Technical Analysis: It is a technique used for the forecast of exchange rate changes.

Temporal Method: It is a method used for translating foreign currency into the reporting currency.

Terms of Trade: Ability of export to make import. It is found out through dividing the export price index by import price index.

Theocratic Legal System: A legal system based on religious precepts.

Third-world Countries: Developing countries not coming under the first-world/second-world countries.

Total Quality Management: A manufacturing system characterised by zero-level defects.

Totalitarianism: A political system where decision-making is centralised.

Trade Creation: Increase in the volume of trade among the members of a regional integration scheme.

Trade Deflection: It occurs in a free trade area (regional grouping) when the goods from a third country enters the market though a country with the lowest tariff rate.

Trade Diversion: It exists when locus of production shifts to a less efficient manufacturing centre due to special tariff arrangements.

Trade Related Aspects of Intellectual Property Rights: It is a provision of the WTO system that requires the member countries to agree to enforce procedures under their national laws to protect intellectual property rights.

Trademark: A name or logo that distinguishes a product from similar products of other manufacturers.

Transaction Exposure: Exchange rate exposure that arises on account of transactions in foreign currencies. Any change in exchange rate influences the present cash flows.

Transfer Price: It is a price charged normally in intra-firm transactions. The price is different from the arm's-length price and is determined arbitrarily for the purpose of minimising tax and tariff burden of the firm as a whole or for working capital management.

Transition Economies: The countries moving out of a centrally planned economic system to a market-based system after the break-up of the former USSR are known as transition economies.

Translation Exposure: Exchange-rate exposure that arises when the parent company translates the figures of the subsidiaries' financial statements into its own currency.

Turn-key Project: An operating facility that is transferred to the owner after it is ready to begin operations.

Unbundling of Prices: It means lower prices for bare-bone items but higher prices for accessories. Bundling of prices is just the opposite.

Unilateral Transfer: Flow of funds across countries with no corresponding movement of goods and services.

United Nations: An international organisation set up in 1945 to foster world peace and security.

United Nations Conference on Trade and Development (UNCTAD): Established in 1964, it is a UN body to look after the interest of the developing countries as far as their trade and development is concerned.

US-Canada Free Trade Agreement: An agreement enacted in 1989 between the USA and Canada for a free trade.

Value-added Tax: Tax imposed on the basis of the value addition at each stage of production or business process.

Value Chain Analysis: Segregating a company's activities into primary and supportive activities and identifying those creating value for the ultimate customers.

Value Density: The value of a product relative to its weight and volume.

Vehicle Currency: A currency that is required for conversion of one currency into the other.

Vertical Integration: Integration between different units manufacturing different parts of the same product.

Voluntary Export Restraints: An agreement restricting the exporter to limit the export to the importing country.

Weak Currency: A currency that is not fully convertible.

Withholding Tax: It is a tax levied on the passive income earned by an individual or a company.

World Bank: It is an amalgam of the International Bank for Reconstruction and Development established in 1945 with its sister institution, International Development Association created in 1960. The purpose is to provide development finance to the member countries.

World Trade Organisation (WTO): An international organisation replacing GATT in 1995 functioning as regulator of multilateral trade.

Zero Defects: The elimination of manufacturing defects.

Zero-sum Game: Any negotiation where none of the parties is at net gain.

AUTHOR INDEX

SUBJECT INDEX

Plate 1 North America

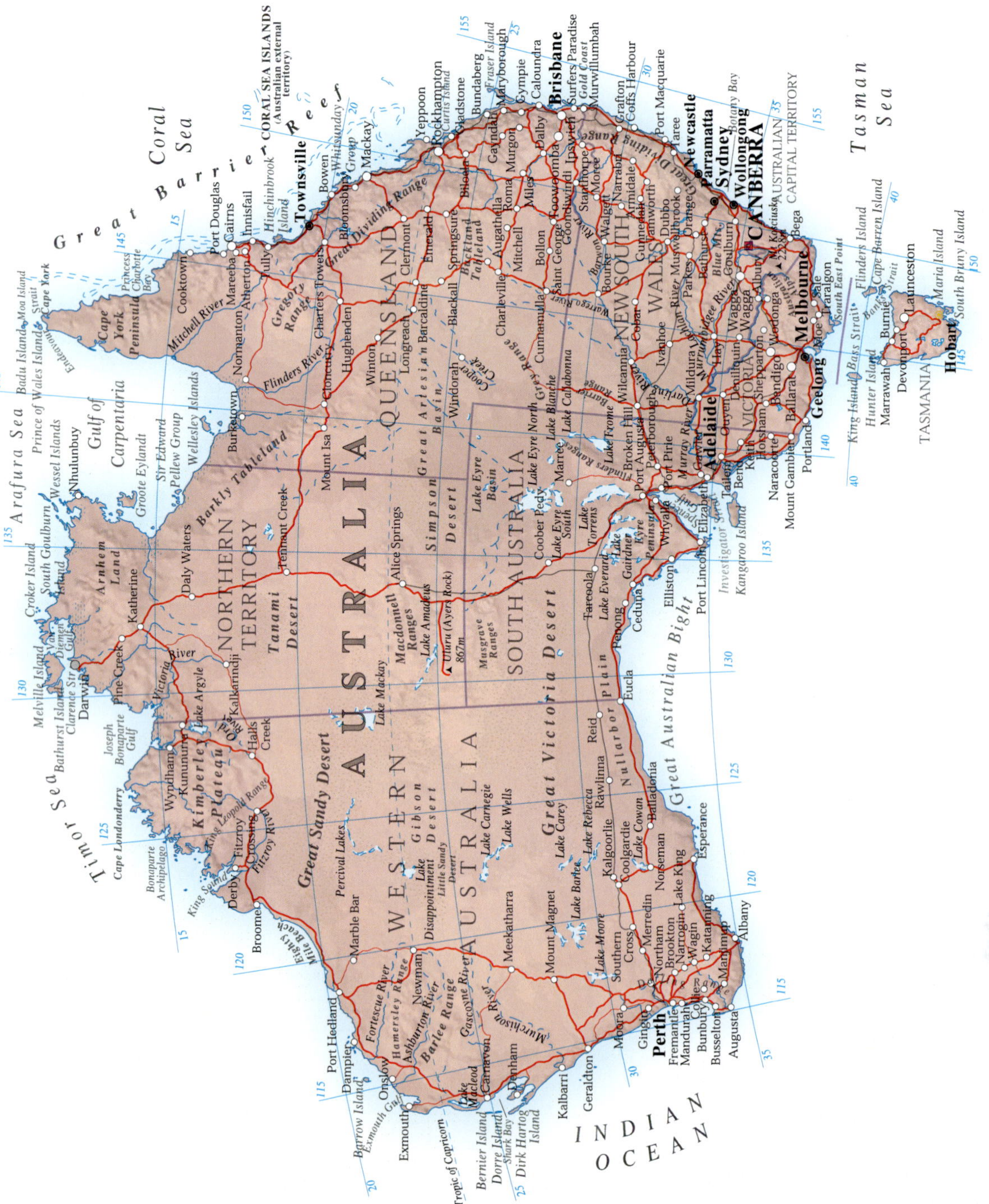

Plate 2 (a) Oceania

Plate 2 (b) New Zealand

Plate 3 South America

Plate 4 Europe

ARCTIC OCEAN
PACIFIC OCEAN
INDIAN OCEAN
EUROPE
AFRICA
RUSSIAN FEDERATION
KAZAKHSTAN
MONGOLIA
CHINA
INDIA
JAPAN
NORTH KOREA
SOUTH KOREA
TAIWAN
PHILIPPINES
INDONESIA
MALAYSIA
SINGAPORE
BRUNEI
THAILAND
CAMBODIA
VIETNAM
LAOS
MYANMAR
BANGLADESH
BHUTAN
NEPAL
SRI LANKA
PAKISTAN
AFGHANISTAN
TAJIKISTAN
KYRGYZSTAN
UZBEKISTAN
TURKMENISTAN
IRAN
IRAQ
SYRIA
TURKEY
GEORGIA
ARMENIA
AZERB.
CYPRUS
LEBANON
ISRAEL
JORDAN
KUWAIT
BAHRAIN
QATAR
U.A.E.
SAUDI ARABIA
OMAN
YEMEN
East Timor
Bering Sea
Gulf of Anadyr
East Siberian Sea
Laptev Sea
Kara Sea
Sea of Okhotsk
Sea of Japan
Yellow Sea
East China Sea
South China Sea
Philippine Sea
Bay of Bengal
Arabian Sea
Andaman Sea
Gulf of Thailand
Java Sea
Flores Sea
Timor Sea
Moluccas
Gulf of Aden
Gulf of Oman
Red Sea
Black Sea
Caspian Sea
Aral Sea
Lake Balkhash
Lake Baikal
Arctic Circle
Tropic of Cancer
Equator
Siberia
Central Siberian Plateau
West Siberian Plain
Ural Mountains
Kolyma Range
Kamchatka
Altai Mountains
Gobi
Inner Mongolia
Kunlun Mountains
Plateau of Tibet
Himalayas
Arabian Peninsula
Kurile Islands
Ryukyu Islands
Shantar Island
Sakhalin
Honshu
Luzon
Mindanao
Borneo
Sumatra
Java
Celebes
Flores
New Guinea
Irian Jaya
Hainan Dao
Andaman Islands (part of India)
Nicobar Islands (part of India)
Socotra (part of Yemen)
Macao (to Portugal)
Ob
Ob'
Yenisey
Lena
Aldan
Indigirka
Kolyma
Vitim
Angara
Amur
Argun
Irtysh
Syr Darya
Amu Darya
Tarim He
Yellow River
Yangtze
Xi Jiang
Mekong
Salween
Irrawaddy
Tsangpo
Ganga
Indus
Narmada
Godavari
Krishna
Tigris
Euphrates
Noril'sk
Yakutsk
Petrovavlovsk-Kamchatskiy
Yuzhno-Sakhalinsk
Khabarovsk
Vladivostok
Yekaterinburg
Krasnoyarsk
Novosibirsk
Novokuznetsk
Bratsk
Irkutsk
Chita
Ulan Ude
Omsk
Barnaul
Petropavlovsk
Pavlodar
ASTANA
Atyrau
Kzyl-Orda
Alma Ata
BISHKEK
TASHKENT
DUSHANBE
ASHGABAT
Choybalsan
ULAN BATOR
Hovd
Bulgan
Saynshand
Urumqi
Yangi
Qiqihar
Harbin
Changchun
Jilin
Shenyang
Anshan
PYONGYANG
Dalian
SEOUL
Pusan
Hohhot
BEIJING
Taiyuan
Jinan
Qingdao
Lanzhou
Zhengzhou
Xi'an
Nanjing
Hangzhou
Shanghai
Ningbo
Wuhan
Nanchang
Chengdu
Chongqing
Changsha
Fuzhou
Guiyang
Nanning
TAIPEI
Kaohsiung
Sapporo
Sendai
TOKYO
Yokohama
Kyoto
Osaka
Hiroshima
Fukuoka
Samsun
ANKARA
Izmir
Adana
NICOSIA
BEIRUT
JERUSALEM
AMMAN
DAMASCUS
TBILISI
YEREVAN
BAKU
Rasht
TEHRAN
Mashhad
Hamadan
BAGHDAD
Esfahan
Yazd
Shiraz
Zahedan
Sakakah
RIYADH
MANAMA
DOHA
Dubai
ABU DHABI
MUSCAT
Madina
Mecca
SANA
Al Mukalla
KABUL
ISLAMABAD
Peshawar
Srinagar
Lahore
Faisalabad
Amritsar
Karachi
Hyderabad
NEW DELHI
Jaipur
Agra
Jodhpur
Lucknow
KATHMANDU
THIMPHU
Guwahati
DHAKA
Ahmadabad
Kolkata
Mumbai
Pune
Vishakhapatnam
Bangalore
Chennai
Kochi
Madurai
Thiruvananthapuram
COLOMBO
Rutog
Chittagong
YANGON
HANOI
VIENTIANE
BANGKOK
PHNOM PENH
Ho Chi Minh City
Long Xuyen
MANILA
Quezon City
Cebu
Davao
Zamboanga
KUALA LUMPUR
BANDAR SERI BEGAWAN
Pontianak
Balikapan
Manado
JAKARTA
Bandung
Semarang
Surabaya
Malang
DILI

Plate 5 Asia

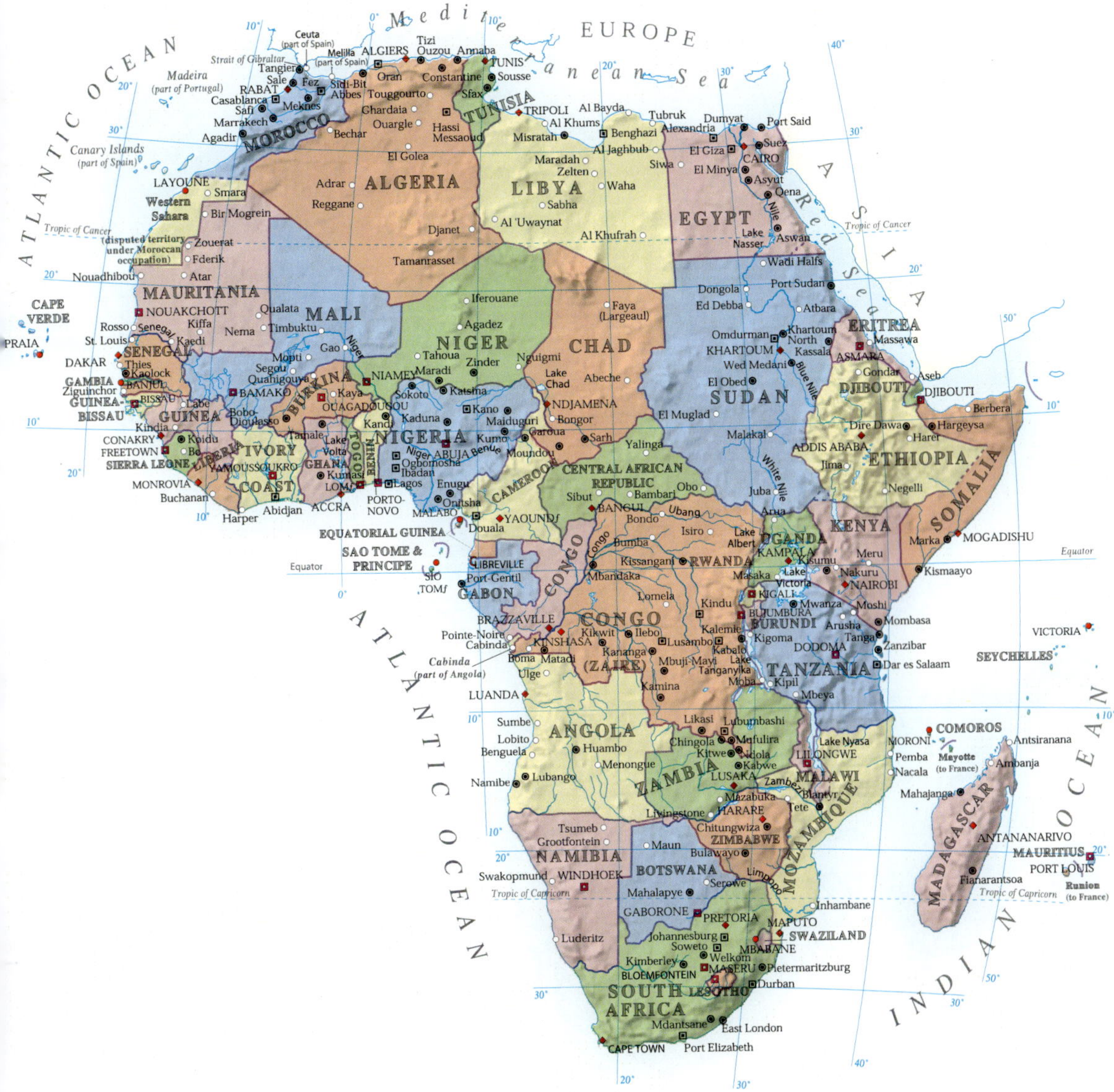

Plate 6 Africa

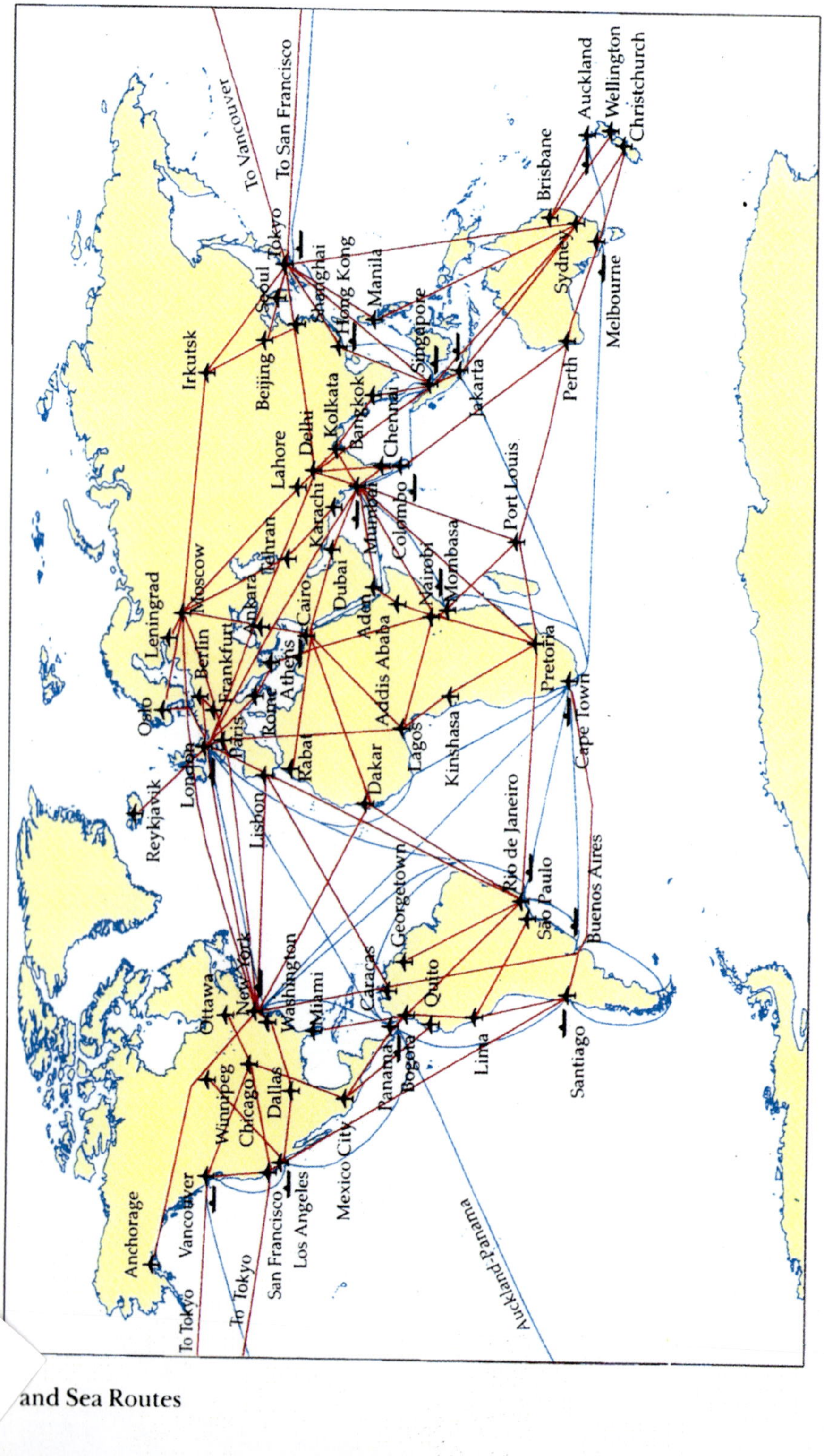

and Sea Routes